WORLD TRADE ORGANIZATION

Dispute Settlement Reports

2012
Volume X

Pages 5303-5748

CAMBRIDGE
UNIVERSITY PRESS

University Printing House, Cambridge CB2 8BS, United Kingdom

Published in the United States of America by Cambridge University Press, New York

Cambridge University Press is part of the University of Cambridge.

It furthers the University's mission by disseminating knowledge in the pursuit of education, learning and research at the highest international levels of excellence.

www.cambridge.org
Information on this title: www.cambridge.org/9781107051447

First published 2014

Printed in the United Kingdom by the CPI Group Ltd, Croydon CR0 4YY

A catalogue record for this publication is available from the British Library

Library of Congress Cataloguing in Publication data

ISBN 978-1-107-05144-7 Hardback

THE WTO DISPUTE SETTLEMENT REPORTS

The *Dispute Settlement Reports* of the World Trade Organization (the "WTO") include panel and Appellate Body reports, as well as arbitration awards, in disputes concerning the rights and obligations of WTO Members under the provisions of the *Marrakesh Agreement Establishing the World Trade Organization*. The *Dispute Settlement Reports* are available in English. Volumes comprising one or more complete cases contain a cumulative list of published disputes. The cumulative list for cases that cover more than one volume is to be found in the first volume for that case.

This volume may be cited as DSR 2012:X

TABLE OF CONTENTS

Page

China - Certain Measures Affecting Electronic Payment Services (WT/DS413)

Report of the Panel 5305

Cumulative List of Published Disputes 5725

CHINA - CERTAIN MEASURES AFFECTING ELECTRONIC PAYMENT SERVICES

Report of the Panel

WT/DS413/R

Adopted by the Dispute Settlement Body on 31 August 2012

TABLE OF CONTENTS

Page

I. INTRODUCTION 5321
- A. Complaint of the United States 5321
- B. Establishment and Composition of the Panel 5322
- C. Panel Proceedings 5322
  - 1. General 5322
  - 2. Preliminary ruling on the consistency with Article 6.2 of the DSU of the United States' request for the establishment of a panel 5323
  - 3. Translation issues 5323

II. FACTUAL ASPECTS 5324

III. PARTIES' REQUESTS FOR FINDINGS AND RECOMMENDATIONS 5326

IV. ARGUMENTS OF THE PARTIES 5326

V. ARGUMENTS OF THE THIRD PARTIES 5326

VI. INTERIM REVIEW 5327

VII. FINDINGS 5335
- A. Preliminary Ruling Under Article 6.2 of the DSU 5335
- B. General Issues 5336
  - 1. Burden of proof 5336
  - 2. Treaty interpretation 5337
- C. The Services at Issue 5339
  - 1. Payment card transactions 5339
  - 2. The services at issue 5344

3. Whether the services at issue cover the three-party model in addition to the four-party model 5349

4. Whether the services at issue include the services supplied by issuer and merchant processors 5352

5. Whether the services at issue are integrated services ... 5354

D. China's Specific Commitments Concerning the Services at Issue 5357

1. Order of analysis of the subsectors identified by the parties.. 5358

2. Interpretation of subsector (d) in China's Schedule 5359

(a) Ordinary meaning 5359

(i) Ordinary meaning of "payment", "money" and "transmission".................. 5360

(b) Context 5367

(i) The rest of subsector (d)......................... 5368

(ii) Other elements of China's Schedule....... 5373

(iii) The GATS Annex on Financial Services 5378

(iv) The structure of the GATS 5388

(v) Schedules of other WTO Members........ 5395

(c) Object and purpose 5397

(d) Conclusion.. 5398

3. Recourse to supplementary means of interpretation 5400

E. The Measures at Issue 5400

1. The specific measures at issue that form part of the United States' challenge 5402

(a) Chinese legal instruments as the basis for the existence of the measures at issue 5402

(b) The repeal or replacement of certain Chinese legal instruments.. 5404

2. Evaluation of the existence of the measures at issue 5407

(a) Requirements on issuers that payment cards issued in China bear the CUP logo ("issuer requirements") 5410

(i) Preliminary translation issue 5411

(ii) Document No. 37 5414

(iii) Document No. 57 5416

(iv) Document No. 129 5418

(v) Document No. 219 5418

(vi) Document No. 76 5419

(vii) Document No. 17 5422

(viii) Yin Lian/UnionPay logo use requirements versus interoperability requirements 5423

(ix) Conclusions and implications 5425

(b) Requirements that all ATM, and POS terminals in China accept CUP cards ("terminal equipment requirements") 5428

(i) Document No. 17 5429

(ii) Document No. 37 5430

(iii) Document No. 57 5431

(iv) Document No. 153 5432

(v) Document No. 149 5432

(vi) Document No. 76 5434

(vii) Conclusions and implications 5434

(c) Requirements on acquiring institutions to post the CUP logo and be capable of accepting all payment cards bearing the CUP logo ("acquirer requirements") 5436

(i) Document No. 153 5437

(ii) Document No. 149 5438

(iii) Document No. 37 5438

(iv) Document No. 76 5439

(v) Conclusions and implications 5440

(d) Requirements pertaining to card-based electronic transactions in China, Hong Kong and Macao ("Hong Kong/Macao requirements") 5441

(i) Document No. 16 5442

(ii) Document No. 8 5444

(iii) Document No. 219 5444

(iv) Document No. 254 5446

(v) Conclusions 5447

(e) Requirements that mandate the use of CUP and/or establish CUP as the sole supplier of EPS for all domestic transactions denominated and paid in RMB ("sole supplier requirement") and prohibitions on the use of non-CUP cards for cross-region or

inter-bank transactions ("cross-region/inter-bank prohibitions") 5448
(i) Document No. 37 5450
(ii) Document No. 57 5451
(iii) Document No. 16 5451
(iv) Document No. 8 5452
(v) Document No. 219 5453
(vi) Document No. 254 5453
(vii) Document No. 103 5454
(viii) Document No. 153 5455
(ix) Document No. 149 5460
(x) Document No. 53 5462
(xi) Document No. 49 5465
(xii) Document No. 129 5466
(xiii) Document No. 76 5468
(xiv) Document No. 17 5474
(xv) Document No. 142 5475
(xvi) Conclusions on the instruments individually 5477
(xvii) Collective assessment of the legal instruments at issue 5479
(f) Overall conclusions on the evaluation of the existence of the measures at issue 5488
F. The United States' Claims Under Article XVI of the GATS ... 5489
1. Whether China has made mode 1 or mode 3 market access commitments covering the supply of EPS 5491
(a) Mode 1 commitments 5491
(b) Mode 3 commitments 5502
2. Whether the measures at issue are inconsistent with Article XVI of the GATS 5517
(a) Whether the relevant requirements fall within the scope of Article XVI:2(a) of the GATS 5519
(b) Whether the issuer, terminal equipment and acquirer requirements are inconsistent with Article XVI:2(a) of the GATS 5523
(c) Whether the requirements pertaining to RMB card-based transactions taking place in China, Macao and Hong Kong are

inconsistent with Article XVI:2(a) of the GATS 5526
(d) Whether China's requirements, when considered jointly, are inconsistent with Article XVI:2(a) of the GATS 5532
(e) Whether the measures at issue are inconsistent with Article XVI:1 of the GATS 5533
3. Conclusions 5535
(a) China's commitment under mode 1 in Sector 7.B(d) of its Schedule 5535
(b) China's commitment under mode 3 in Sector 7.B(d) of its Schedule 5535
(i) Issuer, terminal equipment, acquirer requirements 5535
(ii) Hong Kong/Macao requirements 5535
G. The United States' Claims Under Article XVII of the GATS 5536
1. Analytical approach and scope of Article XVII findings 5537
2. China's requirements considered individually 5538
(a) Whether China has undertaken relevant national treatment commitments 5538
(i) Mode 1 commitments 5538
(ii) Mode 3 commitments 5547
(b) Whether China's requirements affect the supply of services 5550
(c) Whether China's requirements accord less favourable treatment 5551
(i) Issuer requirements 5552
(ii) Terminal equipment requirements 5562
(iii) Acquirer requirements 5565
(d) Overall conclusions 5568
(i) Hong Kong/Macao requirements 5568
(ii) Issuer requirements 5569
(iii) Terminal equipment requirements 5569
(iv) Acquirer requirements 5569
3. China's requirements considered jointly 5570
VIII. CONCLUSIONS AND RECOMMENDATIONS 5571

LIST OF ANNEXES

ANNEX A

EXECUTIVE SUMMARIES OF THE FIRST WRITTEN SUBMISSIONS OF THE PARTIES

Contents		Page
Annex A-1	Executive summary of the first written submission of the United States	5577
Annex A-2	Executive summary of the first written submission of China	5589

ANNEX B

ORAL STATEMENTS OR EXECUTIVE SUMMARIES THEREOF, OF THE PARTIES AT THE FIRST SUBSTANTIVE MEETING

Contents		Page
Annex B-1	Executive summary of the opening oral statement of the United States at the first substantive meeting	5601
Annex B-2	Closing oral statement of the United States at the first substantive meeting	5606
Annex B-3	Executive summary of the oral statement of China at the first substantive meeting	5607

ANNEX C

WRITTEN SUBMISSIONS AND ORAL STATEMENTS, OR INTERGRATED SUMMARIES THEREOF, OF THE THIRD PARTIES

Contents		Page
Annex C-1	Integrated executive summary of the third party written submission and oral statement of Australia	5611
Annex C-2	Third party oral statement of Ecuador at the first substantive meeting	5618
Annex C-3	Integrated executive summary of the third party written submission and oral statement of the European Union	5622
Annex C-4	Integrated executive summary of the third party written submission and oral statement of Japan	5626
Annex C-5	Integrated executive summary of the third party written submission and oral statement of the Republic of Korea	5633

ANNEX D

EXECUTIVE SUMMARIES OF THE SECOND WRITTEN SUBMISSIONS OF THE PARTIES

Contents		Page
Annex D-1	Executive summary of the second written submission of the United States	5637
Annex D-2	Executive summary of the second written submission of China	5649

ANNEX E

ORAL STATEMENTS OR EXECUTIVE SUMMARIES THEREOF, OF THE PARTIES AT THE SECOND SUBSTANTIVE MEETING

Contents		Page
Annex E-1	Executive summary of the oral statement of the United States at the second substantive meeting	5661
Annex E-2	Executive summary of the oral statement of China at the second substantive meeting	5668

ANNEX F

REQUEST FOR A PRELIMINARY RULING

Contents		Page
Annex F-1	Executive summary of China's request for a preliminary ruling	5675
Annex F-2	Executive summary of the United States' submissions in response to China's request for a preliminary ruling	5677
Annex F-3	Executive summary of China's comments on the United States' submissions in response to China's request for a preliminary ruling	5689

ANNEX G

EXCERPT OF CHINA'S SCHEDULE

Contents		Page
Annex G-1	The People's Republic of China - Schedule of Specific Commitments, GATS/SC/135 – excerpt	5691

ANNEX H

TABLE OF TRANSLATIONS OF LEGAL MEASURES AND OTHER INSTRUMENTS

Contents		Page
Annex H-1	Table of translations of legal measures and other instruments referred to by the parties	5695

ABBREVIATIONS OF MEASURES, CERTAIN EVIDENCE, AND OTHER SELECTED INSTRUMENTS REFERRED TO IN THIS REPORT[1]

Short Titles	Full Titles
American Express 2010 Annual Report	US SEC Form 10-K, American Express Company Annual Report, for the fiscal year ended November 30, 2010 (Exhibit US-7)
BIS Red Book 2003	BIS Red Book 2003, Payment Systems in the United States (Exhibit US-11)
CUP's Articles of Association	The Articles of Association of China UnionPay Co., Ltd. (Exhibit US-20, No Chinese Exhibit)
Discover 2010 Annual Report	US SEC Form 10-K, Discover Financial Services Annual Report, for the fiscal year ended November 30, 2010 (Exhibit US-8)
Document No. 8	Announcement of the People's Bank of China on Providing Clearing Arrangements for Banks That Handle Personal RMB Deposits, Exchanges, Bank Cards and Remittance in Macao (PBOC Announcement [2004] No. 8) (Exhibits US-46, CHN-62)

[1] When the relevant exhibits were submitted by the United States and by China, this has been indicated.

Short Titles	Full Titles
Document No. 16	Announcement of the People's Bank of China on Providing Clearing Arrangements for Banks That Handle Personal RMB Deposit, Exchanges, Bank Cards and Remittance in Hong Kong (PBOC Announcement [2003] No. 16) (Exhibits US-44, CHN-60)
Document No. 17	Measures for the Administration of Bank Card Business (Yin Fa [1999] No.17) (Exhibits US-52, CHN-53)
Document No. 37	Circular of the People's Bank of China on Promulgation of the "Opinions on Implementation of the Work in Bank Card Interoperability in 2001" (Yin Fa [2001] No. 37) (Exhibits US-40, CHN-54)
Document No. 49	Circular of China Banking Regulatory Commission concerning Conduction of the Bank Card Business by Wholly Foreign-invested Banks and Chinese-foreign equity joint venture banks (Yin Jian Fa [2007] No. 49) (Exhibits US-62, CHN-68)
Document No. 53	Circular of the State Administration of Foreign Exchange on Standardizing the Administration of Foreign Currency Bank Cards (Hui Fa [2010] No. 53) (Exhibits US-51, CHN-71)
Document No. 57	Circular of the People's Bank of China on Uniform Use of 'Yin Lian'[2] Logo and its Holographic Label for Anti-counterfeiting (Yin Fa [2001] No. 57) (Exhibits US-41, CHN-55)
Document No. 66	Circular of the State Administration of Foreign Exchange on Regulating the Management of Foreign Currency Bank Cards (Hui Fa [2004] No. 66) (Exhibits US-45, CHN-61)

[2] This is without prejudice to the parties' views on the correct translation of the long title of the instrument.

Short Titles	Full Titles
Document No. 76 • Notice of Document No. 76 • Business Practices Appendix of Document No. 76	Notice of the People's Bank of China in Relation to the Issuance of Business Practices for the Interoperable Service of Bank Cards and Appendix on Business Practices for the Interoperable Service of Bank Cards (Yin Fa [2001] No. 76) (Exhibits US-56/US-63, CHN-56)
Document No. 94	Opinions on Bank Card Interoperability Related Work in 2002 by the People's Bank of China (Yin Fa [2002] No.94) (Exhibits US-42, CHN-57)
Document No. 103	Certain Opinions of the People's Bank of China, the National Reform and Development Commission, the Ministry of Public Security, the Ministry of Finance, the Ministry of Information Industry, the Ministry of Commerce, the State Administration of Foreign Exchange, on Promoting the Development of Bank Card Industry (Yin Fa [2005] No. 103) (Exhibits US-1, CHN-65)
Document No. 129	Circular of the People's Bank of China on Further Improving Bank Card Interoperability Related Work (Yin Fa [2003] No.129) (Exhibits US-53, CHN-59)
Document No. 142	Notice of People's Bank of China, the China Banking Regulatory Commission, the Ministry of Public Security and the State Administration for Industry and Commerce on Strengthening the Security Management of Bank Cards and Preventing and Combating Bank Card Crimes (Yin Fa [2009] No. 142) (Exhibits US-55, CHN-69)
Document No. 149	Opinions of the Standing Office of the People's Bank of China on the Circular on Strengthening the Safety Management of Bank Cards and Preventing and Fighting Crimes in Bank Cards by the People's Bank of China, the China Banking Regulatory Commission, the Ministry of Public Security and the State Administration for Industry and Commerce (Yin Ban Fa [2009] No. 149) (Exhibits US-50, CHN-70)

Short Titles	Full Titles
Document No. 153	Guiding Opinions of the People's Bank of China on Regulating and Promoting the Development of Bank Card Acceptance Market (Yin Fa [2005] 153) (Exhibits US-49, CHN-66)
Document No. 219	Notice of the People's Bank of China concerning Relevant Issues on Accepting and Using RMB Bank Cards in Border Areas (Yin Fa [2004] No. 219) (Exhibits US-47, CHN-63)
Document No. 254	Circular on Relevant Issues Concerning the Operation of Individual RMB Business by Mainland Banks and Hong Kong/Macau Banks (Yin Fa [2004] No. 254) (Exhibits US-48, CHN-64)
Document No. 272	Circular Regarding Issues Concerning Bank Card Interoperability Related Work by the People's Bank of China (Yin Fa [2002] No.272) (Exhibits US-43, CHN-58)
Document No. 273	Notice of the People's Bank of China on the Relevant Issues concerning Strengthening the Administration of Overseas Business Acceptance of Bank Cards (Yin Fa [2007] No. 273) (Exhibits US-54, CHN-67)
FFIEC IT Examination Handbook	Federal Financial Institutions Examination Council (FFIEC), "Retail Payment Systems, IT Examination Handbook" (February 2010) (Exhibit US-12)
MasterCard 2010 Annual Report	US SEC Form 10-K, MasterCard Incorporated Annual Report, for fiscal year ended December 31, 2010 (Exhibit US-6)
MasterCard 2009 Annual Report	US SEC Form 10-K, MasterCard Incorporated Annual Report, for fiscal year ended December 31, 2009 (Exhibit US-5)
Notification of Approval of CUP's Business Licence	Shanghai Municipal Administration for Industry and Commerce, Notification of Business Licence Approval and Issuance for China UnionPay Co., Ltd (March 19, 2002) (Exhibit US-29, No Chinese Exhibit)

Short Titles	Full Titles
Visa 2010 Annual Report	US SEC Form 10-K, Visa 2010 Annual Report (as of September 30, 2010) (Exhibit US-4)
Visa IPO Prospectus	US SEC Amendment No. 4 to Form S-1 Registration Statement Under Securities Act of 1933, Visa Inc. IPO Prospectus, February 25, 2008, (Exhibit US-3)

TABLE OF CASES CITED IN THIS REPORT

Short Title	Full Case Title and Citation
Argentina – Textiles and Apparel	Panel Report, *Argentina – Measures Affecting Imports of Footwear, Textiles, Apparel and Other Items*, WT/DS56/R, adopted 22 April 1998, as modified by Appellate Body Report WT/DS56/AB/R, DSR 1998:III, 1033
Australia – Apples	Panel Report, *Australia – Measures Affecting the Importation of Apples from New Zealand*, WT/DS367/R, adopted 17 December 2010, as modified by Appellate Body Report WT/DS367/AB/R
China – Publications and Audiovisual Products	Appellate Body Report, *China – Measures Affecting Trading Rights and Distribution Services for Certain Publications and Audiovisual Entertainment Products*, WT/DS363/AB/R, adopted 19 January 2010
China – Publications and Audiovisual Products	Panel Report, *China – Measures Affecting Trading Rights and Distribution Services for Certain Publications and Audiovisual Entertainment Products*, WT/DS363/R and Corr.1, adopted 19 January 2010, as modified by Appellate Body Report WT/DS363/AB/R
China – Raw Materials	Appellate Body Reports, *China – Measures Related to the Exportation of Various Raw Materials*, WT/DS394/AB/R / WT/DS395/AB/R / WT/DS398/AB/R, circulated to WTO Members 30 January 2012
China – Raw Materials	Panel Reports, *China – Measures Related to the Exportation of Various Raw Materials*, WT/DS394/R / WT/DS395/R / WT/DS398/R / and Corr.1, circulated to WTO Members 5 July 2011

Short Title	Full Case Title and Citation
EC – Approval and Marketing of Biotech Products	Panel Report, *European Communities – Measures Affecting the Approval and Marketing of Biotech Products*, WT/DS291/R, WT/DS292/R, WT/DS293/R, Add.1 to Add.9, and Corr.1, adopted 21 November 2006, DSR 2006:III-VIII, 847
EC – Asbestos	Appellate Body Report, *European Communities – Measures Affecting Asbestos and Asbestos-Containing Products*, WT/DS135/AB/R, adopted 5 April 2001, DSR 2001:VII, 3243
EC – Bananas III	Appellate Body Report, *European Communities – Regime for the Importation, Sale and Distribution of Bananas*, WT/DS27/AB/R, adopted 25 September 1997, DSR 1997:II, 591
EC – Bananas III (Ecuador)	Panel Report, *European Communities – Regime for the Importation, Sale and Distribution of Bananas, Complaint by Ecuador*, WT/DS27/R/ECU, adopted 25 September 1997, as modified by Appellate Body Report WT/DS27/AB/R, DSR 1997:III, 1085
EC - Hormones	Appellate Body Report, *EC Measures Concerning Meat and Meat Products (Hormones)*, WT/DS26/AB/R, WT/DS48/AB/R, adopted 13 February 1998, DSR 1998:I, 135
EEC – Apples I (Chile)	GATT Panel Report, *EEC – Restrictions on Imports of Apples from Chile*, L/5047, adopted 10 November 1980, BISD 27S/98
India – Patents (US)	Appellate Body Report, *India – Patent Protection for Pharmaceutical and Agricultural Chemical Products*, WT/DS50/AB/R, adopted 16 January 1998, DSR 1998:I, 9
Japan - Alcoholic Beverages II	Appellate Body Report, *Japan – Taxes on Alcoholic Beverages*, WT/DS8/AB/R, WT/DS10/AB/R, WT/DS11/AB/R, adopted 1 November 1996, DSR 1996:I, 97
Mexico – Telecoms	Panel Report, *Mexico – Measures Affecting Telecommunications Services*, WT/DS204/R, adopted 1 June 2004, DSR 2004:IV, 1537
Philippines – Distilled Spirits	Appellate Body Reports, *Philippines – Taxes on Distilled Spirits*, WT/DS396/AB/R / WT/DS403/AB/R, adopted 20 January 2012

Short Title	Full Case Title and Citation
Philippines – Distilled Spirits	Panel Reports, *Philippines – Taxes on Distilled Spirits*, WT/DS396/R / WT/DS403/R, adopted 20 January 2012, as modified by Appellate Body Reports WT/DS396/AB/R / WT/DS403/AB/R
Thailand – Cigarettes (Philippines)	Appellate Body Report, *Thailand – Customs and Fiscal Measures on Cigarettes from the Philippines*, WT/DS371/AB/R, adopted 15 July 2011
Thailand – Cigarettes (Philippines)	Panel Report, *Thailand – Customs and Fiscal Measures on Cigarettes from the Philippines*, WT/DS371/R, adopted 15 July 2011, as modified by Appellate Body Report WT/DS371/AB/R
Turkey - Rice	Panel Report, *Turkey – Measures Affecting the Importation of Rice*, WT/DS334/R, adopted 22 October 2007, DSR 2007:VI, 2151
US – Carbon Steel	Appellate Body Report, *United States – Countervailing Duties on Certain Corrosion-Resistant Carbon Steel Flat Products from Germany*, WT/DS213/AB/R and Corr.1, adopted 19 December 2002, DSR 2002:IX, 3779
US – COOL	Panel Reports, *United States – Certain Country of Origin Labelling (COOL) Requirements*, WT/DS384/R / WT/DS386/R, circulated to WTO Members 18 November 2011
US – Countervailing Measures on Certain EC Products	Appellate Body Report, *United States – Countervailing Measures Concerning Certain Products from the European Communities*, WT/DS212/AB/R, adopted 8 January 2003, DSR 2003:I, 5
US – Export Restraints	Panel Report, *United States – Measures Treating Exports Restraints as Subsidies*, WT/DS194/R and Corr.2, adopted 23 August 2001, DSR 2001:XI, 5767
US – Gambling	Appellate Body Report, *United States – Measures Affecting the Cross-Border Supply of Gambling and Betting Services*, WT/DS285/AB/R, adopted 20 April 2005, DSR 2005:XII, 5663 (Corr.1, DSR 2006:XII, 5475)
US – Gambling	Panel Report, *United States – Measures Affecting the Cross-Border Supply of Gambling and Betting Services*, WT/DS285/R, adopted 20 April 2005, as modified by Appellate Body Report WT/DS285/AB/R, DSR 2005:XII, 5797

Short Title	Full Case Title and Citation
US – Gasoline	Appellate Body Report, *United States – Standards for Reformulated and Conventional Gasoline*, WT/DS2/AB/R, adopted 20 May 1996, DSR 1996:I, 3
US – Gasoline	Panel Report, *United States – Standards for Reformulated and Conventional Gasoline*, WT/DS2/R, adopted 20 May 1996, as modified by Appellate Body Report WT/DS2/AB/R, DSR 1996:I, 29
US – Section 301 Trade Act	Panel Report, *United States – Sections 301-310 of the Trade Act of 1974*, WT/DS152/R, adopted 27 January 2000, DSR 2000:II, 815
US - Shrimp	Appellate Body Report, *United States – Import Prohibition of Certain Shrimp and Shrimp Products*, WT/DS58/AB/R, adopted 6 November 1998, DSR 1998:VII, 2755
US – Tuna II (Mexico)	Panel Report, *United States – Measures Concerning the Importation, Marketing and Sale of Tuna and Tuna Products*, WT/DS381/R, circulated to WTO Members 15 September 2011
US – Upland Cotton	Appellate Body Report, *United States – Subsidies on Upland Cotton*, WT/DS267/AB/R, adopted 21 March 2005, DSR 2005:I, 3
US – Wool Shirts and Blouses	Appellate Body Report, *United States – Measure Affecting Imports of Woven Wool Shirts and Blouses from India*, WT/DS33/AB/R, adopted 23 May 1997, and Corr.1, DSR 1997:I, 323
U.S. – Zeroing (EC)	Appellate Body Report, *United States – Laws, Regulations and Methodology for Calculating Dumping Margins ("Zeroing")*, WT/DS294/AB/R, adopted 9 May 2006, and Corr.1, DSR 2006:II, 417

LIST OF ABBREVIATIONS USED IN THIS REPORT

1993 Scheduling Guidelines	1993 Guidelines for the Scheduling of Specific Commitments under the GATS (Document MTN.GNS/W/164)
2001 Scheduling Guidelines	Guidelines for the Scheduling of Specific Commitments under the GATS, S/L/92, March 28, 2001
ATM	Automated Teller Machine
BIN	Bank Identification Number

BIS	Bank for International Settlements
CBRC	China Banking Regulatory Commission
CPC	1991 United Nations Provisional Central Product Classification
CUP	China UnionPay Co., Ltd
DSU	Understanding on Rules and Procedures Governing the Settlement of Disputes
EPS	Electronic payment services
EPS supplier	Electronic payment services supplier
FFI	Foreign Financial Institutions
GATS	General Agreement on Trade in Services
GATT	General Agreement on Tariffs and Trade
PBOC	People's Bank of China
POS	Point-of-Sale
RCBFCC	Rural Credit Banks Funds Clearing Center
RMB	Renminbi
Scheduling Guidelines	1993 Scheduling Guidelines and 2001 Scheduling Guidelines
UNOG	United Nations Office at Geneva
WTO	World Trade Organization
WTO Agreement	Marrakesh Agreement establishing the World Trade Organization

I. INTRODUCTION

A. Complaint of the United States

1.1 On 15 September 2010, the United States requested consultations with China pursuant to Articles 1 and 4 of the Understanding on Rules and Procedures Governing the Settlement of Disputes (DSU) and Article XXII of the General Agreement on Trade in Services (GATS) with respect to the measures and claims set out below.[3]

[3] WT/DS413/1.

B. *Establishment and Composition of the Panel*

1.2 On 11 February 2011, the United States requested the establishment of a panel pursuant to Article 6 of the DSU with standard terms of reference.[4] At its meeting on 25 March 2011, the Dispute Settlement Body (DSB) established a panel pursuant to the request of the United States in document WT/DS413/2, in accordance with Article 6 of the DSU.[5] The Panel's terms of reference are the following:

> To examine, in the light of the relevant provisions of the covered agreements cited by the parties to the dispute, the matter referred to the DSB by the United States in document WT/DS413/2 and to make such findings as will assist the DSB in making the recommendations or in giving the rulings provided for in those agreements.[6]

1.3 On 23 June 2011, the United States requested the Director-General to determine the composition of the panel, pursuant to Article 8.7 of the DSU. On 4 July 2011, the Director-General accordingly composed the Panel as follows:

Chairperson:	Mr Virachai Plasai
Members:	Ms Elaine Feldman
	Mr Martín Redrado

1.4 Australia, Ecuador, the European Union, Guatemala, India[7], Japan, and the Republic of Korea reserved their rights to participate in the Panel proceedings as third parties.

C. *Panel Proceedings*

1. *General*

1.5 On 5 July 2011, China submitted to the Panel a request for a preliminary ruling with respect to the consistency of certain aspects of the United States' panel request with Article 6.2 of the DSU. The Panel issued its preliminary ruling to the parties, with a copy to the third parties, on 7 September 2011. The Panel held a first substantive meeting with the parties on 26-27 October 2011. A session with the third parties took place on 27 October 2011. The Panel held a second substantive meeting with the parties on 13-14 December 2011. On 25 January 2012, the Panel issued the descriptive part of its Panel Report. The Panel issued its Interim Report to the parties on 11 April 2012. The Panel issued its Final Report to the parties on 25 May 2012.

---

[4] WT/DS413/2.

[5] See WT/DSB/M/294.

[6] WT/DS413/3.

[7] India filed its notification of interest to participate in the Panel proceedings as a third party following the date of the Panel's composition. The Panel included India in the list of third parties after consultations with the parties.

2. Preliminary ruling on the consistency with Article 6.2 of the DSU of the United States' request for the establishment of a panel

1.6 China submitted its request for a preliminary ruling to the Panel on 5 July 2011 (see Annex F-1). After consultations with the parties, the Panel decided to issue a preliminary ruling before the date of receipt of the United States' first written submission. The Panel noted that this approach would avoid delay in the proceedings. The Panel provided the United States with an opportunity to submit written comments on China's request and also invited the third parties to submit any written comments they might have in response to the views expressed by the parties. The Panel also provided the parties with an opportunity to request a preliminary ruling hearing to discuss the matter. As neither party requested a hearing on the preliminary ruling issue, the parties were given an opportunity to submit further written comments on the other party's initial written submissions.

1.7 On 29 July 2011, the United States submitted a response to China's request for a preliminary ruling (see Annex F-2). China commented on the United States' submission on 25 August 2011. The United States filed further comments on 30 August 2011. None of the third parties submitted comments on the first set of submissions.

1.8 The Panel issued its ruling to the parties, with a copy to the third parties, on 7 September 2011. The Panel rejected China's preliminary objection of 5 July 2011.[8] After consulting the parties, the Panel requested the Chairperson of the DSB to circulate the ruling to the WTO membership. The ruling was circulated as document WT/DS413/4 on 30 September 2011. The ruling forms an integral part of the findings in Section VII of this report.

3. Translation issues

1.9 The United States submitted translations of certain measures at issue in this dispute in its response of 29 July 2011 to China's request for a preliminary ruling and also in its first written submission of 15 September 2011. In a communication to the Panel on 22 September 2011, China identified a number of issues with these translations, alleging that the United States had incorrectly translated certain words or phrases, thereby affecting the original meaning of the measures.

1.10 In a communication to the parties on 12 October 2011, the Panel indicated that it would discuss the translation issues raised by China during the first substantive meeting with the parties. At that meeting the Panel asked the parties if they would be able to agree on a translation from the outset, or otherwise specify those translation issues on which they could not agree. The Panel suggested that, if the parties were unable to agree, an independent

[8] See WT/DS/413/4, para. 58.

translator could be selected in consultation with the parties to provide expert linguistic advice on the correct translation for outstanding issues. The parties agreed to the selection of an independent translator for any outstanding issues. On 9 December 2011, the parties informed the Panel of the translation issues on which agreement had been reached as well as those that could not be resolved.

1.11 At the second substantive meeting, the parties agreed in principle to the Panel's suggestion to appoint, as the independent translator, UN Geneva's (UNOG) Conference Services Division. At this time, the Panel further requested the parties to provide a brief rationale setting out their views on outstanding translation issues to facilitate the independent translator's work. On 4 January 2012, the parties each submitted a brief rationale setting out their views on outstanding translation issues.

1.12 The Panel appointed UNOG as the independent translator on 26 January 2012. This Report will hereinafter refer to the "independent translator" when discussing advice provided by UNOG. The independent translator provided advice to the Panel on the outstanding issues on 15 February 2012. This advice was promptly forwarded to the parties who submitted written comments thereon on 24 February 2012.

II. FACTUAL ASPECTS

2.1 These proceedings concern a series of legal requirements relating to electronic payment services that the United States alleges are maintained by China. According to the United States, these legal requirements, alone or in combination, "affect electronic payment services for payment card transactions and the suppliers of those services".[9]

2.2 According to the United States, "electronic payment services" involve the following:

> services through which transactions involving payment cards (as defined below) are processed and through which transfers of funds between institutions participating in the transactions are managed and facilitated. Suppliers of electronic payment services supply, directly or indirectly, a system that typically includes the following: the processing infrastructure, network, and rules and procedures that facilitate, manage, and enable transaction information and payment flows and which provide system integrity, stability and financial risk reduction; the process and coordination of approving or declining a transaction, with approval generally permitting a purchase to be finalized or cash to be disbursed or exchanged; the delivery of transaction information among participating entities; the calculation, determination, and

9 WT/DS413/2, p. 1.

reporting of the net financial position of relevant institutions for all transactions that have been authorized; and the facilitation, management and/or other participation in the transfer of net payments owed among participating institutions.[10]

2.3 The United States definition of the term "payment card" includes the following:

a bank card, credit card, charge card, debit card, check card, automated teller machine (ATM) card, prepaid card, and other similar card or payment or money transmission product or access device, and the unique account number associated with that card or product or access device.[11]

2.4 The United States challenges what it alleges to be the following legal requirements:

- requirements that mandate the use of China UnionPay, Co. Ltd. (CUP) and/or establish CUP as the sole supplier of electronic payment services for all domestic transactions denominated and paid in China's domestic currency, renminbi (RMB);
- requirements that payment cards issued in China bear the CUP logo;
- requirements that all automated teller machines (ATM), merchant card processing equipment, and point-of-sale (POS) terminals in China accept CUP cards;
- requirements on acquiring institutions to post the CUP logo and be capable of accepting all bank cards bearing the CUP logo;
- broad prohibitions on the use of non-CUP cards for cross-region or inter-bank transactions; and
- requirements pertaining to card-based electronic transactions in Hong Kong, China and Macao, China.[12]

2.5 The United States considers that these requirements are maintained through a series of instruments that are identified in the request for establishment of a panel:[13]

- Document No. 17;
- Document No. 37;
- Document No. 219;
- Document No. 254;

[10] See WT/DS413/2, fn 1.

[11] See WT/DS413/2, fn 2.

[12] United.States' request for the establishment of a panel, pp. 1-4; United States' submission in response to China's request for a preliminary ruling, 29 July 2011 ("United States' response to China's request for a preliminary ruling"), para. 77; Panel's preliminary ruling, para. 15; and United States'. first written submission, paras. 29-31.

[13] See list "Abbreviations of measures, evidence, and other instruments referred to in this Report", p. viii.

- Document No. 57;
- Document No. 76;
- Document No. 94;
- Document No. 272;
- Document No. 129;
- Document No. 16;
- Document No. 66;
- Document No. 8;
- Document No. 103;
- Document No. 153;
- Document No. 273;
- Document No. 49;
- Document No. 142;
- Document No. 149;
- Document No. 53;
- The "'business specifications' and 'technical standards' that are identified in the instruments above, including in Document No. 17, Document No. 57, Document No. 129, and Document No. 49"; and
- any amendments to date or any related implementing measures "to date".[14]

III. PARTIES' REQUESTS FOR FINDINGS AND RECOMMENDATIONS

3.1 The United States requests that the Panel find that each of the legal requirements identified in the request for the establishment of a panel (and enumerated in paragraph 2.4 above) is inconsistent with China's obligations under Article XVI:1 and XVI:2(a) and Article XVII of the GATS. The United States further requests, pursuant to Article 19.1 of the DSU, that the Panel recommend that China bring its measures into conformity with its WTO obligations.

3.2 China requests that the Panel reject the United States' claims in this dispute in their entirety.

IV. ARGUMENTS OF THE PARTIES

4.1 The arguments of the parties are reflected in their executive summaries provided to the Panel in accordance with paragraph 16 of the Working Procedures adopted by the Panel (see List of Annexes, pages vi and vii).

V. ARGUMENTS OF THE THIRD PARTIES

5.1 The arguments of Australia, Ecuador, the European Union, Japan, and the Republic of Korea, are reflected in their executive summaries provided in

[14] See WT/DS413/2, p. 4.

accordance with paragraph 16 of the Working Procedures adopted by the Panel (see Annex C). Guatemala and India did not submit written or oral arguments to the Panel.

VI. INTERIM REVIEW

6.1 On 11 April 2012, the Panel submitted its Interim Panel Report to the parties. On 25 April 2012, the United States and China each submitted written requests for the review of precise aspects of the Interim Report. On 9 May 2012, the United States submitted comments on China's requests for review. China did not submit any comments on the United States' requests for review. Neither party requested an interim review meeting.

6.2 In accordance with Article 15.3 of the DSU, this section of the Report sets out the Panel's response to the parties' requests made at the interim review stage. The Panel modified aspects of its Report in the light of the parties' comments where it considered these appropriate, as explained below. References to sections, paragraph numbers and footnotes in this section relate to the Interim Panel Report, except as otherwise noted.

6.3 Turning to the parties' requests, both parties asked the Panel to make certain changes of an editorial nature to improve clarity and accuracy. Accordingly, the Panel made changes to paragraphs 7.35, 7.36, 7.58, 7.154, 7.208, 7.227, 7.311, 7.522 and 8.1; footnotes 1, 12, and 91; and the "Table of Abbreviations of Measures, Evidence and Other Instruments Referred to in this Ruling". The Panel made additional editorial corrections and revisions in response to the parties' comments.

6.4 Regarding footnote 30, the United States requests inclusion of a citation, as an example, to paragraphs 35-54 of its submission in response to China's request for a preliminary ruling, given the reference made in that footnote to submissions made by the United States.

6.5 The Panel notes that footnote 30 supports a section containing a description of technical and commercial aspects of payment card transactions based on information and evidence included in the parties' submissions. This section contains a number of references to the evidence presented by the parties. In the Panel's view, in the specific context of footnote 30, it is not necessary to add the citation requested by the United States.

6.6 Regarding paragraph 7.14, China notes that, in describing the steps in a payment card transaction, the Panel states that "[t]he issuer authorizes transactions at POS terminals, collects payment from the card holder, and transmits the funds *to the payment card company's settlement bank for settlement of payment obligations incurred by the card holder*" (emphasis added by China). The italicized portion of this sentence, China argues, is not accurate in all cases. According to China, there are many payment card systems in which the settlement of payment obligations takes place through a mechanism that is operated independently of a "payment card company". China notes that this could include, for example, an inter-bank funds transfer system operated by the central bank, or a clearing and settlement mechanism operated by a different company.[15] On the basis of this argument, China requests that the Panel either (i) indicate that it is describing the operations of a particular "payment card company" (in this case, Visa); or (ii) modify the sentence to reflect more broadly the variety of means by which inter-bank payments are effected (e.g., "transmits the funds through the relevant inter-bank payment channel for settlement ...").

6.7 The United States considers that identifying a particular payment card company is not necessary. Rather, China's alternative suggestion, as indicated in item (ii) of its comment on paragraph 7.14 (i.e., to "modify the sentence to reflect more broadly the variety of means by which inter-bank payments are effected"), may be an acceptable way to modify the sentence should the Panel consider it appropriate to do so.

6.8 The Panel agrees with the United States that identifying a particular payment card company is not necessary. We accept, however, that it is useful to reflect more broadly the variety of means by which inter-bank payments are effected. As a result, the Panel made appropriate changes to paragraph 7.14 along the lines of China's alternative suggestion.

6.9 Regarding paragraph 7.24, China notes that the second sentence states: "Merchants submit transaction information for clearing and payment to acquirers, *which forward their transaction claims to the relevant payment card company*."(emphasis added by China) China argues that, for the same reasons explained by China in relation to paragraph 7.14, the italicized portion of this sentence is not accurate in all cases. In many systems, China argues, the acquiring bank will place a cleared transaction item directly into an inter-bank settlement mechanism that has no connection to a "payment card company". More generally, according to China, the entirety of paragraph 7.24 is describing the particular type of multilateral deferred net settlement system operated by companies like Visa and MasterCard. This is not the only type of settlement system for payment card transactions, contrary to the impression created by this paragraph. China indicates that Australia's EFTPOS system is a case in point. China explains that within that system, issuing and acquiring financial institutions exchange transaction items directly with each other on a bilateral basis.[16] Once a day, financial institutions use these bilateral transaction items to calculate their credit and debit positions in relation to all other financial institutions, and report these positions to the "Collator", which is operated by the Reserve Bank of Australia.[17] The Collator then calculates the multilateral net positions of the financial institutions and transmits these positions to Australia's high-value inter-bank transfer system (known as RITS) for final settlement.[18]

---

15 China refers to Exhibits CHN-101 (Australia), CHN-102 (Canada) and CHI-103 (France).

16 China refers to Exhibit CHN-101, p. 31.

17 China refers to Exhibit CHN-101, pp. 31-33.

18 China refers to Exhibit CHN-101, n. 23.

Within this system, acquiring financial institutions do not "forward their transaction claims to the relevant payment card company." In fact, according to the explanation provided by China in this specific request, there is no "payment card company" involved in the process at all.

6.10 For these reasons, China requests that the Panel (i) indicate that paragraph 7.24 is describing the typical model of operations for global network operators like Visa and MasterCard; or (ii) modify the paragraph to reflect more broadly the variety of back-end clearing and settlement mechanisms that are used in payment card systems.

6.11 The United States indicates that it would not object to the inclusion of clarifying language that confirms that there are variations of both the "four-party model" and the "three-party model". However, the United States observes that a company-specific reference is unnecessary. The United States submits that an accurate and acceptable reference would be to describe the process as a "typical four-party model". The United States also acknowledges that there may be more than one way in which the settlement component of a payment card transaction can be conducted.

6.12 The Panel agrees with the United States that identifying a particular payment card company is not necessary. The Panel also notes that paragraph 7.24 describes the typical back-end processing of payment card transactions in four-party and three-party models. Therefore, we consider that the sentence in question in paragraph 7.24 could be modified along the lines proposed by the United States. As a result, we made relevant changes to the second sentence of paragraph 7.24.

6.13 Regarding paragraph 7.28, the United States requests, for greater accuracy, that the Panel's reference in the second sentence to the United States' definition of "payment cards" be modified to include the phrase "and the unique account number associated with that card or product or access device" as is set forth in the United States' panel request, and as is referred to in paragraph 7.25 of the Interim Report.

6.14 The Panel considers that the requested change would be more faithful to the definition presented by the United States, which is referred to in paragraph 7.28, and therefore the Panel modified paragraph 7.28 accordingly.

6.15 Regarding paragraphs 7.38 to 7.45, China requests that the Panel clarify what the relevant service transaction would be in the case of three-party models. In particular, China requests that the Panel indicate whether it considers that (i) the operators of three-party models supply the services at issue to themselves; (ii) the operators of three-party models supply the services at issue to card holders and/or merchants; or (iii) the Panel has some other understanding of the relevant service transaction in the case of three-party models.

6.16 The United States considers that the particular details China proposes to include regarding three-party models are not necessary to the Panel's analysis. Nor has China offered any explanation as to why these "clarifications" are necessary.

6.17 The Panel notes at the outset that, as pointed out by the United States, China did not offer any explanation as to why the requested clarifications are useful or necessary. It is unclear to us what are the rationale and purpose of those purported clarifications. We recall that paragraphs 7.38 to 7.45 address whether the services at issue cover the three-party model in addition to the four-party model. These paragraphs of the Report should be read in conjunction with the previous sections on payment card transactions and the services at issue. In particular, the main features of three-party models (in contrast with four-party models) are described in paragraphs 7.18 to 7.24 of the Report. In the Panel's view, it is clear from paragraphs 7.23 and 7.24 that operators of three-party models supply their services directly to card holders and merchants. For these reasons, the Panel does not find it necessary or appropriate to make the changes requested.

6.18 Regarding paragraph 7.39, the United States requests that the Panel include a new footnote at the end of the first sentence. The new footnote would refer to United States' responses to Panel question Nos. 25 and 74 and the United States' response to China's request for a preliminary ruling.

6.19 The Panel notes that the United States' responses to Panel question No. 25, paragraphs 81-83, and No. 74, paragraphs 26-28, are referred to in footnote 80, at the end of paragraph 7.39. As regards the requested reference to the United States' response to China's request for a preliminary ruling, in the Panel's view, the United States' arguments cited in paragraph 7.39 do not come from the paragraphs identified by the United States (paragraphs 40-41 and 54)". As a result, the Panel does not find it appropriate to add a new footnote to paragraph 7.39.

6.20 Regarding footnotes 94 and 97, the United States requests that, for completeness, a reference be included to paragraphs 11-14 of its second written submission.

6.21 In the Panel's view, paragraphs 11-14 of the United States' second written submission deal with whether EPS constitute a single integrated service, with a view to substantiating its claim that EPS should be classified in subsector (d) of China's schedule of specific commitments. Having said that, we added a reference to those paragraphs in footnote 94, which contains a summary of the United States' arguments on that issue. As regards footnote 97, we note that the point made in the fifth sentence of paragraph 7.59, to which footnote 97 relates, was not made in paragraphs 11-14 of the United States' second written submission, but in paragraph 17 of that submission. For that reason, we modified footnote 97 to refer to paragraph 17 of the United States' second written submission.

6.22 Regarding paragraph 7.61, the United States requests that the last sentence of this paragraph include a new footnote that refers to specified paragraphs of its submissions and responses to questions.

6.23 The Panel notes that paragraph 7.61 addresses whether the services at issue are integrated services, regardless of their classification in China's schedule of specific commitments. The Panel also notes that paragraphs 35-54 of the United States' response to China's request for a preliminary ruling, as well as paragraph 10 of the United States' first written submission, are not related to the precise issue addressed in paragraph 7.61 of the Report. We also note that the relevant paragraph of the United States' response to Panel question No. 26 is paragraph 84, which is quoted in footnotes 94 and 97 of that section, and that the relevant paragraph of the United States' second written submission is paragraph 17, which we added to footnote 97. For these reasons, the Panel does not find it appropriate or necessary to introduce a footnote to paragraph 7.61 of the Report.

6.24 Regarding paragraph 7.75 and footnote 110, the United States requests that the Report reflect that arguments put forward by the United States regarding the ordinary meaning of the service covered in China's subsector (d) also addresses the plain meaning of the phrase "including credit, charge and debit cards". The United States requests the Panel to add a sentence reflecting this argument in either paragraph 7.75 or footnote 110.

6.25 The Panel notes that the phrase "including credit, charge and debit cards" is discussed subsequently in the Report and therefore the Panel included an appropriate reference in footnote 142. The Panel also added an additional reference to United States' arguments in footnote 110.

6.26 Regarding footnotes 131, 152, 163, 181, 217 and 230, the United States requests the Panel to include references to additional paragraphs in United States' submissions that support the arguments cited by the Panel in the paragraphs concerned.

6.27 The Panel included additional relevant references in footnotes 131, 152, 163, 181, 217 and 230.

6.28 Regarding footnote 142, the United States requests that the citations include references to additional paragraphs in United States' submissions that support the argument cited by the Panel, and also indicate that the United States made arguments regarding the ordinary meaning of this phrase.

6.29 The Panel made appropriate additions to footnote 142.

6.30 Regarding footnote 160, the United States requests that the Panel refer to and cite the United States' rebuttal regarding China's letters of credit argument.

6.31 The Panel included in footnote 160 a reference to the United States' rebuttal argument on China's letters of credit argument.

6.32 Regarding footnote 176, the United States requests that for completeness the Panel include the United States' arguments made in its second written submission at paragraphs 103 to 115.

6.33 The Panel does not find it necessary to reflect the requested references to additional United States' arguments in this particular footnote, as these arguments are not specifically summarized in the paragraph to which footnote 176 is attached.

6.34 Regarding footnote 210, the United States requests that the Panel include a citation to relevant United States' arguments made in its second written submission.

6.35 The Panel does not find it necessary to refer to the United States' second written submission in relation to paragraph 7.157 as this paragraph summarizes the response given by the United States to question No. 39(a) by the Panel. However, the Panel modified footnote 210 so as to include a reference to the United States' complete response to Panel question No. 39(a).

6.36 Regarding paragraph 7.209 (and also paragraphs 7.238, 7.299, 7.334 and 7.360), the United States notes that paragraph 7.209 identifies the alleged requirements challenged by the United States. The United States requests that new footnotes be added for each requirement to reflect the United States' arguments as set forth in its submissions. The United States further requests that the Panel modify its description of the issuer, terminal equipment and acquirer requirements to reflect accurately the scope of the United States' claims concerning these requirements. Finally, the United States requests that the Panel make corresponding changes to the subheadings that appear directly under paragraphs 7.238, 7.299, 7.334 and 7.360.

6.37 The Panel added a new footnote at the beginning of paragraph 7.209 to include appropriate references to the United States' submissions and clarified in the first sub-paragraph that the short names for the requirements were chosen by the Panel. We note that the concise descriptions given in paragraph 7.209 of the issuer, terminal equipment and acquirer requirements are those used by the United States in its own submissions, as is clear from the references included in the new footnote. In the light of this, we decline the request to add further elements to these descriptions along the lines proposed by the United States. We recall in this regard that the precise scope of the United States' claims concerning the issuer, terminal equipment and acquirer requirements is discussed in Section VII.E.2(a)-(c) of the Interim Report. As we did not modify the relevant descriptions in paragraph 7.209, but for one editorial change, we also did not make the consequential changes sought by the United States to paragraphs 7.238, 7.299 and 7.334 (except for one corresponding editorial change). In the subheading following paragraph 7.360, we added a missing word, as requested by the United States.

6.38 Regarding paragraph 7.227, the United States requests that the Panel include the concluding sentence from footnote 282 as the new last sentence in paragraph 7.227, and include a new footnote that refers to the United States' response to Panel question No. 70.

6.39 The Panel modified paragraph 7.227 and included a new footnote to reflect the requested change.

6.40 Regarding paragraph 7.228, the United States requests that the Panel modify the eigth sentence to replace the reference to measures "that are currently in force", with a reference that the measures "were in force at the time of panel establishment". The United States submits that the Panel itself referred in paragraphs 7.227 and 7.228 to the time of the panel's establishment as the relevant point in time. It submits further that the Appellate Body in its recent Report on *China – Raw Materials* (paragraphs 260-261) confirmed that the date of panel establishment is the relevant point in time for a panel's analysis.

6.41 The Panel incorporated the United States' suggested change.

6.42 Regarding paragraph 7.289, the United States requests that, at the end of the second sentence, the Panel add specified references to the United States' panel request and written submissions.

6.43 The Panel added a footnote to paragraph 7.289 to include appropriate references to the United States' panel request and written submissions.

6.44 Regarding paragraph 7.290, China comments that the Panel appears to engage in a substantive examination of Document No. 94. China points out that the Panel in paragraph 7.229 states that it declines to take Document No. 94 into account and will not consider it any further. China submits that it is unclear, therefore, why the Panel engaged in this analysis. China suggests that the Panel omit any discussion of Document No. 94.

6.45 The United States responds that the Panel's discussion of Document No. 94 provides useful and important context for the Panel's analysis of the United States' claims. The United States therefore requests that the Panel not omit this discussion.

6.46 In the light of the parties' comments, the Panel finds it appropriate to clarify the relationship of paragraph 7.290 with paragraph 7.229. We therefore made changes to paragraph 7.290 that take into account more clearly and explicitly the Panel's statements in paragraphs 7.221-7.229. We also made a consequential change to footnote 380 of the Interim Report.

6.47 Regarding paragraphs 7.367, 7.368, 7.371, 7.507(d) and 7.606, China requests that the Panel remove findings on the applicability of certain measures to the processing of RMB-denominated payment cards that are issued *and* used in Hong Kong, or issued *and* used in Macao. China considers that the United States, in its panel request, limited the scope of the relevant claims under Articles XVI and XVII of the GATS to (i) those RMB payment card transactions taking place in Macao or Hong Kong using payment cards issued in China, and (ii) those RMB payment card transactions taking place in China using payment cards issued in China, Hong Kong, or Macao. It considers that the panel request does not refer to those transactions where the payment card is both issued *and* used in either Hong Kong or Macao. China requests that the Panel modify the Report to find that this third category of transactions is not within the terms of reference, or, otherwise, to reflect in the Final Report China's position that these transactions are not within the Panel's terms of reference.

6.48 The United States requests the Panel to reject China's request. As an initial matter, the United States argues that China provides no legal basis under Article 6.2 of the DSU to support its request. In addition, the United States considers that there is no basis to read language in its panel request as excluding transactions where the payment card is both issued *and* used in either Hong

Kong or Macao. In this respect, the United States notes that its panel request specifies that "China ... requires the handling by CUP of all RMB transactions in Macao or Hong Kong using payment cards issued in Mainland China, as well as any RMB transactions in Mainland China using RMB payment cards issued in Hong Kong, China or Macao, China". In addition, the United States notes the statements in its panel request that "China also requires that all cross-bank or inter-bank transactions involving payment cards be handled through CUP. China prohibits the use of non-CUP payment cards for cross-region or cross bank or inter-bank transactions". The United States also submits that its panel request identifies the particular instruments through which China implements the measures.

6.49 The Panel recalls that the United States' panel request supplies a brief narrative description of the impugned measures. As noted by the parties, the panel request states in relevant part that "China ... requires the handling by CUP of all RMB transactions in Macao or Hong Kong using payment cards issued in Mainland China, as well as any RMB transactions in Mainland China using RMB payment cards issued in Hong Kong, China or Macao, China".[19]

6.50 Because the panel request refers only to RMB payment card transactions taking place in Macao or Hong Kong using payment cards issued in China, and to RMB payment card transactions taking place in China using payment cards issued in Hong Kong, or Macao, the Panel modified its findings to clarify that they do not refer to those transactions where the payment card is both issued *and* used in either Hong Kong or Macao. The panel request does not refer explicitly to the latter type of transactions, nor does it indicate, through the use of words such as "e.g.", "in particular", "inter alia", etc., that the types of transactions mentioned are but a subset of the relevant transactions. The United States further argues that its panel request specifies that China also requires that all cross-bank or inter-bank transactions be handled through CUP, and that China prohibits the use of non-CUP payment cards for cross-region or cross-bank or inter-bank transactions. Consistent with the fact that these alleged requirements are specified separately from the "Hong Kong/Macao requirements" in the panel request, the Panel considered allegations of the United States concerning cross-bank or inter-bank transactions and cross-bank or inter-bank prohibitions separately from the alleged Hong Kong/Macao requirements. Consequently, the Panel modified paragraphs 7.367 (including new footnote 469), 7.368, 7.371, 7.507(d), 7.578, 7.606, 7.621, 7.622 (including new footnote 804), 7.623, 7.624, 7.627, 7.636, and 8.1(d) (iv); and footnote 800. In doing so, we consider that our Report adequately reflects the United States' view that transactions where the payment card is both issued *and* used in either Hong Kong or Macao form part of its claims.[20]

---

[19] WT/DS413/2, p. 2.

[20] See Interim Panel Report, paras. 7.364, 7.367, 7.369, 7.378, 7.396, 7.399 and 7.612.

6.51 Regarding paragraphs 7.716, 7.727 and 7.740, the United States requests that the Panel modify them so as to reflect that its claims and arguments concerning the issuer, terminal equipment and acquirer requirements explicitly cover three-party models. The United States notes that in the aforementioned paragraphs, the Panel states that the United States has not specifically addressed three-party networks in the context of issuer, terminal equipment and acquirer requirements. The United States further points out that the Panel in paragraphs 7.38-7.45 recognized that the United States argued that the three-party model was included in the services at issue. Finally, the United States refers the Panel to certain arguments it made in the course of the proceedings.

6.52 The Panel does not see any inconsistency between the statements in paragraphs 7.716, 7.727 and 7.740, on the one hand, and paragraphs 7.38-7.45, on the other. There is no suggestion in paragraphs 7.716, 7.727 or 7.740 that the United States' claims concerning the issuer, terminal equipment and acquirer requirements fail to cover three-party models. Having said this, for greater clarity and accuracy, we slightly modified paragraphs 7.727 and 7.740. In paragraph 7.716, we added one of the arguments to which the United States made reference and made appropriate consequential changes. Further consequential changes were made to paragraphs 7.613 and 7.620.

VII. FINDINGS

A. Preliminary Ruling Under Article 6.2 of the DSU

7.1 As noted in paragraphs 1.6-1.8 above, on 5 July 2011[21] China submitted a request for a preliminary ruling to the Panel with respect to the consistency of certain aspects of the United States' panel request with Article 6.2 of the Understanding on Rules and Procedures Governing the Settlement of Disputes (the "DSU"). China argued that the United States' panel request fails to provide a brief summary of the legal basis of the complaint sufficient to present the problem clearly in two respects: first, by failing to explain how the definition of "electronic payment services" relates to China's specific commitments in any of the three subsectors identified in the panel request; and second, by failing to indicate which mode or modes of supply the United States considers to be at issue.[22] China argued that these deficiencies are central to all of the United States' claims and should be addressed at the earliest opportunity in the interest of due process before either party filed its first submission. The United States requested the Panel to decline China's request to make findings in

[21] China's Letter of 5 July 2011.
[22] China's request for a preliminary ruling.

advance of either party filing its first submission.[23] The United States further challenged the substance of China's request.[24]

7.2 After consulting with the parties, the Panel decided to issue a preliminary ruling to the parties on 7 September 2011, prior to receiving the United States' first written submission. The Panel observed that this would take into account China's concerns regarding the implications of the ruling on the substance of the case without causing additional delays in the proceedings. At the request of the Panel, the Chairperson of the DSB circulated the ruling to the World Trade Organization (WTO) membership on 30 September 2011[25].

7.3 As set out in further detail in its preliminary ruling, the Panel concluded that China had failed to establish that the United States' panel request is inconsistent with Article 6.2 of the DSU on the grounds that it does not provide a brief summary of the legal basis sufficient to present the problem clearly. The Panel found that the text of the panel request makes it clear that each of the requirements allegedly imposed by China is considered by the United States to be in breach of Articles XVI:1 and XVI:2 and Article XVII of the General Agreement on Trade in Services (GATS). The Panel also concluded that the United States' panel request considered as a whole does not need to explain further how the challenged measures are inconsistent with China's commitments under the relevant modes of supply. Accordingly, the Panel rejected China's preliminary objection of 5 July 2011 in its entirety and stated that it would continue its consideration of the case in accordance with the timetable that had been set for these proceedings.

7.4 The Panel's preliminary ruling circulated as document WT/DS413/4 dated 30 September 2011 forms an integral part of the present findings.

B. General Issues

1. Burden of proof

7.5 The general rule on burden of proof in WTO dispute settlement is that a party claiming a violation of a provision of a covered agreement by another Member must assert and prove its claim.[26] Moreover, any party that asserts a fact, whether claimant or respondent, is responsible for providing proof thereof. This conforms to the generally accepted canon of evidence in civil law, common law, and, in fact, in most jurisdictions, that the burden of proof rests upon the party, whether complaining or responding, who asserts the affirmative of a particular claim or defence. If that party adduces evidence sufficient to raise a

---

[23] United States' Letter of 6 July 2011.

[24] United States' response to China's request for a preliminary ruling; United States' comments to China's reply.

[25] WT/DS413/4.

[26] Appellate Body Report, *US – Wool Shirts and Blouses*, p. 16, DSR 1997:I, 323 at p. 337.

presumption that what is claimed is true, the burden then shifts to the other party, who will fail unless it adduces sufficient evidence to rebut the presumption.[27]

7.6 Similarly, in WTO dispute settlement, once a complaining party has made a *prima facie* case, the burden of proof moves to the responding party, which must in turn counter or refute the claimed inconsistency.[28] The Appellate Body has stated that "a *prima facie* case is one which, in the absence of effective refutation by the defending party, requires a panel, as a matter of law, to rule in favour of the complaining party presenting the *prima facie* case."[29] A *prima facie* case must be based on evidence and legal argument put forward by the complaining party in respect of each of the elements of the claim.[30] The amount and type of evidence that will be required will necessarily vary from case to case.[31]

7.7 Generally, the complainant in a given case initially bears the burden of proof to establish a *prima facie* case of inconsistency of a measure with a provision of a WTO covered agreement. In this dispute, therefore, the United States bears the initial burden to establish a *prima facie* case that China's measures are inconsistent with the cited provisions of Articles XVI and XVII of the GATS.

2. *Treaty interpretation*

7.8 Article 3.2 of the DSU directs panels to clarify the existing provisions of the covered agreements "in accordance with customary rules of interpretation of public international law". It is well settled that the rules codified in Articles 31 and 32 of the Vienna Convention on the Law of Treaties (Vienna Convention) are such customary rules.[32] These provisions read as follows:

> Article 31: General rule of interpretation
>
> 1. A treaty shall be interpreted in good faith in accordance with the ordinary meaning to be given to the terms of the treaty in their context and in the light of its object and purpose.
>
> 2. The context for the purpose of the interpretation of a treaty shall comprise, in addition to the text, including its preamble and annexes:
>
> (a) any agreement relating to the treaty which was made between all the parties in connection with the conclusion of the treaty;

---

[27] Appellate Body Report, *US – Wool Shirts and Blouses*, p. 14, DSR 1997:I, 323 at p. 335.

[28] Appellate Body Report, *EC – Hormones*, para. 98.

[29] Appellate Body Report, *EC – Hormones,* para. 104.

[30] Appellate Body Report, *US – Gambling*, para. 140.

[31] Appellate Body Report, *US – Wool Shirts and Blouses*, p. 14, DSR 1997:I, 323 at p. 335.

[32] Appellate Body Reports, *US – Gasoline*, p. 17, DSR 1996:I, 3 at pp. 15-16; *India – Patents (US)*, para. 45; and *US – Shrimp*, para. 114.

(b) any instrument which was made by one or more parties in connection with the conclusion of the treaty and accepted by the other parties as an instrument related to the treaty.

3. There shall be taken into account, together with the context:

(a) any subsequent agreement between the parties regarding the interpretation of the treaty or the application of its provisions;

(b) any subsequent practice in the application of the treaty which establishes the agreement of the parties regarding its interpretation;

(c) any relevant rules of international law applicable in the relations between the parties.

4. A special meaning shall be given to a term if it is established that the parties so intended.

Article 32: Supplementary means of interpretation

Recourse may be had to supplementary means of interpretation, including the preparatory work of the treaty and the circumstances of its conclusion, in order to confirm the meaning resulting from the application of article 31, or to determine the meaning when the interpretation according to article 31:

(a) leaves the meaning ambiguous or obscure; or

(b) leads to a result which is manifestly absurd or unreasonable.[33]

7.9 Article XX:3 of the GATS provides that WTO Members' "Schedules of specific commitments shall be annexed to this Agreement and shall form an integral part thereof." Consistent with Article 3.2 of the DSU, GATS Schedules must be interpreted according to the "customary rules of interpretation of public international law". In *US – Gambling*, the Appellate Body confirmed that:

> [T]he task of identifying the meaning of a concession in a GATS Schedule, like the task of interpreting any other treaty text, involves identifying the *common intention* of Members. […] we consider that the meaning of the United States' GATS Schedule must be determined according to the rules codified in Article 31 and, to the extent appropriate, Article 32 of the Vienna Convention.[34] (emphasis original)

7.10 Accordingly, the Panel shall apply these principles in interpreting the relevant provisions of the covered agreements at issue in this dispute.

[33] The Vienna Convention on the Law of Treaties (the "Vienna Convention"), done at Vienna, 23 May 1969, 1155 U.N.T.S. 331; 8 International Legal Materials 679.

[34] Appellate Body Report, *US – Gambling*, para. 160.

C. *The Services at Issue*

7.11 The Panel begins its analysis with an examination of the services at issue. We first consider the essential features of payment card transactions[35], based on the parties' submissions. Thereafter, we turn to the scope of the services at issue, addressing in particular areas of disagreement between the parties, namely (a) whether the services at issue cover the "three-party model" in addition to the "four-party model"; (b) whether the services at issue include the services supplied by third-party processors; and (c) whether the services at issue are single/integrated services.

1. *Payment card transactions*[36]

7.12 A typical transaction involving the purchase of a good or a service entails a payment to the merchant by the consumer. Transactions often involve payment cards.[37] A "payment card" includes a bank card, credit card, charge card, debit card, check card, automated teller machine (ATM) card, prepaid card, and other similar card or payment or money transmission product or access device, and the unique account number associated with that card or product or access device.[38] Payment cards typically fall into one of three categories, depending on the timing of the payment: "pay later" cards (e.g. credit and charge cards); "pay now" cards (e.g. debit cards); and "pay before" cards (e.g. prepaid or stored-value cards). [39]

---

[35] Both parties have used the expression "payment card transactions" when describing the transactions at issue in this dispute. See, e.g. United States' response to China's request for a preliminary ruling, para. 44 and China's first written submission, para. 15. The Panel will also use this term in its Report.

[36] The information used to prepare this section comes from the parties' submissions. More information about the technical and commercial aspects of payment card transactions is found in the submissions made by the United States than in the submissions made by China, which explains the frequent reference to the sources provided by the former. We note in that regard that in paragraph 15 of its first written submission, China states that "China does not substantially disagree with those descriptions insofar as they go. China will therefore try to avoid repeating what the United States has already described, to the extent that China agrees with those accounts".

[37] The Panel considers that information regarding the different types of cards and their functioning is relevant notably for the discussion of classification of the services at issue (see Section VII.D of this report).

[38] United States' request for the establishment of a panel, fn. 2; response to China's request for a preliminary ruling, para. 35. The United States' response to China's request for a preliminary ruling was incorporated into the United States' first written submission (See United States' first written submission, para. 9). We note that China has used extensively the expression "payment card" in its submissions, and has not contested the definition provided by the United States in its request for the establishment of a panel.

[39] US SEC Amendment No. 4 to Form S-1 Registration Statement Under Securities Act of 1933, Visa Inc. IPO Prospectus, February 25, 2008, (Visa IPO Prospectus), Exhibit US-3, p. 128; US SEC Form 10-K, Visa 2010 Annual Report (as of September 30, 2010), (Visa 2010 Annual Report), Exhibit US-4, pp. 6-7; US SEC Form 10-K, MasterCard Incorporated Annual Report, for fiscal year ended December 31, 2010, (MasterCard 2010 Annual Report), Exhibit US-6, p. 6; and Federal Financial Institutions Examination Council (FFIEC), Retail Payment Systems, IT Examination

7.13 A "pay later" payment occurs after receiving the goods or services, and typically involves the use of a credit card. A credit card enables a consumer to access a credit line account at a financial institution. In general, credit cards have revolving credit arrangements that allow card holders to make purchases and be billed later. Most credit card accounts allow the card holder to carry a balance from one billing cycle to the next and make a minimum payment in each billing cycle, rather than requiring payment of the full balance. A charge card is a specific kind of credit card that has a short-term, fixed-period credit arrangement. The balance on a charge card account is payable in full when the statement is received and cannot be rolled over from one billing cycle to the next.[40] A "pay now" payment, which typically involves the use of a debit card, occurs at the time of purchase of goods or services. A debit card payment is linked to an existing transaction account at a financial institution. Debit cards are either online (i.e. PIN-based)[41] or off-line (i.e. signature-based). Debit card transactions are authorized in real time at the point-of-sale (POS) terminal using the same electronic funds transfer networks that handle ATM transactions.[42] The term "pay before" refers to payments for goods or services with prepaid or stored-value cards, loaded with funds before the purchase of goods or services occurs. The account associated with the prepaid debit card may be the liability of a financial institution. Prepaid cards are generally issued to persons who deposit funds into an account of the issuer, while stored-value cards do not typically involve a deposit of funds as the value is prepaid and stored directly on the cards.[43]

7.14 Payment card transactions involve several entities: issuing institutions (or issuers), acquiring institutions (or acquirers), payment card companies[44], and settlement banks.[45] Issuers, usually banks, are the entities that make payment cards available to card holders. Issuers solicit card holders and establish

Handbook (February 2010), (FFIEC IT Examination Handbook), Exhibit US-12, pp. 17, 20-21, and 24.

40 FFIEC IT Examination Handbook, Exhibit US-12, p. 18; and BIS Red Book 2003, Payment Systems in the United States, (BIS Red Book 2003), Exhibit US-11, p. 440.

41 PIN stands for Personal Identification Number.

42 FFIEC IT Examination Handbook, Exhibit US-12, pp. 20-22; and BIS Red Book 2003, Exhibit US-11, p. 440.

43 FFIEC IT Examination Handbook, Exhibit US-12, p. 24.

44 Throughout this section (paras. 7.13-7.25) on payment card transactions, and only for the sake of this section, the Panel refers to "payment card companies", defined by the Bank for International Settlement as "a company which owns trademarks of payment cards (credit, debit or prepaid cards) and may also provide a number of marketing, processing or other services to institutions issuing its cards." (BIS, Committee on Payments and Settlement Systems, A Glossary of Terms used in Payments and Settlement Systems, March 2003, (« BIS glossary »), Exhibit US-68, p. 16). We are using this term, rather than "EPS suppliers" and "network operators" as done by the United States and China, respectively, in order not to prejudge the discussion in subsequent sections. We are also using the term "payment card services" in this section to refer to the services supplied by these companies, and "payment card networks" to refer to the infrastructure and networks owned and operated by payment card companies.

45 Visa IPO Prospectus, Exhibit US-3, pp. 129-130.

applicable card holder terms, including individual credit limits, fees, interest rates and payment schedules. Payment cards commonly feature the logo or trademark of the issuer as well as the logo or trademark of the relevant payment card company or network. An institution seeking to issue cards must be capable of supplying card-based payment services or must use a payment card company to do so.[46] Issuers agree to adhere to rules specified by the payment card company that allow the payment card company to process transactions that use the cards issued by the bank. The issuer authorizes transactions at POS terminals, collects payment from the card holder, and transmits the funds through the relevant inter-bank payment channel for settlement of payment obligations incurred by the card holder.[47]

7.15 Acquirers sign up merchants to accept payment cards for a specific payment card company. In other words, they "acquire" transactions for a specific payment card company and network. Acquirers, often banks, maintain merchant accounts, handle relations with the merchant, receive all bank transactions from the merchant, ensure that payments are properly credited to the merchant, and provide the merchant with connectivity to the relevant payment network.[48] Like issuers, acquirers must be capable of supplying card-based payment services or must use a payment card company to do so.[49] Acquirers must adhere to specific standards, rules and procedures (typically set by the payment card company) governing the processing of transactions in the payment card network for which transactions have been acquired.

7.16 Issuers and acquirers may choose to partially or totally outsource the services they supply in connection with payment card transactions to so-called "third-party" processors.[50] Broadly speaking, these third-party processors can be categorized as merchant and issuer processors. Merchant and issuer processors provide payment-related services on behalf of acquirers and issuers, respectively. In so doing, they interconnect to, and interact with, the payment card company (or network). Third-party processors provide a potentially broad range of services.[51]

7.17 Payment card companies own, manage and promote payment brands, which they licence to their primary customers (i.e. issuers and acquirers). They approve card design, specifications and other requirements in connection with card issuance and acceptance.[52] Payment card companies establish rules and standards for their product platforms and payment networks, including eligibility

---

[46] United States response to China's request for a preliminary ruling, para. 43.

[47] Visa IPO Prospectus, Exhibit US-3, pp. 129-130.

[48] *Ibid.*

[49] United States response to China's request for a preliminary ruling. para. 43.

[50] Visa IPO Prospectus, Exhibit US-3, p. 130; and China's first written submission, para. 30.

[51] Visa IPO Prospectus, Exhibit US-3, p. 130 (under the title "Functions performed in connection with payment card transactions"); China's first written submission, paras. 31 and 32; and United States' response to Panel question No. 36(a), para. 93.

[52] United States' response to China's request for a preliminary ruling, para. 44.

for participation in the network, product platform features and functionality, merchant acceptance standards, and dispute and arbitration processes. They provide and operate the processing infrastructure and network necessary for the execution of payments via payment cards. They typically transfer authorization and clearing data and help settle funds between issuers and acquirers.[53] Payment card companies also provide issuers and acquirers with certain guarantees, including for example, indemnification for any settlement loss that issuers or acquirers may suffer due to the failure of another issuer or acquirer to fund its daily settlement obligations.[54]

7.18 There are two main business models used in card-based electronic payment transactions. These are often referred to as "open-loop", or "four-party" models, and "closed-loop", or "three-party" models.[55] In the four-party model, different entities handle the issuing of payment cards, the acquisition of transactions and the actual processing of transactions. Payment card companies in this model do not issue payment cards, nor do they acquire transactions with those payment cards. Payment card companies own and operate the networks that connect issuers and acquirers, and process transactions made in connection with payment cards. In the four-party model, the payment card company does not interact directly with either the card holder or the merchant.[56] It is the issuer and the acquirer that interact directly with, respectively, the card holder and the merchant.[57] Moreover, in four-party models, it is the issuer that extends credit to the card holder, not the payment card company.[58]

7.19 In the three-party model, the payment card company itself is responsible for issuing cards, handling the acquisition of transactions, and processing the transactions. In recent years, certain payment card companies that operate three-party models have also developed relationships with banks and other institutions, allowing them to issue these cards and acquire transactions for these cards' networks, thereby emulating certain aspects of the four-party model.[59]

---

[53] Visa IPO Prospectus, Exhibit US-3, p. 131; Visa 2010 Annual Report, Exhibit US-4, pp. 5 and 7-13; *A Time of Change: A World of Opportunities,* MasterCard 2009 Annual Report, Exhibit US-5, pp. 4 and 7-9; UBS Securities LLC, *Visa 201: No Better Way to 'Play the Swipe'* (June 25, 2008), Exhibit US-10, pp. 28-30; and Bank for International Settlements (BIS) Committee on Payment and Settlement Systems (CPSS) *Clearing and Settlement Arrangements for Retail Payments in Selected Countries*, September 2000, Exhibit CHN-1, pages 2-6.

[54] Visa 2010 Annual Report, Exhibit US-4, pp. 30-31; and MasterCard 2010 Annual Report, Exhibit US-6, p. 38.

[55] Visa IPO Prospectus, Exhibit US-3, p. 128.

[56] Visa IPO Prospectus, Exhibit US-3, pp. 128-129; and MasterCard 2010 Annual Report, Exhibit US-6, pp. 4 and 7.

[57] Visa IPO Prospectus, Exhibit US-3, p. 129.

[58] *Ibid.*, p. 128.

[59] Visa IPO Prospectus, Exhibit US-3, p. 128; US SEC Form 10-K, American Express Company Annual Report, for the fiscal year ended November 30, 2010, ("American Express 2010 Annual Report"), Exhibit US-7, pp. 4-11; and US SEC Form 10-K, Discover Financial Services Annual Report, for the fiscal year ended November 30, 2010, ("Discover 2010 Annual Report"), Exhibit US-8, pp. 1-4.

7.20 The processing of transactions, whether in connection with four-party or three-party models, encompasses both (1) "front-end processing" (which serves to authenticate and authorize transactions), and (2) "back-end processing" (which serves, essentially, to clear and settle transactions).[60]

7.21 Front-end processing occurs at the time of the transaction. A card-based payment transaction can be initiated either at a terminal (e.g. a merchant's POS) or remotely via e-mail, telephone or internet. When a card holder presents a payment card to pay for a transaction, the merchant uses its POS terminal to transmit a request for authorization to its acquirer or a merchant (third-party) processor. The acquirer or its third-party processor determines the type of transaction (debit or credit), and the particular payment card network through which the transaction should be routed, and then forwards that request to the relevant payment card company.

7.22 After the payment card company receives the authorization request, it undertakes several tasks. Under a four-party model, it ascertains the type of transaction (e.g. credit or debit), determines various transaction parameters (e.g. location and type of merchant), identifies the issuer, and then routes the authorization request to the issuer. At that point, the issuer identifies the card holder's account and decides whether to authorize the transaction after confirming that the card is authentic, the account is in good standing, and the account limit is not exceeded (in the case of a credit transaction) or that sufficient funds are available (in the case of a debit transaction). The issuer then authorizes or rejects the transaction based on these validations as well as the card holder's record. The authorization (or rejection) information is sent back to the merchant via the payment card network. If the acquirer and the issuer are one and the same, a transaction is referred to as an "on-us" transaction. If the transaction has been authorized, the payment card company receives the approved transaction information. Then the payment card company returns the authorization information to the acquirer, or to the merchant processor or merchant, as the case may be. Finally, when the merchant receives the authorization, it completes the sale.

7.23 Under the three-party model, the payment card company, which is also the issuer and the acquirer, determines various transaction parameters, identifies the card holder's account and decides whether to authorize the transaction. The authorization (or rejection) information is sent by the payment card company directly to the merchant.

7.24 Back-end processing occurs at the time of the transaction or at a later point in time. Merchants submit transaction information for clearing and payment to acquirers, which forward this information to the appropriate entity

[60] United States response to China's request for a preliminary ruling, paras. 49-53; and China's first written submission, para. 20. China also makes reference to "back-end processing" (China's first written submission, para. 31).

(e.g. a payment card company in the case of a typical "four-party model" transaction) for purposes of establishing net settlement positions. The payment card company aggregates and processes all the information and produces a daily report of the net and debit positions of issuing and acquiring financial institutions. The settlement bank relies on the report generated by the payment card company but does not perform any data processing itself. The payment card company organizes this information by the respective card-issuing bank, and then forwards the transaction information to the participating entities specifying those transactions that were cleared and the net amounts to be paid (by issuers) and received (by acquirers). The transfer of money from the card holder to the issuer and from the acquirer to the merchant is carried out in accordance with the contractual agreements between those parties. Under the three-party model, there are no inter-bank transactions, because the payment card company acts as payment card network and processor, card issuer and merchant acquirer. In this case, it is the payment card company that debits the card holder's account and credits the merchant's account. [61]

2. *The services at issue*

7.25 The United States' request for the establishment of a panel specifies that the present dispute concerns "certain restrictions and requirements maintained by China affecting electronic payment services for payment card transactions and the suppliers of those services (electronic payment services suppliers)" (footnotes omitted).[62] It describes "electronic payment services" and a "payment card" as follows:

> "Electronic payment services" involve the services through which transactions involving payment cards (as defined below) are processed and through which transfers of funds between institutions participating in the transactions are managed and facilitated. Suppliers of electronic payment services supply, directly or indirectly, a system that typically includes the following: the processing infrastructure, network, and rules and procedures that facilitate, manage, and enable transaction information and payment flows and which provide system integrity, stability and financial risk reduction; the process and coordination of approving or declining a transaction, with approval generally permitting a purchase to be finalized or cash to be disbursed or exchanged; the delivery of transaction information among participating entities; the calculation, determination, and reporting of the net financial position of relevant institutions for all transactions that have been authorized; and the facilitation,

[61] American Express 2010 Annual Report, Exhibit US-7, pp. 4-11; Discover 2010 Annual Report, Exhibit US-8, pp. 1-4; and China's first written submission, fn. 7.

[62] United States' request for the establishment of a panel, para, 1.

management and/or other participation in the transfer of net payments owed among participating institutions.[63]

A "payment card" includes a bank card, credit card, charge card, debit card, check card, automated teller machine (ATM) card, prepaid card, and other similar card or payment or money transmission product or access device, and the unique account number associated with that card or product or access device.[64]

7.26 According to the United States, electronic payment services (EPS) are at the centre of all payment card transactions, and without these services the transactions could not occur.[65] EPS provide an efficient, timely and reliable means to facilitate the transmission of funds from the holders of payment cards who purchase goods or services to the individuals or businesses that supply them. EPS suppliers receive, check and transmit the information that the parties need to conduct the transactions, and manage, facilitate, and enable the transmission of funds between participating entities. According to the United States, the rules and procedures established by the EPS supplier give the payment system stability and integrity, and enable it to efficiently handle net flows of money among the institutions involved in card payments.[66] EPS suppliers also provide their customers with certain guarantees to ensure the integrity of the electronic payment services, including, for example, instances where customers fail to honour payment cards or where issuers or acquirers fail to fund obligations.[67] In the United States' view, the processing infrastructure, network, and rules and procedures, which facilitate, manage, and enable transaction information and payment flows, and which provide system integrity, stability and financial risk reduction, are key components of electronic payment services.[68]

7.27 China submits that the services at issue, as described in the United States' request for the establishment of a panel, relate to inter-bank payment card transactions, i.e. transactions where the financial institution that issues the payment card to the card holder is unrelated to the financial institution that acquires the payment card transaction from the merchant.[69] These financial institutions (i.e. issuers and acquirers) authorize, clear, and settle inter-bank payment card transactions by obtaining these services from the operators of inter-bank payment card networks.[70] China considers that an inter-bank payment card network is a telecommunications and data-processing infrastructure through which a network operator provides certain authorization, clearing, and settlement

[63] *Ibid.*, fn. 1.

[64] United States' request for the establishment of a panel, fn. 2.

[65] United States' first written submission, para. 25.

[66] United States' response to China's request for a preliminary ruling, para. 40.

[67] *Ibid.*, para. 42.

[68] *Ibid.*, para. 45.

[69] China's first written submission, para. 18.

[70] *Ibid.*, para. 22.

services to participating financial institutions.[71] According to China, the operator of the network is not a party to the payment card transaction (which, it argues, is why it is a "four-party" model, not a "five-party" model),[72] but provides financial institutions with an external network for authorizing, clearing, and settling the payment card transactions to which they are parties.[73] The services at issue are what payment card companies describe as their "transaction processing services", consisting of the operation of a "processing infrastructure" that is used to provide certain "core processing services" relating to the "authorization, clearing, and settlement" of payment card transactions. These are, in China's view, "network services", i.e. the services that network operators provide to financial institutions for the purpose of authorizing, clearing, and settling inter-bank payment card transactions.[74]

7.28 The Panel notes first that the services at issue are "electronic payment services for payment card transactions" or, in other words, electronic payment services for transactions with payment cards. We also note that the definition of services at issue provided by the United States includes transactions with payment cards, which the United States defines as including bank cards, credit cards, charge cards, debit cards, check cards, ATM cards, prepaid cards, and other similar cards or payment or money transmission products or access devices, and the unique account number associated with those cards or products or access devices.[75]

7.29 We also observe that the descriptions provided by the parties of the services involved in the processing of payment card transactions do not differ fundamentally. We find confirmation of this observation in China's first written submission, where China states that "the United States has provided lengthy descriptions of the technical and commercial aspects of payment card transactions. China does not substantially disagree with those descriptions, insofar as they go".[76]

7.30 The Panel further notes that China acknowledged that the services at issue are determined by the United States' description in its request for the establishment of a panel and the scope of the challenged measures.[77] Indeed, China does not challenge the fact that the five "elements" described by the

---

71 *Ibid.*

72 *Ibid.*

73 *Ibid.*

74 *Ibid.*, para. 73.

75 United States' request for the establishment of a panel, fn. 2.

76 China's first written submission, para. 15.

77 "The services at issue in this dispute are determined by two factors. (1) the U.S. definition of the services at issue, as set forth in [its] panel request; and (2) the scope and effect of the challenged measures. It is the overlap of these two factors that determines the services at issue. The services at issue cannot be broader than the services that the United States has described in its panel request, and cannot be broader than the services that are actually affected by the challenged measures". (China's first written submission, para. 61).

United States in its panel request correspond to what EPS suppliers – as the United States calls them – or "network operators" – as China prefers to call them – do. In analysing the five elements, China observes that:

> [T]he first element of the "system" - "the processing infrastructure, network, and rules and procedures" - appears to correspond, at least in part, to what payment card companies describe as their telecommunications and data-processing infrastructure;
>
> the second element of the "system" - "the process and coordination of approving or declining a transaction" - appears to correspond to what payment card companies describe as the authorization component of their core data processing services;
>
> the third and fourth elements of the "system" - "the delivery of transaction information among participating entities" and "the calculation, determination, and reporting of the net financial position of relevant institutions for all transactions that have been authorized" - appear to correspond to what payment card companies describe as the clearing component of their core data processing services; and
>
> the fifth element of the "system" - "the facilitation, management and/or other participation in the transfer of net payments owed among participating institutions" - appears to correspond to what payment card companies describe as the settlement component of their core data processing services.[78]

7.31 Moreover, both parties recognize that other institutions, such as issuers, acquirers and settlement banks, also participate in payment card transactions.[79]

7.32 We observe that China did not request that any element of the definitions of the services at issue provided by the United States be eliminated from the dispute. Indeed, while China emphasizes the clearing and settlement aspect of payment card transaction processing, it does not deny that the services at issue encompass other aspects of payment card transaction processing as well. In China's own words:

> However many other services might be at issue in this dispute, clearing and settlement services are plainly among them … Thus, while the United States makes heroic efforts to avoid using the terms "clearing" and "settlement" in the narrative of its submissions, China believes it should be undisputed that the services at issue include clearing and settlement services.[80]

[78] China's first written submission, para. 72.

[79] United States' response to China's request for a preliminary ruling, para. 43; and China's first written submission, para. 20.

[80] China's first written submission, para. 75.

7.33 We also note that the parties agree that the services at issue, as described in the United States' request for the establishment of a panel, do not include the services supplied by issuing and acquiring institutions.[81]

7.34 However, before proceeding further, the Panel would like to clarify two issues on which the parties differ, namely (i) whether the services at issue relate only to "inter-bank payment card transactions"; and (ii) whether the payment card company is a party to the payment card transaction.

7.35 Regarding the first question, we note China's argument that the services at issue relate to inter-bank payment card transactions, defined by China as transactions where the financial institution that issues the payment card to the card holder is unrelated to the financial institution that acquires the payment card transaction from the merchant.[82] As will become clear in the subsequent sections dealing with the third-party model and third-party processors, we do not agree with this argument by China. In our view, the services at issue relate not only to inter-bank payment card transactions, as defined by China, but also to payment card transactions where the issuing financial institution is related to - or can indeed be the same as - the acquiring financial institution. This is the case, for example, of "on-us" payment card transactions, as well as transactions carried out under the three-party model.

7.36 Turning to the second question, China argues that the "operator of the network" (or the payment card company, as we have called it) is not a party to the payment card transaction (which is why it is a "four-party" model, not a "five-party" model); rather, the "operator of the network" provides financial institutions with an external network for authorizing, clearing, and settling the payment card transactions to which they are parties.[83] We do not agree with this argument by China. In our view, as evidenced by the description of payment card transactions provided in paragraphs 7.13 to 7.24 above, payment card companies or networks are indeed a party to the payment card transaction. This is not only the case with networks operating under the "three-party" model, but also with other networks generally operating under the "four-party" model. Among other things, these operators own the payment card brand; set rules, standards, and procedures by which issuers and acquirers must abide; and provide authorization, clearing and settlement services to issuers and acquirers. More importantly, they guarantee the transactions and get paid by issuers and acquirers for the services supplied.

7.37 In concluding, we recall that the services at issue in this dispute are determined by the description in the United States' panel request. In our view, the services at issue are therefore electronic payment services for all types of

---

[81] In its response to Panel question No. 43, the United States indicated that "[a]s a threshold matter, classification of issuing and acquiring services is not necessary for the panel's resolution of this dispute, as the U.S. claims do not pertain to this service".

[82] China's first written submission, para. 18.

[83] *Ibid.*, para. 22.

payment card transactions. These are the services the Panel must focus on, regardless of the labels used by the parties to refer to them. Hereinafter, we will use the expression "electronic payment services for transactions involving the use of various types of payment cards" (EPS) and "electronic payment service suppliers" (EPS suppliers) to refer to, respectively, the services at issue and the service suppliers supplying those services. We find support for this terminology in the fact that: (i) China does not deny that the dispute is about services related to "payment card transactions"; (ii) transactions with all types of payment cards are envisaged; (iii) these services are currently conducted exclusively through "electronic" means; and (iv) as will become clearer in the discussion on classification (Section E below), the services at issue are, in our view, "payment services".

3. *Whether the services at issue cover the three-party model in addition to the four-party model*

7.38 China argues that the definition of the services at issue proposed by the United States is premised on a four-party model.[84] The services at issue do not include the supply of services in three-party models and, therefore, the Panel should not reach findings on the supply of services under this model. Focusing on the five elements described by the United States, China argues that the definition of the services at issue proposed by the United States is based on the notion that there are "participating institutions" or "participating entities" involved in the "system". The essential feature of this "system", according to China, is to authorize, clear, and settle payment card transactions among "participating institutions". In a three-party model, China argues, there is no need to authorize, clear and settle payment card transactions among different financial institutions, because the issuer and the acquirer are the same entity. Because there are no inter-bank transactions in the three-party model, there is no need for the operator of a three-party payment card system to obtain network services from a network operator.[85]

7.39 The United States argues that the services at issue cover services supplied in three-party models. For the United States, three-party model transactions include both those EPS systems that perform the functions of issuer and acquirer internally and "on-us" transactions occurring in a four-party system where the issuer and the acquirer are the same entity. In a three-party transaction, the role of the EPS supplier may vary by circumstance, but its activities would nevertheless fall within the definition of EPS provided in the panel request. The United States submits that, in some markets and systems, three-party model transactions are processed over the EPS provider's network in the same manner as transactions involving a different issuer and acquirer. Even if the transaction

84 China's second written submission, para. 104.
85 China's second written submission, paras. 104-107.

is processed internally and not over the EPS network, it is the EPS provider that developed the payment product (card program), it is the EPS provider's intellectual property that enables the switching of the transaction and supports the electronic payment process, the transaction is governed by the EPS provider's rules and procedures, and the transaction is secured by the EPS provider's risk management and fraud protections. According to the United States, the fact that certain payment card transactions may occur where the issuing institution and acquiring institution are the same does not change the definition or scope of the service being provided. Even in three-party models, the United States argues, the EPS supplier still must conduct an authorization of the transaction, which includes providing information such as the merchant code, POS terminal ID, country codes of the issuer, acquirer, and merchant, transaction currency, etc. The United States further submits that, in many instances, it "would be virtually impossible to distinguish "on-us" three-party transactions from four-party transactions".[86]

7.40 Replying to a Panel question, Australia, the European Union, Guatemala, and Korea submitted that the services at issue should be classified in the same subsector irrespective of whether they are supplied under the three-party or the four-party model.[87] According to the European Union, China's commitments refer to the services, not to the participants in the transaction; Guatemala is of the view that the participants in the supply of the service do not change the nature of the service.[88]

7.41 The Panel recalls that the services at issue, as defined in the panel request, consist of a "system" that "typically includes" five elements, namely (i) the processing infrastructure, network, and rules and procedures that facilitate, manage, and enable transaction information and payment flows and which provide system integrity, stability and financial risk reduction; (ii) the process and coordination of approving or declining a transaction, with approval generally permitting a purchase to be finalized or cash to be disbursed or exchanged; (iii) the delivery of transaction information among participating entities; (iv) the calculation, determination, and reporting of the net financial position of relevant institutions for all transactions that have been authorized; and (v) the facilitation, management and/or other participation in the transfer of net payments owed among participating institutions.[89] As noted above, China has not challenged this description. Moreover, China agrees that the definition of

86 United States' response to Panel questions No. 25, paras. 81-83; and 74, paras. 26-28.

87 Australia's response to Panel question No. 5; European Union's response to Panel question No. 5, para. 14; Guatemala's response to Panel question No. 5, para. 23; and Korea's response to Panel question No. 5.

88 European Union's response to Panel question No. 5, para. 14, and Guatemala's response to Panel question No. 5, para. 23.

89 United States' request for the establishment of a panel, fn. 1.

the services at issue proposed by the United States includes EPS suppliers operating four-party models.[90]

7.42 We consider important the use of the words "typically includes" in the panel request. By describing the "system" being supplied as "typically" including a number of specified elements, the panel request provides certain general parameters of the system under consideration, rather than seeking to confine the Panel's examination to a "system" that necessarily contains each and every element listed, and only those elements.[91] We note that EPS suppliers operating three-party models provide essentially all the elements of the "system" referred to above, as well as other services, such as card issuing and transaction acquiring, which are not within this system and are thus outside the scope of the services at issue. In particular, three-party model EPS suppliers provide the processing infrastructure, network, and rules and procedures that facilitate, manage, and enable transaction information and payment flows and which provide system integrity, stability and financial risk reduction; the process and coordination of approving or declining a transaction, with approval generally permitting a purchase to be finalized or cash to be disbursed or exchanged; the delivery of transaction information among participants in the transaction; the calculation, determination, and reporting of the net financial position of relevant participants in the transactions (e.g. total debit position of a card holder); and the facilitation, management and/or other participation in the transfer of payments among participants in the transaction. We are aware that in a three-party model, the supply of the fourth and fifth elements of the system[92] would usually involve individuals (e.g. card holders and merchants) rather than "institutions". However, in our view, that aspect does not change the nature of the EPS supplied. Nor does this difference mean that the three-party model falls outside the broadly defined "system" under consideration. In our view, EPS suppliers operating under three- and four-party models provide *in essence* the same services, as argued by the United States and some of the third parties.

7.43 China also argues that the three-party model does not make it necessary to authorize, clear and settle payment card transactions among different financial institutions, because the issuer and the acquirer are the same entity. Therefore, in China's view, there is no need for the operator of a three-party payment card system to obtain network services from a network operator. We agree with the United States that the fact that a payment card transaction is processed by a supplier that is also the issuer and the acquirer (meaning that there is therefore

[90] China's second written submission, para. 104.

[91] We note that, according to the *Shorter Oxford English Dictionary*, typically means symbolically, representatively, characteristically. See *Shorter Oxford English Dictionary*, 6th ed., A. Stevenson (ed.) (Oxford University Press, 2007) (*Shorter Oxford English Dictionary*), Vol. 2, page 3393.

[92] Respectively, the calculation, determination, and reporting of the net financial position of relevant institutions for all transactions that have been authorized; and the facilitation, management and/or other participation in the transfer of net payments owed among participating institutions.

no inter-bank transaction) does not change the fact that such supplier provides the services at issue.

7.44 The Panel also notes the United States' argument that three-party model transactions include both those EPS systems that perform the functions of issuer and acquirer internally and "on-us" transactions occurring in a four-party system where the issuer and the acquirer are the same entity. The Panel observes that, depending on the identity of the issuer and acquirer, payment card transactions processed within – in principle – four-party models may resemble the processing of transactions within three-party models. This is the case of the "on-us" transactions within four-party models, in which the same bank is both the acquirer for the merchant and the issuer to the card holder. In such a case, the transaction is not processed over the network of the EPS supplier, but is handled solely by the bank concerned. In such a case, balances are shifted on the books of that bank, and there are no inter-bank transactions. This is very similar to the processing of payment card transactions by service suppliers operating under three-party models. It would be virtually impossible, in the Panel's view, to distinguish between the processing of a three-party transaction and the processing of an "on-us" four-party transaction, which, China agrees, are undoubtedly within the scope of the services at issue.

7.45 For the above-mentioned reasons, the Panel finds that the services at issue include the services supplied under three-party models, in addition to the services supplied under four-party models.

4. *Whether the services at issue include the services supplied by issuer and merchant processors*

7.46 The parties disagree on whether services supplied by issuer and merchant processors fall within the issues to be decided in this dispute.

7.47 China argues that issuer and merchant processors are providers of outsourced technology services to the issuing and acquiring institutions, respectively. Among other services, merchant processors provide the equipment necessary for the merchant to accept payment cards, route payment card transactions to the correct network, handle transaction authorizations, and undertake the back-end processing necessary for the merchant to obtain payment. Among other services, issuer processors manage and provide the information technology necessary for the card issuer to interact with network operators for the purpose of authorizing, clearing, and settling transactions that are made with the payment cards that it issues. China submits that the description of the services at issue by the United States makes no reference to these types of outsourced services. China further argues that the panel request refers to a "system" provided by "EPS suppliers", that allows for the authorization, clearing and settlement of inter-bank payment card transactions. In China's view, issuer and merchant processors do not supply a "system".[93]

7.48 The United States argues that issuers and acquirers may choose to perform services related to the processing of transactions in-house or may choose to outsource these services to issuer and acquirer processors, that will then handle or transmit electronic payment information to or from an EPS supplier. Issuer and acquirer processors are optional entities for card-based electronic payment transactions. According to the United States, this is in contrast to an EPS supplier that provides necessary infrastructure and services for card-based electronic payment transactions.[94]

7.49 The Panel recalls that the parties agree that the services at issue do not encompass the issuance of payment cards and the acquisition of payment card transactions, activities which are typically handled by banks. Thus, we address only the question of whether or not the services supplied by issuer and merchant processors are included in the services at issue.

7.50 We note that third-party processors have a very broad reach in terms of the services supplied. One global EPS supplier acknowledges that it faces "competition from transaction processors throughout the world, such as FirstData Corporation and Total Systems Services, Inc., some of which seek to enhance their networks that link issuers directly with point-of-sale devices for payment card transaction authorization and processing services. Certain of these transaction processors could potentially displace MasterCard as the provider of these payment processing services".[95]

7.51 The Panel recalls that the definition of the services at issue involves two particular elements relevant to third-party processors, i.e. "services through which transactions involving payment cards are processed", and "services through which the transmission of funds between institutions participating in the transactions are managed and facilitated". Once they are accredited by payment card companies, as noted above, these third-party processors participate in the processing of payment card transactions. As such, they provide "services through which transactions involving payment cards are processed", including, for example, terminal operation, authorization routing, and electronic data capture. They also provide "services through which the transmission of funds between institutions participating in the transactions are managed and facilitated", including the preparation and submission of clearing files, settlement processing, card holder and merchant statement preparation, and charge-back processing.[96]

---

93 China's second written submission, paras. 110-114.

94 United States' response to Panel question No. 36(a), para. 93.

95 MasterCard 2010 Annual Report, Exhibit US-6, p. 22.

96 A "charge back" is a reversal of a payment card transaction, typically initiated by the card issuer at the card holder's request. Charge backs can occur for a number of reasons, including fraud and processing errors.

7.52 We are therefore of the view that, due to their substantial involvement in the process, and considering the overlap between, on the one hand, the services supplied by third-party processors, and, on the other hand, those supplied by electronic payment services suppliers (see discussion regarding the role of EPS suppliers, in paragraphs 7.12 to 7.24 above)[97], third-party processors are part of the payment services loop.

7.53 We turn now to the statement in the United States' request for the establishment of a panel those [s] uppliers of electronic payment services supply, directly or indirectly, a system that typically includes five elements[98]. A textual analysis of this phrase supports our conclusion that the services at issue include the services supplied by third-party processors. We observe first that the definition refers to "suppliers" in the plural (not "a supplier", singular), and makes reference to "a system" in the singular (not "systems", plural). This suggests, in our view, that the services can be supplied by one or several suppliers, who, together, provide "a system". Secondly, the definition indicates that the suppliers supply "directly or indirectly" a system, which suggests that the supplier may supply the system "directly", meaning on its own, or "indirectly", meaning with the participation of other service suppliers. Thirdly, as noted above, many of the services "typically" included in the system are supplied by third-party processors, some of which are seen by global EPS suppliers as competitors.[99] Therefore, we do not consider that there is a need for a service supplier to supply all five elements of the "system" described by the United States to be considered, in terms of the United States' request for the establishment of a panel, as a "supplier of electronic payment services".

7.54 In the light of the foregoing analysis, the Panel concludes that the services at issue include the services supplied by third-party processors.

5. *Whether the services at issue are integrated services*

7.55 The United States argues that electronic payment services for payment card transactions are one integral service – one that is supplied and consumed as such. Moreover, the service is supplied as a coherent whole. According to the United States, each component of the "system" is "critical to effectuate the payment card transaction and EPS suppliers provide the entire package of services to their customers, the institutions that are participating in the payment card transactions." For the United States, each of the elements of the system is integrated and necessary to facilitate a payment card transaction and, as such, constitutes a single service. Indeed, without the entire system supplied by the EPS supplier, no issuer would be able individually to offer a card that is as

---

97 We recall that for the sake of neutrality at that stage of the report, paragraphs 7.12 to 7.24 made reference to "payment card companies" instead of "EPS suppliers".

98 United States' request for the establishment of a panel, fn.1 (emphasis added).

99 MasterCard 2010 Annual Report, Exhibit US-6, p. 22; and Visa IPO Prospectus, Exhibit US-3, table in p. 130.

widely accepted by merchants, and no acquirer could offer merchants a service that can deliver such a large number of card holders. It is necessary for each component element to work collectively for EPS to function properly.[100]

7.56 China argues that the services at issue do not have the nature of a single, integrated service. For China, the argument by the United States is a necessary consequence of its position that all services that "manage", "facilitate", or relate to the "processing" of a payment card transaction (or that are "essential", "integral", or "necessary") must be classified as "payment services". This interpretation, according to China, does not allow for "dividing" the services at issue. While the United States identified five elements of a "system" that "[s]uppliers of electronic payment services supply", it is clear – China argues – that the United States perceives no distinction among these elements for the purpose of classifying the services at issue in this dispute, or in relation to the case that it has decided to present.[101]

7.57 The Panel notes that two different – albeit closely related – issues arise. One is whether the services at issue can be considered an integrated service, which is supplied as such; the other is whether the services at issue should be classified under a single subsector or under more than one subsector in the classification system. We shall examine here the first issue; the discussion related to the classification of the services at issue is found in Section E below.

7.58 The Panel observes that the definition of the services at issue refers to a "system" composed of several elements. Those elements could be considered, individually, as services in their own right, e.g. "the process and coordination of approving or declining a transaction", "the delivery of transaction information among participating entities", "the calculation, determination, and reporting of the net financial position of relevant institutions for all transactions that have been authorized", and "the facilitation, management and/or other participation in the transfer of net payments owed among participating institutions." In the Panel's view, all these elements show that "electronic payment services for payment card transactions" are made up of different services that may be individually identified.

7.59 The United States argues, however, that the various elements of the system are integrated and necessary to facilitate a payment card transaction and, as such, constitute a single service. In our view, all elements of the system, together, are necessary for the payment card transaction to materialize. None of the elements of the "system", individually, would be sufficient to process a payment card transaction. Each of them must be integrated into a whole.[102] Indeed, we agree with the United States' argument that without the entire system

[100] United States' response to Panel question No. 26, para. 84; United States' second written submission, paras. 11-14.

[101] China's response to Panel question No. 29, paras. 22-24.

[102] The *Shorter Oxford English Dictionary*, Vol. 1, p. 1402, defines "integrated" as: "1 Combined into a whole; united; individual, … c Uniting several components previously regarded as separate".

supplied by the EPS supplier, no issuer would be able individually to offer a card that is as widely accepted by merchants, and no acquirer could offer merchants a service that can deliver such a large number of card holders.[103] From that perspective, considering the transaction from beginning to end, electronic payment services for payment card transactions constitute an integrated service.

7.60 A related question is whether "electronic payment services for payment card transactions", despite being made up of several services, are nevertheless supplied as an "integrated" service, or whether those different service components can be supplied – and are in fact supplied – as separate services by different service suppliers. China argues that different "elements" or "components" of "electronic payment services" are routinely supplied as different services by different service suppliers in several countries. One of the examples put forward by China to support this assertion is France, where, according to China, the authorization process for payment card transactions is carried out by the network of "*Groupement des Cartes Bancaires*" (or CB), while the clearing and settlement of transactions is handled by "CompensationREtail" (or CORE).[104] The United States argues that the fact that two separate entities may provide different elements of "electronic payment services" is not inconsistent with the fact that each of the elements is integrated and necessary to facilitate payment card transactions, and as such constitutes a single service. In the United States' view, "electronic payment services" could not be effectuated through the provision of the service provided by STET only, or the service provided by CB only. It is, in the United States' view, the combination that enables the payment card transaction to occur.

7.61 We agree with the United States' view on this matter. How the supply of "electronic payment services" is organized depends on different parameters (e.g. the business models adopted by the entities participating in the payment card transaction). On the one hand, global electronic payment services suppliers provide all the components of the "system" identified by the United States, thus supplying a final product that looks like a "single" service for the direct user (the issuing and acquiring institutions) and for the ultimate beneficiaries of these services (the card holder and the merchant), and that in many countries that is the case. On the other hand, there are jurisdictions where the different components of the "system" are supplied by different service suppliers. Further, as we saw previously, third-party processors may also intervene in the processing of payment card transactions. In the Panel's view, therefore, the services at issue may as a factual matter be supplied by a single service supplier or by more than one service supplier acting in concert.

[103] United States' response to Panel question No. 26, para. 84, United States' second written submission, para. 17.

[104] CORE is a payment processing network developed and operated by the STET company (Systèmes Technologiques d'Echange et de Traitement). Examples of European countries in which the national authorization network is independent of the clearing and settlement mechanism for payment card transactions, Exhibit CHN-103, pp. 2 and 5.

7.62 We conclude therefore that the services at issue include both the instances in which these services are supplied as a single service by a single service supplier, and those instances in which different elements of the "system" described by the United States are supplied by different service suppliers.

D. China's Specific Commitments Concerning the Services at Issue

7.63 The United States claims that, in sector 7.B, under the heading "Banking and Other Financial Services" of its GATS Schedule, China undertook market access and national treatment commitments with respect to subsector (d), which reads "[a]ll payment and money transmission services, including credit, charge and debit cards, travellers cheques and bankers draft (including import and export settlement)" (subsector (d)). According to the United States, subsector (d) includes the electronic payment services supplied in connection with "credit, charge and debit cards", and other payment card transactions.[105]

7.64 China argues that the United States has failed to prove that any of the services at issue, much less all of them, fall within subsector (d) of its Schedule. In China's view, the clearing and settlement services at issue fall under paragraph 5(a), subsector (xiv), of the GATS Annex on Financial Services (subsector (xiv)), which covers "[s]ettlement and clearing services for financial assets, including securities, derivative products, and other negotiable instruments", a subsector for which no commitments have been made in China's Schedule. China maintains that the fact that those clearing and settlement services do not fall within the scope of subsector (d) defeats the United States' assertion that all of the services at issue fall within subsector (d). According to China, the "payment services" referred to in subsector (d) encompass the issuance and acceptance by banks and other types of financial institutions of payment instruments other than cash. However, issuing and acquiring services are not part of this dispute.[106]

7.65 Australia, the European Union and Korea submit that the services at issue fall under subsector (d) of China's Schedule.[107] According to Ecuador, an excessively broad interpretation of specific commitments in GATS schedules would constitute an unacceptable impairment of WTO Members' rights to define the scope and content of such commitments.[108]

7.66 The Panel must determine whether, as claimed by the United States, China has undertaken specific commitments on the services at issue under subsector (d) of its Schedule of Specific Commitments (China's Schedule).[109] To

---

105 United States' first written submission, para. 13.

106 China's first written submission, paras. 78 and 96.

107 Australia's third-party submission, para. 7; European Union's third-party submission, para. 23; and Korea's third-party submission, para. 11.

108 Ecuador's third-party statement, para. 5.

109 Schedule of Specific Commitments of the People's Republic of China, GATS/SC/135 (14 February 2002). The relevant part of China's Schedule is contained in Annex G to this Report.

do so, it will need to interpret China's Schedule as well as relevant provisions of the GATS.

7.67 Article XX:1 of the GATS provides that each Member "shall set out in a schedule the specific commitments it undertakes", notably on market access and national treatment. This schedule, according to Article XX:3, "shall form an integral part" of the GATS[110], and is thus legally part of the WTO Agreement.[111] For that reason, GATS schedules must be interpreted according to the "customary rules of interpretation of public international law", as codified in Articles 31 and 32 of the Vienna Convention.[112]

7.68 As a result, we will interpret China's Schedule and other relevant treaty text in accordance with the ordinary meaning to be given to the terms of the Schedule in their context, and in the light of the object and purpose of the GATS and the WTO Agreement. The Panel will turn to supplementary means of interpretation pursuant to Article 32 of the Vienna Convention as appropriate.

1. *Order of analysis of the subsectors identified by the parties*

7.69 As a preliminary matter, the Panel must decide whether to start its interpretative analysis with subsector (d) of China's Schedule, or with subsector (xiv) of the GATS Annex on Financial Services (Annex).

7.70 China submits that, because clearing and settlement services for payment card transactions are encompassed by subsector (xiv) of the Annex, it is unnecessary for the Panel to examine the United States' assertion that those services are encompassed by subsector (d). According to China, the Panel should begin with an analysis of subsector (xiv) of the Annex – a subsector not listed in China's Schedule – because this subsector offers the more specific description of the clearing and settlement services at issue. Referring to the rules of interpretation contained in the United Nations' Provisional Central Product Classification[113] (CPC), China claims that the category that provides the most specific description is to be preferred to categories providing a more general description.[114] The United States did not offer specific arguments on this issue.

7.71 The Panel notes, first, that this dispute concerns the scope of China's GATS commitments. The issue before us is whether the United States can properly base its claims in respect of the services at issue on China's

[110] Article XX:3 of the GATS provides: "Schedules of specific commitments shall be annexed to this Agreement and shall form an integral part thereof."

[111] Pursuant to Article II:2 (Scope of the WTO) of the Marrakesh Agreement Establishing the World Trade Organization (WTO Agreement), the GATS, which is included in Annex 1B of the WTO Agreement, is an integral part of that Agreement.

[112] DSU Art. 3.2. See also Appellate Body Report, *US – Gambling*, para. 160. For the text of Articles 31 and 32 of the Vienna Convention, see above, para. 7.8.

[113] Provisional Central Product Classification, Statistical Papers, Series M No.77, United Nations (1991).

[114] China's first written submission, para. 89.

commitments under subsector (d). For this reason, we believe that it would be incongruous for the Panel to begin its analysis by interpreting a subsector *not* relied on by the United States and *not* contained in China's Schedule. Furthermore, under the approach proposed by China, the Panel would need to determine at the outset of its examination which of subsectors (d) and (xiv) is "more specific". In our view, the matter is not so obvious that we could confidently determine, without undertaking a detailed examination, that subsector (xiv) is "more specific" in relation to the services at issue.

7.72 For these reasons, we are not persuaded that we must, from the outset, follow the CPC rule of interpretation referred to by China and thus direct our initial analysis away from the provisions of China's Schedule, in particular subsector (d). Naturally, this neither prevents nor dispenses us from subsequently examining subsector (xiv) of the Annex as relevant context for the interpretation of China's Schedule. The Panel will thus start its analysis by examining subsector (d) of China's Schedule.

2. *Interpretation of subsector (d) in China's Schedule*

7.73 The parties have different views on the scope of subsector (d). The United States argues that subsector (d) encompasses the services at issue. China disagrees and submits that this subsector covers issuing and acquiring services, which are not among the services at issue.

7.74 As explained above, we will interpret subsector (d) as described in China's Schedule in accordance with customary rules of interpretation. Therefore, we will first determine the ordinary meaning of relevant terms used to describe the services contained in subsector (d). We shall then turn to the context, which includes, *inter alia*, other elements of China's Schedule, the GATS itself, the GATS Annex on Financial Services, and the schedules of other WTO Members.[115] Finally, we shall consider the object and purpose of the GATS and the WTO Agreement. As indicated above, we may turn to supplementary means of interpretation pursuant to Article 32 of the Vienna Convention as appropriate.

(a) Ordinary meaning

7.75 The United States argues that the services at issue fall within the ordinary meaning of "payment and money transmission services" as one type of "all" such services within subsector (d) of China's Schedule. According to the United States, the ordinary meaning of "payment" and "money transmission", as

---

[115] In *US – Gambling*, a dispute about commitments included in the GATS Schedule of the United States, the Appellate Body found that the context included: (i) the remainder of the Member's Schedule; (ii) the substantive provisions of the GATS; (iii) the provisions of covered agreements other than the GATS; and (iv) the GATS Schedules of other Members. See Appellate Body Report, *US – Gambling*, para. 178.

reflected in definitions from the *Shorter Oxford English Dictionary* and specialized financial sources, demonstrates that subsector (d) covers the action of transferring money from one person to another.[116]

7.76 China argues that subsector (d) is listed in China's Schedule under the heading of "banking services". Consistent with the ordinary meaning of "banking services", all of the services listed under that heading are services that are typically provided by banks, finance companies, and other types of financial institutions. The banks are making a "payment" within the ordinary meaning of that term, i.e. they are engaging in "[a]n act, or the action or process, of paying …". Hence, according to China, the payment services referred to in subsector (d) encompass the issuance and acceptance by financial institutions of payment instruments other than cash, but do not cover the services at issue.[117]

7.77 Australia submits that the ordinary meaning of the terms "all payment and money transmission services" encompasses services which manage and facilitate the transfer of funds, whether for the purpose of payment for a good, service or debt, or for purposes unrelated to payment, from one person or place to another.[118]

7.78 The Panel recalls that subsector (d) in China's Schedule reads as follows:

> All payment and money transmission services, including credit, charge and debit cards, travellers cheques and bankers draft (including import and export settlement)

7.79 We begin our textual analysis of the phrase "all payment and money transmission services" by examining the terms "payment", "money" and "transmission". We shall then turn to the terms "all" and "services".

(i) Ordinary meaning of "payment", "money" and "transmission"

Dictionaries and glossaries

7.80 The Panel observes at the outset that, for the purpose of determining the ordinary meaning of the terms of subsector (d), dictionary definitions of those terms are a useful starting point. However, such definitions are not always sufficient. As the Appellate Body has explained:

> [I]n order to identify the ordinary meaning, a Panel may start with the dictionary definitions of the terms to be interpreted. But dictionaries alone are not necessarily capable of resolving complex questions of interpretation, as they typically aim to catalogue

---

116 United States' response to China's request for a preliminary ruling, paras. 150-155; first written submission, para. 26; and second written submission, paras. 19-32.

117 China's first submission, paras. 95-97.

118 Australia's third-party submission, para. 10.

> *all* meanings of words – be those meanings common or rare, universal or specialized.[119]

7.81 We first consider the term "payment" in subsector (d). The *Shorter Oxford English Dictionary* defines "payment" as "an act, or the action or process, of paying".[120] In turn, the verb "pay" is defined as "give (a person) money etc. that is due for goods received, a service done, or a debt incurred; remunerate. Also, hand over or transfer (money etc.) in return for something."[121] This general definition of "payment" is consistent with definitions in certain glossaries and specialized dictionaries submitted by the United States: (i) a "transfer of funds in any form between two parties";[122] or (ii) the "transfer of money from one party to another with the assent of both parties".[123] We glean from these definitions that the three main elements in a payment are (i) there is a transfer, (ii) what is transferred is money, and (iii) the transferred money is due for goods, services or a debt incurred. The Panel next considers the term "money". The *Shorter Oxford English Dictionary* provides the following general definition:

> ... A current medium of exchange in the form of coins and (in mod. use) banknotes; coins and banknotes collectively. ... Any object or material serving the same purposes as coins. ... Property, wealth, possessions, resources, etc., viewed as convertible into coin or banknotes or having value expressible in terms of these.[124]

7.82 In glossaries and specialized dictionaries, the term "money" is defined as the following: (i) "[a]nything which is immediately and generally acceptable for the discharge of a debt or in exchange for a good or service"[125]; (ii) "the means of facilitating the exchange of goods and services and the accumulation of financial wealth, commonly recognizable as banknotes, coins and bank deposits"[126]; (iii) "[a]nything that is generally acceptable as a means of settling debt. Money is said to have three main functions, being: a store of value; a means of exchange; and a means of debt settlement (cf. fiat money)".[127]

7.83 As one might expect, the definitions found in specialized dictionaries and glossaries are more technical than the general definition found in the *Shorter Oxford English Dictionary;* however, they are consistent with this definition.

---

[119] Appellate Body Report, *US – Gambling*, para. 164 (footnotes omitted, emphasis original).

[120] *Shorter Oxford English Dictionary*, Vol. 2, p. 2130.

[121] *Ibid.*, p. 2129.

[122] *Banking Terminology*, 3rd ed., (American Bankers Association, 1989) (*Banking Terminology*), Exhibit US-59, p. 262.

[123] John V. Terry, *Dictionary for Business & Finance*, 1990, Exhibit US-60, p. 240.

[124] *Shorter Oxford English Dictionary*, Vol. 1, p. 1821.

[125] D. Rutherford, *Dictionary of Economics,* Routledge, 1992, p. 305.

[126] G. Bannock & W. Manser, *The Penguin International Dictionary of Finance*, Penguin Books, 3rd ed., 1999, p. 181.

[127] Peter Moles & Nicholas Terry, *The Handbook of International Financial Terms,* Oxford University Press, 1997.

The definitions suggest that "money" can be characterized as (i) a generally acceptable means of exchange, (ii) that represents wealth, and (iii) is generally acceptable as payment.

7.84 Finally, the Panel considers the term "transmission". The *Shorter Oxford English Dictionary* defines this term as "[c]onveyance or transfer from one person or place to another; the action or process of passing from one person, organism, generation, etc., to another, as by personal contact, stored information, genetic inheritance, etc."[128] This definition suggests that the two main elements characterizing "transmission" are (i) a transfer, (ii) from one person or place to another.

7.85 In sum, our analysis of definitions contained in dictionaries and glossaries suggests that the terms "payment", "money" and "transmission", when used in combination, refer to the transfer of a generally acceptable means of exchange from one person or place to another. The money transferred may be due for goods or services received, or for settling a debt. We continue our consideration of the ordinary meaning of the terms used in subsector (d) with an examination of industry sources.

Industry sources

7.86 The United States argues that the description of the sector at issue drawn from industry sources is relevant to determining the ordinary meaning under Article 31 of the Vienna Convention. According to the United States, industry sources confirm the ordinary meaning of the service and demonstrate that EPS is a payment service that is one type of "all" "payment and money transmission service" falling within subsector (d). The United States contends that, in many instances, the common meaning of a term corresponds to its usage within a particular industry or sector and provides the basis for dictionary definitions. Consequently, the United States suggests, it is appropriate and may be helpful to look at how those involved in the service at issue understand the terms found in a GATS schedule. The United States further submits that sector sources describe the suppliers of the services at issue in this dispute as supplying "electronic payment services" for "payment card" transactions and as operating within the "global payments industry." This confirms, according to the United States, that the services at issue are payment services falling under subsector (d) of China's Schedule.[129]

7.87 China argues that the United States provides no support for the proposition that the manner in which certain service suppliers characterize their services is relevant, as a matter of treaty interpretation, to how those services should be classified in relation to a Member's schedule. Thus, industry sources like company brochures, annual reports, or company websites are not relevant

---

128 *Shorter Oxford English Dictionary*, Vol. 2, p. 3325.

129 United States' first written submission, para. 26; and response to Panel question No. 82, para. 52.

for the purpose of establishing the ordinary meaning of the terms at issue in this dispute, one reason being that they might be biased and self-serving. Moreover, China observes that the United States has not pointed to a single panel or Appellate Body report that uses industry sources as a means of treaty interpretation. China further argues that, even if the industry sources cited by the United were legally relevant to the classification of the services at issue, they would support China's position that these services include clearing and settlement, among other possible services. There are only a handful of references in these sources to the "payment industry" or "payment systems", compared to far more numerous references to the telecommunications, data processing, and clearing and settlement services that these companies describe themselves as providing.[130]

7.88 Ecuador submits that the industry's characterization of a service does not determine the nature of that service and the fact that one or several suppliers describe the services they supply as "payment services" does not necessarily confer that character upon them. The legal value of industry sources is therefore questionable.[131]

7.89 The Panel begins by assessing whether it is appropriate to examine industry sources in addition to dictionaries for the purpose of determining the ordinary meaning of a term appearing in a GATS schedule.[132] We acknowledge that, sometimes, industry sources may define a term in a way that might reflect self-interest and, thus, might be "biased and self-serving", as argued by China. To that extent, we see some merit in China's concerns about relying on such sources, without more. Nevertheless, we see no basis to completely disregard industry sources as potential relevant evidence of an ordinary meaning of a specific term in a particular industry. Indeed, we see no reason why a panel's search for the ordinary meaning of any term should always be confined to regular dictionaries. A panel's initial task in interpreting treaty provisions is to determine the ordinary meaning of the words used. If industry sources can be shown to assist with this task in a particular dispute, we see no reason why a panel should not refer to them. As with a panel's consideration of dictionary definitions, however, panels must be mindful of the limitations, such as self-interest, that industry sources may present and should govern their interpretive task accordingly.

7.90 With these preliminary observations in mind, we now examine the relevance of the terms that appear in the industry sources referred to by the parties for purposes of the interpretation of the terms used in subsector (d). We

---

130 China's first written submission, paras. 117 and 118; and response to Panel question No. 82, paras. 1 and 2.

131 Ecuador's third-party statement, paras. 12, 13 and 15.

132 We observe that, pursuant to Article 31(4) of the Vienna Convention, "[a] special meaning shall be given to a term if it is established that the parties so intended". In the present dispute, no party is relying on this provision. Hence, we shall not consider it.

note that both parties refer to industry sources – sometimes the very same ones[133] – but draw different conclusions from them. [134] The United States argues that the way industry sources describe their own services confirms that EPS is a payment service that is one type of "all" "payment and money transmission service" falling within subsector (d). China has not relied on industry sources to shed light on the meaning of "all payment ...". In China's view, "[r]eading through the various corporate materials and other 'industry sources' that the United States cites as evidence, one is struck not by the handful of references to the 'payment industry' or 'payment systems', but rather by the far more numerous references to the telecommunications, data processing, and clearing and settlement services that these companies describe themselves as providing".[135]

7.91 The Panel notes that industry sources cited in this dispute refer to payment transactions, electronic payments and the various types of cards specifically identified in subsector (d) of China's Schedule.[136] We also note that the usage of these terms in industry sources is consistent with the definitions found in general dictionaries and more specialized glossaries that we examined in the preceding section. We find, however, that industry sources do little to shed further light on the scope of subsector (d).

---

[133] China submits in this regard that "[i]ronically, many of the materials that the United States references and includes as exhibits are materials that China was already planning to cite – and, in fact, has cited above – for the proposition that the services at issue in this dispute include clearing and settlement services." China's first written submission, fn. 69.

[134] For example, both parties refer to MasterCard's 2010 annual report. Our examination of this report indicates that, as argued by the United States, it describes the company as providing "a global payment network" and operating in the "global payment industry". The report also refers to various means of payment, including "credit cards, charge cards, debit cards (including ... [ATM] cards), prepaid cards, ..." and indicates that the company provides "payment services and solutions". We observe however that, as submitted by China, the same report also refers to MasterCard as providing "transaction switching", which includes "authorization, clearing and settlement". MasterCard 2010 Annual Report, Exhibits US-6, pp. 4-10.

[135] China's first written submission, para. 118.

[136] Visa IPO Prospectus, Exhibit US-3, p. 128; MasterCard 2009 Annual Report, Exhibit US-5; MasterCard 2010 Annual Report, Exhibit US-6, p. 6; American Express 2010 Annual Report, Exhibit US-7, pp. 4-11; Discover 2010 Annual Report, Exhibit US-8, pp. 1-4; First Data Corp 10-K Annual Report (March 10, 2011), Exhibit US-9; UBS Investment Research, "Visa 201: No Better Way to 'Play the Swipe', June 25, 2008, Exhibit US-10, pp. 28-30; JCB Corporate Overview: JCB – A Leader in the Payments Industry (as of July 2011), Exhibit US-16; JCB Smart Card Press Release: JCB International and Vital Processing Services Team Up to Introduce JCB Smart Card Capability in the United States (November 2002), Exhibit US-17; JCB History (2001-2009, JCB International Co., LTD), Exhibit US-18; JCB System network: Most Advanced Payment System Network, Exhibit US-19; and CUP's Articles of Association, Articles 11-12, Exhibit US-20. See United States' response to China's request for a preliminary ruling, paras. 55-61 and 164-178; and first written submission, para. 27.

The expression "payment and money transmission *services*"

7.92 Having considered the ordinary meaning of "payment", "money" and "transmission", the Panel notes that these three elements must be examined in conjunction with the term "services", which they qualify. Our understanding is that the phrase "payment and money transmission services" refers to, respectively, "payment services" and "money transmission services". The parties and third parties in this dispute have the same reading. What is thus at stake in this dispute is the scope of the expressions "payment *services*" and "money transmission *services*".

7.93 The United States argues that EPS is the service through which transactions involving payment cards are processed and through which transfers of funds between institutions participating in the transactions are managed and facilitated. It considers that EPS clearly fall within the ordinary meaning of "payment and money transmission services" as one type of "all" such services.[137]

7.94 China submits that a service supplier that is merely "managing" or "facilitating" the supply of this type of payment service, or "processing" payment transactions, is not itself a party to the payment transaction. In China's view, the supplier is neither issuing nor accepting the payment instrument and is never in possession of the funds to be paid. It is not "paying" anyone, and is not providing a "payment service" within the ordinary meaning of that term. China also submits that the United States has not given a proper interpretation to subsector (d) because the United States has failed to acknowledge that network operators are not "paying" or "transmitting money" to anyone.[138]

7.95 The Panel observes that the GATS provides no definition of the word "service", although it defines related concepts, such as the *supply* of a service and a service *supplier*.[139] Paragraph 5(a) of the GATS Annex on Financial Services defines a "financial service" as "any service of a financial nature offered by a financial service supplier of a Member", and contains a list of financial services that comprises "all payment and money transmission services, including …" under subsector (viii).

7.96 It is clear to the Panel that the *supply* of a "payment service" is not the same thing as the act of paying for goods or services. Purchasers who, on their own account, pay merchants for goods or services received are not thereby providing a "payment service" to these merchants. The payment in such case is what a purchaser gives in return for the good or service received, and not a separate service received by the merchant. Thus, "payment services" in our view

[137] United States' response to China's request for a preliminary ruling, para. 147-155; first written submission, paras. 25-26; and second written submission, paras. 19-32.

[138] China's second written submission, para. 40.

[139] Article XXVIII(b) of the GATS defines the "supply of a service" as including "the production, distribution, marketing, sale and delivery of a service" and, pursuant to Article XXVIII(g) of the GATS, a service supplier means "any person that supplies a service".

are supplied, if at all, by a person or entity other than the payer or payee. Typically, when payment instruments other than cash are used, a third party intervenes between the payer and the payee, in order to facilitate or make possible the "act of paying". The same can be said about "money transmission services", since transmitting money normally involves the participation of an intermediary to ensure that the money is transferred from one party to another.

7.97 We consider, therefore, that whoever supplies a "payment service" does not "pay", but makes the payment between payer and payee, for example by processing payment transactions involving the use of credit cards, debit cards, or other such instruments. Similarly, when it comes to "money transmission services", the supplier of the service intervenes between the sender and the recipient (payer and payee) to ensure that the money is transmitted. In our view, a "money transmission service" encompasses, among other situations, those where the supplier either transmits the funds from the payer's account to the payee's account (as in the three-party model) or connects the parties involved in a payment transaction, and ensures that payment instructions are executed and funds are transferred pursuant to the transaction (as in a four-party model). Hence, suppliers of "payment and money transmission services" are providing a "service" that facilitates and enables payments and money transmissions. For that reason, we agree with the United States that "payment and money transmission services" include those services that "manage", "facilitate" or "enable" the act, of paying, or transmitting money.

Ordinary meaning of "all"

7.98 As noted, subsector (d) begins with the word "all". It is the only subsector in the financial services section of China's Schedule that does so. Subsector (viii) of the GATS Annex on Financial Services, on which, according to China, subsector (d) of China's Schedule is based,[140] also starts with the word "all".[141]

7.99 Consistent with the principle of effective treaty interpretation, we consider that the word "all" before "payment and money transmission services" must be given meaning and effect. In our view, the use of the term "all" manifests an intention to cover comprehensively the entire spectrum of "payment and money transmission services". More particularly, this term indicates to us an intention to include all services essential to payment and money transmission, all means of payment and money transmission (i.e. paper-based, card-based and others), and all associated business models (e.g. four-party model, three-party model and any variations thereof).[142]

---

[140] China's first written submission, para. 80.

[141] The *Shorter Oxford English Dictionary*, Vol. 1, p. 55 defines "all" as "the entire number of; the individual constituents of, without exception".

[142] The Panel uses the term "essential" to refer to all component services which are needed to complete a payment transaction or money transmission.

Summary of findings on the ordinary meaning of "all payment and money transmission services"

7.100 Our analysis of the ordinary meaning of the relevant text indicates that "payment and money transmission services" include those services that "manage", "facilitate" or "enable" the act of paying or transmitting money. Finally, we concluded that the use of the term "all" manifests an intention to cover comprehensively the entire spectrum of payment and money transmission services.

7.101 Having determined the ordinary meaning of these terms, we shall turn now to the contextual elements of the phrase "all payment and money transmission services".

(b) Context

7.102 Pursuant to the rule codified in Article 31(2) of the Vienna Convention, the "context" within which a treaty provision shall be interpreted notably comprises the text of the treaty, including its preamble and annexes. For the purpose of interpreting a Member's GATS schedule, the Appellate Body found in *US – Gambling* that the context includes (i) the remainder of the Member's schedule; (ii) the substantive provisions of the GATS; (iii) the provisions of covered agreements other than the GATS; and (iv) the GATS schedules of other WTO Members.[143]

7.103 When looking at the remainder of a Member's schedule as part of a contextual analysis, panels and the Appellate Body have considered several aspects. For instance, in *US – Gambling*, the Appellate Body examined the structure of the schedule.[144] In *China – Publications and Audiovisual Products*, the Appellate Body considered such aspects as the contextual relevance of the sectoral heading at stake; market access, national treatment and additional commitments under the subsector at stake; subsectors adjacent to the services at stake; and commitments scheduled under another related sector.[145]

7.104 In the present dispute, we therefore consider that our examination of the context should, as also reflected in the parties' arguments, cover the following elements: (i) the rest of subsector (d); (ii) the headings in the sector at stake; (iii) market access, national treatment and additional commitments in the sector at stake; (iv) the structure of the GATS; (v) the GATS Annex on Financial Services; and (vi) the schedules of other WTO Members. We shall examine these different contextual elements in turn.

[143] Appellate Body Report, *US – Gambling*, para. 178.
[144] Appellate Body Report, *US – Gambling*, para. 179.
[145] Appellate Body Report, *China – Publications and Audiovisual Products*, paras. 361-372.

(i) The rest of subsector (d)

7.105 We recall that subsector (d) of China's Schedule reads as follows:

> [A]ll payment and money transmission services, including credit, charge and debit cards, travellers cheques and bankers drafts (including import and export settlement)

7.106 The phrase "[A]ll payment and money transmission services" in subsector (d) of China's Schedule is immediately followed by the phrase: "including credit, charge and debit cards, travellers cheques and bankers drafts (including import and export settlement)". We observe that this phrase is similar to that found in subsector (viii) of the Annex on Financial Services[146], on which, according to China, subsector (d) is based.[147] The only difference is the parenthetical addition "(including import and export settlement)" in subsector (d). We shall examine first the phrase "including credit, charge and debit cards, travellers cheques and bankers drafts" and shall then turn to the parenthetical addition.

The phrase "including credit, charge and debit cards, travellers cheques and bankers drafts"

7.107 The United States argues that the explicit reference to credit, charge and debit cards accords with the recognition that EPS is integral to the processing of these types of cards and other payment card-based electronic payment transactions. The United States observes that without EPS, payment card transactions could not occur.[148]

7.108 China submits that, properly interpreted in its context, the "payment services" referred to in subsector (d) encompass the issuance and acceptance by financial institutions of payment instruments other than cash. All of the specific types of payment instruments referenced in subsector (d) are methods of payment that allow the buyers and sellers of goods and services to complete transactions without a direct transfer of cash.[149]

7.109 The Panel first observes that the phrase "including credit, charge and debit cards, travellers cheques and bankers drafts" refers to payment and money transmission instruments, not to services. In our view, this phrase sets out various types of instruments that require payment and money transmission

[146] In paragraph 5(a) of the Annex, subsector (viii) is defined as "[a]ll payment and money transmission services, including credit, charge and debit cards, travellers cheques and bankers drafts".
[147] China's first written submission, para. 80.
[148] The United States also argues that the ordinary meaning of the phrase "including credit, charge and debit cards" supports the position that EPS for payment card transactions fall within subsector (d) in China's Schedule. United States' response to China's request for a preliminary ruling, para. 149 and 156-163; first written submission, paras. 25-26; and second written submission, paras. 19-23 and 33-37.
[149] China's first written submission, para. 96.

services for them to work effectively. We also note that the instruments listed are preceded by the word "including". As explained by the panel in *China – Publications and Audiovisual Products*, "the word 'including' in ordinary usage indicates that what follows is not an exhaustive, but a partial, list of all covered items".[150] In a similar vein, we consider that the phrase "including credit, charge and debit cards, travellers cheques and bankers drafts" in subsector (d) provides a non-exhaustive list of instruments used in connection with payment and money transmission services.[151] In the Panel's view, the explicit reference to "credit, charge and debit cards" in subsector (d) of China's Schedule sheds light on the type of services covered by the phrase "all payment and money transmission services" as it appears in China's Schedule. It notably suggests that the phrase covers payment and money transmission services that are essential for the use of the enumerated instruments.

7.110 Turning to dictionary definitions, a "credit card" is "a card issued by a bank, business, etc., authorizing the acquisition of goods and services on credit".[152] A "charge card" is "a credit card, esp. for use at a particular store or chain of stores or for an account which must be cleared in full on receipt of a statement".[153] A "debit card" is defined as "giving the holder access (through a computer terminal) to an account in order to transfer funds to another's account when making a purchase, etc."[154] These general definitions are confirmed by definitions found in more specialized glossaries, such as the *BIS Glossary of terms used in payment and settlement systems*.[155] Moreover, "credit, charge and debit cards" are commonly associated with EPS suppliers, which own and licence card brands. Finally, we note that definitions of "travellers cheques" and "bankers drafts" also identify them as payment and money transmission instruments involving transmission of money.[156]

---

[150] Panel Report, *China – Publications and Audiovisual Products*, para. 7.294.

[151] In our view, these instruments also include other types of cards, such as ATM cards.

[152] *Shorter Oxford English Dictionary*, Vol. 1, p. 555.

[153] *Ibid.*, p. 385.

[154] *Ibid.*, p. 615.

[155] The BIS defines a "credit card" as "a card indicating that the holder has been granted a line of credit. It enables the holder to make purchases and/or withdraw cash up to a prearranged ceiling; the credit granted can be settled in full by the end of a specified period or can be settled in part, with the balance taken as extended credit. Interest is charged on the amount of any extended credit and the holder is sometimes charged an annual fee." The same glossary defines a "debit card" as "card enabling the holder to have his purchases directly charged to funds on his account at a deposit-taking institution (may sometimes be combined with another function, e.g. that of a cash card or cheque guarantee card)." Finally, the glossary defines a "travel and entertainment card" as "card issued by non-banks indicating that the holder has been granted a line of credit. It enables him to make purchases but does not offer extended credit, the full amount of the debt incurred having to be settled at the end of a specified period. The holder is usually charged an annual fee. Also called charge card." BIS Glossary, Exhibit US-68, pp. 16, 19 and 50.

[156] A travellers cheque is "a cheque for a fixed amount of money which may be cashed or used in payment abroad, on the holder's signature", *Shorter Oxford English Dictionary*, Vo. 2, p. 3331. A "bank draft" is defined as (i) "a check that a bank draws on itself, used when the payee does not wish

7.111 Accordingly, we find that the phrase "including credit, charge and debit cards, travellers cheques and bankers drafts", which sheds light on the types of services covered by the phrase "all payment and money transmission services", refers to an illustrative list of payment and money transmission instruments. Dictionary definitions identify these instruments as instruments enabling the holder to make payments without cash and to transfer money from one person or place to another. Consequently, the list confirms that "[a]ll payment and money transmission services" refers to those services that are essential to the processing and completion of transactions using payment cards. The Panel considers that such transactions include not only those involving, for instance, the use of a credit card at a POS terminal for the purpose of a good or service, but also those involving the use of a credit, debit or ATM card for the purpose of withdrawing cash from an ATM. In the Panel's view, the latter constitutes a form of money transmission service.[157]

The reference to "(including import and export settlement)"

7.112 The United States submits that the parenthetical phrase "(including import and export settlement)" does not appear in subsector (viii) of the GATS Annex on Financial Services, but was added by China to the description of the services covered by subsector (d). According to the United States, the explicit use of "settlement" suggests that there is an element of settlement and clearing that occurs as part of the payment service.[158]

7.113 China submits that the term "import and export settlement" refers to the services that banks provide as payment intermediaries for import and export transactions through letters of credit. Unlike the case of payment cards, there is no third party that provides clearing and settlement services to the financial institutions that are involved in an import/export transaction. The financial institutions deal with each other directly, and use the international inter-bank payment system to complete the necessary transfer of funds. According to China, the reference to "settlement" in subsector (d) in no way suggests that clearing

to accept the credit of the customer as drawer. The customer purchases the bank draft with good funds, which gives the payee confidence that the check will be honoured. Also known as banker's check." *The Palgrave Macmillan Dictionary of Finance, Investment and Banking* (Palgrave MacMillan, New York, 2010) (*The Palgrave Macmillan Dictionary of Finance, Investment and Banking*), p. 44; or as (ii) "a cheque drawn by a bank on itself or its agent. A person who owes money to another buys the draft from a bank for cash and hands it to the creditor who need have no fear that it might be dishonoured. A bank draft is used if the creditor is unwilling to accept an ordinary cheque." *A Dictionary of Finance and Banking*, Oxford Paperback Reference, Exhibit CHN-80, p. 34.

[157] In our view, the use of a credit, debit or ATM card to withdraw cash from an ATM constitutes a form of money transmission service, insofar as, for example, the card issuing institution or card holder's bank authorizes the transmission of money from the card holder's bank account to the location of the ATM or, in the case of a credit card, a cash advance to the location of the ATM.

[158] United States' response to Panel question No. 83, paras. 54-58.

and settlement services are within the scope of this subsector, as there are no clearing and settlement services involved in an import/export transaction. China also submits that it is significant that subsector (d) does not use the word "clearing".[159]

7.114 The Panel notes that, as pointed out above in paragraph 7.106, the words in parenthesis – "including import and export settlement" – do not appear in subsector (viii) of the Annex; they were added by China to its Schedule. Consistent with the principle of effective treaty interpretation, these words must be given meaning.

7.115 In our view, the terms "import and export" suggest that the parenthetical phrase refers to payment services supplied in connection with international trade transactions. China appears to hold a similar view as it considers that the phrase refers to the services that banks provide as payment intermediaries for import and export transactions.[160] We observe that the parenthetical phrase qualifies *inter alia* the expression "bankers drafts", which generally refers to a draft drawn by a bank on itself.[161] Bankers' drafts are payment instruments used in international trade transactions between importers and exporters. Like other payment instruments listed in subsector (d), bankers' drafts must be settled in order to complete the transaction.[162] In our view, the word "settlement" at the end of the phrase refers to the completed transaction. Therefore, the parenthetical phrase serves to confirm that payment services for transactions between importers and exporters where payment occurs by means of bankers' drafts are covered by subsector (d) of China's Schedule.

7.116 We note China's argument that the fact that subsector (d) does not use the word "clearing" should be given interpretative significance.[163] In the Panel's view, the fact that the word "clearing" is not mentioned in the bracketed language does not mean that no clearing is involved in situations where bankers' drafts are used. Bankers' drafts, like any other type of cheque, are normally cleared before they are settled. We also note that various sources suggest that clearing is usually a prior step to settlement: the term "clearing" is defined as "[t]he system of settling payments due from one bank to another"[164] or "[t]he exchange of mutual claims by financial institutions with settlement of the net

---

[159] China's response to Panel question No. 83, paras. 1-3; and comments on United States' response to Panel question No. 83, para. 53.

[160] In response to Panel question No. 83, China submits that "[t]he term 'import and export settlement' refers to the services that banks provide as payment intermediaries for import and export transactions. ... They involve banks acting as trusted payment intermediaries to allow the parties to an import/export transaction to avoid the use of cash." China's response to Panel question No. 83, para. 1.

[161] See above fn. 156 for definitions of "bank draft".

[162] We note in this regard that the BIS definition cited above in fn. 156 likens bankers' drafts to cheques.

[163] China's comments on United States' response to Panel question No. 83, para. 53.

[164] *Oxford Dictionary of Economics,* 3rd ed., Oxford University Press, 2009, Exhibit CHN-4, p. 64.

balance".[165] Settlement marks the final stage in an import/export transaction completed through bankers' drafts. Hence, in our view, "clearing" of a bankers' draft is implied in the parenthetical phrase.

7.117 We understand China's arguments to suggest that the language in parentheses applies primarily to letters of credit.[166] We agree that letters of credit are payment instruments used in international trade transactions and that payment services to complete transactions through letters of credit arguably can fall under subsector (d). Thus the words "including import and export settlement" might also relate to letters of credit. We observe, however, that letters of credit are not mentioned in the illustrative list under subsector (d). Moreover, a parenthetical phrase is a grammatical device often used to link the words in parenthesis to language that precedes them.[167] Here, the parenthetical phrase follows a list of instruments that does not include letters of credit. In our view, it is implausible that the parenthetical phrase relates primarily to letters of credit, i.e. a payment instrument that has not even been included in the list that precedes the parenthetical phrase.

7.118 The Panel therefore concludes that the parenthetical addition "(including import and export settlement)" in China's Schedule confirms that subsector (d) includes settlement, and by implication clearing, e.g. when bankers' drafts are used as payment instruments for transactions between importers and exporters. We perceive no sound basis for assuming that subsector (d) includes settlement, and where appropriate clearing, of transactions involving the use of bankers' drafts, but that it would exclude settlement and clearing of transactions involving the use of the *other* payment instruments listed in subsector (d). In our view, the parenthetical phrase merely seeks to make explicit – in relation to one particular type of transaction – something that the broad phrase "[a]ll payment and money transmission services ..." already contains implicitly.

Summary of findings on the phrase "including credit, charge and debit cards, travellers cheques and bankers drafts (including import and export settlement)"

7.119 Our examination of the phrase "including credit, charge and debit cards, travellers cheques and bankers drafts" in subsector (d) as immediate context for

---

[165] *Banking Terminology*, Exhibit CHN-3, p. 64-65, definition 2. Another source defines "clearing" as "the process of transmitting, reconciling and, in some cases, confirming payment orders or security transfer instructions prior to settlement, possibly including the netting of instructions and the establishment of final positions for settlement." BIS Glossary, Exhibits US-68; CHN-2, p. 13.

[166] China's response to Panel question No. 83, para. 2. United States' rebuttal arguments regarding China's letter of credit arguments are set out in United States' response to Panel question No. 83, paras. 54-58.

[167] The *Shorter Oxford English Dictionary*, Vol. 2, p. 2102 defines "parenthesis" as "a word, clause, sentence, etc., inserted (as an explanation, qualification, aside, or afterthought) into a passage which is already grammatically complete, and usu. marked off by brackets, dashes, or commas."

interpreting the preceding words "[a]ll payment and money transmission services", led us to conclude that this phrase is an illustrative list which provides confirmation that the phrase "[a]ll payment and money transmission services" includes those services that are essential to the processing and completion of transactions using payment cards. Moreover, the parenthetical addition "(including import and export settlement)" confirms that subsector (d) includes settlement, and by implication clearing, when bankers' drafts are used as payment instruments for transactions between importers and exporters. The parenthetical addition also suggests to us that settlement and clearing of transactions involving the use of other payment instruments listed in subsector (d) would likewise be classifiable under this subsector.

7.120 We now proceed to examine whether other contextual elements confirm or undermine these conclusions.

(ii) Other elements of China's Schedule

The subheading "Banking services as listed below" in the sectoral column of China's Schedule

7.121 China argues that subsector (d) is one of six subsectors listed in China's Schedule under the heading "Banking services ...". According to China, the ordinary meaning of "banking services" is services provided by banks. Consistent with this ordinary meaning, all of the services listed under the heading of "Banking services ..." are services that are typically provided by banks, finance companies, and other types of financial institutions. China also submits that China's market access and national treatment inscriptions for mode 3 confirm that the services encompassed by subsectors (a) through (f) are services supplied by banks and other financial institutions, which confirms that subsector (d) does not encompass services that are supplied to banks by non-bank service suppliers. According to China, when interpreted in this context, the "payment services" referred to in subsector (d) encompass the issuance and acceptance by financial institutions of payment instruments other than cash. China also submits that there is no indication in any Member's commitments for subsector (viii) of the Annex that these services are provided by suppliers other than banks or other financial institutions.[168]

7.122 The United States submits that the heading "Banking services..." does not have the effect of limiting the scope of the commitments to "banks" and other "regulated financial institutions". According to the United States, the definition of "financial institution" offered by China is far too narrow. The United States also observes that, in addition to the explicit reference to "non-

[168] China's first written submission, paras. 95-98; and China's response to Panel question No. 60, paras. 108 and 109. The Panel recalls that subsector (viii) of the Annex corresponds to subsector (d) of China's Schedule.

bank financial institutions" in China's Schedule, there are other references to "foreign finance companies" in the market access column and to "foreign financial leasing corporations" in the additional commitments column. The United States further argues that, even if China's approach were correct, suppliers of payment card services would qualify because they were formerly operated as associations of banks and, according to the United States, the nature of the service that an entity supplies does not change merely because that entity assumes a new corporate form. The United States also submits that the characteristics and nature of the service control the classification of that service, and where the identity of the supplier is relevant, the sectoral description must clearly indicate that to be the case.[169]

7.123 Australia, the European Union, Guatemala and Korea are of the view that the subheading "Banking services ..." does not affect the scope of China's commitments under subsector (d).[170]

7.124 The Panel notes that the heading "B. Banking and Other Financial Services ..." in China's Schedule encompasses four categories, namely "Banking services as listed below", "Motor vehicle financing by non-bank financial institutions", "Other financial services as listed below", and "Securities".[171] Subsector (d) is listed under the subheading "Banking services as listed below". The four categories are specific to China's Schedule: they are not present in the GATS Annex on Financial Services and do not appear in other WTO Members' GATS schedules.

7.125 Turning first to the ordinary meaning of "banking", this term is defined as (i) "the provision of payments facilities, credit, and capital to individuals, firms, and the government. ...";[172] (ii) "the business of banks";[173] and (iii) "the area of finance related to taking of deposits, granting of loans, and provision of other financial services, which may include investment, trading, and advisory".[174] We observe that these definitions do not indicate that "banks" are necessarily the exclusive providers of "banking" services.

7.126 We also observe that all of the services listed in subsectors (a) to (f) under the subheading at issue are commonly supplied by banks, but non-bank

[169] United States' second written submission, paras. 118-124; and response to Panel questions No. 60, paras. 151-153 and No. 61, paras. 154 and 155.
[170] Australia's third-party response to Panel question No. 9 (no paragraph numbering provided); European Union's third-party response to Panel question No. 9, para. 29; Guatemala's third-party's response to Panel question No. 9, para. 34; and Korea's third-party's response to Panel question No. 9 (no paragraph numbering provided).
[171] See excerpt of China's Schedule in Annex G to this Report. We note that the last three subheadings are preceded by a hyphen. We view the lack of a hyphen before "Banking services as listed below" as a typographical error.
[172] *Oxford Dictionary of Economics*, 3rd ed., Oxford University Press, 2009, Exhibit CHN-41, p. 26.
[173] *Dictionary of Banking and Finance,* 4th ed., A & C Black, 2010, Exhibit CHN-42, p. 30.
[174] *The Palgrave Macmillan Dictionary of Finance, Investment and Banking*, Exhibit CHN-47, p. 46.

financial services suppliers can also supply them. For example, deposits (subsector (a)) can be taken by post offices; loans (subsector (b)) can be granted by post offices and finance companies; leasing services (subsector (c)) can be supplied by leasing companies; money can be transferred (subsector (d)) by post offices or other specialized suppliers; guarantees (subsector (e)) can be granted by finance companies; and foreign exchange (subsector (f)) can be traded by specialised foreign exchange dealers and brokers. Hence, in practice, different types of entities can supply the services listed in subsectors (a) to (f).

7.127 Moreover, the commitments contained in the market access column, which are relevant context for interpreting the subheading at issue, make reference to "finance companies", which are non-bank entities.[175] Finally, the additional commitments column under the subheading "Banking services ..." contains a reference to "financial leasing corporations" which are also non-bank entities. With these considerations in mind, it is clear to us that "banking services" as that term appears under the subheading at issue includes services supplied by banks and *non*-banks.

7.128 China argues that "[c]onsistent with this ordinary meaning [i.e. the ordinary meaning of banking services, which, according to China, refers to "services provided by banks"], all of the services listed under the heading of 'banking services' are services that are typically provided *by banks, finance companies, and other types of financial institutions*."[176] In other words, China's argument amounts to saying that "services provided by banks" are "services provided by banks *and non*-banks".

7.129 Moreover, as pointed out by the United States, when China wished to undertake a commitment with respect to a certain category of supplier only, it did so explicitly, such as in the subsector "[m]otor vehicle financing by non-bank financial institutions".[177]

7.130 Furthermore, the Panel observes that, as evidenced by the arguments presented by both the United States and China, there is a close historical association between banks and EPS suppliers. Both parties have made reference to the fact that certain United States' EPS suppliers were operated as associations of banks until 2006, i.e. until well after China's accession to the WTO in 2001.[178] If, as argued by China, the identity of the supplier is relevant for purposes of classifying services, then those EPS suppliers were arguably providing "banking services" as China defines that term (i.e. services supplied by banks) until they changed their corporate form in 2006. The Panel has already indicated that it

---

[175] A "finance company" is defined as "a non-bank financial institution ..." See *The Palgrave Macmillan Dictionary of Finance, Investment and Banking*, Exhibit CHN-88, p. 206.

[176] China's first written submission, para. 95 (emphasis added).

[177] United States' response to Panel question No. 60, para. 152.

[178] China's first written submission, para. 50 ("Prior to their initial public offerings in 2006, Visa and MasterCard were operated as associations of banks ... that issued and acquired payment cards under a common brand."); and United States' response to Panel question No. 60, para. 152.

does not share China's narrow interpretation of the term "banking services". Having said that, the Panel agrees with the United States that the classification of a service should not change solely because the suppliers of that service modify their ownership structure or legal form. Such an interpretative approach to classification would undermine the predictability, security and clarity of GATS specific commitments.

7.131 We also find relevant in this respect evidence submitted by China (to which we referred in connection with determining whether the services in question are supplied as integrated services)[179] demonstrating that, in France, for example, the authorization system for payment card transactions is operated by CB, an association of banks. Moreover, clearing and settlement of retail payments transactions, including payment card transactions, is operated by STET Inter-bank Payment Services, an institution created and still owned by five banks in France. In our view, this is further evidence of the continuing link between banks and EPS.[180]

7.132 Finally, as noted above, the heading "B. Banking and Other Financial Services ..." encompasses four subheadings, namely, "Banking services as listed below", "Motor vehicle financing by non-bank financial institutions", "Other financial services as listed below", and "Securities". The subheadings "Banking services as listed below" and "Other financial services as listed below" group together, respectively, six and two subsectors. We note that the pattern of market access and national treatment commitments under each of these four subheadings is different. Hence, in our view, the heading "Banking services as listed below" may also serve a practical purpose, which is to separate China's commitments that apply in the same way to subsectors (a) to (f) from its commitments that apply only to certain categories of services (motor vehicle financing by non-bank financial institutions) or to other services listed further down in China's Schedule (namely, other financial services ... and securities). As indicated, China has undertaken different market access and national treatment commitments under the four subheadings in question.

7.133 In sum, our analysis of the subheading "Banking services as listed below" leads us to conclude that this subheading is not indicative of an intention to circumscribe the commitments under subsectors (a) to (f) to a certain category of services suppliers, namely banks. Rather, this subheading indicates that the services concerned are typically supplied by banks, or were typically provided by banks in the past. This does not detract from the fact, however, that some of these services can be, and are, also provided by other types of financial entities. Additionally, and from a more practical point of view, this subheading may also serve to separate commitments undertaken in respect of subsectors (a) to (f) from

[179] See para. 7.60 above.

[180] See China's response to Panel question No. 75, para. 2 and *Cartes Bancaires* 2010 Annual Report, Exhibit CHN-106, p. 13.

different commitments undertaken in respect of other subsectors listed further down in China's Schedule.

7.134 We conclude therefore that the placement of subsector (d) under the heading "Banking services as listed below" does not contradict our view explained above that subsector (d) encompasses services that are essential to the processing and completion of transactions using payment cards.

The market access commitment under mode 1

7.135 In its arguments concerning the scope of the market access commitment undertaken by China under mode 1[181], the United States submits that the word "Unbound" in China's market access commitment under mode 1 is followed by the qualifying phrase "except for the following," which in turn is further elaborated by two sentences that describe elements of the services within subsector (d) for which China has undertaken mode 1 commitments, namely:

- Provision and transfer of financial information, and financial data processing and related software by suppliers of other financial services;
- Advisory, intermediation and other auxiliary financial services on all activities listed in subparagraphs (a) through (k), including credit reference and analysis, investment and portfolio research and advice, advice on acquisitions and on corporate restructuring and strategy.

7.136 For the United States, China's mode 1 commitment must be understood as recognizing that elements of "payment and money transmission" services include "provision and transfer of financial information" and "advisory, intermediation and other auxiliary services", to the extent that such elements are integral to the core service, and that the service of which they form a part is properly classified within "payment and money transmission" services and not in subsector (k) or (l) of China's Schedule.[182]

7.137 China replies that, in an effort to "jam" all of the services at issue into the exception to China's unbound mode 1 inscription for subsector (d), the United States takes the position that all five of the "components" of the services at issue match the descriptions of subsectors (k) and (l). By doing so, the United States removes everything from the basket of subsector (d) and, as a result, has nothing left in this subsector.[183]

---

181 The Panel will use the term "mode 1" to refer to the supply of a service that is "from the territory of one Member into the territory of any other Member", as provided for in Article I:2(a) of the GATS.

182 United States' response to Panel question No. 45, para. 118; and second written submission, paras. 103-108.

183 China's second written submission, paras. 37 and 38.

7.138 The Panel is of the view that the market access entry under mode 1 constitutes relevant context for the purpose of interpreting the scope of subsector (d). The Panel refers to its detailed discussion of China's market access commitment under mode 1 in Section VII.F.1(a) below. There, the Panel finds that this entry is properly understood as referencing China's mode 1 market access commitment for subsectors (k) and (l). Hence, the context provided by the market access entry under mode 1 does not suggest an interpretation that is different from that suggested by the other contextual elements examined so far. In other words, the mode 1 market access commitment does not contradict our conclusion that subsector (d) encompasses services that are essential to the processing and completion of transactions using payment cards.

(iii) The GATS Annex on Financial Services

The scope of subsector (xiv) in the Annex

7.139 Article XXIX of the GATS (*Annexes*) states that "[t]he Annexes to this Agreement are an integral part of this Agreement". Pursuant to that provision, the GATS Annex on Financial Services is treaty text. Moreover, it constitutes context for purposes of interpreting China's Schedule, which is itself an integral part of the GATS. Paragraph 5 (*Definitions*) of the Annex contains several definitions and a classification of financial services that WTO Members may use – and many of them did use – when scheduling their commitments on financial services. We recall that China stated that it scheduled its financial services commitments by reference to the definition of financial services set forth in the Annex.[184] We shall therefore turn to the Annex as relevant context for the interpretation of China's Schedule.

7.140 Subsector (xiv) in paragraph 5(a) of the Annex, which falls under the heading "Banking and other financial services (excluding insurance)", states as follows:

> Settlement and clearing services for financial assets, including securities, derivative products, and other negotiable instruments[185]

7.141 China argues that the clearing and settlement services at issue in this dispute are classifiable under subsector (xiv) of the Annex, a subsector for which China undertook no commitments. China maintains that every definition of the term "financial assets" points to the conclusion that it refers to "money and claims", including cash and any right to receive cash. Furthermore, the reference to "negotiable instruments" in subsector (xiv) unambiguously includes retail payment instruments, such as cheques and travellers' cheques. It is China's view

---

[184] China's first written submission, para. 80.

[185] We note China's comment that "[b]ecause the process of 'clearing' comes before the process of 'settlement', China will refer to 'clearing and settlement services' even though item (xiv) refers to these two processes in the opposite order" (China's first written submission, fn. 49). Like China and for the same reason, we shall refer to "clearing and settlement services".

that, as context, the illustrative list of examples confirms that the drafters of subsector (xiv) intended to use the term "financial assets" according to its common and ordinary meaning.[186]

7.142 The United States replies that China's position is inconsistent with the ordinary meaning of "settlement and clearing services for financial assets" and fails to recognize that subsector (xiv) constitutes a substantially different financial service than the services at issue. It argues that China's position also fails to interpret the term "financial asset" within its immediate context, which is the full sentence in subsector (xiv).[187]

7.143 Australia argues that subsector (xiv) covers settlement and clearing services for financial assets, other than card based transactions. Settlement and clearing services for financial assets are clearly distinct from the settlement and clearing activity that is part of payment and money transmissions, such as credit card transactions.[188] The European Union submits that the clearing and settlement services involved in the trading (buying and selling) of "securities, derivative products and other negotiable instruments" are separate and distinct from the "payment and money transmission services" which take place when there is a transfer of funds between different persons or entities, in order to settle "credit, charge or debit card" transactions".[189] According to Korea, subsector (xiv) of the Annex addresses mainly paper-based financial asset transactions which, in and of themselves, represent or carry designated monetary value. The term "financial assets" refers to an object or instrument that contains or represents some sort of monetary value to its owner, which can subsequently be sold or negotiated; this is not the case for credit card or credit card transactions.[190]

7.144 The Panel observes that the parties do not dispute that payment card transactions must be cleared and settled. They disagree, however, where the clearing and settlement of payment card transactions should be classified. We recall that our interpretation of subsector (d) thus far has led us to the view that this subsector includes those services that are essential to the processing and completion of transactions using payment cards. We also concluded, in paragraph 7.118 above, that the parenthetical addition "(including import and export settlement)" confirms that subsector (d) includes settlement, and by implication clearing. Consistent with this view, clearing and settlement of payment card transactions should *a priori* be classified under subsector (d),

---

[186] China's first written submission, paras. 79-89; response to Panel question No. 39(a), para. 47; and second written submission, paras. 2-33.

[187] United States' response to Panel question No. 24, paras. 68-80; and second written submission, paras. 42-74.

[188] Australia's third-party submission, para. 17; and third-party response to Panel question No. 1 (no paragraph numbering provided).

[189] European Union's third-party submission, para. 27.

[190] Korea's third-party submission, para. 1; and third-party response to Panel question No. 15(a) (no paragraph numbering provided).

because they are essential services to complete a payment card transaction. We also recall that, although we decided to begin our analysis with subsector (d) of China's Schedule, we also said that we would turn to subsector (xiv) of the Annex before reaching a final conclusion on the scope of subsector (d).[191]

7.145 Starting with an examination of the ordinary meaning of the terms "clearing", "settlement" and "financial assets", the Panel notes the following definitions:

> Clearing: "process of transmitting, reconciling and, in some cases, confirming payment orders or security transfer instructions prior to settlement, possibly including the netting of instructions and the establishment of final positions for settlement"[192] or "(a) the exchange of the payment instrument or of relevant payment information between the payer's and the payee's financial institutions, and (b) the calculation of claims for settlement".[193]
>
> Settlement: "an act that discharges obligations in respect of funds or securities transfers between two or more parties"[194] or "a transfer of funds to complete one or more prior transactions that were made subject to final settlement. Settlement is the point at which underlying claims and obligations are satisfied".[195]
>
> Financial assets: "[m]oney and claims, as distinct from physical assets such as land, buildings, or equipment. Financial assets include money, securities constituting a claim to receive money, such as bills or bonds, and shares giving indirect ownership of the physical assets of companies. The claims held as financial assets include the obligations of individuals, companies, and governments, domestic and foreign. Financial assets include shares in financial institutions, and derivatives such as options."[196] Other definitions describe a "financial asset" as "[a]n asset that is either cash, a contractual right to receive cash, or the right to exchange a financial instrument with another entity under potentially favourable terms or an equity instrument of another entity";[197] or "assets in the form of stocks, bonds, rights, certificates, bank balances, etc., as distinguished from tangible, physical assets …".[198]

[191] See para. 7.72 above.

[192] BIS Glossary, Exhibits US-68 and CHN-2, p. 13.

[193] BIS (CPSS), Clearing and Settlement Arrangements for Retail Payments in Selected Countries, 2000, Exhibit CHN-1, pp. 2-6.

[194] BIS Glossary, Exhibits CHN-2 and US-68, p. 45.

[195] *Banking Terminology*, Exhibit CHN-5, p. 323, definition 3.

[196] *A Dictionary of Economics*, 3rd ed., Oxford University Press, 2009, Exhibit CHN-32, p. 167.

[197] *A Dictionary of Accounting*, Oxford University Press, 1999, Exhibit CHN-38, p. 161.

[198] *Dictionary of Finance and Investment Terms*, 8th ed., Barron's, New York, 2010, Exhibit CHN-34, p. 257.

Financial: "of or pertaining to revenue or money matters".[199]

7.146 An examination of dictionary definitions and other specialized glossaries suggests that the ordinary meaning of the words "clearing" and "settlement" refers to activities that are relevant for both retail payment instruments and securities. The ordinary meaning of the term "financial assets" encompasses virtually all financial instruments. We also observe that definitions of the terms used in subsector (xiv) may overlap with definitions of terms in subsector (d) – for instance, "settlement" and "payment" are almost synonymous.[200] It is difficult, therefore, to ascertain the scope of subsector (d) of China's Schedule and that of subsector (xiv) of the Annex based solely on the ordinary meaning of the terms used in these sector descriptions. We also recall that the Appellate Body has cautioned against using dictionary definitions in a mechanical manner.[201]

7.147 Thus, while we agree with China that an interpretation of the term "financial assets" must begin with the ordinary meaning of the terms, our interpretation cannot end there. We recall that, pursuant to Article 31(1) of the Vienna Convention, the ordinary meaning of "financial assets" must be interpreted "in good faith in accordance with the ordinary meaning to be given to the terms of the treaty *in their context* and in the light of its object and purpose" (emphasis added). With this in mind, we now turn to the phrase "including securities, derivative products, and other negotiable instruments", which follows immediately after the words "settlement and clearing for financial assets" in subsector (xiv) and hence constitutes immediate context.

7.148 The United States argues that illustrative lists may be more than merely non-exhaustive lists of examples. They may also inform the overall scope of a provision and the meaning of a term that they illustrate. An examination of each of the items in the illustrative list in subsector (xiv) demonstrates that retail receipts, such as a claim on a payment card, are not the same type of financial asset as the items included in the illustrative list ("securities", "derivative products" and "other negotiable instruments"). According to the United States, the illustrative list of financial assets in subsector (xiv) indicates that the scope of those assets is limited to tradable investment instruments, which supports the conclusion that the term "financial assets" as used in subsector (xiv) is intended to be limited to these types of instruments.[202]

7.149 China submits that the three examples in the illustrative list do not constitute an exhaustive list of what constitutes a "financial asset" under

---

199 *Shorter Oxford English Dictionary*, Vol. 1, p. 964. The *Shorter Oxford English Dictionary* does not contain a definition for financial asset or for clearing.

200 See, above in section VII.D.2(a) our analysis of the ordinary meaning of the terms used in subsector (d) of China's Schedule.

201 Appellate Body Report, *US – Gambling*, para. 164.

202 United States' response to Panel question No. 42, para. 107; and second written submission, paras. 75-93.

subsector (xiv). Moreover, according to China, the United States tries to work backwards from these examples to limit the ordinary meaning of the term "financial assets" to what it calls "tradeable financial instruments" or, alternatively, "tradeable investment instruments". For China, the reference to "negotiable instruments" in subsector (xiv) unambiguously includes retail payment instruments such as cheques and traveller's cheques. Like securities and derivatives, these are "financial assets" within the ordinary meaning of that term because they give rise to claims for payment. Moreover, China contends that because subsector (viii) of the Annex provides examples of negotiable instruments as types of "payment services", the drafters understood that the clearing and settlement of these instruments under subsector (xiv) is distinct from the issuance and acceptance of these instruments under subsector (viii).[203]

7.150 The Panel is of the view that the list contained in subsector (xiv) sheds light on the type of clearing and settlement services covered under that subsector. In this respect, we recall the view of the panel in *China – Publications and Audiovisual Products* that "the word 'including' in ordinary usage indicates that what follows is not an exhaustive, but a partial, list of all covered items".[204] We find this statement to be correct in the specific context of subsector (xiv), and so, like the parties, we regard the list as illustrative. Accordingly, we conclude that this illustrative list is a non-exhaustive enumeration of the kinds of "financial assets", the clearing and settlement of which are classified under subsector (xiv).

7.151 We observe that although the parties appear to concur that the illustrative list in item (xiv) informs the understanding of the term "financial assets", they reach different conclusions on the meaning and scope of that term. For the United States, illustrative lists "may help to inform the overall scope of a provision and the meaning of a term that they illustrate".[205] For China, the reference to "negotiable instruments" in the illustrative list of subsector (xiv) "necessarily informs the understanding of the term 'financial assets'".[206]

7.152 We now turn to the specific financial instruments listed in the illustrative list of subsector (xiv), i.e. securities, derivative products, and other negotiable instruments, and start with an examination of their ordinary meaning:

> Security: "A document held by a credit as guarantee of his or her right to payment; a certificate attesting ownership of stock, shares, etc.; the financial asset represented by such a document. Also (US), such a document issued to investors to finance a business

[203] China's response to Panel question No. 39(c), paras. 54-62; and second written submission, paras. 15-26. It will be recalled that subsector (viii) states as follows: "[a]ll payment and money transmission services, including credit, charge and debit cards, travellers cheques and bankers drafts" and that China states that subsector (d) was based on subsector (viii). See, para. 7.106 above.

[204] Panel Report, *China – Publications and Audiovisual Products*, para. 7.294.

[205] United States' second written submission, para. 75.

[206] China's response to Panel question No. 39(a), para. 49.

venture";[207] or "A pledge of financial or physical property to be surrendered in the event of failure to repay a loan. Any medium of investment in the money market or capital market, e.g. a money-market instrument, a bond, a share. A term used to refer only to bonds, and shares, as distinct from money-market assets."[208]

Derivative product: "An arrangement or instrument (such as a future, option, or warrant) whose value derives from and is dependent on the value of an underlying asset.";[209] or "a financial contract the value of which depends on the value of one or more underlying reference assets, rates or indices. For analytical purposes, all derivatives contracts can be divided into basic building blocks of forward contracts, options or combinations thereof."[210]

7.153 Definitions found in general and specialized dictionaries suggest that "securities" (i) are a medium of investment, (ii) attest ownership rights and (iii) grant financial returns. Derivative products essentially share these same characteristics.

7.154 We consider now the ordinary meaning of the term "negotiable instruments". The word "negotiable" is defined as follows: "[o]f a bill, draft, cheques, etc.: transferable or assignable in the course of business from one person to another simply by delivery."[211] A "negotiable instrument" is "a document of title that can be freely negotiated ..."[212] or "unconditional order or promise to pay an amount of money, easily transferable from one person to another".[213] The characteristics of "negotiable instruments", as identified in specialized dictionaries, are that they (i) are easily transferable from one person to another, and (ii) can be freely negotiated.

7.155 In our view, the reference to "securities, derivative products and other negotiable instruments" indicates that this subsector deals with financial assets which have in common the characteristic of being "negotiable". Many types of financial instruments are negotiable and some retail payment instruments listed under subsector (d) of China's Schedule, such as traveller's cheques and banker's drafts, may be negotiable. In contrast, we observe, and the parties seem to

---

207 *Shorter Oxford English Dictionary*, Vol. 2, p. 2733.

208 The Economist, *Dictionary of Business*, by Graham, Davis, Trott, Uncles, Bloomberg Press, 2003, Exhibit US-69, p. 334.

209 *Shorter Oxford English Dictionary*, Vol. 1, p. 653.

210 BIS Glossary, Exhibit US-68, p. 20.

211 *Shorter Oxford English Dictionary*, Vol. 2, p. 1905.

212 *A Dictionary of Finance and Banking*, Oxford Paperback Reference, Oxford, 2008, Exhibit CHN-39, p. 303.

213 *Dictionary of Finance and Investment Terms*, 8th ed., Barron's, New York, 2010, Exhibit CHN-40, p. 469.

agree,[214] that plastic payment cards and sales slips signed in connection with payment card transactions are not negotiable instruments because they are neither transferable nor can they be traded on a market. Hence, on this basis we consider that payment cards and sales slips do not fall within the category of "other negotiable instruments" referred to in the illustrative list of subsector (xiv).

7.156 China argues, however, that payment cards have "common features" with bankers' drafts and traveller's cheques in the sense that each of these instruments gives rise to inter-bank claims for payment between acquiring banks and issuing banks, and that such claims need to be cleared and settled. China concludes that, "since it is beyond any reasonable dispute that the clearing and settlement of negotiable instruments is encompassed by item (xiv), it would be arbitrary and illogical to conclude that clearing and settlement services for certain types of retail payment instruments are covered by item (xiv), while clearing and settlement services for other types of retail payment instruments are covered by item (viii) ".[215]

7.157 The United States submits that there are many types of negotiable instruments and, while some are used for payments (for example, cheques), others are used as investment vehicles (for example, commercial paper). The reference to "negotiable instruments" in subsector (xiv) does not include all such instruments. In the United States' view, subsector (xiv) only indicates that there are negotiable instruments that settle and clear like securities and derivative products. However, subsector (xiv) cannot be read properly to mean that all negotiable instruments are settled and cleared like securities and derivative products. Thus, the United States considers that to the extent a negotiable instrument appears in subsector (viii), it is not a negotiable instrument referred to in subsector (xiv).[216]

7.158 The Panel observes that, according to China, the clearing and settling of payment card transactions should be covered under subsector (xiv) because payment cards have "common features" with other payment instruments listed in subsector (d) (for example, bankers' drafts and travellers' cheques), these "common features" being, in China's view, that "(1) each is a type of payment

[214] The United States submits that "[p]ayment cards and the sales slips generated from payment card transactions do not meet the internationally accepted criteria for a negotiable instrument." United States' second written submission, para. 81. China states that "[c]redit, charge, and debit cards are more modern payment instruments, and their relationship to the concept of negotiability is more complicated. It is clear that the cards themselves – the pieces of plastic – are not negotiable instruments. … The slip is a promise to pay, but, in many cases, that promise will be subject to the terms and conditions of a contractual agreement (e.g. the cardholder agreement between the issuer and the cardholder). In these circumstances, the promise to pay may not be "unconditional", which is usually a formal requirement of negotiability." China's response to Panel's question No. 39(a), para. 48.

[215] China's response to Panel question No. 39(a), paras. 49 and 50.

[216] United States' response to Panel question No. 39(a), paras. 99-100.

instrument that is issued by banks; and (2) that each of these instruments gives rise to inter-bank claims for payment between acquiring banks and issuing banks, which such [*sic*] claims need to be cleared and settled."[217] In other words, China's interpretation brings the clearing and settlement of *non*-negotiable payment instruments, such as payment cards, within the scope of subsector (xiv). What appears to matter most, in China's view, is that clearing and settlement services for all financial instruments, whether negotiable or not, be classified in the same subsector.

7.159 It is not clear to us, however, how this interpretative approach can be reconciled with the terms used in subsector (xiv). First, we note that subsector (xiv) does not refer to "all settlement and clearing services", in contrast to the "[a]ll payment and money transmission services" found in subsector (d). Furthermore, we observe that the illustrative list includes two specific terms – "securities and derivative products" – and a broader, residual category – "other negotiable instruments". The adjective "other"[218] ties "negotiable instruments" back to "securities" and "derivative products", thereby establishing a nexus between these three categories of instruments. Reading the term "other negotiable instruments" with reference to the terms "securities" and "derivative products" that precede it supports the conclusion that the term "negotiable instruments" does not include any and all instruments that are "negotiable". We note in this respect that the illustrative list does not say "*any* other negotiable instruments" or "other negotiable instruments *of any kind*". Thus, we consider that the term "other negotiable instruments", read in its context, covers only those instruments that share essentially the same characteristics as securities and derivative products.

7.160 Turning to the term "securities", we noted above that this term is defined as a means of investment attesting ownership rights and granting financial returns. We also noted that derivative products essentially share these same characteristics. In our view, payment cards and other payment instruments listed in subsector (d) do not share these characteristics. In particular, payment instruments are not a means of investment, do not grant ownership rights and do not yield financial returns. Hence, we agree with the United States that instruments listed in subsector (d), such as travellers' cheques, although potentially negotiable, are not among the negotiable instruments falling within subsector (xiv).

7.161 Furthermore, we find convincing the arguments and factual evidence submitted by the United States that there are many practical differences between the systems used to clear and settle investment instruments of the kind referenced in subsector (xiv) and the systems used to clear and settle payment

---

[217] China's response to Panel question No. 39(a), para. 49.

[218] "Other" (adj.) is defined as "4 Existing besides or distinct from that or those already specified or implied; further, additional. …". *Shorter Oxford English Dictionary*, Vol. 2, p. 2035.

instruments, such as those mentioned in subsector (d).[219] These differences relate to the following: (i) the financial instruments involved and the value of typical transactions; (ii) the market participants involved in the transaction and related processing; (iii) the infrastructure needs for such processes to occur safely and efficiently; and (iv) regulatory oversight and systemic risk to the financial system. The distinction between payment systems and securities infrastructure as distinct components of the market infrastructure is common in many countries, including in China.[220]

7.162 China does not contest the differences between clearing and settlement of payment instruments, on the one hand, and securities and derivatives, on the other hand. China argues, however, that these differences are not relevant to the interpretation of the term "financial assets" and do not change the ordinary meaning of the term "negotiable instruments". We disagree. In our view, classification of services is not an abstract exercise; due regard should be had to market and regulatory realities. A classification approach reflecting, and in accord with, those realities contributes to the clarity and, therefore, security and predictability, of GATS specific commitments. Our reading of the scope of subsector (xiv) in the Annex and that of subsector (d) in China's Schedule is consistent with these considerations, because it takes due account of (i) the way payment systems are generally organized and regulated, as well as (ii) the essential differences between the settling and clearing of payment instruments and of securities and other negotiable instruments.

7.163 In sum, we find that subsector (xiv) encompasses the clearing and settlement of financial instruments sharing essentially the same characteristics as securities, derivative products and other negotiable instruments. More particularly, we consider that subsector (xiv) covers the clearing and settlement of financial instruments which have investment attributes, grant ownership rights and yield financial returns. Our conclusion is also based on the important practical differences between, on the one hand, the clearing and settlement of financial assets like securities and, on the other hand, the clearing and settlement of payment transactions. Hence, it is our view that retail payment instruments listed in subsector (d) of China's Schedule are not "financial assets" within the meaning that term has in subsector (xiv) of the Annex and, therefore, transactions based on the payment instruments listed in subsector (d), including payment cards, are not cleared and settled under subsector (xiv).

Subsector (x) of the Annex

7.164 Subsector (x) in paragraph 5(a) of the Annex on Financial Services reads as follows:

---

[219] United States' second written submission, paras. 55 to 74 and Exhibits cited in those paragraphs.

[220] The Panel asked China whether China UnionPay was involved in any stage of the clearing and settlement of securities in China. China replied "[n]o". China's response to Panel question No. 34, para. 35.

(x) Trading for own account or for account of customers, whether on an exchange, in an over-the-counter market or otherwise, the following:

(A) money market instruments (including cheques, bills, certificates of deposits);

(B) foreign exchange;

(C) derivative products including, but not limited to, futures and options;

(D) exchange rate and interest rate instruments, including products such as swaps, forward rate agreements;

(E) transferable securities;

(F) other negotiable instruments and financial assets, including bullion.

7.165 The United States argues that China's interpretation of "financial asset" and "negotiable instruments" as they appear in subsector (xiv) does not accord with how these terms are used elsewhere in the Annex. The United States notes that these terms also appear in paragraph 5(a), subsector (x) of the Annex. The illustrative list of tradable assets under subsector (x) includes "other negotiable instruments and financial assets, including bullion". Thus, according to the United States, "negotiable instruments" and "financial assets" as used in subsector (x) refer to tradable investment assets, rather than "[m]oney and claims." This indicates that "negotiable instruments" and "financial assets" are not retail payment vehicles like credit and debit cards.[221]

7.166 China submits that the United States overlooks the fact that subsector (x)(A) of the Annex explicitly refers to "cheques" as among the "negotiable instruments" and "financial assets" included within this category. According to China, "this fatally undermines the United States' insistence that the drafters of the Annex meant to exclude cheques from the ordinary meaning of the terms 'financial assets' and 'negotiable instruments'".[222]

7.167 The Panel observes that subsector (x) of the Annex contains a list of instruments that can be "traded for own account or for account of customers, ...". The Panel has already observed that cheques are among those retail payment instruments that are potentially negotiable. In our view, the list in subsector (x) confirms this point. Yet we do not consider that the fact that "cheques" are listed in subsector (x) as tradable instruments would support the view that clearing and settlement of cheques and other payment instruments

[221] United States' second written submission, paras. 94 and 95.

[222] China's opening statement at the second substantive meeting, para. 15.

should fall under subsector (xiv) of the Annex. It is only if one assumes that the clearing and settlement of potentially negotiable instruments of any kind falls under subsector (xiv) that this would be so, and we have already explained that we are unable to accept this assumption. Finally, we note that subsector (x) does not refer to payment cards, which also supports our earlier conclusion that payment cards are not negotiable instruments.

7.168 To conclude, we consider that the fact that subsector (x) in the Annex refers to cheques as a kind of tradable instrument does not invalidate our conclusion with respect to the scope of subsector (d) in China's Schedule.

Summary of findings on the GATS Annex on Financial Services

7.169 In our examination of subsector (xiv) of the Annex, we found that payment instruments listed in subsector (d) of China's Schedule, such as payment cards, are not "financial assets" within the meaning of that term as it is used in subsector (xiv) of the Annex. Therefore, in our view, the clearing and settlement of transactions involving the use of the payment instruments listed in subsectors (d) of China's Schedule are not covered under subsector (xiv) of the Annex. In our view, having regard to the broad phrase "[a]ll payment and money transmission services", clearing and settlement services concerning transactions using payment cards are properly classified under subsector (d). As concerns subsector (x) in the Annex, we found that the fact that it refers to cheques as tradable instruments does not invalidate our conclusion with respect to the scope of subsector (d) in China's Schedule.

7.170 Hence, our analysis of the context provided by the GATS Annex on Financial Services does not contradict our finding that subsector (d) of China's Schedule encompasses the services that are essential to the processing and completion of transactions using payment cards.

(iv) The structure of the GATS

7.171 We turn now to a consideration of the structure of the GATS. The United States submits that EPS fall within the ordinary meaning of "payment and money transmission services" as one type of "all" such services. EPS are at the centre of all payment card transactions and without these services the transactions could not occur. According to the United States, EPS involve the services through which transactions involving payment cards are processed and through which transfers of funds between institutions participating in the transactions are managed and facilitated. Moreover, EPS are integral to the processing of credit, charge, debit and other payment card-based electronic payment transactions, and without these services, payment card transactions could not occur.[223]

7.172 China submits that the assertion by the United States that subsector (d) encompasses all of the services at issue is based on an interpretation of this subsector that is "vastly overbroad." This interpretation would lead to the conclusion that this subsector encompasses not only services supplied by banks, but also services supplied to banks. Moreover, in China's view, services that "manage" or "facilitate" the supply of a service, or that relate to the "processing" of another service transaction, are not necessarily classifiable as that other service, but must be classified separately to the extent that they are distinct and separately identifiable services. China points out that, pursuant to the 2001 Scheduling Guidelines, "input" services must be classified and evaluated as distinct services. China further submits that a schedule of specific commitments is based on taxonomy of distinct and mutually exclusive services. Many of those services could be said to "manage" or "facilitate" the provision of other services within the taxonomy, or relate to the "processing" of a distinct service transaction. In China's view, this system of classifying services would collapse if distinct and separately identifiable services could be classified under another sector or subsector merely because they "manage", "facilitate", or relate to the "processing" of that service.[224]

7.173 The United States replies that it has described the entire package provided by an EPS supplier as "managing," "facilitating," or "enabling" the processing of payment card transactions in an effort to capture the "intrinsic linkage" between EPS and payment card transactions. EPS do not "manage," "facilitate," or relate to the "processing" of a payment and money transmission service. EPS are the service at issue. EPS "manage," "facilitate," and relate to the "processing" of payment card transactions – which is one type of payment service falling within "all payment and money transmission services" in subsector (d). According to the United States, EPS for payment card transactions constitute one integral, indivisible service. They are sold in a bundle and the service is a coherent whole, and the service supplier and service consumer are the same for the various component services. Without this integrated service, a payment card transaction could not happen. EPS for payment card transactions is a single service that is "intrinsically linked" to payment card transactions and that, for purposes of classification, should be analysed as a whole. The United States also submits that, if China's position were accepted – that a service must first be disaggregated into subcomponents and each subcomponent separately classified

[223] United States' response to China's request for a preliminary ruling, para. 149; first written submission, paras. 25-26; response to Panel question No. 26, paras. 84-86; and second written submission, paras. 13-18.

[224] China's first written submission, paras. 102-108.

– it would render WTO Members' concessions meaningless for a wide range of services.[225]

7.174 China further submits that network services are at most "inputs" to card issuance and acceptance services, and are better seen as altogether different services. The services supplied by network operators relate to how financial institutions interact with each other, not to how card holders and merchants interact with each other. For China, the United States is trying to imply in subsector (d) a right of market access for a different set of service suppliers who provide input services (at most) at an entirely different level of trade. This is not only inconsistent with the principle of mutual exclusivity, but with WTO Members' express recognition that input services must be classified and evaluated as distinct services. China also takes issue with the argument that EPS is "one integral, indivisible service" and notes that the United States shifted to the singular when referring to EPS. In China's view, the evidence establishes that different "elements" or "components" of what the United States calls "electronic payment services" are routinely supplied as different services by different service suppliers. Hence, these services are not "supplied and consumed as an integrated service".[226]

7.175 In the Panel's view, the arguments by the parties raise three issues: (i) the scope of subsector (d) as it relates to EPS; (ii) whether the fact that different components of EPS can be supplied by different suppliers means that these different components must be classified separately; and (iii) the relevance of the 2001 Scheduling Guidelines for interpreting subsector (d). We shall examine these three issues in turn.

7.176 Turning to the scope of subsector (d) as it relates to EPS, we recall that, in China's view, the "U.S. interpretation of subsector (d) as encompassing 'any service' that is somehow associated with the use of payment cards" is "vastly overbroad and inconsistent with well-established principles of interpreting Schedules of Specific Commitments".[227]

7.177 In addressing this issue, the Panel must first examine the concept of "sector" under the GATS. The Panel recalls that, in *US – Gambling*, the

---

[225] United States' second written submission, paras. 16 and 17.

[226] China's second written submission, paras. 52 and 53; opening statement at the second substantive meeting, para. 20; response to Panel question No. 75, paras. 1-3; and comments on United States' response to the Panel question Nos. 73-77, paras. 3-5 and 12.

[227] China's comments on United States' response to Panel question Nos. 73-77. In this comment, China refers to United States' first written submission, para. 22. We note that the United States referred to by China reads in fact: "China's commitments pertain to 'all payment and money transmission services, including credit, charge and debit cards', indicating that the scope of the commitment covers *any service that is essential to* 'payment and money transmission' including 'credit, charge, and debit cards' payment transactions". United States' first written submission, para. 22 (emphasis added).

Appellate Body referred to the definition of "'sector' of a service" contained in Article XXVIII(e)[228] and explained that:

> … the structure of the GATS necessarily implies two things. First, because the GATS covers *all* services except those supplied in the exercise of governmental authority, it follows that a Member may schedule a specific commitment in respect of *any* service. Second, because a Member's obligations regarding a particular service depend on the specific commitments that it has made with respect to the sector or Subsector within which that service falls, a specific service cannot fall within two different sectors or Subsectors. In other words, *the sectors and subsectors in a Member's Schedule must be mutually exclusive.*[229]

7.178 We also recall that, when referring to Article XXVIII(e)(ii) of the GATS, the panel in *China – Publications and Audiovisual Products*, found that:

> A description of a service sector in a GATS schedule does not need to enumerate every activity that is included within the scope of that service, and is not meant to do so. A service sector or subsector in a GATS schedule thus includes not only every service activity specifically named within it, but also any service activity that falls within the scope of the definition of that sector or subsector referred to in the schedule.[230]

7.179 Hence, the definition of "sector of a service" contained in the GATS and the finding of the Panel in *China – Publications and Audiovisual Products* confirm that a "sector" may include "any service activity that falls within the scope of the definition of that sector", whether or not these activities are explicitly enumerated in the definition of that sector or subsector.

7.180 The Panel observes that, when a card holder pays for a good or a service with a credit card and the merchant accepts that form of payment, both the card holder and the merchant naturally expect that the transaction for which that payment card is used will be completed. The completion of a transaction in which payment cards are used includes, at a minimum, what we referred to as "front-end processing" (which serves to authenticate and authorize transactions) and "back-end processing" (which essentially entails clearing and settlement of

---

[228] Article XXVIII provides that:

"(e) 'sector' of a service means,

(i) with reference to a specific commitment, one or more, or all, Subsectors of that service, as specified in a Member's Schedule,

(ii) otherwise, the whole of that service sector, including all of its Subsectors;"

[229] Appellate Body Report, *US – Gambling*, para. 180 (emphasis added). The Appellate Body further explained that "[i]f this were not the case [i.e. if sectors and subsectors were *not* mutually exclusive], and a Member scheduled the same service in two different sectors, then the scope of the Member's commitment would not be clear where, for example, it made a full commitment in one of those sectors and a limited, or no, commitment, in the other." *Ibid.*, fn. 219.

[230] Panel Report, *China – Publications and Audiovisual Products*, para. 7.1014.

the transaction).[231] In our view, there cannot be any "payment service" and "money transmission service" if the payment is not effected and the money not transferred from the customer's account to the merchant's account. In that sense and referring to the finding cited above, these activities, even though they are not explicitly listed in subsector (d), are necessarily included within the scope of the definition of that subsector because they must operate together for the payment and money transmission service to be supplied. The fact that they are not specifically listed under the subsector at issue does not matter, as stated by the panel in *China – Publications and Audiovisual Products*. Hence, we agree with the United States' characterization of subsector (d) as encompassing "any service that is essential to 'payment and money transmission'".[232] In the view of the Panel, the classification under a single entry, of a service made up of a combination of different services is not incompatible with the principle of mutual exclusivity when these combined services result in a distinct service, which is supplied and consumed as such.[233]

7.181 Finally, contrary to China's view[234], we consider that the fact that the United States switched from plural to singular when referring to "EPS" is immaterial for the purposes of services classification.[235] In our view, in a normal hierarchical classification scheme (like the CPC or the Annex on Financial Services), a service combining different services can be described simply as a "service", or as "services" in the plural. In the latter case, "services" refers to the sum of the different services classified by reference to the "service".

7.182 We examine now whether the fact that different components of the EPS can be supplied by different suppliers means that these different components must be classified separately. We recall that, according to the United States, "EPS for payment card transactions is a single, integrated service – one that is supplied and consumed as such".[236] China submits that different "elements" or "components" of the services at issue are routinely supplied as different services by different service suppliers. In particular, the network and authorization components of the services at issue are frequently supplied by entities other than

---

[231] See paras. 7.20 to 7.24 above.

[232] United States' first written submission, para. 22.

[233] We note that our interpretation is supported by a rule of interpretation in the CPC prov.:

"1. When services are, *prima facie*, classifiable under two or more categories, classification shall be effected as follows, on the understanding that only categories at the same level (sections, divisions, groups, classes or subclasses) are comparable: (a) The category that provides the most specific description shall be preferred to categories providing a more general description; (b) *Composite services consisting of a combination of different services which cannot be classified by reference to 1(a) shall be classified as if they consisted of the service which gives them their essential character, in so far as this criterion is applicable*." Provisional Central Product Classification, Statistical Papers, Series M No.77, United Nations (1991), p. 20 (emphasis added).

[234] China's comments on United States' response to Panel question Nos. 73-77, paras. 4 and 5.

[235] China's comments on United States' response to the Panel question Nos. 73-77, para. 2.

[236] United States' second written submission, para. 11 (citing further references to United States' written submissions). See also United States' second written submission, paras. 13-18.

the entities that provide clearing and settlement services for the same transactions. Hence, according to China, the United States' assertion that the services at issue are "supplied and consumed as an integrated service" is incorrect.[237]

7.183 The Panel observes that the manner in which the supply of integrated services such as the services at issue is organized depends on a number of parameters, including the business models adopted by specific companies, the regulatory framework in the country concerned, and how the direct users of payment services (e.g. issuing and acquiring institutions) organize their supply in specific jurisdictions.[238] Some companies may provide the various components of the services at issue, thus supplying a final product as a "package" for the direct users and for the ultimate beneficiaries of these services (i.e. the card holder, the issuer, the acquirer and the merchant). There may, however, be other circumstances where the different components are supplied by different suppliers.[239] The evidence submitted by China indicates, for instance, that, in the case of France, the authorization process, on the one hand, and clearing and settlement, on the other hand, are provided by two different entities.[240]

7.184 Thus, the evidence before us suggests that, in practice, the services essential to a payment card transaction to be completed may be supplied by one or more service supplier(s). As we have said, while some suppliers provide all the various components of that service in an integrated manner, other suppliers may specialize in one segment of that service. In our view, the fact that some component services may be supplied by different suppliers is not a sufficient basis for classifying each or some of these services under different subsectors. Indeed, as noted by the United States, "[i]t is the combination that enables the payment card transaction to occur".[241] Hence, the mere fact that separate suppliers provide one particular component of a service does not in itself imply that that component should be classified as a distinct service, or that the component is not part of an integrated service. In our view, what is relevant in relation to an integrated service is not whether it is supplied by a single supplier or by several suppliers, but rather whether the component services, when combined together, result in a new and distinct service, the integrated service.

7.185 We note that China itself appears to accept that some services, although supplied by different suppliers, are nonetheless classifiable under the same subsector. Indeed, issuing and acquiring services could be considered as two "distinct and separately identifiable services", to borrow China's terminology. As evidenced by the arguments of the parties, issuing and acquiring are different

---

237 China's opening statement at the second substantive meeting, paras. 20 and 21; response to Panel question No. 75, paras. 1-3; and comments on the United States' response to Panel question Nos. 73 and 77, para. 12.

238 See above section VII.C.1.

239 See our discussion above in para. 7.60.

240 China's response to Panel question No. 75, paras. 1-3, including the evidence indicated therein.

241 *Ibid.*

activities.[242] Moreover, for any given payment card transaction, the issuing and acquiring institutions are not necessarily the same entity; in the four-party model, they are often different entities. Nevertheless, China is not proposing to classify, respectively, issuing services and acquiring services under two separate subsectors, but argues instead that these two services fall under subsector (d).[243]

7.186 We turn now to the third issue raised by the parties, namely whether the services at issue are inputs into a service classified under subsector (d). We recall that, according to China, the 2001 Scheduling Guidelines expressly recognize that a specific commitment does not extend to input services that are separately classifiable within the relevant taxonomy of services. In China's view, the services at issue are at most "inputs" to card issuance and acceptance services, which, according to China, are classified under subsector (d) of its Schedule.[244]

7.187 According to China, the 2001 Scheduling Guidelines are a supplementary means of interpretation falling under Article 32 of the Vienna Convention.[245] We understand, therefore, that China is not proposing that we rely on the 2001 Scheduling Guidelines as context in our interpretation of subsector (d) pursuant to Article 31 of the Vienna Convention. Regardless of whether the 2001 Scheduling Guidelines may be considered as context or as supplementary means

---

[242] United States' response to China's request for a preliminary ruling, para. 43; and first written submission, para. 20.

[243] China submits that "China's *actual* commitment in subsector (d) … was to allow foreign financial institutions to enter its market on a commercial presence basis to issue payment cards to cardholders and acquire payment card transactions from merchants". China's first written submission, para. 8 (emphasis in the original). We recall that issuing and acquiring services are not at stake in this dispute and, hence, we do not need to determine where these services should be classified. We accept China's position merely for the sake of argument on this issue.

[244] China's first written submission, paras. 106-108; and second written submission, paras. 51 and 52. Paragraph 25 of the 2001 Scheduling Guidelines reads as follows: "[i]t is understood that market access and national treatment commitments apply only to the sectors or sub-sectors inscribed in the schedule. They do not imply a right for the supplier of a committed service to supply uncommitted services which are inputs to the committed service." See also paragraph 17 of the 1993 Scheduling Guidelines.

[245] China' response to Panel question No. 58, para. 105 ("The Appellate Body in *U.S. – Gambling* found that the 1993 Guidelines constitute 'supplementary means of interpretation' under Article 32 of the Vienna Convention. China sees no reason to depart from this finding with respect to the 2001 Guidelines.") In response to the same question, the United States submitted that "[w]ith respect to the 2001 Guidelines, there are questions that arise as to timing, such as whether they were actually available when China was negotiating its Services commitments". United States' response to Panel question No. 58, para. 145. We note that the third parties have different views as to whether the 2001 Scheduling Guidelines should be considered under Article 31 or 32 of the Vienna Convention. Australia considers that the 2001 are relevant context pursuant to Article 31 of the Vienna Convention, while the European Union and Guatemala view this document as belonging to supplementary means of interpretation pursuant to Article 32. Australia's third-party response to Panel question No. 6 (no paragraph numbering provided), the European Union's third-party response to Panel question No. 6, para. 18; and Guatemala's third-party response to Panel question No. 6, para. 24.

of interpretation, however, we are not persuaded by China's argument.[246] China has provided no evidence to support its assertion that EPS are "input" services into issuing and acquiring services. Nor has it explained through argument why this is so: it has merely pointed to a rule referring generally to "input" services. It is unclear to us, for example, whether it could be argued that issuing and acquiring services are "inputs" into EPS, as opposed to the other way around.[247] In the absence of supporting evidence or explanation related to EPS as inputs, we are unable to accept China's contention in this respect.

7.188 To summarize our interpretation of subsector (d) based on the structure of the GATS as context, we are of the view that the classification under a single subsector of a service made up of a combination of different services is not incompatible with the principle of mutual exclusivity if these services, when combined together, result in a distinct service that is supplied and consumed as such. Moreover, the mere fact that separate suppliers provide one particular component of a service does not in itself imply that that component should be classified as a distinct service, or that the component is not part of an integrated service. In our view, what is relevant in relation to the classification of an integrated service is not whether it is supplied by a single supplier or by several suppliers, but rather whether the component services, when combined together, result in a new and distinct service, the integrated service. This confirms our view that subsector (d) encompasses the services essential to the processing and completion of transactions using payment cards.

(v) Schedules of other WTO Members

7.189 China submits that other WTO Members consider the services encompassed by subsector (viii) to be limited to services that are supplied by banks and other types of financial institutions. According to China, there is no indication in any WTO Member's commitments for subsector (viii) that these services are provided by suppliers other than banks or other financial institutions.[248]

7.190 The United State submits that a 1998 Background Note by the WTO Secretariat indicates with respect to credit card services that these are "either part of 'all payment and money transmission services'" or "they constitute an independent item." Hence, WTO Members either treated "credit card services"

---

246 China asserts that "[i]n many cases, services that 'manage' or 'facilitate' the provision of another service or that relate to its 'processing' could properly be seen as 'inputs' to the provision of that service". China's first written submission, para. 107.

247 We would observe that, when licensing its brand to a bank, an EPS supplier grants permission to that bank to issue a credit card under a trademark. It is the availability of the card that will allow customers to make payments. Hence, the final service, namely the payment service, is supplied by the EPS supplier, not by the bank. From that point of view, it is at least arguable that issuing and acquiring services constitute input services into EPS. As noted above, this discussion is without prejudice to where issuing and acquiring services should be classified.

248 China's first written submission, para. 99; and response to Panel question No. 60, para. 109.

as part of "all payment and money transmission services" or as a separate, independent entry; and no Member included "credit card services" in 7.B.j (item (xiv) of the annex) – "settlement and clearing services for financial assets, including securities, derivatives, and other negotiable instruments".[249]

7.191 The Panel recalls that, in *US – Gambling* and in *China – Publications and Audiovisual Products*, GATS schedules of other WTO Members were used by the panels and the Appellate Body as relevant context for the interpretation of a Member's Schedule. As noted by the Appellate Body, "this is the logical consequence of Article XX:3 of the GATS, which provides that WTO Members' Schedules are 'an integral part' of the GATS."[250] At the same time, the Appellate Body acknowledged that use of other WTO Members' schedules as context must be tempered by the recognition that"[e]ach Schedule has its own intrinsic logic"; hence, Schedules of other WTO Members may be "of limited utility in elucidating the meaning of the entry to be interpreted".[251] Thus far, they have not figured as a central element in the contextual analysis of a disputed entry.

7.192 We observe that the schedules of other WTO Members cited by China use different names to describe entities supplying services under subsector (d). These include "banks", "commercial banks", "financial institutions", "specialized finance companies" and "credit institutions".[252] China did not submit evidence or make arguments as to the precise nature of these differently named entities in China's and other WTO Members' schedules. For that reason, it is not clear to us whether the schedules of other WTO Members cited by China do indicate that "all payment and money transmission services" can only be supplied by "banks and other types of financial institutions" within the meaning attributed by China to those terms. Indeed, as noted above, each schedule has its own intrinsic logic and we are not in a position to determine, without more, whether, and to what extent, the entities referred to in the schedules cited by China do coincide with "banks and other types of financial institutions". Moreover, as we explain in detail further below (see Section VII.F.1), we consider that China's commitments in subsectors (a) to (f) apply to all foreign financial institutions and that the term "foreign financial institutions" as used in China's Schedule includes EPS suppliers.

7.193 Hence, the context provided by the Schedules of other WTO Members does not point to an interpretation that is different from that suggested by other elements of context examined above.

---

[249] United States' response to Panel question No. 59, para. 150; and second written submission, paras. 40 and 41. The United States refers to the WTO Secretariat Background Note on Financial Services, S/C/W/72 (2 December1998), para. 13.

[250] Appellate Body Report, *US – Gambling*, para 182.

[251] Appellate Body Report, *China – Publications and Audiovisual Products*, para. 383.

[252] China referred to the schedules of Cambodia (GATS/SC/140), FYR Macedonia (GATS/SC/138), India (GATS/SC/42), Jordan (GATS/SC/128), Korea (GATS/SC/48), Macao (GATS/SC/50), Saudi Arabia (GATS/SC/141), Slovak Republic (GATS/SC/77), Venezuela (GATS/SC/92) and Vietnam (GATS/SC/142). China's first written submission, para. 99.

(c) Object and purpose

7.194 China argues that the United States' interpretation of China's Schedule or items in the Annex on Financial Services is "plainly contrary to the object and purpose of the GATS", because it is "arbitrary, illogical, and completely unpredictable". In China's view, the United States' approach is contrary to the "security and predictability of WTO Members' specific commitments, which is an important object and purpose of the GATS". For China, the United States' approach leads to an interpretation of China's Schedule and the Annex list in which "nothing means what it says", services are not clearly defined, and, as a result, it is "impossible to schedule and interpret specific commitments with any degree of security or predictability". According to China, this approach is "manifestly contrary" to the object and purpose of the GATS and must be rejected.[253]

7.195 The United States submits that the "progressive liberalization" called for in the Preamble of the GATS could never be achieved where, as under China's theory, a recognized, integrated service that is supplied and consumed as such, could not be classified in one subsector. Moreover, regarding China's argument that the object and purpose of the GATS calls for greater "transparency," China's own theory would render WTO Members' services schedules "indecipherable and impossible to reconcile with the commercial reality of the services they are supposed to reflect". The United States questions how transparency could be achieved where a Member could purport to liberalize a particular subsector through specific commitments, but then dismantle an integrated service that would otherwise fall within that subsector and argue that various pieces constitute separate "services" for which that Member has undertaken no commitments.[254]

7.196 The Panel begins its consideration of the object and purpose of the GATS and the WTO Agreement by noting one of the key objectives listed in the Preamble to the GATS, namely "the establishment of a multilateral framework of principles and rules for trade in services with a view to the expansion of such trade under conditions of *transparency* and *progressive liberalization*" (emphasis added). We note that, in *US – Gambling*, the Appellate Body found that the purpose of transparency contained in the Preamble to the GATS supported the need for precision and clarity in scheduling GATS commitments, and underlined the importance of having schedules that are readily understandable by all other WTO Members, as well as by services suppliers and consumers.[255] In that dispute, the Appellate Body also recalled that:

> ... the security and predictability of "the reciprocal and mutually advantageous arrangements directed to the substantial reduction of tariffs and other barriers to trade" is an object and purpose of the

---

[253] China's second written submission, paras. 27-29.
[254] United States' opening statement at the second substantive meeting, para. 17.
[255] Appellate Body Report, *US – Gambling*, para. 188.

> WTO Agreement .... This confirms the importance of the security and predictability of Members' specific commitments, which is equally an object and purpose of the GATS.[256]

7.197 We also recall that, in examining the principle of progressive liberalization as an expression of the object and purpose of the GATS, the Appellate Body did not consider that this principle "... lends support to an interpretation that would constrain the scope and coverage of specific commitments that have already been undertaken by WTO Members and by which they are bound."[257] We are also aware that, in both *US – Gambling* and *China – Publications and Audiovisual Products*, the Appellate Body observed that the objectives of the GATS did not provide specific guidance as to the correct interpretation of the entries at stake.[258]

7.198 We find that our interpretation of the scope of China's commitment under subsector (d) is consistent with the objective of transparency because it classifies under a single subsector services which, when combined together, result in a new and distinct service, the integrated service. This integrated service is supplied and consumed as such. Furthermore, by reconciling the classification of EPS with the commercial reality of those services, our interpretation reinforces the predictability, security and clarity of GATS specific commitments. For those same reasons, our interpretation is also consistent with the objective of progressive liberalization contained in the Preamble to the GATS.

7.199 Hence, our conclusion that subsector (d) of China's Schedule encompasses EPS is consistent with the object and purpose of the GATS and the WTO Agreement.

(d) Conclusion

7.200 The Panel has now completed its analysis of the scope of China's commitment in subsector (d) of its GATS Schedule on "all payment and money transmission services, including credit, charge and debit cards, travellers' cheques and bankers' drafts (including import and export settlement)" according to the rules of interpretation codified in Article 31 of the Vienna Convention.

7.201 Our analysis of the ordinary meaning of the terms "payment", "money" and "transmission", when used in combination, refers to the transfer of money from one person or place to another. The transferred money may be due for goods or services, or for settling a debt. When examining the expressions "payment services" and "money transmission services", we determined that "payment and money transmission services" can be characterized as those

---

256 Ibid.

257 Appellate Body Report, *China – Publications and Audiovisual Products*, para. 394.

258 "None of the objectives listed in the GATS preamble provides specific guidance as to the correct interpretation to be given to China's GATS Schedule entry 'Sound recording distribution services'". Appellate Body Report, *China – Publications and Audiovisual Products*, para. 393. See also Appellate Body Report, *US – Gambling*, para. 189.

services that "manage", "facilitate" or "enable" the act of paying, or transmitting money. Finally, we observed that the use of the term "all" manifests an intention to cover comprehensively the entire spectrum of the "payment and money transmission services" encompassed under subsector (d). With regard to the phrase "including credit, charge and debit cards, travellers cheques and bankers drafts" in subsector (d), we concluded that this phrase constitutes an illustrative list that provides confirmation that the phrase "[a]ll payment and money transmission services" refers to those services that are essential to the processing and completion of transactions involving the use of payment cards. Moreover, the parenthetical addition "(including import and export settlement)" confirms that subsector (d) includes settlement, and by implication clearing, when bankers' drafts are used as payment instruments. This, in our view, provides an indication that settlement, and therefore clearing, of transactions involving the use of other payment instruments, such as those listed in subsector (d), is properly classified under subsector (d).

7.202 When examining the remainder of China's Schedule, we found that neither the heading "Banking services as listed below", nor the inscriptions under the mode 1 commitment, pointed to a different interpretation of the scope of subsector (d). Moreover, our analysis of the GATS Annex on Financial Services led us to the conclusion that subsector (xiv) of that Annex does not encompass the clearing and settlement of payment card instruments listed in subsector (d) of China's Schedule. Furthermore, our contextual interpretation of subsector (d) based on the structure of the GATS led us to the view that the classification, under a single subsector, of a service made up of a combination of different services is not incompatible with the principle of mutual exclusivity if these services, when combined together, result in a distinct service, which is necessarily supplied and consumed as such. Also, the mere fact that separate suppliers may provide particular components of a service does not in itself imply that that component should be classified as a distinct service, or that the component is not part of an integrated service. In addition, the arguments submitted with respect to schedules of other WTO Members do not point to an interpretation different from that suggested by other elements of the context. Finally, we found that our interpretation of China's commitment under subsector (d) is consistent with the object and purpose of the GATS and the WTO Agreement.

7.203 We recall that the panel request defines the services at issue as follows:

> [E]lectronic payment services involve the services through which transactions involving payment cards … are processed and through which transfers of funds between institutions participating in the transactions are managed and facilitated.

7.204 Having regard to our examination of the scope of subsector (d) in China's Schedule, the Panel finds that this subsector includes the services at issue.[259]

3. *Recourse to supplementary means of interpretation*

7.205 Pursuant to Article 32 of the Vienna Convention, a treaty interpreter may have recourse to supplementary means of interpretation "in order to confirm the meaning resulting from the application of Article 31, or to determine the meaning when the interpretation according to Article 31 leaves the meaning ambiguous or obscure or leads to a result which is manifestly absurd or unreasonable."

7.206 The parties to the dispute referred to the CPC as supplementary means of interpretation.[260] China also referred to the 2001 Scheduling Guidelines as a source of interpretation under Article 32.[261] The Panel considers that its interpretation of China's Schedule pursuant to Article 31 of the Vienna Convention does not leave the meaning ambiguous or obscure, nor does it lead to a result which is manifestly absurd or unreasonable.

7.207 Accordingly, we do not find it necessary to resort to supplementary means of interpretation under Article 32 of the Vienna Convention.

E. *The Measures at Issue*

7.208 The United States has identified a series of six requirements, or measures, which it claims operate alone or in combination to impose market access restrictions and national treatment limitations on service suppliers of other WTO Members seeking to supply EPS in China. The United States argues that these measures are maintained through a series of legal instruments. As will be discussed in detail in Sections VII.F and VII.G, the United States asserts that these six requirements are inconsistent with China's obligations under Articles XVI:1 and XVI:2(a), and Article XVII of the GATS.

7.209 The United States has alleged the existence of the following requirements[262]:

(a) Requirements that mandate the use of CUP and/or establish CUP as the sole supplier of EPS for all domestic transactions

---

[259] In our view, the services at issue are covered by subsector (d), whether they are provided in connection with payment cards that are used, for instance, at POS terminals to purchase goods or services or in connection with payment cards that are used at ATMs to withdraw cash.

[260] United States' response to Panel question No. 76, paras. 12 and 39.

[261] China's first written submission, paras. 102-108.

[262] The short descriptions of the relevant requirements provided below are identical or closely similar to those that appear in written submissions of the United States. E.g., United States' response to China's request for a preliminary ruling, para. 77; first written submission, para. 12; and second written submission, para. 6.

denominated and paid in Renminbi (RMB) (hereafter referred to by the Panel as "sole supplier requirements");

(b) Requirements on issuers that payment cards issued in China bear the CUP logo ("issuer requirements");

(c) Requirements that all ATMs, merchant card processing equipment and POS terminals in China accept CUP cards ("terminal equipment requirements");

(d) Requirements on acquiring institutions to post the CUP logo and be capable of accepting all payment cards bearing the CUP logo ("acquirer requirements");

(e) Prohibitions on the use of non-CUP cards for cross-region or inter-bank transactions ("cross-region/inter-bank prohibitions"); and

(f) Requirements pertaining to card-based electronic transactions in China, Macao, and Hong Kong ("Hong Kong/Macao requirements")[263].

7.210 The United States considers that these requirements are maintained through a series of Chinese legal instruments that are themselves identified in the United States' request for establishment of a panel.[264]

7.211 China contends that the United States has failed to demonstrate that the alleged measures operate in a manner that is inconsistent with either Article XVI[265] or XVII[266] of the GATS. China submits that the requirements identified by the United States as measures at issue in this dispute do not violate these WTO provisions, as the United States alleges. Rather, it considers that the identified measures establish a national inter-bank network for clearing and settling RMB payment card transactions and otherwise create uniform technical and commercial standards that allow this inter-bank payment card network to function.[267] In the event that the Panel proceeded to consider the United States' claims, China argues that those claims must be based exclusively on the legal instruments specifically identified in the panel request.[268]

7.212 The Panel will consider below the United States' claims that China imposes certain requirements that are inconsistent with its obligations under Articles XVI and XVII of the GATS. In undertaking this task, we must first consider whether China in fact imposes the requirements mentioned above. This necessitates that we evaluate the precise content of the series of legal instruments

[263] Consistent with the views taken by of the parties, this Report refers to the separate customs territories of Hong Kong, China and Macao, China as Hong Kong and Macao, respectively.

[264] WT/DS413/2, pp. 3-4.

[265] China's second written submission, paras. 90-102.

[266] China's first written submission, paras. 151-160; second written submission, paras. 115-121.

[267] China's first written submission, para. 36.

[268] China's second written submission, paras. 83-89.

that have been cited by the United States. Before turning to this assessment, however, we first address the status of three legal instruments that China alleges have been repealed or replaced as well as China's concern that the United States' has broadened the scope of its challenge to include measures that are not specifically identified in the panel request.

1. The specific measures at issue that form part of the United States' challenge

(a) Chinese legal instruments as the basis for the existence of the measures at issue

7.213 We explained above that the United States has identified a series of six requirements that it claims are inconsistent with Articles XVI and XVII of the GATS. For each of these six requirements, the United States has identified an "illustrative list of instruments in which the particular measure is reflected."[269]

7.214 In its rebuttal submission, China argues that the United States has sought to improperly base its claims on measures that are not specifically identified in the panel request.[270] Rather than focusing on those legal instruments, China is of the view that the United States has attempted to improperly shift the basis of its claims to target measures at issue that exist "independently" of any particular legal instrument.[271] Due to the manner in which the United States formulated its panel request, however, China argues that the United States may not shift its challenge so as to allege that the six requirements exist "independently" or as "unwritten 'rules or norms of general and prospective application'".[272] China asserts that the United States has presented "no evidence whatsoever" to meet the "high threshold" that a complaining party must face when challenging an alleged unwritten rule or norm.[273] Accordingly, China requests that the Panel limit its evaluation of the United States' claims to measures that are "specifically" identified in the panel request in accordance with the requirements of Article 6.2 of the DSU.[274]

---

[269] United States' response to Panel question No. 5.

[270] China's second written submission, para. 89. China took issue with the manner in which the United States identified the measures at issue in this dispute in its second written submission, specifically in respect of the United States' claim under Article XVI:2(a) of the GATS. See China's second written submission, paras. 83-89. The United States has framed its claims under Articles XVI and XVII of the GATS in respect of the same measures and identical legal instruments. Accordingly, the Panel considers it appropriate to address this issue generally in relation to all of the United States' claims.

[271] China's second written submission, para. 84; comments on the United States' response to Panel question Nos. 70-72, 86-96, 115-123, para. 62.

[272] China's second written submission, para. 88; comments on the United States' response to Panel question Nos. 70-72, 86-96, 115-123, paras. 63-70.

[273] China's second written submission, para. 88, citing Appellate Body Report, *US – Zeroing (EC)*, para. 198.

[274] China's second written submission, paras. 86 and 87.

7.215 The Panel notes that Article 6.2 of the DSU requires that a complaining party identify the "specific measures at issue" among meeting other requirements. Moreover, Article XXVIII(a) of the GATS defines a "measure" for purposes of the GATS as "any measure by a Member, whether in the form of a law, regulation, rule, procedure, decision, administrative action, or any other form".

7.216 In three narrative paragraphs in its panel request[275], the United States describes those "requirements" or "measures" that it considers are inconsistent with China's obligations under Articles XVI and XVII of the GATS. In addition, the panel request specifies a series of instruments described as those "through which China maintains these measures."[276] The United States has referred to these six requirements throughout the proceedings as well as the identified instruments.[277] For each of the alleged six requirements, the United States explained that it provided an "illustrative list of instruments in which the particular measure is reflected".[278] The United States requested that the Panel make findings "with respect to each of the *measures* that the United States has challenged."[279]

7.217 In the light of the formulation of the United States' panel request and explanations provided in submissions and in response to questions from the Panel, we understand the United States seeks findings on the six alleged requirements, namely those referred to in paragraph 7.209 above. We further understand that the United States has submitted the relevant legal instruments as evidence in support of the existence of the six alleged requirements.

7.218 We note China's concern that the United States sought to establish the existence of the alleged six requirements "independently" from the legal instruments appearing in the panel request. We consider that the United States must establish the existence of the alleged requirements on some concrete evidentiary basis and not simply by asserting their existence. In its first written submission, its opening statement at the first substantive meeting of the Panel, and in response to questions from the Panel following the first substantive meeting, the United States specified that the instruments identified in the panel request establish the basis for the United States' claims with respect to each of the six requirements.[280] Thus, it is our view that the United States based its case

---

[275] WT/DS413/2, pp. 2-3.

[276] WT/DS413/2, pp. 3-4.

[277] See, e.g. United States' first written submission, para. 4; second written submission, para. 6; opening statement at the second meeting of the Panel, para. 38; response to Panel question Nos. 4 and 71.

[278] United States' response to Panel question No. 5.

[279] United States' response to Panel question No. 5 (emphasis original).

[280] United States' first written submission, paras. 55-72, 89-117 and fns. 40-45, 62-67, 81-84; opening statement following the first substantive meeting, paras. 43-44, 48-51 and fns. 37-38, 42-45; response to Panel question No. 5, paras. 24-36.

on those legal instruments. We will therefore consider the United States' claims in light of these instruments.

7.219 Finally, we consider this approach is consistent with the broad definition attributed to a measure under Article XXVIII(a) of the GATS. In our view, the fact that the United States considers that a series of "instruments" "illustrate" or "reflect" the existence of six alleged requirements does not prevent making findings on the six identified requirements as the "measures" at issue in the sense of Article 6.2 of the DSU and Article XXVIII(a) of the GATS. We also observe that this approach is consistent with the United States' request as to how the Panel should consider its case.[281]

7.220 Accordingly, we will examine whether the legal instruments identified in the United States' panel request establish the existence of the six alleged requirements or measures at issue. It is incumbent on the United States as the complaining party to demonstrate their existence.

(b) The repeal or replacement of certain Chinese legal instruments

7.221 China in its first written submission to the Panel submitted evidence that Document Nos. 94[282] and 272[283] were both repealed on 23 March 2010 and ceased to have legal effect prior to the date of the Panel's establishment on 11 February 2011.[284] In response to a question from the Panel, China pointed out that a third instrument, Document No. 66[285], was replaced by Document No. 53 on 1 November 2010, also in advance of the Panel's establishment. China requests that the Panel should decline to make findings with respect to these three instruments.[286] The United States referred to all of these legal instruments in its panel request[287] and subsequently in its submissions to the Panel.

7.222 The issue here is whether the Panel should consider certain instruments – Document Nos. 66, 94 and 272 – in its assessment of the United States' claims. We consider it appropriate to address the status of these instruments first, before

[281] For further discussion on this, see paras. 7.230-7.232 below.
[282] Exhibits US-42; CHN-57.
[283] Exhibits US-43; CHN-58.
[284] China's first written submission, fn. 27, referring to PBOC Announcement [2010] No. 2, Exhibit CHN-15.
[285] Exhibits US-45; CHN-61.
[286] China's first written submission, fn. 27; response to Panel question No. 21. China refers to Article VIII of Document No. 53, which was submitted as Exhibit CHI-54, as evidence of the replacement of Document No. 66. China's translation of Article VIII of this document provides as follows: "This Circular shall come into force as of November, 1 2010. The Circular of the State Administration of Foreign Exchange on Regulating the Administration of Foreign Currency bankcards [Hui Fa (2004) No. 66] … shall be abolished at this time". The translation of Document No. 53 provided by the United States indicates similarly.
[287] WT/DS413/2, p 3.

considering the United States' claims, since these instruments have been cited as evidence of the existence of five of the six alleged requirements at issue.

7.223 The United States indicated in response to a question from the Panel that it "does not contest that Document No. 53 indicates it will come into force simultaneously with the abolition of other instruments, including Document No. 66, and in this sense, [Document No. 53] may be considered to have replaced Document No. [66]".[288] The United States does not specifically comment on the instruments that announced the repeal of Document Nos. 94 and 272. Instead, the United States argues that "separate and apart" from Document Nos. 66, 94 and 272, the other identified instruments at issue adequately "establish a basis" for its claims.[289] Thus, the United States has not rebutted evidence submitted by China concerning the repeal of Document Nos. 94 and 272, nor does the United States contest that Document No. 66 was replaced by Document No. 53.[290] Having regard to the evidence submitted by China and the arguments of both parties, we consider that Document Nos. 94 and 272 were both repealed, and Document No. 66 was replaced by Document No. 53.

7.224 In *US – Upland Cotton*, the Appellate Body noted that "the fact that a measure has expired may affect what recommendation a panel may make" but it is "not dispositive of the preliminary question of whether a panel can address claims in respect of that measure".[291] In previous cases, panels have looked to Article 3.7 of the DSU to determine whether it was appropriate to address claims in respect of such measures. Article 3.7 of the DSU provides that "[t]he aim of the dispute settlement mechanism is to secure a positive solution to a dispute". When deciding whether or not the aim of securing a positive solution warrants findings on measures that expired before a panel's date of establishment, panels have taken into account the particular circumstances of a given dispute.[292] These circumstances included such considerations as the timing of the withdrawal of a

---

[288] United States' response to Panel question Nos. 4-6; response to Panel question No. 70.

[289] United States' response to Panel question No. 6.

[290] We noted in fn. 286 that both the United States' and China's translations of Document No. 53 provide similarly that Document No. 53 replaces Document No. 66.

[291] Appellate Body Report, *US – Upland Cotton*, para. 272. We note as well that in *US – Certain EC Products*, the Appellate Body did not disapprove of the decision by a panel to make a finding concerning a measure that no longer existed at the time of establishment of the panel. Rather, the Appellate Body concluded that the panel erred in recommending that the Dispute Settlement Body request the responding party to bring into conformity with its WTO obligations a measure which the Panel found to no longer exist. See also Appellate Body Report, *US – Countervailing Measures on Certain EC Products*, para. 81.

[292] Appellate Body Report, *US – Countervailing Measures on Certain EC Products*, paras. 60-82; Panel Reports, *EC – Approval and Marketing of Biotech Products*, paras. 7.1648-7.1654; *Argentina – Textiles and Apparel*, para. 6.4-6.15; *US – Gasoline*, para. 6.19.

measure[293], as well as the likelihood that the respondent would later reintroduce the measure.[294]

7.225 In its panel request, the United States identified a series of requirements, which it claims impose market access restrictions and requirements on service suppliers of other WTO Members seeking to supply EPS in China.[295] It indicates in its panel request that each of these "requirements" is "maintained through a series of instruments".[296] The panel request thereafter identifies a list of instruments. The United States subsequently explained that, for each of these "requirements", it identified an "illustrative list of instruments in which the particular measure is reflected".[297]

7.226 In deciding whether to take account of Document Nos. 66, 94 and 272 for purposes of determining whether they support the existence of relevant requirements, we consider it appropriate to determine whether addressing these legal instruments would conform with the aim of securing a positive solution to the present dispute.

7.227 We note that Document Nos. 94 and 272 were repealed more than ten months before the Panel's establishment on 11 February 2011, and more than six months before the date on which consultations were requested on 15 September 2010. Document No. 66 was replaced on 1 November 2010, three days after consultations were held, but five months before the Panel's establishment. We do not know the factors that influenced China's decision to repeal Document Nos. 94 or 272, and to replace Document No. 66, and the timing of these actions. The United States has not expressed the view, or provided any indication, that any of these instruments stand to be reintroduced. Rather, it has made clear that its case stands even without these instruments, as it takes the position that the requirements are still maintained through other instruments.[298] The United States also argued that foreign suppliers did not experience any "changes in the market regarding restrictions, prohibitions, and other impediments on the supply of EPS for payment card transactions" following the entry into force of Document No. 53.[299]

---

[293] Panel Reports, *EC – Biotech*, para. 7.1653; and *Argentina – Textiles and Apparel*, para. 6.1 and 6.13.

[294] Panel Reports, *Argentina – Textiles and Apparel*, para. 6.14; and *US – Gasoline*, para. 6.19. The *US – Gasoline* panel contrasted its decision with that taken by the GATT panel *EEC – Apples (Chile I)* in1980, which ruled on a measure terminated before agreement on the Panel's terms of reference. As noted by the *US – Gasoline* panel, the terms of reference in that case specifically included the terminated measure and, the dispute concerning a seasonal measure, there remained the prospect of its reintroduction. See GATT Panel Report, *EEC – Apples (Chile I)*.

[295] WT/DS413/2, pp. 2-3.

[296] WT/DS413/2, pp. 3-4.

[297] United States' response to Panel question No. 5.

[298] United States' response to Panel question No. 6.

[299] See United States' response to Panel question No. 70.

7.228 On the evidence before us, we have no reason to assume that the three instruments will be re-introduced. Our determination therefore focuses on three elements that are clear. First, Document Nos. 66, 94 and 272 were no longer in force at the time of the Panel's establishment. In other words, they no longer had any legal effect. Secondly, the United States has not put forward any claim or evidence that these instruments might be re-introduced by China. Thirdly, we understand the United States to allege that China currently maintains in place each of the relevant requirements even without these instruments being in effect. For instance, the United States alleges that the requirements exist independently of the content of Document Nos. 66, 94 and 272, such that "there would be no impact on [the United States'] claims relating to the six distinct measures, comprised of instruments operating together"[300], even if the Panel were to decline to take into account Document Nos. 66, 94 and 272. Accordingly, in order to provide a positive solution to this dispute, we consider that our task is to assess the existence of the particular measures in China on the basis of those instruments that were in force at the time of panel establishment. We do not consider that in the particular circumstances of this case there is any need to go further and address also Document Nos. 66, 94 and 272. As indicated, the United States did not argue in this case that a decision by the Panel not to take these instruments into account would effectively deprive the United States of the possibility to have one or more of the challenged requirements considered by the Panel.

7.229 Therefore, for the foregoing reasons, the Panel declines to take Document Nos. 66, 94 and 272 into account in our analysis of the measures at issue. Accordingly, we do not consider them further.

2. *Evaluation of the existence of the measures at issue*

7.230 The United States asks that the Panel assess the six requirements both individually and in conjunction with each other to determine whether they give rise to a breach of Articles XVI and XVII of the GATS. The United States argues that such an approach would be consistent with past practice of panels and the Appellate Body[301], and submits that doing so would help to "ensure the effective resolution of this dispute".[302]

7.231 China recognizes in general that panels may need to consider the overall conformity of a set of measures or legal instruments and how measures interact with each other based on the content of those instruments.[303] In this dispute, however, China submits that the United States has not established that the

[300] United States' response to Panel question No. 6, para. 23.

[301] United States' first written submission, para. 34, citing Appellate Body Report, *EC – Asbestos*, para. 64; Panel Report, *US – Export Restraints*. paras. 8.82-8.131.

[302] United States' first written submission, paras. 30 and 32.

[303] China's second written submission, fn. 48, referring to United States' first written submission, paras. 34 and 35; Panel Reports, *US – Section 301 Trade Act*; *Australia – Apples*.

identified instruments are related to each other as necessary to succeed with its challenge. China submits that the identified instruments "in many cases have no demonstrable relationship to each other", because the instruments were issued "at different times, by different agencies, on different topics".[304] In addition, China asserts that the United States' claims in relation to the first alleged requirement, i.e. "requirements that mandate the use of CUP and/or establish CUP as the sole supplier of EPS for all domestic transactions denominated and paid in RMB", and the fifth alleged requirement, "broad prohibition on the use of non-CUP cards", amount to "drawing a distinction without a difference".[305] Accordingly, China addresses the United States' allegations concerning these requirements together in its submissions.

7.232 The Panel notes that, in previous instances, panels and the Appellate Body have analysed measures or legal instruments not only on an individual basis, but have considered how certain measures or instruments operate collectively, in concert, or in combination, when evaluating the claims of a complainant.[306] We see no reason at the outset to decline to consider the United States' request to consider the requirements both individually and as they operate together. As in previous cases, the need to do so depends on the particular circumstances of the matter before the Panel, including the content of the particular measures before the Panel, the interrelationship of those measures, and the result of the Panel's assessment of the measures considered individually. In our evaluation here, we will assess both the content and interrelationship of those instruments before us.

7.233 We also note that there is overlap in terms of the particular legal instruments that are identified in respect of the six alleged requirements. Specifically, as the United States clarified to the Panel[307], each of the instruments identified in respect of the alleged issuer requirements, terminal equipment requirements, acquirer requirements, cross-region/inter-bank prohibitions and Hong Kong/Macao requirements, i.e. the second through sixth requirements listed in paragraph 7.209 above, are also identified in connection with the alleged sole supplier requirement, i.e. the first requirement listed in paragraph 7.209 above. In cases where the same instrument is identified in respect of more than one requirement, the United States frequently refers to the same provisions of that instrument. In view of the fact that the alleged sole supplier requirements incorporate every legal instrument cited in support of the other five requirements, we consider it appropriate to begin with a review of the issuer, acquirer and terminal equipment requirements before turning to the sole supplier requirement.

---

[304] China's second written submission, fn 48.

[305] China's second written submission, para. 96.

[306] See, e.g. Appellate Body Report, *China – Raw Materials*, paras. 250-255; Panel Reports, *China – Raw Materials*, para. 7.68; *US – Tuna II (Mexico)*, paras. 7.16-7.26.

[307] See United States' response to Panel question No. 4.

7.234 In addition, as pointed out by China, we note that the United States' claim regarding the existence of a sole supplier requirement and its claim regarding the existence of cross-region/inter-bank prohibitions address fundamentally the same concern, namely, whether the measures at issue require the processing of all domestic, RMB inter-bank payment card transactions over the CUP network, and not over the network of any other EPS supplier, including foreign ones. The United States acknowledges that the "ultimate effect" of these two "requirements" is the same on foreign EPS suppliers, but explains that it seeks separate findings in this regard "to ensure that [the Panel's] findings reach the requirement irrespective of whether they are framed in terms of a mandate to use CUP or CUP cards, or a prohibition on the use of non-CUP cards or a prohibition on the use of an EPS supplier other than CUP".[308] Due to the similar nature of these two alleged measures, and because all of the legal instruments identified in connection with the alleged cross-region/inter-bank prohibitions are also identified in connection with the sole supplier requirement, we will analyse the instruments identified in connection with the cross-region/inter-bank prohibitions in the context of our assessment of the alleged sole supplier requirement. In doing so, we will bear in mind the distinction drawn by the United States' between whether the instruments are framed so as to mandate the use of CUP or non-CUP cards, or as a prohibition.

7.235 We also recall our decision set out in paragraphs 7.221 to 7.227 above not to consider Document Nos. 66, 94 and 272. Therefore, these particular instruments are not further considered below to assess whether the six alleged requirements exist.

7.236 Finally, as discussed in paragraph 1.10 and Annex H to this Report, we recall that the parties indicated their disagreement on the correct translation of a number of aspects of the identified legal instruments. As the complaining party, the United States provided its own English language versions of provisions of these instruments. China at times submitted its own English language versions of the same instruments. At the Panel's request, the parties undertook efforts to agree on a single translation. They succeeded in doing so in certain instances. For those occasions in which the parties were unable to agree on a single translation, the Panel, in consultation with the parties, appointed an independent translator – the United Nations Office at Geneva (UNOG) – to provide expert linguistic advice to assist the Panel in determining the correct translation. In general, we will refer to the complaining party's translation, unless the parties specifically agreed to a different translation, or if we elect to follow the advice of the UNOG translator. In all cases, however, we have reviewed both parties' translations. Where appropriate, we refer also to China's versions. Any citation to the United States' translation, or UNOG's suggested translation, of a particular aspect of Chinese law, should not be construed to imply that it is an authoritative translation of China's instruments.

---

[308] United States' response to Panel question No. 2, para. 8.

7.237 Before proceeding to consider the relevant Chinese requirements, it is useful briefly to address the question of whether, as the United States contends[309], CUP is a supplier of the services at issue, i.e. an EPS supplier. In support of its position, the United States points *inter alia* to Article 12 of CUP's Articles of Association and to the definition of CUP's business scope contained in the Notification of Approval of CUP's Business Licence.[310] The two provisions have nearly identical terms, which is why it is sufficient to set out Article 12. It provides:

> Upon being registered according to law, the business scope of the Company is as follows: (1) To establish and operate a single nationwide inter-bank card information switching network; (2) to provide advanced electronic payment technologies and specialized services in connection with the inter-bank bank card information switching; (3) to engage in bankcard technological innovation; (4) to manage and operate the brand of "UnionPay"; (5) to formulate the code and technical standards for inter-bank card transactions, and to mediate and arbitrate any business disputes arising out of inter-bank transactions; (6) to organize trainings for the industry, business seminars and international exchange programs, and to conduct related researches and consulting services; and (7) to conduct such other businesses as may be approved by the People's Bank of China.

7.238 In addition, we note that China has not specifically contested that CUP provides the services at issue, i.e. EPS as defined in the United States' request for the establishment of a panel. In the light of these elements, CUP can in our view properly be considered a supplier of the services at issue.

(a) Requirements on issuers that payment cards issued in China bear the CUP logo ("issuer requirements")

7.239 We turn first to address the issuer requirements. The United States asserts that these requirements are imposed by specific provisions of the following Chinese legal instruments:[311]

- Document No. 37 (Articles 1.2(i), 2 and 3)
- Document No. 57 (Articles 1-6)
- Document No. 129 (Article 3.2(ii))

---

309 United States' first written submission, paras. 1 and 3.

310 United States' response to China's request for a preliminary ruling, paras. 70 and 72 (referring to Article 12 of CUP's Articles of Association, Exhibit US-20, and the Notification of Approval of CUP's Business Licence, Exhibit US-29). See also the 2007 China Payment System Development Report, Exhibit US-15, p. 25.

311 United States' response to Panel question No. 4, para. 17. The United States also relies on Document Nos. 94 and 272. As explained above at paragraphs 7.221-7.229 above, the Panel has decided not to consider the substance of these documents.

- Document No. 219 (Article III)
- Document No. 76 (Chapter I, Article 4)
- Document No. 17 (Articles 5, 7-10 and 64)

7.240 The United States submits that through these instruments, China maintains requirements on issuers that payment cards issued in China bear the CUP logo. More particularly, in the United States' view, China imposes requirements that any bank cards issued in China for RMB purchases in China, as well as any dual currency cards issued in China, must bear the CUP logo. According to the United States, this means that issuers must have access to the CUP system, and must pay CUP for that access.[312]

7.241 China responds that the instruments at issue require all RMB-denominated payment cards issued in China to bear a common logo – the *Yin Lian* logo – and to adhere to certain technical standards so as to be capable of being processed over the CUP network.[313] These instruments allow a national inter-bank payment card network to function. China further submits that the United States fails to identify any aspect of the alleged issuer requirements that would prevent the issuance of payment cards that are capable of being processed over multiple networks.[314] China contends that there are many banks throughout the world that issue cards that are capable of being processed over more than one network.[315] China also argues that nothing in the instruments at issue prevents issuers from placing the logos of EPS suppliers other than CUP on bank cards they issue, provided that they bear the *Yin Lian* logo.[316]

7.242 The Panel will examine one by one the above-mentioned instruments relied on by the United States so as to determine whether they impose the alleged issuer requirements. Before doing so, however, we need to address a translation issue that arises in connection not only with the alleged issuer requirements, but also the alleged terminal equipment and acquirer requirements.

(i) Preliminary translation issue

7.243 According to the United States, the instruments that impose the aforesaid requirements make frequent references to a logo that must be displayed on bank cards issued in China or on terminal equipment operated in China.[317] The United States is of the view that the logo in question is that of China UnionPay Co., Ltd. ("CUP") and accordingly refers to it as the "CUP logo". In contrast, China argues that the relevant instruments refer to the "*Yin Lian* logo", which

---

312 United States' first written submission, paras. 4 and 100; WT/DS413/2, p. 2.

313 China's first written submission, para. 36; China's response to Panel question No. 104(b), para. 51.

314 China's second written submission, para. 93.

315 China's response to Panel question No. 22(c), para. 18.

316 China's response to Panel question No. 104(b), para. 51.

317 The logo in question consists of a tricolour lozenge that contains the phrase "UnionPay" in English as well as the Chinese characters "*Yin Lian*".

China says indicates a bank card's interoperability. In view of the parties' disagreement, it is necessary to determine the correct translation of the Chinese characters that are used in the relevant instruments to describe the logo in question.

7.244 The United States argues that the correct English translation of the logo in all instances at issue is "CUP logo", because internet translation engines commonly translate the characters "*Yin Lian*" as "CUP" and because CUP itself refers to its logo as the "CUP logo" or the "CUP label", or in certain instances as the "UnionPay logo". The United States further submits that contrary to China's suggestion, there is no reason to employ the transliteration "*Yin Lian*". The United States observes in this regard that the logo itself uses the English translation "UnionPay". And it adds that in the case at hand the product of transliteration – "*Yin Lian*" – has no meaning in English. The United States therefore considers that if the Panel does not translate the logo as "CUP logo", there is no basis for translating the logo into English as anything other than "UnionPay".[318]

7.245 China argues that it is incorrect to translate the Chinese term "*Yin Lian*" as CUP. The term "CUP" stands for China UnionPay and is an official abbreviation for the company "China UnionPay Co., Ltd." (CUP). Also, the word "China" is not found in the relevant provisions that use the term "*Yin Lian*". China notes that the *Yin Lian* logo was approved by the People's Bank of China (PBOC) in 2001 as a symbol of bank card interoperability. China notes that CUP was not established until March 2002. China further points out that the logo used by CUP consists of three parts: (1) the logo for bank card interoperability; (2) the Chinese phrase for China UnionPay (Zhong Guo *Yin Lian*); and (3) the English phrase "China UnionPay". According to China, this logo is used as a trademark or company identity symbol. China therefore suggests that the Panel use the term "*Yin Lian*" instead of CUP.[319]

7.246 The UNOG translator asked to advise the Panel points out that there is no ready means of distinguishing between "*Yin Lian*" when used as an idiomatic short form meaning "bank card network interoperability", and "*Yin Lian*" when used to stand for UnionPay or even, again idiomatically, the company CUP. The UNOG translator further observes that the English term "UnionPay" is itself a convenient but necessarily approximate equivalent for "*Yin Lian*" in its application as a term for "bank card network interoperability".[320] Moreover, the same term has been incorporated in the name of the relevant company. As a result, in the view of the UNOG translator, the use of the English term

[318] United States' translation comments of 4 January 2012, pp. 1-2; comments on the UNOG evaluation of 24 February 2012, pp. 1 and 3.

[319] China's translation comments of 4 January 2012, pp. 1-3.

[320] The UNOG translator notes that the English equivalent of "UnionPay" bears only tangential relation to the original Chinese meaning and that a more appropriate choice would have been "BankCardNet".

"UnionPay" as shorthand for the concept of interoperability and for the company gives rise to confusion. In the light of this ambiguity, the UNOG translator advises that the Panel use the compound form "*Yin Lian*/UnionPay", except where the Chinese uses the fuller "China UnionPay" or "China UnionPay Co. Ltd.".[321]

7.247 In considering this translation issue, we first note the Business Practices Appendix contained in Document No. 76, which in an annex defines the term "network logo" as "[t]he [...] logo compris[ing] the uniform brand name for domestic bank cards (the Chinese characters "*Yin Lian*") and the design symbolizing the united network, as registered with the trademark office. All rights of ownership and use belong to the [United Association]...".[322] Document No. 76 was promulgated by the PBOC and dates from 2001.[323] In 2002, CUP obtained its business licence. According to that licence, the activities that are within the company's business scope include the establishment and operation of a single nationwide inter-bank card information switching network, and the management and operation of the brand "UnionPay".[324] Thus, the nationwide inter-bank network to which Document No. 76 and the Notification of Approval of CUP's Business Licence refer are one and the same. As the parties have explained, CUP as of 2002 took over the responsibility of that network from the United Association.[325]

7.248 We understand from the UNOG translator's evaluation that what the parties have referred to in their translations of Chinese instruments as the "CUP logo" or the "*Yin Lian* logo" is generally the aforementioned network logo, except for certain instances where the Chinese original refers to CUP. Based on the UNOG translator's advice, we accept that the network logo that uses the Chinese characters "*Yin Lian*" symbolizes interoperability, as China contends.[326] But the network logo is not a generic logo that indicates that a particular bank card is interoperable with *a* nationwide inter-bank payment card network in China. Rather, as is clear from Document No. 76 and the Notification of Approval of CUP's Business Licence, the network logo indicates that a particular

[321] UNOG evaluation, pp. 3-4 and 16.

[322] See the UNOG translator's linguistic advice as set out in Annex H. Article 4.2 of Chapter I of the Business Practices Appendix contains a very similar definition.

[323] See also the press release by the People's Bank of China entitled "Central Bank Introduces Bankcard Network Logo" (Exhibit US-26).

[324] Exhibit US-29 uses the term "UnionPay". Article 12 of CUP's Articles of Association. describes the company's business scope in the same terms as the Notification of Approval of CUP's Business Licence. According to the United States, CUP's Articles of Association also date from 2002. United States' response to Panel question No. 88(a), para. 71.

[325] United States' second written submission, para. 160; response to Panel question Nos. 71, para. 7; 115, para. 104; China's response to Panel question No. 99, para. 40.

[326] Specifically, China has said that the *Yin Lian* logo designates that the RMB bank card on which the logo appears can be used on an inter-bank, interoperable basis. China's response to Panel question No. 105(a), para. 54.

bank card is interoperable with the specific network that is currently operated by CUP.

7.249 We understand from China that the company China UnionPay (CUP) has its own company logo, which incorporates the network logo. To the right of that logo, the company logo adds the term "China UnionPay" in both Chinese and English.[327] To that extent, as noted by the UNOG translator, a distinction can, in principle, be made between the network logo and the company logo. However, as also confirmed by China in response to a question from the Panel, CUP on its own CUP-branded cards issued in China does not use the full company logo, but only the network logo.[328] Plainly, this blurs the distinction between the network logo and the company logo.

7.250 In the light of the foregoing, we find persuasive the UNOG translator's suggestion that we refer to the network logo as the "*Yin Lian*/UnionPay" logo. The suggested compound form usefully distinguishes the network from the company CUP. In addition, the compound form reflects the fact that both terms appear on the network logo – "*Yin Lian*" in Chinese and "UnionPay" in English – and that the English term "UnionPay" "bears only tangential relation"[329] to the meaning of the Chinese characters "*Yin Lian*". Consequently, throughout the remainder of this Report, we will use the UNOG-suggested translation, except where the Chinese original refers to CUP or where we summarize arguments put forward by the parties.

7.251 Using the suggested translation helps to clarify that, formally speaking, the relevant legal texts generally refer to the network logo as opposed to the company logo. We hasten to recall, however, that it is CUP that currently operates the network in question, and that CUP appears to use only the network logo on its own CUP-branded cards. As a result, it is virtually inevitable, in our view, that the average bank card user whose card displays the network logo will associate that logo with CUP or the nationwide inter-bank network operated by CUP. We therefore consider that as long as CUP is the company charged with operating the relevant nationwide inter-bank network, it makes little practical difference whether the relevant Chinese instruments formally refer to the network logo or the CUP logo. We will revert to this point further below.[330]

(ii) Document No. 37

7.252 The Panel now addresses the Chinese legal instruments cited by the United States as sources of the alleged issuer requirements. We begin with Document No. 37.

---

327 China's response to Panel question No. 105(b), para. 55.

328 China's response to Panel question No. 105(b) and (c), paras. 55-57. Evidence submitted by China demonstrates that there are CUP-branded credit and debit cards that display only the network logo (Exhibit CHN-105).

329 UNOG evaluation, p. 16.

330 See, below para. 7.696.

7.253 In relation to Document No. 37, the United States refers the Panel to the text of Articles 1.2(i) and 2.[331] In one footnote, the United States also cites Article 3 as a provision requiring the use of the CUP logo.[332] Regarding Article 2, the United States observes that it prohibits the use of non-CUP cards for cross-region or cross-bank transactions.[333]

7.254 China states that Document No. 37 establishes uniform technical standards for inter-bank payment cards. It also establishes the *Yin Lian* logo as the common logo for inter-bank payment cards that conform to these standards. It requires commercial banks that issue inter-bank payment cards to use the *Yin Lian* logo and to join the national inter-bank payment card network.[334]

7.255 The Panel notes that the United States identified Articles 1.2(i), 2 and 3 of Document No. 37 as the relevant provisions. Article 1.2(i) imposes a requirement on all commercial banks to complete, by the end of 2001, the transformation of their internal bank card processing system according to the uniform standards and specifications for bank cards, and to make technical preparations for accepting bank cards bearing the *Yin Lian*/UnionPay logo.[335] This provision does not impose a requirement that all bank cards issued in China must bear the *Yin Lian*/UnionPay logo. Rather, it appears to require that all commercial banks, which include issuers, be capable of processing transactions involving bank cards bearing the *Yin Lian*/UnionPay logo.

7.256 Article 2.1(i) provides in relevant part that "bank cards issued by all commercial banks with inter-bank usability in China must bear the [*Yin Lian*/UnionPay] logo" on the front of the cards.[336] Article 2.2(i) stipulates that by the end of 2003, commercial banks had to replace all bank cards that did not conform to the *Yin Lian*/UnionPay logo use requirement. As from 2004, bank cards not bearing the *Yin Lian*/UnionPay logo could no longer be used for cross-region or inter-bank transactions.

7.257 Article 2.1(iii) states that all cards bearing the *Yin Lian*/UnionPay logo must abide by the unified technical specifications, and that all issuers of bank cards must provide corresponding cross-region and inter-bank services pursuant to the unified business specifications. Moreover, pursuant to Article 2.2(i), by the end of 2003 commercial banks had to replace all bank cards that did not conform to the unified requirements. These Articles do not require that all bank cards issued in China must bear the *Yin Lian*/UnionPay logo. But they do impose requirements on issuers that relate to bank cards issued in China and bearing the *Yin Lian*/UnionPay logo.

331 United States' first written submission, para. 94.

332 United States' second written submission, fn. 201.

333 United States' preliminary ruling submission, para. 106.

334 China's first written submission, para. 45.

335 See the UNOG translator's linguistic advice as set out in Annex H.

336 Pursuant to Article 2.1(i), "special cards" are not subject to this requirement. Articles 7 and 8 of Document No. 17 suggest that "special cards" are one type of debit card.

7.258 Regarding Article 3, the United States states that it requires the use of the *Yin Lian*/UnionPay logo. We see nothing in Article 3 that would support this assertion. We note, however, that Article 3.1 requires commercial banks that engage in bank card business in China to join the nationwide bank card inter-bank exchange network.[337]

7.259 Based on the foregoing, we consider that Articles 2.1(i) and 2.2(i) require issuers to ensure that all bank cards issued in China for use in connection with domestic inter-bank transactions bear the *Yin Lian*/UnionPay logo. In contrast, Article 1.2(i) requires issuers to transform their processing systems so that they can process transactions involving bank cards bearing the *Yin Lian*/UnionPay logo. Article 2.1(iii) imposes requirements on issuers that appear intended to ensure that bank cards bearing the *Yin Lian*/UnionPay logo are interoperable, i.e. that they can be used in domestic inter-bank and cross-region transactions. Article 3.1 requires issuers to join the national inter-bank bank card network.

(iii) Document No. 57

7.260 The United States submits that Document No. 57 contains several requirements – set out in Articles 1-6 – that mandate that payment cards bear the CUP logo.[338]

7.261 China argues that Document No. 57 elaborates on the requirements set forth in Document No. 37. It requires payment cards issued for domestic inter-bank use to bear the *Yin Lian* logo, and requires commercial banks that issue inter-bank payment cards to adhere to the business specifications for bank card interoperability contained in Document No. 76.[339]

7.262 The Panel notes that the provisions of Document No. 57 identified as relevant by the United States are Articles 1 through 6. Article 1 stipulates that bank cards issued by all commercial banks solely for domestic interoperable use must bear the uniform *Yin Lian*/UnionPay logo, and RMB credit cards must also bear the *Yin Lian*/UnionPay holographic anti-counterfeiting logo.[340] Article 2 makes it mandatory for "dual-account" (i.e. dual currency) bank cards issued by all commercial banks in China for both domestic and foreign interoperable use to bear the uniform *Yin Lian*/UnionPay logo.[341]

---

[337] The United States has referenced Article 3.1 in the context of a discussion concerning applicable technical specifications. United States' response to Panel question No. 119, para. 118.

[338] United States' first written submission, para. 93; second written submission, fn. 201.

[339] China's first written submission, para. 45.

[340] Credit card logos, like the *Yin Lian*/UnionPay bank card logo, appear in the lower right corner of the front side of the card. They serve to identify the card's brand. Holographic anti-counterfeiting logos also appear on the front side of the card, on the right-hand side, above the card logo. They serve a security function. We note that the United States' description of the issuer requirements makes no mention of the *Yin Lian*/Union Pay anti-counterfeiting logo. United States' first written submission, para. 4.

[341] Regarding the translation of Articles 1 and 2, see the UNOG translator's linguistic advice as set out in Annex H.

7.263 Article 3 provides that bank cards issued for cross-region or inter-bank use must comply with the unified business specifications and technical standards. It further stipulates that commercial banks must provide card samples to the PBOC that comply with the *Yin Lian*/UnionPay logo use requirements. Neither of these two elements of Article 3 imposes a requirement that bank cards issued in China bear the *Yin Lian*/UnionPay logo. The former element – that bank cards must comply with the unified business specifications and technical standards – nonetheless imposes a requirement on issuers that relates to bank cards bearing the *Yin Lian*/UnionPay logo. Regarding the second element of Article 3 – that commercial banks must provide card samples to the PBOC that comply with the *Yin Lian*/UnionPay logo use requirements – the United States asserts that this means that issuers must submit any cards to be issued for approval by the PBOC.[342] China responds that the United States misinterprets Article 3.[343] We are not persuaded on the basis of the text of Article 3 and in the absence of other evidence that this article confers on the PBOC the power to deny issuance of a bank card that complies with the logo use requirements of Document No. 57.

7.264 Article 4 is concerned with the *Yin Lian*/UnionPay holographic anti-counterfeiting logo, which is different from the *Yin Lian*/UnionPay logo. Also, Article 4 does not impose a requirement on issuers or require the use of the *Yin Lian*/UnionPay logo.

7.265 Article 5 states in relevant part that commercial banks must take the job of promoting the use and acceptance of the *Yin Lian*/UnionPay seriously[344], and that they were gradually to reduce the role of their own bank card brands in the market. Article 6 provides *inter alia* that as from 2002, no bank cards were allowed to bear a regional interoperability logo.

7.266 Based on the above, we consider that Articles 1, 2, 5 and 6 impose a requirement that all bank cards, including dual currency cards, issued in China for use in connection with domestic inter-bank transactions bear the *Yin Lian*/UnionPay logo. Article 3 also imposes a requirement on issuers. However, it concerns ensuring that bank cards bearing the *Yin Lian*/UnionPay logo are interoperable, i.e. that they can be used in domestic inter-bank and cross-region transactions.

---

342 United States' response to Panel question No. 15, para. 57.

343 China's second written submission, fn. 51.

344 The parties have provided no elaboration on the meaning of this requirement, other than to confirm that it is a requirement. United States' response to Panel question No. 123, para. 122; China's response to Panel question No. 123, para. 89.

(iv) Document No. 129

7.267 The United States submits that Article 3.2(ii) of Document No. 129 requires that all newly issued bank cards must bear the CUP logo and must conform to unified business specifications and meet technical CUP standards.[345]

7.268 China does not specifically address Document No. 129.

7.269 The Panel notes that Article 3.2(ii) relates to the "universal use of bank cards bearing the [*Yin Lian*/UnionPay] logo". It provides in relevant part that all RMB bank cards newly issued by commercial banks must conform to the unified business specifications and technical standards, and must bear the unified *Yin Lian*/UnionPay logo. It further states that commercial banks must formulate and submit to PBOC specific plans for replacement of remaining bank cards not bearing the *Yin Lian*/UnionPay logo.

7.270 In the light of this, we consider that Article 3.2(ii) imposes a requirement that all RMB bank cards issued in China for use in connection with domestic inter-bank transactions must bear the *Yin Lian*/UnionPay logo. The Article further imposes a requirement on issuers that seeks to ensure that bank cards bearing the *Yin Lian*/UnionPay logo are interoperable.

(v) Document No. 219

7.271 The United States argues that Article III of Document No. 219 provides for both the use of CUP to process authorized card transactions and also that no supplier of EPS can process a card transaction that is not authorized (i.e. cards not bearing the CUP logo).[346]

7.272 China states that Article III regulates acquirers in China's border areas and is designed to combat payment card fraud. It requires that the acquiring agreement between an acquirer and merchant stipulate that the merchant must not use the *Yin Lian* logo for purposes outside the scope of the agreement.[347]

7.273 The Panel notes that Article III is addressed to RMB bank card acquiring institutions.[348] It provides that the RMB card acquisition agreements that such institutions conclude with merchants are to stipulate, *inter alia*, that merchants must not use the *Yin Lian*/UnionPay logo or POS terminals for purposes outside the scope of the acquisition agreement.[349] Thus, Article III is concerned with RMB bank card acquirers and the merchants with whom they enter into acquisition agreements. It is not concerned with issuers or the issuance of bank cards.

---

[345] United States' first written submission, para. 95.

[346] United States' first written submission, para. 95; United States' response to China's request for a preliminary ruling, para. 107.

[347] Exhibit CHI-74.

[348] As its title indicates, Document No. 219 concerns "Relevant Issues on Accepting and Using RMB Bankcards in Border Areas" (Exhibit US-47).

[349] See the UNOG translator's linguistic advice as set out in Annex H.

7.274 In the light of this, we consider that Article III does not impose a requirement on issuers that bank cards issued in China must bear the *Yin Lian*/UnionPay logo.

(vi) Document No. 76

7.275 The United States draws the Panel's attention to Chapter I, Article 4 of Document No. 76, which assigns to the "United Association" ownership of the "UnionPay" logo and gives it the use and management rights of the logo. As the rights of the United Association were eventually transferred to CUP, CUP has exclusive control over the UnionPay logo. According to the United States, CUP can therefore refuse permission for the logo to appear on any bank cards that carry the logo of a competing EPS supplier. The United States argues that if CUP does so, the bank cards carrying the logo of the competing supplier cannot be issued and the competing supplier is effectively barred from the market.[350]

7.276 China points out that Document No. 76 sets forth detailed specifications concerning the technical and commercial aspects of inter-bank payment card transactions.[351] China argues that the United States has failed to identify anything in the instruments at issue that would give CUP the "negative" power to prevent banks from placing other logos on a bank card that bear the *Yin Lian* logo.[352]

7.277 The Panel begins by recalling that CUP was given the role of operating the "United Association" when CUP was established in 2002.[353] We further observe that pursuant to Article 4.2 of Chapter I of the Business Practices Appendix of Document No. 76, the United Association does indeed possess the ownership in and the use and management rights of the *Yin Lian*/UnionPay network logo.[354] However, Article 4.2 must in our view be read together with the Article that follows it, Article 4.3. Article 4.3 is entitled "Right to use the logo". It stipulates that "Interoperating Members" "automatically obtain" the right to use the logo as from the date on which they officially engage in the inter-bank business upon approval by the United Association.[355] Document No. 76 makes clear that "Interoperating Members" include issuing banks that participate in the bank card interoperating business.[356] To become an "Interoperating Member", an

[350] United States' response to Panel question No. 71, para. 7.

[351] China's first written submission, para. 45.

[352] China's response to Panel question Nos. 106, para. 58; 117, para. 81.

[353] See para. 7.247 above.

[354] We also recall that the Notification of Business License Approval and Issuance (Exhibit US-29) makes clear that CUP's business scope includes the management and operation of the network brand "UnionPay/*Yin Lian*".

[355] The United States has provided two exhibits with translated versions of Document No. 76. In this instance, we rely on Exhibit US-63. The translation provided of Article 4.3 in Exhibit US-56 is slightly different. It reads: "The members are automatically granted the rights to use the logo when they are approved by the Association to initiate the cross-bank business".

[356] Articles 2.3 and 5.2.3 of Chapter I as well as the Appendix (Definition of Terms and Phrases) of the Business Practices Appendix contained in Document No. 76.

issuing bank must be approved as such by the United Association following an examination by a testing team.[357] As we understand Article 4.3, once an issuing bank officially becomes an "Interoperating Member", it as a consequence has the right to use the network logo.[358] We therefore fail to see how Article 4.2 could provide a basis for the United Association, or CUP, to refuse permission for the network logo to appear on bank cards bearing the logo of competing EPS suppliers.[359] In other words, Article 4.2 in our view does not demonstrate that the logo use requirements enable CUP to prevent issuers from issuing bank cards of competing EPS suppliers.

7.278 We observe as an additional matter that the United States also refers to a provision of the CUP's Operating Regulations in support of its argument based on Article 4.2.[360] The United States submitted the relevant provision of the Operating Regulations as part of its response to a Panel question that was posed after the second substantive meeting.[361] According to the United States, the Operating Regulations prohibit the logo of a competing EPS supplier from appearing on the surface of "UnionPay Cards".[362] China responds that the United States' assertion that CUP does not licence the *Yin Lian*/UnionPay network logo for use on bank cards that carry the logo of competing EPS suppliers is contradicted by the evidence on record. Specifically, China points to the prevalence of dual logo cards that bear the *Yin Lian*/UnionPay network logo as well as the logo of other EPS suppliers.[363]

7.279 We note that the relevant provision of the Operating Regulations, submitted very late in the proceedings, raises a number of questions that the United States did not address. For instance, it is not clear to us from the text of the relevant provision whether the bank cards on which other logos may not

---

[357] Articles 2.1, 2.3, 5.2.1, 5.3.1.1 and 5.3.4 of Chapter I of the Business Practices Appendix contained in Document No. 76.

[358] The United States itself appears to share this understanding. In response to Panel question No. 92 (para. 86), it states in relation to acquirers that "[o]nce an acquiring institution has been approved as a member of CUP, the acquiring institution gains the right to the CUP logo" according to Article 4.3 of the Business Practices Appendix contained in Document No. 76.

[359] The United States' argument based on Article 4 is that CUP could refuse permission to use the network logo, not that CUP could bar an issuing bank from becoming an "Interoperating Member". It is pertinent to note in this respect that according to the parties, several foreign banks are currently members of CUP. United States' response to Panel question No. 15, para. 108 (citing six foreign banks as examples); China's response to Panel question No. 115, para. 76; Exhibit CHN-105.

[360] United States' response to Panel question No. 94, para. 94 (citing Document No. 76 and the Operating Regulations together); and also response to Panel question Nos. 86, para. 64, and No. 117, para. 113.

[361] We note that the Operating Regulations date from April 2011, which is before this Panel was composed. Also, the United States did not submit the entire text of the Operating Regulations, but only the relevant provision.

[362] The United States identifies Article 2.5.3.2 of the Operating Regulations (Exhibit US-115).

[363] China's comments on the United States' response to Panel question Nos. 70-72, 86-96, 115-123, para. 67. China also points out that the document in question was not identified in the request for establishment of a panel. China's comments on the United States' response to Panel question Nos. 70-72, 86-96, 115-123, para. 68.

appear – referred to in the relevant provisions as "UnionPay Cards" – are only CUP-branded bank cards (China UnionPay cards) or also perhaps any bank card issued in China supported by a foreign EPS supplier and that in addition to the logo of the foreign EPS supplier, would have to bear the *Yin Lian*/UnionPay network logo. Nor do we have a response from the United States to China's argument about the existence of dual logo bank cards that are issued in China. Moreover, the United States, in its response to the Panel's question, has not tried to reconcile its interpretation of the Operating Regulations with Article 4.3 of the Business Practices Appendix, which indicates that the right to use the *Yin Lian*/UnionPay logo is automatically granted to "Interoperating Members". The United States merely asserts, without elaboration, that the Operating Regulations implement the mandate regarding the requirements in the Business Practices Appendix related to the use and non-use of the UnionPay/*Yin Lian* logo.[364] For these reasons, we are not persuaded that the relevant provision of the Operating Regulations supports the United States' assertion that the logo use requirements allow CUP to prevent issuers from issuing bank cards of competing EPS suppliers.

7.280 Finally, we note that in response to another question from the Panel concerning CUP's alleged power to refuse permission to use the network logo, the United States asserts that CUP at times did not approve EPS suppliers' applications for new dual-branded, dual-logo cards, and that it achieved this "essentially through the card approval process".[365] According to the United States, this is demonstrated in various press reports that date from 2006 and 2007.[366] We note, initially, that the United States provides no elaboration on what the relevant "card approval process" entails and what the governing rules and procedures are.[367] Furthermore, and without entering into a discussion of the evidentiary value of these press reports, we observe that the press reports do not refer to either Article 4 of the Business Practices Appendix or the Operating Regulations, or another instrument cited by the United States in support of the issuer requirements. Nor do they indicate that CUP denied or prevented approval of a card programme specifically by refusing permission to use the network logo.[368] In the light of this, the press reports in question in our view do not assist the United States in demonstrating that by virtue of the logo use requirements CUP can prevent issuers from issuing bank cards of competing EPS suppliers.

---

[364] United States' response to Panel question No. 86, para. 64.

[365] United States' response to Panel question No. 117, para. 113.

[366] Exhibits US-119, US-120, US-121, US-122 and US-123.

[367] The only card approval process that we have been made aware of is that provided for in Article 3 of Document No. 57. It states in relevant part that commercial banks must submit to PBOC a card sample which complies with the requirements of the *Yin Lian*/UnionPay logo as laid down in Document No. 57. On its face, Article 3 does not provide for any involvement of CUP in the approval process.

[368] For example, one of the press reports indicates merely that CUP refused the request of a commercial bank for card issuance (Exhibit US-120).

(vii) Document No. 17

7.281 The United States observes that the issuer requirements concern "bank cards" and that Document No. 17 defines that term. According to the United States, Document No. 17 in Articles 5 and 7-10 defines "bank cards" as encompassing the range of payment cards that are broadly used in card-based electronic payment transactions.[369] The United States further asserts that Article 64 of Document No. 17 requires the use of the unified standards of the Business Practices Appendix of Document 76, which are CUP-only.[370]

7.282 China does not specifically address the provisions identified by the United States, except to note that Document No. 17 was issued in 1999 and that subsequent instruments have established additional requirements.[371]

7.283 The Panel notes that Articles 5 and 7-10 of Document No. 17 do not impose any requirements. Rather, they provide legal definitions. They notably indicate that the term "bank cards", which appears in several of the instruments at issue, comprises both credit cards and debit cards, and that the latter category includes cards for transferring accounts and stored-value cards (Articles 5 and 7). It is further stipulated that bank cards may be classified into both domestic currency cards – RMB cards – and foreign currency cards (Article 5).

7.284 The United States' claims in this case concern EPS for "payment card" transactions and not EPS for "bank card" transactions.[372] However, "payment cards" as defined by the United States include bank cards, credit cards, debit cards and prepaid cards. Thus, the term "bank card" as defined in Document No. 17 covers at least some important types of "payment card".

7.285 The United States suggests that the definition of "bank cards" provided in Document No. 17 is also applicable when this term appears in other instruments at issue. China has not asserted anything to the contrary. We see nothing in Document Nos. 37, 57, 129, 219 or 76 to indicate that we should not take that definition into account in our analysis of these instruments.[373]

7.286 As regards Article 64, it provides in relevant part that a commercial bank in China, when issuing any variety of bank cards (other than those of an international credit card organization), must implement the technical standards prescribed by the State.[374] In our view, Article 64 does not require that all bank

[369] United States' response to China's request for a preliminary ruling, fn. 153.

[370] United States' second written submission, para. 170 and fn. 201.

[371] China's response to Panel question No. 122, para. 88.

[372] WT/DS413/2, p. 1.

[373] Document No. 76 in Chapter 10 specifically refers to Document No. 17.

[374] In response to a question from the Panel concerning the reference to international credit card organizations, China has said that Document No. 17 dates from 1999 and that subsequent instruments have established that all RMB payment cards must have the technical capability of being processed over the CUP network. China's response to Panel question No. 122, para. 88. We do not understand this response to mean that Document No. 17 does not require compliance with technical standards prescribed by the State that post-date Document No. 17. The United States similarly responded that Article 64 predates the creation of CUP and that it does not mean that banks in China can issue RMB

cards issued in China must bear the *Yin Lian*/UnionPay logo. Nor does Article 64 itself require the use of the unified standards set out in the Appendix on Business Practices contained in Document No. 76. But we agree that the Business Practices Appendix includes technical standards prescribed by the State that are applicable to issuers.[375] In the light of this, we consider that Article 64 in conjunction with Document No. 76 requires issuers to implement technical standards when issuing bank cards that must bear the *Yin Lian*/UnionPay logo.

(viii) Yin Lian/UnionPay logo use requirements versus interoperability requirements

7.287 Before reaching overall conclusions, it is necessary to address an additional point that was made by the United States. According to the United States, the fact that issuers in China are subject to *Yin Lian*/UnionPay logo use requirements means that they must have access to the CUP system and pay CUP for that access. As this contention concerns two distinct elements, we first consider the issue of access to the CUP system.

7.288 In our view, the *Yin Lian*/UnionPay logo use requirements do not in and of themselves mean that issuers must have access to the CUP system.[376] As the preceding analysis shows, however, China does maintain related requirements on issuers that are designed to ensure that issuers join CUP and that the bank cards that must bear the *Yin Lian*/UnionPay logo meet uniform business specifications and technical standards and thus be interoperable with CUP.[377] The specific provisions and instruments that impose these requirements are the following: Articles 1.2(i), 2.1(iii), 2.2(i) and 3.1 of Document No. 37; Article 3 of Document No. 57; Article 3.2(ii) of Document No. 129; and Article 64 of Document No. 17 in conjunction with Document No. 76. Having regard to these

cards that carry only the logo of an international credit card organization. United States' response to Panel question No. 122, para. 121.

375 See, e.g. Articles 5.2.2 and 5.2.3 of Chapter I and paragraph 3 of the Notice.

376 The United States appears to acknowledge this when it states, in response to Panel question No. 119 (para. 118), that Article 2.1 of Document No. 37 "requires that all cards bearing the UnionPay/*Yin Lian* logo (which, by virtue of measures described elsewhere, includes all cards issued in China for domestic use) 'must strictly abide by the unified technical specification and all bank card issuers must provide [...] services pursuant to the unified business specifications.'"

377 The United States has itself distinguished these two requirements. United States' response to Panel question No. 15, para. 57. According to the United States, the uniform business specifications include relevant provisions of the Business Practices Appendix contained in Document No. 76. With regard to the uniform technical specifications, the United States points out that they include a variety of technical documents (including Document No. 76), some of which have been issued by CUP and some of which have been issued by the PBOC or other agencies. United States' response to Panel question Nos. 15, para. 57; and 72, paras. 14 and 15.

provisions, it is in our view correct to say that issuers must have access to the CUP network.[378]

7.289 The United States in response to a question from the Panel referred to this category of issuer requirements as "interoperability requirements".[379] As the United States has raised the element of access to the CUP system from the beginning in connection with the requirements on issuers that bank cards bear the *Yin Lian*/UnionPay logo[380], we will proceed on the basis that there are two categories of issuer requirements for us to address: those that relate to the *Yin Lian*/UnionPay logo use and those that relate to interoperability.

7.290 We now turn to the issue of payment for access to the CUP network. The United States alleges that in order to join the network, issuers must pay fees to CUP.[381] Here again, it appears that what triggers the alleged fees are not the *Yin Lian*/UnionPay logo use requirements per se, but rather the interoperability requirements imposed on issuers. In response to a question from the Panel, the United States identifies two types of fee that may need to be paid to CUP: membership fees and testing fees.[382] In support of its allegation, the United States refers the Panel to Article 3.1(iii) of Document No. 94. That Article states in relevant part that CUP must "regulate fee charging methods and standards for inter-bank transactions at all city centers". We recall that Document No. 94 was repealed and ceased to have legal effect prior to the date of the Panel's establishment. As indicated above[383], we therefore decline to take this document into account in our analysis of the measures at issue, which include the issuer requirements. In any event, even if Document No. 94 were relevant for our purposes, it is not clear that it supports the United States' allegation regarding fees payable for joining the CUP network. The United States does not address whether the fees referred to in Article 3.1(iii) are fees payable to CUP for access to the network. As the United States points out, Article 3.1(iii) is concerned with the regulation of inter-bank transactions, including fee-setting.[384] China has explained that inter-bank transactions often involve so-called interchange fees that are usually paid by acquirers to issuers.[385]

---

[378] China appears to agree that its instruments require that all inter-bank bank cards adhere to a common technical standard and that all issuers of such cards in China must be members of CUP. China's response to Panel question No. 22(c), para. 17.

[379] United States' response to Panel question Nos. 15, para. 55; 92, para. 88.

[380] WT/DS413/2, p. 2; United States' response to China's request for a preliminary ruling, paras. 102 and 111; first written submission, paras. 12, 50 and 100; and second written submission, para. 201.

[381] United States' response to Panel question No. 94, para. 96.

[382] United States' response to Panel question No. 93, para. 93.

[383] See paras. 7.221 et seq. above.

[384] United States' response to Panel question No. 93, para. 91. We also note that Article 2.4.1 of Document No. 76 refers to obligations to be met by Interoperating Members that include "abiding by relevant regulations governing interoperation fees".

[385] China's first written submission, para. 52. We note that the Visa IPO Prospectus (Exhibit US-3), at page 146, confirms China's explanation. It also states that Visa sets default interchange rates in the

7.291 The United States also relies on Articles 11 and 12 of CUP's Articles of Association.[386] However, these Articles do not mention any fees that CUP charges issuers. Additionally, the United States in response to a Panel question posed after the second substantive meeting submitted the previously mentioned CUP Operating Regulations.[387] They include provisions on membership and testing fees payable to CUP.[388] However, as also pointed out by China, the Operating Regulations are not identified as a relevant legal instrument in the United States' request for the establishment of a panel.[389] Moreover, unlike in the context of the logo use requirements where the United States also refers to the Operating Regulations, in the present context the United States does not specifically contend that they implement a requirement contained in one of the instruments cited by it in support of the issuer requirements.[390] We note in this respect that the provisions on membership and testing fees provided to us by the United States do not, by their terms, establish a link to any of the aforementioned instruments.[391] In the absence of further explanation on the Operating Regulations, it is therefore not clear to us that its provisions on membership and testing fees are linked to any of the specific provisions and instruments cited by the United States in support of the issuer requirements. We are therefore not persuaded that the Operating Regulations demonstrate what the United States asserts, i.e. that as a result of Document Nos. 37, 57, 129, 219, 76 or 17, issuers in China must pay fees to CUP for access to the CUP network.

7.292 For these several reasons, the United States in our view has not established that the issuer requirements entail, or are associated with, access fees payable to CUP.

(ix) Conclusions and implications

7.293 Having regard to the preceding analysis, we reach the following conclusions in respect of the United States' assertions concerning the issuer requirements. First, China maintains requirements on commercial banks as issuers of bank cards. The term "bank cards" as defined in Document No. 17 covers at least some types of what the United States has defined as "payment cards".

United States and other regions, and that in certain jurisdictions interchange rates are subject to government regulation.

386 Exhibit US-20.

387 United States' response to Panel question No. 93, para. 93.

388 The United States identifies Chapter 7 of the Operating Regulations (Exhibit US-116).

389 China's comments on the United States' response to Panel question Nos. 70-72, 86-96, 115-123, para. 68.

390 United States' response to Panel question Nos. 86, para. 64; and 93, para. 93. We note that CUP's Articles of Association are not among the instruments cited in support of the issuer requirements.

391 Exhibit US-116. We observe in this connection that the Panel's question asked the United States to indicate, "in any of the instruments before the Panel", the specific provisions concerning access fees for issuers. The Operating Regulations were not among these instruments at the time the question was put to the United States.

7.294 Secondly, all RMB bank cards issued in China by commercial banks for use in domestic inter-bank RMB transactions must bear the *Yin Lian*/UnionPay logo on the front of the card. This requirement is maintained through Articles 2.1(i) and 2.2(i) of Document No. 37; Articles 1, 5 and 6 of Document No. 57; and Article 3.2(ii) of Document No. 129. Similarly, dual currency (dual account) bank cards issued by commercial banks in China for use *inter alia* in domestic inter-bank or cross-region RMB transactions must also bear the *Yin Lian*/UnionPay logo on the front of the card. This requirement is imposed through Article 2 of Document No. 57. Additionally, all RMB credit cards must bear the *Yin Lian*/UnionPay holographic anti-counterfeiting logo. This requirement is imposed by Article 1 of Document No. 57.

7.295 Thirdly, China requires that issuers join CUP, and that the bank cards which they issue and which must bear the *Yin Lian*/UnionPay logo meet uniform business specifications and technical standards. These interoperability requirements are maintained through the following provisions: Articles 1.2(i), 2.1(iii), 2.2(i) and 3.1 of Document No. 37; Article 3 of Document No. 57; Article 3.2(ii) of Document No. 129; and Article 64 of Document No. 17 in conjunction with Document No. 76.

7.296 Finally, and in contrast, we have determined that Article 4 of Document No. 57, Article III of Document No. 219 and Article 4.2 of Document No. 76, when considered individually, either do not impose requirements on issuers or do not constitute relevant issuer requirements. We find no basis to modify our conclusion when considering these provisions either together or with the other provisions and instruments cited by the United States in connection with the issuer requirements.

7.297 It remains for us to address an assertion made by China regarding the implications of the issuer requirements. China asserts that the United States has not demonstrated that the issuer requirements would prevent the issuance in China of bank cards that are capable of being processed over more than one network and that bear both the *Yin Lian* logo and the logo of an EPS supplier other than CUP. Thus, the issue to be addressed is whether the issuer requirements would prevent commercial banks from issuing single or dual currency bank cards in China that could be used in domestic inter-bank RMB transactions and that would be capable of being processed over a network in China that is not the CUP network.

7.298 We understand that it is technically possible for a single bank card to be capable of being processed over more than one network.[392] We can therefore proceed to consider the issuer requirements. We begin with the *Yin Lian*/UnionPay logo use element of these requirements. The relevant provisions

[392] The parties have, for instance, provided the example of dual-branded (dual-logo), dual-currency bank cards. Additionally, China contends that it is technically possible for POS terminals to give card holders or merchants a choice as to the network over which a payment card transaction will be processed. China's response to Panel question No. 7, para. 61.

of Document Nos. 37, 57 and 129 concern the requirement to bear the *Yin Lian*/UnionPay logo. They do not state that bank cards cannot be issued in China if they are capable of being processed over a network in China other than that of CUP. Nor do they say that bank cards can bear the logo of only one – CUP's – network.[393] The United States contends, however, that the *Yin Lian*/UnionPay logo use requirement is incompatible with logo use requirements of competing EPS suppliers.[394] China responds that the United States has cited no evidence of this incompatibility and points out that bank cards in China frequently bear more than one logo.[395] China notably provided unrefuted evidence of the existence of dual-logo bank cards.[396] For these reasons, we see no basis on which to conclude that the provisions in question would prohibit the issuance of relevant cards that would be capable of being processed over more than one inter-bank network in China, provided these cards also bear the *Yin Lian*/UnionPay logo.[397] We note that the United States itself appears to view the issuance of such cards as a possible, if unlikely, scenario.[398] Specifically, the United States has said that "[e]ven if a foreign supplier of EPS was to convince an issuer to issue a card, [the issuer] requirements ensure that it will not be able to compromise CUP's prominent logo or obtain any market share to the certain exclusion of CUP."[399]

7.299 Turning to the interoperability element of the issuer requirements, China submits that these requirements do not preclude issuers from being members of networks other than the CUP network, and do not prevent bank cards from adhering at the same time to technical standards that are not those of CUP.[400] In support of its view, China points to the issuance of dual-branded, dual-currency bank cards issued in China.[401] To us, the existence of dual-branded (dual-logo), dual-currency bank cards issued in China suggests that it is technically possible for bank cards simultaneously to comply with different sets of business specifications and technical standards. Moreover, nothing in the relevant provisions of Document Nos. 37, 57, 129 or 17 (in conjunction with No. 76) indicates that issuers who are members of CUP may not join other networks in China, or that bank cards that meet CUP's uniform business specifications and technical standards must not, or cannot, simultaneously meet those of other

[393] We note that Exhibit CHN-112 shows examples of dual-branded (dual-logo), dual-currency bank cards issued in China.

[394] United States' response to Panel question No. 86, para. 62.

[395] China's comments on the United States' response to Panel question Nos. 70-72, 86-96, 115-123. , paras. 56 and 73.

[396] Exhibit CHN-112.

[397] We recall that we have already rejected relevant arguments developed by the United States on the basis of Article 4.2 of Document No. 76 and CUP's Operating Regulations. See paras. 7.275 to 7.279 above.

[398] Para. 7.360 below addresses the United States' claim that the logo use requirements modify the conditions of competition to the detriment of EPS suppliers of other Members.

[399] United States' first written submission, para. 101. See also first written submission, para. 80.

[400] China's response to Panel question Nos. 22(c), para. 18; 112, para. 73; and 119, para. 84.

[401] China's comments on the United States' response to Panel question Nos. 70-72, 86-96, 115-123, para. 56; response to Panel question No. 116, para. 78; Exhibit CHN-112.

networks. The United States refers to paragraph 5 of the Notice of Document No. 76.[402] It states that bank card business rules that are inconsistent with the Business Practices contained in Document No. 76 must be abolished as from the date of implementation of Document No. 76. As we understand it, paragraph 5 means that bank card business rules that differ from those of the Business Practices can be implemented, provided they do not conflict with the Business Practices.[403] The United States has not demonstrated that any of the aforementioned provisions are inconsistent with central issuer-related bank card business rules that have been adopted by EPS suppliers other than CUP. Consequently, we find no basis to conclude that the issuer requirements that relate to interoperability would prevent the issuance of single or dual currency cards that would be capable of being processed over more than one inter-bank network in China. But if any such cards are issued by commercial banks in China, they must bear the *Yin Lian*/UnionPay logo.

(b) Requirements that all ATM, and POS terminals in China accept CUP cards ("terminal equipment requirements")

7.300 The requirements to which the Panel turns next are the alleged terminal equipment requirements. The United States asserts that these requirements are maintained through specific provisions of the following Chinese legal instruments:[404]

- Document No. 17 (Article 64)
- Document No. 37 (Articles 1.2(i); 2.1(ii) and (iii))
- Document No. 57 (Articles 3, 5 and 6)
- Document No. 153 (Article 2.2)
- Document No. 149 (Article 2(5)(iii))
- Document No. 76 (Chapter II, Article 1.2)

7.301 The United States submits that through these instruments China requires that all ATMs, merchant card processing equipment and POS terminals in China be capable of accepting CUP cards.[405]

7.302 China responds that the measures at issue require that all POS terminals used for domestic inter-bank transactions denominated in RMB in China be capable of accepting bank cards that bear the *Yin Lian* logo and they must adhere

[402] United States' second written submission, para. 163.

[403] Paragraph 5 does not say that any and all bank card business rules that differ from those contained in the Business Practices are to be abolished.

[404] United States' response to Panel question Nos. 4, para. 18; and 6, para. 32. The United States also relies on Document Nos. 94 and 272. As explained above at paras. 7.221-7.229, the Panel has decided not to consider the substance of these documents.

[405] United States' first written submission, paras. 4 and 102; WT/DS413/2, p. 2.

to certain technical standards.[406] These measures create uniform technical and commercial standards that allow a national inter-bank payment card network to function. China further submits that the United States fails to identify any aspect of the alleged terminal equipment requirements that would prevent the acceptance of payment cards that are capable of being processed over multiple networks.[407] China observes in this respect that most POS terminals are capable of processing any type of bank card.[408]

7.303 Below, the Panel will examine the above-listed instruments so as to determine whether they impose the requirements alleged by the United States. It is important to point out in this respect that the United States has described the terminal equipment requirements as mandating that terminal equipment in China – ATMs and POS terminals used by merchants or other operators such as banks – be capable of accepting *Yin Lian*/UnionPay bank cards. The alleged requirements are not about whether the *Yin Lian*/UnionPay logo must be posted on terminal equipment.[409] The issue of the posting of the *Yin Lian*/UnionPay logo has been raised by the United States only in the context of its challenge to the alleged acquirer requirements.[410]

(i) Document No. 17

7.304 The United States submits that Document No. 17 mandates the use of unified, CUP-only standards. It asserts that this in turn means that any POS terminal must be capable of accepting CUP cards for any payment card transaction in China.[411]

7.305 China does not address the specific requirement on which the United States relies.

7.306 The Panel notes that the requirement referred to by the United States may be found in Article 64 of Document No. 17, which has been addressed earlier.[412] Article 64 requires commercial banks in China to implement technical standards prescribed by the State when issuing bank cards. It makes no reference to terminal equipment, or to acceptance of bank cards. In the absence of any elaboration by the United States, it is not clear to us why and how Article 64,

---

406 China's first written submission, para. 36; response to Panel question Nos. 22(c), para. 17; 101, para. 43.

407 China's second written submission, para. 93.

408 China's response to Panel question No. 101, para. 43.

409 In the context of the Chinese instruments before us, the two issues – the posting of the UnionPay/*Yin Lian* logo and the capability of terminal equipment to accept bank cards bearing the logo – are not one and the same. As will be clear from the analysis below and that concerning the alleged acquirer requirements, the relevant instruments address these two issues in separate requirements.

410 See, e.g. United States' first written submission, paras. 4, 12, 102 and 111; WT/DS413/2, p. 2.

411 United States' second written submission, para. 177.

412 See para. 7.286 above.

which on its face focuses on the activity of bank card issuance, "means that any POS terminal must be capable of accepting CUP cards".[413]

7.307 In the light of this, we do not consider that Article 64 of Document No. 17 imposes a requirement that all ATMs, merchant card processing equipment and POS terminals must be capable of accepting bank cards bearing the *Yin Lian*/UnionPay logo.

(ii) Document No. 37

7.308 The United States also refers the Panel to the text of Articles 1.2(i) and 2.1(ii) and (iii) of Document No. 37.[414]

7.309 China states that Document No. 37 establishes uniform technical standards for POS terminals that accept inter-bank payment cards.[415]

7.310 The Panel notes that Article 1.2(i) does not specifically mention ATMs or POS terminals.[416] However, it requires commercial banks to make "technical preparations for accepting bank cards bearing the [*Yin Lian*/UnionPay] logo".[417] We note the references to "technical preparations" and "acceptance" of bank cards. ATMs or POS terminals of commercial banks constitute technical equipment used for accepting bank cards. In our assessment, these elements support the view that Article 1.2(i) requires, *inter alia*, that terminal equipment of commercial banks must be capable of accepting cards bearing the *Yin Lian*/UnionPay logo.

7.311 Article 2.1(ii) prescribes in relevant part that "[a]ll terminals (such as ATMs and POS) which join the nationwide bank card inter-bank processing network must be capable of accepting all bank cards bearing the [*Yin Lian*/UnionPay] logo". As regards Article 2.1(iii), as pointed out above, this provision is concerned with bank cards bearing the *Yin Lian*/UnionPay logo and the services to be supplied by issuers of bank cards pursuant to the unified business specifications.[418] In the absence of an explanation by the United States on how this provision lays down a requirement concerning terminal equipment , we are not persuaded that this is the case.

7.312 Based on the foregoing, we consider that Articles 1.2(i) and 2.1(ii) require that all terminal equipment of commercial banks that join China's national inter-bank bank card network be capable of accepting bank cards bearing the *Yin Lian*/UnionPay logo. China has clarified in response to a question from the Panel that there is terminal equipment in China that does not

---

413 United States' second written submission, para. 177.

414 United States' first written submission, paras. 103 and 105.

415 China's first written submission, para. 45.

416 Article 1.2(i) was discussed above in connection with the issuer requirements. See para. 7.255 above.

417 See the UNOG translator's linguistic advice as set out in Annex H.

418 See para. 7.257 above.

need to be connected to the national inter-bank network. Such terminal equipment is used exclusively for foreign currency transactions.[419]

(iii) Document No. 57

7.313 The United States also relies on Document No. 57, specifically its Articles 3, 5 and 6.[420]

7.314 China argues that Document No. 57 requires payment cards issued for domestic inter-bank use to bear the *Yin Lian* logo, and requires commercial banks that issue inter-bank payment cards to adhere to the business specifications for bank card interoperability contained in Document No. 76.[421]

7.315 As the Panel explained above, Article 3 provides that bank cards issued for domestic inter-bank use must comply with the unified business specifications and technical standards. It further provides that commercial banks must provide card samples to the PBOC that comply with the *Yin Lian*/UnionPay logo use requirements.[422] Article 5 provides in relevant part that POS terminals must have the *Yin Lian*/UnionPay logo posted. Article 6 mandates the abolition of regional bank card interoperability logos and requires that terminal equipment such as ATMs and POS terminals not bear any regional bank card interoperability logo.[423] In our view, none of these Articles imposes a requirement that terminal equipment in China be capable of accepting bank cards bearing the *Yin Lian*/UnionPay logo. Article 3 deals with bank cards. Only Articles 5 and 6 mention terminal equipment. Article 5 requires the posting of the *Yin Lian*/UnionPay logo on POS terminals, while Article 6 is concerned with regional interoperability logos that terminal equipment may not display. Neither Article 5 nor Article 6 addresses the issue of whether terminal equipment in China must be capable of accepting bank cards bearing the *Yin Lian*/UnionPay logo.[424] This is consistent with the title of Document No. 57, which is "Circular on Uniform Use of CUP Logo and its Holographic Label for Anti-Counterfeiting".[425] As we have explained earlier the terminal equipment requirements as described by the United States are not concerned with the posting of the *Yin Lian*/Union Pay logo on such equipment.

---

419 China's response to Panel question No. 101, para. 43. The United States has confirmed that there are a small number of POS terminals that can only accept foreign-issued bank cards and that are not required to be connected to the CUP network. United States' comments on China's response to Panel question No. 101, para. 37.

420 United States' second written submission, para. 179; response to Panel question Nos. 6, para. 32; 71, para. 8.

421 China's first written submission, para. 45.

422 See para. 7.263 above.

423 Article 5 contains a corresponding requirement that all POS terminals in the bank card acceptance market must have the UnionPay/*Yin Lian* logo posted.

424 We recall in this connection that there are other provisions, e.g. in Document No. 37, that specifically require that terminal equipment be capable of accepting bank cards bearing the UnionPay/*Yin Lian* logo.

425 Exhibit US-41, heading.

7.316 Based on the above, we consider that Articles 3, 5 and 6 of Document No. 57 do not impose a requirement that all terminal equipment in China be capable of accepting bank cards bearing the *Yin Lian*/UnionPay logo.

(iv) Document No. 153

7.317 The United States identifies Document No. 153 as another instrument that imposes a terminal equipment requirement. According to the United States, the relevant provision is Article 2.2.[426]

7.318 China does not specifically address Document No. 153 in connection with the alleged terminal equipment requirements.

7.319 The Panel notes that Article 2 of Document No. 153 is entitled "Principles to be complied with in the merchant acquiring business". Article 2.2 requires that POS terminals placed by acquirers or third-party service providers conform to the business specifications and technical standards of cross-network interoperability, be posted with the unified *Yin Lian*/UnionPay logo, and be capable of accepting all bank cards bearing the *Yin Lian*/UnionPay logo.

7.320 In the light of this, we consider that Article 2.2 imposes a requirement that merchant POS terminals in China that have been placed by acquirers or third-party providers be capable of accepting bank cards bearing the *Yin Lian*/UnionPay logo.

(v) Document No. 149

7.321 The United States submits that Document No. 149 contains a clear prohibition on accepting non-CUP cards. According to the United States, Article 2(5)(iii) prevents acquirers and merchants from accepting prepaid bank cards that do not bear the CUP logo.[427]

7.322 China argues that Article 2(5)(iii) relates to prepaid cards issued by non-financial institutions, including cards issued by a retailer that are meant to be used only at that retailer. China states that the point of this provision is that these types of non-interoperable payment cards should not be processed through the same POS terminals used to process interoperable payment cards that bear the *Yin Lian* logo. According to China, Article 2(5)(iii) is intended to prevent payment card crimes. Specifically, it seeks to prevent a situation in which someone tries to use a prepaid card issued by a retailer, for example, to complete a transaction with someone other than that retailer. China points out that this would be a form of fraud since the merchant that accepts the card is unlikely to be able to obtain payment from the retailer that issued the prepaid card. China maintains, therefore, that Article 2(5)(iii) merely reflects the fact that all interoperable RMB payment cards must be capable of being processed over the

426 United States' second written submission, para. 176.
427 United States' second written submission, para. 175.

CUP network and bear the *Yin Lian* logo. China also states that Article 2(5)(iii) does not prohibit accepting cards that bear the *Yin Lian* logo and the logo of another network operator (i.e. dual-logo cards).[428]

7.323 The Panel notes that Document No. 149 is about security management of bank cards and preventing and fighting crime in bank cards.[429] Article 2(5)(iii) of Document No. 149 relates to access to bank card terminals, and to prepaid cards. Prepaid cards are among the payment cards at issue in this dispute. Moreover, according to linguistic advice provided by the UNOG translator, Article 2(5)(iii) concerns prepaid cards issued by "non-financial social enterprises". The UNOG translator indicates that "non-financial social enterprises" are social enterprises that are not financial institutions, such as charitable institutions or social enterprises that provide prepaid debit cards to their clientele.[430] China states that the relevant enterprises would also include retailers. Even if this means that China argues for a broader category of non-financial enterprises, China's position does not contradict the fundamental point that the relevant prepaid cards are issued by *non-financial* enterprises.[431]

7.324 Article 2(5)(iii) states that acquirers may not allow prepaid cards to be accepted at bank card terminal equipment (POS terminals) if these cards do not bear the *Yin Lian*/UnionPay logo or do not meet the PBOC 2.0 standard. In our view, this Article is not about which prepaid cards POS terminals must be capable of accepting. Rather, the Article is about which prepaid cards such terminals must *not* accept. This view is consistent with the purpose of Document No. 149, which is to prevent bank card crime. In the case of Article 2(5)(iii), as China has explained, the specific concern is to prevent fraud involving prepaid cards issued by relevant enterprises.

7.325 In our view, the fact that prepaid cards without the *Yin Lian*/UnionPay logo are not allowed to be accepted at bank card POS terminals does not imply that all prepaid cards bearing the *Yin Lian*/UnionPay logo must be allowed.[432] It implies merely that the relevant terminals may allow such cards to be accepted.[433] We also note that no evidence other than the text of Article 2(5)(iii)

[428] China's response to Panel question Nos. 104(b), paras. 52 and 53; 110, para. 68; Exhibit CHN-74.

[429] Exhibit US-50, heading.

[430] UNOG evaluation, p. 13.

[431] This view also draws support from the fact that Article 2(5)(iii) refers to prepaid "cards" rather than to prepaid bank cards.

[432] We note that prepaid cards bearing the *Yin Lian*/UnionPay logo would appear to include dual-logo prepaid cards that at the same bear the logo of another EPS supplier.

[433] In response to a Panel question, the United States itself states that Article 2(5)(iii) "means that only CUP cards may be used at such terminals". United States' response to Panel question No. 91, para. 85.

itself has been provided to assist us in determining the legal effect of this provision.[434]

7.326 As a result, we are not persuaded that Article 2(5)(iii) imposes a requirement that all merchant POS terminals be capable of accepting prepaid cards issued by relevant enterprises and bearing the *Yin Lian*/UnionPay logo.

(vi) Document No. 76

7.327 The United States cites Document No. 76 as a further source of the alleged terminal equipment requirements. The United States refers the Panel to Article 1.2 of Chapter II of the Business Practices Appendix.[435]

7.328 China points out that Document No. 76 sets forth detailed specifications concerning the technical and commercial aspects of inter-bank payment card transactions.[436]

7.329 The Panel notes that in accordance with Article 1.2 of Chapter II, the "Unified Network Logo"[437] must be posted on the machines and equipment of any merchant in accordance with relevant regulations of interoperability, and must be posted on the merchant's cash register machines. This requirement mandates the posting of the *Yin Lian*/UnionPay logo. It does not address the issue of whether merchants' terminal equipment must be capable of accepting bank cards bearing the *Yin Lian*/UnionPay logo.[438] As mentioned above, the alleged terminal equipment requirements as described by the United States are not about the posting of logos.

7.330 In the light of this, we do not consider that Article 1.2 of Chapter II imposes a requirement that all merchant terminal equipment be capable of accepting bank cards bearing the *Yin Lian*/UnionPay logo.

(vii) Conclusions and implications

7.331 Having regard to the preceding analysis, we agree that China maintains terminal equipment requirements with regard to bank cards for use in domestic

---

434 Given this, it is important, in our view, not to read into Article 2(5)(iii) more than it says, or necessarily implies, all the more so as there are provisions of other Chinese instruments, notably Document Nos. 37 and 153, which explicitly require that bank cards bearing the UnionPay/*Yin Lian* logo be accepted at relevant terminals.

435 United States' response to China's request for a preliminary ruling, para. 113.

436 China's first written submission, para. 45.

437 The Business Practices Appendix to Document No. 76 defines this term as meaning the uniform brand name for domestic bank cards (the Chinese characters *yinlian*) and the design symbolizing the united network, as registered with the trademark office. See the UNOG's translator's linguistic advice as set out in Annex H.

438 As is clear from our findings so far, there are provisions of other Chinese instruments – such as Document Nos. 37 and 153 – which explicitly require that bank cards bearing the UnionPay/*Yin Lian* logo be accepted at relevant terminals. Therefore, we are not persuaded that we can infer that a logo posting requirement amounts at the same time to a requirement that terminal equipment be capable of accepting bank cards bearing the relevant logo.

inter-bank RMB transactions. More specifically, in our view China requires that terminals (ATMs, merchant processing devices and POS terminals) in China that are part of the national bank card inter-bank processing network be capable of accepting all bank cards bearing the *Yin Lian*/UnionPay logo.[439] This requirement is maintained through Articles 1.2(i) and 2.1(ii) of Document No. 37 (for terminal equipment of commercial banks) and also through Article 2.2 of Document No. 153 (for merchant terminal equipment).

7.332 However, we are not convinced that Article 64 of Document No. 17, Articles 3, 5 or 6 of Document No. 57, Article 2(5)(iii) of Document No. 149, or Article 1.2 of Chapter II of the Business Practices Appendix contained in Document No. 76, when considered individually, require that all terminal equipment in China be capable of accepting bank cards bearing the *Yin Lian*/UnionPay logo. We find no basis to modify our conclusion when considering these provisions together, or with the other provisions cited by the United States in connection with the terminal equipment requirements.

7.333 Finally, we recall that Document Nos. 37 and 153 use the term "bank card". The term "bank card" as defined in Document No. 17 covers at least some types of "payment card", which is the term used by the United States in its request for the establishment of a panel.[440]

7.334 Having reached these conclusions, we now consider China's argument concerning the implications of the terminal equipment requirements. According to China, the United States has not identified any aspect of the terminal equipment requirements that would prevent the acceptance of bank cards that are capable of being processed over multiple networks. China submits that POS terminals can accept bank cards that bear different logos.[441] We also understand that modern ATMs and POS terminals are typically capable of accepting not just bank cards with the logo of one particular EPS supplier, but also bank cards with the logo of other EPS suppliers. Furthermore, the relevant provisions of Document Nos. 37 and 153 do not state that the terminal equipment that must be capable of accepting bank cards bearing the *Yin Lian*/UnionPay logo must not be capable of accepting, at the same time, bank cards bearing the logo of different EPS suppliers. Hence, in the absence of other evidence, we see no basis for concluding that the terminal equipment requirements would prevent the acceptance of bank cards that would be capable of being processed over an inter-bank network in China other than that of CUP.[442]

---

[439] The terminals in question are those that are used for domestic inter-bank RMB transactions. China's response to Panel question No. 101, para. 43.

[440] See para. 7.284 above.

[441] China's response to Panel question No. 22(c), para. 18; comments on the United States' response to Panel question Nos. 70-72, 86-96, 115-123, para. 73.

[442] We note that the United States itself appears to suggest that terminal equipment in China could in principle accept relevant bank cards. The United States points out that "a foreign EPS [supplier] must build that network [of merchants that accept its card] by marketing itself to merchants and acquiring banks" (United States' first written submission, para. 110). Similarly, the United States observes that

(c) Requirements on acquiring institutions to post the CUP logo and be capable of accepting all payment cards bearing the CUP logo ("acquirer requirements")

7.335 We now consider the alleged acquirer requirements. The United States asserts that these requirements are maintained through specific provisions of the following Chinese legal instruments:[443]

- Document No. 153 (Article 2.2)
- Document No. 149 (Article 2(5)(iii))
- Document No. 37 (Article 1.2(i))
- Document No. 76 (Notice, paragraphs 2 and 3; Chapter I, Articles 2.1 and 5.2.1)

7.336 The United States submits that through these instruments China requires that all acquirers in China post the CUP logo and be capable of accepting CUP cards.[444]

7.337 China responds that the measures at issue require POS terminals in China to adhere to certain technical standards and to bear a common logo indicating their ability to be used for domestic inter-bank transactions.[445] These measures create uniform technical and commercial standards that allow a national inter-bank payment card network to function. China further submits that the United States fails to identify any aspect of the alleged acquirer requirements that would prevent the acceptance of payment cards that are capable of being processed over multiple networks.[446]

7.338 The Panel begins its analysis by noting that the acquirer requirements as defined by the United States comprise two distinct elements (i) requirements that acquirers post the *Yin Lian*/UnionPay logo, and (ii) requirements that acquirers be capable of accepting payment cards bearing the *Yin Lian*/UnionPay logo. We gather from the specific provisions relied on by the United States that the second element includes alleged requirements that terminal equipment operated or provided by acquirers (ATMs and merchant POS terminals) must be capable of accepting payment cards bearing the *Yin Lian*/UnionPay logo. To that extent, there is overlap between the acquirer and the above-discussed terminal equipment requirements. The United States itself has pointed out, however, that

"[t]o the extent a foreign supplier of EPS was to create or secure access to a POS, then CUP would also gain as well because of the [terminal equipment] requirement" (United States' first written submission, para. 80).

[443] United States' response to Panel question No. 4, para. 19. The United States also relies on Document Nos. 94 and 272. As explained above at paras. 7.221-7.229, the Panel has decided not to consider the substance of these documents.

[444] United States' first written submission, paras. 4 and 111.

[445] China's first written submission, para. 36.

[446] China's second written submission, para. 93.

there is a "significant degree of overlap" among the six categories of requirements it has distinguished.[447] In addition, the United States has stated that the acquirer requirements include alleged requirements on acquirers to join CUP and to comply with business standards and technical specifications of inter-bank interoperability.[448] The United States has explained that these requirements concern the capabilities of acquirers themselves, regardless of the type of terminal equipment located at merchants' places of business.[449] Consequently, the alleged requirements that acquirers be capable of accepting *Yin Lian*/UnionPay logo payment cards appear to comprise both terminal equipment and interoperability requirements. With this in mind, we now proceed to determine whether the four instruments identified by the United States impose the alleged acquirer requirements.

(i) Document No. 153

7.339 The United States cites Article 2.2 of Document No. 153 as one source of the alleged acquirer requirements.[450]

7.340 China does not specifically address Document No. 153 in connection with the alleged acquirer requirements.

7.341 As previously noted by the Panel[451], Article 2.2 states that merchant POS terminals in China that have been placed by qualified merchant acquirers[452] or third-party providers must: (i) conform to the business specifications and technical standards of cross-network interoperability, (ii) be capable of accepting bank cards bearing the *Yin Lian*/UnionPay logo, and (iii) be posted with the unified *Yin Lian*/UnionPay logo.[453] Thus, Article 2.2 establishes a requirement that acquirers be capable of accepting bank cards bearing the *Yin Lian*/UnionPay logo (interoperability requirement (i) and terminal equipment requirement (ii)). It also requires that acquirers post the *Yin Lian*/UnionPay logo on the POS terminals they provide to merchants (requirement (iii)).

7.342 In the light of this, we consider that Article 2.2 imposes a requirement that qualified acquirers in China post the *Yin Lian*/UnionPay logo and be capable of accepting, through the merchant POS terminals they place with merchants, all bank cards bearing the *Yin Lian*/UnionPay logo.

---

[447] United States' response to Panel question Nos. 4, para. 14; 1, para. 1.

[448] United States' second written submission, para. 181; response to Panel question No. 92, para. 90.

[449] United States' response to Panel question No. 1, para. 1.

[450] United States' first written submission, para. 112.

[451] See para. 7.319 above.

[452] According to Article 1.1 of Document No. 153, merchant acquiring institutions comprise financial institutions and qualified professional acquiring institutions.

[453] See para. 7.320 above.

(ii) Document No. 149

7.343 The United States submits that Article 2(5)(iii) of Document No. 149 also sets forth acquirer requirements.[454]

7.344 China argues that Article 2(5)(iii) simply reflects the fact that all POS terminals must be capable of accepting prepaid payment cards that bear the *Yin Lian* logo. It does not prohibit accepting cards that also bear other logos.[455]

7.345 As explained above[456], the Panel is not persuaded that this Article *requires* that prepaid cards bearing the *Yin Lian*/UnionPay logo must be accepted at any POS bank card terminals.[457] As a result, we find that the United States has failed to demonstrate that Article 2(5)(iii) imposes a requirement that acquirers be capable of accepting all prepaid cards that have been issued by the relevant non-financial enterprises and bear the *Yin Lian*/UnionPay logo.

(iii) Document No. 37

7.346 The United States considers that acquirer requirements are also laid down in Article 2.1(i) of Document No. 37. According to the United States, Article 2.1(i) requires all commercial banks to make technical preparations for accepting bank cards bearing the CUP logo, and requires acquirers to join CUP for accepting cards.[458]

7.347 China states that Document No. 37 establishes uniform technical standards for POS terminals that accept inter-bank payment cards. It also requires commercial banks that acquire inter-bank payment cards to use the *Yin Lian* logo and to join the national inter-bank payment card network.[459]

7.348 The Panel notes that the United States has identified the wrong provision of Document No. 37. Article 2.1(i) imposes neither of the two alleged requirements. However, as explained above, Article 1.2(i) of Document No. 37 imposes an interoperability requirement addressed to all commercial banks, which include acquiring banks[460], and also a requirement that terminal equipment operated by acquiring banks and merchant terminal equipment provided by acquiring banks be technically capable of accepting cards bearing the *Yin Lian*/UnionPay logo.[461] Moreover, Article 3.1(i) requires that commercial banks, which include acquiring banks, join the national inter-bank exchange network, i.e. the CUP network.

---

454 United States' first written submission, para. 113.
455 Exhibit CHN-74.
456 See para. 7.323 above.
457 *Ibid.*
458 United States' second written submission, para. 182.
459 China's first written submission, para. 45.
460 See para. 7.255 above.
461 See para. 7.310 above.

7.349 For these reasons, we agree that, by imposing a terminal equipment requirement (Article 1.2(i)) and interoperability requirements (Articles 1.2(i) and 3.1(i)), Articles 1.2(i) and 3.1(i) require that acquiring banks be capable of accepting all bank cards bearing the *Yin Lian*/UnionPay logo.

(iv) Document No. 76

7.350 The United States also relies on Document No. 76. The United States asserts that in accordance with Document No. 76, any financial institutions seeking to acquire merchant bank card transactions must join CUP and process transactions according to CUP's rules and procedures, including the logo requirements and the unified CUP standards.[462]

7.351 China points out that Document No. 76 sets forth detailed specifications concerning the technical and commercial aspects of inter-bank payment card transactions.[463]

7.352 The Panel notes that in connection with the alleged acquirer requirements, the United States has referred to the following provisions of Document No. 76: paragraphs 2 and 3 of the Notice; Articles 2.1, 5.2.1, 5.2.2 and 5.2.3 of Chapter I of the Business Practices Appendix.[464] Paragraph 2 provides in relevant part that the Business Practices contained in Document No. 76 apply to all commercial banks participating in bank card service in China. Paragraph 3 states *inter alia* that acquiring banks that have been participating in the bank card acceptance business must meet the relevant requirements of the Business Practices Appendix. Articles 2.1 and 5.2.1 of Chapter I are among these requirements. These Articles make clear that commercial banks that conduct bank card business in China must join the United Association (i.e. CUP) before they can apply to participate in bank card interoperable service. To qualify as interoperating banks, applying banks must meet technical specifications and business requirements laid down in Articles 5.2.2 and 5.2.3 of Chapter I. In our view, the provisions identified by the United States mean that acquiring banks must join CUP and comply with United Association (CUP) business standards and technical specifications of inter-bank interoperability.

7.353 In the light of this, we consider that, together, paragraphs 2 and 3 of the Notice, as well as Articles 2.1 and 5.2.1-5.2.3 of Chapter I of the Business Practices Appendix, impose a requirement that all acquiring banks must be capable of accepting bank cards bearing the *Yin Lian*/UnionPay logo.

---

462 United States' second written submission, para. 182.

463 China's first written submission, para. 45.

464 United States' response to Panel question No. 71, para. 11 (referring to second written submission, paras. 153-165); second written submission, paras. 155 and 157; response to Panel question No. 72, para. 17; response to Panel question No. 92, para. 86 (referring to business standards and technical specifications).

(v) Conclusions and implications

7.354 Based on the above analysis, we conclude that China imposes a requirement that acquirers post the *Yin Lian*/UnionPay logo. This requirement is maintained through Article 2.2 of Document No. 153 (for all qualified acquirers). In addition, we find that China maintains requirements that acquirers be capable of accepting all bank cards bearing the *Yin Lian*/UnionPay logo. These requirements are maintained through Article 2.2 of Document No. 153 (for all qualified acquirers); Articles 1.2(i) and 3.1(i) of Document No. 37 (for acquiring banks); and paragraphs 2 and 3 of the Notice as well as Articles 2.1 and 5.2.1-5.2.3 of Chapter I of the Business Practices Appendix, both of which are contained in Document No. 76 (for acquiring banks).

7.355 Furthermore, and in contrast, we are not convinced that Article 2(5)(iii) of Document No. 149, considered on its own, imposes a requirement that acquirers must be capable of accepting all bank cards that bear the *Yin Lian*/UnionPay logo. We find no basis to modify our conclusion when considering this provision together with the other provisions cited by the United States in connection with the acquirer requirements.

7.356 Finally, we recall that Document Nos. 153, 37 and 76 use the term "bank card". The term "bank card" as defined in Document No. 17 covers at least some types of "payment card", which is the term used by the United States in its request for the establishment of a panel.[465]

7.357 As regards the implications of the acquirer requirements, we note China's argument that the United States has not identified any aspect of the acquirer requirements that would prevent the acceptance of bank cards that are capable of being processed over multiple networks. China submits that acquirers can accept bank cards that bear different logos.[466]

7.358 We first consider the terminal equipment element of the acquirer requirements. For the same reasons as those we have enunciated above in connection with the terminal equipment requirements[467], in the absence of other evidence we see no basis for concluding that these acquirer requirements would prevent the acceptance by acquirers of bank cards capable of being processed over an inter-bank network in China other than that of CUP.

7.359 As concerns the interoperability element of the acquirer requirements, we understand that it would be technically possible for acquirers simultaneously to comply with different sets of business standards and technical specifications. Also, the relevant provisions of Document Nos. 153, 37 and 76 do not indicate that acquirers that are members of CUP may not join other networks in China, or that acquirers complying with CUP's uniform business standards and technical

---

[465] See para. 7.284 above.

[466] China's response to Panel question No. 22(c), para. 18; comments on the United States' response to Panel question Nos. 70-72, 86-96, 115-123, para. 73.

[467] See para. 7.334 above.

specifications must not simultaneously abide by those of other networks. With regard to paragraph 5 of the Notice of Document No. 76[468], we note that the United States has not demonstrated that the relevant provisions are inconsistent with key acquirer-related bank card business rules of EPS suppliers other than CUP. As a result, there are no reasonable grounds to conclude that the acquirer requirements pertaining to interoperability would prevent the acceptance of bank cards that are capable of being processed over more than one inter-bank network in China.

7.360 We address, lastly, the *Yin Lian*/UnionPay logo element of the acquirer requirements. Document No. 153 does not say that terminal equipment provided by acquirers must not post the logos of EPS suppliers other than CUP. The United States contends, however, that the requirement to post the *Yin Lian*/UnionPay logo is incompatible with requirements of competing networks that do not use the *Yin Lian*/UnionPay logo.[469] China responds that the United States cited no evidence in support of this contention and avers that merchants in China frequently post more than one logo.[470] In the light of this, we have no basis, given the absence of evidence, to conclude that the acquirer requirement that mandates the posting of the *Yin Lian*/UnionPay logo prevents the posting of other EPS suppliers' logo, much less the acceptance by acquirers of bank cards that are capable of being processed over an inter-bank network in China other than that of CUP.

(d) Requirements pertaining to card-based electronic transactions in China, Hong Kong and Macao ("Hong Kong/Macao requirements")

7.361 The United States argues that China requires that CUP handle the clearing of all RMB bank card transactions in Hong Kong or Macao using bank cards issued in China, and that CUP handle the clearing of any RMB bank card transaction in China using bank cards issued in Hong Kong or Macao.[471] It asserts that these requirements are reflected in and imposed by the following Chinese legal instruments:

- Document No. 16 (Article 6)
- Document No. 8 (Article 6)
- Document No. 219 (Article 3)
- Document No. 254 (Articles 3, 4 and 17)

---

[468] See para. 7.299 above.

[469] United States' response to Panel question No. 86, para. 62.

[470] China's comments on the United States' response to Panel question Nos. 70-72, 86-96, 115-123, para. 56.

[471] United States' response to China's request for a preliminary ruling, para. 132; first written submission, para. 4; United States' second written submission, paras. 147 and 189.

7.362 China rejects the view that this requirement or any of the identified legal instruments are relevant to the modes of supply at issue in this dispute, on the basis that the measures concern the clearing of RMB transactions taking place in either Hong Kong or Macao, both of which are separate customs territories. Therefore, China requests the Panel to reject the United States' claims concerning alleged Hong Kong and Macao requirements.

7.363 The Panel will examine in this section whether the above-mentioned instruments impose the alleged requirements. We will address China's arguments regarding the status of Hong Kong and Macao as separate customs territories and the relevance of the measures and the modes of supply at issue in the context of the United States' Article XVI claims in Section VII.F below.

(i) Document No. 16

7.364 The United States argues that Document No. 16 establishes CUP as the sole entity responsible for clearing any RMB bank card transaction taking place in Hong Kong using a bank card issued in China, and any RMB bank card transactions taking place in Hong Kong or China using a bank card issued in Hong Kong. Therefore, the United States considers this provision precludes foreign suppliers from processing these transactions.[472]

7.365 China argues that this measure relates to the clearing and settlement of RMB bank card transactions that take place in the separate customs territory of Hong Kong and, therefore, there is no "legal basis" for the claims advanced by the United States in relation to EPS services in Hong Kong under the modes of supply at issue.[473] China considers its commitments relate only to the supply of services in China.

7.366 The Panel notes that Document No. 16 governs "clearing arrangements" for various RMB-related matters in Hong Kong, including individual bank card matters. Article 6 indicates that "[t]he clearance of individual RMB bankcards is organized and handled by the clearing banks and [CUP]". This provision provides that Chinese residents may use individual RMB bank cards issued by the domestic banks to pay for expenses including shopping, meals and lodging in Hong Kong, or to withdraw small amounts of cash in Hong Kong dollars from ATMs in Hong Kong. In addition, RMB bank cards issued to Hong Kong individual residents by participating banks can be used to pay for individual expenses in China and to withdraw small amounts of RMB cash from ATMs in China. Article 1 of Document No. 16 specifies that PBOC in conjunction with the Hong Kong Monetary Authority will select and authorize "a licensed bank in Hong Kong" to serve as a clearing bank for related Hong Kong banks in handling RMB bank card services. Pursuant to Article 2, this clearing bank will

---

[472] United States' response to China's request for a preliminary ruling, para. 91; first written submission, paras. 55 and 58; response to Panel question No. 89, para. 81.

[473] China's second written submission, para. 97 (citing Exhibit CHN-74).

enter into "business clearing agreements" with other banks that wish to participate in the RMB bank card business.

7.367 Based on the text of Article 6, as identified by the United States, we understand that Document No. 16 expressly governs the clearance of RMB bank card transactions that take place in Hong Kong.[474] Based on the second and third sentences of Article 6, this Article expressly covers transactions that involve either an RMB bank card issued in China and used in Hong Kong, or a bank card issued in Hong Kong that is used in China in an RMB bank card transaction. Article 6 explicitly requires that CUP, as the EPS supplier working in conjunction with designated "clearing banks", is to handle the clearing of these RMB bank card transactions involving individual RMB bank cards issued in Hong Kong. It is thus not possible, based on the text of this instrument, for any clearing channel other than CUP – be it a foreign-based channel or a domestic-based provider other than CUP – to clear any of the aforementioned types of RMB bank card transactions.[475] We note that China does not contest that the measure operates as contested by the United States; rather, it disagrees as to the relevance of this provision in light of the status of Hong Kong as a separate customs territory.

7.368 We therefore conclude that Article 6 of Document No. 16 requires that CUP and no other EPS supplier is to handle the clearing of RMB bank card transactions that involve an RMB bank card issued in China and used in Hong Kong, or an RMB bank card issued in Hong Kong that is used in China in an RMB bank card transaction.

---

[474] The Panel notes that the United States provided an English translation of Article 6 of Document No. 16. See Exhibits US-44 and US-46; United States' response to Panel question No. 12. China provided an English translation of the full text of Document No. 16 as Exhibit CHN-60.

[475] In response to Panel question No. 9, the United States identified three scenarios in which it considers Document Nos. 8, 16, 219 and 254 operate together to ensure CUP's exclusivity in respect of card-based RMB transactions taking place in China, Macao and Hong Kong. These include: (i) the case of a Chinese national travelling to Hong Kong and making a purchase with a card issued in China; (ii) the case of a Hong Kong or Macao national travelling to China and making a purchase with a card issued in Hong Kong or Macao; and (iii) the case of a Hong Kong or Macao national making an RMB purchase in either of these territories with an RMB payment card issued in either Hong Kong or Macao. However, the Panel considers only the United States' claim in the case of the first and second scenarios. The United States' panel request provides a brief narrative description that explicitly covers these two scenarios, but does not refer, either explicitly or implicitly, to a third scenario in which an RMB-denominated bank card is both issued and used in either Hong Kong or Macao. We recognized above that, through narrative paragraphs in its panel request, the United States described those "requirements" or "measures" that it considers are inconsistent with China's obligations under Articles XVI and XVII of the GATS. Accordingly, the Panel considers that the two types of transactions that are specified in the relevant narrative paragraph fall within its terms of reference. In contrast, the third type of transaction – those involving cards issued and used in Hong Kong or Macao – is nowhere specified in the relevant narrative paragraph. For this reason, we consider that the Hong Kong/Macao requirements as described in the panel request do not include the third scenario. Put differently, we consider that the United States' claim in respect of the third scenario falls outside our terms of reference. We therefore reject this claim.

(ii) Document No. 8

7.369 The United States argues that Document No. 8 establishes CUP as the sole entity responsible for clearing any RMB bank card transaction taking place in Macao using a bank card issued in China, and any RMB bank card transaction taking place in Macao or China using a bank card issued in Macao. Therefore, the United States considers this provision precludes foreign suppliers from processing these transactions.[476]

7.370 China argues that this measure relates to the clearing of RMB payment card transactions in the separate customs territory of Macao and, therefore, there is no "legal basis" for the claims advanced by the United States in relation to EPS services in Macao under the modes of supply at issue.[477] China considers its commitments relate only to the supply of services in China.

7.371 The Panel notes that the content of Document No. 8 is identical to that of Document No. 16, except that it concerns "clearing arrangements" for various RMB-related matters in Macao instead of Hong Kong.[478] Taking this into account, for the same reasons as those set out in paragraphs 7.367 and 7.368 above, we conclude that Article 6 of Document No. 8 requires that CUP and no other EPS supplier is to handle the clearing of RMB bank card transactions that involve an RMB bank card issued in China and used in Macao, or a bank card issued in Macao that is used in China in an RMB bank card transaction.

(iii) Document No. 219

7.372 The United States argues that Article 3 of Document No. 219 prohibits EPS suppliers other than CUP from processing RMB card transactions based on the fact that this provision mandates that merchants shall not authorize "third parties" to handle RMB card business or otherwise transfer such business to a third party.[479] The United States additionally submits that this measure is applicable in "border areas", which includes Macao and Hong Kong.[480]

7.373 China argues that this provision addresses RMB card fraud in connection with the acquiring of RMB card transactions in border areas within China and does not prohibit EPS suppliers from processing RMB card transactions as the United States alleges. In addition, China argues that Hong Kong and Macao are not "border areas" within the meaning of the term as it is used in Document No. 219. It argues that this term refers to "regions within [China] that neighbour

[476] United States' response to China's request for a preliminary ruling, para. 91; first written submission, paras. 55 and 58; response to Panel question No. 89, para. 81.

[477] China's second written submission, para. 97 (citing Exhibit CHN-74).

[478] The United States provided an English translation of Article 6 of Document No. 16. See Exhibits US-44 and US-46; United States' response to Panel question No. 12. China provided an English translation of the full text of Document No. 16 as Exhibit CHN-62.

[479] United States' first written submission, para. 58; second written submission, para. 152; comments on China's response to Panel question No. 109, para. 51.

[480] United States' response to Panel question No. 16.

a foreign country (such as Russia) or region (such as Hong Kong or Macao)".[481] China further notes that the only reference to CUP is the requirement that acquiring agreements require merchants not to use the *Yin Lian* logo for purposes outside the scope of the acquiring agreement.[482]

7.374 The Panel notes, as reflected in the title of Document No. 219 ("Notice of the People's Bank of China concerning Relevant Issues on Accepting and Using Renminbi Bank Cards in Border Areas"), that Article 3 requires *inter alia* that acquiring institutions handling RMB transactions in "border areas" enter into "card acquisition agreements" with merchants. In accordance with these agreements, merchants are prohibited from using sales documentation, the *Yin Lian*/UnionPay logo or POS for purposes falling outside the acquisition agreement. Under Article 3, merchants are also prohibited from "entrust[ing] or transfer[ing] the handling of RMB card business to a third party", or otherwise falsely reporting transactions or using POS terminals to fraudulently withdraw RMB cash.

7.375 Based on these elements, the Panel understands that Article 3 contains various anti-fraud measures applicable in "border areas". The focus on fraud, money laundering and other criminal concerns is further evident in other provisions of the document. In our view, this focus informs the interpretation of the principal language in contention within this provision, namely that of "entrust[ing] or transfer[ing] the handling of RMB card business to a third party". There is no textual basis elsewhere in the provision of Document No. 219 to conclude that EPS suppliers should be considered as a "third party" and thus be prevented from handling RMB bank card inter-bank information, clearing and settlement. On this basis, we do not agree with the United States' interpretation that Article 3 of Document No. 219 prevents EPS suppliers other than CUP from handling RMB transactions in "border areas" in China. Like China, we consider this provision prohibits a merchant from outsourcing any aspect of its core *acquisition* business to a third party, such as a third-party "acquirer processor". To that extent, we do not understand this provision to reserve certain transactions to CUP.

7.376 Turning to the parties' arguments regarding the meaning of the term "border areas", we noted, the title of this instrument makes clear that the scope of Article 3 relates to bank card acceptance in border areas. The United States asserts that Hong Kong and Macao qualify as border areas within the meaning of this instrument. However, the United States has not provided any evidence in support of its assertions in this respect. China has argued that "border areas" refers to regions within China that neighbour a foreign country such as Russia or a region such as Hong Kong or Macao. . Thus, it argues that Hong Kong and Macao are not border regions themselves. To us, it is not readily apparent from the evidence before us, namely the text of Document No. 219, that Hong Kong

[481] China's second written submission, fn. 53.
[482] China's second written submission, para. 97 (citing Exhibit CHN-74).

and Macao should be considered border areas for the purposes of Document No. 219. In the absence of any supporting evidence on this issue, we consider we lack the necessary elements to determine the precise scope of application of Document No. 219 As noted, however, we are not persuaded that his provision reserves certain transactions to CUP.

7.377 For the foregoing reasons, in the absence of additional evidence, we are unable to conclude that Article 3 of Document No. 219 prohibits EPS suppliers other than CUP from processing RMB card transactions taking place in Hong Kong or Macao using RMB cards issued in either Hong Kong, Macao or China, or RMB card transactions taking place in China using RMB cards issued in Hong Kong or Macao.

(iv) Document No. 254

7.378 The United States argues that Document No. 254 establishes and maintains CUP as the sole EPS supplier that may handle the processing of RMB bank card transactions taking place in Hong Kong and Macao using bank cards issued in either Hong Kong, Macao or China, or RMB bank card transactions taking place in China using RMB bank cards issued in Hong Kong and Macao.[483]

7.379 As with Document Nos. 16 and 8, China argues that there is no "legal basis" for the claims advanced by the United States as this instrument relates to the clearing of RMB bank card transactions in the separate customs territories of Hong Kong and Macao.[484]

7.380 The Panel notes that United States refers to Articles 3, 4 and 17 of Document No. 254 in support of its claim. Article 3 states that, "[w]here RMB bank cards issued by domestic banks are used for paying expenses or withdrawing cash in Hong Kong dollars or Macao dollars in Hong Kong or Macao, the issuers shall process clearing in RMB with [CUP]". In addition, it provides that CUP shall process clearing in Hong Kong dollars or Macao dollars with acquiring banks in Hong Kong and Macao after purchasing foreign exchange from designated foreign exchange banks. Article 4 provides that CUP shall handle clearing in RMB between issuers and acquiring banks "[w]here the RMB bank cards issued by Hong Kong or Macao participating banks are used for paying expenses or withdrawing RMB cash in Mainland China". Finally, Article 17 provides that banks in China shall clear all transactions with CUP and "shall not directly carry out RMB transactions with the other Hong Kong or Macao Institutions".

7.381 The Panel notes that, much like Document Nos. 16 and 8, Articles 3, 4 and 17 of Document No. 254 govern particular bank card transactions that

---

[483] United States' response to China's request for a preliminary hearing, para. 93; first written submission, para. 58; second written submission, para. 147.

[484] China's second written submission, para. 97 (citing Exhibit CHN-74).

involve RMB bank cards issued in China and used in Hong Kong or Macao, and bank cards issued in Hong Kong or Macao and used in China in RMB-denominated transactions. These transactions concern payments for consumption or tourism or limited cash withdrawals. In each case, Articles 3, 4 and 17 specify that CUP is to handle clearing of these transactions through purchasing foreign currency (Hong Kong dollars or Macao dollars) from designated foreign exchange banks and clearing with the relevant acquirer in either Hong Kong or Macao, or in China. As with Document Nos. 16 and 8, these provisions of Document No. 254 expressly require that CUP is to handle the clearing of these RMB bank card transactions as the EPS supplier working in conjunction with issuers and acquirers.

7.382 Based on the clear language in Articles 3, 4 and 17, we therefore conclude that Document No. 254 requires that CUP and no other EPS supplier is to handle the clearing of RMB bank card transactions that involve an RMB bank card issued in China and used in Hong Kong or Macao, or a bank card issued in Hong Kong that is used in China in an RMB payment card transaction.

(v) Conclusions

7.383 Based on the above analysis of Document Nos. 16, 8 and 254[485], we conclude that China requires that CUP and no other EPS supplier shall handle the clearing of certain RMB bank card transactions that involve either an RMB bank card issued in China and used in Hong Kong or Macao, or a bank card issued in Hong Kong or Macao that is used in China in an RMB transaction. These bank card transactions concern payment for expenses incurred through purchases, meals and accommodation, or limited cash withdrawals. We recall from above[486] that the term "bank cards" as defined in Document No. 17 covers at least some types of what the United States has defined as "payment cards". We further conclude that Article 3 of Document No. 219 does not require that CUP is the sole supplier to handle the clearing of these RMB bank card transactions. We found that Article 3 is directed at third parties involved with the outsourcing of any aspect of a merchant's acquisition business, rather than EPS suppliers.

7.384 Because we have already concluded that the identified provisions of Document Nos. 16, 8 and 254 individually mandate the use of CUP to process the clearing of the particular RMB bank card transactions discussed above, we do not consider it necessary to assess these instruments further in combination with each other. Regarding the applicability or relevance of Document No. 219 to RMB matters taking place in Hong Kong or Macao, we find nothing in Document Nos. 16, 8 or 254 that modifies our conclusions in respect of

---

485 The Panel specifically refers to Article 6 of Document No. 16, Article 6 of Document No. 8 and Articles 3, 4 and 17 of Document No. 254. See paras. 7.364-7.368, 7.369-7.371 and 7.378-7.382 above.

486 See para. 7.283 above.

Document No. 219. Accordingly, we do not consider Document No. 219 further in respect of requirements pertaining to Hong Kong or Macao.

(e) Requirements that mandate the use of CUP and/or establish CUP as the sole supplier of EPS for all domestic transactions denominated and paid in RMB ("sole supplier requirement") and prohibitions on the use of non-CUP cards for cross-region or inter-bank transactions ("cross-region/inter-bank prohibitions")

7.385 The United States asserts that China imposes measures that mandate the use of or establish CUP as the sole supplier of EPS for all domestic transactions denominated and paid in RMB through the following Chinese legal instruments:[487]

- Document No. 37 (Articles 1.2(i), 2.1(i)-(iii), 2.2(i), and 3.1)
- Document No. 57 (Articles 1, 2, 3, 5, and 6)
- Document No. 16 (Article 6)
- Document No. 8 (Article 6)
- Document No. 219 (Article 3)
- Document No. 254 (Articles 3,4, and 17)
- Document No. 103 (Section II.5(1) and Section III)
- Document No. 153 (Articles 1.2, 1.3, 2.2, 4, 5, and 6)
- Document No. 149 (Article 2(5)(iii))
- Document No. 53 (Articles V.2, and VII.3)
- Document No. 49 (Article 4)
- Document No. 129 (Articles 3.2 and 3.4)
- Document No. 76 (Notice, paragraph 5, Business Practices Appendix, Chapter I, Articles 1.1, 2.1, 4, and Chapter 10)
- Document No. 17 (Article 64)
- Document No. 142 (Articles 2.3, 4, 5, and 6)

7.386 The United States argues that the preceding legal instruments interact to establish and maintain CUP as the sole supplier in three ways: (i) certain instruments explicitly state that CUP must be used to process specific types of bank card transactions; (ii) certain instruments establish and/or require the use of business specifications and technical standards which mandate the use of CUP;

[487] United States' response to China's request for a preliminary ruling, para. 77; first written submission, para. 49; response to Panel question No. 4. The United States also relies on Document Nos. 94 and 272. As explained above at paragraphs 7.221-7.229, the Panel has decided not to consider the substance of these documents.

and (iii) certain instruments implicitly recognize that CUP is the sole supplier of EPS services for RMB denominated transactions.[488]

7.387 The United States argues that in the Notification of Approval of CUP's Business Licence, China's State Council and the PBOC explicitly approved and authorized only CUP to "establish and operate a single nationwide inter-bank bank card information switching network".[489] The United States argues that the use of the word "single" in this document, in addition to similar language appearing in CUP's Articles of Association, confirms that CUP was established to operate an exclusive nationwide inter-bank card information switching network.[490]

7.388 China rejects that the identified legal instruments operate to establish CUP as sole supplier for the clearing and settlement of all RMB domestic inter-bank bank card transactions.[491] Rather, China submits that the identified measures operate to establish a common national network for processing RMB domestic inter-bank bank card transactions. In its view, this does not equate to establishing an exclusive provider of network services in China.[492] Under a common network, China submits that inter-bank bank cards and POS devices must adhere to certain technical standards. However, it does not consider the above instruments preclude adherence to other technical standards. Similarly, it argues that issuers that participate in the CUP network are not precluded from being members of other networks.[493] Thus, China argues, there is nothing in any of these instruments that would prevent a foreign provider of network services from establishing a domestic clearing channel in China.[494]

7.389 The Panel will examine the above-mentioned instruments to determine whether they impose the alleged requirements in respect of bank card transactions denominated and paid in RMB. In other words, in conducting our analysis, we need to assess, not whether as a factual matter there is a single supplier operating in China, but whether the instruments in question require that CUP is the sole EPS supplier for RMB bank card transactions involving bank cards issued and used in China. We first examine the instruments individually and thereafter, we consider them in conjunction. We recall also that certain of the instruments identified in connection with the sole supplier requirement have also been identified in relation to the other requirements that are alleged in this dispute. Where this is the case, we will refer to our preceding analysis as appropriate. In addition, we recall[495] that we will analyse the instruments

---

[488] United States' second written submission, para. 144.

[489] United States' first written submission, para. 46.

[490] United States' comments on China's response to Panel question No. 121, para. 62; see also second written submission, para. 184

[491] China's second written submission, paras. 90-102.

[492] China's first written submission, para. 64; response to Panel question No. 121, para. 87.

[493] China's response to Panel question No. 22(c), paras. 17 and 18.

[494] China's response to Panel question No. 103, para. 45.

[495] See para. 7.234 above.

identified in connection with the cross-region/inter-bank prohibitions in the context of our assessment of the sole supplier requirement, bearing in mind the distinction drawn by the United States between whether the instruments are framed so as to mandate the use CUP or CUP cards, or as a prohibition.

(i) Document No. 37

7.390 As discussed in paragraphs 7.253, 7.308, and 7.346 above, the United States submits that Document No. 37 establishes and entrenches CUP as the exclusive EPS supplier for inter-bank transactions by requiring the use of the CUP logo for inter-bank bank cards, requiring that all ATM and POS terminals in China accept CUP cards, and by requiring that acquiring banks be capable of accepting all bank cards bearing the CUP logo.[496]

7.391 China responds[497] that Document No. 37 requires the use of the *Yin Lian*/UnionPay logo as the common logo for inter-bank bank cards, ATMs and POS terminals, and otherwise, this document requires that commercial banks that issue and acquire inter-bank bank cards meet business and technical standards. However, China argues that the identified provisions do not preclude banks from becoming members of other networks.[498] As a general matter, in its view, the fact that bank cards and POS devices must adhere to certain technical standards does not preclude adherence to other technical standards.[499]

7.392 The Panel concluded in paragraphs 7.256-7.259, 7.311, 7.312, and 7.349 above that Articles 1.2(i), 2.1(ii) and 3.1 of Document No. 37 mandate the use of the *Yin Lian*/UnionPay logo and impose certain interoperability requirements. As stated previously[500], however, we see nothing in these requirements themselves or elsewhere in Document No. 37 that precludes bank cards issued in China from bearing logos of other EPS suppliers in addition to the *Yin Lian*/UnionPay logo, nor do the identified provisions prohibit the use of bank cards on other networks with the same or different technical/interoperability requirements, so long as the cards meet CUP interoperability requirements. Therefore, we do not identify anything on the face of these provisions that establishes or maintains CUP as the exclusive EPS supplier for all RMB bank card transactions involving bank cards issued and used in China. In the absence of specific evidence demonstrating otherwise, we reject the assertion that this instrument on its own establishes or maintains CUP as a sole supplier.

---

496 United States' response to China's request for a preliminary ruling, para. 126; second written submission, paras. 186 and 187.

497 See paras. 7.254, 7.297, 7.309, 7.334, 7.347 and 7.357 above.

498 China's first written submission, para. 45; response to Panel question No. 22(c), para. 18.

499 China's response to Panel question No. 22(c), para. 18.

500 See paras. 7.299, 7.334 and 7.358- 7.360 above.

(ii) Document No. 57

7.393 As discussed in paragraphs 7.260 and 7.265 above, the United States argues that Document No. 57 requires that all regional non-CUP logo bank card interoperability logos be gradually eliminated[501], and that commercial banks promote the use of the CUP logo.[502] In addition, it argues that Document No. 57 requires that newly issued bank cards with cross-region or inter-bank functionality comply with relevant technical standards and with unified "Business Specifications for Interoperable Service of Bank Cards" in Document No. 76.[503]

7.394 China states that Document No. 57 elaborates on requirements set forth in Document No. 37 and discussed above, namely, it requires bank cards issued for domestic inter-bank use to bear the *Yin Lian*/UnionPay logo, and requires that commercial banks that issue and acquire inter-bank bank cards to meet business and technical standards.[504] China disputes that these requirements preclude banks from becoming members of other networks.[505]

7.395 The Panel concluded in paragraph 7.266 above that Articles 1, 2, 5 and 6 of Document No. 57 mandate the use of the *Yin Lian*/UnionPay logo and impose certain interoperability requirements. However, as mentioned above in respect of Document No. 37 and as stated previously[506], we do not identify anything on the face of this document that precludes bank cards issued in China from bearing logos of other EPS suppliers in addition to the *Yin Lian*/UnionPay logo. Nor do the identified provisions prohibit the use of bank cards on other networks with the same or different technical/interoperability requirements, so long as the cards meet CUP interoperability requirements. Therefore, we do not identify anything on the face of these provisions that establishes or maintains CUP as the exclusive EPS supplier for all RMB bank card transactions involving bank cards issued and used in China. In the absence of specific evidence demonstrating otherwise, we reject the assertion that this instrument on its own establishes or maintains CUP as a sole supplier.

(iii) Document No. 16

7.396 As discussed in paragraph 7.364 above, the United States argues that Article 6 of Document No. 16 establishes CUP as the sole entity responsible for clearing and settling RMB bank card transactions taking place in Hong Kong using bank cards issued in China, and RMB bank card transactions taking place in Hong Kong or China using bank cards issued in Hong Kong. The United States considers this instrument demonstrates that CUP is the sole supplier for

501 United States' response to Panel question No. 2, para. 10; second written submission, para. 186.
502 United States' response to Panel question No. 6, para. 36.
503 China's comments on the United States' response to Panel question Nos. 70-72, 86-96, 115-123.
504 China's first written submission, para. 45.
505 China's comments on the United States' response to Panel question Nos. 70-72, 86-96, 115-123.
506 See para. 7.299 above.

all RMB bank card transactions involving bank cards issued and used in China.[507]

7.397 China maintains its position that this measure relates to the clearing of RMB bank card transactions that take place in the separate customs territory of Hong Kong and, therefore, there is no "legal basis" for the claims advanced by the United States in relation to EPS services in Hong Kong under the modes of supply at issue.[508] China considers its commitments relate only to the supply of services in China.

7.398 The Panel recalls from paragraphs 7.364-7.368 above its conclusion that Article 6 requires that CUP and no other EPS supplier is to be involved in the clearing of RMB bank card transactions that involve either an RMB bank card issued in China and used in Hong Kong, or a bank card issued in Hong Kong that is used in Hong Kong or China in an RMB transaction. As Document No. 16 is limited in scope to bank card transactions that involve bank cards issued in China and used in Hong Kong, or alternatively, bank cards issued in Hong Kong and used either in Hong Kong or China, we fail to see how this instrument establishes CUP as the sole supplier of EPS for *all* domestic transactions denominated and paid in RMB. Therefore, we do not consider that Article 6 establishes CUP as the sole supplier of EPS for *all* domestic transactions denominated and paid in RMB. Below, we further consider this instrument as it operates in relation to other identified instruments, in the context of the United States' assertion that the measures at issue establish CUP as the sole supplier of EPS for *all* domestic transactions.

(iv) Document No. 8

7.399 As discussed in paragraphs 7.369 above, the United States argues that Article 6 of Document No. 8 also establishes CUP as the sole entity responsible for clearing and settling RMB bank card transactions taking place in Macao using bank cards issued in China, and RMB bank card transactions taking place in Macao or China using bank cards issued in Macao. The United States considers this instrument demonstrates that CUP is the sole supplier for *all* RMB bank card transactions involving bank cards issued and used in China.[509]

7.400 China again maintains that this measure relates to the clearing of RMB bank card transactions in the separate customs territory of Macao and, therefore, there is no "legal basis" for the claims advanced by the United States in relation to EPS services in Macao under the modes of supply at issue.[510] China considers its commitments relate only to the supply of services in China.

[507] United States' response to China's request for a preliminary ruling, para. 91; first written submission, paras. 55 and 58; response to Panel question No. 89, para. 81.
[508] China's second written submission, para. 97 (citing Exhibit CHN-74).
[509] United States' response to China's request for a preliminary ruling, para. 91; first written submission, paras. 55 and 58; response to Panel question No. 89, para. 81.
[510] China's second written submission, para. 97 (citing Exhibit CHN-74).

7.401 The Panel recalls its conclusion from paragraphs 7.369-7.371 that the content of Document No. 8 is identical to that of Document No. 16, except that it concerns "clearing arrangements" for various RMB-related matters in Macao, instead of Hong Kong. Taking this into account, for reasons set out in paragraphs 7.367 and 7.368 above, we are unable to conclude that Document No. 8 establishes CUP as the sole supplier of EPS for *all* domestic transactions denominated and paid in RMB. As with Document No. 16, we further consider below this instrument as it operates in relation to other identified instruments, in addressing the United States' claim that the measures at issue establish CUP as the sole supplier of EPS for *all* domestic transactions.

(v) Document No. 219

7.402 As discussed in paragraphs 7.372 above, the United States argues that Article 3 of Document No. 219 prohibits processing of RMB card transactions by EPS suppliers other than CUP based on the fact that this provision mandates that merchants shall not authorize "third parties" to handle RMB card business or otherwise transfer such business to a third party.[511] The United States submits that this measure is applicable in "border areas", which specifically refers to the "special administrative regions" of Macao and Hong Kong.[512]

7.403 China maintains that this provision does not establish CUP as a sole supplier as the United States alleges, but rather, this provision addresses RMB card fraud in connection with the acquiring of RMB card transactions in border areas within China. China asserts that the only reference to CUP is the requirement that acquiring agreements require merchants not to use the *Yin Lian*/UnionPay logo for purposes outside the scope of the acquiring agreement.[513]

7.404 The Panel recalls from paragraphs 7.372-7.376 above its conclusion that Article 3 is concerned with RMB bank acquirers and the merchants with whom they enter into acquisition agreements and, as such, it is not evident on its face that this provision prohibits processing of bank card transactions by EPS suppliers other than CUP. Accordingly, we do not consider that this provision on its own establishes or maintains CUP as the exclusive EPS supplier for all RMB card transactions involving bank cards issued and used in China

(vi) Document No. 254

7.405 As discussed in paragraphs 7.378 above, the United States argues that Document No. 254 establishes CUP as the sole entity responsible for processing RMB bank card transactions using bank cards issued in China and used in Hong

[511] United States' first written submission, para. 58; second written submission, para. 152; comments on China's response to Panel question No. 109, para. 51.

[512] United States' response to Panel question No. 16.

[513] China's second written submission, para. 97 (citing Exhibit CHN-74).

Kong or Macao, or RMB bank cards issued in Hong Kong and Macao and used in China.[514]

7.406 China maintains that this measure relates to the clearing of RMB bank card transactions taking place in the separate customs territory of Hong Kong and Macao and, therefore, there is no "legal basis" for the claims advanced by the United States in relation to EPS services in Hong Kong and Macao under the modes of supply at issue.[515] China considers its commitments relate only to the supply of services in China.

7.407 The Panel recalls its conclusion from paragraphs 7.378-7.381 above that Articles 3, 4 and 17 of Document No. 254 expressly require that CUP is to handle the clearing of RMB bank card transactions that involve RMB bank cards issued in China and used in Hong Kong or Macao, and bank cards issued in Hong Kong or Macao and used in China in an RMB transaction. Due to the fact that Document No. 254 is limited in scope to bank card transactions that involve bank cards issued in China and used in Hong Kong or Macao, or alternatively, bank cards issued in Hong Kong or Macao and used in China, we fail to see how this instrument establishes CUP as the sole supplier of EPS for *all* domestic transactions denominated and paid in RMB. Below, we further consider this instrument as it operates in relation to other identified instruments, in the context of the United States' assertion that the measures at issue establish CUP as the sole supplier of EPS for *all* domestic transactions denominated and paid in RMB.

(vii) Document No. 103

7.408 The United States argues that Section III of Document No. 103 provides explicit recognition by multiple Chinese government agencies of China's awareness that any purported limitations on market access to the RMB "bank card industry" were to be eliminated by 2006. Moreover, it argues that Document No. 103 sets out a requirement that banks competing in the RMB bank card business use uniform business specifications and technical standards that mandate the use of CUP.[516]

7.409 China considers this provision to reflect that issuers and acquirers would be permitted to enter the Chinese market beginning in 2006, but not EPS suppliers. In general, China maintains that a requirement to comply with one set of business rules and technical standards does not preclude a bank card issuer

---

[514] United States' response to China's request for a preliminary ruling, para. 93; first written submission, para. 58; second written submission, para. 147.

[515] China's second written submission, para. 97 (citing Exhibit CHN-74).

[516] United States' response to China's request for a preliminary ruling, para. 100; first written submission, paras. 43, 44, 83; second written submission, para. 154.

from issuing cards that also comply with other rules and standards, which would enable that card to operate over other networks.[517]

7.410 The Panel observes that Article III provides that "[t]he RMB bankcard business opens fully to the outside world at the close of 2006, posing greater challenges to the China bankcard industry; the limited time remaining must be used to boost that industry's competitiveness". The United States also points to Section II.5(1), which provides that any newly issued RMB bank cards shall comply with applicable technical standards.

7.411 The Panel takes note of the identified provisions of Document No. 103, including the statement that newly issued RMB bank cards shall comply with applicable technical standards. Following the advice we received from the UNOG translator[518], we do not understand this provision to impose a normative mandate that establishes CUP as the sole supplier of EPS in China. In the absence of further information, it is also not clear to us from reading the text of Document No. 103 what is encompassed by the term "RMB bankcard business" and specifically whether this term covers the provision of EPS, or whether it refers only to other relevant business activities, such as issuing bank cards and acquiring bank card transactions. Concerning Section II.5(1), as we stated in respect of other instruments that impose interoperability requirements[519], in the absence of evidence demonstrating otherwise, we cannot conclude that Section II.5(1) on its own maintains or establishes CUP as the sole supplier of EPS in respect of domestic transactions denominated or paid in RMB. Accordingly, we are not persuaded that this instrument alone maintains or establishes CUP as the sole supplier in China.

(viii) Document No. 153

7.412 The United States argues that Article 1.2 of Document No. 153 explicitly establishes CUP as the sole supplier of EPS for RMB bank card transactions in China through its invocation that "[CUP] is *the* domestic clearance organization" (emphasis added). The United States submits that this conclusion is supported in other provisions of Document No. 153. It argues that Article 1.3 prohibits EPS suppliers other than CUP from clearing RMB bank card transactions in China as this provision states that "[n]o third party service provider shall engage in bank card information exchange services".[520] In addition, according to the United States, Article 5 establishes CUP as the only entity that is permitted to promote

---

[517] China's response to Panel question No. 22(c), para.18; comments on the United States' response to Panel question Nos. 70-72, 86-96, 115-123, para. 56.

[518] See Annex H.

[519] See the Panel's discussion of Document Nos. 37 and 57 above.

[520] United States' response to China's request for a preliminary ruling, para. 88; second written submission, para. 148; response to Panel question No. 2, para. 8; response to Panel question No. 90, para. 84.

bank card acceptance[521] and Article 6 prevents any "organizations" from interfering with bank card processing by CUP.[522] Finally, it asserts that Articles 2.2 and 4 require that POS terminals and merchant acquirers comply with the business specifications and technical standards for cross-network interoperability, and inter-bank business, respectively.[523]

7.413 China disputes the United States' translation of Article 1.2, arguing instead that this provision states that "[CUP] is *a* domestic clearing organization" (emphasis added), and that, as such, it does not establish CUP as the sole supplier of EPS. Even accepting the translation provided by the United States, China submits that Document No. 153 does not support the United States' claims.[524] China argues that the context in Article 1.3 makes clear that Document No. 153 prohibits acquiring institutions from outsourcing their switching functions to third-party service providers, but it does not prevent the establishment of other inter-bank card networks.[525] In its view this is clear from the fact that this provision addresses security of financial information[526] as well as the fact that "third-party service providers" are clearly defined in the text. China argues that the definition of third-party service providers in Document No. 153 refers to merchant or acquirer "processors" at the point of interconnection between the acquirer and EPS suppliers, and not EPS suppliers themselves.[527] Thus, China does not prevent the establishment of other inter-bank EPS networks.[528] Finally, China argues that Article 6 is not relevant to the United States' claims as it relates to use of bank cards outside China. In particular, it asserts that Article 6 was a response to efforts by international EPS suppliers to prevent acceptance of *Yin Lian* bank cards outside of China, particularly dual logo cards.[529] Regardless, China contends that this provision only requires that Chinese issuers are capable of processing transactions over the CUP network, but does not require them to process transactions over the CUP network.[530]

7.414 The Panel recalls at the outset its conclusion in paragraphs 7.319, 7.341, and 7.342 above, that Articles 2.2 and 4 mandate the use of the *Yin*

[521] United States' response to Panel question No. 6, paras. 25 and 27; response to Panel question No. 88(a), para. 76 (quoting the second and third paragraphs of Article 5 of Document No. 153).

[522] United States' second written submission, para. 150; response to Panel question No. 90, para. 84.

[523] United States' second written submission, para. 154; response to Panel question No. 71(c), para. 9.

[524] China's comments on United States' response to Panel question Nos. 70-72, 86-96, 115-123, para. 78.

[525] China's second written submission, paras. 97 (citing Exhibit CHN-74) and 98; response to Panel question No. 109, para. 65.

[526] China's response to Panel question No. 109, para. 65.

[527] China's response to Panel question No. 102, para. 44; response to Panel question No. 109, para. 66; comments on the United States' response to Panel question No. 90, para. 57.

[528] China's second written submission, paras. 97 (citing Exhibit CHN-74) and 98.

[529] China's response to Panel question No. 100.

[530] China's second written submission, para. 97 (citing Exhibit CHN-74); response to Panel question No. 100.

Lian/UnionPay logo and impose certain interoperability requirements. We further note that Document No. 153, which was issued in 2005, set outs responsibilities directed at agencies to promote the development of a bank card acceptance market in China. Following the advice we received from the UNOG translator, Article 1.2 of this document, labelled "Regarding bank card clearance organizations", specifies that CUP is "currently the domestic clearing organization" that specializes in the supply of EPS for RMB bank card inter-bank transactions. CUP is designated to formulate specifications and standards for this inter-bank network. Article 1.3 defines "third party service providers of merchant acquiring business" as "the legal person enterprises which engage in non-core businesses of the bank card acquiring business entrusted by merchant acquiring institutions on the basis of making their own operation decisions..." Article 1.3 states further that "[n]o third party service provider shall engage in bank card information exchange services".

7.415 Article 1.3 further explains that the bank card exchange system concerns the security of financial information and payment systems and is subject to strict access and management. We further note that Article 3 sets out that merchant acquiring institutions may "freely decide" whether to outsource to third party services providers their non-core business such as "equipment placement and services, system construction and maintenance, and customer service and training". Merchant acquiring institutions can choose third-party providers that meet security management requirements and technical standards of PBOC.

7.416 Article 5 expressly authorizes CUP to establish branches in certain areas of China "in accordance with the company's overall plan to provide bank card information exchange and clearance services". This "engagement in inter-bank POS transaction information transfer shall be directly managed and operated by [CUP], and shall not be indirectly managed or operated through authorization". Finally, Article 6 of Document No. 153 provides that "Chinese issuing banks should support routing through the CUP network" and "[n]o organizations should set any obstacles or cause any interference".

7.417 With this in mind, we address the United States' contention that Article 1.2 explicitly recognizes CUP as the sole supplier of EPS for RMB bank card transactions in China, and that Articles 1.3, 5 and 6 support this conclusion.

7.418 Beginning with Article 1.2, as we noted above, it is not in dispute that this provision acknowledges that CUP was an EPS supplier for RMB bank card transactions before June 2005, the date on which Document No 153 was published. Through the use of the term "currently", this provision refers to the situation as it existed at that time, but does not, by its terms, impose a limitation going forward.[531] As the parties' submissions highlight[532], there was no

[531] In stating this, we note that the advice provided by the UNOG translator indicates that the context provided by the Chinese text "strongly implies that the situation (whatever it is) may change". See Annex H.

nationwide EPS supplier operating in China before June 2005. Article 1.2 appears to recognize this. Against this background, it is at least understandable that Document No. 153 would have designated CUP to formulate the specifications regarding relevant inter-bank processing (as discussed in Article 1.2). Taking this into account, it follows logically that CUP was authorized to establish branches in certain areas of China (as discussed in Article 5, which states that "[a]fter being approved by PBOC, [CUP] may set up branches in regions where there is a market demand"), as well as expand RMB bank card acceptance in overseas markets (as discussed in Article 6). China would not have been in a position to direct an entity or EPS supplier outside of China to do this.

7.419 We do not consider the authority granted to CUP under Article 5 to set up new branches in China precludes other EPS suppliers from establishing a network in China. In our view, this language instructs CUP to manage and operate the network that it is tasked to establish, and CUP should not delegate this authority.

7.420 In addition, we do not understand the guidance found in Article 6 that CUP expand RMB bank card acceptance in overseas markets to mean that other suppliers of EPS are prohibited from establishing a network in China. We note that Article 6 addresses setting up an international network for acceptance of RMB bank cards bearing the *Yin Lian*/UnionPay logo. This provision indicates that Chinese-based issuing banks "should support" inter-bank EPS processing for dual currency credit and debit card transactions that take place abroad and "should open the RMB accounts related transactions and settlements to the CUP network". We note first that, in certain respects, Article 6 employs the use of the term "should" differently from the use of the word "shall" that appears elsewhere in Document No. 153. This suggests that the guidance to support routing through the CUP network is not mandatory. By stating that issuing banks "should support" this routing, the provision does not appear to prevent them from routing transactions through other networks. Moreover, we do not read the guidance that "[n]o organizations should set any obstacles or cause any interference" to mean that other suppliers of EPS are prohibited from establishing a network in China. In our view, the fact that Article 6 provides that issuing banks should support routing through the CUP network, and should open RMB accounts to the network, with the further guidance that other organizations should not interfere,

---

[532] United States' response to China's request for a preliminary ruling, paras. 64-71; citing Steve Worthington, The Chinese payment card market: an exploratory study, 21 Int'l J. of Bank Marketing, pp. 324, 325, 327 (2003), Exhibit US-21; Pecht, Michael, China's Electronics Industry: The Definitive Guide for Companies and Policy (2006), pp. 82-83, Exhibit US-22; Strong Measures to be Taken to Achieve the Target of Commecting Bank-Card Networks This Year, PBOC (March 27, 2002), available at http://www.pbc.gov.cn/publish/english/955/1965/19655.html , Exhibit US-25; Marina Yu Zhang & Mark Dodgson, High Tech Entrepreneurship in Asia: Innovation, Industry and Institutional Dynamics in Mobile Payments, Edward Elgar Publishing Limited (2007), pp. 215-216, Exhibit US-30; China's first written submission, paras. 38-46.

does not preclude any bank or entity from additionally having relationships with other EPS suppliers or routing transactions through other networks. We further do not understand this provision would prohibit another supplier of this service from establishing a network in China.[533]

7.421 Finally, we do not agree that Article 1.3 can be read to prohibit the use of EPS suppliers other than CUP. Article 1.3 refers to and defines "third party service providers" as those entities that may engage in "non-core business of the bank card acquiring business" as entrusted by merchant acquiring institutions. We note in this respect that third-party providers are discussed separately from provisions addressing "bank card clearing organizations" (Article 1.2), suggesting that these entities are different in nature. In addition, since the "main business" in which CUP specializes is the supply of EPS for RMB bank card transactions and not the acquisition of bank card transactions (i.e. acquirer services), the fact that third-party service providers may only engage in the "non-core business of the bank card acquiring business" would seem to indicate that third-party providers would not handle any of those activities falling within the principal activities of CUP.

7.422 We further consider that the language referred to by the United States in Article 1.3 must be read in the light of Article 3 of Document No. 153, which addresses "Rules of merchant acquiring business' outsourcing". As indicated above, this provision indicates which is the "non-core business" that a merchant acquiring institution may outsource to a third party service provider. These activities include "equipment placement and services, system construction and maintenance, and customer service and training", none of which are primary activities in respect of RMB bank card inter-bank information routing and exchange. Reading these provisions together, we understand that Document No. 153 seeks to prevent third party service providers of merchant acquiring business from addressing core aspects related to supply of EPS in such a way that would compromise the security of sensitive financial information exchange. It would seem, therefore that this provision seeks to limit the number of actors including third parties that work in conjunction with acquirers that have access to sensitive information, so as to prevent fraudulent misuse of information. For these reasons, we are not convinced that Article 1.3 effectively bans other EPS suppliers – which are different from third party service providers of merchant acquiring business – from the marketplace in China, taking into account the focus of this provision.

533 According to China, Article 6 of Document No. 153 relates to the development of a payment card acceptance network outside of China for RMB cards that bear the *Yin Lian*/UnionPay logo and is therefore not relevant to this dispute. China submits that Article 6 is a response to efforts by international EPS suppliers to prevent the acceptance of payment cards bearing the *Yin Lian*/UnionPay logo outside of China. China's response to Panel question No. 100, paras. 41 and 42, citing Exhibits CHN-108 and CHN-109.

7.423 Accordingly, for the reasons set out above, we conclude that Articles 1.2, 1.3, 5 or 6 of Document No. 153 do not establish or maintain CUP as the sole supplier of EPS for RMB bank card transactions in China or otherwise prohibit the use of EPS suppliers other than CUP. In concluding this, we take into account the reference in Article 1.2 that "[CUP] is currently the domestic clearing organization". As we discuss further in paragraphs 7.431-7.441 below, we note that our conclusion is consistent with the reference to "domestic clearing channels" that appears in the plural form in Document No. 53. It is pertinent to note in addition that Document No. 53 postdates Document No. 153.

(ix) Document No. 149

7.424 The United States argues that Article 2(5)(iii) of Document No. 149 prohibits acquirers from allowing "non-CUP" and "non-PBOC 2.0 prepayment cards" to be accepted at POS terminals.[534] In its view, this provision effectively limits the number of suppliers of EPS in China, and establishes and maintains CUP's monopoly on EPS for RMB bank card transactions in China.[535]

7.425 China argues, as indicated in paragraph 7.322 above, that Document No. 149 as a whole addresses RMB bank card crimes in respect of prepayment cards and that the purpose of Article 2(5)(iii) is to prevent the card holder from fraudulently using a non-interoperable card on an interoperable basis.[536] In China's view, it does not prohibit the acceptance of cards bearing other logos in addition to the *Yin Lian* logo.[537]

7.426 The Panel observes, as indicated by the UNOG translator[538], that Article 2(5)(iii) provides that "[n]o acquiring institutions may allow non-"*Yin Lian*/UnionPay" and non-PBOC 2.0 standard prepaid cards issued by non-financial social enterprises to be accepted at bankcard terminal equipment". We understand this provision prevents acquirers from allowing non-YinLian/UnionPay *prepaid* cards issued by non-financial enterprises to access bank card terminals.[539] In other words, this provision relates to access to terminal equipment by prepaid cards that were issued by relevant enterprises[540] and that do not bear the *Yin Lian*/UnionPay logo. This provision is itself limited in focus to a narrow subset of bank cards.

7.427 Setting aside this particular provision, we recall that Document No. 149 broadly relates to security management of bank cards and preventing bank card-

---

[534] United States' second written submission, para. 151; response to Panel question No. 71(c)(iii), para. 10; response to Panel question No. 72, para. 19; response to Panel question No. 91, para. 85.

[535] United States' comments on China's response to Panel question No. 104, para. 41.

[536] China's comments on the United States' response to Panel question No. 91, para. 58.

[537] China's response to Panel question No. 110, para. 68.

[538] See Annex H.

[539] As noted above in paragraph 7.323, the exact nature of the relevant enterprises is not entirely clear. We understand, though, that the relevant prepaid cards are issued by *non-financial* enterprises.

[540] As explained in fn. 430 above, "non-financial social enterprises" refer to entities that are not financial institutions.

related crimes. This is reflected in the title of the instrument, which refers to "Strengthening the Safety Management of Bank Cards and Preventing and Fighting Crimes in Bank Cards". It is also reflected in other references in the document. Notably, Article 1 refers to the objective of "stabilizing the market order of bank cards". Article 2(4) addresses issues related to card holder identity fraud. CUP is designated to participate in reporting on identity-related crimes.[541]

7.428 In our assessment of Article 2(5)(iii) in paragraphs 7.323 and 7.325 above, we noted that this provision addresses specifically those cards that may not be accepted at bank card POS terminals, which we found to be consistent with the purpose of preventing bank card-related crimes. These include non-"*Yin Lian*/UnionPay" and "non-PBOC 2.0" prepaid cards. We noted as well that the United States did not provide evidence other than the text of Article 2(5)(iii) to elucidate the legal effect of this provision.

7.429 We have explained in Section VII.E.2(a) above that China imposes requirements on issuers that bank cards issued in China bear the *Yin Lian*/UnionPay logo, and furthermore, China requires that issuers become members of the CUP network, and that the payment cards they issue in China meet certain uniform business specifications and technical standards. In addition, China requires acquirers to post the *Yin Lian*/UnionPay logo, become members of the CUP network and be capable of accepting all bank cards bearing the *Yin Lian*/UnionPay logo. In our assessment of these instruments, we have explained that the requirement that a given bank card bear the *Yin Lian*/UnionPay logo would not preclude bank cards issued in China from bearing logos of other EPS suppliers in addition to the *Yin Lian*/UnionPay logo. Moreover, such a requirement would not preclude the use of a bank card on other networks with the same or different technical/interoperability requirements, so long as it was at the same time compatible with the CUP network.

7.430 We see nothing on the face of Article 2(5)(iii) that would prevent acceptance at a bank card terminal of a prepaid card issued by a relevant enterprise that bears the logo of another EPS supplier and is interoperable with that supplier's network, provided the card also bears the *Yin Lian*/UnionPay logo and is interoperable over the CUP network. In our view, Article 2(5)(iii) is about access to bank card terminal equipment. At that level, there is no exclusive access for CUP. Article 2(5)(iii), by its terms, does not speak to the processing of the transactions that involve the use of the relevant prepaid cards. In the absence of any argument and evidence on this, we have no basis for assuming that any transaction would have to be processed over the CUP network. Therefore, the United States in our view has not demonstrated that Article 2(5)(iii) establishes or maintains CUP as the exclusive supplier in respect of prepaid cards.

[541] See, e.g. Articles 2(4)(xii)-(xiii).

(x) Document No. 53

7.431 The United States argues that the references to "domestic clearing channels" and "domestic RMB card clearing organizations" in Articles V.2 and VII.3 of Document No. 53, respectively, have the effect of guaranteeing that CUP processes all RMB-denominated transactions in China that involve bank cards issued in China. It considers this to be further evident when these provisions are read in conjunction with Article 1.2 of Document No. 153, which refers to CUP as the "domestic clearing organization".[542] The United States does not consider that the references to "domestic clearing channels" and "domestic RMB card clearing organizations" in their plural forms alters the fact that CUP exclusively processes all RMB bank card transactions.[543] To the extent this language alone is not clear, the United States argues that additional language in Article V.2 regarding payment of overdrafts in RMB provides further evidence that only CUP may process domestic RMB bank card transactions.[544] Moreover, it considers that the requirement in Article VII.3 that bank card issuers report the bank identification numbers (BINs) of their cards "to the domestic RMB card clearing organization" facilitates and ensures that transactions will automatically be processed over the CUP network.[545]

7.432 China argues that the purpose of Document No. 53 is to require that RMB card transactions are cleared and settled in RMB to avoid unnecessary foreign exchange transactions in cases where a dual- or foreign-currency card is used in China.[546] Setting aside the purpose of this document, China argues that the references to "domestic clearing channels" and "domestic RMB card clearing organizations" do not establish that CUP will be the only domestic clearing organization in China going forward in time.[547] It considers this to be clear, based on the fact that the terms appear in the plural, and because Document No. 53 does not expressly refer to CUP by name.[548]

7.433 The Panel notes that Document No. 53 is entitled "Notice of the State Administration of Foreign Exchange on the Management of Foreign Currency Bank Cards". Article I of this document defines "foreign currency bank cards" as

---

542 United States' second written submission, para. 167; response to Panel question No. 6, para. 28

543 United States' response to Panel question No. 88(b), para. 78.

544 United States' first written submission, paras. 59 and 60; response to Panel question No. 15, paras. 58 and 59.

545 United States' response to Panel question No. 1, paras. 58 and 59; response to Panel question No. 6, para. 28; response to Panel question No. 15, paras. 58 and 59; response to Panel question No. 87, para. 68; response to Panel question No. 95, para. 100; response to Panel question No. 116, para. 112; comments on Chinese replies to Panel question No. 106, para 48 (citing CUP's Operating Regulations, Volume III, Rules on UnionPay Card, BIN and Logo, April 2011, Section 2.5.3.2, Exhibit US-115).

546 China's second written submission, para. 99; response to Panel question No. 111, paras. 69 and 70; comments on the United States' response to Panel question Nos. 70-72, 86-96, 115-123, para.77.

547 China's comments on the United States' response to Panel question Nos. 70-72, 86-96, 115-123, para.78.

548 China's second written submission, paras. 97 (referencing Exhibit CHN-74) and 100.

"domestic foreign currency cards ... issued by domestic financial institutions ... and foreign bank cards ... issued by overseas institutions ... except ... RMB cards issued by [domestic financial institutions and overseas institutions]". Article II.3 states that "domestic cards are classified into foreign currency cards, which refers to those denominated in only one foreign currency, and home-foreign currency cards, which refers to those denominated in both RMB and one or more foreign currencies".[549]

7.434 Article V.2 of Document No. 53 specifies that "[d]omestic card transactions inside China shall be settled in RMB through domestic clearing channels...".[550] It provides further that "[a]ny overdraft arising from domestic transactions shall be paid by the cardholder in RMB". According to the translation advice provided by the UNOG translator[551], Article V.3 in turn identifies two circumstances in which international bank card organizations may clear transactions involving domestically issued bank cards. These are:

> (1) where domestic foreign currency card transactions occurring within China are cleared through an international bankcard organization; and (2) "wrong hand-off" transactions, in which domestic dual-currency cards, which should be treated as RMB cards, are mistakenly identified by the acquiring financial institution as foreign currency cards and are thus handed off to an international bankcard organization for clearance.

7.435 Article VII.3 provides that "[d]omestic RMB card clearing organizations shall do a good job in the RMB clearing of domestic transactions of home-foreign currency cards". As noted above[552], home-foreign currency cards are dual-currency cards. In addition, Article VII.3 requires that card issuers report the BIN of cards that are issued to "the domestic RMB card clearing organizations".

7.436 Articles V.2, V.3 and VII.3, when read together, make clear that domestically based EPS suppliers are to handle the clearing and settlement of RMB payment transactions involving domestically issued RMB cards. Article V.2 provides that "*domestic* card transactions *inside* China shall be settled in RMB through *domestic* clearing channels" (emphasis added). Article V.3 characterizes "wrong hand-off" transactions as those cases in which domestic dual-currency cards are "mistakenly identified" as foreign currency cards and are thus handled by an "international bankcard organization". Articles I and II.3 indicate that "foreign currency bank cards" include single-currency, foreign currency cards issued by domestic institutions, as well as single-currency, foreign currency cards issued by overseas institutions. However,

---

549 We note that this dispute concerns exclusively bank cards issued in China.

550 United States' second written submission, para. 145; response to Panel question No. 87, para. 67.

551 See Annex H.

552 In paragraph 7.433, we note that Article II.3 defines "home-foreign currency cards" as "those denominated in both RMB and one or more foreign currencies".

"domestic cards" include dual-currency cards denominated in RMB and any other currency that are issued jointly by domestic financial institutions and overseas institutions. These do not qualify as foreign currency cards. Thus, any transaction made in China with a card that is denominated in part or in whole in RMB should not as a rule be handled by an international bank card organization. The requirement in Article VII.3 for issuers to report BINs appears directed at avoiding "wrong hand-off" transactions as described in Article V.2 that arise when dual-currency cards are mistakenly treated as foreign-currency-only cards, and are thereby cleared and settled by international bank card organizations.[553]

7.437 Taking into account the operation of these provisions together, we understand that any transaction made in China with an RMB bank card that is issued in China or a card with an RMB component must be handled by a domestic clearing channel. It is evident on the face of Articles V.2, V.3 and VII.3 that a domestic clearing channel may not be an international bank card organization. China itself explains that an international bank card organization or "international network operator" should be distinguished from a "domestic network" or "RMB clearing channel".[554] Therefore, we understand a domestic clearing channel must be based in China in accordance with Document No 53. We further understand from China that Document No. 53 is directed at avoiding unnecessary foreign exchange transactions; this is why the relevant transactions must be cleared through domestic RMB clearing channels, and not over the networks of international bank card organizations.

7.438 Setting aside the purpose behind this instrument, it is clear that foreign-based EPS suppliers are excluded from handling the clearing of RMB payment transactions involving domestically issued cards. This would seem to be the case regardless of whether it were possible for a foreign-based EPS supplier to clear such a transaction abroad in RMB, i.e. without involving foreign exchange, since Article V.2 states that all such transactions "*shall* be settled in RMB through *domestic* clearing channels" (emphasis added).

7.439 Nevertheless, we have not identified any language in Articles V.2, V.3 or VII.3 that specifies that CUP alone must be that domestic clearing channel, or

---

553 In stating this, we understand the United States' position to be that an EPS supplier would sort through different transactions based on the card-specific BIN, enabling it to distinguish between transactions that are initiated with a dual-currency card or a foreign-currency card. It considers that, when a transaction is initiated at a merchant POS terminal, the transaction will automatically be processed over the CUP network as the card's BIN will match the BIN transferred to, and stored in, CUP's BIN table. See United States' response to Panel question Nos. 1, paras. 58 and 59; 6, para. 28; and 87, para. 68

554 In response to Panel question No. 116, China explained that a number of "complex" factors affect the network over which a dual-logo card is processed. For international transactions, where the issuing bank is not located in the country in which the transaction occurs, China explains that certain transactions will be permitted to be processed over "domestic" networks, while in other cases, they may need to be processed over an external network, such as "VisaNet". See China's response to Panel question No. 116, para. 79 and fns. 39 and 40. See also Visa International Operating Regulations, Core Principle 7.4, Exhibit CHN-113.

that EPS suppliers of other WTO Members could not meet the definition of domestic clearing channels or domestic RMB card clearing organizations. For one thing, the language seems to acknowledge the possibility of more than one domestic clearing channel, through the reference to "channels" in the plural form. In addition, there is no explicit indication in any of these provisions that CUP specifically must process all RMB payment transactions involving domestically issued cards.[555]

7.440 Turning to the United States argument that the reference to CUP in Article 1.2 of Document No. 153 confirms that CUP is the only entity that may process domestic RMB bank card transactions, we recall that Article 1.2 of Document No. 153 provides that "[CUP] is currently the domestic clearing organization specializing in RMB bank card inter-bank information routing and exchange".[556] This document dates from June 2005. We recall our conclusion that, while CUP may have been the only domestic clearing channel operating in China in 2005, and may still be the sole domestic channel operating in China that clears domestic RMB bank card transactions, the relevant language in Document No. 153 does not grant CUP the exclusive privilege to clear and settle RMB for transactions involving domestic foreign currency and dual currency bank cards.

7.441 Therefore, having addressed the foregoing aspects of Document No. 53, as well as the United States' argument regarding Document No. 153, we conclude that Document No. 53 does not impose a requirement or otherwise maintain or establish CUP as the sole supplier of EPS in respect of domestic RMB bank card transactions.

(xi) Document No. 49

7.442 The United States argues that Document No. 49 requires that a wholly foreign-funded bank or a Chinese-foreign equity joint bank that plans to issue bank cards comply with the bank card business and technical standards formulated by the PBOC. In its view, this requirement to follow uniform business specifications and technical standards establishes a mandate that CUP be used to process all RMB bank card transactions.[557]

7.443 China did not specifically address Document No. 49. In general, China argues that a requirement to comply with one set of business rules and technical standards does not preclude a bank card issuer from issuing cards that also

---

[555] We also recall that Document No. 53, which was promulgated on 11 October 2010 and entered into force on 1 November 2010, replaced Document No. 272. We stated above that we would not consider Document No. 272 in our analysis in part due to its repeal prior to the establishment of the panel. See paras. 7.221-7.227 above. We do not wish to make any findings in respect of Document No. 272 here, but find it pertinent to note that, differently from Document No. 53, Article 4.1 of Document No. 272 expressly required that all domestic RMB transactions involving domestic foreign currency and dual currency bank cards be handled through CUP.

[556] See also discussion in paras. 7.412-7.421 above.

[557] United States' second written submission, para. 154 (citing Article 4 of Document No. 49).

comply with other rules and standards that enable that card to operate over other networks. China submits that many such cards exist around the world.[558]

7.444 The Panel notes that Article IV, in a translation agreed between the parties, requires a wholly foreign-funded bank or Chinese-foreign equity joint bank that plans to issue bank cards to abide by the business and technical standards formulated by the PBOC and to ensure that issued bank cards meet the general requirements regarding the network for bank card interoperability.[559]

7.445 In our view, this provision intends to ensure *inter alia* that bank cards issued in China can be used in domestic inter-bank transactions. Similarly to what we have said above in respect of other instruments that impose interoperability requirements[560], we do not identify anything on the face of this document that requires that all cross-region or inter-bank transactions occur over the CUP network, or that prohibits the use of cards on other networks with different technical/interoperability requirements. Accordingly, in the absence of evidence demonstrating otherwise, we cannot conclude that this instrument on its own mandates or establishes CUP as the sole supplier of EPS in respect of domestic bank card transactions denominated or paid in RMB.

(xii) Document No. 129

7.446 The United States argues that Article 3.2 of Document No. 129 mandates that all RMB bank cards newly issued by commercial banks and postal savings and remittance bureau comply with unified business specifications and technical standards of the CUP network and bear the CUP logo. Based on adherence to these standards, the United States argues, therefore, that this provision mandates and establishes CUP as the sole supplier to process all RMB bank card transactions issued and used in China.[561] The United States notes as well that Article 3.4 of this document requires commercial banks to work with CUP to "improve procedures for dealing with errors".[562] It submits that, if suppliers other than CUP were permitted in the market, then all other EPS suppliers would be subject to similar requirements. The fact that other suppliers are not subject to the same requirements demonstrates that CUP is a sole supplier, in its view.

7.447 China does not specifically refer to Document No. 129. In general, China argues that a requirement to comply with one set of business rules and technical standards does not preclude a bank card issuer from issuing cards that also comply with other rules and standards, which would enable that card to operate

558 China's response to Panel question No. 22(c), para.18; comments on the United States' response to Panel question Nos. 70-72, 86-96, 115-123, para. 56.

559 See Translation Issues in DS413, Table I: Translation Issues Agreed by China and the United States, dated 6 December 2011.

560 See paras. 7.299, 7.334 and 7.358- 7.360 above; see also the Panel's discussion of Document Nos. 37, 57, 103 and 149 in this section of the Report.

561 United States' second written submission, para. 154; response to Panel question Nos. 88(a), para. 73; 119, para. 118.

562 United States' second written submission, para. 168.

over other networks. China submits that many such cards exist around the world.[563]

7.448 The Panel concluded above[564] that Article 3.2(ii) requires that all RMB bank cards issued in China must bear the *Yin Lian*/UnionPay logo and must be interoperable with the CUP network. In addition, Article 3.4(i) provides that "[CUP] shall, in conjunction with all commercial banks, further supplement and perfect error processing management measures and implementation rules, establishing a scientific and effective error processing procedures, clarify the responsibilities of the parties involved in error processing and specify the task assignment".

7.449 We have indicated in respect of Document No. 129 above[565], and in respect of other instruments at issue[566] our view that the requirement to comply with logo and business and technical requirements for interoperability does not preclude banks from issuing cards that meet other technical or business requirements and also bear the logo of a foreign EPS supplier. Similarly here, we consider the requirement to bear the *Yin Lian*/UnionPay logo and meet interoperability requirements does not on its own establish or maintain CUP as a sole supplier. We find nothing on the face of this measure that would prevent cards from bearing the logo of another EPS supplier or operating over the network of another EPS supplier, so long as that card also bears the *Yin Lian*/UnionPay logo and is interoperable with the CUP network.

7.450 We note that Article 3.4 refers to CUP by name, and directs CUP to work together with all commercial banks to develop and perfect error processing related to bank card transactions. Document No. 129 dates from July 2003. As we have discussed above[567], CUP may have been the only EPS supplier operating in China in 2003, and may today still be the sole EPS supplier operating in China, that clears domestic RMB-denominated bank card transactions for cards issued in China. If this is the case, then this could explain the reference in Document No. 129 to CUP in its direction to work with commercial banks to handle error processing. That is, in referring to CUP, Document No. 129 does not exclude other suppliers; it merely reflects the fact that CUP was and perhaps still is the only supplier. Moreover, if the CUP network was and is the only EPS supplier in China, any errors in bank card processing would occur on CUP's network. In other words, we have not identified any language in Articles 3.2(ii) and 3.4(i) of Document No. 129 that grants CUP the exclusive privilege to process RMB transactions on a continuing basis. There is also no evidence before this Panel that other EPS suppliers were

563 China's response to Panel question No. 22(c), para. 18; comments on the United States' response to Panel question Nos. 70-72, 86-96, 115-123, para. 56.
564 See para. 7.270 above.
565 See para. 7.299 above.
566 See the Panel's discussion of Document Nos. 37, 57, 103, 149 and 49 in this section of the Report.
567 See para. 7.440 above.

prevented from establishing alternative networks to process RMB transactions. In the absence of additional evidence, we are unable to conclude that Document No. 129 mandates or establishes CUP as the sole supplier of EPS in respect of domestic transactions denominated or paid in RMB.

(xiii) Document No. 76

7.451 The United States contends that Document No. 76 requires that all entities participating in the bank card business comply with a series of "business practices" and implement technical standards as set out in the Business Practices Appendix to Document No. 76. Consistent with the way that laws are typically written, the United States considers that these rules and procedures must be followed to the exclusion of other rules.[568] It argues that all entities participating in the bank card business participate in the common network, process all RMB bank card transactions over the network, and process transactions according to uniform rules and procedures, including conforming to CUP logo requirements.[569] The United States considers the net effect is to mandate the use of CUP for all RMB bank card transactions, and otherwise prohibit the use of EPS suppliers other than CUP.[570] Moreover, the United States submits that CUP's own operating regulations "implement the mandate in Document No. 76", and similarly prohibit logos of competing EPS suppliers from appearing on CUP cards.[571]

7.452 According to the United States, a number of elements in Document No. 76 support the conclusion that CUP alone may handle RMB bank card transactions. It considers that references to a "countrywide", "unified logo" or "standardize[d]" system throughout Document No. 76 reinforce that CUP alone may process RMB transactions taking place in China.[572] It argues that the reference to the establishment of a "unified" network in CUP's Articles of Incorporation and Notification of Approval of CUP's Business Licence support this interpretation.[573] It further submits that the "precise" ways in which Document No. 76 describes how transactions must be processed and how participating banks must organize themselves further supports the intention that all issuers and acquirers must comply with uniform standards which are exclusive to CUP and necessitate that all RMB transactions will be processed by CUP.[574]

568 United States' second written submission, para. 163.

569 United States' response to Panel question No. 88(a), para. 72.

570 United States' second written submission, paras. 153, 159 and 161.

571 United States' response to Panel question No. 8; comments on China's response to Panel question No. 104.

572 United States second written submission, para. 164 (referring to Chapter I, Articles 1.1, 2.1 and 4.1 of the Business Practices Appendix to Document No. 76); comments on China's response to Panel question No. 119, para. 60.

573 United States' second written submission, para. 165.

574 United States' second written submission, paras. 157-171.

7.453 In addition, the United States considers the fact that Chapter 10 of the Business Practices Appendix to Document No. 76 excludes application of the business practices to foreign currency cards issued outside China, conversely demonstrates that the business practices are intended to apply to all transactions involving domestically issued cards in China.[575] The United States also notes that paragraph 5 of the Notice to Document No. 76 requires that all "bankcard business rules that are inconsistent with the Specifications shall be abolished"[576]. In its view, this limitation contradicts any assertions by China that bank cards may conform to other standards and rules, and consequently, that other EPS suppliers may process RMB transactions.[577] Finally, the United States submits that Article 4 of the business practices assigns exclusive ownership and management rights of the network logo to CUP.[578] The United States argues that CUP is thus capable of protecting its exclusivity in the marketplace by refusing permission to use the CUP logo to issuers of cards carrying the logo of competing EPS suppliers.[579]

7.454 China agrees that Document No. 76 sets forth detailed rules and technical specifications pertaining to bank card interoperability.[580] However, as repeated throughout its submissions and reflected in preceding sections, China argues that compliance with one set of business rules does not preclude compliance with another set of business rules, the latter of which would enable bank cards to operate over other networks. China considers that many bank cards in the marketplace are capable of operating over numerous networks.[581]

7.455 The Panel concluded in paragraph 7.330 above that Article 1.2 of Chapter II of the Business Practices Appendix does not impose a requirement that all merchant terminal equipment be capable of accepting bank cards bearing the *Yin Lian*/UnionPay logo. The Panel further concluded in paragraphs 7.352 and 7.353 that paragraphs 2 and 3 of the Notice to Document No. 76 as well as Articles 2.1 and 5.2.1-5.2.3 of Chapter I of the Business Practices Appendix do impose a requirement that all acquiring banks must be capable of accepting bank cards bearing the CUP logo. We understand that Document No. 76 establishes clear business and technical standards to facilitate the processing of transactions over the CUP network. With this in mind, we assess the United States' contention that Document No. 76 requires that all domestic RMB transactions on domestically issued cards be processed over the CUP network.

7.456 We begin with the United States' argument that paragraph 5 of the Notice and Chapter 10 of the Business Practices Appendix to Document No. 76 support

575 United States' response to Panel question No. 88(a), para. 74.

576 United States' response to Panel question No. 88(a), para. 74; comments on China's response to Panel question No. 119, para. 69.

577 United States' second written submission, para. 163.

578 United States' response to Panel question No.15, para. 57.

579 United States response to Panel question No. 71(b)(i), para. 7.

580 China's first written submission, para. 45.

581 China's response to Panel question No. 119, para. 84.

the United States' allegation that only CUP may process domestic RMB transactions on domestically issued cards, and that other EPS suppliers may not do so. The United States contends that the requirement in paragraph 5 to abolish all business rules that are inconsistent with the Business Practices Appendix to Document No. 76 following the entry into force of Document No. 76 effectively grants CUP sole supplier status. Given the context provided by Articles 1.1 and 2.1 and elsewhere in Document No. 76, we understand paragraph 5 serves to ensure that entities participating in the bank card business do not apply business rules that are inconsistent with the Business Practices Appendix, thereby effectively preventing the establishment of a unified, interoperable network. As we have indicated above[582], the United States has provided no evidence to demonstrate that it would not be possible for a bank card issuer to issue a card, or an acquirer or terminal equipment to accept a card, that is at the same time interoperable with the business rules of EPS suppliers of other WTO Members and the rules of the Business Practices Appendix to Document No. 76. In the absence of any such evidence, we are not persuaded that it can be inferred from paragraph 5 that all cross-region or inter-bank transactions must occur over the CUP network, or that it would not be technically or legally possible to issue and use cards in China on other networks that apply different business rules, while at the same time ensuring their consistency with the Business Practices Appendix. Accordingly, we cannot conclude that paragraph 5 mandates that CUP is the sole supplier of EPS in respect of domestic transactions denominated or paid in RMB.

7.457 We next turn to Chapter 10 of the Business Practices Appendix, which provides that Document No. 76 does not apply to foreign currency cards issued outside China that are used in China. The United States' claims are directed toward all RMB cards issued *and* used in China. In our view, when read in isolation, it is not clear to us that this statement means that Document No. 76 is applicable to all RMB-denominated payment cards issued in China. Regardless, we do not consider that this statement alone would support the conclusion that the business and technical standards set out in the Business Practices Appendix must apply to all cards issued in China to the exclusion of other rules. As we have already stated above[583], we do not consider the requirement to bear the *Yin Lian*/UnionPay logo and meet business and technical requirements for interoperability on its own establishes or maintains CUP as a sole supplier. We are thus not persuaded that the United States' reference to Chapter 10 supports its allegations.

7.458 We have found throughout Section VII.E.2(e) that the requirement to bear the *Yin Lian*/UnionPay and meet certain business and technical requirements for interoperability does not preclude issuers from issuing bank

582 See paras. 7.299 and 7.358- 7.360 above.

583 See the Panel's discussion of Document Nos. 37, 57, 103, 149, 49 and 129 in this section of the Report.

cards that are also interoperable with the business and technical rules of EPS suppliers of other WTO Members. In view of this, we similarly reject the United States' contention that the "way" in which Document No. 76 is written as a regulation means that the rules and procedures in Document No. 76 must be followed to the exclusion of other procedures.[584] We therefore consider whether any other elements identified by the United States in Document No. 76 mandate the use of CUP for all RMB-denominated transactions.

7.459 We next consider the United States' contention that references to a "unified logo" or "standardize[d]" system throughout Document No. 76 support the conclusion that CUP is intended to be a sole supplier of EPS services for RMB bank card transactions in China. The United States argues that the use of the phrase "to set up and operate a single nationwide inter-bank card information switching network" and particularly the word "single", that is used both in CUP's Articles of Association[585] and Notification of Approval of CUP's Business Licence[586], confirm that CUP alone may supply EPS services for RMB transactions in China for those cards issued in China. It argues that "China's decision early on to position CUP as the monopoly supplier of EPS in China is reflected in these foundational documents".[587]

7.460 We first note that the Article 2.1 of the Business Practices Appendix to Document No. 76 provides that the "bank card united association" that was to be established pursuant to this document, (and that later became CUP) means a "countrywide bank card united operational organization". In discussing the meaning of "bank card interoperation", Article 2.2 provides that bank card institutions and merchants should "link themselves with the countrywide… system to achieve the sharing of information …and interoperation". Article 4.2 of the Business Practices Appendix states that the logo of the network consists of "the Chinese character of 'UnionPay' and a graph symbolising the *united* network" (emphasis added). In our view, the references to the establishment of a "countrywide" network, or the provision mentioning that the logo of the network should symbolize that the network is "united", reflects foremost an intention to establish a common, nationwide network. Evidence on record indicates that, prior to 2001, when Document No. 76 was issued, no EPS supplier had in place a nationwide, interoperable network.[588] The fact that a nationwide network did not exist in China previously meant that bank cards were not guaranteed to be usable throughout China. Hence, we understand the focus in Document No. 76 was to create a network that is "united" and "countrywide". In reaching this view, however, we do not agree with the United States that one can properly

[584] In this respect, we respond to the United States' argument as set out in paragraph 163 of its second written submission.

[585] See CUP's Articles of Association, Articles 11 and 12, Exhibit US-20.

[586] Notification of Approval of CUP's Business Licence, Exhibit US-29.

[587] United States' response to Panel question No. 121.

[588] See United States' response to China's request for a preliminary ruling, paras. 64-71; China's first written submission, paras. 38-46. See also fn. 532 above.

infer from this effort to create a nationwide network an intention to create an exclusive network in China, wherein all other EPS suppliers except the association that would later become CUP would be prohibited from operating. We do not find the inference drawn by the United States is supported by the aforementioned references, nor do we find such support elsewhere in Document No. 76. As we explained above, we have found nothing in Document No. 76 that prevents issuers from incorporating logos of other EPS suppliers, or issuing cards that comply with the rules of other EPS suppliers, so long as those cards bear the *Yin Lian*/Union Pay logo and are interoperable with the CUP network.

7.461 As noted, the United States also refers to the reference to the establishment of a "single" network in CUP's Articles of Association and Notification of Approval of CUP's Business Licence in support of its interpretation of what was intended through Document No. 76, in particular the references to a "unified logo" or a "standardize[d]" system. We note that the term "single" does not appear in Document No. 76 itself. One meaning of the term "single" is "consisting of only one part", as a limitation in number.[589] However, we note that the term "single" may also be understood to mean "undivided, united".[590] In addition to the meaning of this term, we also note that the phrase "to set up and operate a single nationwide inter-bank card information switching network" uses the indefinite article "a", and not the definite article "the", and to that extent does not appear to indicate an intention to limit the number of EPS suppliers in the marketplace to one. Moreover, we note that Article 11 of CUP's Articles of Association specifies that the purpose of CUP is "to set up a unified, highly efficient and safe inter-bank card information exchange network across the country". In view of the different meanings of "single" and its use in CUP's foundational documents, we do not agree with the United States that these documents should inform the conclusion that CUP is a sole supplier of EPS services for RMB bank card transactions in China. Rather, we find the use of "single" in these identical phrases in CUP's Articles of Association and Notification of Approval of CUP's Business Licence is consistent with the stated objective in Articles 1.1 and 2.1 of Document No. 76 to establish a "countrywide", "interoperable" bank card network in China. In our view, therefore, the stated objective to establish a "single" network is not indicative of an intention to create an exclusive network.

7.462 Finally, we turn to the United States' contention that CUP's control of the ownership and management rights of the *Yin Lian*/UnionPay logo enables it to prohibit other EPS suppliers from operating in China. We concluded in paragraph 7.277 above that Article 4.2 of the Appendix grants the United Association (now CUP) exclusive ownership and use and management right of the *Yin Lian*/UnionPay logo. However, we observed that, pursuant to Article 4.3 of the Business Practices Appendix, "Interoperating Members" (which include

[589] *Shorter Oxford English Dictionary*, Vol. 2, p. 2843.
[590] *Ibid.*

issuing banks) "automatically obtain" the right to use the logo from the date they officially engage in inter-bank business upon approval by the United Association/CUP. Therefore, we stated[591] that we were not persuaded that Article 4.2, when read together with Article 4.3, provides a basis for CUP to refuse permission for the logo to appear on bank cards bearing the logo of competing EPS suppliers. Rather, banks that already engage in the bank card business would be permitted to incorporate additional logos of EPS suppliers.

7.463 In its responses to several of the Panel's questions following the second substantive meeting of the parties[592], the United States submitted the text of CUP's Operating Regulations[593] as well as reports from China's press[594] in support of its allegation that CUP uses its control over the CUP logo to prevent other logos from appearing on the cards and thereby limits the ability of other EPS suppliers to enter the Chinese market. According to the United States, CUP's Operating Rules state in relevant part:

> The following logos cannot appear on UnionPay Card surface (including card face and card back).
>
> - Name/logo/trademark of credit card or debit card of the companies and their subsidiaries that are deemed to have competitive relationship with UnionPay by UnionPay Board of Directors …

7.464 As we noted above[595], CUP's Operating Regulations are not identified as a relevant legal instrument in the United States' panel request. We are unclear why the United States did not identify these regulations earlier. We recall China's view that evidence on record does not support the United States' assertion that CUP does not licence the *Yin Lian*/UnionPay logo for use on cards that also carry the logo of other EPS suppliers.[596] China submits Exhibit CHN-112 as evidence that a large number of cards in China are "dual logo" cards.[597]

7.465 We set out reasons in paragraph 7.279 above why we are not convinced that the identified provisions of CUP's Operating Regulations support the United States' assertion that the logo use requirements enable CUP to prevent an issuer from issuing bank cards of competing EPS suppliers. We noted that the

[591] See paras. 7.277-7.279

[592] United States' response to Panel question No. 117. See also United States' response to Panel question Nos. 86 and 94.

[593] CUP's Operating Regulations, Volume III, Rules on UnionPay Card, BIN and Logo, April 2011, Section 2.5.3.2, Exhibit US-115

[594] See Exhibits US-119, US-120, US-121, US-122, and US-123.

[595] See para. 7.291 above.

[596] See para. 7.278 above.

[597] China's comments on United States' response to Panel question Nos. 70-72, 86-96, 115-123, para. 67.

Regulations, submitted very late in the proceedings, raise a number of questions concerning their operation that the United States did not address. In particular, the Operating Regulations do not specify whether the bank cards on which other logos may not appear – referred to above – are only CUP-branded bank cards, or also bank cards issued in China that bear more than one logo. We also took note of evidence submitted by China that numerous cards issued in China – "one quarter of all bank cards issued in China in 2010" – carry the logo of other EPS suppliers.[598] In our view, the United States failed to reconcile its interpretation of CUP's Operating Regulations with this evidence. The United States also failed to explain its interpretation of the language taking into account that Article 4.3 of the Business Practices Appendix to Document No. 76 indicates that the right to use the logo is automatically granted to interoperating members to the CUP network.[599] For these reasons, we reject the United States' contention that CUP's control of the ownership and management rights of the *Yin Lian*/UnionPay logo enables it to prohibit other EPS suppliers from operating in China.

7.466 Accordingly, for the reasons set out above, we conclude that Document No. 76 does not establish CUP as the sole supplier of EPS for RMB-denominated transactions in China or otherwise prevent the use of EPS suppliers other than CUP.

(xiv) Document No. 17

7.467 The United States submits that Article 64 of Document No. 17 requires issuing banks to "implement technical standards prescribed by the State" when issuing bank cards.[600] The United States argues that "many" of the technical standards are developed by CUP, and as a result, the requirement to implement CUP standards "enhances CUP's position as sole supplier".[601]

---

598 Exhibit CHN-112.

599 In respect of its claim that China limits EPS suppliers other than CUP from entering the Chinese market, the United States' asserts that CUP at times has not approved EPS suppliers' applications for new dual logo cards, as it argues is demonstrated in various press reports (Exhibits US-119, US-120, US-121, US-122, US-123). Without entering into a discussion of the evidentiary value of these press reports, as explained in paragraph 7.280, we do not understand how the United States' assertion that CUP undertakes approval of applications to issue dual logo cards can be reconciled with Article 4.3. Also, the United States has not explained to us how its allegation that CUP restrains the issuance of dual branded cards to a "certain threshold percentage (e.g. 80%)" (stated in response to Panel question No. 117, para. 114) supports the contention that CUP is therefore the "sole supplier" of EPS for RMB transactions. In addition, we note the United States' argument in response to Panel question No. 94 (para. 95) that CUP has the authority to deny or delay the issuance of BIN numbers to competing EPS suppliers, thereby preventing EPS suppliers from competing in the Chinese market. Like China, we note that the United States has not provided any specific reference in the instruments at issue to substantiate its assertion. We are therefore unable to agree that the above elements support the United States' claim that China limits EPS suppliers other than CUP from entering the Chinese market.

600 United States' second written submission, para. 154.

601 United States' response to Panel question No. 71(a), para. 6.

7.468 China does not specifically address the provision identified by the United States. We recall that, in general, China maintains that a requirement to comply with one set of business rules and technical standards does not preclude a bank card issuer from issuing cards that also comply with other rules and standards, which would enable that card to operate over other networks.[602]

7.469 The Panel concluded in paragraph 7.286 above that Article 64, when read in conjunction with Document No. 76, requires issuers to implement business and technical standards when issuing bank cards that bear the *Yin Lian*/UnionPay logo.[603] It is not clear that "many" of the technical standards prescribed by the State are those standards developed by CUP. But even if it were, as we stated in respect of Document No. 17 above[604], and in respect of other instruments that impose interoperability requirements[605], we do not consider the requirement to comply with certain business and technical interoperability requirements alone precludes banks from issuing cards that meet other technical or business requirements that enable these cards to operate on another network. Given our conclusions, we do not consider that Article 64 individually could be considered to mandate the use of CUP or establish CUP as the sole supplier of EPS for all domestic transactions denominated and paid in RMB, and hence we do not agree with the United States that Article 64 results in "enhanc[ing] CUP's position as sole supplier".

(xv) Document No. 142

7.470 The United States argues that Article II.3 of Document No. 142 requires that issuers of bank cards prioritize issuance of cards that adopt the PBOC 2.0 Standards, a chip standard developed by the PBOC and CUP. It submits that China "intends to require that all cards comply with this standard.[606] The United States submits that this standard is China-specific and incompatible with the "EMV" chip standard used by non-Chinese EPS suppliers.[607] As a result, the United States argues that non-Chinese EPS suppliers have to redesign their chips to allow their cards to be used in China.[608] The United States considers that this requirement contributes to establishing CUP as a sole supplier in the processing of RMB bank card transactions. In addition, it notes that various provisions in Document No. 142 – notably Articles III, V and VI – designate CUP to

[602] China's response to Panel question No. 22(c), para.18; comments on the United States' response to Panel question Nos. 70-72, 86-96, 115-123, para. 56.

[603] We concluded, however, that Article 64 does not require that all bank cards in China must bear the *Yin Lian*/UnionPay logo and that it does not require the use of the unified standards in all cases.

[604] See para. 7.299 above.

[605] See the Panel's discussion of Document Nos. 37, 57, 103, 149, 49, 129 and 76 in this section of the Report.

[606] United States' response to Panel question No. 94, para. 97.

[607] United States' response to Panel question No. 72, para. 17.

[608] United States' response to Panel question No. 94, para. 97 (citing Article 2.3 of Document No. 142); see also response to Panel question No. 88, para. 73.

participate with other Chinese institutions in an effort to enhance bank card security. The United States submits that, if suppliers other than CUP were permitted in the market, then all other EPS suppliers would similarly be subject to the requirements set out in Articles III, V and VI of Document No. 142. The fact that other suppliers are not so subject demonstrates that CUP is a monopoly, in its view.[609]

7.471 China contends that the United States provides no support for its assertion that EPS suppliers will need to significantly redesign their chip to be allowed to operate in the Chinese market.[610] Setting this aside, as noted above[611], China maintains that a requirement to comply with CUP's business rules and technical standards does not preclude bank card issuers from issuing cards that also comply with other rules and standards that enable that card to operate over other networks.

7.472 The Panel notes that Article II.3 directs card issuers to ensure that all cards issued meet the requirements of the "Bank Card Specifications (JR0052-2009)" and the "Technical Specifications on Bankcard Interoperability (JR-55-2009)". The United States suggests that this standard will be implemented at a future point in time.[612] Issuers are directed to give priority to the issuance of bank cards which adopt the "PBOC 2.0 Standards" to improve "the anti-counterfeiting ability of bank cards." Article II.5 and Articles III.7 and III.8 direct card issuers to submit risk information on bank cards to the bank card information sharing system of CUP to aid in preventing bank card fraud. Article V.15 directs CUP, *inter alia*, to improve its "bank card risk prevention and control system", including setting up a "uniform national merchant information registration and risk prevention and control system"; and to "work out the business rules and technical standards for inter-bank payment services … that are not specified in the current networking business standards".

7.473 We note the United States' assertion that the PBOC 2.0 standard is not compatible with the EMV chip standard used in other parts of the world, and that EPS suppliers will have to "significantly redesign their chips" to allow their cards to be used in China. Although stating that this redesign would be a "significant" one, the United States does not provide explanation or evidence about what would be involved in such redesign. Hence we have nothing on which to assess the significance, difficulty or otherwise of any redesign procedures.. Nor does the United States assert that a redesign to conform to the PBOC 2.0 standard would be so difficult such that EPS suppliers would opt not to enter the market. In the absence of any supporting evidence, we are unable to

[609] United States' second written submission, para. 168.

[610] China's comments on the United States' response to Panel question Nos. 70-72, 86-96, 115-123, para. 69.

[611] See, e.g. China's response to Panel question No. 22(c), para.18; comments on the United States' response to Panel question Nos. 70-72, 86-96, 115-123, para. 56.

[612] As we noted, the United States argues that "China intends to require that all cards comply with the new chip standard…" See United States' response to Panel question No. 94, para. 97.

accept the United States' assertion that a requirement to comply with this standard in the future would ensure that CUP would remain in the market as a sole supplier. In addition, the United States does not assert that compliance with the PBOC 2.0 standard would preclude simultaneous compliance with the EMV or any other standard, such that we cannot conclude that a given card would be prevented from operating over more than one network.

7.474 We indicated above in respect of other instruments[613] that the requirement to comply with technical/interoperability requirements does not preclude banks from issuing cards that meet other technical requirements. Thus, we are not persuaded that the initiative set out in Article II.3 to require compliance with PBOC 2.0 standards prevents cards from complying with other standards such that they might operate over other networks. Accordingly, we are unable to conclude that a requirement to comply with PBOC 2.0 standards establishes or maintains CUP as a sole supplier.

7.475 We note, finally, the United States' argument that the designation of CUP in Articles III, V and VI in Document No. 142 to participate with other Chinese institutions in an effort to enhance bank card security demonstrates that CUP is a sole supplier. We concluded in paragraph 7.450 above that the mere fact that Document No. 129 designates card issuers or acquirers to work together with CUP, so as to develop error processing related to bank card transactions, does not by itself establish or maintain CUP as a sole supplier.[614] We consider our conclusions in that context to be relevant here and conclude similarly. Document No. 142 entered into force in 2009. Given CUP's position in the Chinese marketplace, the fact that CUP is identified by name may simply reflect the prevailing market situation in China at that time. Hence, Document No. 129 designates CUP to participate in reducing bank card-related crimes. Apart from this specific role, there is no language in Document No. 142 that grants CUP the exclusive privilege to provide RMB inter-bank information exchange and processing on a continuing basis. In the absence of additional evidence, we are unable to conclude that references to CUP in Document No. 142 have the effect of mandating or establishing CUP as the sole supplier of EPS in respect of domestic transactions denominated or paid in RMB.

(xvi) Conclusions on the instruments individually

7.476 Based on the above analysis, the Panel concludes that none of the identified legal instruments considered individually mandates or establishes CUP as sole supplier of EPS in respect of domestic RMB bank card transactions or otherwise prohibits the use of EPS suppliers other than CUP.

7.477 Specifically, we concluded that certain provisions in Document Nos. 17, 37, 49, 57, 76, 129, 142, 149 and 153 require that all bank cards issued in China,

[613] See the Panel's discussion of Document Nos. 37, 57, 103, 149, 49, 129, 76 and 17 above.

[614] See also para. 7.440.

including dual currency bank cards, for use in connection with domestic inter-bank transactions bear the *Yin Lian*/UnionPay logo. In various respects, these documents further require, *inter alia*, that terminal equipment operated by acquirers and merchant terminal equipment provided by acquirers be technically capable of accepting all bank cards bearing the *Yin Lian*/UnionPay logo. Finally, these documents require that acquirers themselves be capable of accepting bank cards bearing the *Yin Lian*/UnionPay logo. We found, however, that nothing in the cited provisions of these instruments precludes the issuance or acceptance of bank cards that would operate on any inter-bank networks other than that of CUP, or precludes the use, or the acceptance at terminals, of bank cards bearing logos of other EPS suppliers, so long as those cards also bear the *Yin Lian*/UnionPay logo and are also interoperable over the CUP network. Accordingly, we found that the cited provisions of these instruments do not establish or maintain CUP as the exclusive EPS supplier for all RMB bank card transactions, where a bank card is issued and used in China. We similarly concluded that Document No. 103 does not establish or maintain CUP as the sole supplier.

7.478 We further concluded that Document No. 153 does not grant CUP the exclusive privilege to provide EPS in relation to RMB bank card transactions taking place in China on the basis that it refers to CUP as the domestic clearing channel, or because it regulates third-party service providers. We similarly concluded that Document No. 53 does not require that CUP alone may serve as a domestic clearing channel to process RMB transactions.

7.479 Finally, in our analysis of Document Nos. 16, 8 and 254, we recalled our previous conclusions[615], that China requires that CUP and no other EPS supplier is to handle the clearing of certain RMB bank card transactions that involve either an RMB bank card issued in China and used in Hong Kong or Macao, or a bank card issued in Hong Kong or Macao that is used in either of these territories, or in China in an RMB transaction. We additionally recalled our conclusion that Document No. 219 does not establish or maintain CUP as sole EPS supplier for RMB transactions in respect of the clearing of these RMB card transactions in Hong Kong, Macao and China, specifically, or in relation to RMB transactions in China generally.[616]

7.480 As we explained, Document Nos. 16, 8 and 254[617] establish CUP as the exclusive EPS provider for RMB bank card transactions concerning Chinese, Hong Kong or Macao nationals who travel in China, Hong Kong or Macao. In this section of the Report, we specifically address the question of whether legal instruments at issue in this dispute explicitly establish or maintain CUP as sole supplier in respect of *all* RMB bank card transactions in China. As Document

[615] See paras. 7.383-7.384 above.

[616] See paras. 7.372-7.377 and 7.402-7.404.

[617] The Panel specifically refers to Article 6 of Document No. 16, Article 6 of Document No. 8 and Articles 3, 4 and 17 of Document No. 254. See paras. 7.372-7.377 and 7.402-7.404 above.

Nos. 16, 8 and 254 are limited in scope to bank card transactions that involve bank cards issued in China and used in Hong Kong or Macao or, alternatively, payment cards issued in Hong Kong or Macao and used in China, we explained above that we do not see how any of these instruments establish CUP as sole supplier of EPS for *all* domestic transactions occurring throughout China that are denominated and paid in RMB. As these measures pertain to transactions concerning Chinese, Hong Kong or Macao nationals who travel in China, Hong Kong or Macao, we thus do not consider them as a direct indication of the establishment or maintenance of CUP as the sole supplier for *all* RMB transactions taking place in China.[618]

7.481 Therefore, in respect of the various instruments identified in connection with the alleged sole supplier requirements, we are unable to conclude that any of the legal instruments, when considered individually, maintains or establishes CUP as the exclusive EPS supplier for RMB bank card transactions, or otherwise prohibit the use of EPS suppliers other than CUP.

(xvii) Collective assessment of the legal instruments at issue

7.482 We recall that the United States has requested the Panel to consider the "measures" at issue in this dispute both individually and in combination with each other. It submits that these measures, or six requirements, reflected or embodied in the various legal instruments affect "every element of the electronic payment system and all of the key participants", including issuers, acquirers, merchants and EPS suppliers themselves.[619] In particular, it argues that all entities participating in the bank card business in China participate in the CUP network, process all RMB bank card transactions over the network, and process transactions according to uniform rules and procedures, including conforming to logo requirements.[620] The United States considers that the net effect of these measures is to "create a system in which CUP is the only entity that can supply EPS for RMB transactions", or that the measures "ensure and consolidate CUP's monopoly position"[621].

7.483 The United States maintains that the various legal instruments interact to establish and maintain CUP as the sole supplier in three principal ways: (i) certain instruments explicitly state that CUP must be used to process specific types of bank card transactions; (ii) certain instruments establish and/or require the use of business specifications and technical standards which mandate the use of CUP; and (iii) certain instruments implicitly recognize that CUP is the sole

618 The Panel addresses below, at paras. 7.482 and 7.576, whether this requirement is inconsistent with Articles XVI and XVII of the GATS.

619 United States' first written submission, para. 48.

620 United States' response to Panel question No. 88(a), para. 72.

621 United States' first written submission, para. 63; second written submission, paras. 153, 159, and 161.

supplier of EPS services for RMB denominated transactions.[622] It argues that the various requirements "ensure CUP's privileged position", both "explicitly" and "effectively".[623]

7.484 The United States argues that no EPS supplier other than CUP benefits from issuer requirements, terminal equipment requirements and acquirer requirements. The United States argues that because of the need to fulfil these requirements, issuers and acquirers must have access to the CUP system, and must pay for that access.[624] It contends that it is thus "economically unviable" for any foreign supplier of EPS to participate in the market.[625] The United States explains:

> Document Nos. 37, 57, 94, 272, 129, and 219 contain requirements that banks that issue payment cards in China must bear the CUP logo at a specified position, and that all ATMs and POS terminals must be capable of processing cards that bear the CUP logo. No foreign suppliers are eligible for this privilege. As banks and processing parties are already required to provide CUP such access (as well as pay for it), it makes no economic sense for such banks to pay for the additional privilege of using a foreign EPS. In other words, these types of privileges do not simply discriminate against foreign suppliers in the marketplace; they effectively deny them access altogether.[626]

7.485 The United States submits that the requirement to pay fees to join CUP's network "creates an unlevel playing field with other suppliers, even in those small areas where other suppliers are permitted to operate (e.g. dual currency cards)."[627] Elsewhere, the United States argues that each of the six requirements help "entrench CUP's position as the sole service supplier in the market".[628] It explains, "[t]hese requirements gave CUP automatic and universal acceptance of its RMB payment card products by banks and merchants in China and permitted and supported CUP becoming the sole supplier of EPS in China".[629]

7.486 As we noted above, China maintains that the six alleged requirements do not operate in such a way as to establish CUP as sole supplier for the clearing and settlement of all RMB domestic inter-bank bank card transactions.[630] Rather, China submits that the identified measures establish a common national network

---

622 United States' second written submission, para. 144.
623 United States' first written submission, para. 46
624 United States' first written submission, paras. 50-52.
625 United States' first written submission, para. 66.
626 United States' first written submission, para. 69.
627 United States' response to Panel question No. 94, para. 96..
628 United States' second written submission, paras. 173, 180, and 183; response to Panel question No. 86, para. 63; 92, para. 88.
629 United States' second written submission, para. 190.
630 China's second written submission, paras. 90-102.

for processing RMB domestic inter-bank bank card transactions.[631] China further submits that the above instruments do not preclude adherence to other technical standards, such as the rules and operating procedures of other EPS suppliers. Similarly, it argues that issuer banks are not prevented from being members of other EPS suppliers' networks.[632] Thus, it maintains that there is nothing in any of these instruments that would prevent a foreign EPS supplier from establishing a domestic clearing channel in China.[633]

7.487 Taking into account the United States' arguments, we understand the United States considers that the six requirements, as reflected in the legal instruments at issue, operate together in several respects to establish and maintain CUP as the sole or exclusive EPS supplier. [634] First, the United States maintains that various legal instruments work together in ways to explicitly or implicitly restrict entry into the Chinese market. Second, the United States' arguments suggest that it considers that certain instruments work together in ways that impose technical barriers to entry. Third, the United States considers that the measures operate together in a way that makes it "economically unviable" to enter the market. We address each of these three arguments in turn.

7.488 As an initial matter, the parties dispute whether CUP is currently the only EPS supplier in the market. China contends that the Rural Credit Banks Funds Clearing Center (RCBFCC) operates throughout China as a second EPS supplier for RMB bank card transactions, and processes inter-bank bank card transactions independently of CUP.[635] In reference to the Center's website and related materials, the United States considers that the RCBFCC is a "clearing and settlement center used by rural commercial banks in China",[636] but that rural commercial banks using the RCBFCC "issue bank cards bearing the CUP logo and transactions using these cards are processed by CUP."[637] As bank cards issued by rural commercial banks for use on the RCBFCC network must carry the CUP logo, issuers of these cards must be members of CUP, which entails following all applicable CUP rules and regulations.

7.489 The website reference provided by the United States is entirely in Chinese. However, as the United States contends, the RCBFCC website contains a series of images of bank cards, each of which includes a depiction of the CUP

---

631 China's first written submission, para. 64; response to Panel question No. 121, para. 87.

632 China's response to Panel question No. 22(c), paras. 17, 18.

633 China's response to Panel question No. 103, para. 45.

634 In this respect, we note that the European Payments Council, "SEPA Cards Framework," refers to "technical", "legal" and "commercial" barriers when discussing requirements or regulations governing co-branding or limiting international EPS suppliers to offering services only for transactions outside of the SEPA area. See United States' response to Panel question No. 73; European Payments Council, "SEPA Cards Framework," Version 2.1, 16 December 2009, Section 1.2, Exhibit US-110, page 4.

635 China's response to Panel question No. 114, para. 75; comments on United States' response to Panel question Nos. 70-72, 86-96, 115-123, fn. 43.

636 United States' response to Panel question No. 88(b), para. 79.

637 *Ibid.*

logo. In this respect, it would appear that bank cards depicted on the RCBFCC website also conform to the issuer requirements at issue in this dispute. However, we cannot be sure of this as we have not been provided with evidence explaining the origin of this site, its date, or its contents. Nor are we able to verify China's assertion that the RCBFCC is a second EPS supplier operating in China because we do not have access to a version of the website in an official WTO language. Accordingly, we reach no findings in respect of the RCBFCC that would inform or alter our analysis.

Explicit and implicit legal operation of the instruments when considered collectively

7.490 As reflected in our discussion above, China's instruments affect all aspects of the market for bank card transactions and affect all entities in the process, including issuers, acquirers, merchants, EPS suppliers and potentially third parties involved in the handling of bank card transactions. Our analysis above also confirms that requirements imposed by the instruments are mandatory.

7.491 However, as we stated before, with the exception of RMB bank card transactions involving Hong Kong and Macao nationals that travel to China, and Chinese nationals that travel to Hong Kong or Macao, we found that the United States had failed to identify anything in the identified legal instruments that explicitly grants CUP the exclusive privilege to supply EPS in respect of all RMB bank card transactions taking place in China. In addition, the United States did not point to anything in the identified provisions of the instruments at issue that prevents issuers from incorporating logos of other EPS suppliers, in addition to the *Yin Lian*/UnionPay logo, or issuing cards that comply with the rules of other EPS suppliers, so long as those cards also bear the *Yin Lian*/UnionPay logo and are also interoperable with the CUP network. In this sense, despite the fact that the measures are mandatory and may lead to opportunities for CUP that other suppliers do not enjoy, we found that the United States did not identify anything on the face of these instruments that legally prohibits EPS suppliers other than CUP from operating in China's market.

7.492 The United States maintains that, in the event that the instruments individually do not demonstrate that CUP is a sole supplier, collectively, the instruments operate in this way. Primarily, the United States bases its collective assessment on references to the text of the instruments themselves. For instance, in response to question No. 87 from the Panel, the United States argues:

> The logo requirements work in conjunction with one another and are reinforced and complemented by the mandate to conform to CUP's rules and procedures contained in Document No. 76. These requirements work together to reinforce CUP's monopoly over payment card transactions in China by ensuring that only CUP cards can be issued for RMB denominated accounts, that all merchants accept those cards when they are presented for purchases, and that the transactions will be processed in

> accordance with CUP's rules and procedures. Consequently, no other supplier of EPS may conduct domestic RMB transactions in China.[638]

7.493 As set out in our assessment of the instruments individually, we found that none of the instruments, such as Document No. 76, individually supports the proposition that "only CUP cards can be issued for RMB denominated accounts". Having concluded as such, we find no basis to conclude that merely reading the various instruments together, as the United States seems to suggest that we do, leads us to modify our conclusions regarding the United States' assertion. Beyond asserting that particular cited provisions of instruments or requirements "work together", we find no explanation that varies from that provided in the United States' assessment of the instruments individually.[639] In other words, in relying on the texts of the provisions and without more, the United States has not in our view established that the provisions taken together effectively create a monopoly in favour of CUP.

7.494 We recall the United States' view that the stated purpose set out in both CUP's Articles of Association[640] and in the Notification of Approval of CUP's Business Licence [641] "to set up and operate a single nationwide inter-bank card information switching network" and particularly the word "single", confirms that CUP alone may supply EPS services for RMB transactions in China for those cards issued in China. In view of the different meanings of "single" and its use in CUP's foundational documents, we concluded in paragraph 7.461 above that the references to the establishment of such a "single" network does not establish that CUP is the sole supplier of EPS services for RMB bank card transactions in China. Rather, we explained that this statement is consistent with the objective stated elsewhere in Document No. 76 to establish a "countrywide", "interoperable" bank card service in China.

7.495 We note as well that the United States has identified certain instruments that pertain to transactions involving Hong Kong and Macao, in arguing that the legal instruments at issue in this dispute explicitly establish or maintain CUP as a sole supplier in respect of *all* RMB bank card transactions. We explained in paragraph 7.473 above that these instruments do not establish CUP as the sole

---

[638] United States' response to Panel question No. 87, para. 69.

[639] We note that, in response to question No. 115, the United States similarly argues the following:

> The requirement on issuing banks to issue only cards that carry the CUP logo, when combined with the requirements on acquiring banks to be capable of accepting CUP cards (as discussed in response to question No. 92), and the mandate to use CUP processing rules (as discussed in response to question No. 86) establishes CUP's monopoly over RMB denominated cards. No other EPS supplier can establish a competing interoperative bank card network.

United States' response to Panel question No. 115, para. 107. Again, in a statement such as this, which serves as a mere recitation of the requirements individually, we find no support for the conclusion that no other EPS supplier can establish itself in China.

[640] See CUP's Articles of Association, Articles 11 and 12, Exhibit US-20.

[641] Notification of Approval of CUP's Business Licence, Exhibit US-29.

supplier of EPS for *all* domestic RMB bank card transactions occurring throughout China, since the measures are limited in scope to bank card transactions that involve bank cards issued in China and used in Hong Kong or Macao, or alternatively, bank cards issued in Hong Kong or Macao and used in China.

7.496 Finally, we note the United States' refrain that its interpretation of various provisions is "consistent" with the fact that CUP's network is the exclusive network for all RMB bank card transactions. In support of this view, the United States has referred to the fact that certain provisions at issue refer singularly to CUP. For instance, it asserts that Article 5 of Document No. 153 expressly authorizes CUP to establish branches in certain areas of China "in accordance with the company's overall plan to provide bank card information exchange and clearance services". It submits that Article 3.4 of Document No. 129 requires commercial banks to work with CUP to "improve procedures for dealing with errors". It also considers that Articles III, V and VI of Document No. 142 direct CUP to participate with other Chinese institutions in an effort to enhance bank card security. In respect of instances such as these, in our assessment above, we stated how references to CUP, or recognition of CUP's role, do not necessarily confirm that CUP operates exclusively in China. Rather, we indicated that these references may inform a different interpretation. In the absence of further evidence that would eliminate reasonable alternative interpretations, we consider the United States has not met its burden to establish that the instruments operate collectively in this way, so that we should conclude in favour of the United States' interpretation. The Appellate Body in *US – Carbon Steel* has explained:

> The party asserting that another party's municipal law, as such, is inconsistent with relevant treaty obligations bears the burden of introducing evidence as to the scope and meaning of such law to substantiate that assertion. Such evidence will typically be produced in the form of the text of the relevant legislation or legal instruments, which may be supported, as appropriate, by evidence of the consistent application of such laws, the pronouncements of domestic courts on the meaning of such laws, the opinions of legal experts and the writings of recognized scholars. The nature and extent of the evidence required to satisfy the burden of proof will vary from case to case.[642]

7.497 In the absence of evidence other than the texts of the instruments, such as on how the relevant provisions have been applied or opinions of legal experts, we consider the United States has not met its burden to establish that the net, or combined, legal effect of these instruments is to preclude EPS suppliers other than CUP from operating in China's market for RMB bank card transactions.

[642] Appellate Body Report, *US – Carbon Steel*, para. 157.

Technical barriers imposed through the instruments

7.498 The United States has also alleged that the rules and standards imposed under certain of the instruments at issue make it technically difficult for foreign EPS suppliers to operate in the market, thereby effectively "entrenching" CUP as the sole supplier.[643] We explained in paragraph 7.477 above that nothing in the identified provisions in Document Nos. 17, 37, 49, 57, 76, 129, 142, 149 and 153 impose technical barriers that cannot be met by EPS suppliers other than CUP so as to completely prevent those EPS suppliers from entering and operating in the market for RMB bank card transactions in China. In particular, we found that nothing in the identified provisions of the instruments at issue prevents issuers from issuing cards that comply with the rules of other EPS suppliers, so long as those cards are also interoperable with the CUP network.

7.499 In addition to the requirements just mentioned, the United States, asserts that Document No 142 requires that all RMB bank cards incorporate the PBOC 2.0 standard which, in the United States' view, would force EPS suppliers to significantly redesign their chips in order to allow their cards to be used in China. Allegedly, this is because the PBOC 2.0 and EMV chip standards are incompatible.[644] As we noted in paragraph 7.473 above, the United States does not provide any evidence to indicate that the redesign would be so "significant" so as to effectively "lock" EPS suppliers out of the market entirely.[645] Accordingly, in the absence of any evidence that an EPS supplier would not be able to take such steps to make its cards compatible with this standard due to costs or other reasons, or that competing standards are inherently incompatible, we consider that the United States has failed to establish that the need to comply with this standard would ensure that CUP is the sole supplier. We consider this to be the case even when we assess this, in the light of current evidence, together with other elements identified in the instruments.

Economic barriers imposed by the instruments

7.500 Lastly, we address the United States' contention that the instruments in question make it "economically unviable" for any foreign EPS supplier to participate in that market, thereby entrenching CUP as the sole supplier in the market for RMB bank card transactions. The United States argues that, because issuers and acquirers are required to join the CUP network, and pay for that access, it makes "no economic sense" for these entities to additionally pay to use the services of a foreign EPS supplier. In other words, we understand the United States to argue that foreign EPS suppliers have no incentive to enter the market

---

[643] See, e.g. United States' second written submission, paras. 153-165; response to Panel question No. 106, para. 47.

[644] United States' response to Panel question No. 94, para. 97.

[645] *Ibid.*

because potential customers (i.e. issuers and acquirers) would not demand their services since they are obliged already to pay for the services of CUP.

7.501 In response to questions from the Panel following the second substantive meeting[646], the United States referred to the text of CUP's Operating Regulations, which set out one-time membership fees and testing fees. We explained in paragraph 7.291 that CUP's Operating Regulations were not identified in the United States' panel request and do not constitute measures at issue in this dispute. We further explained that the United States failed to establish a link between these regulations and any of the legal instruments under discussion. That concern aside, we observe that the cited provisions of CUP's Operating Regulations provide insufficient information on membership fees and testing fees to enable us to ascertain the additional costs or indeed the total costs that would be incurred by an issuer seeking services from particular EPS suppliers. Even if there are no additional costs, we do not have information on how significant any CUP fees are relative to the profits that issuers and acquirers may earn in the marketplace. Nor has the United States explained what fees participating institutions would incur if they wished to join the networks of other EPS suppliers. In the absence of such evidence, we are unable to gauge whether those costs are significant enough to discourage issuers. Despite asserting that the membership and testing fees have this "discouraging" effect, the United States has not provided evidence that issuers, acquirers or merchants are or would in fact be unwilling to join the network of other EPS suppliers and pay additional fees required for such access. Due to the variety of factors that might influence the decision of an EPS supplier to enter the market for RMB payment transactions, we cannot merely accept the assertion that the mere imposition of the fees in question has had or will have the effect of preventing foreign EPS suppliers from entering and establishing themselves in China. We also note that there is evidence on record that a number of "dual-branded, dual logo" cards exist in the Chinese market, as noted by China[647], which suggests that EPS suppliers have in fact been willing to enter the market in some form. In the absence of other evidence, the fact that these cards exist in the market suggests that the fees have not dissuaded issuers or acquirers from seeking the services of other EPS suppliers.

7.502 We additionally note that, while it is foreseeable that there may be a cost associated with complying with the technical and business standards imposed by Document Nos. 17, 37, 49, 57, 76, 129, 142, 149 and 153, the United States has not provided evidence of the costs of compliance, beyond suggesting that compliance might prove difficult or burdensome. In the absence of concrete evidence, we are again not persuaded that the cost associated with these or other business or technical requirements has dissuaded or would in the future dissuade

[646] See United States' response to Panel question Nos. 86, 94 and 117.

[647] Exhibit CHN-112. See China's comments on the United States' response to Panel question Nos. 70-72, 86-96, 115-123, para. 67 and fn. 38; Exhibit CHN-112.

issuers or acquirers from seeking the services of other EPS suppliers, thereby effectively establishing or maintaining CUP as the only supplier in the market.

7.503 We have pointed out that the instruments in question place CUP in a unique position in the Chinese EPS market. Through the issuer requirements, CUP is effectively assured that every card that might be issued by an EPS supplier other than CUP is effectively a "CUP" card, i.e. a card that is capable of operating over the CUP network. In other words, only dual-logo cards that bear the *Yin Lian*/UnionPay logo in addition to the logo of another EPS supplier may be issued. At the same time, the acquirer requirements oblige all acquiring institutions to be capable of acquiring transactions from cards bearing the *Yin Lian*/UnionPay logo, and terminal equipment requirements mandate that all merchants be capable of accepting these cards. Even though the relevant instruments would not prevent acquirers or merchants from accepting other cards, CUP has a significant foothold in the market. The fact that CUP does not have to invest in promoting its brand to issuing institutions (because issuer requirements are mandatory), and does not have to invest in persuading banks to acquire transactions for the CUP brand (because acquirer requirements are also mandatory) further solidifies CUP's privileged position.

7.504 Nevertheless, in the absence of specific legal provisions designating a company as the single supplier in a market, the United States in our view needs to provide evidence to sustain the assertion that the instruments produce economic effects that are so significant that they preclude other EPS suppliers from operating in the market.[648] In the present case, we have no evidence, e.g. economic analyses of profitability, price-cost margins, or demand elasticity, including in comparison with other markets, that would allow us to assess whether indeed the instruments at issue make it economically unviable for other EPS suppliers to establish themselves and operate in China. We note that parties in previous disputes have submitted economic analyses and econometric studies when alleging actual economic and trade effects of particular measures, and to support allegations that those effects are attributable to the measures.[649] Additional information on the conduct of CUP (e.g. price discrimination or evidence that CUP charges different customers different prices for the same

[648] In competition policy enquiries, for instance, monopoly power is found to exist if (i) the firm has a high share of a relevant market and (ii) there are entry barriers – perhaps ones created by the company's conduct itself – that allow the company to exercise substantial market power for an appreciable period of time. See U.S. Department of Justice (2008) "Competition and Monopoly: Single-Firm Conduct Under Section 2 of the Sherman Act". In assessing the existence of a monopoly, competition authorities typically evaluate a company's market share and the durability of market power, i.e. the ability to price substantially above the competitive level for a significant period of time without erosion of the position by new entrants.

[649] For instance, the panel in *US – COOL* noted in this respect that the function of panels does not exclude, but may in fact require, the review of economic and econometric evidence and arguments. See Panel Reports, *US – COOL*, para. 7.452 and paras. 7.507-7.546. See also *Thailand – Cigarettes (Philippines)*, paras. 136-138; and *Philippines – Distilled Spirits*, para. 7.55, 7.109-7.113; and Appellate Body Report, *Thailand – Cigarettes (Philippines)*, paras. 136-138.

service) could have assisted us in our analysis, but no such information was submitted. We are aware that relevant data may be difficult to obtain. However, given the lack of concrete evidence, we are unable to conclude that CUP is the sole supplier. Assertion without more is simply not enough.

Conclusions on collective assessment

7.505 Accordingly, for the reasons set out here and above, we find that the United States has not substantiated its claim that the instruments at issue collectively mandate the use of CUP or establish CUP as the sole supplier of EPS for all domestic RMB bank card transactions. The United States carries the burden to demonstrate that the measures operate together to establish or maintain CUP as the exclusive supplier. That is, the United States must demonstrate that CUP is the only supplier permitted to operate in the Chinese market. It is not clear to us, in the absence of any concrete evidence, that the consequence of the instruments in question is to reduce the number of suppliers in the market to one. As we explained, in our view, the United States has failed to demonstrate that the instruments impose a legal barrier to entry, explicit or otherwise. We also found that the United States has failed to demonstrate that the technical requirements that must be met to operate in China preclude other EPS suppliers from operating in the market. Finally, we explained that we did not have sufficient evidence before us to accept the United States' allegation that the operation of the instruments makes it "economically unviable" to enter the market, such that no other EPS supplier would be willing to enter the market.

7.506 In reaching this conclusion, we are uncertain whether CUP currently operates in the market as the sole supplier for RMB bank card transactions. Although it is possible that this is the case, including for reasons unrelated to the instruments we have addressed above, we are not persuaded based on the arguments of the United States and the evidence before the Panel that the instruments in question establish or maintain CUP as the only EPS supplier in the market.

(f) Overall conclusions on the evaluation of the existence of the measures at issue

7.507 The Panel concluded above, as reflected in various legal instruments, as follows that:

(a) China, through Document Nos. 37, 57 and 129, imposes requirements on issuers that bank cards issued in China bear the *Yin Lian*/UnionPay logo, and furthermore, China, through Document Nos. 17, 37, 57, 76 and 129, requires that issuers become members of the CUP network, and that the bank cards they issue in China meet certain uniform business specifications and technical standards;

(b) China, through Document Nos. 37 and 153, imposes requirements that all terminals (ATMs, merchant processing devices and POS terminals) in China that are part of the national bank card inter-bank processing network be capable of accepting all bank cards bearing the *Yin Lian*/UnionPay logo;

(c) China, through Document No. 153, imposes requirements on acquirers to post the *Yin Lian*/UnionPay logo and furthermore, China, through Document Nos. 37, 76 and 153, imposes requirements that acquirers join the CUP network and comply with uniform business standards and technical specifications of inter-bank interoperability, and that terminal equipment operated or provided by acquirers be capable of accepting bank cards bearing the *Yin Lian*/UnionPay logo;

(d) China, through Document Nos. 16, 8 and 254, imposes requirements that CUP and no other EPS supplier handle the clearing of certain RMB bank card transactions that involve either an RMB bank card issued in China and used in Hong Kong or Macao, or an RMB bank card issued in Hong Kong or Macao that is used in China in an RMB-denominated transaction;

(e) The United States failed to establish that China, through Document Nos. 37, 57, 16, 8, 219, 254, 103, 153, 149, 53, 49, 129, 76, 17 and/or 142, imposes requirements that mandate the use of CUP or establish CUP as the sole supplier of EPS for all domestic transactions denominated and paid in RMB; and

(f) Having regard to our assessment of the instruments in connection with the sole supplier requirement, the United States failed to establish that China, through Document Nos. 37, 57, 153, 219 and/or 76, imposes broad prohibitions on the use of "non-CUP" cards for cross-region or inter-bank transactions.

F. The United States' Claims Under Article XVI of the GATS

7.508 The United States argues that the six alleged requirements imposed by China on the supply of EPS are inconsistent with Article XVI of the GATS. The United States submits that China made mode 1 and mode 3[650] commitments in its Schedule covering the supply of EPS, wherein China committed not to maintain any limitations on the number of foreign EPS suppliers. Through the imposition of these six requirements, the United States asserts, China established and maintains a monopoly structure to ensure that CUP is the exclusive supplier of EPS for all RMB bank card transactions in China whenever a bank card is issued

[650] The Panel will use the term "mode 3" to refer to the supply of a service that is "by a service supplier of one Member, through commercial presence in the territory of any other Member", as provided for in Article I:2(c) of the GATS.

in China and used in China.[651] It further argues that the measures are not justified by any limitations, conditions or qualifications on market access in China's Schedule. As a result of this, the United States considers that the measures at issue are inconsistent with China's obligations under Articles XVI:1 and XVI:2(a) of the GATS.[652]

7.509 China argues that the United States has failed to prove that China made relevant market access and national treatment commitments under subsector (d) in relation to mode 1 and mode 3, and therefore requests the Panel to dismiss the United States' claims. According to China, claims under Article XVI are limited to the sectors and subsectors in which the responding Member has made market access commitments.[653] Even if the Panel were to conclude that China made specific commitments in respect of the particular services and suppliers at issue, China contends that the United States has failed to demonstrate that the alleged measures maintain or adopt limitations on the number of service suppliers in the form of monopolies or exclusive service suppliers to prove its claim under Article XVI of the GATS.[654]

7.510 Article XVI of the GATS, entitled "Market Access", provides in relevant part:

> 1. With respect to market access through the modes of supply identified in Article I, each Member shall accord services and service suppliers of any other Member treatment no less favourable than that provided for under the terms, limitations and conditions agreed and specified in its Schedule.
>
> 2. In sectors where market-access commitments are undertaken, the measures which a Member shall not maintain or adopt either on the basis of a regional subdivision or on the basis of its entire territory, unless otherwise specified in its Schedule, are defined as:
>
> > (a) limitations on the number of service suppliers whether in the form of numerical quotas, monopolies, exclusive service suppliers or the requirements of an economic needs test

7.511 The Panel recalls that in the United States' view, the measures at issue are inconsistent with Articles XVI:1 and XVI:2(a) of the GATS. In the specific context of Article XVI:2(a), the Appellate Body in *US – Gambling* explained that a complaining party must do two things to establish a *prima facie* case of

[651] United States' second written submission, paras. 137-143; see also response to China's request for a preliminary ruling, Sections V.B to V.I; first written submission, paras. 12, 31, 37-72, and 79-92; opening statement at the first meeting of the Panel, para. 43; response to Panel question Nos. 4, 6, 17 and 23.

[652] See, e.g. United States' first written submission, paras. 37-40 and 70-72.

[653] China's first written submission, paras. 123 and 124; second written submission, para. 81.

[654] China's second written submission, paras. 90-102.

violation. First, it must establish that a responding party has undertaken relevant market access commitments in its GATS Schedule and thereafter, it must "identify[] with supporting evidence, how the challenged laws constitute impermissible 'limitations'" falling within the meaning of one of the subparagraphs of Article XVI:2.[655] This same approach was followed by the panel in *China – Publications and Audiovisual Products*.[656]

7.512 We see no reason to depart from this approach and therefore, we begin by addressing whether China made market access commitments under mode 1 or mode 3 in respect of the services at issue. Only if we determine that China has made a commitment will we consider whether the requirements at issue impose limitations that are inconsistent with Article XVI of the GATS.

1. *Whether China has made mode 1 or mode 3 market access commitments covering the supply of EPS*

7.513 Consistent with Appellate Body guidance, we begin our analysis under Article XVI by determining whether China has undertaken relevant market access commitments in its GATS Schedule for subsector (d) and the two modes of supply relied on by the United States, i.e. modes 1 and 3. As China's Schedule contains different entries for these two modes, we first address China's mode 1 market access entry.

(a) Mode 1 commitments

7.514 The United States argues that China has undertaken mode 1 market access commitments with respect to subsector (d) in its Schedule. Under mode 1, the word "Unbound" is followed by the qualifying phrase "except for the following," which in turn is further elaborated by two sentences that describe elements of the services within subsector (d). According to the United States, China's mode 1 commitment must be understood as recognizing that "payment and money transmission" services include aspects of "provision and transfer of financial information" and "advisory, intermediation and other auxiliary services" to the extent that such aspects are integral to the core service, and that such aspects are properly classified within "payment and money transmission" services and not in subsector (k) or (l). In the United States' view, the fact that there are elements of "provision and transfer of financial information, and financial data processing" and "auxiliary, intermediation, and advisory services" embedded in the core "payment and money transmission" services is not inconsistent with the principle that sectors must be scheduled in a mutually exclusive manner.[657]

---

[655] Appellate Body Report, *US – Gambling*, para. 143.

[656] Panel Report, *China – Publications and Audiovisual Products*, para. 7.1354.

[657] United States' first written submission, para. 41; and response to Panel question Nos. 45, para. 118 and 46(b), para. 127.

7.515 China recalls its view that the services at issue are not properly classifiable under subsector (d) of its Schedule. China submits that its market access entry for subsectors (a) through (f) repeats, verbatim, the descriptions of subsectors (k) and (l), which appear under the heading of "[o]ther financial services as listed below".[658] In China's view, the identical language in the same Schedule cannot have two different meanings. The meaning of this portion of China's Schedule is that China undertook no market access commitments under mode 1 with respect to subsectors (a) through (f), including subsector (d).[659]

7.516 China states that there are two possible ways of reading the "except" language in the mode 1 market access entry. The first is as a cross-reference to China's mode 1 market access commitment for subsectors (k) and (l). The second is as a description of the exception to China's unbound market access entry for subsectors (a) through (f) in mode 1. According to China, the "embedded services" theory proposed by the United States is contrary to the principle of mutual exclusivity and runs afoul of the principle of effective treaty interpretation. China argues that, in order to give effect to its unbound market access entry for subsectors (a) through (f), it is critically important to distinguish between those activities that are unbound in mode 1 and those activities that fall within the exception. If the United States has met its burden of proving that the services at issue in this dispute are classifiable under subsector (d), then, in China's view, the United States cannot simultaneously maintain that China undertook mode 1 market access commitments in respect of those services. For China, the services at issue cannot be covered in subsector (d), and also in subsectors (k) and (l).[660]

7.517 Australia submits that the commitment at issue is unclear, but is not unbound.[661] According to the European Union, China is unbound under mode 1 for subsectors (a) to (f), except for parts of the subsectors described in the two hyphens; China has then committed the actual service of "provision and transfer of financial information" and "advisory, intermediation and other auxiliary services" as stand-alone services under subsectors (k) and (l). The European Union is of the view that, if China had intended this entry to be a cross-reference, it should have been explicitly set out in the Schedule.[662] Guatemala submits that the two subsectors listed, respectively, under the mode 1 entry at issue and under subsectors (k) and (l) cover the same services, but refer to

[658] China notes that there is a minor difference consisting of a plural form in the mode 1 entry, which refers to "suppliers of other financial services" while subsector (k) states "by supplier of other financial services". In China's view, the latter appears to be a typographical error. China's response to Panel question No. 50, fn. 50.

[659] China's first written submission, paras. 126 and 127.

[660] China's response to Panel question No. 50(a), para. 76; and second written submission, paras. 58-62.

[661] Australia's third-party response to Panel question No. 11.

[662] European Union's third-party response to Panel question No. 4, para. 13; and third-party response to Panel question No. 11, para. 34.

different commitments. According to Guatemala, there is no cross-reference among the subsectors.[663] Japan is of the view that, by inscribing "unbound except for the following", China intended to make no commitment and that the question to be addressed is whether EPS correspond to "provision and transfer of financial information [...]".[664] Korea submits that the two subsectors committed under mode 1 of subsector (d) relate only to the services described under the latter subsector. In contrast, subsectors (k) and (l) are separate and distinct subsectors which are not confined to subsector (d). For Korea, China's cross-reference argument is misplaced because subsectors (a) to (f) on the one hand and subsectors (k) and (l) on the other are found under different subheadings.[665]

7.518 The relevant section of China's Schedule is reproduced below (emphasis added):

[...]	
B. Banking and Other Financial Services (excluding insurance and securities) Banking services as listed below: (a) ... (b) ... (c) ... *(d) All payment and money transmission services, including credit, charge and debit cards, travellers cheques and bankers drafts(including import and export settlement);* (e) ... (f) ...	*(1) Unbound except for the following:* - *Provision and transfer of financial information, and financial data processing and related software by suppliers of other financial services;* - *Advisory, intermediation and other auxiliary financial services on all activities listed in subparagraphs (a) through (k), including credit reference and analysis, investment and portfolio research and advice, advice on acquisitions and on corporate restructuring and strategy.* (2) [. ..] (3) [...] (4) [...]

[663] Guatemala's third-party response to Panel question No. 4, para. 20; and third-party response to Panel question No. 11, para. 36.

[664] Japan's third-party response to Panel question No. 23, para. 3.

[665] Korea's third-party response to Panel question No. 4; and third-party response to Panel question No. 11.

- Motor vehicle financing by non-bank financial institutions	(1) Unbound except for the following: - Provision and transfer of financial information, and financial data processing and related software by suppliers of other financial services; - Advisory, intermediation and other auxiliary financial services on all activities listed in subparagraphs (a) through (k), including credit reference and analysis, investment and portfolio research and advice, advice on acquisitions and on corporate restructuring and strategy. (2) [...] (3) [...] (4) [...]
- Other financial services as listed below: *(k) Provision and transfer of financial information, and financial data processing and related software by supplier of other financial services;* *(l) Advisory, intermediation and other auxiliary financial services on all activities listed in subparagraphs (a) through (k), including credit reference and analysis, investment and portfolio research and advice, advice on acquisitions and on corporate restructuring and strategy.* - Securities	 *(1) None* (2) [...] (3) [...] (4) [...] | (1) [...] (2) [...] (3) [...] (4) [...]

7.519 The Panel notes that the market access entry under mode 1 contains the term "Unbound", which is qualified by the words "except for the following". In GATS schedules, the term "Unbound" means that, for a given sector and mode of supply, a Member undertakes no commitment.[666] The qualifying phrase "except for the following" suggests that there follows an exception to the general

[666] Paragraph 46 of the 2001 Scheduling Guidelines stipulates: "..., the Member remains free in a given sector and mode of supply to introduce or maintain measures inconsistent with market access or national treatment. In this situation, the Member must record in the appropriate column the word: UNBOUND. [...]." See also paragraph 27 of the 1993 Scheduling Guidelines. Moreover, in *US – Gambling*, the Appellate Body, when examining the term "None" scheduled in the entry at issue in that dispute, found that "[t]his notation is the opposite of the notation 'Unbound', which means that a Member undertakes *no* specific commitment." Appellate Body Report, *US – Gambling*, fn. 257 (emphasis original).

"Unbound" entry. The expression "Unbound except for the following" is then followed by the descriptions of two services listed in the two hyphens. These services are (i) "[p]rovision and transfer of financial information, and financial data processing and related software by suppliers of other financial services"; and (ii) "[a]dvisory, intermediation and other auxiliary financial services on all activities listed in subparagraphs (a) through (k), including credit reference and analysis, investment and portfolio research and advice, advice on acquisitions and on corporate restructuring and strategy". The descriptions of these two services are nearly identical to the descriptions of subsectors (k) and (l) that, in the case of China's Schedule, appear under the subheading "[o]ther financial services as listed below"; the only difference is that the description in the first hyphen under the mode 1 entry at issue refers to "suppliers" in the plural, whereas the description in subsector (k) uses the singular form of the same term.[667] The mode 1 market access commitment assumed by China for subsectors (k) and (l) is full ("None").

7.520 The Panel observes that WTO Members commonly use the inscription "Unbound except for" in their GATS schedules. China has made use of it in other sectors listed in its Schedule.[668] Moreover, China employs this inscription for its mode 4 commitments as well, as have most other WTO Members.[669] What is particular about and sets apart the mode 1 entry in question, however, is the fact that the two services referred to are textually nearly identical to subsectors (k) and (l) for which China has undertaken specific commitments. Pursuant to Article 31 of the Vienna Convention, the Panel will examine the ordinary meaning of the text of the relevant mode 1 entry in its context and in the light of the object and purpose of the GATS and the WTO Agreement.

7.521 We turn first to an examination of the ordinary meaning of the terms used to describe the services that fall within the first hyphen. The description reads: "[p]rovision and transfer of financial information, and financial data processing and related software *by suppliers of other financial services*" (emphasis added). As there is no comma after "related software", the question arises whether the phrase "by suppliers of other financial services" relates only to the phrase "financial data processing and related software" which immediately precedes the reference to suppliers of other financial services, or whether that reference also

---

[667] We agree with China that the singular form of the term "supplier" in subsector (k) appears to be a typographical error (see fn. 658 above). We note, first, that this singular form results in a grammatically incorrect phrase. In addition, subsector (xv) of the GATS Annex on Financial Services, on which China said its Schedule is based (China's first written submission, para. 80), refers to "suppliers" in the plural. The French and Spanish versions of subsector (xv) of the Annex on Financial Services also use the plural form for this particular term, as do the French and Spanish versions of China's Schedule.

[668] See, for instance, China's mode 1 commitments with respect to "Retailing services (excluding tobacco)" ("Unbound except for mail order") and "Environmental services" ("Unbound except for environmental consultation services").

[669] We also recall in this regard paragraph 45 of the 2001 Scheduling Guidelines and paragraph 26 of the 1993 Scheduling Guidelines.

qualifies the phrase "provision and transfer of financial information". In addressing this question, we note that the description of subsector (xv) of the GATS Annex , on which China's Schedule is based, does not contain a comma after the equivalent of "related software". However, the equally authentic French and Spanish versions of subsector (xv) of the Annex, which are relevant context for interpreting China's Schedule, shed useful light on this issue. In both of these versions, a comma has been added after the phrase "related software".[670] The French and Spanish versions of China's Schedule also include that comma. Moreover, we fail to discern a plausible rationale for why the services described as "financial data processing and related software" would warrant a reference to the suppliers of such services that was not equally warranted in the case of the services described as "provision and transfer of financial information". For these reasons, we consider that the phrase "by suppliers of other financial services" in the mode 1 entry at issue qualifies both the phrase "financial data processing and related software" and the phrase "provision and transfer of financial information".

7.522 We turn now to the word "other" in the phrase "by suppliers of other financial services". The ordinary meaning of the word "other" suggests that the services provided by the relevant suppliers are different from the services listed in the sectoral column with respect to subsectors (a) to (f).[671] In other words, a distinction appears to be made between two different categories of financial services suppliers: (i) the suppliers of financial services listed under subsectors (a) to (f) in the sectoral column of the Schedule, and (ii) the suppliers of "other financial services" which undertake the "provision and transfer of financial information, and financial data processing and related software" to other suppliers of financial services. If the phrase "provision and transfer of financial information […]" concerned suppliers providing the financial services at issue in subsectors (a) to (f), or components thereof, it would be incongruous to refer to a category of suppliers supplying "other" financial services. Conversely, if there were an intention to refer to services other than those classifiable under subsectors (a) to (f), it would be necessary to make this intention clear, and the word "other" would serve that purpose. In our view, therefore, a textual analysis of the entry in the first hyphen supports the view that "suppliers of other financial services" supply services that are not simply integral components of the services listed in the sectoral column (or, to use the United States' terms, an element "embedded" in a "core" service), but rather services that are separate and distinct from the services classifiable in subsectors (a) to (f).

[670] The French version reads "[f]ourniture et transfert d'informations financières, et traitement de données financières et logiciels y relatifs, par les fournisseurs d'autres services financiers", and the Spanish version "[s]uministro y transferencia de información financiera, y procesamiento de datos financieros y soporte lógico con ellos relacionado, por proveedores de otros servicios financieros".

[671] "Other" is defined, *inter alia*, as "[e]xisting besides or distinct from that or those already specified or implied; further, additional. […]", *Shorter Oxford English Dictionary*, Vol. 2, p. 2035.

7.523 We now examine the ordinary meaning of the terms used to describe the services that fall within the second hyphen, "[a]dvisory, intermediation *and other auxiliary financial services on all activities listed in subparagraphs (a) through (k)*, including credit reference and analysis, investment and portfolio research and advice, advice on acquisitions and on corporate restructuring and strategy" (emphasis added). First, that the reference to "and other auxiliary ... services" suggests to us that the services covered in this hyphen are considered "auxiliary". The ordinary meaning of the word "auxiliary"[672] indicates that these services are separate and different from the services falling within subsectors (a) to (f), rather than "embedded"[673] in them. Furthermore, the second hyphen uses the phrase "auxiliary financial services *on all activities listed in subparagraphs (a) through (k)*" (emphasis added). This clear textual distinction between, on the one hand, the services listed in the sectoral column and, on the other hand, services that are "auxiliary" to them reinforces our view that auxiliary services cannot properly be considered to be the same as the services described in the sectoral column under subsectors (a) to (f), or integral components thereof. As an additional matter, it is noteworthy that the second hyphen refers to services which are "auxiliary" to all activities "listed in subparagraphs *(a) through (k)*" (emphasis added). China's sectoral column concerning "banking services" lists only subsectors (a) through (f), not (a) through (k). If the second hyphen were intended to set out services that are "embedded" in their entirety in services listed in the sectoral column with respect to subsectors (a) to (f), it would have referred to "activities listed in subparagraphs (a) through (f)", for China has not listed any other subsectors under "[b]anking services".[674]

7.524 Therefore, our analysis of the ordinary meaning of the terms used to describe the services under the mode 1 entry at issue does not allow us to conclude that these services are "elements" of "all payment and money transmission services" in subsector (d), as contended by the United States. It suggests, to the contrary, that these services are separate and distinct from the services listed in the sectoral column with respect to subsectors (a) to (f). To that extent, the text in the two hyphens is consistent with the view that this entry refers to the full market access commitment on mode 1 for subsectors (k) and (l).[675]

7.525 We turn now to an examination of relevant contextual elements, which include the remainder of China's Schedule and the Annex. The first element we take note of is China's sectoral commitments under mode 4, which generally read

---

672 "Auxiliary" is defined, *inter alia*, as "[h]elpful; giving support or succour; [...] Subsidiary, additional, ancillary; [...]", *Shorter Oxford English Dictionary*, Vol, 1, p. 158.

673 "Embed" (verb), is defined, *inter alia*, as "[p]lace or secure within something else, esp. within a larger or firmer entity; cause to be wholly contained within." *Ibid.*, p. 816.

674 While the reference to "subparagraphs (a) through (k)" may reflect an error, we must not lightly assume that this is the case. Neither party has suggested that the second hyphen contains an error.

675 China's response to Panel question No. 50(a), para. 76.

"[u]nbound, except as indicated in horizontal commitments". These inscriptions are found under both the market access and national treatment columns, and refer to the horizontal section of China's Schedule where the scope of China's mode 4 commitments is defined.[676] Hence, these mode 4 entries tell us that, as a general matter, China's Schedule does contain cross-references to another part of the same Schedule. We recognize, however, that the mode 1 entry at issue does not specifically refer to commitments undertaken under subsectors (k) and (l).[677]

7.526 Continuing our contextual analysis, we note the United States' argument that the limitations inscribed in the market access and national treatment columns "cannot change the scope of the sector description itself".[678] Hence, according to the United States:

> China's mode 1 commitment must be understood as recognizing that 'payment and money transmission' services include aspects of 'provision and transfer of financial information' and 'advisory, intermediation and other auxiliary services' to the extent that such aspects are integral to the core service, and that such aspects are properly classified within 'payment and money transmission' services and not in subsector (k) or (l).[679]

7.527 The Panel observes that subsectors (k) and (l) in China's Schedule are relevant contextual elements for the interpretation of the mode 1 entry at issue. As noted above, the descriptions of these two subsectors are almost identical to the descriptions of the services in the two hyphens. Thus, although the United States submits that limitations in the market access and national treatment columns cannot modify the scope of the sector description, it appears to us that the United States' proposed approach to interpreting the excepted language in the mode 1 entry at issue would do precisely that. By carving out elements of the services listed in the two hyphens on the grounds that these elements are "aspects" of the services described under subsector (d), the United States' approach would correspondingly remove these same elements from subsectors (k) and (l) which are committed in the sectoral column of China's Schedule.

7.528 We now consider the United States' view that there are "elements" of the services listed in the two hyphens that are "embedded" in the "core" "payment and money transmission services". In considering this argument, we determine first whether it is possible to identify clearly, on the one hand, the "core" service

---

676 As noted above, the technique of cross-referencing mode 4 commitments is acknowledged in the 2001 Scheduling Guidelines. See fn. 669 above.

677 We note, however, that the services described in the second hyphen reference "activities listed in subparagraphs (a) through (k)"

678 United States' response to Panel question No. 45, para. 118; second written submission para. 107.

679 United States' response to Panel question No. 45, para. 118. Therefore, according to the United States, the services in the two hyphens are "an integral part" of the provision of "payment and money transmission services", while subsectors (k) and (l) encompass services "that facilitate but are not integral to" the provision of "payment and money transmission services". *Ibid.*, paras. 118 and 119.

and, on the other hand, the "elements" of, respectively, "provision and transfer of financial information" and "advisory, intermediation and other auxiliary services" that, according to the United States, are included in the "core" service under subsector (d). We note that, in a response to a question by the Panel, the United States provided a chart illustrating, for each of the five components referred to in its panel request, the "aspects of EPS" which, according to the United States, are covered by the mode 1 market access commitment.[680] In the United States' view, these "aspects" include such elements as the provision of the underlying physical network and wiring; fraud protection; authorization routing, authorization decision solutions, global clearing management, exception handling solutions, automated calculation of the net financial position of a sender/receiver of financial transactions based on the desired currency and settlement service option selected by each party; and, the creation and execution of the transfer order for each financial institution participating in the value day payment activity. Moreover, when asked by the Panel to indicate those services that would fall within subsector (d), but would fall *outside* the mode 1 commitment, the United States cited the establishment of settlement accounts as "an example of an aspect of the service at the 'back end' of EPS processing ... that falls outside China's mode 1 commitment".[681] As evidenced by this response, the United States was able to provide one example of what it considers to be a "core" service that falls within subsector (d), but falls outside of the two services described under mode 1. This contrasts with its detailed description of the "elements" of the two services that, according to the United States, are "embedded" in the "core" service.

7.529 In the Panel's view, these responses by the United States reveal the difficulty entailed by the United States' approach. It is rather counter-intuitive that, under the taxonomy provided by the United States, the "core" appears largely to coincide with the "embedded elements". In other words, were we to accept the United States' position, subsector (d) would appear to be composed overwhelmingly of the services described in subsectors (k) and (l).[682] Moreover, in the case of subsector (d), these services would be "integral to a core service", while, in the case of subsectors (k) and (l), the same services would be supplied "independently", as the United States put it.[683] In our view, the result of the approach proposed by the United States is difficult to reconcile with the

[680] United States' response to Panel question No. 46(a), para. 121.

[681] United States' response to Panel question No. 77, para. 43.

[682] We recall that the United States' panel request (WT/DS413/2) also referred to subsectors (k) and (l) of China's Schedule. However, in the course of these proceedings, the United States did not put forward any claims on the basis of commitments in these subsectors.

[683] As we explained above in Section VII.D, para. 7.188, the mere fact that separate suppliers provide one particular component of an integrated service does not in itself imply that that component should be classified as a distinct service. While in our view a composite service may consist of component services supplied by one or more supplier(s), all these components belong to the "integrated" service and are classified as such. To that extent, those same component services are not classifiable under other subsectors even when supplied "independently".

Appellate Body's clarification that a specific service cannot fall within two different sectors or subsectors.[684]

7.530 Furthermore, in response to a question from the Panel, the United States submits that the GATS framework itself recognizes the interrelated nature of financial services. According to the United States, this "interrelated nature" is illustrated by the fact that the GATS Annex on Financial Services covers (i) services that are "auxiliary" to "the activities listed in subparagraphs (v) through (xv)" in subsector (xvi), as well as (ii) "provision and transfer of financial information" provided by suppliers of "other financial services" in subsector (xv).[685] In the United States' view, "whether an aspect of a service falls into one of these separate subsectors as an independent service or whether it falls into one of the other subsectors depends on how central that aspect is to the provision of the service described".[686]

7.531 We recall that the Annex is relevant context for the interpretation of China's Schedule and that subsectors (xv) and (xvi) of the Annex correspond to, respectively, subsectors (k) and (l) in China's Schedule. We agree that various financial services subsectors listed in the Annex may be "interrelated" in practice. As we have said, the reading proposed by the United States is in our view difficult to reconcile with the principle that sectors and subsectors must be mutually exclusive. In view of this principle, the fact that the financial services described in subsectors (xv) and (xvi) of the Annex may be "interrelated" with other financial services in the Annex does not mean that they can be properly classified as those other services. By the same token, it may well be that the services in subsectors (k) and (l) in China's Schedule are "interrelated" with the services committed under subsectors (a) to (f). However, this does not mean that the services in subsectors (k) and (l) – or aspects thereof – are classifiable under subsectors (a) to (f). Furthermore, the United States has not provided a principled basis for evaluating how "central" an aspect of a service is to the provision of a particular service described in a schedule, nor has it explained what degree of centrality would warrant classifying that aspect as one or other service.

7.532 The United States additionally refers to paragraph 8 of the Understanding on Commitments in Financial Services in support of its view that a service may include elements of "provision and transfer of financial information, and financial data processing".[687] According to the United States, this provision

---

[684] The Appellate Body found that "[b]ecause a Member's obligations regarding a particular service depend on the specific commitments that it has made with respect to the sector or subsector within which that service falls, a specific service cannot fall within two different sectors or Subsectors. In other words, *the sectors and subsectors in a Member's Schedule must be mutually exclusive*." Appellate Body Report, *US – Gambling*, para. 180 (emphasis added).

[685] United States' response to Panel question No. 46(b), para. 128.

[686] Ibid.

[687] Paragraph 8 of the Understanding on Commitment in Financial Services stipulates: "No Member shall take measures that prevent transfers of information or the processing of financial information,

means that "the provision and transfer of financial information and data processing is central to the supply of many different financial services, and, according to the Understanding, signatory WTO Members cannot frustrate their commitments by, for example, blocking the ability to communicate and process information."[688] We observe, first, that, as acknowledged by the United States, China is not a party to the Understanding.[689] Hence, paragraph 8 of the Understanding is not applicable to China. Second, we do not question that, in many, if not most cases, "transfers of information or the processing of financial information, including transfers of data by electronic means" may be an important part in the provision of financial services. However, even if paragraph 8 of the Understanding on Financial Services were relevant to this dispute, we do not see how this provision could detract from our interpretation, which is based on the text of the entry in the first hyphen and which led us to the conclusion that "suppliers of other financial services" supply services that are separate and distinct from the services classifiable in subsectors (a)-(f).

7.533 To sum up our analysis so far, we note that, unlike China's mode 4 commitments, the mode 1 commitment at issue does not refer explicitly to another section of China's Schedule. Our textual analysis led us to the view that the services described in the two hyphens are distinct from the services listed in the sectoral column under subsector (a) through (f), and that they involve different suppliers. Therefore, the services referred to in the two hyphens cannot constitute "elements" of the services encompassed under subsector (d). Furthermore, the interpretation proposed by the United States is difficult to reconcile with the principle that a specific service must not fall within two different sectors or subsectors.

7.534 Based on the preceding analysis, we consider that the mode 1 entry at issue does not result in a market access commitment under mode 1 for "all payment and money transmission services". In our assessment, China's mode 1 market access entry concerning subsectors (a) to (f) should be understood instead as referencing China's mode 1 market access commitment for subsectors (k) and (l), which, as noted above, is fully bound. To our minds, the meaning and effect of this entry is to indicate that, although there are no mode 1 commitments for subsectors (a) to (f), there are commitments under mode 1 for services falling within subsectors (k) and (l), which services are often provided in connection with services classified under subsectors (a) to (f). In other words, it is our view that in this particular instance, the phrase "except for the following" has not been used to undertake a market access commitment under

including transfers of data by electronic means, or that, subject to importation rules consistent with international agreements, prevent transfers of equipment, where such transfers of information, processing of financial information or transfers of equipment are necessary for the conduct of the ordinary business of a financial service supplier".

[688] United States response to Panel question No. 46(b), para. 131; and second written submission, paras. 114 and 115.

[689] Ibid.

mode 1 for subsectors (a) to (f). Rather, it serves to alert the reader to other relevant content in China's Schedule – in this case, the full mode 1 commitment undertaken by China under subsectors (k) and (l) of its Schedule.

7.535 Our interpretation of the mode 1 entry at issue must also be considered in the light of the object and purpose of the GATS and the WTO Agreement. We identified the relevant object and purpose of the agreements in Section VII.D.2(c) above. We consider that our conclusion that the entry at issue references China's market access entry commitments for subsectors (k) and (l) is not inconsistent with the object and purpose of those two agreements. In giving the words contained in the two hyphens the meaning they can be reasonably understood to bear in their context, our interpretation ensures security and predictability of specific commitments.

7.536 From a strictly legal perspective, it may seem unusual to reference services classifiable under subsectors (k) and (l) in an entry that concerns subsectors (a) to (f). However, as explained above, we do find it difficult to read the mode 1 entry at issue as creating a market access commitment for subsector (d). We consider that, on balance, our reading is the better reading of this particular entry. As we have said, the services listed in the two hyphens are often supplied in connection with services listed under subsectors (a) to (f). To that extent and taking a broader perspective, it is not unreasonable to read in the words used in their context a desire on the part of the negotiators to clarify that, although China was not prepared to make any mode 1 market access commitments for services classifiable under subsectors (a) to (f), it did make unqualified market access commitments for other relevant services.

7.537 We consider that our interpretation of the mode 1 entry at issue pursuant to Article 31 of the Vienna Convention does not leave the meaning ambiguous or obscure, nor does it lead to a result which is manifestly absurd or unreasonable. Accordingly, we do not find it necessary to resort to supplementary means of interpretation under Article 32 of the Vienna Convention. We also note that the parties did not provide any evidence of the negotiating history that could help to confirm our interpretation of this entry.[690]

7.538 Based on the above considerations, we conclude that China has no market access commitments under mode 1 with respect to the services encompassed under subsector (d) of its Schedule.

(b) Mode 3 commitments

7.539 The Panel now examines what market access commitments China has undertaken in subsector (d) and mode 3, and if so, whether these commitments apply to EPS suppliers of other WTO Members. The Panel notes that China's

[690] See notably China's response to Panel question No. 50(b), para. 79.

Schedule contains a relevant entry in the column entitled "Limitations on market access".[691]

7.540 The United States argues that under the market access commitments for mode 3, China scheduled certain limitations regarding geographic coverage, potential clients, and licensing, all of which were to be eliminated within five years after China's accession, i.e. in December 2006. Therefore, since December 2006, China's Schedule provides no market access limitations under mode 3 with respect to EPS.[692]

7.541 China argues that its market access commitments for subsector (d) and mode 3 are limited to foreign financial institutions (FFIs) and did not expire five years after China's accession. As regards the heading "clients" in its mode 3 market access entry, China submits that no limitations expired in December 2006. Rather, it is on that date that China's commitment became effective. China argues that as of that date, FFIs were to "be permitted" to provide relevant services "to all Chinese clients". China made no commitment to permit entities that are not FFIs to provide these services, at any point in time. Referring to another heading in its mode 3 entry concerning "licensing", China observes that its commitment to eliminate existing non-prudential measures was similarly limited to FFIs. And with regard to the qualifications for engaging in local currency business that are also specified under the heading "licensing", China intended that only FFIs meeting these qualifications would engage in local currency business.[693]

7.542 China notes that the term "financial institutions" has been widely used by various WTO Members in their Schedules, without a definition of the term.[694] China further points out that its mode 3 market access entry pervasively refers to FFIs, and that it does not refer to "financial service suppliers" or "foreign service suppliers".[695] China submits that consistent with the principle of effective treaty interpretation, this difference in terminology must be given effect. According to China, the ordinary meaning of the term "FFIs" is narrower than the term "financial service suppliers". In China's view, financial institutions are banks and other types of regulated financial institutions. According to China, dictionary definitions reflect that there are two essential attributes of a financial institution: (1) that it collects funds from the public (whether as deposits or investments), and (2) that it is subject to some type of regulation or supervision.[696] China observes that this general definition is consistent, *inter alia*, with the definition

[691] For the text of the entry, see Annex G to this Report.

[692] United States' first written submission, para. 19.

[693] China's first written submission, paras. 134-136.

[694] China provides relevant excerpts from the Schedules of Angola, Australia, Côte d'Ivoire, El Salvador, Guatemala, Honduras, Korea, Malta and Singapore in Exhibit CHN-85.

[695] China notes, however, that the term "foreign service supplier" appears approximately thirty different times throughout China's Schedule. China's response to Panel question No. 63, para. 116.

[696] China's first written submission, paras. 140-142; response to Panel question Nos. 49, para. 71; 51, para. 80; and 52(a), para. 82.

given to the term "foreign financial institutions" in its own domestic financial service regulations.[697] China considers that in the particular context of China's Schedule, the term "FFIs" refers to foreign banks and finance companies.[698]

7.543 China additionally points out that limiting its commitments to FFIs is consistent with the fact that the services classifiable under subsectors (a) to (f) are core banking and finance services provided by regulated financial institutions. China adds that the United States' position on FFIs would have absurd consequences. For example, it would mean that non-bank foreign service suppliers could enter the Chinese market and begin accepting deposits or making loans, while foreign banks – the types of entities that actually supply these services – would need to establish a branch or subsidiary in China and engage in foreign currency business for three years before obtaining a bank licence. Also, non-FFIs would then have had a right of market access since 2001, which is the date of China's accession to the WTO. China observes that like other WTO Members, it plainly did not intend entities that are not financial institutions subject to comprehensive supervision by their home countries to enter the Chinese market to provide these types of banking services.[699]

7.544 China argues, lastly, that the United States failed to demonstrate that EPS suppliers of other WTO Members are FFIs. China contends that they are not FFIs under any understanding of the term and notes that they go out of their way to disavow any such status.[700] China considers that the United States has therefore failed to demonstrate that China's commitments are relevant to the services and service suppliers at issue.[701]

7.545 The United States responds that China's mode 3 market access commitments are not limited to FFIs. Although China includes certain limitations with regard to FFIs, this does not mean that its commitments are limited to FFIs. It would have been necessary to impose such a limitation explicitly by prefacing the commitments with language like "unbound except" or "the service may only be supplied by ...". The United States argues that the only limitations China may impose are prudential authorization criteria and the now defunct restrictions on geographic scope and use of domestic currency as well as on-going requirements applicable to banks. Nothing in China's Schedule supports the view that China may condition the supply of a service on the aforementioned criteria and restrictions listed in the market access column *and* in

[697] China refers to the Regulations of the People's Republic of China on Administration of Foreign-Funded Banks of 2006, Exhibit CHN-45.

[698] China's response to Panel question No. 49, para. 72.

[699] China's first written submission, para. 143; second written submission, paras. 71-73.

[700] China refers e.g. to MasterCard Worldwide Terms of Use and to Visa Gift Card Holiday Guide, Exhibit CHN-84. See China's response to Panel question No. 49, para. 72.

[701] China's first written submission, paras. 145 and 146; response to Panel question Nos. 49, para. 72; and 53, para. 95.

addition require that another Member's service supplier meet unspecified criteria to be recognized as a "financial institution".[702]

7.546 The United States further argues that even if China's commitments were somehow limited to FFIs, the definition of that term offered by China is much too narrow. The United States notes that many dictionary definitions of the term "financial institutions" are much broader. In the United States' view, EPS suppliers of other WTO Members would qualify as financial institutions.[703] The United States also points out that in 2002 CUP was referred to by the PBOC as a joint-stock "financial institution" that provides an inter-bank bank card information switching network and associated specialized services.[704] The United States further notes that a CUP executive during a press event similarly referred to CUP as a "financial institution for offering cross-bank information exchange network and specialized services for bankcards".[705]

7.547 Australia submits that, although China included certain limitations with respect to foreign financial institutions, this does not mean that its commitments are limited to foreign financial institutions. If this were the case, China would have included the words "unbound except", or "otherwise unbound" in its Schedule, as it has with respect to mode 1. According to Australia, a Member wishing to limit the service suppliers that are permitted to provide a particular service must explicitly inscribe such a limitation in its schedule.[706] The European Union argues that there is no "*chapeau*" along the lines of "unbound except for the following" preceding the limitations listed under subsector (d), mode 3 in China's Schedule. This is different from the text preceding the limitations on market access for modes 1 and 4, which clearly state "Unbound except ...". In the European Union's view, therefore, anything that is not explicitly included in the scheduled limitation (which has already run its course), would fall under China's commitment to provide market access.[707] Japan submits that the absence of any "Unbound except ..." or similar language with respect to the market access and national treatment commitments under mode 3 strongly indicates that China's commitments are not limited to "financial institutions".[708]

7.548 The Panel notes that both parties agree that China has market access commitments in subsector (d) and mode 3 that apply to FFIs. The parties disagree, however, on whether these commitments are limited to FFIs and on whether EPS suppliers are FFIs. As it is common ground (and we agree with the parties on this) that China has commitments that apply to FFIs, we first determine whether, for the purposes of China's commitments concerning

---

702 United States' second written submission, paras. 116 and 121-123.
703 United States' second written submission, paras. 117 and 124.
704 Paragraph 2 of the Reply of PBOC on the Opening of CUP, Exhibit US-27.
705 "China Unionpay Executive Met the Press", Answer to Question 5 of 26 March 2002, Exhibit US-101.
706 Australia's third-party submission, para. 24-25; third-party statement, para. 10.
707 European Union's third-party submission, para. 36.
708 Japan's third-party statement, para. 9; response to Panel question No. 23(b), para. 4.

subsector (d) and mode 3, EPS suppliers of other WTO Members are FFIs. The first point to be noted is that the term "FFIs" is not defined in China's Schedule. Nor is it defined in the GATS or any of its annexes. However, section C of the relevant mode 3 market access entry in China's Schedule makes it clear, in our view, that the term includes, at a minimum, foreign banks and foreign finance companies. Section C is entitled "Licensing" and specifies that FFIs that meet certain conditions "are permitted to establish a subsidiary of a foreign bank or a foreign finance company in China". This implies that foreign banks and finance companies are considered FFIs for the purposes of China's Schedule. If a foreign finance company were not an FFI, it could not "establish a subsidiary of ... a foreign finance company in China". Finance companies are defined as "non-bank financial institution[s] that provide[] credit to customers that are either purchasing or leasing a product".[709] We thus deduce from the relevant mode 3 entry itself that, for purposes of China's Schedule, FFIs include at least foreign banks and foreign finance companies. We also understand that the latter are a type of non-bank financial institution.

7.549 To determine whether EPS suppliers of other WTO Members constitute non-bank FFIs, we must first ascertain the ordinary meaning of the term "FFIs". We note that the parties have submitted several dictionary definitions of the term "financial institutions". It emerges from these materials that the term "institutions" refers to organizations, companies or other entities.[710] The definitions provided to us also confirm that banks and finance companies are financial institutions.[711] We further observe that some of the definitions before us are quite narrowly drawn, e.g. one dictionary describes a financial institution as any organization "... that collects funds ... and invests these funds or lends them on to borrowers".[712] Other dictionaries or reference sources define the covered activities more broadly and suggest that the term is not limited to banks and finance companies. Specifically, these sources state that a financial institution is (a) "[a]n organization whose core activity is to provide financial

709 *The Palgrave Macmillan Dictionary of Finance, Investment and Banking*, Exhibit CHN-88, p.206. This dictionary also states that finance companies "generate[] revenues based on the differential between [their] own rate of borrowing and the rate at which [they] lend to customers". China further explains that the principal difference between a bank and a finance company is that a bank has a licence to borrow money in the form of demand deposits and other repayable funds from the public, while a finance company borrows money from other sources. China's response to Panel question No. 53, fn. 58.

710 E.g. Oxford Dictionary of Finance and Banking, Exhibit US-76; Webster's New World, Finance and Investment Dictionary, Exhibit CHN-90; Black's Law Dictionary, 9th Edition, (West Publishing 2010) (Black's Law Dictionary), Exhibit CHN-91.

711 E.g. *A Dictionary of Finance*, Exhibit CHN-48, which refers to banks and finance houses. A "finance company" is defined as "a non-bank financial institution [...]", *The Palgrave Macmillan Dictionary of Finance, Investment and Banking*, Exhibit CHN-88.

712 *A Dictionary of Finance*, Exhibit CHN-48. Similar definitions are provided in Barron's Dictionary of Finance and Investment Terms, Exhibit CHN-49; and Webster's Finance and Investment Dictionary, Exhibit CHN-90.

services or advice in relation to financial products"[713]; (b) "[a] firm that handles financial transactions or gives financial advice" or "[a]n establishment responsible for … facilitating transmission of funds"[714]; or (c) "[a] business organization[] that offer[s] a broad base of financial services or specialize[s] in specific functions, products or services, e.g., commercial banks, … and others that deal in money or equivalents".[715]

7.550 We find that some of the above-quoted dictionary definitions are sufficiently broad to capture EPS suppliers. Indeed, looking at these particular definitions, we consider that EPS suppliers can be reasonably described as (a) organizations whose core activity is to provide specific financial services; (b) establishments that handle financial transactions and facilitate the transmission of funds; or (c) business organizations that specialize in specific financial service functions or financial services, or that deal in money equivalents (electronic retail payment instruments).

7.551 As always, the ordinary meaning to be given to a treaty term must fit the specific context within which that term appears. We recall in this respect that the term "FFIs" appears in an entry that relates to China's commitments concerning certain financial services, specifically those classified under subsectors (a) to (f). This fact, together with the aforementioned dictionary definitions, suggests to us that in the specific context of China's Schedule, "FFIs" are any foreign organizations, companies or other business entities that provide financial services classified under subsectors (a) to (f).

7.552 China argues that financial institutions are, in addition, regulated, or supervised, organizations.[716] In support of this assertion, China submitted a dictionary definition and legal definitions contained in certain free trade agreements to which the United States is a party, e.g. the North American Free Trade Agreement (NAFTA).[717] Regarding the definitions provided in free trade agreements, we note that they are not applicable to all WTO Members or even the two parties to the present dispute. Moreover, they are definitions that were agreed on by the parties to that agreement. The parties' agreement need not necessarily accord with the ordinary meaning of the term "financial institutions".

---

713 Oxford Dictionary of Finance and Banking, Exhibit US-76.

714 *Banking Terminology*, Exhibit US-113.

715 The Dictionary of Banking, Exhibit US-114.

716 China's first written submission, para. 140.

717 *The Palgrave Macmillan Dictionary of Finance, Investment and Banking*, Exhibit CHN-46. The free trade agreements cited by China are: the North American Free Trade Agreement, Exhibit CHN-50; the United States – Australia Free Trade Agreement, Exhibit CHN-51; and the Korea – United States Free Trade Agreement, Exhibit CHN-52. According to China, a standard definition of "financial institution" found in these agreements is a "financial intermediary or other enterprise that is authorized to do business and regulated or supervised as a financial institution under the law of the Party in whose territory it is located". China's first written submission, fn 82.

As concerns the dictionary definition[718], we note that other definitions provided to us do not suggest that financial institutions are by definition regulated organizations. We do not dispute that financial institutions are commonly subject to some domestic regulation or supervision. We understand that the extent to which this is the case varies depending on the country and the type of financial institution and may even vary over time for a given country and type of financial institution. In our view, the existence, nature and extent of any regulation and supervision reflect policy choices, and we do not consider that regulation or supervision is a defining characteristic of financial institutions. We are therefore unable to accept China's argument on this point.

7.553 Other evidence placed on the record includes US and Chinese domestic legal documents. The United States submitted a law of the United States, Section 5312(a)(2)(L) of the United States' Code.[719] That section, which relates to reporting requirements on monetary transactions, bank secrecy and money laundering, provides a legal definition of the term "financial institution". Among the entities listed is "an operator of a credit card system". Thus, Section 5312(a)(2)(L) characterizes EPS suppliers that process credit card transactions as "financial institutions". China has pointed out, however, that another United States law, the Hiring Incentives to Restore Employment Act, defines "financial institutions" more narrowly as including essentially all entities accepting deposits, holding financial assets for the account of others or engaged in the business of investing or trading in securities.[720]

7.554 China also refers the Panel to documents issued by the China Banking Regulatory Commission (CBRC) in 2003, i.e. after China's accession to the WTO.[721] The documents indicate that CBRC rescinded the "financial institution" licence that had been issued to CUP when it was established in 2002.[722] The regulatory responsibility over CUP was to be transferred in December 2003 from the "non-bank financial institution regulatory department" of CBRC to PBOC. The reason provided for this transfer of regulatory functions was that the business scope of CUP "does not include financial services" and that it "therefore is not a financial institution".[723] We note as an initial matter that these

[718] *The Palgrave Macmillan Dictionary of Finance, Investment and Banking*, Exhibit CHN-46, defines "financial institution" as "[a] regulated organization that provides a range of banking and investment services" (Exhibit CHN-46, p. 207).

[719] 31 U.S.C. 5312(a)(2)(L), Exhibit US-102.

[720] United States Hiring Incentives to Restore Employment Act, H.R. 2847, 111th Congress §1471 (2010), Exhibit CHN-94.

[721] Transfer of Regulatory Function with Respect to China UnionPay (2003), Exhibit CHN-97, and Notice regarding relevant issues on the transfer of the regulatory responsibilities of China UnionPay Co., Ltd. (2003), Exhibit CHN-97.

[722] Regarding the "financial institution" licence from 2002, we note paragraph 2 of the Reply of PBOC on the Opening of CUP, Exhibit US-27. It provides that "China UnionPay Co., Ltd. is a joint-stock financial institution that provides an inter-bank bankcard information switching network and specialized services in connection therewith".

[723] It remains unclear on what definition of "financial services" the CBRC based this assessment.

documents concern CUP, not EPS suppliers of other WTO Members.[724] Furthermore, they suggest that CUP *was* considered, and authorized as, a non-bank financial institution before its financial institution licence was revoked in 2003. Finally, we recall that the basis for rescinding CUP's licence as a financial institution was the CBRC's view that CUP did not provide the specific financial services that are regulated and supervised by the CBRC, i.e. China's banking regulator.[725]

7.555 China further draws the Panel's attention to its Regulations on Administration of Foreign-Funded Banks which define a "foreign financial institution" as "a financial institution that is registered outside the People's Republic of China and approved or licensed by the financial regulatory authorities of the country or region where it originated".[726] This definition is provided for the purposes of these particular Regulations, and the Regulations talk about FFIs in the specific context of establishment of foreign-funded banks.[727]

7.556 In considering the above-mentioned United States and Chinese legal documents, we observe that they emanate from, and reflect the particular objectives and needs of, the domestic legal systems of the United States and China. It is therefore important to be cautious when interpreting the treaty term "FFIs" that we do not attribute undue weight to these documents for the purposes of our interpretative task. In particular, as regards the legal definitions provided in some of these documents, we consider that it would be inappropriate to draw, from these context-specific definitions, general conclusions as to the meaning and scope of the term "FFIs" as it appears in China's Schedule. At any rate, these various documents do not suggest to us that there is anything inherently questionable about conceiving of EPS suppliers as non-bank financial institutions.

7.557 Evidence submitted by the parties shows that certain EPS suppliers – specifically those that have adopted a four-party business model – refer to their

---

[724] Nonetheless, as we have explained above in Section VII.E of this Report, CUP in our view is an EPS supplier.

[725] We understand that CUP is now subject to the supervision and regulation of another financial agency, the PBOC. We also recall that we have found above in Section VII.D that, for the purposes of China's GATS Schedule, the services provided by EPS suppliers *are* financial services and are properly classified under subsector (d) of that Schedule.

[726] Article 3 of the Regulations of the People's Republic of China on Administration of Foreign-Funded Banks, Exhibit CHN-45.

[727] See Article 2 of the Regulations of the People's Republic of China on Administration of Foreign-Funded Banks. Article 3, which sets out the definition, opens with the phrase: "A foreign financial institution referred to in these Regulations shall mean ...". Also, Article 3 provides exactly the same definition for "foreign banks", except that it defines these as commercial banks rather than financial institutions.

clients as financial institutions.[728] This is not surprising, as issuers and acquirers are often banks. In contrast, these EPS suppliers do not appear to refer to themselves as financial institutions.[729] We have said above that industry sources may sometimes shed useful light on the ordinary meaning of terms.[730] In this instance, we do not consider that much weight can be attributed to the EPS industry's usage of the term "financial institutions". We would not find it unusual if companies in a given industry did not claim to be subject to what often amounts to burdensome regulation as financial institutions, unless it is important for business reasons to be considered a financial institution (as in the case of banks, for instance). Moreover, what ultimately matters are the views of regulators. Hence, it was open to the drafters of China's Schedule to bring EPS suppliers of other WTO Members within the ambit of the Schedule term "FFIs" even if EPS suppliers did not refer to themselves as financial institutions. For these reasons, we consider that the EPS industry's usage of the term "financial institutions" does not demonstrate that, despite the broad ordinary meaning of the term "FFIs", EPS suppliers of other WTO Members are not FFIs for the purposes of China's mode 3 entry.

7.558 At the end of our analysis of the ordinary meaning of the term "FFIs", we thus remain of the view that the term "FFIs" as it appears in China's Schedule is reasonably susceptible of meaning any foreign institutions that provide financial services classifiable under subsectors (a) to (f). This would notably include EPS suppliers of other WTO Members. But our analysis so far has shown that the term "FFIs" likewise bears the narrower meaning argued for by China, according to which the term covers only foreign banks and finance companies providing these services.

7.559 We therefore need to examine further and in more detail whether the relevant context confirms or puts in doubt either of the above-noted ordinary meanings. We begin this task by noting that the relevant mode 3 entry lists temporary or permanent (i) geographic restrictions (section A), (ii) client limitations on local currency business (section B), and (iii) licensing requirements, including general authorization criteria[731] and qualifications for engaging in local currency business (section C). These elements are applicable to

---

[728] See, e.g. Visa 2008 IPO Prospectus, Exhibit US-3, pp. 128-129; MasterCard 2010 Annual Report, Exhibit US-6, p. 4; MasterCard Worldwide Terms of Use and Visa Gift Card Holiday Guide, Exhibit CHN-84.

[729] China has submitted print-outs from the websites of two EPS suppliers of the United States that have adopted the four-party model (Exhibit CHN-84). In these print-outs, the EPS suppliers state that they are not financial institutions and do not issue payment cards. China further provided a submission by one of these suppliers to Canada's Competition Tribunal in which a similar statement is made (Exhibit CHN-84, para. 11).

[730] See para. 7.89 above.

[731] Among these are prudential authorization criteria. China has stated that the term "prudential regulation" is generally understood to relate only to the regulation of deposit-taking financial institutions (e.g. to capital adequacy requirements). China's response to Panel question No. 55, para. 100.

all FFIs. We perceive no basis to conclude that it would be unreasonable to impose these limitations on EPS suppliers of other WTO Members.

7.560 Additionally, we note that the licensing requirements in section C include minimum asset requirements. They apply to FFIs wishing to establish "a subsidiary of a foreign bank or a foreign finance company in China", "a branch of a foreign bank in China" or "a Chinese-foreign joint bank or a Chinese-foreign joint finance company in China". Or, to put it differently, these requirements apply to foreign banks or finance companies that wish to establish in China in one of the specified forms of commercial presence.[732] As noted above, these requirements confirm that foreign banks and finance companies are FFIs. But if the term "FFIs" encompassed solely foreign banks and finance companies, it would have been simpler and more natural, in our view, for section C to refer to FFIs wishing to establish a "subsidiary in China" rather than "a subsidiary of a foreign bank or a foreign finance company in China", and to "a Chinese-foreign joint venture enterprise in China" rather than "a Chinese-foreign joint bank or a Chinese-foreign joint finance company in China". Conversely, if the term "FFIs" included, but was not limited to, foreign banks and finance companies, it would have been necessary to specify to which type of FFI the relevant asset requirements applied. For this reason, we consider, first, that the asset requirements support the view that foreign banks and finance companies are not the only institutions covered by the term "FFIs". Secondly, and contrary to China's contention, the asset requirements do not indicate, in our view, that only foreign banks and finance companies may establish a commercial presence in China to provide the services under subsectors (a) to (f).[733]

7.561 It should also be recalled that China's mode 3 market access entry relates to services that appear under the subheading "Banking services...". As we have determined in Section VII.D above that subsector (d) covers EPS, the subheading "Banking services" in our view does not support China's contention that the term "FFIs" covers foreign banks and finance companies, but not EPS suppliers of other WTO Members.

7.562 We also note that China's Schedule under "Banking and Other Financial Services" contains a separate subsectoral description which reads "motor vehicle financing by non-bank financial institutions". The parties agree that the non-bank financial institutions referred to in this description cover finance companies and/or other types of non-bank financial institutions.[734] China has explained that scheduling this commitment separately ensured that non-bank financial institutions would be able to provide motor vehicle financing immediately upon China's accession to the WTO in December 2001, without the limitations on

[732] It appears to us that in order to establish a subsidiary "of a foreign bank", for instance, the FFI must be a foreign bank.

[733] China's response to Panel question Nos. 52(a), para. 87, and 80, para. 16.

[734] United States' response to Panel question No. 84(a), para. 59; China's response to Panel question No. 84(a), para. 32.

market access inscribed for subsectors (a) to (f).[735] In our view, China's explanation concerning the separate commitment relating to motor vehicle financing by non-bank financial institutions is consistent with the view that FFIs include non-bank financial institutions. China's explanation would appear to imply that if China had wished to subject motor vehicle financing by non-bank financial institutions to the limitations inscribed for subsectors (a) to (f), China would have classified it under "Banking services" (subsectors (a) to (f)). We recall in this respect that China's mode 3 commitments concerning subsectors (a) to (f) apply to FFIs.

7.563 We further find relevant China's mode 3 market access entry concerning subsectors (k) and (l). This entry is also part of the commitments concerning "Banking and Other Financial Services". It specifies that "[b]ranches of foreign institutions are permitted". While this entry refers to "foreign institutions", thus omitting the word "financial", we attach no particular significance to this omission as the entry relates to subsectors listed under the heading "other financial services". We recognize that some of the services falling within subsectors (k) and (l) are provided by e.g. banks – such as advice on acquisitions and on corporate restructuring. But we do not consider that the services described in subsectors (k) and (l) are exclusively provided by banks and/or finance companies. For instance, the United States has noted that subsector (k) includes such information services supplied by financial news providers like Reuters and Bloomberg.[736] Similarly, subsector (l) includes the services provided by what are known as credit rating agencies.[737]

7.564 Also worthy of note are China's financial services commitments in the subsectors concerning insurance and securities services. The relevant entries use the terms "foreign insurance institutions" and "foreign securities institutions", respectively. Accordingly, the reference to foreign "institutions" is not unique to China's commitments in the subsector concerning banking services. China's Schedule does not provide much guidance as to the meaning and coverage of the term "foreign securities institutions". In contrast, it is clear from the Schedule that the term "foreign insurance institutions" is used broadly to cover not just foreign life and non-life insurers, but also insurance brokers.[738] Moreover, whereas outside the context of China's Schedule the term "financial institutions" is often used to refer narrowly to banks and finance companies (as some of the dictionary meanings indicate), the terms "insurance institutions" and "securities institutions" to our knowledge are less commonly encountered. They do not

[735] China's response to Panel question No. 84(b), para. 33.

[736] United States' response to Panel question No. 45, para. 119. Subsector (k) refers *inter alia* to "[p]rovision and transfer of financial information".

[737] Subsector (l) refers *inter alia* to "credit reference and analysis, investment and portfolio research and advice".

[738] See notably section D of China's mode 3 market access entry concerning insurance and insurance-related services.

suggest a narrow meaning.[739] To us, the use of parallel terms – financial institutions, insurance institutions and securities institutions, respectively – in China's financial services commitments provides further support for the view that the word "institution" may be understood to refer notably to companies that provide the relevant services.[740] We note that the EPS suppliers of other WTO Members to which the parties have referred in these proceedings are all companies.

7.565 Finally, China refers the Panel to the GATS Schedules of eight other WTO Members.[741] As they are all integral parts of the GATS, they also form part of the relevant context. The excerpts from other WTO Members' Schedules that China has provided to us use the term "foreign financial institutions" or "financial institutions", and do not offer a formal definition of either term. Several Schedules provide confirmation that banks and finance companies would be considered financial institutions for the purposes of these Schedules. We note, though, that the excerpts provided do not specifically indicate that EPS suppliers are financial institutions, or that they are not.[742] In the light of this, we do not find these other Schedules to be particularly instructive. As we have explained, the term "FFIs" in our view can refer to a variety of foreign institutions, including, but not limited to, banks and finance companies. Therefore, the fact that in some WTO Members' Schedules this term might possibly have been used in a narrower sense does not demonstrate that it would be improper, in the context of China's Schedule, to give it the meaning its words

---

[739] We note that while e.g. the above-mentioned *Oxford Dictionary of Finance and Banking*, Exhibit US-76, and the *Barron's Dictionary of Finance and Investment Terms*, Exhibit CHN-49, contain an entry for "financial institution", they do not contain entries for either "insurance institution" or "securities institution".

[740] It is pertinent to note that section D of China's mode 3 market access commitments concerning insurance services specifically states that the qualifications for establishing a "foreign insurance institution" include the requirement that the investor be a foreign insurance company with 30 years of establishment experience in a WTO Member. Thus, this particular entry appears to indicate that only companies can be foreign insurance institutions. We further note that one of the dictionaries that has been referred to by China has an entry concerning "insurance company" that says "[s]ee insurer". The word "insurer" is in turn defined as "[a] regulated institution that accepts the risks of insureds or cedants through the insurance mechanism ...". See *The Palgrave Macmillan Dictionary of Finance, Investment and Banking*, pp. 272-273.

[741] "Use of the term 'financial institution" in other WTO Members' Schedules" (Exhibit CHN-85). The eight WTO Members are: Angola, Australia, Côte d'Ivoire, Honduras, Korea, Malta, Singapore and Venezuela.

[742] In contrast, Brazil's Schedule, which was not provided to us by China, contains the following definition: "Financial institutions subject to this commitment are classified as commercial bank, investment bank, consumer finance company, financial leasing company, brokers and dealers". See the horizontal note on financial services of Brazil's Schedule (GATS/SC/13). This definition appears to imply that EPS suppliers are not financial institutions for the purposes of Brazil's Schedule. We note, however, that unlike Brazil, China has not included a definition of the term "FFIs" in its Schedule. China itself has stated that in the absence of an explicit definition in its Schedule, treaty terms must be interpreted in accordance with customary rules of interpretation of public international law. China's response to Panel question No. 54, para. 97.

are capable of bearing. As the Appellate Body has observed, each Schedule has "its own intrinsic logic" and must be interpreted on its own merits.[743]

7.566 To sum up, the preceding contextual considerations either support or do not contradict the view that the term "FFIs" covers any foreign institutions that provide financial services classifiable under subsectors (a) to (f). Thus, on the basis of the ordinary meaning of the term "FFIs" read in the specific context provided by China's Schedule, we see no reason to construe that term in such a way that it would exclude EPS suppliers of other WTO Members.

7.567 The result of our interpretative analysis so far needs to be considered also in the light of the object and purpose of the GATS and the *WTO Agreement*. We have previously identified relevant objects and purposes of these two agreements.[744] With specific reference to the term "FFIs", we do not consider that interpreting that term so as to include EPS suppliers of other WTO Members would be at variance with the object and purpose of either the GATS or the *WTO Agreement*. In our view, the purpose of ensuring the security and predictability of commitments is served by giving the words used in China's Schedule the meaning that they are fairly capable of bearing in their context.

7.568 As an additional matter, we note that China has adverted to the importance of avoiding any interpretation of its mode 3 market access entry that would produce what it considers unreasonable results. Essentially, China submits that any interpretation of the entry in question must take full account of the fact that China was allowed to maintain geographic, client and non-prudential limitations for the first five years after its accession to the WTO, and that it is still allowed to impose prudential authorization criteria and qualifications requirements for engaging in local currency business. Under our interpretation of the term "FFIs", foreign non-bank financial institutions other than finance companies were, and are, subject to the same limitations as foreign banks and finance companies (which China accepts are FFIs). Our interpretation therefore steers clear of a result whereby, e.g. for the first five years, non-bank financial institutions other than finance companies could enter China's market without being subjected to the aforementioned limitations, while foreign banks and finance companies would have faced these limitations.

7.569 China further appears to suggest that any interpretation of the term "FFIs" that would cover institutions other than foreign banks and finance companies would mean that non-bank foreign service suppliers with little industry experience could enter the Chinese market and begin accepting deposits or making loans. That is not the case, however. As indicated above, in accordance with section C of China's mode 3 market access entry, China may impose prudential authorization criteria. Additionally, as confirmed by the preamble to the GATS, China retains the right to regulate, and to introduce new regulations

743 Appellate Body Report, *US – Gambling*, para. 182.

744 See paras. 7.196-7.197 above.

on the supply of services to meet domestic policy objectives. Articles VI:1 and VI:5 of the GATS further confirm that even in sectors in which a WTO Member has undertaken specific commitments, that WTO Member may, subject to certain disciplines, apply measures of general application affecting trade in services, including e.g. non-discriminatory licensing, qualification and technical requirements. Finally, paragraph 2(a) of the GATS Annex on Financial Services provides that, notwithstanding any other provisions of the GATS, a WTO Member may take measures for prudential reasons, including for the protection of e.g. investors and depositors, or to ensure the integrity and stability of the financial system.

7.570 For all these reasons, we conclude that the term "FFIs" as it appears in China's commitments concerning banking services covers foreign companies that supply financial services classifiable under subsectors (a) to (f).[745] Accordingly, it is our view that, as used in China's relevant commitments, the term "FFIs" covers foreign banks, foreign finance companies, as well as other foreign non-bank financial institutions, including EPS suppliers.

7.571 Having found that EPS suppliers of other Members are FFIs for the purposes of China's market access commitments, there is no need to go on to determine whether China has any market access commitments in subsector (d) and mode 3 that would apply to any foreign service suppliers that are not FFIs. We thus proceed to examine China's current market access commitments in respect of FFIs that provide their services through mode 3.

7.572 We note that the claims put forward by the United States in the present dispute concern the provision of EPS for domestic RMB payment card transactions in China.[746] Consequently, it would appear that for purposes of China's mode 3 entry, the relevant business in which EPS suppliers of other WTO Members would engage in China is local currency (RMB) business.[747] China's mode 3 entry expressly states that for local currency business, and after expiry of the phase-out period of five years, FFIs – which in our view include EPS suppliers of other WTO Members – may provide their services to all

[745] It is not necessary in this dispute to determine whether, for the purposes of China's Schedule, the term "FFIs" covers only companies, or whether they also include other organizations and entities.

[746] The United States alleges, for instance, that China refuses to allow EPS suppliers of other WTO Members "to process payment card transactions in China denominated and paid in China's domestic currency, Renmimbi ('RMB')". United States' first written submission, para. 3.

[747] The Panel asked the United States whether its Article XVI claims that are based on China's mode 3 market access entry related to foreign or local currency business. The United States did not provide a direct answer to the question. It pointed out that whether the purchase is RMB-denominated or whether the payment card is RMB-denominated, a payment card transaction would, in its view, be processed by CUP when the card is issued and used in China. United States' response to Panel question No. 65, para. 168. China, for its part, understands the United States to be claiming a right of market access to engage in local currency business. China states that although the United States in its view avoided answering Panel question No. 65, the subject matter of this dispute is what the United States calls "domestic transactions denominated and paid in RMB", which China understands to be part of local currency business. China's second written submission, para. 69.

Chinese enterprises and natural persons, without being subject to geographic restrictions or non-prudential authorization criteria restricting their ownership, operation or juridical form.[748] The enterprises and natural persons that EPS suppliers serve are issuers, acquirers, merchants and private or corporate card holders.[749]

7.573 Significantly, China's mode 3 entry does not set out any limitations on the number of service suppliers in the form of a monopoly or exclusive service suppliers.[750] The entry nonetheless specifies that China's market access commitment is subject to a limitation concerning qualifications for FFIs to engage in local currency business.[751] Pursuant to the limitation in question, prior to applying for authorization to engage in local currency business, FFIs must have three years of business operation in China and be profitable for two consecutive years. In other words, as also pointed out by China[752], FFIs must engage in foreign currency business through commercial presence in China before they can apply for authorization to conduct local currency business.

7.574 It should be added that, as a general matter, China's Schedule might possibly set out additional relevant limitations on market access in the section that concerns horizontal commitments. Neither party argues that this is the case, however. Having reviewed these horizontal commitments, we consider that they do not modify the result we have reached on the basis of the mode 3 entry in question.

7.575 Accordingly, we come to the conclusion that in respect of services classified under subsector (d) and provided by FFIs – which we consider include EPS provided by EPS suppliers of other WTO Members – China has made a commitment on market access concerning mode 3. That commitment is not subject to any limitations on the number of service suppliers. But it is subject to a limitation with regard to the qualifications that FFIs must meet to be permitted to engage in local currency (RMB) business. As a consequence, China is obligated to give EPS suppliers of other WTO Members access to its market, through commercial presence, so that they may engage in local currency business in China, subject to such suppliers meeting the aforementioned qualifications requirement.

---

[748] See sections A, B and C of the relevant mode 3 market access entry. We also note that China's mode 3 national treatment entry further specifies that with the expiry of the phase-out period of five years, China may no longer maintain any limitations on national treatment in respect of FFIs. As stated in the relevant entry, FFIs may do business, without restrictions or need for case-by-case approval, with foreign invested enterprises or non-Chinese natural persons, or with Chinese clients.

[749] The enterprises or persons with which EPS suppliers do business vary according to the type of network EPS suppliers use (four-party vs. three-party model).

[750] We do not understand the parties to argue otherwise. E.g. United States' second written submission, para. 116; China's first written submission, paras. 133-139.

[751] See section C of the relevant mode 3 market access entry.

[752] China's response to Panel question No. 52(a), para. 86.

2. *Whether the measures at issue are inconsistent with Article XVI of the GATS*

7.576 The United States asserts that China made relevant commitments in its Schedule not to maintain any limitations on the number of EPS suppliers of other WTO Members in respect of the services at issue. As a result of these commitments, the United States considers the measures at issue are inconsistent with China's obligations under Articles XVI:1 and XVI:2(a) of the GATS.[753] In respect of Article XVI:2(a), the United States claims that each of the six requirements establishes and maintains CUP as both a "monopoly" supplier and an "exclusive service supplier" within the meaning of Article XVI:2(a) of the GATS for all RMB bank card transactions.[754]

7.577 China asserts that the United States has failed to demonstrate that the measures at issue maintain or adopt limitations on the number of service suppliers that are inconsistent with Article XVI:1 or XVI:2(a) of the GATS.[755] China argues that the legal instruments which form the basis of the United States' claims establish a common national network for processing domestic inter-bank bank card transactions. In its view, this does not equate to a "monopoly" network.[756] It submits that there is nothing in the instruments that would prevent the issuance or acceptance of bank cards bearing more than one logo and capable of being processed over multiple networks.[757] Moreover, it considers the fact that bank cards, POS devices and ATMs must adhere to certain technical standards does not preclude their adherence to other technical standards.[758] Finally, in respect of requirements identified in relation to Hong Kong and Macao, China argues that its own obligations under the covered agreements do not extend to separate customs territories, and therefore there is no "legal basis" for the claims advanced by the United States relating to services in Hong Kong or Macao under the modes of supply at issue in this dispute.[759]

7.578 The Panel recalls its conclusions that certain Chinese legal instruments require that bank cards issued in China bear the Yin Lina/UnionPay logo, and furthermore, China, requires that issuers become members of the CUP network, and that the bank cards they issue in China meet certain uniform business specifications and technical standards.[760] We found that China also imposes requirements that all terminals (ATMs, merchant processing devices and POS

[753] United States' first written submission, para. 61.

[754] United States' first written submission, para. 65; response to Panel question No. 64, para. 165.

[755] China's response to Panel question No. 22; second written submission, para. 90.

[756] China's first written submission, paras. 54, 92-93, and 101; opening statement at the first meeting of the Panel, para. 20; response to Panel question No. 22; comments on United States' response to Panel question Nos. 70-72, 86-96, 115-123, paras. 72 and 73.

[757] China's second written submission, para. 93; comments on United States' response to Panel question Nos. 70-72, 86-96, 115-123, para. 73.

[758] China's response to Panel question No. 22.

[759] China's response to Panel question No. 18, paras. 1-5.

[760] See Section VII.E.2(a) above.

terminals) in China that are part of the national bank card inter-bank processing network be capable of accepting all bank cards bearing the *Yin Lian*/UnionPay logo.[761] We also concluded that China requires acquirers to post the *Yin Lian*/UnionPay logo, become members of the CUP network and be capable of accepting all bank cards bearing the *Yin Lian*/UnionPay logo.[762] In addition, we found that certain instruments mandate that CUP and no other EPS supplier handle the clearing of certain RMB bank card transactions that involve either an RMB bank card issued in China and used in Hong Kong or Macao, or an RMB bank card issued in Hong Kong or Macao that is used in China in an RMB transaction.[763] We did not conclude, however, that there is a general requirement that mandates the use of CUP or otherwise establishes CUP as the sole supplier of EPS for all domestic RMB bank card transactions that take place in China.[764] Similarly, we did not conclude that there are broad prohibitions on the use of "non-CUP cards" for cross-region or inter-bank transactions.

7.579 As we have concluded that there is no requirement that establishes CUP as the "sole supplier" (i.e. the alleged "sole supplier requirements"), and that there are no broad prohibitions on the use of non-CUP cards for cross-region or inter-bank transactions (the alleged "cross-region/-bank requirements"), we do not address the United States' claims under Article XVI in respect of these two alleged "requirements". By contrast, we have concluded that China maintains in place certain issuer, terminal equipment and acquirer requirements (the "issuer requirements", "terminal requirements" and "acquirer requirements", respectively), and that CUP enjoys exclusivity as the EPS supplier in respect of transactions concerning Chinese nationals travelling in Hong Kong or Macao, and Hong Kong or Macao nationals travelling in China (the "Hong Kong/Macao requirements"). Therefore, we consider below whether these four requirements are inconsistent with China's obligations under Article XVI of the GATS, as claimed by the United States.

7.580 With this in mind, we recall our conclusion above[765] that China has not undertaken any market access commitments under mode 1 in Sector 7.B(d) of its Schedule in respect of the services at issue in this dispute. In light of this finding, the Panel further finds that the issuer, terminal equipment, acquirer and Hong Kong/Macao requirements are not inconsistent with Article XVI of the GATS.

7.581 In addition, we concluded above[766] that China has undertaken a market access commitment under mode 3 in Sector 7.B(d) of its Schedule in respect of the services at issue in this dispute. In light of this finding, we therefore proceed to consider whether the issuer, terminal equipment, acquirer and Hong

---

761 See para. 7.239 above.

762 See Section VII.E.2(c) above.

763 See paras. 7.361-7.383 above.

764 See paras. 7.385-7.504 above.

765 See para. 7.538 above.

766 See paras. 7.539-7.575 above.

Kong/Macao requirements are inconsistent with any of China's market access obligations in respect of this commitment. Additionally, in the light of the United States' assertion that each of the four requirements at issue maintains limitations on the number of service suppliers in the form of a "monopoly" and "exclusive service supplier" within the meaning of Article XVI:2(a) of the GATS, we begin our assessment under Article XVI:2(a) of the GATS.

(a) Whether the relevant requirements fall within the scope of Article XVI:2(a) of the GATS

7.582 The United States argues that each of the requirements at issue is inconsistent with Article XVI:2(a) of the GATS because they limit the number of foreign suppliers of EPS for bank card transactions. The United States considers these measures establish and maintain CUP as both a "monopoly" supplier and an "exclusive service supplier" within the meaning of Article XVI:2(a) of the GATS for all RMB bank card transactions.[767] In accordance with statements by the Appellate Body in *US – Gambling*, the United States submits that the terms "monopolies" and "exclusive service suppliers" should be interpreted to include not only limitations that are "in the form" of monopolies or exclusive service suppliers, but also those that are "in effect" such limitations.[768]

7.583 China argues that the Appellate Body made clear in *US – Gambling* that the scope of Article XVI:2(a) extends only to "quantitative" or "quantitative-type measures" and therefore, Article XVI does not extend to measures that "merely have the effect of limiting the number of services suppliers".[769] China argues that, if Article XVI were understood to encompass measures that "have the effect" of limiting the number of service suppliers, then measures that are permitted under other provisions of the GATS would need to be considered to fall within the scope of Article XVI due to their limiting effect. China argues that the subject matter of Article XVI would thus "begin to overlap" with other GATS disciplines, and this would inappropriately "blur the distinction" between different disciplines and would "intrude upon" Members' rights.[770] Furthermore, China disagrees with the United States that the terms "monopoly" and "exclusive service suppliers" should be interpreted to have the same meaning.[771]

7.584 The Panel will consider the scope of Article XVI:2(a) of the GATS before assessing the United States' particular claims. We first note that the

---

767 United States' first written submission, para. 65; response to Panel question No. 64, para. 165.

768 United States' response to Panel question No. 67; see also second written submission, paras. 132-136.

769 China's response to Panel question No. 67 (quoting Appellate Body Report, *US – Gambling*, para. 248).

770 See China's response to Panel question No. 67 (citing Panel Report, *US – Gambling*, para. 6.305).

771 China's response to Panel question No. 66.

parties provided several definitions and explanations of the terms "monopoly" and "exclusive service suppliers".

7.585 Article XXVIII(h) of the GATS defines "monopoly supplier of a service" as "any person, public or private, which in the relevant market of the territory of a Member is authorized or established formally or in effect by that Member as the sole supplier of that service". Article VIII:5 states: "The provisions of this Article shall *also* apply to cases of exclusive service suppliers, where a Member, formally or in effect, (a) authorizes or establishes a small number of service suppliers and (b) substantially prevents competition among those suppliers in its territory" (emphasis added).

7.586 Referring to dictionary definitions[772] and the meaning given to the term "monopoly supplier of a service" in Article XXVIII(h) of the GATS, the United States emphasizes that a monopoly supplier is a single or sole supplier that has an exclusive right to operate in a market. China similarly refers to the definition in Article XXVIII(h) in arguing that a monopoly encompasses a sole supplier. Regarding "exclusive service suppliers", the United States observes that they are not granted sole access, but rather, more than one exclusive service supplier will be granted rights to operate in a market that protects them from competition. China appears to agree, based on Article VIII:5 of the GATS, that the term "exclusive service suppliers" entails a small number of service suppliers that are protected from competition.

7.587 As a general textual matter, the definitions of the term "monopoly" provided by the United States support the view that the notion of a monopoly service supplier may overlap with that of an exclusive service supplier. However, Article XVI:2(a) of the GATS draws a distinction between these two terms. We must give meaning to all terms and cannot therefore assume that the terms mean one or the same thing.[773] Taking into account the different meaning given to these terms in the text of the Articles VIII:5 and XXVIII(h) of the GATS, and the distinction made in Article XVI:2(a), we consider that a monopoly supplier is a sole supplier authorized or established formally or in effect by a Member, whereas an exclusive service supplier is one of a small number of suppliers in a situation where a Member authorizes or establishes a small number of service suppliers, either formally or in effect, and that Member substantially prevents competition among those suppliers. We have not identified anything in the definitions provided by the parties, or elsewhere, that would lead us to conclude differently. Thus, for the purposes of Article XVI:2,

[772] As also pointed out by the United States, a monopoly can be defined as "exclusive possession or control of the trade in a commodity or service ... the condition of having no competitor in one's trade or business..." or as "an exclusive privilege to carry on a business, traffic, or service granted by a government". See United States' first written submission, para. 65, citing *New Shorter Oxford English Dictionary* (1993), p. 1819.

[773] See Appellate Body Report, *US – Gasoline*, p. 23, DSR 1996:I, 3, at p. 29.

we do not consider that a monopoly supplier is at the same time an exclusive service supplier.

7.588 Due to the formulation of the United States' panel request and its subsequent argumentation[774], we understand the United States to claim that, in the event that the Panel was to determine that CUP operates as the sole supplier in the Chinese market, then CUP constitutes a monopoly within the meaning of Article XVI:2(a). We note, in this respect, the United States alleges specifically that CUP is the "sole supplier" of EPS for RMB bank card transactions.[775] In the event that the Panel was to determine that CUP is one of a small number of EPS suppliers, then we understand it is the United States' view that CUP operates as an exclusive service supplier within the meaning of that provision. Thus, whether the requirements at issue establish CUP as the *sole* supplier of EPS services, or whether they establish CUP as one of a small number of EPS suppliers and substantially prevent competition[776], the United States considers that the requirements are inconsistent with Article XVI:2(a). We will assess the United States' claims with this understanding in mind.

7.589 We next address the parties' arguments concerning the scope of Article XVI:2(a), namely, whether Article XVI:2(a) extends to cover measures that impose "quantitative" or "quantitative-type" limitations, and whether it should be interpreted to include not only limitations that are "in the form" of monopolies or exclusive service suppliers, but also those that are "in effect" such limitations.

7.590 As noted by both parties, the Appellate Body in *US – Gambling* considered the meaning of the terms "monopoly" and "exclusive service suppliers" that appear in Article XVI:2(a). It stated:

> [T]he reference, in Article XVI:2(a), to limitations on the number of service suppliers "in the form of monopolies and exclusive service suppliers" should be read to include limitations that are in

[774] See, e.g. United States' first written submission, para. 65. The United States argues that the "types of privileges afforded CUP by the measures, including the ability to set prices, fall within the definition of both 'monopoly' and 'exclusive service supplier'".

[775] The United States specifically alleges in this dispute that China maintains certain measures, including requirements that mandate the use of CUP and/or establish CUP as the *sole supplier* of EPS for all domestic transactions denominated and paid in RMB. The United States also considers that CUP is the sole supplier for transactions pertaining to the particular RMB card-based transactions taking place in China, Macao and Hong Kong at issue in this dispute. See, e.g. United States' first written submission, para. 4.

[776] In respect of whether CUP would constitute an exclusive service provider, we recall that China asserts that a second domestic RMB clearing organization, the RCBFCC, currently supplies EPS in the Chinese market. See China's response to Panel question Nos. 98, 113 and 114. The United States disputes that the RCBFCC handles the processing of RMB payment card transactions. As we explained above, we are unable to verify China's assertion that the RCBFCC is a second EPS supplier operating in China, or the United States' contention in this regard. See paras. 7.488 and 7.489 above.

> form *or in effect*, monopolies or exclusive service suppliers.[777] (emphasis original)

7.591 Looking at the remaining context of Article XVI:2(a), the Appellate Body concluded that the thrust of Article XVI:2(a) is not on the "form" of a measure, but on its "numerical, or quantitative, nature", stating:

> This is not to say that the words "in the form of" should be ignored or replaced by the words "that have the effect of". Yet, at the same time, they cannot be read in isolation. Rather, when viewed as a whole, the text of sub-paragraph (a) supports the view that the words "in the form of" must be read in conjunction with the words that precede them—"limitations on the *number* of service suppliers" — as well as the words that follow them, including the words "*numerical* quotas". (emphasis added) Read in this way, it is clear that the thrust of sub-paragraph (a) is not on the *form* of limitations, but on their *numerical*, or *quantitative*, nature.[778] (emphasis original)

7.592 Therefore, as these statements reflect, whether a limitation is "in the form of" a monopoly or exclusive service supplier within the meaning of Article XVI, turns notably on whether it is "numerical" or "quantitative" in nature. We understand the Appellate Body to mean that even a measure that is not, for instance, called a "quota" can fall within the scope of Article XVI:2(a), if it is quantitative in its thrust and therefore, limits the supply of a service as a quota would do. Regarding the form of such a measure, it may be any type of government-imposed law or regulation.[779]

7.593 Accordingly, we consider that in our Article XVI:2 analysis of the four requirements at issue we must focus, not on whether they formally or explicitly institute a monopoly or an exclusive service supplier, but on whether they constitute a limitation that is numerical and quantitative in nature. More particularly, we must examine whether they are of such a nature that they limit to one, or a small number, the number of authorized EPS suppliers in China.

7.594 With the foregoing considerations in mind, we proceed to consider whether the issuer, terminal equipment, acquirer and Hong Kong/Macao requirements constitute such "limitations on the number of service suppliers" "in

---

777 Appellate Body Report, *US – Gambling*, para. 230.

778 Appellate Body Report, *US – Gambling*, para. 232.

779 Regarding the "effect" of a measure, unlike Article XVI:2(a) of the GATS, we note that Article XV of the GATS, entitled "Subsidies" refers to the "distortive effects on trade in services" that subsidies may have. Article XV:2 indicates that a Member may request consultations with another Member in instances where it considers itself to be "adversely affected" by a subsidy of that other Member. Thus, this provision contemplates the "effect" a measure may have. Article XVI:2(a) does not expressly refer to the "effects" that arise from a limitation such as a monopoly or exclusive service provider.

the form of" a monopoly or an exclusive service supplier as those terms are used in Article XVI:2(a) of the GATS.

(b) Whether the issuer, terminal equipment and acquirer requirements are inconsistent with Article XVI:2(a) of the GATS

7.595 The United States argues that, in accordance with its GATS Schedule, China committed not to maintain any limitations on the number of foreign service suppliers of EPS. We recall that the United States argues that the imposition of various requirements "ensure CUP's privileged position", both "explicitly" and "effectively".[780] Specifically, the United States argues that no EPS supplier other than CUP benefits from requirements imposed on issuers and acquirers of bank cards, or terminal equipment requirements. Due to the need to fulfil these requirements, the United States argues that issuers and acquirers must have access to the CUP system, and must pay for that access.[781] It contends that it is thus "economically unviable" for any foreign supplier of EPS to participate in the market.[782] This is so, it argues, because it does not make "economic sense" for banks and processing entities to pay for the privilege of using a foreign EPS supplier in addition to what it pays to have access to CUP's network.[783] Broadly, it argues that each of these requirements help "entrench CUP's position as sole service supplier in the market".[784] In addition, it argues that the collective effect of these requirements establish CUP as the sole entity able to provide EPS for bank card transactions in China.[785] In this respect, it argues that the requirements gave CUP automatic and universal acceptance of its RMB bank cards by banks and merchants.[786]

7.596 China contends that none of these three requirements "have anything to do with the maintenance or adoption of a limitation on market access 'in the form of' of a monopoly or exclusive service supplier arrangement".[787] In addition, as discussed in Section VII.E.2(b) above, China argues that the United States failed to identify any aspect of these alleged requirements that would prevent the issuance or acceptance of bank cards that are capable of being processed over multiple networks, and therefore, it failed to establish that these measures impose "quantitative" or "quantitative-type" limitations on market access such

780 United States' first written submission, para. 46
781 United States' first written submission, paras. 50-52.
782 United States' first written submission, para. 66.
783 United States' first written submission, para. 69.
784 United States' second written submission, paras. 173, 180 and 183.
785 For further explanation on the United States' arguments concerning the collective effect of the requirements at issue, see paras. 7.482-7.506 above.
786 United States' second written submission, para. 190.
787 China's second written submission, para. 92.

that they would violate Article XVI:2(a) of the GATS.[788] Accordingly, China requests the Panel to reject the United States' claims under Article XVI.

7.597 The Panel concluded in Section VII.E.2(a) above that, China, through Document Nos. 37, 57 and 129 imposes requirements on issuers that bank cards issued in China bear the *Yin Lian*/UnionPay logo, and furthermore, China, through Document Nos. 17, 37, 57, 76 and 129 requires that issuers become members of the CUP network, and that the bank cards they issue in China meet certain uniform business specifications and technical standards. In reaching findings on these issuer requirements, we further indicated that none of the legal instruments reflecting these requirements indicates that issuers who are members of CUP may not join other networks in China (with the result that the bank cards issued work over those other networks), or that bank cards that meet CUP's uniform business specifications and technical standards must not, or cannot, simultaneously meet those of other networks.[789]

7.598 We further concluded in Section VII.E.2(b) above that China, through Document Nos. 37 and 153, imposes requirements that all terminals (ATMs, merchant processing devices and POS terminals) in China that are part of the national bank card inter-bank processing network must be capable of accepting all bank cards bearing the *Yin Lian*/UnionPay logo. In reaching findings on these terminal equipment requirements, we further indicated that none of the legal instruments reflecting these requirements indicates that terminal equipment that must be capable of accepting bank cards bearing the *Yin Lian*/UnionPay logo could not also be capable of accepting, at the same time, bank cards bearing the logo of different EPS suppliers. Hence, we saw no basis to conclude that the terminal equipment requirements would prevent the acceptance of bank cards that would be capable of being processed over an inter-bank network in China other than that of CUP.[790]

7.599 Finally, we concluded in Section VII.E.2(c) above that China, through Document No. 153, imposes requirements on acquirers to post the *Yin Lian*/UnionPay logo and furthermore, China, through Document Nos. 37, 76 and 153, imposes requirements that acquirers join the CUP network and comply with uniform business standards and technical specifications of inter-bank interoperability, and that terminal equipment operated or provided by acquirers be capable of accepting bank cards bearing the *Yin Lian*/UnionPay logo. In reaching findings on these acquirer requirements, we further concluded that none of the legal instruments reflecting these requirements indicates that acquirers may not also accept bank cards that would be capable of being processed over an inter-bank network in China other than that of CUP.[791]

---

788 China's second written submission, para. 93.

789 See paras. 7.297-7.299 above.

790 See para. 7.334 above.

791 See paras. 7.359-7.360 above.

7.600 It is clear from our conclusions as to the nature of these requirements that none of them imposes a limitation on the supply of EPS services that is quantitative in nature, i.e. they do not require that CUP shall be established and maintained as a "monopoly" or an exclusive service supplier. In addition, in view of our conclusions, we find that none of the provisions in the legal instruments that reflect these three requirements imposes an express limitation on the number of EPS suppliers that is numerical or quantitative in nature, be it in the form of a monopoly or exclusive service supplier. As we explained, we perceive no limitation on the number of EPS suppliers that could support the issuance of bank cards bearing their own logo. Similarly, we see no limitation on the number of EPS suppliers resulting from the fact that terminal equipment in China must be capable of accepting all bank cards bearing the *Yin Lian*/UnionPay logo. Finally, we see no limitation on the number of EPS suppliers that arises from the fact that acquirers must post the *Yin Lian*/UnionPay logo and be capable of accepting all bank cards bearing the *Yin Lian*/UnionPay logo.

7.601 We also recall that, in our evaluation of the existence of a "sole supplier" requirements above, we assessed the instruments at issue in this dispute not only individually, but also together.[792] We consider our conclusions above equally relevant to our assessment here.

7.602 As is clear from our assessment above, we concluded that the United States did not identify anything in the requirements that would lead us to conclude that the issuer, terminal and acquirer requirements considered alone or in combination, have the "effect" of limiting the number of services suppliers so as to maintain or establish CUP as a monopoly or exclusive service provider. As explained above, we noted that the imposition of these requirements places CUP in a unique position and may grant CUP certain advantages in the EPS market. Despite this, we nevertheless concluded that the United States has not identified anything in the instruments, when considered individually or together, that would explicitly establish CUP as the sole supplier of *all* RMB bank card transactions. In addition, we indicated that the fact that the various measures (such as Document Nos. 17, 37, 49, 57, 76, 129, 142, 153) mandate compliance with CUP business and technical standards does not mean that issuers or acquirers are prevented from operating over other networks. We explained that the fact that the stated objective for CUP is to establish a "countrywide", "unified" or single network is not indicative of an intention to create an exclusive network.

7.603 We further concluded that the United States has not submitted evidence beyond mere assertions to support its conclusion that the rules and requirements imposed under certain of the instruments at issue make it technically difficult for foreign EPS suppliers to operate in the market, thereby effectively "entrenching"

---

[792] See paras. 7.385-7.481 and 7.482-7.506 above.

CUP as the sole supplier. We found that the United States did not submit any evidence to support its assertion that, due to costs or other reasons, such as the fact that competing standards are inherently incompatible, other EPS suppliers would not enter the market.

7.604 Finally, we rejected the United States' assertion that the collective "economic" effect of the imposition of the requirements is to entrench CUP's status as a sole supplier in China.[793] In reaching this conclusion, we noted that the United States did not establish that the economic effect of any of the requirements was to prevent foreign EPS suppliers from entering and establishing themselves in China. Finally, we noted that we have no direct evidence to assess whether the instruments at issue make it economically unviable for other EPS suppliers to establish themselves and operate in China.

7.605 Accordingly, we are unable to conclude that the imposition of issuer, acquirer and terminal equipment requirements imposes a limitation on the number of EPS suppliers in China in the form of a monopoly or exclusive service supplier. For these reasons, we are unable to conclude that the issuer, terminal equipment and acquirer requirements, considered either separately or in combination, are inconsistent with Article XVI:2(a) of the GATS.[794]

(c) Whether the requirements pertaining to RMB card-based transactions taking place in China, Macao and Hong Kong are inconsistent with Article XVI:2(a) of the GATS

7.606 In Section VII.E.2(a) above, we concluded that, as reflected in various legal instruments, certain instruments mandate that CUP and no other EPS provider handle the clearing of certain RMB bank card transactions that involve either an RMB bank card issued in China and used in Hong Kong or Macao, or an RMB bank card issued in Hong Kong or Macao that is used in in China in an RMB transaction.[795] These bank card transactions concern payment for expenses including shopping, meals and accommodation, or small cash withdrawals from ATMs.

7.607 The United States argues that this requirement establishes and maintains CUP as a "monopoly" supplier or an "exclusive service supplier" within the meaning of Article XVI:2(a) of the GATS in respect of the services at issue. On the basis that China made specific market access commitments not to maintain any limitations on the number of foreign EPS suppliers, the United States

[793] See paras. 7.500-7.504 above.

[794] We consider in Section G, whether these same requirements are inconsistent with China's obligations under Article XVII of the GATS.

[795] See paras. 7.361-7.383 above. We recall our conclusion above that Document No. 219 does not require that CUP be the sole supplier of EPS services in respect of RMB card-based transactions taking place in China, Macao and Hong Kong. See, specifically, paras. 7.372-7.376 above.

considers these requirements are inconsistent with China's obligations under Article XVI:2(a) of the GATS.

7.608 China contends that there is no legal basis for the claims advanced by the United States in relation to EPS services in Hong Kong or Macao under the modes of supply at issue. Pursuant to Article XVI:2 of the GATS, China argues that a Member's schedule only implicates the provision of services in the territory of that Member. [796] China submits that Hong Kong and Macao are separate customs territories for purposes of the covered WTO agreements, and that each maintains their own rights and obligations in respect of these agreements. In consideration of their status, China argues that its own obligations under the covered agreements therefore do not extend to Hong Kong and Macao. Accordingly, it requests that the Panel reject these claims.[797]

7.609 As an initial point, the Panel notes that the four legal instruments identified in connection with this requirement – Document Nos. 8, 16, 219 and 254 – were also identified in connection with the alleged "sole supplier" requirements. In addition, Document No. 219 was also identified in connection with cross-region/inter-bank prohibitions. The United States argues that these four instruments "entrench"[798], or enforce, the existence of the sole supplier requirement and cross-region/inter-bank prohibitions. Because we found above[799] that no "sole supplier" requirement has been demonstrated in respect of the supply of EPS for *all* domestic RMB bank card transactions taking place in China, and that there are no cross-region/inter-bank prohibitions, we do not reach conclusions on these instruments in respect of either of these "requirements". Rather, our analysis focuses on these instruments as they concern RMB bank card-based transactions taking place in China, Macao and Hong Kong. We therefore address the United States' Article XVI claims in this respect only.

7.610 The Panel finds it useful to begin with China's contention that there is no legal basis for the claims advanced in relation to Hong Kong and Macao due to their status in the WTO as separate customs territories. The WTO status of Hong Kong and Macao *per se* is not in question in this dispute, nor is the fact that each of these territories maintains its own rights and obligations in respect of the WTO Agreements. What is at issue is whether or not the particular requirements in question relate to China's WTO obligations.

7.611 We understand that China invokes the language in Article XVI:2 to support its contention that its WTO obligations do not extend to Hong Kong or Macao. Pursuant to Article XVI:2 of the GATS, a Member's market access commitments impose limitations on certain measures that a Member may

[796] China's second written submission, para. 95.

[797] China's first written submission, fn. 27; response to Panel question No. 18, paras. 1-5; second written submission, para. 95.

[798] United States' second written submission, paras. 141 and 190.

[799] See paras. 7.385-7.481 and 7.482-7.506.

maintain or adopt "either on the basis of a regional subdivision or on the basis of its entire territory, unless otherwise specified in its Schedule". On its face, we understand this language to indicate merely that a measure of a Member may be subject to obligations under Article XVI not only in cases where it is applicable or enforced across the entire territory of a Member, but also in cases where it is applicable or enforced in only a part of that Member's territory.

7.612 The United States identifies different scenarios in which it considers Document Nos. 8, 16 and 254 operate together to ensure CUP's exclusivity in respect of the RMB card-based transactions taking place in China, Macao and Hong Kong. In the case of a Chinese national travelling to Hong Kong and making a purchase, according to the United States, CUP would mandatorily provide services to the issuing bank in China and the acquiring bank in either Hong Kong or Macao. Hence, EPS suppliers of other WTO Members would be prohibited from establishing a local presence in China to supply EPS services to either the issuing bank located in China or the acquiring bank located in either Hong Kong or Macao.[800] In a situation where either a Hong Kong or Macao national travels to China and makes a purchase, the United States argues that CUP would also mandatorily provide services to the issuing bank in either Hong Kong or Macao as well as the acquiring bank in China. Here again, the United States submits that a foreign EPS supplier would be prohibited from providing services to either the issuing or acquiring bank.[801] Finally, the United States contends that a foreign EPS supplier is prohibited from providing its services from China to an issuing or acquiring bank even, for instance, where the issuing bank is located in Hong Kong and issues a card to a Hong Kong national who then makes a purchase in Hong Kong.[802]

7.613 In our discussion of the services at issue above[803], we indicated that the clearing and settlement of a given bank card transaction involves participation by various actors. Under a four-party model, typically a card holder, an acquirer, an issuing bank/institution and an EPS supplier would all be involved in a transaction.[804] Under a three-party model or other similar variations, at a minimum, a card holder and an EPS supplier would be involved in a given transaction.

[800] United States' response to Panel question No. 9, para. 46. We recall our conclusion in paragraphs 7.538 above that China has no market access commitment under mode 1 in respect of the services at issue.

[801] United States' response to Panel question No. 9, para. 47.

[802] United States' response to Panel question No. 9, para. 48.

[803] See paras. 7.14-7.24 above.

[804] In the case a card holder uses a payment card to make a purchase, a merchant would be involved in the transaction. If a card holder uses a payment card to withdraw cash, for instance from an ATM, a merchant would not be involved. In either case, an acquiring institution would be involved in the transaction, either having supplied a POS terminal to the merchant or by servicing the ATM. As discussed in paras. 7.46-7.54 above, third party "processors" may also participate in the transaction.

7.614 We also found above[805] that China's Schedule contains a mode 3 market access commitment that covers the supply of EPS. This includes the supply of EPS provided under both the three-party and four-party models. This commitment requires that foreign EPS suppliers are permitted to establish operations in China and supply their services from within China to the relevant customers.

7.615 It is clear to us from Document Nos. 8, 16 and 254, and as illustrated through the examples presented by the United States, that both actors located in China and actors outside of China, in either Hong Kong or Macao, would be involved in the types of transactions which are governed by these three instruments. In the first two scenarios described in paragraph 7.612, at least one of the actors involved in the transaction – be it the issuer or acquirer – will be located in China. As we understand, in the third example outlined above, the United States contends that the RMB bank card holder, issuer of such a card, acquirer and merchant would all be located outside of China, in either Hong Kong or Macao, while the EPS supplier and settlement bank would be located in China.

7.616 The issue arises whether the supply of services through commercial presence under China's mode 3 commitment includes the supply of services to all actors under these three scenarios, including actors located outside of China, in either Hong Kong or Macao. In assessing this issue, we note that the supply of a service through commercial presence (mode 3) is defined in Article I:2(c) of the GATS as the supply of a service "by a service supplier of one Member, through commercial presence in the territory of any other Member". "Commercial presence" is defined in Article XXVIII, as follows:

> (d) "commercial presence" means any type of business or professional establishment, including through
>
> > (i) the constitution, acquisition or maintenance of a juridical person, or
> >
> > (ii) the creation or maintenance of a branch or a representative office,
> >
> > within the territory of a Member for the purpose of supplying a service

7.617 As the panel noted in its report in *Mexico – Telecoms*, this definition is silent with respect to any other territorial requirement (as is the case in cross-border supply under mode 1) or the nationality of the service recipient (as is the case in consumption abroad under mode 2). The definition of services supplied through commercial presence addresses only the location of the foreign service supplier, not that of the recipient of the relevant service, nor the nationality of the recipient. It indicates that for purposes of the GATS a service is supplied

[805] See paras. 7.539-7.575 above.

through mode 3 if a service supplier of a Member supplies its service through commercial presence in the territory of another Member.[806] The definition does not state that a foreign service supplier may supply its services only to recipients that are in the territory of the Member in which the service supplier has established a commercial presence and are nationals of that Member. Nor does the definition state that a foreign service supplier may not supply its services to recipients that are outside the territory of the Member in which the service supplier has established a commercial presence. Taking into account the absence of any territorial qualification as to the location of the recipient of a service, the panel in *Mexico – Telecoms* concluded that Mexico's commitment under mode 3 covered the supply of basic telecommunications services at issue both within Mexico and from Mexico into any other country.[807]

7.618 We agree with the reasoning of the panel in *Mexico – Telecoms*. Nothing in the GATS suggests that the supply of a service through commercial presence in the territory of a Member does not extend to the "export" of services from that Member's territory to a recipient in the territory of another Member or to a foreign recipient located in the "exporting" Member's territory. A foreign service supplier may therefore, subject to any limitations set out in the Member's schedule, supply a committed service to a foreign recipient wherever located, and of whatever nationality or origin.[808]

7.619 In view of our interpretation, and in the absence of a specific mode 3 limitation in China's Schedule that restricts the supply of EPS from within China into the territory of other WTO Members, we consider that China's commitment under mode 3 covers not only the supply of EPS to clients within China, but also the supply of EPS to clients located in the territory of other WTO Members.[809]

7.620 Having concluded that China's mode 3 commitment for EPS covers the supply of EPS into the territory of any other WTO Member, we do not agree

---

[806] Panel Report, *Mexico – Telecoms*, para. 7.375.

[807] In reaching this view, the panel in *Mexico – Telecoms* also took into account the fact that the Chairman's Note for Scheduling Basic Telecommunications Services Commitments makes specific reference to "local, long distance and international services", as well as the fact that Mexico did not exclude international services in the sector column, or elsewhere in its schedule, from the scope of services that commercial agencies may supply. The panel concluded that the Chairman's Note was an important part of the circumstances of the conclusion of the negotiations of the GATS, and should be given considerable weight in its assessment. See Panel Report, *Mexico – Telecoms*, paras. 7.376-7.377.

[808] This means, for example, that a mode 3 commitment on data processing services would allow a foreign company established in the territory of a Member to supply data processing services to a consumer located in the territory of another Member. Similarly, a mode 3 commitment on "hotel services" would allow a foreign-owned hotel established in the territory of that Member to supply hotel services to foreign tourists.

[809] It is useful to note that the supply of EPS from China into the territory of another Member could potentially be subject to market access or national treatment limitations in China and/or that other Member. For instance, the supply of services could be limited by the mode 3 market access commitments of China. Or it could be limited by the mode 1 (cross-border supply) commitments of the other Member.

with China that there is no legal basis for the claims advanced in relation to Hong Kong and Macao. Having so concluded, we therefore turn to consider whether China has fulfilled its obligations in Section 7.B(d) of its Schedule to ensure that EPS suppliers of any other Member may supply their services from China to issuers and acquirers, in a four-party model, or to the card holder and merchant, in a three-party model or other similar variations, in order to comply with its obligations under Article XVI:2(a) of the GATS.

7.621 We recall again, the measures require that only CUP handle the processing of the relevant transactions taking place in Hong Kong or Macao, or China. These transactions include situations in which (i) a Chinese national travels to Hong Kong or Macao and initiates an RMB bank card transaction with a card issued in China; and (ii) a Hong Kong or Macao national travels to China and initiates an RMB bank card transaction there with a card issued in either Hong Kong or Macao.

7.622 In the light of our understanding of what the supply of EPS under mode 3 may entail, we conclude that China's mode 3 commitment for EPS is applicable to the two scenarios described in the preceding paragraph.[810] Due to the requirement that only CUP handle the processing, in the event a foreign EPS supplier established itself in China through commercial presence, that foreign EPS supplier would be prevented from providing its services with respect to any such transaction. This would be the case despite the fact that China committed to allow foreign EPS suppliers to provide these services, subject to their meeting the qualifications requirements specified in China's mode 3 market access entry.

7.623 We recall that we need to determine whether the requirements at issue impose a limitation on the number of EPS suppliers, be it in the form of a monopoly or exclusive service suppliers. As we have explained in this section, Document Nos. 8, 16 and 254[811] mandate that only CUP handle the processing of RMB bank card transactions that involve either an RMB bank card issued in China and used in Hong Kong or Macao, or a bank card issued in Hong Kong or Macao that is used in China in an RMB transaction. Thus, the Hong Kong/Macao requirements limit the number of suppliers of EPS to one, namely to CUP. Plainly, this limitation is of a numerical and quantitative nature. We recall that a monopoly supplier is a sole supplier authorized or established formally or in effect by a Member. Due to the exclusivity that CUP enjoys as the

[810] We recall, in footnote 475 above, we explained that we would address the United States' claim only in relation to Document Nos. 8, 16 and 254 in (i) the case of a Chinese national travelling to Hong Kong and making a purchase with a card issued in China; (ii) the case of a Hong Kong or Macao national travelling to China and making a purchase with a card issued in Hong Kong or Macao. We stated that we would not consider a third scenario involving a Hong Kong or Macao national making an RMB purchase in either of these territories with an RMB payment card issued in either Hong Kong or Macao because we consider that the United States' claim in respect of the third scenario falls outside our terms of reference.

[811] The Panel specifically refers to Article 6 of Document No. 16, Article 6 of Document No. 8 and Articles 3, 4 and 17 of Document No. 254. See paras. 7.372-7.377 and 7.402-7.404 above.

sole EPS supplier in respect of the relevant transactions, we conclude that with regard to these transactions CUP is a monopoly within the meaning of Article XVI:2(a) of the GATS.[812]

7.624 Therefore, and for the foregoing reasons, we find that the Hong Kong/Macao requirements impose a limitation on the number of service suppliers in the form of a monopoly within the meaning of Article XVI:2(a) of the GATS for the supply of EPS for RMB bank card transactions that involve either an RMB bank card issued in China and used in Hong Kong or Macao, or an RMB bank card issued in Hong Kong or Macao that is used in China in an RMB-denominated transaction. This limitation on the number of suppliers is imposed even in respect of EPS suppliers of other WTO Members that meet the qualifications requirements specified in China's mode 3 market access entry. Because China has not "otherwise specified in its Schedule" that it may maintain such a limitation, we conclude that the Hong Kong/Macao requirements imposed by China are inconsistent with Article XVI:2(a) of the GATS.

(d) Whether China's requirements, when considered jointly, are inconsistent with Article XVI:2(a) of the GATS

7.625 The Panel recalls that the United States requested that the Panel consider the Chinese requirements at issue not only individually, but also in conjunction with each other, as it considers the requirements at issue are not just WTO-inconsistent when analysed individually, but operate together in a manner that is also WTO-inconsistent.[813] . The United States argues that this would help to ensure the effective resolution of this dispute.[814]

7.626 We concluded above that we would not address the United States' claims under Article XVI in respect of the sole supplier requirement or cross-region/inter-bank-bank prohibitions, as we concluded on the evidence before us that China does not maintain in place either of these "requirements". Having concluded that China maintains in place certain issuer requirements, terminal equipment requirements, acquirer requirements and Hong Kong/Macao requirements, however, we considered whether these four requirements are inconsistent with China's obligations under Article XVI of the GATS, as claimed by the United States. Ultimately, we concluded above[815] that the United States failed to establish that the issuer, terminal equipment and acquirer requirements, considered either separately or in combination, are inconsistent with

812 In our view, the relevant markets in which CUP is a monopoly within the meaning of Article XXVIII(h) of the GATS are the supply of EPS for RMB bank card transactions that involve a bank card issued in China and used in Hong Kong or Macao, and for RMB bank card transactions that involve a bank card issued in Hong Kong or Macao that is used in China in an RMB-denominated transaction.

813 United States' first written submission, para. 29; response to Panel question No. 4.

814 United States' first written submission, para. 32

815 See paras. 7.600-7.605 above.

Article XVI:2(a) of the GATS. Separately, we concluded that the Hong Kong/Macao requirements impose a limitation on the number of service suppliers in the form of a monopoly within the meaning of Article XVI:2(a) of the GATS. Because China has not "otherwise specified in its Schedule" that it may maintain such a limitation in respect of its mode 3 market access commitment, we concluded that the Hong Kong/Macao requirements imposed by China are inconsistent with Article XVI:2(a) of the GATS.[816]

7.627 In the light of the United States' request, we consider whether an assessment of the requirements in conjunction with each other would modify our conclusions. We have noted above on various occasions[817] that the Hong Kong/Macao requirements are limited in scope to bank card transactions that involve bank cards issued in China and used in Hong Kong or Macao, or alternatively, bank cards issued in Hong Kong or Macao and used in China. Due to their limited scope, we do not see how consideration of the Hong Kong/Macao requirements in conjunction with the issuer, terminal equipment and acquirer requirements would lead us to conclude that the issuer, terminal equipment and acquirer requirements impose a type of limitation that is inconsistent with Article XVI:2(a) of the GATS. In other words, it is not clear to us how combining the Hong Kong/Macao requirements with any of the other requirements would have the effect of converting any of the other requirements into the type of measure referred to in Article XVI:2(a). We therefore conclude that the United States has not established that the Hong Kong/Macao, issuer, terminal equipment and acquirer requirements, when considered in conjunction, give rise to a separate and independent breach of Article XVI:2(a) of the GATS.

(e) Whether the measures at issue are inconsistent with Article XVI:1 of the GATS

7.628 We recall that the United States has raised claims in respect of both Articles XVI:1 and XVI:2(a) of the GATS. Several panels have discussed the relationship between Articles XVI:1 and XVI:2. The panel in *US – Gambling* found "[t]he ordinary meaning of the words, the context of Article XVI, as well as the object and purpose of the GATS confirm that the restrictions on market access that are covered by Article XVI are only those listed in paragraph 2 of this Article".[818] On this basis, finding that the measures at issue were inconsistent with Articles XVI:2(a) and (c), the panel in that dispute did not consider it necessary to reach findings in respect of Article XVI:1 of the GATS. The Appellate Body in that dispute did not specifically address what is required to establish a violation of Article XVI:1.[819]

816 See para. 7.624 above.

817 See paras. 7.398, 7.401, 7.407, 7.480 and 7.491 above.

818 Panel Report, *US – Gambling*, paras. 6.318, 6.298-6.299.

819 Appellate Body Report, *US – Gambling*, para. 256. On appeal, the Appellate Body noted that Antigua conditionally appealed whether the measures at stake were also inconsistent with

7.629 In *China – Publications and Audiovisual Products*, the panel concluded similarly to the panel in *US – Gambling*, as follows:

> Paragraph 1 of Article XVI sets out the general principle that a Member must accord to services and service suppliers of other Members treatment no less favourable than that specified under the "terms, limitations and conditions" contained in its schedule. Paragraph 2 is more specific. It defines, in six sub-paragraphs, the measures that a Member, having inscribed a specific sectoral commitment, must not adopt or maintain "unless otherwise specified in its Schedule". The six types of measures form a closed or exhaustive list, as indicated by the wording of the chapeau to paragraph 2 ("the measures ... are defined as"). Under Article XVI, a Member undertakes a minimum standard of treatment, and is thus free to maintain a market access regime less restrictive than set out in its schedule, as confirmed in paragraph 1 which refers to a standard of "no less favourable" treatment.[820]

7.630 Bearing the approaches of these panels in mind, we similarly do not consider it necessary to proceed in our analysis under Article XVI:1. We first recall our finding above that the issuer, terminal equipment and acquirer requirements are not among the measures which Article XVI:2 says a Member may not maintain, and more specifically that they do not constitute market access limitations within the meaning of Article XVI:2(a) of the GATS. That being so, as the United States has directed its arguments toward alleging a market access limitation of the type described in Article XVI:2(a), it is difficult to see how the relevant requirements could be subject to Article XVI:1. In any event, in the absence of any meaningful attempt by the United States to demonstrate that the issuer, terminal equipment and acquirer requirements, taken either individually or together, are separately inconsistent with Article XVI:1, we consider that the United States has failed to meet its burden to present a *prima facie* case in respect of its Article XVI:1 claim.

7.631 In addition, we recall our finding above that the Hong Kong/Macao requirements imposed by China pursuant to Document Nos. 8, 16 and 254[821] are inconsistent with Article XVI:2(a). In the light of this finding, there is in our view no need to offer additional findings on these requirements under Article XVI:1 and we therefore decline to consider this claim further.

Article XVI:1 of the GATS, "in the event the Appellate Body were to agree with the United States' argument that GATS Articles XVI:2(a) and (c) only apply to limitations that are in form specified exactly and expressly in terms of numerical quotas." Having upheld the panel's interpretation of sub-paragraphs (a) and (c) of Article XVI:2, the Appellate Body decided to "leave the issue of the relationship between the first and the second paragraphs of Article XVI for another day" (Appellate Body Report, *US – Gambling*, para. 256).

[820] Panel Report, *China – Publications and Audiovisual Products*, para. 7.1353.

[821] The Panel specifically refers to Article 6 of Document No. 16, Article 6 of Document No. 8 and Articles 3, 4 and 17 of Document No. 254. See paras. 7.372-7.377 and 7.402-7.404 above.

3. *Conclusions*

7.632 Having completed its analysis, we recall our main conclusions on the United States' claims under Article XVI of the GATS.

(a) China's commitment under mode 1 in Sector 7.B(d) of its Schedule

7.633 The Panel finds that China has not undertaken a market access commitment under mode 1 in Sector 7.B(d) of its Schedule in respect of the services at issue. Therefore, the Panel concludes that the issuer, terminal equipment, acquirer and Hong Kong/Macao requirements are not inconsistent with Article XVI of the GATS in this respect.

(b) China's commitment under mode 3 in Sector 7.B(d) of its Schedule

7.634 The Panel finds that China has undertaken a market access commitment under mode 3 in Section 7.B(d) of its Schedule in respect of the services at issue in this dispute. That commitment is not subject to a limitation on the number of service suppliers in the form of monopolies.

(i) Issuer, terminal equipment, acquirer requirements

7.635 The Panel finds that the United States failed to establish that the issuer, terminal equipment and acquirer requirements are inconsistent with Article XVI:2(a) of the GATS, as these requirements do not impose a limitation that falls within the scope of Article XVI:2(a). The Panel further finds that the United States failed to meet its burden to present a *prima facie* case in respect of its Article XVI:1 claims concerning the issuer, terminal equipment and acquirer requirements.

(ii) Hong Kong/Macao requirements

7.636 The Panel finds that China, through Document Nos. 8, 16 and 254[822], imposes a limitation on the number of service suppliers in the form of a monopoly for CUP concerning the supply of EPS for RMB bank card transactions that involve either an RMB bank card issued in China and used in Hong Kong or Macao, or an RMB bank card issued in Hong Kong or Macao that is used in China in an RMB transaction. That limitation on the number of service suppliers is imposed even in respect of EPS suppliers of other WTO Members that meet the qualifications requirements specified in China's mode 3 market access entry. Accordingly, we find that the Hong Kong/Macao requirements imposed by China are inconsistent with Article XVI:2(a) of the GATS. In the

[822] *Ibid.*

light of this finding, the Panel exercised judicial economy with respect to the United States' claims under Article XVI:1 of the GATS regarding the Hong Kong/Macao requirements.

G. *The United States' Claims Under Article XVII of the GATS*

7.637 The Panel now turns to assess the United States' claims under Article XVII of the GATS. The United States claims that each of the challenged Chinese requirements (measures) are inconsistent with Article XVII in view of commitments taken by China under subsector (d) and modes 1 and 3. Article XVII is entitled "National Treatment" and provides as follows:

> 1. In the sectors inscribed in its Schedule, and subject to any conditions and qualifications set out therein, each Member shall accord to services and service suppliers of any other Member, in respect of all measures affecting the supply of services, treatment no less favourable than that it accords to its own like services and service suppliers.
>
> 2. A Member may meet the requirement of paragraph 1 by according to services and service suppliers of any other Member, either formally identical treatment or formally different treatment to that it accords to its own like services and service suppliers.
>
> 3. Formally identical or formally different treatment shall be considered to be less favourable if it modifies the conditions of competition in favour of services or service suppliers of the Member compared to like services or service suppliers of any other Member. (footnote omitted)

7.638 As noted, the United States claims that all six of China's requirements at issue are inconsistent with Article XVII both individually and in conjunction with each other. It bases these claims on national treatment commitments which it alleges were assumed by China under subsector (d) and modes 1 and 3. The United States submits that these requirements treat foreign suppliers of EPS services less favourably than CUP.[823]

7.639 China requests the Panel to dismiss the United States' claims under Article XVII in their entirety. With regard to its national treatment commitments, China argues that the United States failed to demonstrate that these commitments are relevant to the services and service suppliers at issue. More specifically, China contends that the United States failed to demonstrate that EPS suppliers of other WTO Members are "foreign financial institutions" within the meaning of China's GATS Schedule.[824] As concerns China's national treatment commitments in mode 1, China submits that the United States improperly bases its claims

[823] United States' first written submission, para. 76; second written submission, para. 215.
[824] China's first written submission, para. 146.

under Article XVII on the same aspects of the same requirements that are the foundation of the United States' claims under Article XVI of the GATS.[825] China argues that it reserved the right to introduce market access limitations for subsector (d) and mode 1, including limitations under Article XVI:2 that might be seen as discriminatory. China is of the view that its right to introduce such measures cannot be taken away by a finding that the exact same aspects of the requirements at issue are inconsistent with Article XVII. According to China, this would defeat the choice that it made by leaving market access unbound in mode 1.[826]

7.640 The Panel begins its assessment of the United States' Article XVII claims by setting out its analytical approach and determining the scope of its Article XVII findings.

1. Analytical approach and scope of Article XVII findings

7.641 As has been pointed out by the United States, the panel in *China – Publications and Audiovisual Products* effectively applied a three-part test to assess whether a Member's measure is inconsistent with Article XVII.[827] The United States suggests that we follow the same analytical approach.[828] We find it appropriate to do so, noting also that China has not specifically opposed the United States' suggestion. Accordingly, in order to sustain its claim that China's measures are in breach of Article XVII, the United States as the complaining party needs to establish all of the following three elements:

(i) China has made a commitment on national treatment in the relevant sector and mode of supply, regard being had to any conditions and qualifications, or limitations[829], set out in its Schedule;

(ii) China's measures are "measures affecting the supply of services" in the relevant sector and mode of supply; and

(iii) China's measures accord to services or service suppliers of any other Member treatment less favourable than that China accords to its own like services and service suppliers.

---

[825] China's first written submission, para. 148.

[826] China's first written submission, para. 159.

[827] The panel in *China – Publications and Audiovisual Products* at one point in its report distinguished four elements. But elsewhere in its report, the panel combined two of the four elements into one, thus effectively applying a three-part test. See Panel Report, *China – Publications and Audiovisual Products*, paras. 7.1272, 7.942 and 7.956.

[828] United States' first written submission, paras. 74 and 75.

[829] Regarding the term "limitations", we note that Article XX:1 of the GATS refers specifically to "terms, limitations and conditions" to market access, and "conditions and qualifications" to national treatment. This accords with the wording of Articles XVI:2 (on market access), XVII:1 (on national treatment) and XX:1(b) (on schedules of specific commitments). For simplicity, we adopt the term "limitations", which is used in the column headings in China's Schedule (and those of other Members), and throughout the 1993 and 2001 Scheduling Guidelines.

7.642 We separately examine these three elements below. The Chinese requirements we will review in this section include the issuer requirements, the terminal equipment requirements and the acquirer requirements. As concerns the remaining three requirements at issue, we recall our conclusion that the United States has not established the existence of the alleged sole supplier requirements or the alleged cross-region/inter-bank prohibitions. We consequently do not examine these requirements under Article XVII. Furthermore, as we have determined above that the Hong Kong/Macao requirements are inconsistent with Article XVI of the GATS in respect of foreign EPS suppliers supplying EPS through mode 3, in the interest of judicial economy we refrain from determining whether these requirements are also inconsistent with Article XVII for mode 3 suppliers. We do, however, examine whether the Hong Kong/Macao requirements are inconsistent with Article XVII in respect of foreign EPS suppliers supplying EPS through mode 1.

7.643 Having clarified which requirements are to be the subject of our Article XVII findings, we can commence our three-part analysis of the relevant requirements.

2. *China's requirements considered individually*

(a) Whether China has undertaken relevant national treatment commitments

7.644 The first element of our three-part analysis is to determine whether China has made commitments on national treatment in the relevant sector and modes of supply, regard being had to any limitations set out in its Schedule. The Panel recalls that the United States in this case has identified subsector (d) as the relevant inscribed sector, and modes 1 and 3 as the relevant modes of supply. We first consider whether China has undertaken national treatment commitments under mode 1.

(i) Mode 1 commitments

General

7.645 The United States argues that China has made a full national treatment commitment for subsector (d) in mode 1, having inscribed "None" (no limitations) for this mode in the national treatment column of its Schedule.[830]

7.646 China responds that the United States improperly bases its national treatment claims on "the same aspects of the same measures" that are the foundation of its market access claims under Article XVI of the GATS.[831] In China's view, the measures described in Article XVI:2 cannot simultaneously be

[830] United States' first written submission, paras. 20 and 77.
[831] China's first written submission, paras. 148 and 150.

subject to Article XVII, without wholly disregarding the basis upon which market access and national treatment commitments were scheduled.[832] For China, the United States' approach is contrary to the "order of precedence" that Article XX:2 establishes in favour of Article XVI, as well as the principle of effectiveness of treaty interpretation (*effet utile*).[833] According to China, Article XVI governs "all aspects" of the measures described in Article XVI:2(a)-(f), including any respect in which such a measure is potentially discriminatory.[834] Articles XVI and XVII are thus "mutually exclusive" in their respective spheres of application.[835] To interpret these provisions otherwise would make it impossible for China to remove a national treatment inconsistency, while leaving in place its market access limitation.[836] It would defeat entirely the policy choice that China made by leaving market access unbound in mode 1.[837]

7.647 The United States disagrees with China's argument that the inscription of "Unbound" for market access in mode 1 affects the scope of its national treatment commitment for that mode.[838] Article XVI:2, for the United States, does not extend to restrictions that are discriminatory.[839] A measure limiting the number of foreign suppliers only would not, for example, limit "the number of services suppliers" under Article XVI:2(a), since the measure is silent as to how many domestic persons can supply the service.[840] As for Article XX:2, the United States argues that it is simply a scheduling rule that exists because measures may be inscribed in a Member's schedule that are inconsistent with both Articles XVI and XVII.[841] For the United States, Article XX:2 does not make Articles XVI and XVII "mutually exclusive" in their respective spheres of application, as argued by China.[842] Thus, an "Unbound" inscription for market access, combined with a "None" for national treatment, "carves out" only overall quantitative limitations, not limitations that discriminate against foreign suppliers.[843]

7.648 According to the European Union, an inscription of "Unbound" in the market access column of a schedule logically implies that a Member has retained the right to impose any of the limitations under Article XVI:2, and that those limitations, in accordance with Article XX:2, extend to its national treatment obligations under Article XVII, despite the absence of limitations scheduled

[832] China's first written submission, para. 150.
[833] China's first written submission, para. 156.
[834] *Ibid.*
[835] China's first written submission, para. 156.
[836] China's second written submission, para. 119.
[837] China's first written submission, para. 159.
[838] United States' second written submission, para. 194.
[839] United States' response to Panel question No. 69, para. 196.
[840] *Ibid.*
[841] United States' second written submission, para. 195.
[842] *Ibid.*
[843] United States' second written submission, para. 196.

under this provision.[844] Japan, Australia and Ecuador agree that China's unbound entry for market access allows it to maintain market access limitations that are discriminatory.[845] Guatemala, on the other hand, argues that the inscription of "Unbound" for market access means that China must respect any national treatment commitments that it has made under Article XVII.[846]

7.649 The Panel notes that the parties disagree on the scope of China's national treatment commitment in mode 1, as it applies to the measures at issue. Their disagreement focuses on the effect, if any, of China's market access inscription of "Unbound" on the scope of its national treatment commitment, the entry for which is inscribed as "None".[847] To resolve this issue, we begin by examining Article XX:1 of the GATS, which sets out the basic rule for a Member inscribing commitments in its schedule:

> 1. Each Member shall set out in a schedule the specific commitments it undertakes under Part III [including Articles XVI and XVII] of this Agreement. With respect to sectors where such commitments are undertaken, each Schedule shall specify:
>
> (a) terms, limitations and conditions on market access;
>
> (b) conditions and qualifications on national treatment;
>
> ...

7.650 We observe that Article XX:1 requires a Member to inscribe, for the sectors it has committed in its Schedule, the limitations ("terms, limitations and conditions") it intends to maintain for market access, and the limitations ("conditions and qualifications") it wishes to maintain for national treatment. Each inscription of a limitation (or absence thereof) is normally entered in the appropriate market access or national treatment column of the Schedule by inscribing "None" (no limitations), "Unbound" (no commitment), or the measure or measures that limit the commitment.[848] This terminology and usage is drawn from the Scheduling Guidelines.[849]

---

[844] European Union's response to Panel question No. 7(a), para. 22.

[845] Japan's response to Panel question No. 24; Australia's response to Panel question No. 7(a) and 7(b); Ecuador's oral statement, para. 17.

[846] Guatemala's response to Panel question No. 7(a), para. 28.

[847] Since we have found that China's market access inscription of "Unbound, except ..." amounts to unbound market access, for the sake of simplicity we use the term "Unbound" in this part of the Report.

[848] Occasionally, Members use variations of these basic inscriptions. A common example is the inscription "Unbound except ...", an example of which is found in China's market access inscription for mode 4 in subsector (d).

[849] 1993 Scheduling Guidelines, paras. 24, 25, and 27; 2001 Scheduling Guidelines, paras. 42, 44, and 46. The original 1993 Scheduling Guidelines were updated and formally agreed in a 2001 Decision by the Council for Trade in Services. The 1993 Scheduling Guidelines are considered a supplementary source of interpretation for the GATS. See Appellate Body Report, *US – Gambling*, para. 196.

7.651 In the light of the basic rule set out in Article XX:1, supplemented by the Scheduling Guidelines, we now examine the relevant entries in China's Schedule. We start with China's inscription for national treatment in mode 1. We recall that China has inscribed the term "None" in the column entitled "Limitations on National Treatment". Although no specific definition exists in the GATS of the term "None", its ordinary meaning is clear when read in conjunction with the title of the column in which the term appears. It indicates that China has undertaken "no" limitations – in other words, a full commitment – with respect to national treatment in this mode, unless otherwise inferred from its Schedule.[850] Hence, as regards the supply of services in subsector (d) through mode 1, the entry of "None" in the national treatment column suggests that China would be committed to providing full national treatment. This national treatment would extend to "all measures affecting the supply of services", the scope of Article XVII as defined in that provision.

7.652 We continue our analysis by examining China's inscription for market access in mode 1, which we have found in paragraph 7.538 to amount to "Unbound". Although there is no specific definition in the GATS of this term, we note that a general dictionary meaning of the term "bound" is to be "compelled or obliged".[851] This sense is supported by a specialized legal dictionary, which gives a meaning of "constrained by a contractual or other obligation".[852] Thus the term "unbound" would indicate an absence of constraint or obligation.[853] In the same vein, the Scheduling Guidelines instruct a Member wishing to retain the freedom to introduce measures inconsistent with market access or national treatment to record the term "Unbound" in its GATS Schedule.[854] Since we have found subsector (d) to be unbound for market access, this suggests that China is under no constraint or obligation to grant market access within the terms of Article XVI:2. Unlike Article XVII, however, the scope of the market access obligation does not extend generally to "all measures affecting the supply of services". Instead, it applies to six carefully defined categories of measures of a mainly quantitative nature. The issue thus arises whether the scope of these measures, and thus the extent of China's absence of

---

[850] The interpretation of "None" as meaning a full commitment has been confirmed, in the context of a market access commitment, by the Appellate Body (Appellate Body Report, *US – Gambling,* para. 215).

[851] *Shorter Oxford English Dictionary*, Vol.1, p. 236.

[852] *Black's Law Dictionary*, p. 210.

[853] We note as additional context that the term "unbound" is also used in connection with GATT 1994 goods schedules to indicate, with respect to a particular tariff line, absence of obligation. See, for example, usage in China's WTO goods schedule (Schedule CLII, People's Republic of China, Part I – Most-favoured-nation Tariff, Section II – Other Products) in which "bound rate of duty" is indicated in one column, and "Base rate of duty U/B" in another. The structure of a WTO goods schedules is described generally in a Secretariat Note on "Preparation of the Uruguay Round Schedules of Concession on Market Access", MTN.GNG/MA/W/25 of 22 December 1993.

[854] 1993 Scheduling Guidelines, para. 11; 2001 Scheduling Guidelines, para. 18. See also Appellate Body Report, *US – Gambling*, fn. 257, which states: "This notation is the opposite of the notation 'Unbound', which means that a Member undertakes *no* specific commitment."

obligation with respect thereto, extends to discriminatory measures in the sense of Article XVII.

7.653 On this matter, the United States takes the position that discriminatory quantitative restrictions are not within the scope of Article XVI:2.[855] The Panel, in assessing the scope of the six categories of measures in Article XVI:2, observes at the outset that subparagraph (f), concerning foreign equity limitations, is expressly discriminatory, and that the limitation on joint ventures in subparagraph (e) is inherently so since this business form is very likely applicable only to foreign service suppliers. Nonetheless, while the wording of subparagraphs (e) and (f) suggests that discriminatory measures are not completely excluded from the scope of Article XVI:2, it does not, in the Panel's view, indicate whether the other four subparagraphs also extend to discriminatory measures.

7.654 Pursuing our examination of the scope of Article XVI:2, we note that the wording of the quantitative measures described in subparagraphs (a)-(d) contains nothing that would suggest that measures having discriminatory aspects are for this reason excluded. This view finds contextual support in the wording of Article XX:2 (examined in paragraph 7.657 below), which is premised on the existence of measures "inconsistent with both Articles XVI and XVII", and thus on the existence of measures within the scope of Article XVI:2 that have discriminatory aspects. Since nothing in the generality of the wording of Article XX:2 indicates that it applies only to measures within the scope of subparagraphs (e) and (f), which are expressly or inherently discriminatory in nature, we view Article XX:2 as a further indication that measures within the scope of any of the subparagraphs of Article XVI:2 can have discriminatory aspects. This view is also supported by the Scheduling Guidelines, in which the generality of the discussion on measures inconsistent with both Articles XVI and XVII reflects the view that, overall, Article XVI:2 extends to measures with discriminatory aspects.[856] For these reasons, the Panel finds that the obligations in Article XVI:2 can extend to measures that are also within the scope of Article XVII. With respect to China's inscription of "Unbound" for market access in mode 1, our finding would therefore suggest that China may introduce or maintain any measures falling within Article XVI:2, including those that may be discriminatory within the meaning of Article XVII.

7.655 The Panel notes, however, that its analysis of the scopes of Articles XVI and XVII leads to an apparent ambiguity in China's inscriptions in mode 1 for market access and national treatment. On the one hand, China's full national treatment commitment under Article XVII extends to "all measures affecting the supply of a service", which would appear to include measures within the scope of its unbound market access commitment. On the other, China's unbound market access commitment under Article XVI would appear to extend to

[855] United States' second written submission, para. 196.

[856] 1993 Scheduling Guidelines, para. 11; 2001 Scheduling Guidelines, para. 18.

measures that are also discriminatory, and within the scope of its full national treatment commitment. The United States argues that China's full national treatment commitment implies that measures inconsistent with both Articles XVI and XVII are subject to China's obligations under Article XVII. China, on the other hand, argues that its absence of market access commitment means that such measures are *not* subject to any obligations it may have under Article XVII.

7.656 In resolving this difference of view, the Panel considers that the main issue is not an ambiguity over the scope of Article XVI and the scope of Article XVII. The main issue is rather a lack of clarity about the scope of the *inscriptions* "Unbound" and "None" when applied, in China's Schedule, to measures that conflict with both market access and national treatment obligations. In considering this more specific question, we observe that the basic scheduling rule in Article XX:1, referred to above, does not determine how a Member should inscribe a limitation in such a case. Instead, we note that a special scheduling rule in Article XX:2 aims to resolve this lack of clarity:

> Measures inconsistent with both Articles XVI and XVII shall be inscribed in the column relating to Article XVI. In this case the inscription will be considered to provide a condition or qualification to Article XVII as well.

7.657 The wording of Article XX:2 indicates that it applies when a measure is (a) inconsistent with both Article XVI and Article XVII, and (b) inscribed in the market access column of a Member's Schedule. As long as these two requirements are met, then the inscription under market access will provide a "condition or qualification" or, in the simpler usage we adopt, a "limitation", to Article XVII as well. In other words, the single inscription of a measure conflicting with both Articles XVI and XVII in the market access column of a schedule provides a limitation for both discriminatory and non-discriminatory aspects of the measure.

7.658 The Panel draws several inferences from the wording of Article XX:2. First, the provision confirms the basic point that measures exist that are inconsistent with both market access and national treatment obligations. In that sense, the scope of Article XVI and the scope of Article XVII are not mutually exclusive, as China appears to argue. Both provisions can apply to a single measure. As Article XX:2 makes clear, a single measure can contain or give rise to two simultaneous inconsistencies: one with respect to a market access obligation, the other with respect to a national treatment obligation. To maintain or introduce such a measure, the normal rule for inscribing commitments in Article XX:1 might suggest that a Member needs to enter an explicit limitation in both the market access and national treatment columns. In such cases however, the special rule in Article XX:2 provides a simpler requirement: a Member need only make a single inscription of the measure under the market access column, which then provides an implicit limitation under national treatment.

7.659 Secondly, the Panel observes that the wording of Article XX:2 indicates that what is inscribed in the market access column is a "measure" which, in the situation of conflict contemplated by Article XX:2, must encompass aspects that are inconsistent with both Articles XVI and XVII. In this way, a single inscription under Article XVI of a "measure" will provide a limitation as well under Article XVII.

7.660 The United States argues that the term "Unbound" cannot be viewed as the inscription of "measures" and therefore cannot provide a condition or qualification to Article XVII through the operation of Article XX:2.[857] In contrast, China says that the term "Unbound" is "simply a shorthand device for inscribing all measures, present or future" that are inconsistent with Article XVI:2.[858] The Panel notes that Article XX:2 states that "*[m]easures* inconsistent with both Articles XVI and XVII shall be inscribed ..." (emphasis added). We see nothing in the text of Article XX:2 that would constrain the latitude of a Member to inscribe the "measures" excluded from Article XVI:2 either individually or collectively. In our view, it would be incongruous if an inscription of "Unbound" had an effect different from that of inscribing individually all possible measures within the six categories foreseen under Article XVI:2. To take a different interpretation would be to elevate form over substance. In our assessment, therefore, an inscription of the term "Unbound" in the market access column should be viewed as an inscription of "measures", specifically of all those defined in Article XVI:2, which a Member may not maintain or adopt, unless otherwise specified in its schedule. For this reason, we find that Article XX:2 does apply to situations where a Member has inscribed "Unbound" in the market access column of its schedule. In the Panel's view, the inscription of "Unbound" in the market access column of China's Schedule has the equivalent effect of an inscription of all possible measures falling within Article XVI:2.

7.661 Having found that the special scheduling rule in Article XX:2 applies to China's inscription of "Unbound", the Panel must now consider what effect this has on the scope of China's national treatment commitment. The Panel recalls that Article XX:2 provides, in the case of measures inconsistent with both Articles XVI and XVII, that the measure inscribed in the market access column encompasses aspects inconsistent with *both* market access and national treatment obligations. Consequently, an "Unbound" inscription in the market access column encompasses inconsistencies with Article XVII as well as those arising from Article XVI. The inscription of "Unbound" will therefore, in the terms of Article XX:2, "provide a condition or qualification to Article XVII as well", thus permitting China to maintain measures that are inconsistent with both Articles XVI and XVII. With an inscription of "Unbound" for subsector (d) in mode 1 under Article XVI, and a corresponding "None" for Article XVII, China has

[857] United States' response to Panel question No. 69, para. 173.

[858] China's response to Panel question No. 69, para. 125.

indicated that it is free to maintain the full range of limitations expressed in the six categories of Article XVI:2, whether discriminatory or not.

7.662 The Panel recalls that China's overall argument is that the United States improperly cites "the same aspects of the same measures" to support claims that China both maintains a monopoly inconsistent with Article XVI:2(a) and violates its national treatment commitment under Article XVII.[859] China submits that Article XVI "governs all aspects of the measures identified in Article XVI:(a)-(f), including the maintenance of a monopoly", and that this is in accordance with Article XX:2 and necessary to give effect to China's "Unbound" entry in the market access column.[860] Our findings respond to China's argument on this point, in that they imply that a measure that is inconsistent with both Articles XVI and XVII, and that is inscribed in the market access column of China's Schedule, could not be found to be in breach of China's full national treatment commitment. The relevant measure would not be subject to China's full national treatment commitment as it would be covered by the market access limitation.

7.663 In the present case, we consider that our interpretation of the meaning of "Unbound" when inscribed in the market access column of a schedule gives full meaning to that term. By inscribing "Unbound" under market access, China reserves the right to maintain any type of measure within the six categories falling under Article XVI:2, regardless of its inscription in the national treatment column. We observe, however, that our interpretation also gives meaning to the term "None" in the national treatment column. Due to the inscription of "None", China must grant national treatment with respect to any of the measures at issue that are not inconsistent with Article XVI:2. China's national treatment commitment could thus have practical application should China, for example, choose to allow in practice the supply of services from the territory of other WTO Members into its market, despite the fact that it has not undertaken any market access commitments in subsectors (a) to (f) of its Schedule.

7.664 We point out that our conclusion on the relationship of the inscription "Unbound" under Article XVI with that of "None" under Article XVII preserves the freedom of WTO Members, when taking services commitments, to choose the combination of market access and national treatment limitations, if any, that they wish to maintain. Our conclusion does not narrow the range of options available to WTO Members to limit their market access and national treatment commitments. It focuses solely on how to interpret through scheduling rules, notably Article XX:2, the inscriptions that a WTO Member has chosen to enter in its schedule. We emphasize as well that we do not find that either of Articles XVI or XVII is substantively subordinate to the other. We find simply that Article XX:2 establishes a certain *scheduling* primacy for entries in the market access column, in that a WTO Member not wishing to make any commitment

[859] China's first written submission, para. 150.

[860] China's first written submission, paras. 149-159.

under Article XVI, discriminatory or non-discriminatory, may do so by inscribing the term "Unbound" in the market access column of its schedule.

7.665 For all these reasons, the Panel finds that China's market access entry concerning subsector (d) and mode 1 allows it to maintain any measures in that subsector and mode that are inconsistent with both Articles XVI and XVII.

Whether China has mode 1 national treatment commitments that apply to China's relevant requirements

7.666 Having considered the mode 1 market access and national treatment entries in China's Schedule, we address whether China has mode 1 national treatment commitments that apply to China's relevant requirements. We first examine the Hong Kong/Macao requirements. At the outset of our examination we recall that we have already found above at paragraph 7.624 that these requirements are inconsistent with Article XVI:2(a) because China has undertaken market access commitments in mode 3 for subsector (d) and because these requirements constitute limitations on the number of service suppliers in the form of a monopoly – a limitation not included in China's schedule. The question arises whether these same requirements constitute limitations on the number of service suppliers only with regard to mode 3 or whether they also limit the number of service suppliers with regard to mode 1.

7.667 We recall that the instruments that impose the Hong Kong/Macao requirements – Document Nos. 8, 16 and 254 – mandate that only CUP handle the processing of RMB payment card transactions that involve either an RMB payment card issued in China and used in Hong Kong or Macao, or an RMB card issued in Hong Kong or Macao and used in China. Therefore, it is clear to us that in respect of such transactions EPS suppliers of other WTO Members are precluded from providing their services on a cross-border basis to consumers (i.e. issuers or acquirers), that are based in China. In the light of this, the Hong Kong/Macao requirements in our view constitute limitations on the number of service suppliers in the form of a monopoly, including with regard to EPS suppliers of other WTO Members that would supply their services on a cross-border basis to Chinese consumers (mode 1 supply). In other words, we consider that these requirements impose an Article XVI:2(a)-type limitation on market access through mode 1.

7.668 As such, the Hong Kong/Macao requirements are covered by China's market access entry for mode 1 and subsector (d). We have determined above that due to the inscription of "Unbound" in that entry and Article XX:2, China is allowed to maintain the full range of limitations expressed in Article XVI:2, whether discriminatory or not. More particularly, Article XX:2 makes clear that even if the Hong Kong/Macao requirements, in addition to being market access limitations, are also "measures affecting the supply of services" within the meaning of Article XVII:1 and result in EPS suppliers of other WTO Members being treated less favourably than like Chinese services and service suppliers when supplying through mode 1, the inscription of "Unbound" in China's market access entry provides "a condition or qualification to Article XVII". In turn, Article XVII:1 states that a Member's national treatment obligations apply "subject to any conditions and qualifications set out [in its Schedule]". Accordingly, despite the inscription of "None" in its national treatment column concerning subsector (d) and mode 1, China has no obligation in respect of the Hong Kong/Macao requirements to accord to EPS supplied through mode 1, and EPS suppliers of other WTO Members supplying through mode 1, treatment no less favourable than that it accords to its own like services and service suppliers.

7.669 For these reasons, we conclude that the Hong Kong/Macao requirements, to the extent that they affect the cross-border supply of EPS (mode 1), are not inconsistent with China's obligations under Article XVII:1 of the GATS.

7.670 With respect to the issuer, terminal equipment and acquirer requirements, we have previously found that, contrary to the United States' assertion, these requirements are not subject to Article XVI because they do not impose any market access limitations of the type specified in Article XVI:2(a). As a result, the inscription of "Unbound" in China's market access column does not apply to these requirements. We recall, however, that China has inscribed in its national treatment column a full national treatment commitment in mode 1 for subsector (d). The issuer, terminal equipment and acquirer requirements are covered by this commitment if they are "measures affecting the supply" of EPS through mode 1. We will address this issue further below.[861]

(ii) Mode 3 commitments

General

7.671 The Panel must now examine whether China has undertaken national treatment commitments in subsector (d) concerning mode 3. China's Schedule in the column entitled "Limitations on national treatment" contains a relevant entry. It reads as follows:

> (3) Except for geographic restrictions and client limitations on local currency business (listed in the market access column), foreign financial institution [*sic*] may do business, without restrictions or need for case-by-case approval, with foreign invested enterprises, non-Chinese natural persons, Chinese natural persons and Chinese enterprises. Otherwise, none.[862]

7.672 The United States notes that this entry provides for no national treatment limitations concerning subsector (d) and mode 3 other than the geographic and client limitations inscribed in the mode 3 market access column. The United States argues that because those market access limitations expired in December

---

861 See paras. 7.680 et seq. below.

862 For the geographic restrictions and client limitations on local currency business that are listed in the market access column of China's Schedule, see Annex G.

2006, there are no longer any national treatment limitations with regard to subsector (d) and mode 3. In the United States' view, China must therefore provide national treatment within the meaning of Article XVII to foreign EPS suppliers supplying services on a commercial presence basis.[863]

7.673 China responds that its mode 3 national treatment commitments for subsector (d) mirror the corresponding limitation on market access inscribed by China in its Schedule for the same subsector and mode. Thus, China submits that its mode 3 national treatment commitments are limited to "foreign financial institutions". In other words, China contends that the only types of entities that may provide relevant services on a commercial presence basis are foreign financial institutions.[864] China argues that contrary to the United States' assertion, this limitation of its commitments to foreign financial institutions did not expire five years after China's accession to the WTO. China also contends that the United States failed to demonstrate that EPS suppliers of other WTO Members are foreign financial institutions.[865]

7.674 The Panel observes that China's national treatment entry concerning mode 3 ends with the phrase "otherwise, none". This indicates that there are no limitations on China's national treatment commitment concerning subsector (d) and mode 3 other than those set out in the preceding sentence of the entry. Having regard to that sentence, we note that it refers to geographic restrictions and client limitations on local currency business conducted by foreign financial institutions that are listed in the corresponding mode 3 market access column of China's Schedule. However, these restrictions and limitations were only in effect until December 2006.[866] As a consequence, under the terms of the entry in question, foreign financial institutions must no longer face any limitations on national treatment.

7.675 The next issue we consider is whether EPS suppliers of other WTO Members constitute foreign financial institutions within the meaning of the entry in question. We recall that we addressed the same question in the context of our analysis of China's market access commitments concerning subsector (d) and mode 3. We determined there that EPS suppliers of other WTO Members – i.e. WTO Members other than China – can be properly considered foreign financial institutions.[867] We find no basis to conclude differently in the context of the present inquiry. Indeed, we note that the mode 3 national treatment limitations specifically refer to the mode 3 market access limitations.

7.676 In our view, the entry at issue therefore supports the conclusion that China has committed to allow EPS suppliers of other WTO Members to carry

863 United States' first written submission, paras. 20 and 77.
864 China's first written submission, para. 137.
865 China's first written submission, paras. 131-132.
866 The relevant restrictions and limitations expired five years after China's accession to the WTO.
867 See para. 7.570 above.

out local currency business[868] in China with issuers, acquirers, merchants and card holders[869], without restrictions that would constitute limitations on national treatment, except for any national treatment limitations inscribed by virtue of Article XX:2 in the mode 3 market access column concerning subsector (d). A relevant limitation that is inscribed in the market access column concerns qualifications for foreign financial institutions to engage in local currency business.[870]

7.677 We are mindful that there are limitations on national treatment contained in the section of China's Schedule that sets out horizontal commitments. However, we discern nothing in the horizontal section of China's Schedule that would lead us to modify the conclusion we have reached on the basis of the columns on national treatment limitations and market access limitations.

7.678 For all these reasons, we conclude that, with regard to EPS provided by suppliers of other WTO Members, China has made a commitment on national treatment concerning mode 3. That commitment is subject to a limitation concerning qualifications to engage in local currency business. China is therefore obligated to accord national treatment to like EPS and EPS suppliers of other WTO Members in respect of local currency (RMB) business, subject to such suppliers meeting the aforesaid qualifications requirement.

Whether China has mode 3 national treatment commitments that apply to China's relevant requirements

7.679 With respect to the issuer, terminal equipment and acquirer requirements, we found earlier that these requirements are not subject to Article XVI because they do not impose any market access limitations of the type specified in Article XVI:2(a). However, in our view these requirements are covered by China's aforementioned national treatment commitment for mode 3, provided they are "measures affecting the supply" of EPS through mode 3. We address this issue below.[871]

---

868 As explained at para. 7.572 above, we understand that for the purposes of the requirements at issue the relevant business in which EPS suppliers of other WTO Members would engage is local currency (RMB) business.

869 We recall that the enterprises or persons with which EPS suppliers do business vary according to the type of network that EPS suppliers use (four-party vs. three-party model).

870 Pursuant to the entry in question, prior to applying for authorization to engage in local currency business, foreign financial institutions must have three years of business operation in China and be profitable for two consecutive years.

871 See paras. 7.680 et seq. below.

(b) Whether China's requirements affect the supply of services

7.680 The second element of our Article XVII inquiry calls for an analysis of whether China's requirements (measures) affect the supply of services.[872] We recall that in this particular Article XVII inquiry, we are concerned with EPS services provided by service suppliers of other WTO Members through modes 1 and 3, because the United States bases its Article XVII claims on China's relevant commitments under these two modes of supply.

7.681 The Appellate Body has provided the following relevant clarification regarding the meaning of the term "affect":

> [T]he term "affecting" [as it appears in Article I:1 of the GATS] reflects the intent of the drafters to give a broad reach of the GATS. The ordinary meaning of the word "affecting" implies a measure that has "an effect on", which indicates a broad scope of application. This interpretation is further reinforced by the conclusions of previous panels that the term "affecting" in the context of Article III of the GATT is wider in scope than such terms as "regulating" or "governing".[873]

7.682 Accordingly, we need to determine whether the Chinese requirements to be examined regulate or at least have an effect on the supply of EPS services by service suppliers of other Members through modes 1 and 3.

7.683 Turning now to the requirements to be examined under the second element of our Article XVII inquiry, we recall that in respect of the Hong Kong/Macao requirements we have already reached the conclusion that they are not inconsistent with Article XVII to the extent that they affect the cross-border supply of EPS. We do not, therefore, need to examine these requirements further. In contrast, we do need to determine whether the issuer, terminal equipment and acquirer requirements affect the supply of EPS.

7.684 The United States submits that these three requirements affect the supply of EPS by foreign suppliers because they directly regulate the terms on which they may be provided in China. The United States argues that they are requirements that promote CUP's position in the marketplace by imposing certain requirements on every key player in a card-based electronic payment transaction, including issuers, merchants and acquirers.[874] More specifically, the United States notes that, due to the issuer requirements, bank cards in China

---

[872] To recall, Article XVII states that WTO Members must provide national treatment "in respect of all measures affecting the supply of services".

[873] Appellate Body Report, *EC – Bananas III*, para. 220. As indicated, the Appellate Body made this statement in relation to the term "affecting" as it appears in Article I:1 of the GATS. We find the statement to be equally relevant and persuasive when looked at in the context of our Article XVII analysis, not least in view of the Appellate Body's explicit reference to Article III of the GATT, which is the GATT-equivalent of Article XVII of the GATS.

[874] United States' first written submission, paras. 79 and 81.

used for RMB purchases in China, as well as dual currency cards issued in China, must bear the CUP logo, while no foreign EPS supplier is afforded a similar privilege.[875] Similarly, the United States argues that as a consequence of the terminal equipment and acquirer requirements, all terminal equipment must accept CUP cards and acquirers in China must post the CUP logo and accept all bank cards bearing that logo. According to the United States, no foreign EPS supplier is afforded a similar privilege.[876]

7.685 China does not specifically address the issue of whether the requirements at issue affect the supply of services.

7.686 The Panel notes that the issuer, terminal equipment and acquirer requirements are addressed, *inter alia*, to issuers, merchants and acquirers, but not to EPS suppliers. However, all three requirements explicitly relate to one – and only one – EPS supplier, CUP. As noted by the United States and as further explained by our findings below concerning the issue of less favourable treatment, these requirements have an effect on the terms on which CUP can supply its services in the Chinese market. We have not been made aware of any parallel requirements that would specifically relate to EPS suppliers other than CUP. Therefore, due to the fact that the three requirements in question have an effect on the terms on which CUP can supply its services, they also have a consequential effect on the terms on which CUP's potential competitors, which include EPS suppliers of other Members, can supply their services in China, e.g. on a cross-border basis or through commercial presence. In the light of this, we conclude that the issuer, terminal equipment and acquirer requirements "have an effect" on, and hence affect, the mode 1 and 3 supply of EPS by suppliers of other Members. In other words, we consider that the three requirements at issue each constitute "measures affecting the [mode 1 and 3] supply of services" within the meaning of Article XVII:1.

(c) Whether China's requirements accord less favourable treatment

7.687 It remains for us to address the third and last element of our Article XVII inquiry. This involves determining whether China's requirements (measures) accord to services or service suppliers of any other Member "treatment less favourable" than that China accords to its own "like services and service suppliers". We note that the GATS provides no definition of the phrase "like services and service suppliers". In contrast, as regards the concept of "less favourable treatment", Article XVII:3 provides useful clarification. It states that formally identical or different treatment is deemed less favourable "if it modifies the conditions of competition in favour of services or service suppliers of the Member compared to like services or service suppliers of any other Member".

875 United States' first written submission, para. 80.

876 *Ibid.*

We deduce from this that, subject to all other Article XVII conditions being fulfilled, formally identical or different treatment of service suppliers of another Member constitutes a breach of Article XVII:1 if and only if such treatment modifies the conditions of competition to their detriment.

7.688 The only requirements at issue in respect of which we reach the third element of our Article XVII inquiry are the issuer, terminal equipment and acquirer requirements. In respect of these requirements, the United States alleges that on their face they confer an advantage, or privilege, on CUP that is not afforded EPS suppliers of another Member.[877] We therefore understand the United States to allege that China provides formally different treatment to CUP, on the one hand, and like EPS suppliers of other Members, on the other hand, and that the different treatment modifies the conditions of competition to the detriment of the latter.

7.689 Accordingly, our examination of the third Article XVII element will proceed in two steps for each of the relevant requirements. First we will analyse whether, and if so, how the requirements provide for different treatment between CUP and "like" EPS suppliers of other Members. We note in this respect that these requirements are not addressed to CUP, but at such entities as issuers or acquirers. Then we will examine whether any different treatment of like services and service suppliers that we might find amounts to less favourable treatment.

(i) Issuer requirements

Different treatment of like services and service suppliers

7.690 The United States points out that the issuer requirements mandate that any payment cards used only for RMB purchases in China, as well as any dual currency cards issued in China, bear the CUP logo. The United States submits that no other EPS provider is afforded such a privilege.[878]

7.691 The United States argues in addition that the issuer requirements, as well as the other requirements at issue in this dispute, provide disparate treatment solely according to the identity of the EPS supplier: CUP or not CUP. In the United States' view, it is evident from China's own documents that China was concerned about the potential competition its domestic supplier of EPS would face from foreign suppliers of EPS as a result of China's WTO commitments. The United States considers that it is therefore unsurprising that the requirements at issue are meant to favour the domestic Chinese entity and accordingly discriminate on that basis. The United States further observes that outside of its protected Chinese home market, CUP is being described by other EPS suppliers

[877] United States' first written submission, paras. 80 and 109; second written submission, paras. 201-203 and 207.

[878] United States' first written submission, para. 80.

as an active competitor in the global market for card-based electronic payment transactions. The United States also points out that CUP's Articles of Association are explicit that the company is "[T]o provide advanced electronic payment technologies and specialized services in connection with the inter-bank card information switching."[879] To the United States, it is clear that CUP provides services for payment card transactions "like" those provided by foreign suppliers of EPS for payment card transactions and that the basis for the differential treatment by China is ultimately one of origin. Referring to the panel report in *China – Publications and Audiovisual Products*[880], the United States submits that the "like service suppliers" requirement of Article XVII is therefore satisfied.[881]

7.692 China does not specifically address whether the issuer requirements result in different treatment of CUP and its services, on the one hand, and "like" services and service suppliers of other Members, on the other hand. China considers that it is unnecessary to resolve this question. In China's view, the United States' claims under Article XVII should be dismissed because the United States did not distinguish its national treatment claims from its market access claims.[882]

7.693 The Panel first addresses the issuer requirements that relate to the *Yin Lian*/UnionPay logo use. These requirements mean that bank cards issued by commercial banks in China must bear the *Yin Lian*/UnionPay logo. In contrast, there is nothing in the record to indicate that bank cards must bear the logos of other EPS suppliers. Thus, the requirements in question give rise to formally different treatment between CUP and its network, on the one hand, and other EPS suppliers and their networks, on the other.

7.694 As concerns the other relevant type of issuer requirements – those relating to interoperability – we recall that they require issuers in China to join CUP, and bank cards issued in China to be interoperable with the CUP network. The parties have not made us aware of any comparable requirement whereby issuers would have to join other networks and bank cards would need to be interoperable with them. We consequently determine that the relevant requirements also result in formally different treatment between CUP and other EPS suppliers.

7.695 The question we need to consider next is whether the issuer requirements accord different treatment to "like services and service suppliers". We note in this regard the United States' reliance on the following statement by the panel in *China – Publications and Audiovisual Products*:

---

[879] Article 12 of CUP's Articles of Association.

[880] Panel Report, *China – Publications and Audiovisual Products*, para. 7.975.

[881] United States' first written submission, paras. 82-87.

[882] China's response to Panel question No. 124, para. 91.

> When origin is the only factor on which a measure bases a difference of treatment between domestic service suppliers and foreign suppliers, the "like service suppliers" requirement is met, provided there will, or can, be domestic and foreign suppliers that under the measure are the same in all material respects except for origin. We note that similar conclusions have been reached by previous panels. We observe that in cases where a difference of treatment is not exclusively linked to the origin of service suppliers, but to other factors, a more detailed analysis would probably be required to determine whether service suppliers on either side of the dividing line are, or are not, "like".[883]

7.696 The United States argues that the basis for the differential treatment resulting from the issuer requirements, as well as the other Chinese requirements at issue in this dispute, is "ultimately one of origin".[884] We are not persuaded. As an initial matter, we recall that some of the relevant provisions of the instruments through which these requirements are maintained refer to the network logo – the *Yin Lian*/UnionPay logo – as opposed to the logo of the company China UnionPay (CUP). For reasons we have stated earlier, however, we consider that it makes no significant practical difference whether the relevant Chinese instruments formally refer to the network logo or the CUP logo, as long as CUP remains the company charged with operating the relevant nationwide inter-bank network.[885] We also accept, of course, that CUP is a Chinese EPS supplier. But the issuer requirements do not provide for different treatment between Chinese EPS suppliers, on the one hand, and EPS suppliers of other Members, on the other. Rather, they distinguish between CUP, including via the references to the network logo, and all other EPS suppliers. The "all other" category comprises actual or potential EPS suppliers of other Members as well as actual or potential Chinese EPS suppliers. Indeed, the United States itself has stated that the treatment of EPS suppliers varies "according to the identity of the EPS supplier: CUP or not CUP."[886]

7.697 According to the panel in *China – Publications and Audiovisual Products*, in a case "where a difference of treatment is not exclusively linked to the origin of service suppliers, but to other factors, a more detailed analysis [of 'likeness'] would probably be required." As our case fits this situation, consistent with the view expressed by that panel, we undertake a more detailed analysis of the likeness issue.

7.698 We address first the reference in Article XVII to "like services". As there is a particular framework for analyzing the "likeness" of products in the context

883 Panel Report, *China – Publications and Audiovisual Products*, para. 7.975 (original footnote omitted).

884 United States' first written submission, para. 87.

885 See para. 7.251 above.

886 United States' first written submission, para. 82.

of Article III of the GATT 1994[887], we requested the parties to provide their views on any relevant criteria for establishing the "likeness" of services in the context of Article XVII. Neither party provided the Panel with such criteria, however, or suggested a particular analytical framework.[888] In approaching this matter, we do not assume that without further analysis we may simply transpose to trade in services the criteria or analytical framework used to determine "likeness" in the context of the multilateral agreements on trade in goods. We recognize important dissimilarities between the two areas of trade – notably the intangible nature of services, their supply through four different modes, and possible differences in how trade in services is conducted and regulated.

7.699 We thus begin our interpretative analysis by considering the ordinary meaning of "like". The dictionary defines the adjective "like" as "[h]aving the same characteristics or qualities as some other person or thing; of approximately identical shape, size, etc., with something else; similar".[889] To us, this range of meanings suggests that for services to be considered "like", they need not necessarily be exactly the same, and that in view of the references to "approximately" and "similar", services could qualify as "like" if they are essentially or generally the same.[890] The aforementioned definition highlights another point: something or someone is like in some respect, such as – in the terms of the definition – the "shape, size, etc." of a thing or person. To determine in what respect services need to be essentially the same for them to be "like", we turn to consider the context of the phrase "like services".

7.700 We note that Article XVII:1 requires that a Member accord to services of another Member "treatment no less favourable" than that it accords to its own like services. Article XVII:3 clarifies in relevant part that a Member would be deemed to provide less favourable treatment if it "modifies the conditions of competition in favour of services ... of [that] Member compared to like services ... of any other Member". We deduce from these provisions that Article XVII seeks to ensure equal competitive opportunities for like services of other Members. These provisions further suggest that like services are services that are in a competitive relationship with each other (or would be if they were allowed to be supplied in a particular market). Indeed, only if the foreign and domestic services in question are in such a relationship can a measure of a Member modify the conditions of competition in favour of one or other of these services.

7.701 Furthermore, we note that Article XVII is applicable to all services[891], in any sector, and that services – which are intangible – may be provided through

---

[887] E.g. Appellate Body Report, *EC – Asbestos*, para. 102.

[888] United States' response to Panel question No. 124, para.124; China's response to Panel question No. 124 para. 91.

[889] *Shorter Oxford English Dictionary*, Vol. 1, p. 1601.

[890] We note in this regard that another panel based a likeness determination on a finding that the services at issue were "virtually the same". Panel Report, *EC – Bananas III (Ecuador)*, para. 7.322.

[891] Except for services supplied in the exercise of governmental authority. See Article I:3(b) of the GATS.

any of the four modes of supply. As well, Article XVII refers to "like services and service suppliers". In the light of this complexity, "like services and service suppliers" analyses should in our view take into account the particular circumstances of each case. In other words, we consider that determinations of "like services", and "like service suppliers", should be made on a case-by-case basis.[892]

7.702 In the light of the above, we consider that a likeness determination should be based on arguments and evidence that pertain to the competitive relationship of the services being compared.[893] As in goods cases where a panel assesses whether a particular product is a "like product", the determination must be made on the basis of the evidence as a whole.[894] If it is determined that the services in question in a particular case are essentially or generally the same in competitive terms, those services would, in our view, be "like" for purposes of Article XVII.[895]

7.703 With the foregoing observations in mind, we turn to assess whether EPS supplied by CUP are like those supplied by EPS suppliers of other Members. To that end, we must review any relevant evidence. To begin with, evidence submitted by the United States indicates that CUP is perceived by other global EPS suppliers as a competitor in the global marketplace.[896] Additional evidence submitted by the United States indicates that CUP and EPS suppliers of other Members provide a data-processing infrastructure.[897] Both CUP and EPS suppliers of other Members also provide services in connection with inter-bank bank card information switching.[898] Specifically, both categories of suppliers are

---

[892] For a similar view with regard to "like products" determinations in the context of Article III of the GATT 1994, see Appellate Body Reports, *EC – Asbestos*, para. 101; and *Japan – Alcoholic Beverages II*, DSR 1996:I, 97, at p. 113.

[893] This is also consistent with the approach taken in the goods context. See Appellate Body Reports, *EC – Asbestos*, paras. 99 and 103; and *Philippines – Distilled Spirits*, fn. 211.

[894] See Appellate Body Report, *EC – Asbestos*, para. 103.

[895] It is important to note that even if relevant services are determined to be "like" and a measure of a Member is found to result in less favourable treatment of "like" services of another Member, it may still be possible to justify that measure under one of the general exceptions set out in Article XIV of the GATS.

[896] Visa IPO Prospectus, Exhibit US-3, p. 147; MasterCard 2009 Annual Report, Exhibit US-5, p. 20. We understand that there are currently no EPS suppliers of other WTO Members providing EPS in China for domestic inter-bank RMB transactions. We also note that the 2007 China Payment System Development Report of the PBOC compares CUP's inter-bank transaction volume to that of Visa, MasterCard and American Express (2007 China Payment System Development Report, Financial Service Report of the People's Bank of China, No. 5, 2008, Exhibit US-15, p. 59). Moreover, we note that American Express, in its 2010 annual report, indicates that it "competes in the global payment industry with other card networks, including, among others, Visa, MasterCard, Diners Club International … and Discover…" (American Express 2010 Annual Report, Exhibit US-7, p. 13).

[897] Article 12 of CUP's Articles of Association; MasterCard 2009 Annual Report, Exhibit US-5, p. 7; and Visa IPO Prospectus, Exhibit US-3, p. 138.

[898] Article 12 of CUP's Articles of Association; Visa IPO Prospectus, Exhibit US-3, p. 135; and MasterCard 2009 Annual Report, Exhibit US-5, pp. 78.

engaged in the authorization[899] and clearing[900] of payment card transactions and also facilitate their settlement[901]. They are further involved in any related transfer of data and information.[902] Moreover, both CUP and EPS suppliers of other Members establish common standards, rules and procedures that enable transaction information and data processing for the purpose of processing payment card transactions.[903] Finally, CUP and EPS suppliers of other Members mediate or arbitrate any business disputes arising out of payment card transactions.[904] Thus, evidence placed on record by the United States shows that CUP and EPS suppliers of other Members offer essentially the same description of their business scope and of the specific services that they provide.

7.704 While the evidence provided by the United States is not extensive, it is sufficient to raise a presumption that the services supplied by CUP and those supplied by EPS suppliers of other Members are essentially the same in competitive terms. China has not adduced any evidence to rebut the United States' assertion, nor has China asserted that the services supplied by CUP, on the one hand, and by foreign EPS suppliers, on the other, are not "like" services.[905] Moreover, evidence submitted by China regarding the existence of dual-logo bank cards – i.e. bank cards bearing the *Yin Lian*/UnionPay logo and the logo of an EPS supplier of another Member and that are interoperable with the networks of both suppliers – lends support to the view that EPS supplied by CUP and suppliers of other Members are closely competitive services.[906] Furthermore, in the particular circumstances of this case, we do not see how our

---

[899] Article 2.4.A of Chapter III of the Business Practices Appendix of Document No. 76; MasterCard 2010 Annual Report, Exhibit US-6, p. 8; and Visa IPO prospectus, Exhibit US-3, p. 136.

[900] Article 2.4.B of Chapter III, and Article 1.4.1 of Chapter IV, of the Business Practices Appendix of Document No. 76; MasterCard 2010 Annual Report, Exhibit US-6, p. 9; and Visa IPO prospectus, Exhibit US-3, pp. 136-137.

[901] Article 2.4.B of Chapter III, and Articles 1.4.3 and 2 of Chapter IV, of the Business Practices Appendix of Document No. 76; MasterCard 2010 Annual Report, Exhibit US-6, p. 9; and Visa IPO prospectus, Exhibit US-3, pp. 136-137.

[902] Article 12 of CUP's Articles of Association; Article 3 of Chapter I, and Article 1.2 of Chapter III, of the Business Practices Appendix of Document No. 76; Visa IPO prospectus, Exhibit US-3, pp. 130-131.

[903] Article 12 of CUP's Articles of Association; MasterCard 2010 Annual Report, Exhibit US-6, pp. 4 and 18; and Visa IPO prospectus, Exhibit US-3, p. 131.

[904] Article 12 of CUP's Articles of Association; Visa IPO prospectus, Exhibit US-3, pp. 129 and 131; and Visa 2010 Annual Report, Exhibit US-4, p. 8.

[905] China notes that the creation of CUP reflected a desire to "establish alternatives to the global networks". China's first written submission, para. 54. Similarly, China states that CUP operates China's national inter-bank payment card network. In establishing a nationwide network, China wanted to achieve the network effects associated with inter-bank payment cards, "but without having the Chinese market taken over by the same [global] network operators that had come to dominate other markets". China's first written submission, paras. 54, 44 and 57. Finally, China states that the United States has not identified anything in the instruments at issue that prevents other EPS suppliers from processing inter-bank payment card transactions, and that there is nothing in these instruments that establishes a "monopoly". China's opening statement at the first meeting of the Panel, para. 20.

[906] "Dual-logo bankcards bearing the *Yin Lian* logo and the logo of an international network operator", Exhibit CHN-112.

conclusion on "likeness" of services could be different depending on whether EPS suppliers of other Members supply EPS through mode 1 or through mode 3. In the light of this, we consider that EPS supplied by CUP are like EPS supplied by EPS suppliers of other Members.

7.705 Turning now to the issue of "likeness" of service suppliers, we note that in a different dispute, a panel has found that entities may be considered like service suppliers if, and to the extent that, they provide like services.[907] We agree that the fact that service suppliers provide like services may in some cases raise a presumption that they are "like" service suppliers. However, we consider that, in the specific circumstances of other cases, a separate inquiry into the "likeness" of the suppliers may be called for. For this reason, we consider that "like service suppliers" determinations should be made on a case-by-case basis.

7.706 In the present case, we have already found that CUP and EPS suppliers of other Members provide like services. Furthermore, the evidence before us indicates that CUP and EPS suppliers of other Members describe their business scope in very similar terms, and that CUP is perceived by EPS suppliers of other Members as a competitor in the global marketplace. This suggests that these suppliers compete with each other in the same business sector. Also, in the particular circumstances of this case, we see no basis for reaching a different conclusion on "likeness" of service suppliers depending on whether EPS suppliers of other Members supply EPS through mode 1 or through mode 3.

7.707 Additionally, we recall that in our case the treatment in China of EPS suppliers varies according to the identity of the EPS supplier or its network, namely according to whether or not the EPS supplier is CUP or the network is that of CUP. We consider that the fact that EPS suppliers of other Members are not CUP, and that their networks are not that of CUP, does not render EPS suppliers of other Members or their networks "unlike" CUP or its network. In our view, to accept otherwise would make it easy to circumvent the national treatment obligation and would deprive Article XVII of any useful effect.

7.708 Based on these elements and considerations, and in the absence of any evidence from China suggesting that CUP is different from EPS suppliers of other Members, we consider that for purposes of this case CUP and EPS suppliers of other Members are "like" suppliers of EPS, at least to the extent that they provide "like" services.

7.709 In the light of our findings above, we thus come to the conclusion that the issuer requirements result in different treatment of "like" EPS and EPS suppliers of other Members.

Less favourable treatment

7.710 In relation to the "less favourable treatment" condition, the United States argues that due to the issuer requirements, issuing banks may not use the CUP

[907] Panel Report, *EC – Bananas III (Ecuador)*, para. 7.322.

logo unless they have access to the CUP network, paid CUP for that access, and meet CUP's technical standards. The United States considers that issuing banks have no reason to seek an alternative EPS supplier, as any issuing bank is required to have access to the CUP system and to pay for that access. According to the United States, the issuer requirements have three competitive effects – they guarantee CUP an income stream from every credit card issued for domestic use within China, they give issuers an incentive to control costs by using CUP as their exclusive supplier, and they provide free branding to CUP. The United States submits that, in contrast, foreign suppliers of EPS are forced to secure such access and promote their brand on their own. The United States contends that even if a foreign supplier of EPS were to convince an issuer to issue a card, these requirements ensure that it will not be able to compromise CUP's prominent logo or obtain any market share to the certain exclusion of CUP. In its view, the value, if any, of co-branding or having a non-CUP supplier of EPS is extremely limited in any event, because only CUP can handle inter-bank or cross-region card-based electronic transactions.[908]

7.711 China does not specifically address whether the issuer requirements accord less favourable treatment to like EPS and EPS suppliers of other Members. China contends, however, that the requirement that all RMB-denominated cards bear the *Yin Lian* logo does not require banks to purchase network services from CUP. China further states that CUP charges for network services on a transaction-by-transaction basis.[909]

7.712 The Panel first addresses the *Yin Lian*/UnionPay logo element of the issuer requirements. To recall our earlier finding, China requires that RMB bank cards, and dual currency bank cards, that are issued in China by commercial banks and usable in domestic inter-bank RMB transactions must bear the *Yin Lian*/UnionPay logo on the front of the card.[910] We have also found no basis on which to conclude that the provisions in question would prohibit the issuance of relevant cards that would be capable of being processed over a network in China that is not that of CUP. As a result, any EPS supplier of another Member that wishes to have a commercial bank in China issue a bank card on its network would have no choice but to accept that the *Yin Lian*/UnionPay logo feature prominently on the front of that card. Holders of the relevant bank card would thus be constantly reminded of the availability of CUP, a competing EPS supplier, and its network. There is a further way in which CUP benefits from the Chinese requirements that bank cards issued in China bear the *Yin Lian*/UnionPay logo. As a consequence of these requirements, issuers must give publicity to the *Yin Lian*/UnionPay logo by putting it on all cards that they issue, and they must do so for free, whereas EPS suppliers of other Members are not

[908] United States' first written submission, paras. 80 and 100-101.

[909] China's response to question No. 104(b), para. 51.

[910] In the case of credit cards issued solely for domestic use in China the CUP anti-counterfeiting logo must also be displayed.

entitled to have their logo put on CUP-branded cards. The attention that is drawn in this way to the CUP network raises its profile.[911] Based on these elements, we consider that China's requirements that RMB and dual currency bank cards bear the *Yin Lian*/UnionPay logo modify the conditions of competition in favour of CUP. Pursuant to Article XVII:3, these requirements can therefore be considered to result in like EPS suppliers of other Members being treated less favourably than CUP.

7.713 We now consider the interoperability element of the issuer requirements. The United States asserts in this context that issuers must have access to the CUP network and must pay fees to CUP for that access. The United States also refers to a guaranteed income stream for CUP from every credit card that is issued. However, the United States has not established that the issuer requirements entail, or are associated with, access fees payable to CUP, let alone their level and other modalities.[912] Nor has the United States provided evidence to substantiate its assertion that the issuer requirements guarantee CUP an income stream from each and every credit card issued in China. In contrast, we agree that issuers in China must have access to the CUP network, and that bank cards that must display the *Yin Lian*/UnionPay logo must also be interoperable with CUP. Accordingly, we confine our analysis to these particular requirements. We recall in this connection that these requirements do not appear to prevent issuers who are members of CUP from joining other networks in China, or that bank cards that meet CUP's uniform business specifications and technical standards must not, or cannot, simultaneously be interoperable with other EPS suppliers' networks.

7.714 In effect, these interoperability requirements guarantee that all commercial banks that issue bank cards for use in domestic inter-bank RMB transactions in China are members of CUP. They further guarantee that all bank cards that are issued for such use by commercial banks – CUP cards as well as non-CUP cards – are capable of being processed over CUP's network. In contrast, EPS suppliers of other Members have to convince issuers to join their networks.[913] They might be unsuccessful in that endeavour, or at least they might

[911] We note that according to one global EPS supplier, brand recognition is one of the principal competitive factors in the global payments industry. See American Express 2010 Annual Report, Exhibit US-7, p. 13.

[912] For instance, it is not clear whether fees would need to be paid for every bank card that is issued or whether access fees would have to be paid by issuers for access to CUP independently of the number of bank cards they issue on that network. This information would also be important for any assessment of the United States' assertion that the alleged access fees give issuers an incentive to control costs by using CUP as their exclusive supplier. We add in this regard that, in our understanding, it is not uncommon for issuing banks to issue bank cards on the networks of different EPS suppliers' networks, to meet bank clients' demand. See, e.g. MasterCard 2009 Annual Report, Exhibit US-5, p. 21.

[913] We recall in this respect that issuers play an essential part in the business model of EPS suppliers. They issue the bank cards that are used in transactions that will be processed over a particular EPS supplier's network.

fail to achieve the same level of membership of relevant issuing banks.[914] And even if they could achieve the same level of membership, unlike CUP, EPS suppliers of other Members would need to expend time and effort in the process.[915] Moreover, if issuers in China were to issue relevant bank cards that are interoperable with the networks of EPS suppliers of other Members, those bank cards would also need to be interoperable with the CUP network. In contrast, in cases where CUP-branded bank cards are issued, they would not need to be interoperable with networks of EPS suppliers of other Members.[916] Based on these elements, we consider that the interoperability requirements in question modify the conditions of competition in favour of CUP. By virtue of Article XVII:3, they thus result in like EPS suppliers of other Members being treated less favourably than CUP.

7.715 In the particular case of the issuer requirements, we do not see how our conclusions on the issue of less favourable treatment could be affected by whether a like EPS supplier of another Member provides its services under mode 1 or mode 3. In our view, the conditions of competition of EPS suppliers of other Members are adversely modified irrespective of whether the relevant services are provided under mode 1 or 3. In relation to mode 3, it is nonetheless necessary to add that the issuer requirements result in less favourable treatment of like EPS suppliers of other Members even if these suppliers meet the qualifications for engaging in local currency business that are stipulated in China's mode 3 limitation.

7.716 We observe, finally, that with regard to three-party networks, the United States argues that, due to the issuer requirements, three-party EPS suppliers are not able to issue their own branded bank cards.[917] As also indicated by the United States, three-party EPS suppliers ordinarily issue cards directly to card holders.[918] We note that the issuer requirements concern commercial banks as issuers and bank cards issued by such banks. We consider that to the extent that EPS suppliers, such as those that implement a three-party model, use institutions authorized as commercial banks in China to issue bank cards, or are themselves authorized as commercial issuing banks, the issuer requirements result in less favourable treatment of such EPS suppliers.

---

[914] Evidence submitted by the United States suggests that a relevant factor in this regard is the economic attractiveness to bank card issuers of an EPS supplier's network. See American Express 2010 Annual Report, Exhibit US-7, p. 13; Discover 2010 Annual Report, Exhibit US-8, p. 10.

[915] Evidence provided by the United States indicates that the success of marketing and promotional campaigns is a relevant competitive factor for EPS suppliers. See American Express 2010 Annual Report, Exhibit US-7, p. 13.

[916] We note in this regard that according to one EPS supplier, one of the main competitive factors in the global payments industry is the number of cards in force and the amount of spending on these cards. See American Express 2010 Annual Report, Exhibit US-7, p. 13.

[917] United States' response to Panel question No. 25, para. 82.

[918] *Ibid.*, para. 81.

(ii) Terminal equipment requirements

Different treatment of like services and suppliers

7.717 The United States recalls that under the terminal equipment requirements all ATMs, merchant card processing equipment and POS terminals must accept cards bearing the CUP logo. According to the United States, there is no equivalent requirement for other cards, and no foreign EPS supplier is afforded a similar privilege.[919]

7.718 The United States further argues that the terminal equipment requirements, as well as the other requirements at issue in this dispute, provide disparate treatment solely according to the identity of the EPS supplier: CUP or not CUP. The United States considers that CUP provides services for payment card transactions "like" those provided by foreign suppliers of EPS for payment card transactions and that the basis for the differential treatment by China is ultimately one of origin. Referring to the panel report in *China – Publications and Audiovisual Products*, the United States submits that the "like service suppliers" requirement of Article XVII is therefore satisfied.[920]

7.719 China does not specifically address whether the terminal requirements result in different treatment of CUP and its services, on the one hand, and "like" services and service suppliers of other Members, on the other hand. China considers that it is unnecessary to resolve this question because the United States national treatment claims in its view should be dismissed in their entirety.[921]

7.720 The Panel notes that pursuant to the terminal equipment requirements, terminal equipment that joins the national bank card inter-bank processing network must be capable of accepting bank cards bearing the *Yin Lian*/UnionPay logo. In contrast, the record does not indicate that China imposes a requirement whereby terminal equipment must be capable of accepting bank cards bearing the logos of other EPS suppliers. In the light of this, we determine that the terminal equipment requirements result in formally different treatment between CUP and other EPS suppliers.

7.721 The next issue for us to examine is whether the terminal equipment requirements accord different treatment to "like services and service suppliers". As with the issuer requirements, the terminal equipment requirements in our view draw a distinction between CUP and other EPS suppliers that is not based on origin, but on the identity of the EPS supplier, or the network it operates. Therefore, as in the context of our analysis of the issuer requirements, we consider it appropriate to undertake a more detailed analysis of the likeness issue than the one that was conducted by the panel in *China – Publications and*

[919] United States' first written submission, paras. 80 and 109.
[920] United States' first written submission, paras. 82-87.
[921] China's response to Panel question No. 124, para. 91.

Audiovisual Products. We recall that we have already conducted such an analysis above. Thus, for the reasons set out in paragraphs 7.698 - 7.708 above, we consider that for purposes of this case EPS supplied by CUP are "like" EPS supplied by EPS suppliers of other Members, and that CUP and EPS suppliers of other Members are "like" suppliers of EPS, at least to the extent that they provide "like" services.[922]

7.722 In the light of the above, we conclude that the terminal equipment requirements result in different treatment of "like" EPS and EPS suppliers of other Members.

Less favourable treatment

7.723 The United States argues that the terminal equipment requirements modify the conditions of competition in favour of CUP. CUP is guaranteed access to all merchants in China who accept credit cards, while foreign EPS must market themselves to each POS terminal user. The United States observes that the main value that an EPS supplier has to offer issuing banks and card holders is the ability to use a card at a large number of locations, and the larger the network of merchants that use the card, the greater the attractiveness of the EPS supplier to its customers. The United States argues that the terminal equipment requirements give CUP automatic and universal acceptance of its bank cards by banks and merchants. In contrast, in China a foreign EPS supplier must build that network by marketing itself to merchants and acquiring banks. The United States notes in this respect that EPS suppliers must ordinarily invest heavily and incur substantial expense to build acceptance of their payment products by merchants, often in vigorous competition with other suppliers of EPS.[923]

7.724 China does not specifically address whether the terminal equipment requirements accord less favourable treatment to like EPS and EPS suppliers of other WTO Members.

7.725 The Panel recalls that pursuant to the terminal equipment requirements all terminals in China that are part of the national bank card inter-bank processing network must be capable of accepting all bank cards bearing the *Yin Lian*/UnionPay logo. This guarantees that all bank cards that bear the *Yin Lian*/UnionPay logo can be accepted by commercial bank and merchant terminal equipment in China and processed over CUP's network. As regards EPS suppliers of other WTO Members, we recall that the terminal equipment requirements do not appear to preclude terminals from accepting at the same time bank cards that would be capable of being processed over a network in

[922] As we indicated earlier, in the particular circumstances of this case, we see no basis for reaching a different conclusion on "likeness" of services or service suppliers depending on whether EPS suppliers of other WTO Members supply EPS through mode 1 or through mode 3.

[923] United States' first written submission, paras. 102 and 110; second written submission, para. 207; response to Panel question No. 15, para. 56.

China other than that of CUP. Consequently, EPS suppliers of other WTO Members could seek to obtain access to the terminals that must be capable of accepting bank cards bearing the *Yin Lian*/UnionPay logo. These terminals could then process transactions also over their networks. However, EPS suppliers of other WTO Members may not be able to get access to all these terminals because, unlike in the case of bank cards bearing the *Yin Lian*/UnionPay logo, commercial banks, acquirers and merchants could refuse access.[924] Also, even if the same level of access to terminal equipment could be achieved by EPS suppliers of other WTO Members, they would need to expend time and effort, which is not the case for CUP.[925] As pointed out by the United States, the level of access to bank and merchant terminals that an EPS supplier has is an important determinant of its attractiveness to issuers as well as bank card users and thus of its competitive position.[926] Based on these elements, we consider that the terminal equipment requirements modify the conditions of competition in favour of CUP. Having regard to Article XVII:3, they therefore accord to like EPS suppliers of other WTO Members less favourable treatment than to CUP.

7.726 In the particular case of the terminal equipment requirements, we do not consider that our conclusions on the issue of less favourable treatment are affected by whether a like EPS supplier of another WTO Member provides its services under mode 1 or mode 3. In our view, the conditions of competition of EPS suppliers of other WTO Members are adversely modified irrespective of whether the relevant services are provided under mode 1 or 3. In relation to mode 3, it is nonetheless important to add that the terminal equipment requirements result in less favourable treatment of like EPS suppliers of other WTO Members even if these suppliers meet the qualifications for engaging in local currency business that are stipulated in China's mode 3 limitation.

7.727 Finally, we note that the United States has not specifically addressed how the terminal equipment requirements affect three-party networks. It is clear to us, however, that EPS suppliers operating such networks would find themselves in substantially the same position as EPS suppliers operating four-party networks as regards the issue of access to terminal equipment in China. We therefore consider that our finding of less favourable treatment applies to EPS suppliers, regardless of whether they adopt a three- or a four-party model or some variation of either model.

---

[924] Evidence submitted by the United States suggests that a relevant factor in this regard is the economic attractiveness to merchants of participating in an EPS supplier's network. See American Express 2010 Annual Report, Exhibit US-7, p. 13.

[925] As noted earlier, EPS suppliers suggest that the success of marketing and promotional campaigns is a relevant competitive factor for them. See American Express 2010 Annual Report, Exhibit US-7, p. 13.

[926] We note in this regard that according to evidence submitted by the United States the quantity and quality of establishments where bank cards can be used ranks among the principal competitive factors in the global payments industry. See American Express 2010 Annual Report, Exhibit US-7, p. 13.

(iii) Acquirer requirements

Different treatment of like EPS suppliers

7.728 The United States notes that under the acquirer requirements all acquiring institutions in China must post the CUP logo and accept all bank cards bearing that logo. According to the United States, no foreign EPS supplier is afforded a similar privilege.[927]

7.729 The United States further argues that the acquirer requirements, as well as the other requirements at issue in this dispute, provide disparate treatment solely according to the identity of the EPS supplier: CUP or not CUP. The United States considers that CUP provides services for payment card transactions "like" those provided by foreign suppliers of EPS for payment card transactions and that the basis for the differential treatment by China is ultimately one of origin. Referring to the panel report in *China – Publications and Audiovisual Products*, the United States submits that the "like service suppliers" requirement of Article XVII is therefore satisfied.[928]

7.730 China does not specifically address whether the acquirer requirements result in different treatment of CUP and its services, on the one hand, and "like" services and service suppliers of other WTO Members, on the other hand. China considers that it is unnecessary to resolve this question because the United States national treatment claims in its view should be dismissed in their entirety.[929]

7.731 The Panel recalls that pursuant to the acquirer requirements acquirers must (i) post the *Yin Lian*/UnionPay logo and (ii) be capable of accepting bank cards bearing the *Yin Lian*/UnionPay logo. The latter requirements relate both to terminal equipment and interoperability. In contrast, the parties have not made us aware of any requirements whereby acquirers would have to post the logos of other EPS suppliers or be capable of accepting bank cards bearing their logos. We therefore consider that the acquirer requirements result in formally different treatment between CUP and other EPS suppliers.

7.732 We now address whether the acquirer requirements accord different treatment to "like services and service suppliers". As with the issuer and terminal equipment requirements, the acquirer requirements in our view draw a distinction between CUP and other EPS suppliers that is not based on origin, but on the identity of the EPS supplier, or the network it operates. Therefore, as in the context of our analysis of the issuer and terminal equipment requirements, we consider it appropriate to undertake a more detailed analysis of the likeness issue than the one that was conducted by the panel in *China – Publications and Audiovisual Products*. We recall that we have already conducted such an analysis above. Thus, for the reasons set out in paragraphs 7.698 - 7.708 above,

927 United States' first written submission, para. 80.
928 United States' first written submission, paras. 82-87.
929 China's response to Panel question No. 124, para. 91.

we consider that for purposes of this case EPS supplied by CUP are "like" EPS supplied by EPS suppliers of other WTO Members, and that CUP and EPS suppliers of other WTO Members are "like" suppliers of EPS, at least to the extent that they provide "like" services.[930]

7.733 Based on the foregoing considerations, we conclude that the acquirer requirements result in different treatment of "like" EPS and EPS suppliers of other WTO Members.

Less favourable treatment

7.734 The United States argues that the acquirer requirements distort the competitive relationship between CUP and foreign EPS suppliers for the same reasons as the terminal equipment requirements. The United States adds that acquirers have important relationships with merchants, often providing POS terminal and processing equipment to merchants so that they can process payment cards. Acquirers also maintain merchants' accounts, handle relations with merchants, and ensure that payments are properly credited to merchants.[931]

7.735 China does not specifically address whether the acquirer requirements accord less favourable treatment to like EPS and EPS suppliers of other Members.

7.736 The Panel first addresses the acquirer requirements that relate to terminal equipment. Pursuant to these requirements, terminal equipment operated by acquiring banks and merchant terminal equipment provided by acquirers must be technically capable of accepting cards bearing the *Yin Lian*/UnionPay logo. We also recall our view that these requirements would not prevent the acceptance by acquirers, or merchants, of bank cards that would be capable of being processed over a network in China other than that of CUP. To that extent, the analytical starting point for these acquirer requirements is not substantially different from that for the terminal equipment requirements we have examined earlier.[932] Consequently, our considerations in paragraphs 7.717 to 7.727 above concerning the terminal equipment requirements are applicable, with the necessary modifications, to the acquirer requirements in question. Accordingly, on the basis of the factual situation described in this paragraph and the considerations set out in paragraphs 7.728 to 7.734, we consider that the acquirer requirements that relate to terminal equipment modify the conditions of competition in favour of CUP. That being the case, we also consider that they result in like EPS suppliers of other Members being treated less favourably than CUP.

[930] As we indicated earlier, in the particular circumstances of this case, we see no basis for reaching a different conclusion on "likeness" of services or service suppliers depending on whether EPS suppliers of other WTO Members supply EPS through mode 1 or through mode 3.

[931] United States' second written submission, para. 203.

[932] The main difference is that in this case, we are concerned only with those terminals that are operated or provided by acquirers.

7.737 We now proceed to address the interoperability element of the acquirer requirements. Pursuant to these acquirer requirements, acquirers must join CUP and comply with uniform business standards and technical specifications of inter-bank interoperability. We also recall that these requirements do not appear to prevent acquirers from complying with business standards and technical specifications adopted by EPS suppliers of other Members. Thus, if EPS suppliers of other Members wish acquirers to join their networks and to be able to accept bank cards that are interoperable with their networks, they must take the initiative. It is uncertain, however, whether any such initiative would result in the same level of membership of relevant acquirers and the same number of acquirers meeting the business standards and technical specifications of EPS suppliers of other Members, because acquirers are not required to respond favourably. And even if EPS suppliers of other Members could achieve the same result, they would need to invest time and effort.[933] We note in this respect that acquirers are important to EPS suppliers because they acquire merchant transactions and provide merchants with terminal equipment that can process transactions over a particular EPS supplier's network. Based on these elements, we consider that the acquirer requirements that relate to interoperability modify the conditions of competition in favour of CUP. In view of Article XVII:3, we further determine that they result in like EPS suppliers of other Members being treated less favourably than CUP.

7.738 The final element of the acquirer requirements to be examined is the *Yin Lian*/UnionPay logo element. Pursuant to this requirement, acquirers must post the *Yin Lian*/UnionPay logo on merchant terminals. We also recall that this requirement does not appear to prevent the posting of the logo of competing EPS suppliers. Thus, while the *Yin Lian*/UnionPay logo is automatically posted, EPS suppliers of other Members who wish acquirers to post their logo need to invest time and effort to achieve this. In our view, the posting of an EPS supplier's logo on merchant terminals is relevant inasmuch as it alerts card holders to the option of using their bank card rather than paying in cash, for instance. The logo may thus generate additional transactions that the EPS supplier whose logo is posted can process. Also, since merchant terminals are frequently capable of accepting bank cards with a variety of logos, the fact that one EPS supplier's logo is posted while another's is not might mislead holders of cards bearing the latter's logo, in the sense that the absence of a particular logo might suggest that cards bearing that logo would not be accepted. As a result, such cards might either not be used by card holders or card holders might not seek to get such bank cards in the first place. Based on these elements, the requirement that acquirers must post the *Yin Lian*/UnionPay logo in our view modifies the conditions of competition in favour of CUP. In accordance with Article XVII:3, the requirement can thus be

---

933 As noted earlier, EPS suppliers suggest that the success of marketing and promotional campaigns is a relevant competitive factor for them. See American Express 2010 Annual Report (Exhibit US-7), p. 13.

considered to result in like EPS suppliers of other Members being treated less favourably than CUP.

7.739 In the particular case of the acquirer requirements, we do not see how our conclusions on the issue of less favourable treatment could be affected by whether a like EPS supplier of another Member provides its services under mode 1 or mode 3. In our view, the conditions of competition of EPS suppliers of other Members are adversely modified irrespective of whether the relevant services are provided under mode 1 or 3. In relation to mode 3, it is nevertheless important to add that the acquirer requirements result in less favourable treatment of like EPS suppliers of other Members even if these suppliers meet the qualifications for engaging in local currency business that are stipulated in China's mode 3 limitation.

7.740 We also observe that the United States has not specifically addressed how the acquirer requirements affect three-party networks. As described by the United States, these networks ordinarily serve merchants directly. As regards the acquirer requirements that relate to terminal equipment and the logo posting, we do not see how EPS suppliers of other Members would be impacted differently, depending on whether they operate a three- or a four-party network or some variation of either type of network. With regard to the interoperability element of the acquirer requirements, we consider that to the extent that EPS suppliers, such as those that implement a three-party model, operate as acquiring banks in China, the interoperability element of the acquirer requirements results in less favourable treatment of such EPS suppliers.

(d) Overall conclusions

7.741 As we have completed our analysis of the three Article XVII elements, we can come to overall conclusions on the United States' claims that the Hong Kong/Macao requirements as well as the issuer, terminal equipment and acquirer requirements are inconsistent with Article XVII.

(i) Hong Kong/Macao requirements

7.742 We found above that the Hong Kong/Macao requirements impose an Article XVI:2(a)-type limitation on market access through mode 1 and that they are therefore subject to China's "Unbound" market access entry for that mode and subsector (d). We further found that Article XX:2 indicates that even if the Hong Kong/Macao requirements are also "measures affecting the supply of services" within the meaning of Article XVII:1 and result in EPS suppliers of other Members being treated less favourably than like Chinese services and service suppliers when supplying through mode 1, the inscription of "Unbound" in China's market access entry provides "a condition or qualification to Article XVII". We determined on that basis that China has no obligation in respect of the Hong Kong/Macao requirements to accord national treatment to EPS supplied through mode 1, and EPS suppliers of other Members supplying through mode 1. For these reasons, we conclude that the Hong Kong/Macao requirements, to the extent that they affect the cross-border supply of EPS (mode 1), are not inconsistent with Article XVII:1 of the GATS.[934]

(ii) Issuer requirements

7.743 We also found that the issuer requirements (relating to both the *Yin Lian*/UnionPay logo and interoperability elements) are subject to commitments set out in China's mode 1 and 3 national treatment entries concerning subsector (d); that they are measures affecting the supply of services; and that they result in like EPS and EPS suppliers of other Members being treated less favourably than CUP and its EPS, irrespective of whether the relevant services are provided under mode 1 or 3 and even in cases where those other suppliers would meet the qualifications for engaging in mode 3 local currency business. For these reasons, we conclude that the issuer requirements are inconsistent with Article XVII:1 of the GATS. The issuer requirements that relate to the *Yin Lian*/UnionPay logo use are maintained through Articles 2.1(i) and 2.2(i) of Document No. 37; Articles 1, 2, 5 and 6 of Document No. 57; and Article 3.2(ii) of Document No. 129. Those that relate to interoperability are maintained through Articles 1.2(i), 2.1(iii), 2.2(i) and 3.1 of Document No. 37; Article 3 of Document No. 57; Article 3.2(ii) of Document No. 129; and Article 64 of Document No. 17 in conjunction with Document No. 76.

(iii) Terminal equipment requirements

7.744 We further found that the terminal equipment requirements (relating to both the *Yin Lian*/UnionPay logo and interoperability elements) are subject to commitments set out in China's mode 1 and 3 national treatment entries concerning subsector (d); that they are measures affecting the supply of services, and that they result in like EPS and EPS suppliers of other Members being treated less favourably than CUP and its EPS, irrespective of whether the relevant services are provided under mode 1 or 3 and even in cases where those other suppliers would meet the qualifications stipulated in China's Schedule for engaging in mode 3 local currency business. For these reasons, we conclude that they are inconsistent with Article XVII:1 of the GATS. These requirements are maintained through Articles 1.2(i) and 2.1(ii) of Document No. 37 and also Article 2.2 of Document No. 153.

(iv) Acquirer requirements

7.745 Finally, we found that the acquirer requirements (relating to both the posting of the *Yin Lian*/UnionPay logo and the capability of accepting bank cards bearing the *Yin Lian*/UnionPay logo) are subject to commitments set out

[934] We recall that we exercised judicial economy in respect of the United States' claim that the Hong Kong/Macao requirements are also inconsistent with Article XVII to the extent that they affect the supply of EPS through commercial presence in China (mode 3).

in China's mode 1 and 3 national treatment entries concerning subsector (d); that they are measures affecting the supply of services, and that they result in like EPS and EPS suppliers of other Members being treated less favourably than CUP and its EPS, irrespective of whether the relevant services are provided under mode 1 or 3 and even in cases where those other suppliers would meet the qualifications stipulated in China's Schedule for engaging in mode 3 local currency business. For these reasons, we conclude that they are inconsistent with Article XVII:1 of the GATS. The acquirer requirement that relates to the posting of the *Yin Lian*/UnionPay logo is maintained through Article 2.2 of Document No. 153. The requirements that relate to the capability of acquirers to accept bank cards bearing the *Yin Lian*/UnionPay logo (terminal equipment and interoperability elements) are maintained through Article 2.2 of Document No. 153; Article 1.2(i) of Document No. 37; and paragraphs 2 and 3 of the Notice as well as Articles 2.1 and 5.2.1-5.2.3 of Chapter I of Document No. 76.

3. *China's requirements considered jointly*

7.746 The Panel now addresses the United States' request that the Chinese requirements at issue should be considered not only individually, but also when operating in conjunction. The United States argues that this would help to ensure the effective resolution of this dispute.[935]

7.747 According to the United States, the requirements at issue are not just WTO-inconsistent when analysed individually, but operate together in a manner that is also WTO-inconsistent.[936] The United States submits in this respect that the effect of the requirements at issue is to distort competition in China's market for EPS. The United States submits that these requirements maintain CUP as the sole entity able to provide the full range of EPS. The United States further observes that under these requirements, banks in China must join CUP in order to issue bank cards or acquire bank card transactions, and only cards bearing the CUP logo can be issued as RMB denominated cards. According to the United States, these requirements also mean that all banks that wish to acquire merchant transactions or operate ATMs and all merchants that wish to accept bank cards must join CUP and process transactions in accordance with CUP's rules and procedures. In the United States' view, these requirements gave CUP significant leverage and automatic and universal acceptance of its RMB payment card products by banks and merchants in China and permitted and supported CUP becoming the sole EPS supplier in China. The United States points out that no foreign EPS supplier enjoys any of these advantages.[937]

7.748 In considering the United States' request, the Panel recalls that it found above that the issuer, terminal equipment and acquirer requirements are each

[935] United States' first written submission, para. 32.
[936] United States' first written submission, para. 29; response to Panel question No. 4.
[937] United States' second written submission, para. 207; response to Panel question No. 71, para. 7.

inconsistent with Article XVII:1 for modes 1 and 3. We further found that the Hong Kong/Macao requirements are inconsistent with Article XVI:2(a) for mode 3, and not inconsistent with Article XVII:1 for mode 1 (due to the absence of a national treatment obligation covering these requirements). In our view, these findings help to secure a positive solution to this dispute. That being so, we see no need to determine whether the same requirements, when considered in conjunction with each other, would give rise to an independent breach of Article XVII:1 for mode 1 or 3. We therefore decline to offer a separate conclusion on whether the issuer, terminal equipment, acquirer and Hong Kong/Macao requirements, when considered jointly, are also inconsistent with Article XVII:1.[938]

VIII. CONCLUSIONS AND RECOMMENDATIONS

8.1 For the reasons set forth in this Report, the Panel concludes as follows:

(a) In respect of the United States' panel request:[939]

(i) the Panel finds that China has failed to establish that the United States' panel request is inconsistent with Article 6.2 of the DSU on the grounds that it does not provide a brief summary of the legal basis sufficient to present the problem clearly.

(b) In respect of the services at issue:

(i) the Panel finds that the services at issue as defined by the United States in its request for the establishment of a panel are classifiable under Sector 7.B(d) of China's Schedule, which reads "[a]ll payment and money transmission services, including credit, charge and debit cards, travellers cheques and bankers draft (including import and export settlement)".

(c) In respect of repealed or replaced Chinese legal instruments:

(i) the Panel finds that Document Nos. 94 and 272 were repealed prior to the date of establishment of the panel and,

---

[938] This approach is consistent with that followed by the panel in *Turkey – Rice*. The panel in that case found two Turkish measures to be individually inconsistent with Turkey's WTO obligations. The panel then stated that "[i]n the light of these findings, and under the guidance of the principle of judicial economy, we do not see the need to reach a separate conclusion on these measures considered jointly, for the resolution of this dispute" (Panel Report, *Turkey – Rice*, para. 7.281). We further note that the United States itself has drawn our attention to this particular statement. See United States' first written submission, fn 49.

[939] The Panel's conclusions incorporate those set forth in its preliminary ruling, which is contained in document WT/DS413/4 circulated on 30 September 2011 and which forms an integral part of this Report.

therefore, do not figure in the Panel's findings or recommendations; and

(ii) the Panel finds that Document No. 66 was replaced by Document No. 53 prior to the date of establishment of the panel and, therefore, does not figure in the Panel's findings or recommendations.

(d) In respect of China's measures at issue:

(i) the Panel finds that China, through Document Nos. 37, 57 and 129, imposes requirements on issuers that bank cards issued in China bear the *Yin Lian*/UnionPay logo, and furthermore, China, through Document Nos. 17, 37, 57, 76 and 129, requires that issuers become members of the CUP network, and that the bank cards they issue in China meet certain uniform business specifications and technical standards;

(ii) the Panel finds that China, through Document Nos. 37 and 153, imposes requirements that all terminals (ATMs, merchant processing devices and POS terminals) in China that are part of the national bank card inter-bank processing network be capable of accepting all bank cards bearing the *Yin Lian*/UnionPay logo;

(iii) the Panel finds that China, through Document No. 153, imposes requirements on acquirers to post the *Yin Lian*/UnionPay logo, and furthermore, China, through Document Nos. 37, 76 and 153, imposes requirements that acquirers join the CUP network and comply with uniform business standards and technical specifications of inter-bank interoperability, and that terminal equipment operated or provided by acquirers be capable of accepting bank cards bearing the *Yin Lian*/UnionPay logo;

(iv) the Panel finds that China, through Document Nos. 16, 8 and 254, imposes requirements that CUP and no other EPS supplier handle the clearing of certain RMB bank card transactions that involve either an RMB bank card issued in China and used in Hong Kong or Macao, or an RMB bank card issued in Hong Kong or Macao that is used in China in an RMB-denominated transaction;

(v) the Panel finds that the United States failed to establish that China, through Document Nos. 37, 57, 16, 8, 219, 254, 103, 153, 149, 53, 49, 129, 76, 17 and/or 142, imposes requirements that mandate the use of CUP and/or establish CUP as the sole supplier of EPS for all domestic RMB payment card transactions; and

(vi) the Panel finds that the United States failed to establish that China, through Document Nos. 37, 57, 153, 219 and/or 76, imposes broad prohibitions on the use of "non-CUP" cards for cross-region or inter-bank transactions.

(e) In respect of the United States' claims under Article XVI of the GATS:

(i) in relation to the United States' claims concerning China's Sector 7.B(d) mode 1 market access commitment, the Panel finds that the issuer, terminal equipment, acquirer and Hong Kong/Macao requirements are not inconsistent with Article XVI of the GATS, as China has not undertaken a market access commitment under this mode and in this sector in respect of the services at issue in this dispute;

(ii) the Panel finds that the United States failed to establish that the issuer requirements are inconsistent with Article XVI:2(a) of the GATS, in respect of China's Sector 7.B(d) mode 3 market access commitment, as these requirements do not impose a limitation that falls within the scope of Article XVI:2(a);

(iii) the Panel finds that the United States failed to establish that the terminal equipment requirements are inconsistent with Article XVI:2(a) of the GATS, in respect of China's Sector 7.B(d) mode 3 market access commitment, as these requirements do not impose a limitation that falls within the scope of Article XVI:2(a);

(iv) the Panel finds that the United States failed to establish that the acquirer requirements are inconsistent with Article XVI:2(a) of the GATS, in respect of China's Sector 7.B(d) mode 3 market access commitment, as these requirements do not impose a limitation that falls within the scope of Article XVI:2(a);

(v) the Panel finds that the Hong Kong/Macao requirements are inconsistent with Article XVI:2(a) of the GATS because, contrary to China's Sector 7.B(d) mode 3 market access commitments, they maintain a limitation on the number of service suppliers in the form of a monopoly;

(vi) the Panel finds that the United States failed to establish that the Hong Kong/Macao, issuer, terminal equipment and acquirer requirements, when considered jointly, give rise to a separate and independent breach of Article XVI:2(a) of the GATS;

(vii) the Panel finds that the United States failed to present a *prima facie* case that the issuer, terminal equipment or acquirer requirements, considered either individually or jointly, are inconsistent with Article XVI:1 of the GATS in respect of China's Sector 7.B(d) mode 3 market access commitment; and

(viii) the Panel exercised judicial economy with respect to the United States' Sector 7.B(d) mode 3 market access claims under Article XVI:1 of the GATS regarding the Hong Kong/Macao requirements.

(f) In respect of the United States' claims under Article XVII of the GATS:

(i) the Panel finds that the issuer requirements are inconsistent with Article XVII:1 of the GATS, because contrary to China's Sector 7.B(d) mode 1 and mode 3 national treatment commitments, these requirements fail to accord to services and service suppliers of any other Member treatment no less favourable than China accords to its own like services and service suppliers;

(ii) the Panel finds that the terminal equipment requirements are inconsistent with Article XVII:1 of the GATS, because contrary to China's Sector 7.B(d) mode 1 and mode 3 national treatment commitments, these requirements fail to accord to services and service suppliers of any other Member treatment no less favourable than China accords to its own like services and service suppliers;

(iii) the Panel finds that the acquirer requirements are inconsistent with Article XVII:1 of the GATS, because contrary to China's Sector 7.B(d) mode 1 and mode 3 national treatment commitments, these requirements fail to accord to services and service suppliers of any other Member treatment no less favourable than China accords to its own like services and service suppliers;

(iv) the Panel finds that the Hong Kong/Macao requirements are not inconsistent with Article XVII:1 of the GATS, as China has no Sector 7.B(d) mode 1 national treatment obligation in respect of these requirements;

(v) the Panel exercised judicial economy with respect to the United States' Sector 7.B(d) mode 3 national treatment claims under Article XVII:1 of the GATS regarding the Hong Kong/Macao requirements; and

(vi) the Panel declined to conclude separately on whether the issuer, terminal equipment, acquirer and Hong Kong/Macao requirements, when considered jointly, are also inconsistent with Article XVII:1 of the GATS.

8.2 Under Article 3.8 of the DSU, in cases where there is an infringement of the obligations assumed under a covered agreement, the action is considered *prima facie* to constitute a case of nullification or impairment. We conclude that, to the extent that the measures at issue are inconsistent with the GATS, they have nullified or impaired benefits accruing to the United States under that agreement.

8.3 Pursuant to Article 19.1 of the DSU, we recommend that the Dispute Settlement Body request China to bring its measure into conformity with its obligations under the GATS.

ANNEX A

EXECUTIVE SUMMARIES OF THE FIRST WRITTEN SUBMISSIONS OF THE PARTIES

Contents		Page
Annex A-1	Executive summary of the first written submission of the United States	5577
Annex A-2	Executive summary of the first written submission of China	5589

ANNEX A-1

EXECUTIVE SUMMARY OF THE FIRST WRITTEN SUBMISSION OF THE UNITED STATES

I. INTRODUCTION

1. Operating from a protected home market monopoly position, China UnionPay, Co. Ltd. ("CUP") has thrived since its creation nearly a decade ago. With competitors shut out of China, CUP has solidified its complete domestic market dominance. CUP has also experienced explosive growth abroad. While serving as China's domestic champion, CUP, has been expanding its payment card issuance and acceptance internationally and enjoys full and unencumbered access to the domestic payment card market in a growing number of foreign countries in which it has chosen to operate (now numbering more than 110).

2. Back in 2001, China made important commitments with respect to electronic payment services ("EPS") for payment card transactions when it joined the World Trade Organization ("WTO"). EPS enable, facilitate, and manage the transfer of funds between cardholders and merchants and are essential to processing the several hundred million card-based electronic payment transactions that occur daily around the world. In the financial services sector, as set out in China's Schedule of Specific Commitments on Services, China undertook to provide by December 2006 both market access and national treatment for "all payment and money transmission services, including credit, charge and debit cards."

3. Yet, at the same time as CUP expands aggressively abroad, China maintains a government-mandated domestic monopoly, enabling only CUP to provide these services in China. China refuses to allow foreign suppliers of EPS

to process payment card transactions in China denominated and paid in China's domestic currency, renminbi ("RMB"). China has also enacted and maintains numerous barriers to prevent foreign suppliers of EPS from establishing the processing infrastructure, network, rules, and procedures that are essential to the processing of card-based electronic payment transactions in China. In addition, China maintains measures that also impact the other key entities in payment card transactions, including the institutions that issue payment cards ("issuing institutions"), acquiring institutions (those that seek to "acquire" transactions using payment cards and that have relationships with merchants), and merchants in terms of requirements pertaining to payment card-processing equipment and point-of-sale ("POS") terminals.

4. These measures have entrenched CUP's monopoly position in China and accord less favorable treatment to foreign suppliers of EPS.

II. PROCEDURAL HISTORY

5. On September 15, 2010, the United States requested consultations with China pursuant to Articles 1 and 4 of the *Understanding on Rules and Procedures Governing the Settlement of Disputes* ("DSU"), and Article XXII of the *General Agreement on Trade in Services* ("GATS") with respect to certain restrictions and requirements maintained by China pertaining to electronic payment services for payment card transactions and the suppliers of those services. The United States and China held consultations on October 27 and 28, 2010, but those consultations did not resolve the dispute. The United States submitted its request for the establishment of a panel on February 11, 2011, the Dispute Settlement Body ("DSB") established a panel on March 25, 2011, and the Panel was composed on July 4, 2011.

6. On July 5, 2011 China filed a request for a preliminary ruling on the consistency of the U.S. panel request with DSU Article 6.2. On July 29, 2011, the United States filed a submission in response to China's request for a preliminary ruling ("U.S. July 29, 2011 Response"). (The U.S. July 29, 2011 Response, in its entirety and including all of the exhibits attached thereto, was subsequently incorporated by express reference into the U.S. First Written Submission, dated September 13, 2011.) On September 7, 2011, the Panel issued its preliminary ruling in which it rejected all of China's claims that the U.S. panel request failed to satisfy the requirements of Article 6.2 of the DSU.

III. FACTUAL BACKGROUND

A. Electronic Payment Services for Payment Card Transactions

7. Card-based electronic payments take many forms, including credit cards, charge cards, debit cards, deferred debit cards, ATM cards, prepaid cards, private label cards and other types of general-purpose and limited-use payment cards. A supplier of EPS enables cardholders' banks to pay merchants' banks the

amount they are owed. Suppliers of electronic payment services supply, directly or indirectly, a system that typically includes the following:

- the processing infrastructure, network, and rules and procedures that facilitate, manage, and enable the transmission of transaction information and payments, and which provide system integrity, stability and financial risk reduction;
- the process and coordination of approving or declining a transaction, with approval generally permitting a purchase to be finalized or cash to be disbursed or exchanged;
- the delivery and transmission of transaction information among participating entities;
- the calculation, determination, and reporting of the net financial position of relevant institutions for all transactions that have been authorized in a given period; and
- the facilitation, management and/or other participation in the transfer of net payments owed among participating institutions.

8. Electronic payment services provide an efficient, timely and reliable means to facilitate the transmission of funds from the holders of payment cards who purchase goods or services to the individuals or businesses that supply them. The network, rules and procedures, and operating system that are part of the EPS architecture that allow payment card transactions to be processed to enable merchants to be paid promptly the amounts they are owed, and to ensure that customers pay what they owe. EPS suppliers receive, check and transmit the information that the parties need to conduct the transactions, and manage, facilitate, and enable the transmission of funds between participating entities. The rules and procedures established by the EPS supplier give the payment system stability and integrity, and enable it to efficiently handle net flows of money among the institutions involved in card payments. EPS suppliers also provide their customers with certain guarantees to ensure the integrity of the electronic payment services, including, for example, instances where customers fail to honor payment cards or where issuers or acquirers fail to fund obligations.

9. EPS, whether provided in connection with open-loop (four-party) systems or closed-loop (three party) systems, encompass both (1) "front-end processing" (which determines whether a payment card user has sufficient funds or is otherwise authorized to make a purchase and provides that information to the merchant or ATM owner), and (2) "back-end processing" (which, among other things, determines, calculates, and instructs banks regarding net payments owed among participating institutions).

B. The Evolution of China's Payment Card System and the Creation of CUP

10. China's payment card system was inefficient and fragmented, and limited to local regional transactions. Chinese banks' independent and uncoordinated

efforts undermined the efficacy of payment card use. Bank cards were inconvenient for individual consumers to use because they were not widely accepted by merchants, and the networks' ad hoc development resulted in some merchants having multiple terminals and others having none. Additionally, consumers could access cash and purchase items only from the POS terminals bearing their respective bank's logo. Incompatibility between the various bank networks also prevented cross-bank or inter-bank transactions at the national level.

11. Instead of allowing these market inefficiencies to be remedied with the opening of its market to competition, including from foreign suppliers of EPS consistent with its WTO commitments, the Chinese government took steps to consolidate the industry under a domestic champion. First, in January 2001, the PBOC issued a series of measures that standardized bank cards and mandated the use of the "UnionPay" logo. Second, in March 2002, the PBOC approved and authorized the establishment of CUP, a private limited liability corporation whose shares were primarily held by four of China's state-owned commercial banks.

12. From its inception, CUP was envisioned not only as a means to create a uniform national platform for electronic payment services for card-based electronic transactions, but also as a homegrown company championing a national brand. The Chinese government has taken a deep interest in the development and progress of CUP, and the corporation has hired as its top executives key former PBOC officials.

13. With China's accession to the WTO in 2001, the Chinese government worked to build CUP's core capabilities and to prepare it for the arrival of China's deadline to complete liberalization of the financial sector in 2006. The Chinese government's efforts to strengthen CUP coincided with measures that resulted in the systematic exclusion of foreign suppliers of EPS from the market.

14. By 2010, CUP had grown its network outside of China, and CUP cards could be used in well over 100 countries, including in Australia, Canada, Malaysia, Singapore, the United Arab Emirates, and the United States. In the years since its inception in 2002, CUP has emerged as a dominant domestic and international player in the EPS market. CUP controls the merchant services network and owns half of the POS terminals in China. In 2007, just five years after CUP was created, PBOC reported on the company's explosive growth and its mammoth transaction volume (placing it then fourth within the world). Because of its success, CUP briefly considered an initial public offering ("IPO") in 2008, with President Xu Luode stating that he remained open to considering an IPO again if the conditions were right. China continues to sustain CUP's growth and to maintain a regulatory environment that has entrenched CUP's hold over the Chinese payment card market.

C. China's Measures That Maintain CUP's Monopoly on the Supply of EPS and that Affect the Supply of EPS By Foreign Suppliers

15. China maintains the following measures:

- **Requirements that mandate the use of CUP and/or establish CUP as the sole supplier of EPS for all domestic transactions denominated and paid in RMB.** China requires that all transactions denominated and paid in RMB in China be processed and cleared in RMB through CUP, and that where there is a choice, all domestic transactions on dual currency cards be routed in RMB through CUP. See U.S. July 29, 2011 Response, sections V.B, V.C, V.D

- ***Requirements that RMB denominated payment cards issued in China bear the CUP logo.*** China requires that any bank cards issued in China for RMB purchases in China, including dual currency payment cards issued in China, must bear the CUP logo. This means that issuers – the institutions that issue payment cards to consumers – must have access to the CUP system, and must pay CUP for that access. *See* U.S. July 29, 2011 Response, sections V.B, V.C, V.E.

- ***Requirements that all automated teller machines ("ATM"), merchant card processing equipment, and POS terminals in China accept CUP cards.*** China requires that all ATMs, merchant card processing equipment, and POS terminals in China be capable of accepting CUP cards. There are no equivalent requirements for non-CUP cards. See U.S. July 29, 2011 Response, sections V.B, V.C, V.F.

- ***Requirements on acquiring institutions to post the CUP logo and be capable of accepting all payment cards bearing the CUP logo.*** China requires that all acquiring institutions – the institutions that sign up merchants to accept payment cards – in China post the CUP logo and be capable of accepting all payment cards bearing the CUP logo. An acquiring institution, often a bank, provides POS terminal and processing equipment to merchants so it can process payment cards, maintains the merchant's account, handles relations with the merchant, and ensures that payments are properly credited to the merchant. *See* U.S. July 29, 2011 Response, sections V.B, V.C, V.G.

- ***Broad prohibitions on the use of non-CUP cards.*** China prohibits the use of domestically issued non-CUP payment cards where the issuing bank and acquiring bank are different. China also requires that all inter-bank transactions for all bank cards be handled through CUP. *See* U.S. July 29, 2011 Response, sections V.B, V.C, V.H.

- ***Requirements pertaining to card-based electronic transactions in China, Macao and Hong Kong.*** China requires that CUP be used to handle all RMB transactions in Macao or Hong Kong using bank cards issued in China. China also requires that CUP be used to handle any RMB transactions in China using RMB cards issued in Hong Kong or Macao. *See* U.S. July 29, 2011 Response, sections V.B, V.C, V.I.

IV. CHINA'S SPECIFIC COMMITMENTS IN ITS GATS SCHEDULE

A. China's Schedule of GATS Commitments Covers "All payment and money transmission services, including credit, charge and debit cards..." (item d)

16. In Sector 7B, under the Banking and Other Financial Services heading of China's Services Schedule, the services listed include:

> (d) All payment and money transmission services, including credit, charge and debit cards, travellers cheques and bankers drafts (including import and export settlement).

17. China undertook market access and national treatment commitments with respect to "[a]ll payment and money transmission services," which includes the electronic payment services supplied in connection with "credit, charge and debit cards," and other payment card transactions.

B. EPS Fall Within the Ordinary Meaning of "All payment and money transmission services, including credit, charge and debit cards..." (Item d)

18. China's commitments pertain to "*all* payment and money transmission services, including credit, charge and debit cards," indicating that the scope of the commitment covers any service that is essential to "payment and money transmission" including "credit, charge, and debit cards" payment transactions. EPS suppliers are at the heart of this service.

19. EPS are at the center of all payment card transactions and without these services the transactions could not occur. EPS fall within the ordinary meaning of payment and money transmission services, within item (d) of China's Schedule. The language of item (d) itself makes this abundantly clear.

20. First, EPS involve the services through which transactions involving payment cards are processed and through which transfers of funds between institutions participating in the transactions are managed and facilitated. EPS clearly fall within the ordinary meaning of "payment and money transmission services" as one type of "*all*" such services.

21. Second, the phrase "all payment and money transmission services" is modified with an illustrative list that explicitly provides that it "include[s] credit,

charge and debit cards." This explicit reference is in line with the recognition that EPS are integral to the processing of credit, charge, debit and other payment card-based electronic payment transactions, and without these services, payment card transactions could not occur. EPS suppliers such as Visa, MasterCard, and American Express are names recognized around the world as credit cards and charge cards. The reference to debit cards covers suppliers of EPS for debit card transactions like Visa, MasterCard, Discover, First Data, Pulse, NYCE, STAR, and PLUS.

V. CHINA'S MEASURES SHOULD BE CONSIDERED BOTH INDIVIDUALLY AND IN CONJUNCTION WITH OTHER MEASURES

22. China maintains a monopoly structure that ensures that CUP is the sole entity that can provide EPS for RMB transactions in China – the vast majority of all transactions in China. Chinese measures that provide for the monopoly structure and restrict the supply of EPS by foreign suppliers affect every aspect of a payment card transaction and all of the key participants in such transactions.

23. As the Panel confirmed in its preliminary ruling, the United States has challenged measures that establish or maintain requirements that fall within six categories. The United States requests the Panel to analyze China's measures both individually and in conjunction with one another as indicated by the United States.

VI. CHINA'S MEASURES ESTABLISHING AND SUPPORTING CHINA UNIONPAY'S MONOPOLY ON THE SUPPLY OF EPS ARE INCONSISTENT WITH ARTICLE XVI OF THE GATS

A. GATS Article XVI (Market Access)

24. The measures imposed by China on the supply of electronic payment services are inconsistent with Article XVI of the GATS because they limit the number of suppliers of EPS for RMB-denominated transactions that are paid in RMB.

25. Article XVI:2(a) provides that where a Member has made a market access commitment in its Services Schedule, that Member is prohibited from imposing limitations on the number of service suppliers, including through the use of monopolies, quotas, and exclusive service suppliers, unless the Member has included that limitation in its Schedule. Thus, in order to show that a measure is inconsistent with Article XVI:2, it is necessary first to demonstrate that a Member has undertaken a market access commitment and then establish that the measure in question imposes the type of limitation prohibited by Article XVI:2.

B. China Made Extensive Market Access Commitments Covering the Supply of Electronic Payment Services

26. China made mode (1) and mode (3) market access commitments with respect to "All payment and money transmission services, including credit, charge and debit cards...," a category that encompasses electronic payment services for payment card transactions.

27. China's own pronouncements confirm its recognition that its WTO accession commitments included providing market access for foreign suppliers of EPS and that any purported limitations on such access were to be eliminated by 2006:

> By 2006, the RMB bank card operation shall be opened to the outside world in an all-around manner, and accordingly the bank card industry of our country is facing a comparatively big challenge and we should make use of the limited time to enhance the international competitiveness of our industries.

C. China's Measures Related to China UnionPay and the Use of CUP Payment Cards Operate to Limit The Number Of Foreign Suppliers of EPS

28. First, China imposes requirements that mandate the use of CUP and/or establish CUP as the sole supplier of EPS for all domestic transactions denominated and paid in RMB. These measures require that all transactions denominated and paid in RMB in China must processed and cleared in RMB through CUP, and where there is a choice, all domestic transactions on dual currency cards must be routed in RMB through CUP.

29. Second, China imposes requirements on issuers of payment cards that any payment cards issued in China must bear the CUP logo. No other payment card logo benefits from such a mandate. Any dual currency card issued in China also must bear the CUP logo. This means that issuers must have access to the CUP system, and pay CUP for that access.

30. Third, China requires that all ATM, merchant card processing devices, and POS terminals in China post the CUP logo and be capable of accepting CUP cards. These requirements extend to all such processing equipment and POS terminals in China and there is no equivalent requirement mandating acceptance for any other card.

31. Fourth, China imposes requirements on acquiring institutions that they post the CUP logo and be capable of accepting all bankcards bearing the CUP logo.

32. Fifth, China imposes broad prohibitions on the use of non-CUP cards for cross-region or inter-bank (or cross-bank) transactions. China also requires that all inter-bank (or cross-bank) transactions for all bankcards be handled through CUP.

33. Finally, China requires that CUP be used to handle all RMB transactions in Macao or Hong Kong using bankcards issued in China. China also requires that CUP be used to handle any RMB transactions in China using RMB cards issued in Hong Kong or Macao.

VII. CHINA'S MEASURES ESTABLISHING AND SUPPORTING CHINA UNIONPAY'S MONOPOLY ON THE SUPPLY OF EPS ARE INCONSISTENT WITH ARTICLE XVII OF THE GATS BECAUSE THEY ACCORD LESS FAVORABLE TREATMENT TO FOREIGN EPS SUPPLIERS

A. GATS Article XVII (National Treatment)

34. The measures imposed by China affecting foreign suppliers of electronic payment services are also inconsistent with Article XVII of the GATS. A national treatment commitment under Article XVII of the GATS obligates a WTO Member to accord services and service suppliers of other Members "treatment no less favorable than that it accords to its own like services and services suppliers." Article XVII:2 specifies that a Member may accord foreign services or suppliers different treatment to achieve this objective. Article XVII:3 defines treatment as "less favorable" if it "modifies the conditions of competition in favour of services or service suppliers of the Member."

B. China Made National Treatment Commitments Regarding The Supply of Electronic Payment Services

35. China made mode (1) and mode (3) national treatment commitments with respect to "All payment and money transmission services, including credit, charge and debit cards..." which clearly encompass the electronic payment services at issue here. China thereby committed to provide national treatment within the meaning of Article XVII to foreign suppliers of EPS.

C. China's Measures Affect the Supply of Electronic Payment Services

36. China maintains numerous measures affecting the supply of electronic payment services under modes (1) and (3). The measures operate to prevent market access irrespective of the mode. The terms "affecting" and "supply of services" have been construed broadly by the Appellate Body.

37. The measures at issue affect the supply of services in two principal ways.

38. First, there are measures that impose a limitation such that CUP is the sole entity that can process certain transactions, such as domestic RMB transactions. This of course means that foreign suppliers of EPS are prevented from supplying the service at all.

39. Second, there are measures that promote CUP's position in the marketplace such as by imposing certain requirements on every key player in a

card-based electronic payment transaction, including issuers (all cards issued in China for domestic RMB transactions must bear the CUP logo), merchants (all merchant card processing equipment and POS terminals must accept CUP cards), and acquiring institutions (which must post CUP logo and accept CUP cards).

40. The following measures affect every aspect of a card-based electronic payment transaction and the key players – issuers, acquiring institutions, merchants, and EPS suppliers – involved in such transactions.

- China's measures ensure that CUP is the sole supplier of certain transactions such as interbank transaction, transactions denominated and paid in RMB, and transactions in certain border areas such as Hong Kong and Macau. These provisions discriminate against foreign suppliers of EPS by either categorically precluding their participation in the market, and/or by adversely modifying the conditions of competition among the key participants – issuers, acquiring institutions, merchants, and the EPS supplier – in card-based electronic payment transactions.
- China's measures requiring that any payment cards used only for RMB purchases in China, as well as any dual currency cards issued in China, bear the CUP logo. No other EPS provider is afforded such a privilege. Since any issuer of payment cards in China is required to have access to the CUP system (and to pay for that privilege), the issuer has no reason to seek an alternative supplier of EPS. The requirement also means that even if a card was issued for a foreign EPS supplier, CUP would also gain as the CUP logo would be on the card as well.
- China's measures requiring all automatic teller machines, merchant card processing equipment and point of service terminals accept CUP cards. No foreign EPS supplier is afforded a similar privilege. To the extent a foreign supplier of EPS was to create or secure access to a POS, then CUP would also gain as well because of this requirement.
- China's measures requiring that all acquiring institutions in China post the CUP logo and to accept all bankcards bearing that logo. No foreign EPS supplier is afforded a similar privilege.

41. These measures affect the supply of electronic payment services within the meaning of Article XVII because they directly regulate the terms on which they may be provided in China.

D. *China's Measures Treat Suppliers of Electronic Payment Services of Other Members Less Favorably than CUP, China's Like Supplier of EPS*

42. The measures at issue provide disparate treatment solely according to the identity of the EPS supplier: CUP or not CUP. The Panel in *China - Publications and Audiovisual Products* found that:

> When origin is the only factor on which a measure bases a difference of treatment between domestic service suppliers and foreign suppliers, the "like service suppliers" requirement is met, provided there will, or can, be domestic and foreign suppliers that under the measure are the same in all material respects except for origin. We note that similar conclusions have been reached by previous panels. We observe that in cases where a difference of treatment is not exclusively linked to the origin of service suppliers, but to other factors, a more detailed analysis would probably be required to determine whether suppliers on either side of the dividing line are, or are not, "like."

43. Here, it is self-evident from China's own documents that China was concerned about the potential competition its domestic supplier of EPS faced from foreign suppliers of EPS and was determined to enhance its industry's position because, as the Chinese Government stated, it was "facing a comparatively big challenge and we should make use of the limited time to enhance the international competitiveness of our industries."

44. Therefore, it is unsurprising that the measures at issue here are meant to favor the domestic Chinese entity and accordingly discriminate on that basis.

45. Outside of China, with the ability to operate from its protected home market, CUP has become a significant and increasingly active participant in this competition and EPS suppliers describe CUP as a competitor. CUP's Articles of Association are explicit that the company is "to provide advanced electronic payment technologies and specialized services in connection with the inter-bank bank card information switching." CUP itself recently noted the global reach of its "payment services" around the world.

46. It is clear that CUP provides services for payment card transactions "like" those provided by foreign suppliers of EPS for payment card transactions and that the basis for the differential treatment by China in its measures is ultimately one of origin, and the "like service suppliers" requirement of Article XVII is therefore satisfied.

47. The Panel in *China – Publications and Audiovisual Products* explained:

> a measure that prohibits foreign service suppliers from supplying a range of services that may, subject to satisfying certain conditions, be supplied by the like domestic supplier cannot constitute treatment 'no less favourable,' since it deprives the foreign service supplier of any opportunity to compete with like domestic suppliers. In terms of paragraph 3 of Article XVII, such treatment

> modifies conditions of competition in the most radical way, by eliminating all competition by the foreign service supplier with respect to the service at issue.

48. On their face, many of the measures at issue explicitly prohibit any entity other than CUP from supplying services in the Chinese market. China's measures thus categorically exclude foreign suppliers of EPS from providing EPS on RMB and interbank transactions. Because these measures categorically prohibit foreign EPS suppliers from participating in certain transactions, their treatment is less favorable than that afforded CUP, a Chinese entity, and therefore inconsistent with China=s obligations under GATS Article XVII.

49. China's measures include those that prevent competition against CUP altogether in regards to certain transactions. Other measures, however, while not *per se* banning competition modify the conditions of competition to disfavor foreign suppliers of EPS as opposed to CUP. These measures include:

- requirements on issuers that payment cards issued in China bear the CUP logo;
- requirements that all ATM and POS Terminals in China Accept CUP cards;
- requirements on acquiring institutions to post the CUP logo; and
- broad prohibitions on the use of non-CUP cards.

50. These measures are inconsistent with Article XVII of the GATS because they accord less favorable treatment to foreign suppliers of EPS than to CUP.

VIII. CONCLUSION

51. The United States respectfully requests that the Panel find that China's measures, as set out above, are inconsistent with China's obligations under Article XVI:1 and XVI:2(a) and Article XVII of the GATS. The United States further requests, pursuant to Article 19.1 of the DSU, that the Panel recommend that China bring its measures into conformity with its WTO obligations.

ANNEX A-2

EXECUTIVE SUMMARY OF THE FIRST WRITTEN SUBMISSION OF CHINA

I. INTRODUCTION AND OVERVIEW

1. The Panel should dismiss the U.S. claims in their entirety, because the United States has failed to prove that China undertook relevant market access and national treatment commitments in the cross-border and commercial presence modes of supply for the services at issue in this dispute.

2. The services at issue are those services that fall within the U.S. definition of what it has described as "electronic payment services", and that are actually affected by the measures at issue. As China will demonstrate, the services at issue in this dispute are those services that operators of interbank payment card networks supply to financial institutions, including clearing and settlement services.

3. Once the services at issue have been identified, the task before the Panel is to classify those services in relation to China's Schedule and identify the commitments, if any, that China made in respect of those services. The U.S. claims fail completely at this juncture, because the United States has failed to prove its assertion that the services at issue in this dispute are encompassed by subsector (d), "all payment and money transmission services", and because the United States has failed to prove that China undertook relevant commitments in subsector (d) for Modes 1 and 3.

4. In the absence of any relevant commitments, there is no legal basis for the Panel to proceed to what would otherwise be the next task before it, namely, determining whether the measures at issue are inconsistent with the specific commitments that China actually made. China will, however, conclude this submission by demonstrating that the U.S. national treatment claims under Article XVII do nothing more than repeat the "monopoly" allegations that are the basis of its market access claims under Article XVI. This approach is inconsistent with the fact that Article XVI provides the sole basis for evaluating measures of the types listed in Article XVI:2(a)-(f), including monopolies under Article XVI:2(a). Thus, in all events, there is no legal basis for the U.S. national treatment claims in this dispute.

II. BACKGROUND

A. Payment Cards and Interbank Payment Card Networks

5. The measures and services at issue in this dispute, and the alleged "monopoly" that is the centrepiece of the U.S. claims, relate to *interbank*

payment card transactions. Interbank payment card transactions are based on what is commonly referred to as the "four-party" (or "open loop") model. The defining characteristic of the four-party model is that there is more than one financial institution involved in the payment card transaction. This means that the financial institutions participating in the payment card transactions (the "participating financial institutions") must have some method of *authorizing* the transactions, *clearing* transaction data, and *settling* their financial claims in respect of each other.

6. In most cases, financial institutions authorize, clear, and settle interbank payment card transactions by obtaining these services from the operators of interbank payment card networks. An interbank payment card network is a telecommunications and data processing infrastructure through which the network operator provides certain authorization, clearing, and settlement services to participating financial institutions. Throughout this dispute, China will refer to operators of interbank payment card networks as "network operators", and will refer to the services that network operators provide to financial institutions as "network services". This terminology is consistent with how governments and antitrust authorities have referred to these services, as well as service suppliers like Visa, MasterCard, and American Express. Moreover, unlike the term "electronic payment services", the terms "network operator" and "network services" are objectively based on prior usage, were not invented for the purpose of this dispute, and are not designed to prejudge either the number of distinct services at issue or their classification in relation to China's Schedule.

7. The market for network services is distinct from the market in which financial institutions issue payment cards and acquire payment card transactions. This has been the consistent finding of antitrust authorities and other government regulators. The two markets also differ in terms of the nature and identity of the relevant service suppliers. Suppliers of network services are not financial institutions and are not regulated as such. They are, as one observer notes, "primarily technology-based processing companies". Issuers and acquirers, on the other hand, are almost always banks or other types of regulated financial institutions. Most issuers and acquirers provide these payment services as part of an array of other banking services. In short, these two markets are the polar opposites of each other, from the standpoint of economics, regulation, and the identity of the service suppliers.

B. The Measures at Issue

8. The measures at issue in this dispute establish a national interbank network for clearing and settling RMB-denominated payment card transactions. In addition to establishing this domestic network, the measures require interbank payment cards issued in China, as well as POS terminals, to adhere to certain technical standards and to bear a common logo indicating their ability to be used for domestic interbank transactions.

9. As the United States has summarized, the challenged measures emerged from a period in which Chinese commercial banks were issuing proprietary, three-party payment cards bearing their own logos. Merchants that wanted to accept more than one type of payment card had to maintain a separate POS terminal for each type of card. Consumers who wanted the convenience of payment cards often carried different payment cards from different banks, in order to increase the likelihood that any given merchant would accept one of their cards.

10. Beginning in 1993, the People's Bank of China ("PBOC") began a series of efforts to develop a functional interbank payment card network. In March 2002, the project was transferred to China Union Pay ("CUP"), a legal entity established to run this network. Today, CUP operates China's interbank payment card network under the direct supervision and regulation of the PBOC.

11. Some of the measures that gave rise to China's interbank payment card network are among the measures that the United States has challenged in this dispute. Document No. 37, for example, established uniform technical standards for interbank payment cards and for POS terminals that accept interbank payment cards, and established the "Yin Lian" logo as the common logo for interbank payment cards and POS terminals that conform to these standards. Document No. 57 requires payment cards issued for domestic interbank use to bear the Yin Lian logo, and requires commercial banks that issue and acquire interbank payment cards to adhere to the Business Specifications for Bankcard Interoperability in Document No. 76. These and other measures finally allowed China to realize the network effects of a genuine interbank payment card system, and, as demonstrated below, are entirely consistent with its WTO commitments.

III. THE SERVICES AT ISSUE ARE NETWORK SERVICES SUPPLIED BY OPERATORS OF INTERBANK PAYMENT CARD NETWORKS

12. The services at issue in this dispute are determined by two factors: (1) the U.S. definition of the services at issue, as set forth in its panel request; and (2) the scope and effect of the challenged measures. The services at issue cannot be broader than the services that the United States has described in its panel request, and cannot be broader than the services that are actually affected by the challenged measures.

13. The panel request describes the services at issue as "the services through which transactions involving payment cards … are processed and through which transfers of funds between institutions participating in the transactions are managed and facilitated." The next sentence describes "a system" that "[s]uppliers of electronic payment services supply, directly or indirectly". This "system," according to the United States, "typically includes" what appear to be five distinct elements, which the United States separates with semicolons. These are: (1) "the processing infrastructure, network, and rules and procedures that facilitate, manage, and enable transaction information and payment flows and

which provide system integrity, stability and financial risk reduction;" (2) "the process and coordination of approving or declining a transaction, with approval generally permitting a purchase to be finalized or cash to be disbursed or exchanged;" (3) "the delivery of transaction information among participating entities;" (4) "the calculation, determination, and reporting of the net financial position of relevant institutions for all transactions that have been authorized;" and, (5) "the facilitation, management and/or other participation in the transfer of net payments owed among participating institutions."

14. There are several noteworthy features of this description. First, it does not encompass the issuance of payment cards or the acquisition of payment card transactions. That is, it does not encompass payment card services that are typically provided by banks or other types of financial institutions. Second, the description seems to relate exclusively to four-party payment card models, since it contemplates the participation of more than one financial institution in the "system" (*e.g.*, in its references to "participating institutions"). Finally, at least three of the five elements of the "system" that it describes relate to the clearing and settlement of interbank payment card transactions – the third and fourth elements relate to clearing, while the fifth element relates to settlement.

15. Turning to the scope and effect of the challenged measures, the measures at issue in this dispute establish a national network for clearing and settling RMB-denominated interbank payment card transactions. These measures affect the ability of other network operators to provide network services to financial institutions in China for the purpose of authorizing, clearing, and settling RMB-denominated interbank payment card transactions. The measures do *not* affect the ability of financial institutions to enter and compete in the market for issuing payment cards and acquiring payment card transactions, and do not affect their ability to provide proprietary (three-party) payment card services. Nor do the challenged measures affect the ability of companies to enter and compete in the market for issuer processing or merchant processing services.

16. Based on the description of the services at issue in the panel request and the scope of the challenged measures, China concludes that the services at issue in this dispute are the network services that China has described above. Fundamentally, these services relate to the operation of a telecommunications and data processing infrastructure through which network operators supply authorization, clearing, and settlement services to banks and other financial institutions.

17. As China noted above, a minimum of three of the five elements of the "system" described by the United States in its panel request relate to clearing and settlement. However many other services might be at issue in this dispute, clearing and settlement services are plainly among them. Thus, while the United States makes heroic efforts to avoid using the terms "clearing" and "settlement" in the narrative of its submissions, China believes it should be undisputed that the services at issue include clearing and settlement services. Moreover, as the United States acknowledges, these clearing and settlement services are "central" to what it calls "electronic payment services".

IV. THE UNITED STATES HAS FAILED TO DEMONSTRATE THAT CHINA MADE MARKET ACCESS AND NATIONAL TREATMENT COMMITMENTS IN RESPECT OF THE SERVICES AT ISSUE IN THIS DISPUTE

A. The Clearing and Settlement Services at Issue in this Dispute Are Classifiable Under Item (xiv) of the Annex on Financial Services, Which Is Unbound in China's Schedule

18. Given the "central" importance of clearing and settlement services to the services at issue in this dispute, China will begin with the classification of these services in relation to China's Schedule. As China will proceed to demonstrate, China made no market access or national treatment commitments in respect of clearing and settlement services. The Panel must therefore reject the U.S. claims as they relate to these services.

19. Section 5 of the *Annex on Financial Services* lists 16 distinct types of financial services that fall within the definition of a "financial service." China made no market access or national treatment commitments in respect of item (xiv) in the *Annex*, "settlement and clearing services for financial assets, including securities, derivative products, and other negotiable instruments". Had China made a commitment in respect of this service, it would have been subsector (j) in China's Schedule. China's Schedule skips over this subsector in its sequence of commitments, jumping from subsector (f) to subsector (k), and not elsewhere referring to "settlement and clearing services for financial assets".

20. The term "financial assets", as used in item (xiv) in the *Annex*, refers broadly to cash or any sort of monetary claim. Looking at the words "financial" and "assets" separately, the ordinary meaning of the term "financial" is "[o]f or pertaining to revenue or money matters", while an "asset" is "a thing or person of use or value". Putting these two definitions together, a "financial asset" can be understood as any revenue or monetary item ("financial") that has value to its possessor ("asset"). The same ordinary meaning is supported by referring to sources that define "financial assets" as a single term. The *Oxford Dictionary of Economics*, for example, defines "financial assets" as "[m]oney and claims, as distinct from physical assets such as land, buildings, or equipment." This definition includes cash and any right to receive cash.

21. Interbank payment card transactions involve the clearing and settlement of cash or contractual rights to receive cash, and therefore involve the clearing and settlement of financial assets within the ordinary meaning of item (xiv). An interbank payment card transaction gives rise to a claim by the acquiring bank against the issuing bank in the amount of the transaction, to be paid in cash. Operators of interbank payment card networks provide clearing and settlement services for these cash claims and positions. Whether one views these clearing and settlement services as relating to cash or rights to receive cash, in either event these services are encompassed by item (xiv) because they involve the clearing and settlement of financial assets.

22. Because clearing and settlement services for payment card transactions are encompassed by item (xiv), it is unnecessary for the Panel to examine the U.S. assertion that these clearing and settlement services are encompassed by subsector (d). It is a well-established rule of classification that the heading or subsector that provides the most specific description shall be preferred to more general headings or subsectors that might otherwise encompass the good or service at issue. As compared to subsector (d), item (xiv) would clearly provide the more specific description of the clearing and settlement services at issue in this dispute, even if there were otherwise a basis to interpret subsector (d) as encompassing clearing and settlement services – which, as China will proceed to demonstrate, there is not.

B. The United States Has Not Met Its Burden of Proving that Subsector (d) Encompasses the Services at Issue

23. The United States has staked its entire case on the proposition that *all* of the services at issue in this dispute should be classified under subsector (d), "all payment and money transmission services". Because the United States agrees that the sectors and subsectors in a Member's Schedule are mutually exclusive, it follows that, in the United States' view, none of the services at issue in this dispute can be classified under another sector or subsector. That is the case that the United States has decided to present.

24. China has just demonstrated that the *clearing and settlement* services at issue in this dispute are encompassed by a subsector that China left unbound. Accordingly, these services are *not* classifiable under subsector (d), and the U.S. claims in respect of these services must fail. Nevertheless, the United States has failed to prove that *any* of the services at issue in this dispute – much less *all* of the services that might be at issue – are encompassed by subsector (d). Subsector (d) encompasses payment services that banks and other financial institutions provide to their cardholder and merchant customers. The United States argues, in effect, that subsector (d) encompasses not only card issuance and acquisition services provided *by banks*, but also services provided *to* banks by *non-bank* service suppliers. This interpretation is in error.

25. Subsector (d) is one of six subsectors listed in China's Schedule under the heading of "banking services". The ordinary meaning of "banking services" is services provided by banks. Consistent with this ordinary meaning, all of the services listed under the heading of "banking services" are services that are typically provided by banks, finance companies, and other types of financial institutions.

26. Properly interpreted in this context, the "payment services" referred to in subsector (d) encompass the issuance and acceptance by financial institutions of payment instruments other than cash. These are characteristically "banking services" because they involve banks acting as payment intermediaries. At some point in the transactional chain, the banks are in possession of the relevant funds and are paying these funds to another party. The banks are making a *payment*

within the ordinary meaning of that term, *i.e.*, they are engaging in "[a]n act, or the action or process, *of paying* … ."

27. China believes the United States would agree with the conclusion that issuance and acquisition are banking services encompassed by subsector (d). However, issuance and acquisition are not among the services at issue in this dispute, among other reasons because these services are not within the U.S. description of the services at issue. Instead, the cornerstone of the U.S. interpretation of subsector (d) is that the term "payment and money transmission services" includes any service that could be said to "manage" or "facilitate" a payment card transaction, or that relates to the "processing" of a payment card transaction. The U.S. interpretation is untenable as a matter of treaty interpretation.

28. To begin with, as discussed above, the ordinary meaning and context of subsector (d) support the conclusion that a "payment service" is a banking service in which the service supplier (*i.e.*, the bank or other financial institution) becomes a party to the payment transaction, having rights and obligations of payment in relation to the payer and payee (or their respective financial institutions). A service supplier that is merely "managing" or "facilitating" the supply of this type of payment service, or "processing" payment transactions, is not itself a party to the payment transaction. It is neither issuing nor accepting the payment instrument and is never in possession of the funds to be paid. It is not "paying" anyone, and is not providing a "payment service" within the ordinary meaning of that term.

29. More generally, services that "manage" or "facilitate" the supply of a service, or that relate to the "processing" of another service transaction, are not necessarily classifiable *as that other service*. The Members have expressly affirmed that services that help to "manage" or "facilitate" the supply of another service, or that relate to its "processing", must be classified separately to the extent that they are distinct and separately identifiable services. In this regard, the 2001 Scheduling Guidelines state that "[i]t is understood that market access and national treatment commitments apply only to the sectors or sub-sectors inscribed in the schedule. *They do not imply a right for the supplier of a committed service to supply uncommitted services which are inputs to the committed service.*"

30. Equally untenable is the proposition that any service that relates to the "processing" of a service transaction (such as a payment card transaction) is necessarily the same as the service to which the processing relates. Different types of processing services are recognized as distinct services throughout China's Schedule, and throughout the taxonomy of W/120 generally. For example, item (xv) in the *Annex* list of financial services, corresponding to subsector (k) in China's financial services commitments, refers to "financial data processing and related software by suppliers of other financial services". Subsector 2.C.n in the Services Sectoral Classification List refers to "on-line information and/or data processing (*incl. transaction processing*)". These processing services are clearly distinct from any other service that they happen

to support (*e.g.*, the "other financial service" referred to in subsector (k) or the "transaction" referred to in subsector 2.C.n). The contention that services relating to the "processing" of payment card transactions are necessarily "payment services" under subsector (d) would obliterate these distinctions.

31. For all of these reasons, the Panel must reject the U.S. assertion that subsector (d) encompasses all services that "manage", "facilitate", or "process" payment card transactions. As this assertion is the foundation of the U.S. position that all of the services at issue in this dispute are classifiable under subsector (d), the U.S. claims that are based on this interpretation must fail.

C. Conclusion to Section IV

32. The failure of the United States to meet its burden of proof in respect of the classification of the services at issue brings this matter to an end. Because the United States has failed to prove its proposed classification of the services at issue, there is no legal basis for the Panel to proceed to an evaluation of whether the challenged measures are inconsistent with relevant specific commitments. The remainder of this submission is advanced entirely on an *arguendo* basis, accepting the erroneous premise that some or all of the services at issue are classifiable under subsector (d). As the next two sections will demonstrate, the Panel would still need to reject the entirety of the U.S. claims, even under this erroneous premise.

V. EVEN IF SOME OR ALL OF THE SERVICES AT ISSUE WERE COVERED BY SUBSECTOR (D), THE UNITED STATES HAS FAILED TO ESTABLISH RELEVANT MARKET ACCESS AND NATIONAL TREATMENT COMMITMENTS IN MODE 1 AND MODE 3

33. The United States has staked its case on the proposition that all of the services at issue in this dispute are encompassed by subsector (d), a proposition that the United States has failed to prove. But even if some or all of the services at issue in this dispute *were* classifiable under subsector (d), the United States has failed to prove that China made relevant market access and national treatment commitments under this subsector in the cross-border and commercial presence modes of supply. This is a separate and independent reason why the Panel must reject all of the U.S. claims in this dispute.

A. China's Mode 1 Market Access Entry for Subsector (d) Is Unbound

34. China's entry in the market access column for subsectors (a) through (f) states that the cross-border mode of supply is "unbound except for the following". The entry then repeats, verbatim, the descriptions of subsectors (k) and (l), which appear in China's Schedule under the heading of "[o]ther financial services".

35. The meaning of this portion of China's Schedule could not be clearer: China undertook no market access commitments under Mode 1 with respect to subsectors (a) through (f), including subsector (d). Notwithstanding the fact that subsector (d) is unbound in Mode 1, the United States makes no effort whatsoever to explain the logical or legal basis for its Mode 1 claims in this dispute. The failure of the United States to make this showing means that it has failed to establish a *prima facie* case of violation in respect of its Mode 1 claims, and the Panel must reject these claims in their entirety.

B. China's Mode 3 Market Access and National Treatment Commitments for Subsector (d) Are Limited to Foreign Financial Institutions

36. The U.S. claims under Mode 3 are based on a single premise: that all of the market access and national treatment limitations inscribed in China's Schedule for subsector (d), Mode 3, "were to be eliminated within five years after China's accession." The United States has provided no interpretative support for this conclusion whatsoever – it is sheer assertion, wholly unsupported by the actual text of China's Mode 3 market access and national treatment commitments.

37. For example, under the heading of "Clients", China's market access inscription for subsectors (a) through (f) states that "[w]ithin five years after accession, foreign financial institutions will be permitted to provide services to all Chinese clients." This is an express limitation on China's market access commitment: the only types of entities that "will be permitted" to provide the services under subsectors (a) through (f) are "foreign financial institutions". It follows that China made no market access commitment under subsectors (a) through (f) in respect of entities that are not "foreign financial institutions".

38. By its express terms, this limitation on market access applied after the five-year phase-in period, and continues to apply to this day. China committed to allow "foreign financial institutions" to "provide services to all Chinese clients" on a commercial presence basis no later than 11 December 2006. Contrary to the implicit U.S. suggestion that this limitation *expired* on 11 December 2006, in fact that is the date on which the commitment became *effective*. As of that date – and going forward thereafter – "foreign financial institutions" would "be permitted" to provide the services under subsectors (a) through (f) "to all Chinese clients." China made no commitment to permit entities that are *not* foreign financial institutions to provide these services, at any point in time.

39. The ordinary meaning of the term "financial institution" is "[a] regulated organization that provides a range of banking and investment services". It is "[a]ny organization, such as a bank, building society, or finance house, that collects funds from individuals, other organizations, or government agencies and invests these funds or lends them on to borrowers." As these definitions reflect, the essential attributes of a financial institution are (1) that it collects funds from the public (whether as deposits or investments), and (2) that it is subject to some

type of prudential regulation or supervision. These are the types of entities to which China has opened its market for the services listed in subsectors (a) through (f), in accordance with China's commitments.

40. China has fully adhered to the commitments that it actually made under subsector (d). With regard to payment card acquisition services, China allowed foreign financial institutions to engage in this business even before it acceded to the WTO. With regard to the issuance of payment cards, China promulgated a number of measures that allowed foreign financial institutions to enter this market in line with China's commitments. Foreign financial institutions in China issue payment cards and acquire payment card transactions, and do so on an equal footing with Chinese financial institutions. The United States has not alleged otherwise in this dispute.

41. Nor has the United States made any effort to demonstrate that what it calls "electronic payment services suppliers" are foreign financial institutions – either in general, or in the case of the specific service suppliers that it has identified by name in its submissions. Presumably, this is because it has erroneously concluded that the limitations on market access and national treatment inscribed in China's Schedule for Mode 3 expired five years after accession.

42. Having failed to demonstrate that "electronic payment services suppliers" are foreign financial institutions, the United States has necessarily failed to demonstrate that China's commitments in Mode 3 are relevant to the services and service suppliers at issue in this dispute and do not preclude the rights of market access and national treatment to which it claims to be entitled. The Panel must therefore reject the U.S. claims of violation under Articles XVI and XVII of the GATS, even accepting the erroneous proposition that subsector (d) encompasses the network services at issue in this dispute.

VI. IN ALL EVENTS, THE U.S. NATIONAL TREATMENT CLAIMS MUST FAIL BECAUSE THE UNITED STATES RELIES UPON THE SAME ASPECTS OF THE SAME MEASURES THAT IT RELIES UPON IN SUPPORT OF ITS MARKET ACCESS CLAIMS

43. This section accepts, *arguendo*, that some or all of the services at issue in this dispute are classifiable under subsector (d), *and* that China made relevant market access and national treatment commitments in the cross-border and commercial presence modes of supply. Even if both of these assumptions were true, the U.S. national treatment claims must still fail, because the United States improperly bases its national treatment claims on the same aspects of the same measures that are the foundation of its market access claims.

44. Article XVI:2 of the GATS lays out the six types of measures that a Member may not maintain or adopt in any sector in which it has undertaken a market access commitment, unless that measure is identified in its Schedule.

These measures, identified in Article XVI:2(a)-(f), can be either discriminatory or non-discriminatory. The United States claims that the same aspects of the measures that allegedly confer a monopoly on CUP in violation of China's market access commitments also violate China's national treatment commitments under Article XVII of the GATS, which governs the imposition of discriminatory measures.

45. Even accepting the faulty U.S. argument that the provision of a monopoly is discriminatory, the text of the GATS plainly requires that monopolies be addressed under Article XVI:2(a), and not Article XVII. Article XX:2 of the GATS explains that "[m]easures inconsistent with both Articles XVI and XVII shall be inscribed in the column relating to Article XVI", in which case the measure "will be considered to provide a condition or qualification to Article XVII as well." By virtue of this provision, the inscription in the market access column of a discriminatory limitation on market access will also be considered a limitation on national treatment. This would include any respect in which the existence of a monopoly could be considered "discriminatory".

46. According to the Scheduling Guidelines, a Member's entry of "unbound" in its Schedule means that the Member is "free in a given sector and mode of supply to introduce or maintain measures inconsistent with market access or national treatment", as the case may be. Because Article XX:2 provides that measures inconsistent with both Article XVI and Article XVII are to be inscribed in the market access column, an entry of "unbound" in the market access column means that a Member is free to introduce measures of the types specified in Article XVI:2, without regard to whether those measures are discriminatory or non-discriminatory. What the United States is doing in this dispute – invoking the same aspects of the same measures to establish *both* a market access and national treatment violation – would render *inutile* a Member's entry of "unbound" in the market access column.

47. The current dispute presents a perfect example of the flaw in the U.S. approach. China's market access entry in Mode 1 for subsector (d) is "unbound", with a cross-reference to subsectors (k) and (l). By inscribing "unbound" in Mode 1, China elected not to undertake market access commitments with respect to the cross-border supply of the services in subsectors (a)-(f). Therefore, for the supply of those services in Mode 1, China reserved the right to maintain and introduce measures of the types listed in Article XVI:2, including a monopoly under Article XVI:2(a).

48. China's national treatment commitment for the cross-border supply of the services under subsectors (a) through (f) is "none". The United States claims that the same aspects of the measures that allegedly confer a monopoly upon CUP also violate China's national treatment commitments. This contention, if accepted, would entirely defeat the choice that China made by leaving market access unbound in Mode 1. China reserved the right to introduce market access limitations for this subsector and mode of supply, including limitations under Article XVI:2 that might be seen as discriminatory, and its right to introduce

such measures cannot be taken away by a finding that the exact same aspects of the measures are inconsistent with Article XVII.

49. The essence of the U.S. claim in this dispute is that China is maintaining a monopoly in the supply of network services, which it erroneously believes to be inconsistent with China's market access commitments. The United States has presented no evidence or legal argument that *other* aspects of the challenged measures are inconsistent with China's national treatment commitments. Accordingly, the Panel must reject the U.S. national treatment claims in this dispute, without regard to its disposition of any other issue before it.

VII. CONCLUSION

50. For the reasons set forth in this submission, China respectfully requests that the Panel reject the U.S. claims in this dispute in their entirety.

ANNEX B

ORAL STATEMENTS OR EXECUTIVE SUMMARIES THEREOF, OF THE PARTIES AT THE FIRST SUBSTANTIVE MEETING

Contents		Page
Annex B-1	Executive summary of the opening oral statement of the United States at the first substantive meeting	5601
Annex B-2	Closing oral statement of the United States at the first substantive meeting	5606
Annex B-3	Executive summary of the oral statement of China at the first substantive meeting	5607

ANNEX B-1

EXECUTIVE SUMMARY OF THE OPENING ORAL STATEMENT OF THE UNITED STATES AT THE FIRST SUBSTANTIVE MEETING

I. INTRODUCTION

1. When China joined the World Trade Organization ("WTO") in 2001, it made important commitments with respect to electronic payment services ("EPS") for payment card transactions. China explicitly acknowledged its commitments in 2005 and recognized that by 2006 its payment card market would be "opened to the outside world in an all-around manner." Simply put, China has not honored its WTO commitments.

2. Under the terms of China's Schedule of Specific Commitments on Services, China committed to provide both market access and national treatment for "all payment and money transmission services, including credit, charge and debit cards" for domestic currency transactions. Yet, despite these commitments, China continues to maintain a government-mandated domestic monopoly, enabling only its national champion, China UnionPay, Co. Ltd. ("CUP"), to provide these services, thereby blocking foreign service suppliers. The measures at issue establish a monopoly and systematically discriminate against and restrict foreign EPS suppliers while favoring China's own supplier of EPS.

II. EPS FOR PAYMENT CARD TRANSACTIONS FALL WITHIN THE ORDINARY MEANING OF "ALL PAYMENT AND MONEY TRANSMISSION SERVICES, INCLUDING CREDIT, CHARGE AND DEBIT CARDS..." (SUBSECTOR (D))

3. EPS is the service through which transactions involving credit, charge, debit and other payment cards are processed and through which transfers of funds between institutions participating in the transactions are managed and facilitated. China's commitments pertain to "*all* payment and money transmission services, including credit, charge and debit cards," indicating that the scope of the commitment covers the service that is essential to payment card transactions. EPS suppliers are at the heart of this service. Without EPS, these payment card transactions could not occur.

4. First, EPS clearly falls within the ordinary meaning of "payment and money transmission services" as one type of "*all*" such services. Second, the phrase "all payment and money transmission services" is modified with an illustrative list that explicitly provides that it "include[s] credit, charge and debit cards." This explicit reference is in line with the recognition that EPS is integral to the processing of credit, charge, debit and other card-based electronic payment transactions, and without this service, payment card transactions could not occur.

III. CHINA'S MODE 1 AND MODE 3 COMMITMENTS FOR "ALL PAYMENT AND MONEY TRANSMISSION SERVICES, INCLUDING CREDIT, CHARGE AND DEBIT CARDS..."

5. China argues that its mode 3 commitments in subsector (d) apply only to services supplied *by* banks because subsector (d) falls under the heading of "banking services." The term "banking services" is not limited in this manner. As even China has recognized, major U.S. EPS suppliers, as well as CUP, were formally operated as associations of banks – and from their inception they were clearly performing "banking services." The nature of the service that an entity supplies does not change merely because that entity assumes a new corporate form. In analyzing a service for purposes of a GATS commitment, one must look at the characteristics and nature of the service to classify that service.

6. It is also evident from China's Schedule itself that the term "banking services" listed in China's Schedule, including those listed in subsector (d) are not limited to those provided by banks as China claims. In addition to the explicit reference to "non-bank financial institutions" in China's Schedule, there are references to "foreign finance companies" in the market access column and to "foreign financial leasing corporations" in the additional commitments column. Moreover, the definition of "financial service supplier" in the Annex on Financial Services to the GATS covers not only banks but other suppliers of financial services, which supply or wish to supply financial services within the meaning of the Annex.

7. For similar reasons, China's argument that its mode 3 market access and national treatment commitments for subsector (d) are limited to foreign financial institutions, and that EPS suppliers do not qualify, must also fail. Although China includes certain limitations with respect to foreign financial institutions, this does not mean that its commitments are limited to foreign financial institutions. Such a limitation would have needed to be imposed explicitly. China's the Schedule states that "[c]riteria for authorization to deal in China's financial services sector are solely prudential." Thus, under China's Schedule, the only limitations China may impose are prudential restrictions and the explicitly listed limitations – defunct restrictions on geographic scope and use of domestic currency, and ongoing requirements applicable to banks. Finally, the definition of "financial institution" offered by China is far too narrow. There are many definitions that are much broader, and some explicitly include "an operator of a credit card system."

8. It is also plain from the text that China has taken mode 1 commitments for "all payment and money transmission services, including credit, charge and debit cards..." The word "Unbound" is followed by the qualifying phrase "except for the following," which in turn is further elaborated by two sentences that describe elements of the services within subsector (d) for which China has taken mode 1 commitments. A fundamental tenet of treaty interpretation requires that the qualifying phrase "except for the following" and the further specific elaboration following the word "Unbound" should be given meaning. China focuses solely on the term "Unbound." If China wished to in fact be fully "Unbound," that is, not to have any commitments, it would have left the word "Unbound" unqualified. However, as the Schedule reflects, China did not do so.

9. Much of the activity involved in the supply of EPS for payment card transactions entails the transfer of financial information and financial data processing, and much of this occurs on a cross-border basis. It is therefore not surprising that China made cross-border commitments for subsector (d) for EPS for payment card transactions to the extent that the activities entail the provision and transfer of financial information and financial data processing.

IV. THE SERVICE AT ISSUE IS NOT "SETTLEMENT AND CLEARING SERVICES FOR FINANCIAL ASSETS, INCLUDING SECURITIES, DERIVATIVE PRODUCTS, AND OTHER NEGOTIABLE INSTRUMENTS"

10. In classifying EPS for payment card transactions under item (xiv), China ignores the ordinary meaning of the provision, the scope of which is limited to investment instruments, such as securities, derivatives, and other negotiable instruments. The context-specific nature of these terms is evident from the international institutional framework that establishes separate regimes for payment systems and securities settlement systems. The Committee on Payment and Settlement Systems ("CPSS"), a part of the Bank for International Settlements ("BIS"), is charged with developing the multilateral framework that

governs payment systems, on the one hand, and securities settlement systems, on the other hand – two very distinct systems.

11. The CPSS provides guidance concerning payment systems (which include suppliers of EPS for payment card transactions) and securities settlement systems. The CPSS "glossary of terms used in payments and settlement systems" clearly illustrates that the terms "clearing" and "settlement" each have different meanings in the respective payment and securities contexts. The definitions relating to payments systems, including EPS for payment card transactions, are drawn from different source documents than those for securities settlement systems.

12. It is clear that "settlement and clearing services for financial assets," as explicitly qualified in item (xiv) of the GATS are clearing and settlement services for assets like derivative products, stocks, or bonds. In contrast, EPS for payment card transactions are used to clear and settle payments associated with the transfer of goods and services, *not* financial assets. This is also entirely consistent with the explicit reference to "credit, charge and debit card" payment transactions in item (viii) ("all payment and money transmission services…") and the lack of any similar reference to card transactions in item (xiv).

V. CHINA'S MEASURES ESTABLISHING AND SUPPORTING CHINA UNIONPAY'S MONOPOLY ON THE SUPPLY OF EPS ARE INCONSISTENT WITH ARTICLE XVI OF THE GATS

13. The measures imposed by China on the supply of EPS are inconsistent with Article XVI of the GATS because they limit the number of suppliers of EPS for RMD-denominated payment card transactions in China. China maintains numerous measures that ensure CUP's privileged position by explicitly and effectively limiting the number of foreign EPS suppliers. China's State Council and the People's Bank of China ("PBOC") approved and authorized only one entity, CUP, to process inter-bank card-based payment transactions.

14. The terms of certain measures are explicit in their requirements or prohibitions that establish CUP as the exclusive supplier of EPS for RMB denominated domestic payment card transactions in China. Other measures establish requirements or prohibitions that effectively preclude foreign EPS suppliers from being in the market. China's measures that create the monopoly structure and restrict the supply of EPS by foreign suppliers affect every element of the electronic payment system and all of the key participants (issuers, acquiring institutions, merchants, and EPS suppliers themselves) and card-based electronic payment transactions. China has chosen not to offer substantive rebuttal to U.S. claims related to the challenged measures or to the CUP monopoly.

VI. CHINA'S MEASURES ESTABLISHING AND SUPPORTING CHINA UNIONPAY'S MONOPOLY ON THE SUPPLY OF EPS ARE INCONSISTENT WITH ARTICLE XVII OF THE GATS

15. The measures at issue affect the supply of services in two principal ways. First, there are measures that impose a limitation such that CUP is the sole entity that can process certain transactions, such as domestic RMB transactions. This of course means that foreign suppliers of EPS are prevented from supplying the service at all. Second, there are measures that promote CUP's position in the marketplace such as by imposing certain requirements on every key player in a card-based electronic payment transaction, including issuers (all cards issued in China for domestic RMB transactions must bear the CUP logo), merchants (all merchant card processing equipment and POS terminals must accept CUP cards), and acquiring institutions (which must post the CUP logo and accept CUP cards).

16. It is important to note that the measures at issue provide disparate treatment solely according to the identity of the EPS supplier: CUP or not CUP. The EPS supplied is the same, and therefore is "like services."

17. China's own documents demonstrate China's concern about the potential competition its domestic supplier of EPS would face from foreign EPS suppliers:

> By 2006, the RMB bank card operation shall be opened to the outside world in an all-around manner, and accordingly the bank card industry of our country is facing a comparatively big challenge and we should make use of the limited time to enhance the international competitiveness of our industries.

18. It is unsurprising that the measures at issue here are meant to favor the domestic Chinese entity and accordingly discriminate on that basis.

VII. CONCLUSION

19. The United States respectfully requests that the Panel find that China's measures are inconsistent with China's obligations under Article XVI:1 and XVI:2(a) and Article XVII of the GATS.

ANNEX B-2

CLOSING ORAL STATEMENT OF THE UNITED STATES AT THE FIRST SUBSTANTIVE MEETING

1. The United States would first like to thank the Panel and the Secretariat staff assisting it. The United States would also like to thank China for its participation in this meeting. The United States found that the Panel's written and oral questions were very helpful in fostering a very focused discussion. We also found the third party session useful and consider the third party statements and our meeting confirm our concerns with China's measures.

2. The United States notes that China's defense rests entirely on a series of truly implausible arguments. For example:

3. China expects you to believe that there are no restrictions on foreign EPS suppliers handling RMB card transactions, but no foreign supplier has chosen to enter its market. Is that because foreign suppliers are not eager to enter the Chinese market? Or because the Chinese market is not lucrative enough?

4. China expects you to believe that it took commitments under subsector (d) for "credit, charge and debit cards" but took no commitments for the "payment and money transmission services" we all associate with the use of those cards and that are the heart of the service.

5. China expects you to believe that it restricted the supply of foreign services to "financial institutions" without having used language to indicate that, without any definition of that term, and despite stating in its Schedule that criteria for authorization are solely "prudential."

6. China expects you to believe that it included extensive language qualifying the word "Unbound" under mode 1 for subsector (d), but that those words are entirely redundant of other subsectors, (k) and (l), and that it does not even know why it included those words under mode 1.

7. In contrast, the United States has provided explanations grounded in the text of China's Schedule and the GATS and that are legally sound and fully consistent with the commercial reality of the way EPS for card transactions are supplied.

8. We look forward to further engaging in the process with you and again thank you for your service on the panel.

ANNEX B-3

EXECUTIVE SUMMARY OF THE ORAL STATEMENT OF CHINA AT THE FIRST SUBSTANTIVE MEETING

I. INTRODUCTION

1. In the interest of moving expeditiously to the Panel's questions, and in order to avoid repeating the arguments laid out in China's first written submission, I will limit my opening remarks this afternoon to three key issues. These are: (1) the fact that China made no market access or national treatment commitments in respect of clearing and settlement services; (2) the contention by the United States that services that "manage" or "facilitate" the supply of a service, or that relate to the "processing" of another service transaction, are classifiable as that other service; and (3) China's limitation of its Mode 3 market access and national treatment commitments for subsector (d) to foreign financial institutions.

II. CLEARING AND SETTLEMENT SERVICES

2. Item (xiv) of the *Annex*, which would have been subsector (j) in China's Schedule had China made a commitment for this service, refers to "settlement and clearing services for financial assets, including securities, derivative products, and other negotiable instruments". Pursuant to Article 31 of the Vienna Convention, any analysis of this provision must begin with the ordinary meaning of its terms.

3. There can be no question that "electronic payment service suppliers" like Visa and MasterCard provide clearing and settlement services. As China demonstrated in its first written submission, these clearing and settlement services are for "financial assets" within the ordinary meaning of that term. The *Oxford Dictionary of Economics*, for example, defines "financial assets" as "[m]oney and claims, as distinct from physical assets such as land, buildings, or equipment", a definition that includes cash and any right to receive cash. In its oral statement, the United States offered *nothing* to contradict this understanding. Because interbank payment card transactions involve the clearing and settlement of cash or rights to receive cash, these transactions necessarily involve the clearing and settlement of financial assets within the ordinary meaning of item (xiv).

4. The United States has taken the position that *all* of the services at issue in this dispute should be classified under subsector (d), "all payment and money transmission services". Furthermore, the United States has agreed that the sectors and subsectors in a Member's Schedule are mutually exclusive. Accordingly, the U.S. claims with respect to clearing and settlement services must fail, because

these services cannot fall into a subsector that China left unbound and simultaneously fall into subsector (d).

III. SERVICES THAT "MANAGE", "FACILITATE", OR RELATE TO THE "PROCESSING" OF A SERVICE

5. The cornerstone of the U.S. interpretation of subsector (d) is that the term "payment and money transmission services" includes any service that could be said to "manage" or "facilitate" a payment card transaction, or that relates to the "processing" of a payment card transaction. But subsector (d), properly interpreted, only encompasses payment services that banks and other financial institutions provide to their cardholder and merchant customers. It does not encompass the U.S. notion of "electronic payment services", which are services provided *to* banks by *non-bank* service suppliers.

6. Subsector (d) falls under the heading of "banking services" in China's Schedule, and the ordinary meaning of "banking services" is services provided by banks. Consistent with this heading, China limited its commitments for subsectors (a) through (f) to banks and other types of financial institutions. Properly interpreted in this context, subsector (d) encompasses the issuance and acceptance by financial institutions of payment instruments other than cash.

7. The problem for the United States is that issuance and acquisition are *not* among the services at issue in this dispute, leaving the United States in the untenable position of having to argue that services which help "manage", "facilitate", or "process" the services actually covered by subsector (d) are likewise properly classified in the same subsector. Taken to its logical extreme, this interpretation would sweep into subsector (d) a large array of telecommunications, data processing, and clearing and settlement services – among other potential services – that are typically supplied to banks and other financial institutions by non-bank service suppliers.

8. The 2001 Scheduling Guidelines state, "[i]t is understood that market access and national treatment commitments apply only to the sectors or sub-sectors inscribed in the schedule. They do not imply a right for the supplier of a committed service to supply uncommitted services which are inputs to the committed service." In many cases, services that "manage" or "facilitate" the provision of another service or that relate to its "processing" could properly be seen as "inputs" to the provision of that service. But a Member's decision to make different commitments (or no commitments) for these "input" services must be given effect.

9. Because clearing and settlement services are properly classified in a subsector that China left uncommitted, and because the United States has failed to prove, in any event, that services that "manage", "facilitate", or "process" payment card transactions are properly classified in subsector (d), the U.S. claims fail at the threshold. However, even accepting the erroneous premise that some or all of the services at issue are classifiable under subsector (d), the U.S.

argument with respect to China's commitments in this subsector would require the Panel to reject the U.S. claims in this dispute.

IV. CHINA'S MODE 3 COMMITMENTS FOR SUBSECTOR (D)

10. The United States claims that all of the market access and national treatment limitations inscribed in China's Schedule for subsector (d) in Mode 3 "were to be eliminated within five years after China's accession." Incredibly, however, the United States has failed to provide any textual support for this assertion in its first submission or its oral statement. What China's market access inscription for subsectors (a) through (f) *actually* says is that "[w]ithin five years after accession, foreign financial institutions will be permitted to provide services to all Chinese clients." The only plausible reading of China's commitments is that China agreed to allow "foreign financial institutions" to "provide services to all Chinese clients" on a commercial presence basis *no later than* December 11, 2006.

11. China can only imagine that the reason why the United States has now forgotten the obvious meaning of China's Mode 3 limitations is because the U.S. claims must fail unless the United States can convince the Panel that these restrictions have disappeared entirely. Per the clear terms of China's Mode 3 commitments, the only types of entities that "will be permitted" to provide the services under subsectors (a) through (f) are "foreign financial institutions". But the United States has not demonstrated that its "electronic payment services" suppliers are financial institutions. In fact, Visa and MasterCard, whose documents the U.S. cites frequently as relevant "industry sources", go out of their way to make clear that they are *not* financial institutions. As such, China's market access and national treatment commitments in subsector (d) would not extend to these entities, either before or after December 2006.

12. The absence of any relevant commitments brings this dispute to an end. As a final matter, however, China wishes to correct the U.S. mischaracterization of the measures at issue. The United States has failed to identify anything in the challenged measures that would require all interbank payment card transactions to be processed over the CUP network, or that would prevent other networks from processing interbank payment card transactions. Contrary to the U.S. assertion, there is nothing in the challenged measures that establishes any sort of "monopoly". The measures at issue ensure that every interbank payment card in China is capable, at a minimum, of being processed over the CUP network. But establishing a *common* network is not the same as establishing a *monopoly* network.

13. China reiterates, however, that there is neither a need nor a legal basis for the Panel to reach this issue. As prior panels have recognized, the first task before the Panel is to classify the services at issue and determine the extent of the commitments, if any, that China undertook in respect of those services. Because the United States has failed to demonstrate the existence of any such commitments, the U.S. claims fail at the threshold and must be dismissed in their entirety.

14. China thanks the Panel for its attention, and looks forward to answering its questions.

ANNEX C

WRITTEN SUBMISSIONS AND ORAL STATEMENTS, OR INTERGRATED SUMMARIES THEREOF, OF THE THIRD PARTIES

Contents		Page
Annex C-1	Integrated executive summary of the third party written submission and oral statement of Australia	5611
Annex C-2	Third party oral statement of Ecuador at the first substantive meeting	5618
Annex C-3	Integrated executive summary of the third party written submission and oral statement of the European Union	5622
Annex C-4	Integrated executive summary of the third party written submission and oral statement of Japan	5626
Annex C-5	Integrated executive summary of the third party written submission and oral statement of the Republic of Korea	5633

ANNEX C-1

INTEGRATED EXECUTIVE SUMMARY OF THE THIRD PARTY WRITTEN SUBMISSION AND ORAL STATEMENT OF AUSTRALIA

I. INTRODUCTION

1. These proceedings, initiated by the United States, present Members with an important opportunity to consider the interpretation of Members' obligations under the Schedule of Specific Commitments under the General Agreement on Trade in Services (GATS).

2. Australia has identified the following key matters, which raise issues of legal importance:

a. The meaning of the words "all payment and money transmission services" in subsector 7B(d) of China's Schedule of Specific Commitments under the GATS (China's Schedule);[1]

b. The scope of China's GATS commitments under subsector 7B(d); and

c. Interpretation of the sectoral classifications used by Members in their GATS Schedules.

II. THE GENERAL AGREEMENT ON TRADE IN SERVICES

A. The Meaning of "All Payment and Money Transmission Services"

3. A material issue in this matter is the meaning of the words "all payment and money transmission services" in subsector 7B(d) of China's Schedule, and whether the services at dispute are captured by this provision.

4. The United States contends that subsector 7B(d) of China's Schedule captures "electronic payment services" (as defined by the United States in its Request for Establishment of a Panel).[2] China submits that the services at dispute are correctly characterised as "network operator" and "network services".[3] China's view is that these services are classified under an alternative subsector, which China has left unbound in its Schedule – namely, "settlement and clearing services for financial assets" as set out in sub-paragraph 5(a)(xiv) of the *Annex on Financial Services* (Annex).[4]

5. Australia submits that, having regard to the ordinary meaning of the terms, the phrase "all payment and money transmission services" should be interpreted broadly to encompass services which are integral to payment and money transmission services, including services which manage and facilitate credit card based payments.

6. Australia therefore submits that the services described by both the United States and China in their submissions may be correctly classified under subsector 7B(d) of China's Schedule. In particular, the services that the United States refers to as "electronic payment services", involve services through which transactions involving payment cards are processed, and through which transfers of funds between institutions participating in the transaction are managed and

---

[1] Section II, 7 (Financial Services), B (Banking and Other Financial Services) of China's Schedule (circulated in WT/ACC/CHN/49/Add.2 and WT/MIN(01)/3/Add.2), item (d).

[2] See page 1 and note 2 of *China – Certain Measures Affecting Electronic Payment Services,* WT/DS413, U.S. Request for the Establishment of a Panel, February 11, 2011.

[3] See para 24 of *China – Certain Measures Affecting Electronic Payment Services,* WT/DS413, First Submission of China, October 11 2011 (China 11 October First Submission).

[4] See para 11 of China 11 October First Submission.

facilitated.[5] By managing and facilitating the transfer of money or payment from one person or place to another, Australia agrees that credit card based payment service suppliers engage in both "payment and money transmission services" and thus fall under subsector 7B(d).

7. Similarly, Australia submits that the meaning of "all payment and transmission services" correctly captures the services described by China. That is, the services described by China, including clearing and settlement services as they relate to credit card based payments, are fundamental components of card based transactions. Indeed, without the processing infrastructure, network and rules and procedures, which China refers to as "telecommunications and data processing infrastructure",[6] card based payment transactions could not occur. These services are fundamental to the transmission of funds in a card based transaction.

8. The Appellate Body has found that under Article 31 of the Vienna Convention on the Law of Treaties (1969) (Vienna Convention), the ordinary meaning of treaty terms may be ascertained only in their context, and in light of the object and purpose of the treaty.[7] The Appellate Body has accepted that Members may therefore refer inter alia to a Member's GATS Schedule, provisions of the GATS, and the GATS Schedules of other Members as relevant context in determining the meaning of a scheduled commitment.[8]

9. To this end, Australia notes that China has included the words "including credit, charge and debit cards, travellers cheques and bankers drafts (including import and export settlement)" in its Schedule, as examples of activities envisaged under "all payment and money transmission services". The inclusion of these additional words in "all payment and money transmission services", further supports the view that subsector 7B(d) was at least intended to cover the services under dispute. In particular, inclusion of these words makes it clear that services which manage and facilitate the transmission and processing of money and payment transactions, such as through the use of payment cards (i.e. credit and debit cards), fall within the confines of China's market access and national treatment commitments.

10. In addition, Australia submits that reference to the provisions of the GATS provides further relevant context for interpretation of subsector 7B(d) of China's Schedule. Paragraph 5(a) of the Annex sets out a detailed list of activities falling under the meaning of financial services, which evidences the

---

[5] See para 155 of *China – Certain Measures Affecting Electronic Payment Services,* WT/DS413, Submission of the United States of America in Response to China's Request for a Preliminary Ruling, July 29, 2011 (including Exhibits US-1 - US-62) (U. S. July 29 Response) sections V.B, V.C, V.D.

[6] See para 72 of China 11 October First Submission.

[7] See para 348 of *China – Measures Affecting Trading Rights and Distribution Services for Certain Publications and Audiovisual Entertainment Products,* WT/DS363/AB/R (*China – Publications and Audiovisual Products*), citing article 31, *Vienna Convention on the Law of Treaties, 1969.*

[8] Ibid, at para. 358.

intention of the negotiators to cover comprehensively the activities of the financial sector. In particular, sub-paragraph 5(a)(viii) of the Annex refers to "credit, charge or debit cards" as examples of activities envisaged under "all payment and money transmission services". This clarifies that members intended that credit card and debit card transmission services are categories of financial services, for which Members may choose to make commitments.

11. Reference to the other categories under paragraph 5(a) of the Annex also provides additional context informing the meaning of "all payment and transmission services". China submits that the services relating to card based transactions at dispute, including clearing and settlement services, more appropriately fall under sub-paragraph 5(a)(xiv) of the Annex, which relates to "settlement and clearing services for financial assets". Australia submits that this subsector concerns settlement and clearing services for financial assets, other than card based transactions. Australia notes that sub-paragraph 5(a)(xiv) includes the words "securities, derivative products and other negotiable instruments", as examples of the subject of the transactions envisaged by "settlement and clearing services for financial assets". The distinguishing quality of sub-paragraph 5(a)(xiv) is that it concerns services relating to financial assets.

12. In addition, unlike sub-paragraph 5(a)(viii), sub-paragraph 5(a)(xiv) does not make specific reference to "credit, charge and debit cards". Australia submits that inclusion of the words "credit, charge or debit cards" under "all payment and money transmission services" in sub-paragraph 5(a)(viii), further supports the view that credit and debit card transactions, including clearing and settlement services in so far as they are integral to card based transactions, more appropriately fall under sub-paragraph 5(a)(viii) of the Annex, rather than sub-paragraph 5(a)(xiv).

13. Article 32 of the Vienna Convention provides that recourse may be had to supplementary means of interpretation, including the preparatory work of the treaty and the circumstances of its conclusion in order to confirm the meaning resulting from the application of Article 31.[9] In the US-Gambling dispute, the Appellate Body noted that the Services Sectoral Classification List (MTN.GNS/W/120, 10 July 1991) "constitutes supplementary means of interpretation, including the preparatory work of the treaty."[10] W/120 appears to have been the starting point for China's Schedule, which sets out its categories and entries, under the heading of "B. Banking and Other Financial Services (excluding insurance and securities)", by using similar entries, including numbering and letters, as those contained in the "Banking and other Financial Services (EXCL. insurance)" section of W/120. Importantly, subsector 7(B)(d)

---

[9] See paras 404 and 405 of Appellate Body Report, *China – Publications and Audiovisual Products*.

[10] See para 196 of Appellate Body Report in *United States – Measures Affecting the Cross Border Supply of Gambling and Betting Services*, WT/DS285/AB/R, adopted 20 April 2005, DSR 2005:XII, 5663 (Corr.1, DSR 2006:XII, 5475)

of W/120 only refers to "all payment and money transmission services", such that China's inclusion of the additional words "including credit, charge and debit cards, travellers cheques and bankers drafts" clarifies that services which facilitate the transmission of money and payment transactions, such as through the use of payment cards (i.e. credit and debit cards), fall within subsector 7B(d) in China's Schedule.

14. It therefore follows that the services at dispute, described by the United States and China respectively as "electronic payment services" and/or "network services", are correctly classifiable under subsector 7B(d) of China's Schedule.

B. China's GATS Commitments on Financial Services

15. Another important matter in this dispute is the interpretation of China's scheduled services commitments under subsector 7B(d). Australia notes that this is a complex area, not least because not all Members have followed the scheduling Guidelines in all instances.

16. Australia notes the WTO Secretariat takes the view that all commitments in a Member's Schedule are bound unless otherwise specified.[11] If a member wishes to remain free in a given sector and/or mode of supply (i.e. where it wishes to retain the flexibility to introduce or maintain limitations on market access or national treatment) the Member will enter the term "unbound" in its Schedule of Specific Commitments. Conversely, where a Member wishes to bind itself to a market access and/or national treatment commitment, for which it maintains no limitations, it will enter "none" with respect to the relevant sector or mode. A Member may also make a commitment with limitations by providing specific explanation in the text of the Schedule.

17. In addition, Australia recognises the point made by the European Union in its submission, that Article I:2(c) of the GATS defines mode 3 services as the supply of a service "by a service supplier of one member, through commercial presence in another Member".[12] Importantly, if a Member wishes to limit the service suppliers that are permitted to provide a particular service, then it must explicitly inscribe such a limitation in its schedule of commitments.

18. Australia is of the view that a proper interpretation of China's commitments with regard to subsector 7B(d) is as follows. Under the "market access" column for subsector 7B(d), China has inscribed neither "Unbound" nor "None" with respect to mode 3. Australia submits that other than the prudential licensing limitations on foreign financial entities, China's Schedule should be interpreted as "otherwise, none" as to any further limitations relating to subsector 7B(d). Similarly, given the expiry of the geographic and client

---

[11] See WTO's "Guide to reading the GATS schedules of specific commitments and the list of article II (MFN) exemptions" at *http://www.wto.org/english/tratop_e/serv_e/guide1_e.htm*

[12] See para 34 of *China – Certain Measures Affecting Electronic Payment Services,* WT/DS413, Third Party Submission of the European Union, October 18 2011.

restrictions in 2006, there are no limitations relating to China's national treatment commitments. This is confirmed by the inclusion of the words "otherwise, none" under "national treatment".

19. It is therefore Australia's view that the commitments made by China with respect to subsector 7B(d) are not limited to foreign financial institutions, as claimed by China, as no such limitation has been inscribed in its Schedule. Australia submits that although China has inscribed certain limitations and clarifications under "market access" and "national treatment", which relate to foreign financial institutions, this does not mean that its commitments are limited to foreign financial institutions. If this were the case, China would have included the words "unbound except" or "otherwise unbound" in its Schedule, as indeed it has with respect to mode 1.

C. *Interpretation of The Sectoral Classification Used in GATS Schedules*

20. In its submission, China highlights the importance of interpreting GATS Schedules in line with the 2001 Scheduling Guidelines. Australia agrees with China's position that the system of classifying services would "collapse" if distinct and separately identifiable services could be classified under another sector or subsector, simply because they manage or facilitate or relate to the processing of that service. Australia acknowledges that sectors and subsectors in a Member's Schedule are mutually exclusive, and agrees that preserving this reading of the architecture of the Schedules is fundamental to a meaningful interpretation of Members' commitments

21. Australia remains of the view, however, that "electronic payment services" or "network services" are a fundamental component of credit card based payment services, and should properly be included under the definition of "all payment and money transmission services". To this end, Australia reiterates that, based on the application of Article 31 of the Vienna Convention, "all payment and money transmission services" should be interpreted to encompass services that are integral to payment and money transmission services, including services which manage and facilitate credit card based payments.

III. CONCLUSION

22. Central to this dispute are a number of important systemic issues concerning the interpretation of Members' GATS Schedules. As set out above, Australia submits that subsector 7B(d) "all payment and money transmission services, including credit, charge and debit cards, travellers cheques and bankers drafts (including import and export settlement)" should be interpreted broadly, so as to include services essential to card based payment services, including services which manage and facilitate credit card based payments, and clearing and settlement services insofar as they relate to card transactions. Further, Australia has offered some views on how China's GATS Schedule should be interpreted, noting the importance of interpreting GATS Schedules consistently with the 2001 Scheduling Guidelines.

ANNEX C-2

THIRD PARTY ORAL STATEMENT OF ECUADOR AT THE FIRST SUBSTANTIVE MEETING

I. INTRODUCTION

1. Members of the Panel: The Government of Ecuador thanks the Panel and the Parties for this opportunity to present its views on certain issues involved in this dispute. Ecuador is participating in this case given its systemic concerns with regard to the correct interpretation of the Schedules of specific commitments in services undertaken by Members and, hence, the correct legal interpretation of the General Agreement on Trade in Services (GATS).

2. In this oral submission, the Government of Ecuador will focus on briefly highlighting two legal aspects relating to: (i) specific guidelines for interpreting commitments under the General Agreement on Trade in Services (GATS); and (ii) the scope of the obligations under Articles XVI and XVII of the GATS in relation to monopolies.

II. GUIDELINES FOR INTERPRETING GATS COMMITMENTS

A. Commitments in Services are the Result of Positive List Negotiations

3. A reading of the GATS reveals that Members decided that their services commitments were contingent upon public policy spaces in the area concerned that they had chosen to protect. Parallel to this, in their positive lists, they established independently the level and scope of and restrictions on those spaces. The fourth recital of the preamble to the GATS confirms the importance attached by Members to the link between public policies and specific commitments by recognizing the right of Members to "... regulate, and to introduce new regulations on, the supply of services within their territories in order to meet national policy objectives".

4. It is evident from a review of a number of GATS provisions, for example Articles XVI, XVII, XVIII, XIX and XX, that Members have decided to grant market access and non-discriminatory treatment to foreign services suppliers *solely and exclusively* in the sectors or subsectors included in their schedules of specific commitments. Members may, in full compliance with GATS rules, undertake, amend or eliminate commitments, notably on market access and non-discrimination, on the basis of public policies the definition of which corresponds to each individual Member. In short, as far as trade in services is concerned, market access and non-discrimination are restricted to the level of the commitments that Members agreed to undertake.

5. As a result, there is no room for interpretation as regards the scope of specific services commitments in the schedules of original commitments when, in spite of the complexity of the issue, these commitments have been clearly specified by a Member. To seek to broaden the scope to cover other sectors by means of an expansive interpretation of the schedule of specific commitments would constitute an unacceptable impairment of Members' right to define its scope and content.

6. The interpretation of specific commitments should take into account the context and the object and purpose of the GATS, which indicate that specific commitments are established solely on the basis of the positive list of commitments, and thereby avoid attempts, by means of interpretation, to broaden the range of these commitments to cover sectors that are not included.

B. In the Event of the Existence of Two Specific Commitments on the Same Service, the More Specific Commitment Takes Precedence

7. A general legal principle is that a special law prevails over a general law. This principle is applied, *mutatis mutandis*, to the disciplines of the various covered agreements set forth in Appendix 1 to the Understanding on Rules and Procedures Governing the Settlement of Disputes. In the context of the interpretation of specific services commitments, there is no reason why this general legal principle should not apply to the legal relationship between the specific commitments that a Member has undertaken in respect of the other Members of this Organization, all the more so since the rules on the classification of services state that the most specific description of the sectors or subsectors that could correspond to a services commitment shall prevail over a more general description.[1] The criterion of the primacy of the special law over the general law forms a constituent part of legal hermeneutics, which cannot be left unaddressed in the review of the scope of specific GATS commitments.

C. The Terms of Commitments Must be Interpreted Stricto Sensu

8. The **specific** commitments undertaken by Members are based *ab initio* on a number of **specific** trade concessions which **facilitate** market access or **reduce** or **eliminate** discrimination between domestic and foreign suppliers in relation **only** to committed sectors of trade in services. This involves the voluntary imposition of self-restraint with regard to the power to implement national policies relating to these sectors or subsectors, through the regulation of the supply of services or the establishment of new regulations.

9. In light of the above, a broad and unrestricted interpretation of the specific services commitments undertaken by Members could lead, in practice,

[1] United Nations Provisional Central Product Classification (CPC), Rule of interpretation 1(a).

to Members disregarding the specificities that characterize the supply of services of a different nature. This would not only weaken the predictability of the multilateral trading system but would undermine Members' power to regulate trade in services on the basis of the self-restraint imposed, where this exists.

10. An excessively broad interpretation of, for example, the descriptors established in the classification of the schedules of specific commitments could therefore open the way for attempts to include commitments where they do not exist, which means covering more than what it was voluntary agreed upon to liberalize.

11. For instance, the term "payment" is defined as the "handover of money or kind that is owed".[2] This term is clear in its common usage and should therefore be interpreted *stricto sensu* with regard to the effective transfer of resources, which means excluding from its coverage any step or action that facilitates or administers a "payment", even if it is a related service.

D. The Characterization of a Service by the Industry Does Not Necessarily Determine the Nature of the Service

12. In Ecuador's view, the industry's characterization of a service does not determine the nature of that service. It is clear that when negotiating their schedules of specific commitments Members established the scope of the specific sectors or subsectors that they were prepared to liberalize, i.e. they defined the types of services for which they would open up markets and grant national treatment. It is therefore up to the Members to define what is meant by a specific service.

13. The fact that one or several companies decide to describe the services they supply as "payment services" does not necessarily confer that character upon them. In defining what they do internally, companies may be guided by categories or definitions that will not necessarily coincide with Members' understanding as established and assumed in the schedules of specific commitments. Moreover, these categories or definitions may vary from company to company, sector to sector, or even country to country.

14. In order to determine the nature of services, an assessment should be made of the objective characteristics of the facts, and of the services provided by the service supplier and their customers or consumers. If, for example, the services offered by a service supplier consist of data transmission, digital trade facilitation or data storage, it is difficult to argue that they can be characterized as "payment services".

15. The legal value of the characterization of a service in the light of the opinion of its suppliers is therefore questionable, as not only would subjective

---

[2] *Diccionario de la Lengua Española*, 22nd edition, volume 2, p. 1647.

criteria and private interests be privileged, but there would also be a risk of impairing rights which the Members are responsible for defining.

III. SCOPE OF THE OBLIGATIONS UNDER ARTICLES XVI AND XVII OF THE GATS IN RELATION TO MONOPOLIES

A. Services Provided by a Member's Monopolies and Exclusive Service Suppliers Are Only Limited by the Specific Commitments Undertaken by That Member

16. In Ecuador's view, it is important to note that the services provided by a Member's monopolies and exclusive service suppliers will only be limited by the level of the specific commitments that this Member has included in its schedule of commitments. In this respect, the provisions of Articles VIII, XVI and XVII converge in specifying that the monopolies and exclusive service suppliers of a Member may operate without any restriction unless market access commitments are undertaken in the sectors in which they operate and/or where national treatment has been granted "in the sectors inscribed in its Schedule [in that of the Member], and subject to any conditions and qualifications set out therein ...".

17. In conclusion, it should be noted that if a Member has not undertaken any commitment in its schedules of commitments, i.e. if it has entered the term "unbound" for the sector, or left the sector blank, it will be taken to mean that there is no commitment in favour of either foreign suppliers (market access) or domestic suppliers (national treatment) and that, as a result, both types of supplier will be equally impeded from supplying the services that Members have reserved for designated monopolies or exclusive service suppliers.

ANNEX C-3

INTEGRATED EXECUTIVE SUMMARY OF THE THIRD PARTY WRITTEN SUBMISSION AND ORAL STATEMENT OF THE EUROPEAN UNION

I. THE MEASURES AT ISSUE

1. The EU agrees with the US that measures can be subject to challenge individually as well as collectively and that, when this is necessary to assist the DSB in discharging its duties, the panel should review both.

2. When provisions of certain individual measures together and collectively amount to a general scheme and that scheme nullifies or impairs the benefit of a Member, such a scheme can be construed as a measure. The scheme as a whole is therefore susceptible to review, provided it can be defined with sufficient precision in the panel request.

II. WHETHER CHINA'S SPECIFIC COMMITMENTS IN ITS GATS SCHEDULE INCLUDE ELECTRONIC PAYMENT SERVICES FOR PAYMENT CARD TRANSACTIONS

3. China argues in favour of a narrow reading of its scheduled commitment for "all payment and money transmission services" and a broad reading of a sector as defined in the *Annex on Financial Services* to the GATS, with respect to which it did not schedule any commitments; namely "settlement and clearing services for financial assets".

4. In the view of the EU the ordinary meaning of China's commitments relating to "all payment and money transmission services" does not support the narrow reading advanced by China and consequently does not warrant the conclusion that the services at issue are excluded from its commitments.

5. Firstly, China's Schedule uses the term "banking services" not "services of banks". Explicit terminology used by China in its Schedule fully supports the view that China's commitments under "Banking services" are not solely and exclusively related to banks, but also "suppliers of other financial services" (Section II.7.B, Subsector (d), second column, Mode 1, first indent) and "foreign financial institutions" (Section II.7.B, Subsector (d), second column, Mode 3, points B and C).

6. Secondly, China has undertaken specific commitments with respect to a category of "services", as opposed to a category of "service providers". This is clear from the text of the individual commitment under Section II.7.B, Subsector (d), as well as its heading and subheading. Nothing in the text of China's Schedule of Specific Commitments supports China's argument that the supply of

"payment and money transmission services" pursuant to China's GATS Schedule is limited to certain entities. It may therefore be concluded that these services can be offered by any financial service supplier. In fact, Article 5(b) of the GATS *Annex on Financial Services* makes it clear that the Annex introduces a very wide definition of financial service suppliers. Furthermore, in order to be a financial service supplier under the GATS the natural or judicial person does not, in principle, need to be previously or solely engaged in the supply of financial services.

7. Thirdly, the Panel may consider and examine the differences in meaning between sub-paragraphs (viii) and (xiv) of Paragraph 5 of the GATS *Annex on Financial Services*.

8. In the opinion of the EU, "payment and money transmission services" cannot take place without the actual transfer of money between one party and another. This would necessarily entail a process of "clearing" and "settlement", or basically the removal or debiting of funds from the accounts of one person or entity, in order to pay or credit the accounts of another person or entity. This process is an essential part of the operations of any credit, charge or debit card system, and without this transfer of funds the system simply will not work.

9. The EU is of the opinion that the term "electronic payment services", the services at issue in this dispute, falls within the meaning of sub-paragraph (viii) of paragraph 5 of the GATS *Annex on Financial Services* and within paragraph (d) listed in China's GATS Schedule of Specific Commitments. The meaning of "all payment and money transmissions services" is wide enough to include "electronic payment services" that the US refers to. Moreover, the fact that this phrase is then followed by the words "including credit, charge and debit cards", also clearly indicates that the term "electronic payment services" would also fall under this definition.

10. The term "clearing and settlement for financials assets", does not relate to "credit, charge and debit cards", which clearly and specifically fall under the definition of paragraph 5 (viii) of the GATS *Annex on Financial Services*. Moreover, paragraph 5 (xiv) gives examples of the "financial assets" which could fall within its definition, namely "securities, derivative products and other negotiable instruments". Credit cards, debit cards or charge cards which are the subject of this present dispute are very distinct from the "financial assets" that paragraph 5(xiv) is referring to. The "clearing and settlement services" involved in the trading (buying and selling) of "securities, derivative products and other negotiable instruments", are separate and distinct from the "payment and money transmission services" which take place when there is a transfer of funds between different persons or entities, in order to settle "credit, charge or debit card" transactions.

III. WHETHER CHINA'S MEASURES ARE INCONSISTENT WITH ARTICLE XVI OF THE GATS

11. Article XVI of the GATS sets forth the obligations on market access, which apply where a WTO Member has taken specific commitments in a given service sector. In its second paragraph it inter alia prohibits WTO Members from maintaining or adopting "limitations on the number of service suppliers", unless appropriate reservations have been made in their Schedule of Specific Commitments.

12. It is clear from China's Schedule of Specific Commitments that China made market access commitments with respect to Section II.7.B, Subsector (d) of its Schedule. It is also evident from the text of the commitment that certain limitations exist (or existed) with respect to Mode 1 and Mode 3.

13. The parties disagree on the exact scope of the commitments. In the view of the EU, anything that is not explicitly included in the scheduled limitation falls under China's commitment to provide market access. Nothing in the text of the reservations previously mentioned provides for a limitation on the number of service suppliers scheduled by China; not in general terms, nor specifically in favour of China Union Pay. China did not argue otherwise in its First Written Submission. Furthermore, the EU notes that China does not seem to dispute the fact that the measures at issue in this dispute result in a privileged position for China Union Pay (China's First Written Submission, paras 36-46, 54-57). It is therefore clear that in the absence of a scheduled limitation, China is subject to the obligations under Article XVI.

IV. WHETHER CHINA'S MEASURES ARE INCONSISTENT WITH ARTICLE XVII OF THE GATS

14. In order to review a claim under Article XVII of the GATS, one must assess: Firstly, whether China's Schedule of Specific commitments includes national treatment commitments on electronic payment services. Secondly, whether there are "like" services/suppliers. And thirdly, whether maintaining such measures amounts to less favourable treatment than that granted to domestic services and suppliers; that is (a) whether the measure modifies the conditions of competition and (b) whether this modification is in favour of domestic services and suppliers.

15. In the few cases in which the term "like" as it appears in the GATS has been interpreted so far, the services and suppliers at issue were found to be "like". This was done essentially by looking at the similarity of the activity performed and of the result of such activity (that is the service itself).

16. The EU agrees with the reasoning of the panel in China – Publications and Audiovisual Products, also referred to by the US in its First Written Submission. In that case the panel took the view that when origin is the only factor on which a measure bases a difference of treatment between domestic

service suppliers and foreign suppliers, the "like service suppliers" requirement is met, provided there will, or can, be domestic and foreign suppliers that under the measure are the same in all material respects except for origin. On the basis of the information presently before it, the EU observes that the measures at issue in this dispute appear to differentiate solely on the basis of the identity of the service supplier.

V. RELATIONSHIP BETWEEN ARTICLES XVI AND XVII OF THE GATS AGREEMENT

17. In the absence of scheduled limitations, Article XVII GATS prohibits any form of discrimination, de facto or de iure, against foreign services and foreign service suppliers. As this provision applies to all measures affecting service supply, it also covers any discriminatory measure of the types mentioned under Article XVI:2 GATS. In that respect it overlaps with Article XVI. More specifically, any measure that falls under Article XVI:2(a)-(d) that restricts market access and that is discriminatory, and all discriminatory restrictions concerning legal entity or foreign equity participation that fall under Article XVI:2(e)-(f), would then be covered by the Articles XVI and XVII.

18. The text of Article XX:2 GATS confirms that there is a potential overlap between Articles XVI and XVII GATS and provides guidance on avoiding problems and unintentional commitments when scheduling limitations. Following Article XX:2, Members that have scheduled as limitations in their market access column any of the measures listed under Article XVI:2, do not need to schedule such limitations twice. But in order to exempt themselves from obligations under Article XVII, they would still have to schedule in the national treatment column any discriminatory measure that does not fall under the categories set out in Article XVI:2.

19. Article XX:2 establishes a hierarchy with respect to the scheduling of limitations to specific commitments under Articles XVI and XVII GATS. However, it does not establish a hierarchy as to the substance of those provisions.

ANNEX C-4

INTEGRATED EXECUTIVE SUMMARY OF THE THIRD PARTY WRITTEN SUBMISSION AND ORAL STATEMENT OF JAPAN

I. THE SERVICES AT ISSUE

1. The United States describes the services at issue as "electronic payment services" ("EPS") supplied either on a cross-border (Mode 1) or commercial presence (Mode 3) basis. In its panel request, the United States indicates that EPS involve "[…] the services through which transactions involving payment cards […] are processed and through which transfers of funds between institutions participating in the transactions are managed and facilitated."[1]

2. In response, China contends in its First Written Submission ("FWS) that the services at issue must be determined by taking into account the overlap of two factors: (1) the United States' definition of the services at issue, as set out in the panel request; and (2) the scope and effect of the challenged measures.[2] Thus, China concludes that the services at issue are limited to what China describes as "network services".[3] Since the definition of the services at issue can influence all issues related to the application of the GATS, Japan would request the Panel to carefully examine the definition of the service at issue.

II. CHINA'S GATS COMMITMENTS

A. The Relevant Sector or Sectors

3. The United States claims that the EPS it has identified are covered by sub-sector 7.B(d) of China's GATS Schedule.[4] In response, China contends that there is no specific commitment in its Schedule which is relevant to the services at issue, and rather that they are classifiable under item (xiv) of the Annex on Financial Services which is unbound in China's Schedule.

4. Although what the relevant service sub-sector or sectors are in this dispute is still not definitive, Japan would recall that, as the Appellate Body in US-Gambling made clear, the meaning of a GATS Schedule of a Member must be determined according to the rules contained in Article 31 of the Vienna

---

1 See footnote 1 of U.S. Request for the Establishment of a Panel, *China – Certain Measures Affecting Electronic Payment Services*, WT/DS413/2, February 11, 2011.

2 First Submission of China, October 11, 2011 (China FWS), para. 61.

3 *Ibid.*, paras. 63-65.

4 Sub-sector 7.B(d) of China's GATS Schedule provides that "All payment and money transmission services, including credit, charge and debit cards, travellers cheques and bankers drafts (including import and export settlement)".

Convention on the Law of Treaties ("Vienna Convention") and, if necessary, Article 32.[5]

1. Sub-sector 7.B(d) of China's GATS Schedule

5. Two parties have drawn different conclusions regarding the meaning and scope of its commitments in sub-sector 7.B(d) of China's Schedule. The main point of contention is whether the phrase "All payment and money transmission services" only covers services which actually involve making a payment or transmitting money, or whether the commitment also extends to any services which are "essential" to the execution of those services.[6]

6. In this regard, Japan notes that item (xiv) of the Annex on Financial Services concerning "settlement and clearing services for financial assets" is one source of relevant context. The question is whether the service at issue involves "settlement" and/or "clearing services" within the meaning of item (xiv) which is unbound in China's Schedule.

2. China's all or nothing proposition

7. In its FWS, the United States argues that all of the services at issue fall within the scope of sub-sector 7.B(d). Further, the United States recalls that, as the Appellate Body stated in US-Gambling, a specific service cannot fall within the two different sectors or sub-sectors since they are "mutually exclusive".[7] In response, China argues that the Panel must refuse to find that any of the services at issue fall within the scope of sub-sector 7.B(d) if it agrees that three of the five services cited by the United States in its panel request fall within "settlement" and/or "clearing" services within the meaning of item (xiv) of the Annex on Financial Services.[8]

8. To the extent that any of the services do fall within the scope of "settlement and clearing services", it must be determined which service sector or sub-sector (or sectors) is applicable to the remaining services. In Japan's view, no Vienna Convention principle would permit the Panel to find that the remaining services also fall within the scope of item (xiv) solely on the basis that the "majority" of the other services challenged fall within the scope of that provision. Moreover, along the same lines, if the Panel finds that any of the services at issue are classifiable under sub-sector 7.B(d) of China's Schedule, the mere fact that the United States claims that all such services fall within the scope of China's commitment cannot preclude the Panel from analyzing the United

[5] Appellate Body Report in *United States – Measures Affecting the Cross-Border Supply of Gambling and Betting Services*, WT/DS285/AB/R, para. 160.

[6] First Submission of the United States, September 13, 2011 (US FWS), para. 22.

[7] US FWS, para. 24.

[8] China FWS, paras. 89-93.

States' claims with respect to any services which do fall within the scope of that sub-sector.

3. *Limitations on China's "payment and money transmission services" commitment*

9. If the EPS which the United States describes in its panel request fully or partially fall within the scope of sub-sector 7.B(d) of China's GATS Schedule, a further issue is whether China has inscribed market access and national treatment limitations on the services at issue.

10. The United States has clarified that it is pursuing claims in relation to both Mode 1 and Mode 3 services for both Article XVI and Article XVII claims. Furthermore, it has also frequently stated that China imposes no relevant limitations on both Mode 1 and 3 services in sub-sector 7.B(d) of its Schedule.[9] In response, China claims that it has no relevant commitment in sub-sector 7.B(d). As regards Mode 1, it states that it has inscribed "unbound" in the market access column for those services. As regards Mode 3, China argues that its commitments only apply with respect to financial institutions.

11. In relation to Mode 1, Japan requests the Panel to carefully consider the precise scope of China's sub-sector 7.B(d) commitment. For Mode 3, Japan specifically requests the Panel to consider whether the interpretation by China is consistent with entries in other parts of its Schedule, especially those concerning "All Insurance and Insurance-Related Services" and "Securities" which are also contained in Sector 7 on Financial Services. The question is whether any entity that provides a financial service covered by those commitments is necessarily included in the concept of "financial institution" under China's commitments.

III. ARTICLE XVI OF THE GATS

12. The United States considers that the measures imposed by China on the supply of EPS are inconsistent with Article XVI:2(a) of the GATS because they limit the number of suppliers of EPS for renminbi ("RMB")-denominated transactions that are paid in RMB.[10]

13. China does not contend that the measures at issue would not violate Article XVI:2(a) of the GATS, even if the relevant measures are bound by its market-access commitments. Nevertheless, should the Panel determine that Article XVI is applicable to the measures in question, it needs to be specifically considered whether the United States has demonstrated a prima facie case.[11] Thus, if the services which the United States complains about are only partially

---

9 See, e.g., US FWS, paras. 41,77.

10 US FWS, para. 37.

11 See Appellate Body Report, *US-Gambling*, paras. 140-141.

covered by China's commitments, the Panel should ensure that the United States has demonstrated that the relevant measure (or set of measures) affects the supply of the covered service and otherwise has the Article XVI:2(a) impact which the United States claims (e.g. a monopoly) with respect to the covered service.

IV. ARTICLE XVII OF THE GATS

14. China contends that the Article XVII national treatment claims of the United States must fail on the basis that (1) they are the same measures that are the foundation of its market access claims; and (2) Articles XVI and Article XVII are mutually exclusive.[12] In other words, China seems to claim that any measure which violates Article XVI cannot constitute the violation of Article XVII.

15. To support its view that Articles XVI and XVII are mutually exclusive, China points to Article XX:2 of the GATS. In China's view, finding that measures which confer a monopoly contrary to Article XVI are also discriminatory under Article XVII would be directly contrary to this order of precedence established by Article XX:2. China also notes that, if a monopoly could be discriminatory under Article XVII, separate and apart from the effect that it has on market access under Article XVI, a Member would need to schedule the "discriminatory" aspects of a monopoly in its national treatment column, even if it had left market access unbound and thereby reserved the right to maintain exactly the same monopoly.[13]

16. In Japan's view, the Chinese claim that Articles XVI and XVII are mutually-exclusive needs to be examined by taking into account Article XX:2 of the GATS and paragraph 18 of the 2001 Scheduling Guidelines(S/L/92).[14] Japan also ask the Panel to take into account the following: (1) whether the scope of the measures challenged by the United States under both Article XVI and Article XVII in fact overlap; and (2) whether the possibility for a measure to violate both Article XVI and Article XVII may depend on the way of committing market access and limitations applicable to the measure at issue.

---

[12] China FWS, paras. 148, 154-156.

[13] China FWS, para. 155.

[13] *Ibid.*, paras. 155, 157.

[14] Guidelines for the Scheduling of Specific Commitments Under the General Agreement on Trade in Services(GATS), adopted by the Council for Trade in Services on 23 March 2001, S/L/92, 28 March 2001.

V. ORAL STATEMENT

A. Introduction

17. Mr. Chairman, members of the Panel: Thank you for the opportunity to present the views of Japan in this third party session. Today, Japan will focus on one point: namely, the extent of China's Mode 3 commitments for "All payment and money transmission services".

18. If the Panel finds that all or part of the services at issue fall within the scope of "All payment and money transmission services", as contained in sub-sector 7.B(d) of China's GATS Schedule, China takes the view that the Panel should dismiss all of the United States' claims related to Mode 3 on the basis that its Mode 3 commitments are limited to "financial institutions".[15] Japan will address whether China has in fact limited its Mode 3 "All payment and money transmission services" commitments to "financial institutions".

19. It is worth noting, before arguing this issue in detail, that the China's argument is without merit if the term "financial institution" in China's Schedule refers to all entities which supply financial services within the meaning of China's sector 7.B "[…] Financial Services" commitments on a "Mode 3" basis.[16] In that case, it is, thus, unnecessary for the Panel to examine whether China has limited its Mode 3 commitments on "All payment and money transmission" only to "financial institutions".

B. Whether China's "All payment and money transmission services" commitments are limited to services supplied by "financial institutions"

20. Regarding the existence of a "financial institution" limitation, Japan understands China to argue that it has limited its "All payment and money transmission" Mode 3 commitments to a particular type of "service supplier" of a WTO Member, namely those which are "financial institutions".

21. In Japan's view, there is nothing in the GATS which would prohibit China from limiting the scope of its Mode 3 "All payment and money transmission services" commitment to services supplied by "financial institutions". The important question is whether China has in fact done this in its Schedule. In US-Gambling, the Appellate Body recognized that the 1993

15 China FWS, para. 132.

16 One reason for this is that "financial institution" is not defined. Absent a definition or any other commonly understood meaning, it seems that the term could be interpreted in a number of ways and, moreover, if China's suggested understandings are accepted, the scope of China's commitment could change over time depending on the evolving regulatory systems of other WTO Members. Japan doubts that China would have wanted to formulate its commitments in such a manner.

Scheduling Guidelines[17] serve to assist parties in reviewing offers made by others Members and, moreover, that they constitute a supplementary source of interpretation within the meaning of Article 32 of the Vienna Convention on the Law of Treaties.[18] Likewise, in Japan's view, the 2001 Scheduling Guidelines constitute a supplementary source of interpretation.[19]

22. Japan notes that the 2001 Scheduling Guidelines set out the principle that GATS schedules should contain clear descriptions of limitations. Thus, paragraph 3 of those Guidelines states that a schedule contains, inter alia, a clear description of limitations to market access and to national treatment. Furthermore, paragraph 22 explains that since "[s]chedules record, for each sector, the legally enforceable commitments of each Member", "[i]t is therefore vital that schedules be clear, precise and based on a common format and terminology."[20] Moreover, Japan notes that the Guidelines seem to specifically contemplate the precise situation where a Member only wants to bind its commitments with respect to a certain category of suppliers for a particular mode. In this circumstance, the Guidelines state that this "may be achieved through an indication [...] such as 'Unbound except for measures affecting [the category of suppliers which the Member wishes to exclude]'".[21]

23. In scheduling its GATS commitments, there can be little doubt that China applied the principles set out in the 2001 Scheduling Guidelines and that other WTO Members assessed China's offers in light of the Guidelines. Therefore, in Japan's view, these Guidelines are an important source for interpreting China's GATS Schedule, i.e. for determining what China meant to schedule and what other Member's understood China's Schedule to mean. In this regard, Japan recalls that the task of ascertaining the meaning of a Schedule involves identifying the "common intention" of Members which is to be achieved by the customary rules of interpretation of public international law codified in the Vienna Convention.[22]

24. Following this guidance, therefore, one would expect some part of China's Schedule to state that its Mode 3 commitments for "All payment and money transmission services" are "unbound" to the extent that any measures affect service suppliers which are not "financial institutions". China's Schedule does not contain this or any similar language. Japan therefore agrees with Australia and the European Union that the absence of any "unbound except" or

---

[17] 1993 Guidelines for the Scheduling of Specific Commitments under the GATS (Document MTN.GNS/W/164) (hereinafter "1993 Scheduling Guidelines").

[18] See Appellate Body Report, *US-Gambling*, paras. 196 and 204.

[19] 2001 Guidelines for the Scheduling of Specific Commitments under the GATS (Document S/L/92), (hereinafter "2001 Scheduling Guidelines).

[20] In light of this fundamental need, the Guidelines are therefore devoted to clarifying not only what items should be scheduled, but also how they should be scheduled.

[21] 2001 Scheduling Guidelines, para. 45.

[22] See Appellate Body Report, *EB- Computer Equipment*, para. 84; Appellate Body Report, *US-Gambling*, para. 159.

similar language strongly indicates that China's commitments are not limited to "financial institutions", as China contends[23]

25. In this regard, Japan notes that China did use such language in other parts of its Schedule to effectuate limitations on the type of service suppliers covered by a commitment. For example, in the horizontal section of its Schedule, for Mode 4 China explicitly inscribed "Unbound except for measures concerning the entry and temporary stay of natural persons who fall into one of the following categories […]." In Japan's view, this fact can also be "context" that strongly suggests that China's "All payment and money transmission services" Mode 3 commitments are not limited to "financial institutions", as China contends.

26. Although the use of "unbound except for" language would seem to be the expected means for limiting the scope of a commitment to a particular type of supplier, Japan would not exclude that China could have limited its Mode 3 commitments to suppliers which are "financial institutions" in another manner. However, in order to respect the "common" intention of the Members, any such limitation would need to be "clear" as the 2001 Scheduling Guidelines require. In Japan's view, China did not do so by any means. Thus, for example, if China had wanted to limit its commitments to "financial institutions", China could have stated – as it did when noting limitations on forms of commercial presence in other parts of its Schedule – that its commitments were "only for service suppliers which are financial institutions".[24] China did not. Moreover, it seems that China could have made a distinct category for such a limitation as it did with respect to "geographic coverage" and "clients", for example. Again, China did not.

27. Therefore, Japan submits that China's Schedule cannot be interpreted, as China claims, as limiting its commitments only to a particular type of service supplier, namely "financial institutions", and that China has no limitations on "All payment and money transmission" Mode 3 commitments with respect to entities which are not "financial institutions".

---

23 See EU TPS, paras. 35-36; Australia TPS, para. 24 (see also paras. 25-26 of Australia's TPS).

24 For example, in numerous parts of its Schedule and with respect to Mode 3 commitments, China often inserted the sentence that "*Only* in the form of joint ventures, with foreign majority ownership permitted" (emphasis added).

ANNEX C-5

INTEGRATED EXECUTIVE SUMMARY OF THE THIRD PARTY WRITTEN SUBMISSION AND ORAL STATEMENT OF THE REPUBLIC OF KOREA

1. This dispute raises an important issue regarding the proper meaning of the entries contained in the Schedules of Specific Commitments that China submitted at the time of its accession to the WTO in 2001. It also raises a critical issue regarding how the terms contained in the *Annex on Financial Services* of the GATS should be interpreted in terms of credit card or debit card transactions, which are indispensable to modern daily commercial activities.

2. The measure challenged by the complainant is China's requirement that all Electronic Payment Services ("EPS"), such as transactions using credit cards or debit cards, denominated in RMB should go through a designated bank - China UnionPay, Co. Ltd. ("CUP"). The complainant alleges that the respondent's measure constitutes discriminatory treatment of foreign electronic payment services providers in terms of both market access and national treatment in a way that deviates from China's obligations under its Schedules of Specific Commitments. These measures are therefore inconsistent with China's obligations under Articles XVI:1, XVI:2 and XVII of the GATS.

3. In its third party submission, Korea offers its views on two issues: (i) the interpretation of the term "settlement and clearing services for financial assets" as it appears in Item (xiv) of the *Annex on Financial Services* and (ii) identification of a measure at the WTO panel proceeding when multiple measures exert a single effect, both individually and collectively.

4. *First*, Korea discusses interpretation of key terms raised in this dispute. Korea notes that the parties present two completely different interpretations of the terms. The difference between the positions of the two parties hinges upon whether the EPS should be categorized as "payment and money transmission services" under Item (d) of China's schedule (which is also identical with Item (viii) of the Financial Services Annex of the GATS) or instead "settlement and clearing services for financial assets" under Item (xiv) of the *Annex on Financial Services*. The United States supports the former view while China does the latter one.

5. More specifically, China argues that the EPS at issue in this dispute constitute one form of clearing and settlement services for financial assets and thus should be classified under Item (xiv) of the *Annex on Financial Services*. In Korea's view, China's point warrants a careful scrutiny from the Panel. Korea submits, however, that the ordinary meaning of the relevant terms in Item (d) and Item (xiv) together with their context apparently lead to a different conclusion than the one China presents. In a nutshell, it seems that Item (xiv) of the *Annex on Financial Services* addresses mainly paper-based financial asset

transactions which, in and of themselves, represent or carry designated monetary value and which always require settlement and clearing process to complete the transactions. To the contrary, Item (d) apparently addresses payments through the utilization of credit cards or debit cards. Item (xiv) is about "clearing" while Item (d) is about "payment." Korea believes credit card and debit card are more directly related to "payment." Thus, in Korea's view the U.S. interpretation seems more persuasive and reasonable under the general usage of the terms as they are used in daily commercial activities.

6. The term "financial assets" in Item (xiv) should mean something of a financial value when we follow the ordinary meaning of the term. To borrow the definition of the term proposed by China, it means "any revenue or monetary item that has value to its possessor." In other words, it refers to an object or instrument that contains or represents some sort of monetary value to the owner. It is not clear whether EPS such as "credit card transactions or debit card transactions" fall under this category. Most notably, credit card transactions or debit card transactions, in and of themselves, do not contain or represent some sort of monetary value in them. More properly understood, these are simply "payment" methods – a type of delayed payment depending on the credit of the card-holders, where the card-holders purchase products first, and the actual payments are made afterwards.

7. This conclusion is also supported when we consider the interpretation suggested by China. As noted above, China interprets the term "financial asset" as any revenue or monetary item ("financial") that has value to its possessor ("asset"). But, again, it is difficult to accept that a credit card transaction constitutes revenue or monetary item that has value to the merchant. If anything, revenue or monetary gain is only provided when the payment is actually made, either through cash or credit card payment; thus a credit card transaction is one method of such commercial payment.

8. In addition, Korea draws the Panel's attention to the examples that immediately follow the term "financial assets" in Item (xiv) of the *Annex on Financial Services*: they are securities, derivative products and other negotiable instruments. Obviously, as noted above, they all constitute financial assets. At the same time, they all share one important commonality, in that they are all written documents that signify or carry some sort of monetary value. At the same time, all of them can change hands, from one person to another (thus "negotiable"). But, again, the credit card or credit card transaction does not fall under this category: it does not carry any instrument that signifies the entitlement to cash payment afterwards. The credit card or credit card transaction itself does not signify or carry some sort of monetary value: the monetary value lies in the product that the card-holder purchases with the credit card. Nor does the credit card transaction involve "changing hands" as other examples do in Item (xiv). Thus, Korea sees a significant difference between the two.

9. As the EPS should be covered by Item (d) of the China's schedule, China is under the obligation to comply with the terms and conditions set out in its schedule regarding the market access and national treatment.

10. Korea's second point concerns the identification of a measure in this dispute. The United States presents a series of legal instruments that, individually and collectively, indicate China's policy that all transactions denominated and paid in RMB in China must be processed and cleared in RMB through CUP.

11. If individual measures are inter-related and complement and supplement each other in a way that introduces one general scheme, Korea submits that both individual measures and collective measures should constitute the challenged measures, respectively.

12. This approach is also supported by the Appellate Body precedents. In *U.S.-Zeroing (EC) (21.5)*, the Appellate Body explicitly upheld the nexus based approach while rejecting a "formalistic reliance on the date of issuance of the [individual measures]." Although the Appellate Body in that dispute discussed this matter in terms of an implementation dispute, such an analysis should equally apply to original disputes where, as here, all individual measures individually and collectively constitute one single scheme of CUP-only EPS system. Arguably, there seems to exist a sufficient close nexus among the individual measures identified in the U.S. First Written Submission.

13. Also, in a recent dispute, a WTO panel adopted a similar approach. The panel in *U.S.-Tuna II* stated in recent finding that it "must therefore consider whether these various instruments taken together may be described as constituting the measures before us." The panel also stated that the question it must consider "is whether it is appropriate to consider these measures jointly in our analysis of Mexico's claims, and make findings based on their combined operation, rather than on the basis of each individual measure separately." The same rationale should be equally applicable to the present dispute.

14. In conclusion, Korea respectfully submits that in reaching its decision in this important dispute, the Panel should ensure that the provisions of the GATS are construed in their proper context, which will give effect to the ordinary meaning of the terms consistently with the context, object and purpose of the agreements as a whole.

ANNEX D

EXECUTIVE SUMMARIES OF THE SECOND WRITTEN SUBMISSIONS OF THE PARTIES

Contents		Page
Annex D-1	Executive summary of the second written submission of the United States	5637
Annex D-2	Executive summary of the second written submission of China	5649

ANNEX D-1

EXECUTIVE SUMMARY OF THE SECOND WRITTEN SUBMISSION OF THE UNITED STATES

I. INTRODUCTION

1. China created and maintains a monopoly for China UnionPay, Co. Ltd. ("CUP") to supply the service necessary for credit, charge, debit and other payment card transactions to occur in China for all transactions where the card is issued in China and used in China. Such transactions, whether RMB-payment card transactions or transactions using foreign currency denominated payment cards issued in China, constitute the overwhelming number of all payment card transactions in China.

2. The evidence and arguments advanced by the United States also establish that the service at issue is a single, integrated service falling within subsector (d) of China Schedule of Specific Commitments: "All payment and money transmission services, including credit, charge and debit cards..." China undertook both mode 1 (cross-border) and mode 3 (commercial presence) commitments with respect to subsector (d). Finally, China's measures are inconsistent with China's obligations under Articles XVI:1 and XVI:2 of the General Agreement on Trade in Services ("GATS") not to adopt or maintain measures of the types listed in Article XVI:2, and with China's obligations under GATS Article XVII to accord to services and service suppliers of any other Member treatment no less favorable than that it accords to its own like services and service suppliers, in respect of all measures affecting the supply of services.

II. EPS FOR PAYMENT CARD TRANSACTIONS IS A SINGLE, INTEGRATED SERVICE THAT FALLS WITHIN THE ORDINARY MEANING OF SUBSECTOR (D) OF CHINA'S SCHEDULE ("ALL PAYMENT AND MONEY TRANSMISSION SERVICES, INCLUDING CREDIT, CHARGE AND DEBIT CARDS...")

3. As the United States has demonstrated, EPS for payment card transactions is a single, integrated service – one that is supplied and consumed as such. The extensive evidence provided by the United States demonstrates that EPS is at the center of all payment card transactions and without this service the transactions could not occur. EPS fall within the ordinary meaning of payment and money transmission services, within subsector (d) of China's Schedule. The language of subsector (d) itself makes this abundantly clear. EPS clearly fall within the ordinary meaning of "payment and money transmission services" as one type of "all" such services. In addition, the phrase "all payment and money transmission services" is modified with an illustrative list that explicitly provides that it "include[s] credit, charge and debit cards." The explicit reference to these types of cards is in line with the recognition that EPS is integral to the processing of credit, charge, debit and other payment card-based electronic payment transactions, and without EPS, payment card transactions could not occur.

4. China tries to delink and disaggregate certain components of EPS that are central to payment card transactions. China combines its disaggregation strategy with an exceedingly narrow interpretation of its commitments, arguing that only issuing and acquiring services are covered by subsector (d). Indeed, China has declined even to provide a response to the question of where – even under its flawed disaggregation theory – remaining elements of EPS should be classified, underscoring the difficulty of its position. Simply, China's arguments cannot be reconciled with the text of its commitments or how the service at issue operates in practice.

5. Contrary to China's assertions, EPS for payment card transactions constitutes one integral service. The service is supplied as coherent whole. A supplier of EPS enables cardholders' banks to pay merchants' banks the amount they are owed. EPS suppliers provide an efficient, timely and reliable means to facilitate the transmission of funds from the holders of payment cards who purchase goods or services to the individuals or businesses that supply them. The network, rules and procedures, and operating system that are part of the EPS architecture allow merchants to be paid the amounts they are owed and ensure that cardholders pay what they owe. EPS suppliers receive, check and transmit the information that the parties need to conduct the transactions, and manage, facilitate, and enable the transmission of funds between participating entities. The rules and procedures established by the EPS supplier give the payment system stability and integrity, and enable it efficiently to handle net flows of money among the institutions involved in card payments. Each component is

critical to effectuate the payment card transaction and EPS suppliers provide the entire package of services to their customers, the institutions that are participating in the payment card transactions.

6. Regarding China's assertion that the approach described by the United States (and endorsed by several third parties) would somehow undermine the GATS and the principle of mutual exclusivity, this argument is also misplaced. To the contrary, if China's position were accepted – that a service must first be disaggregated into subcomponents and each subcomponent separately classified – it would render Members' concessions meaningless for a wide range of services.

III. EPS FOR PAYMENT CARD TRANSACTIONS DOES NOT FALL WITHIN ITEM (XIV) ("SETTLEMENT AND CLEARING SERVICES FOR FINANCIAL ASSETS, INCLUDING SECURITIES, DERIVATIVE PRODUCTS AND OTHER NEGOTIABLE INSTRUMENTS")

7. China relies on an exceedingly narrow reading of subsector (d) that essentially reads the qualifying word "all" out of the sectoral description of "all payment and money transmission services, including credit, charge, and debit cards…" and on arguments that fail to account for the fact that EPS are at the heart of credit, charge and debit card transactions. Moreover, China's exceedingly narrow reading of subsector (d) stands in stark contrast to China's exceedingly broad interpretation of item (xiv) of the Annex. China's broad reading is combined with an incorrect understanding of the services in item (xiv) that places China's interpretation at odds with fundamental, recognized differences in the operation and risk profile of financial services under item (xiv) and services related to retail payment processing, such as EPS for payment card transactions.

8. The same rules of treaty interpretation that compel the conclusion that EPS for payment card transactions fall within subsector (d) also compel the conclusion that EPS for payment card transactions do not fall within item (xiv). In this regard, Article 31(1) of the Vienna Convention requires that the terms "settlement and clearing services for financial assets, including securities, derivatives and other negotiable instruments" be interpreted "in good faith in accordance with the ordinary meaning to be given to the terms of the treaty in their context and in the light of its object and purpose." Various commentaries on the Vienna Convention point out that "ordinary meaning" cannot be analyzed independently from the other interpretive elements described in Article 31, including "context."

9. China's position is inconsistent with the ordinary meaning of "settlement and clearing services for financial assets" and also fails to recognize that item (xiv) is a substantially different financial service than EPS for payment card transactions, which is a type of retail payment service. The BIS CPSS has explained that "[r]etail payments are generally classified as cash payments or

non-cash payments," which are subclassified into "cheque payments, direct funds transfers and card payments." Indeed, there are many practical differences between the systems used to settle and clear investment instruments of the kind referenced in item (xiv) and the systems used to settle and clear retail payment instruments, like payment cards. These differences relate to: (1) the financial instruments involved and the value of typical transactions, (2) the market participants involved in the transaction and related processing; (3) the infrastructure needs for such processes to occur safely and efficiently; and (4) regulatory oversight and the relative risks presented to the financial system as a whole.

10. China's position also fails to interpret the term "financial asset" within its immediate context, i.e., the full sentence in item (xiv). An examination of each of the items in the illustrative list demonstrate that retail receipts, such as a claim on a payment card, are not of the same type of financial assets as the items included in the illustrative list – "securities, derivative products and other negotiable instruments." This further supports the conclusion that they are not within the scope of "financial assets" referenced in the provision.

11. A "security" is generally defined as "an instrument that signifies an ownership position in a corporation (a stock), a creditor relationship with a corporation or government body (a bond) or rights to ownership..." Securities are, in short, ownership and investment instruments. Credit and debit cards are not similar to securities. Payment cards are retail payment instruments. They provide a non-cash alternative for consumers to use when making purchases. A payment card does not provide a pledge of property to secure a loan, it is not an investment instrument, and it is not tradeable on money markets or capital markets.

12. Derivatives are also investment instruments. A derivative is "a financial contract the value of which depends on the value of one or more underlying reference assets, rates or indices" such as futures contracts and options. A payment card is not a contract whose value is dependent of the performance of some other asset or investment. It is simply an instrument for making retail purchases.

13. Payment cards and the sales slips generated from payment card transactions do not meet the internationally accepted criteria for a negotiable instrument. A payment card transaction does not involve a written promise or order to pay that satisfies the definition above and, thus, does not involve a negotiable instrument. Some payment card transactions are processed entirely electronically, without the cardholder signing a sales slip and, thus, do not result in the creation of any writing, signed by the cardholder, either promising to pay or ordering the payment of an amount to the merchant. Other payment card transactions require the cardholder to sign a sales slip instructing the bank that issued the payment card to pay the merchant for the transaction, but the sales slips created in connection with such transactions are not payable to bearer, but rather, are payable only to the identified merchant. Finally, payment cards are not similar to the types of negotiable instruments referenced in Item (xiv), such

as commercial paper, which a type of investment instrument that is processed through settlement and clearing. As noted, in context, the types of negotiable instruments referenced in item (xiv) are tradeable assets, and do not include instruments that are used for retail payments.

IV. CHINA'S MODE 1 AND MODE 3 COMMITMENTS FOR SUBSECTOR (D) "ALL PAYMENT AND MONEY TRANSMISSION SERVICES, INCLUDING CREDIT, CHARGE, AND DEBIT CARDS..."

A. China's Mode 1 Commitments for "All Payment and Money Transmission Services, Including Credit, Charge and Debit Cards..."

14. It is plain from the text that China has taken mode 1 commitments for "all payment and money transmission services, including credit, charge and debit cards..." The word "Unbound" is followed by the qualifying phrase "except for the following," which in turn is further elaborated by two sentences that describe elements of the services within subsector (d) for which China has taken mode 1 commitments. Proper treaty interpretation requires that the qualifying phrase "except for the following" and the further specific elaboration following the word "Unbound" should be given meaning. In response to the Panel's questions, the United States prepared a chart in which it identified several aspects of EPS that are covered by the mode 1 market access commitment undertaken by China.

15. China's responses to the Panel's questions regarding the meaning of the extensive language qualifying the term "Unbound..." essentially reduces to the single point that all of the extensive language qualifying the term "Unbound" in its market commitments was provided simply to confirm language already existing elsewhere. In short, according to China, that the additional wording should be given no meaning. This is not credible. If China wished to in fact be fully "Unbound," that is, not to have any commitments, it would have left the word "Unbound" unqualified. However, as the Schedule reflects, China did not do so. It is not credible to argue that this language is merely for greater certainty to repeat China's commitments in subsectors (k) and (l). Such an argument fails to give meaning to this treaty language.

16. The services defined by the sector and subsector descriptions cannot be altered by the commitments made in the market access or national treatment columns. While a WTO Member may place limitations on the scope of its commitment with respect to a given sector, limitations inscribed in the market access and national treatment columns cannot change the scope of the sector description itself.

17. Elements of CUP's own activities are described in terms similar to the "excepted" elements that are set out in China's mode 1 market access commitments. The Chinese regulatory system similarly describes a primary activity of CUP as exchanging information among financial institutions. This is

all of course consistent with the recognition that the ability to "transfer financial information" and supply "advisory, intermediation and other auxiliary financial services" cross-border with respect to an integrated service (when the service supplier is located in a particular country) is often necessary for corporate risk management purposes and typically occurs in the ordinary course of business.

18. Finally, the concept that a service may include elements of "provision and transfer of financial information, and financial data processing" was recognized, for example, in paragraph 8 of the Uruguay Round Understanding on Commitments in Financial Services. The provision and transfer of financial information and data processing is central to the supply of many different financial services, and, according to the Understanding, signatory WTO Members cannot frustrate their commitments by, for example, blocking the ability to communicate and process information.

B. China's Mode 3 Commitments for "All Payment and Money Transmission Services, Including Credit, Charge and Debit Cards..."

19. China has mode 3 market access and national treatment commitments for subsector (d). The presence of the term "financial institution" in China's schedule does not create a separate and independent limitation. There is nothing in China's Schedule that indicates it may condition the supply of a service on the criteria listed in column 2 and in addition require that another Member's supplier meet additional (and unspecified) criteria to be recognized as a "foreign financial institution." The Schedule states that "[c]riteria for authorization to deal in China's financial services sector are solely prudential." Thus, under China's Schedule, the only limitations China may impose are in connection with legitimate prudential regulation and the limitations explicitly listed in China's Schedule – the now defunct restrictions on geographic scope and use of domestic currency, and ongoing requirements applicable to banks. The additional references to the term "financial institution" in the paragraphs that follow the explicit statement that the criteria are "solely prudential" does not alter that unequivocal statement as to the sole criteria for authorization to deal in China's financial services sector.

20. The fact that subsector (d) falls under the heading of "banking services" does not operate to limit China's commitments to "banks" or other "regulated financial institutions" as China argues. The "banking services" heading does not operate in this manner. The characteristics and nature of the service control the classification of that service.

21. It is also evident from China's Schedule itself that the term "banking services" listed in China's Schedule, including those listed in subsector (d) are not limited to those provided by banks as China claims. The definition of "financial service supplier" in the Annex on Financial Services provides additional support in this regard: "A financial service supplier means any natural or juridical person of a Member wishing to supply or supplying financial

services but the term 'financial service supplier' does not include a public entity." This definition covers not only banks but other suppliers of financial services, which supply or wish to supply financial services within the meaning of the Annex.

22. China also argues that its mode 3 market access and national treatment commitments for subsector (d) are limited to foreign financial institutions. Although China includes certain limitations with respect to foreign financial institutions, this does not mean that its commitments are limited to foreign financial institutions. Such a limitation would have needed to be imposed explicitly, and China did not do so. Finally, even if it were the case that the term "financial institution" somehow served as a limitation in China's Schedule (and it is clear from the above that it does not), the definition of "financial institution" offered by China is far too narrow. Many definitions are much broader, and some explicitly include "an operator of a credit card system."

V. CHINA'S MEASURES ESTABLISHING AND SUPPORTING CHINA UNIONPAY'S MONOPOLY ON THE SUPPLY OF EPS ARE INCONSISTENT WITH ARTICLE XVI OF THE GATS

23. The measures imposed by China on the supply of EPS are inconsistent with Article XVI:2 of the GATS because they limit the number of suppliers of EPS for RMB-denominated transactions that are paid in RMB. The evidence provided by the United States demonstrates that China's measures limit the number of suppliers of EPS for payment card transactions. China requires that all RMB-denominated payment card transactions in China be processed by CUP, and that CUP process all foreign currency denominated card transactions where the card is issued in China. In short, China requires that CUP process all payment card transactions where the card is issued in China and used in China.

24. During the Panel's first meeting with the Parties, China asserted several times that the United States had failed to demonstrate that foreign EPS suppliers could not supply EPS for payment card transactions in China. The Panel has now asked China Question 22(b) from the Panel to China:

25. Could China confirm that operators other than China UnionPay could be authorised to establish their own network and process domestic RMB-denominated payment card transactions independently from China UnionPay's network? If relevant, please identify legal instruments and provisions that address this.

26. China did not answer the Panel's question. This is not surprising because, as the United States has demonstrated, in fact and as China's measures mandate, EPS suppliers other than China UnionPay cannot process domestic RMB-denominated payment card transactions in China. EPS suppliers other than CUP cannot process any payment card transactions in China where the card is issued in China and used in China.

27. Requirements that mandate the use of CUP and/or establish CUP as the sole supplier of EPS for all domestic transactions denominated and paid in RMB.

28. Even without considering Documents Nos. 94, 272 and 66, which China argues have either been repealed or replaced, the remaining instruments establish and maintain the CUP monopoly in essentially three ways. First, certain instruments explicitly state that CUP must be used to process specific types of transactions. Second, certain instruments establish and/or require the use of business specifications and technical standards which mandate the use of CUP. Finally, certain instruments implicitly recognize that CUP is the sole supplier of EPS services for RMB denominated transactions.

29. Several instruments independently designate CUP as a sole supplier. Document No. 53 (Exhibit US-51) is a primary example. Article V.2 of Document 53 states that "[d]omestic card transactions inside China shall be settled in RMB through domestic clearing channels . . . ." CUP is the only "domestic clearing channel" and, therefore, the only entity that can settle domestic card transactions. Article V.3 sets forth procedures for correcting the erroneous processing of such transactions through an international bank card organization. Moreover, Article VII.3 then states that "[d]omestic RMB card clearing organizations shall do a good job in the RMB clearing of domestic transactions of home-foreign currency cards." These are foreign denominated currency payment cards that are issued in China.

30. Document No. 16 (Exhibit US-44) states that, with respect to Hong Kong, "[m]atters in relation to individual RMB bank card clearing shall be organized and handled by the clearance banks and China UnionPay Joint Stock Co., Ltd." Document No. 254 (Exhibit US-48) requires that CUP process RMB transactions involving RMB cards issued in China and used in Hong Kong or Macao, or involved RMB cards issued in Hong Kong or Macao and used in China. Document No. 8 (Exhibit US-46) requires that CUP be used to clear RMB denominated transactions in Macao. China does not deny that CUP has a monopoly over such services. Section 1.2 of Document 153 (Exhibit US-49) appears to explicitly recognize that "China UnionPay is the domestic clearance organization which specializes in the RMB bank inter-bank information routing and exchange" (emphasis supplied). Other provisions of Document No. 153 appear to confirm the designation of CUP as the sole supplier.

31. Section 2.2 of Document No. 37 (Exhibit US-40) states that cards that do not comply with "the unified requirements and the CUP logo usage requirements" must be replaced and that, "[s]tarting in 2004, all bank cards not bearing a CUP logo will not be used for cross-region or inter-bank transactions." Article 6 of Document 57 (Exhibit US-41) requires that all "regional bank card interoperability logos produced and designed regionally shall be gradually abolished." Also, Article 6 of Document 153 (Exhibit US-49) states that, in any country where dual currency cards are used, "the Chinese issuing banks should support routing through the CUP network and open RMB accounts related transactions and settlements to the CUP network." Document 149 (Exhibit US-

50) states that "acquiring organizations may not allow the non-CUP and non-PBOC 2.0 pre-payment cards to be accepted at any POS terminals." Document No. 219, Article III, prohibits processing of payment card transactions by third-parties, mandating that "no merchant shall... authorize a third party to handle Renminbi card business or transfer such business to a third party."

32. In addition, certain instruments establish and/or require the use of business specifications and technical standards which mandate the use of CUP. Document No. 76 (Exhibit US-56/US-63) includes the "Notice of People's Bank of China in Relation to Issuance of Business Practices for the Interoperable Services of Bank Cards," and an accompanying Appendix, which includes the "Business Practices for the Interoperable Services of Bank Cards" ("Business Practices Appendix"). The Business Practices Appendix requires that all domestic transactions on domestically issued cards be processed over the network that was to become CUP. Several of the 19 instruments explicitly require the use of uniform business specifications and technical standards, including: Document No. 37 (Exhibit US-40); Document 57 (Exhibit US-41); Document 153 (Exhibit US-49); Document 129 (Exhibit US-53); Document 142, (Exhibit US-55); Document 49 (Exhibit US-62); Document 17 (Exhibit US-52); and Document 103 (Exhibit US-1)

33. Another category of instruments recognizes that CUP is the sole supplier of EPS services for transactions on cards issued and used in China. These measures include, for example, measures related to fraud protection and similar regulation which is explicitly directed only to CUP.

34. Logo requirements on issuing institutions, requirements related to POS terminals and ATMs, requirements on acquiring institutions, prohibitions on the use of non-CUP cards and non-CUP EPS suppliers, and requirements for certain transactions involving RMB denominated cards issued and/or used in Macau and Hong Kong

35. The collective effect of these measures is to establish CUP as the sole entity able to provide EPS for payment card transactions in China where the card is issued in China and used in China. Banks in China must use CUP's network in order to issue or acquire bank card transactions. Only CUP cards can be issued as RMB denominated cards. The logo and interoperability requirements mean that that all banks that wish to acquire merchant transactions or operate ATMs and all merchants who wish to accept bank cards must join CUP and process transactions in accordance with CUP's rules and procedures as set out in Document No. 76 (Exhibit US-56/US-63). These requirements gave CUP automatic and universal acceptance of its RMB payment card products by banks and merchants in China and permitted and supported CUP becoming the sole supplier of EPS in China. These measures have entrenched CUP's monopoly position. Suppliers of EPS must ordinarily invest heavily and incur substantial expense to build acceptance of their payment card products by merchants, often in vigorous competition with other suppliers of EPS. All transactions that take place involving cards issued in China and used for transactions in China must be

processed over CUP's network as well as transactions involving RMB denominated cards issued and/or used in Macau and Hong Kong.

VI. CHINA'S MEASURES ACCORD LESS FAVORABLE TREATMENT TO FOREIGN EPS SUPPLIERS

36. A national treatment commitment under Article XVII of the GATS obligates a WTO Member to accord services and service suppliers of other Members "treatment no less favorable than that it accords to its own like services and services suppliers." Article XVII:2 specifies that a Member may meet this requirement in instances in which it accords foreign services or suppliers formally different treatment. Article XVII:3 defines treatment as "less favorable" if it "modifies the conditions of competition in favour of services or service suppliers of the Member."

37. The measures at issue affect the supply of services in two principal ways. First, there are measures that impose a limitation such that CUP is the sole entity that can process certain transactions, such as domestic RMB transactions. This of course means that foreign suppliers of EPS are prevented from supplying the service at all. Second, there are measures that promote CUP's position in the marketplace such as by imposing certain requirements on every key player in a card-based electronic payment transaction, including issuers (all cards issued in China for domestic RMB transactions must bear the CUP logo), merchants (all merchant card processing equipment and POS terminals must accept CUP cards), and acquiring institutions (which must post CUP logo and accept CUP cards).

38. The United States has explained how China's measures affect every aspect of a card-based electronic payment transaction and the key players – issuers, acquiring institutions, merchants, and EPS suppliers – involved in such transactions.

39. China's measures ensure that CUP is the sole supplier of EPS for payment card transactions in China where the card is issued in China and used in China, and for certain payment card transactions involving Hong Kong and Macau. The description of the scope of CUP's business in CUP's Articles of Association, CUP's "Notification of Business License Approval and Issuance," and PBOC's reply with respect to the establishment of CUP clearly establish that CUP is to be the single nationwide inter-bank card network. Additional provisions prohibit processing of transactions by third-parties (i.e., any network other than CUP). China's measures discriminate against foreign suppliers of EPS by either categorically precluding their participation in the market, or by modifying the conditions of competition among the key participants – issuers, acquiring institutions, merchants, and the EPS supplier – in card-based electronic payment transactions.

40. China's measures require that any payment cards used only for RMB purchases in China, as well as any dual currency cards issued in China, bear the

CUP logo. No other EPS provider is afforded such a privilege. Any issuer of payment cards in China is required to have access to the CUP system (and to pay for that privilege) and, as a result, issuers have no reason to seek alternative suppliers of EPS. The logo requirements also operate such that even if a card was issued with the logo of a foreign EPS supplier, CUP would also obtain an advantage as the CUP logo would have to appear on the card as well.

41. Similarly, China's measures require all ATMs, POS terminals, and merchant card processing equipment accept CUP cards. Once again, no foreign EPS supplier is afforded a similar privilege. Moreover, even were a foreign supplier of EPS able to create or secure access to a POS terminal, then China's measures would still provide CUP with an advantage because of the requirement that all ATMs, POS terminals, and merchant card processing equipment accept CUP cards.

42. For the same reasons, China's measures requiring that all acquiring institutions in China post the CUP logo and accept all cards bearing that logo distort the competitive relationship between CUP and foreign suppliers. No foreign EPS supplier is afforded a similar privilege. Acquiring institutions have important relationships with merchants, often providing POS terminal and processing equipment to merchants so it can process payment cards. Acquiring institutions also maintain the merchant's account, handle relations with the merchant, and ensures that payments are properly credited to the merchant.

43. The broad prohibitions on the use of non-CUP cards and that prevent foreign suppliers of EPS have similar adverse effects on competition and operate to accord less favorable treatment to foreign EPS suppliers. China requires that all inter-bank transactions for all bank cards be handled through CUP.

44. Finally, the requirements pertaining to card-based electronic transactions in China, Macao and Hong Kong also modify the conditions of competition and operate to accord less favorable treatment to foreign EPS suppliers. China requires that CUP be used to handle all RMB transactions in Macao or Hong Kong using bank cards issued in China. China also requires that CUP be used to handle any RMB transactions in China using RMB cards issued in Hong Kong or Macao.

45. These measures affect the conditions of competition in the supply of EPS within the meaning of Article XVII because they directly regulate the terms on which they may be provided. The measures at issue provide different treatment solely according to the identity of the EPS supplier: CUP or not CUP

46. The effect of these measures is to completely distort competition in China's market for EPS for payment card transactions. These measures establish and maintain CUP the sole entity able to provide the full range of EPS for payment card transactions in China where the card is issued in China and used in China. Banks in China must join CUP in order to issue or acquire bank card transactions. Only CUP cards can be issued as RMB denominated cards. The logo and interoperability requirements mean that all banks that wish to acquire merchant transactions or operate ATMs and all merchants who wish to accept

bank cards must join CUP and process transactions in accordance with CUP's rules and procedures as set out in Document No. 76 (Exhibit US-56/US-63). These requirements gave CUP automatic and universal acceptance of its RMB payment card products by banks and merchants in China and permitted and supported CUP becoming the sole supplier of EPS in China. No foreign EPS supplier enjoys any of these advantages and CUP is not constrained in the ways in which foreign EPS suppliers are constrained.

47. The measures at issue were meant to favor the domestic Chinese entity and accordingly discriminate on that basis. They have been effective in this regard and outside of China, with the ability to operate from its protected home market, CUP has become a significant and increasingly active competitor. CUP's Articles of Association are explicit that the company is "to provide advanced electronic payment technologies and specialized services in connection with the inter-bank bank card information switching" and CUP's success in the global market for card-based electronic payment transactions reflects and is in accord with the "purpose of the company," which is to foster "and promote the rapid development of China's bank card industry."

48. Finally, it is clear that CUP provides services for payment card transactions "like" those provided by foreign suppliers of EPS for payment card transactions and that the basis for the differential treatment by China in its measures is ultimately one of origin, and the "like service suppliers" requirement of Article XVII is therefore satisfied.

VII. CONCLUSION

49. The United States respectfully requests that the Panel find that China's measures are inconsistent with China's obligations under Article XVI:1 and XVI:2(a) and Article XVII of the GATS. The United States further requests, pursuant to Article 19.1 of the DSU, that the Panel recommend that China bring its measures into conformity with its WTO obligations.

ANNEX D-2

EXECUTIVE SUMMARY OF THE SECOND WRITTEN SUBMISSION OF CHINA

I. THE UNITED STATES HAS FAILED TO MEET ITS BURDEN OF PROOF IN RESPECT OF THE CLASSIFICATION OF THE SERVICES AT ISSUE

A. The Clearing and Settlement Services at Issue in this Dispute Are Classifiable Under Item (xiv) of the Annex List

1. Item (xiv) of the Annex list encompasses "settlement and clearing services for financial assets, including securities, derivative products, and other negotiable instruments". The United States acknowledges that clearing and settlement services are "central" to the services at issue in this dispute, and that these clearing and settlement services relate to interbank claims for payment. The only interpretative issue that remains is whether these clearing and settlement services are "for financial assets" within the ordinary meaning of that term, in its context and in light of the object and purpose of the agreement.

1. Ordinary meaning

2. It is axiomatic that "the words of the treaty form the foundation for the interpretive process". "The meaning of a treaty provision, properly construed, is rooted in the ordinary meaning of the terms used". As China demonstrated in its first written submission, every definition of the term "financial assets" points to the same conclusion: it refers to "money and claims", including cash and any right to receive cash.

3. The United States has offered nothing that is relevant under Article 31 of the Vienna Convention that would contradict the ordinary meaning of the term "financial assets" that China has put forward. The *only* definition of the term "financial assets" to which the United States refers is the definition of this term in Article 8 of the U.S. Uniform Commercial Code ("UCC"). But the United States fails to explain how the municipal law of a single Member is relevant to the process of treaty interpretation under Article 31 of the Vienna Convention.

4. The inability of the United States to identify a coherent understanding of the term "financial assets" becomes most evident in its response to Question 38(b) from the Panel, concerning asset-backed securities. The United States acknowledges, as common sense dictates, that the "assets" in "asset-backed securities" are claims that an issuing bank has against cardholders. It then asserts, however, that "[t]he contractual obligation to pay is only with respect to the issuing bank", and, for this reason, "only the issuing bank can securitize

receivables." According to the United States, it is only when credit card receivables are securitised that they "could be deemed a financial asset."

5. The United States seems to be suggesting that issuing banks have no obligation to pay acquiring banks. Obviously, this is incorrect – in the four-party model, the acquiring bank has a valid claim against the issuing bank, just as the issuing bank has a valid claim against the cardholder. The U.S. solution to this flaw in its reasoning is to assert that the claim to payment only becomes a financial asset once it is bundled into an asset-backed security. Again, this makes no sense – it is the fact that the claim to payment is *already* a financial asset that allows it to be bundled into an "*asset*-backed" security.

6. The last refuge for the United States is to assert that interbank claims for payment "are not transferable". The notion that "transferability" is relevant to the interpretation of the term "financial assets" is connected to the U.S. assertion that item (xiv) is limited to instruments that "settle and clear like securities and derivative products", an assertion that China rebuts below. But in any event, the assertion that an acquiring bank's claim against an issuing bank is not transferable is just that – an assertion. The United States presents no evidence to support this claim.

7. For these reasons, China considers that the ordinary meaning of the term "financial assets" is uncontested in this dispute. The ordinary meaning of this term includes cash and any right to receive payment. The services at issue in this dispute include clearing and settlement services "for financial assets".

2. Context

8. Lacking any support for its interpretation of item (xiv) in the ordinary meaning of the term "financial assets", the United States insists that its interpretation is supported by the illustrative list of financial assets that appears in item (xiv): "securities, derivative products, and other negotiable instruments". Even though the parties agree that these are merely three examples of what constitutes a "financial asset", the United States tries to work backwards from these examples to limit the ordinary meaning of the term "financial assets" to what it calls "tradeable financial instruments" or, alternatively, "tradeable investment instruments".

9. As China has previously explained, the reference to "negotiable instruments" in item (xiv) unambiguously includes retail payment instruments such as cheques and traveller's cheques. Like securities and derivatives, these are "financial assets" within the ordinary meaning of that term because they give rise to claims for payment. As context, the illustrative list of examples therefore confirms that the drafters of item (xiv) intended to use the term "financial assets" according to its common and ordinary meaning. Moreover, because item (viii) of the *Annex* list provides examples of negotiable instruments as types of "payment services", the drafters understood that the clearing and settlement of these instruments under item (xiv) was distinct from the issuance and acceptance of these instruments under item (viii).

10. Faced with these circumstances, the United States had only one option: to deny the ordinary meaning of the term "negotiable instruments". In response to the Panel's questions, the United States takes the extraordinary position that "[i]tem (xiv) only indicates that there are negotiable instruments that settle and clear like securities and derivative products … [and] to the extent a negotiable instrument appears in item (viii), it is not a negotiable instrument referred to in item (xiv)."

11. The objections to this line of reasoning are obvious. First, why is the test whether a particular instrument is "settled and cleared like securities and derivative products"? Securities and derivative products are two of the three examples provided in the illustrative list: why do these two examples govern the meaning of the third example? The relevant question is what these three examples have *in common* that makes them non-exhaustive examples of the term "financial assets". What they have in common, of course, is that they all give rise to claims for payment that need to be cleared and settled – not that they are "investment instruments".

12. Second, and relatedly, what does it even mean for a particular type of financial asset to be "settled and cleared like securities and derivative products"? It is undisputed that cheques and other types of negotiable instruments need to be cleared and settled. While the United States insists that clearing and settlement services for securities and derivatives "differ in crucial ways", it offers no explanation of why these alleged differences are relevant to the interpretation of the term "financial assets" or somehow change the ordinary meaning of the term "negotiable instruments".

13. Finally, why would the drafters of the *Annex* list refer to certain types of negotiable instruments in item (viii), but then not intend to have these instruments covered by the reference to negotiable instruments in item (xiv)? The United States asks the Panel to believe that the drafters drew an arbitrary distinction between different types of negotiable instruments – a distinction that is nowhere evident in the text. Among other absurdities, the U.S. theory leads to the result that clearing and settlement services for certain types of negotiable instruments are expressly covered by item (xiv), while clearing and settlement services for other types of negotiable instruments are somehow implied by "necessity" in item (viii).

14. In sum, the overall U.S. interpretation of item (xiv) is unmoored from any objective understanding of the ordinary meaning of terms and from the context in which those terms are used. According to the United States, the term "financial assets" does not mean "financial assets" as that term is commonly understood, and neither does the term "negotiable instruments". The United States purports to use the context of the illustrative list to inform its interpretation of the term "financial assets", but then gives the terms in the illustrative list their own special (and erroneous) understanding. As a result, the U.S. interpretation becomes hopelessly circular: the term "financial assets" is limited to "investment instruments", which is demonstrated by interpreting the

term "negotiable instruments" to be limited to "investment instruments". Neither term means anything other than what the United States wants it to mean.

3. *Object and purpose*

15. It is well established that "the security and predictability of Members' specific commitments" is an important object and purpose of the GATS. The interpretative approach taken by the United States is neither "secure" nor "predictable". It is arbitrary, illogical, and completely *un*predictable. The U.S. approach leads to an interpretation of China's Schedule and the *Annex* list in which nothing means what it says, services are not clearly defined, and, as a result, it is impossible to schedule and interpret specific commitments with any degree of security or predictability. This approach is manifestly contrary to the object and purpose of the GATS, and must be rejected.

4. *Conclusion to Part A*

16. In China's view, the inability of the United States to rebut China's interpretation of item (xiv) should bring this dispute to an end. China will nonetheless proceed to discuss the U.S. interpretation of subsector (d) on its own terms. As China will demonstrate, the U.S. interpretation of subsector (d) has effectively collapsed. This confirms that the United States has failed to meet its burden of proof in respect of the classification of the services at issue.

B. *The United States Has Failed to Establish that the Services at Issue Are Classifiable Under Subsector (d)*

17. It is hard to know what is left of the U.S. interpretation of subsector (d) following its answers to the Panel's questions. In an effort to jam all of the services at issue into the exception to China's unbound Mode 1 inscription for subsector (d), the United States now takes the position that *all five* of the "components" of what it calls "electronic payment services" match the descriptions of subsectors (k) and (l). The question that naturally arises is this: what is left of subsector (d)? The United States continues to insist that the services described by subsectors (k) and (l) are "embedded in the core 'payment and money transmission' services", but there does not appear to be any "core" left.

18. As best as China can understand the U.S. theory, the United States believes that the services described by any given subsector can become "embedded" in another subsector if they are "central" to the provision of services under that other subsector. That is, any service that is "central" to the provision of another service (or "necessary", "essential", "at the heart of", etc.) ceases to exist as an independent subsector and merges into the other subsector. The U.S. theory would apply not only to subsectors (k) and (l), but to any subsector within the taxonomy of services that could be seen as "essential" or "central" to the provision of some other service.

19. It is absurd for the United States to contend that this theory of "embedded" services is consistent with the principle of mutual exclusivity. Its theory leads directly and inevitably to the collapsing of distinct subsectors into an indiscriminate mass of services. Consider the reference in subsector (k) to "financial data processing and related software by suppliers of other financial services". As the United States acknowledges, this subsector "applies only to suppliers who provide 'other financial services.'" It is, by its express terms, a subsector that supports the provision of services that are covered by other subsectors, and applies only in cases where the same service supplier is providing both sets of services. Yet under the U.S. theory, subsector (k) automatically collapses into other subsectors whenever the services that subsector (k) describes are "integral" or "necessary" to the provision of another financial service. Under what circumstances would that *not* be the case? When would subsector (k) ever apply as a distinct subsector? The same problem would arise for countless other sectors and subsectors across the entire taxonomy of services that have relationships of "necessity" to each other.

20. It is *solely* on the basis of this "embedding" theory that the United States finds any of the services at issue in this dispute to be classifiable under subsector (d). As discussed above, the United States fails to identify any service at issue in this dispute that is *actually* a "payment and money transmission service", as opposed to what it alleges to be an "aspect" of subsector (k) or (l) that is "embedded" in "payment and money transmission services". The United States has therefore failed to satisfy its burden of proving that the services at issue in this dispute are classifiable under subsector (d).

C. Conclusion to Section I

21. "[T]he absence of any relevant commitment … would suffice to dismiss this case." That is the situation before the Panel. China considers that there is no legal basis for the Panel to proceed to an evaluation of any other issue in this dispute. For this reason, China sets forth the remainder of this submission on an *arguendo* basis, accepting the U.S. position that the services at issue in this dispute are classifiable under subsector (d).

II. THE UNITED STATES HAS FAILED TO ESTABLISH THE EXISTENCE OF RELEVANT MARKET ACCESS AND NATIONAL TREATMENT COMMITMENTS FOR MODE 1 AND MODE 3 OF SUBSECTOR (D)

A. Mode 1

22. In its response to Question 7 from the Panel, the United States has revealed its true agenda in this dispute: to make it possible for companies like Visa and MasterCard to provide network services in China *entirely* on a cross-border basis. The United States asserts, unabashedly, that "[t]he U.S. EPS supplier would have no or a very limited physical presence in China". It then

provides a lengthy description of how every aspect of what it calls "electronic payment services" would be provided on a cross-border basis. In stark contrast, in response to Question 8 from the Panel, the United States offers a single perfunctory sentence about services that might be provided on a commercial presence basis in China.

23. To suggest that the United States is trying to have it both ways would be an understatement. The United States wants to prove its central assertion that all of the services at issue in this dispute are classifiable under subsector (d). At the same time, it wants to establish an unfettered right of market access for these services in the cross-border mode of supply. The small wrinkle in the U.S. plan is that China's Mode 1 market access entry for subsector (d) is *unbound*, except for the description of subsectors (k) and (l). Therefore, the United States needs the services at issue to be in two places at once: in subsector (d), and in subsector (k) or (l). This is the genesis of its "embedded services" theory, discussed above.

24. The absurd consequences of this theory could hardly be more evident than in the case of China's Mode 1 market access entry for subsector (d). In order to give effect to China's unbound market access entry for subsectors (a) through (f), it is critically important to be able to distinguish between those activities that are unbound in Mode 1 and those activities that meet the exception.

25. As China described above, the United States associates all five of the "components" of what it calls "electronic payment services" with the descriptions of subsectors (k) and (l). As a result, there appears to be nothing left in subsector (d). It is understandable why the United States does not want to identify the "core" services that, in its view, make subsector (d) the linchpin of this dispute – the necessary implication would be that China has no Mode 1 market access commitment in respect of those services. But for subsector (d) to be relevant at all, there must be something in subsector (d) to begin with.

26. In sum, the United States cannot have it both ways – the services cannot be in subsector (d), and also in subsectors (k) and (l). If the services at issue are so "integral" or "essential" to subsector (d) that they become "embedded" in subsector (d) under the U.S. theory, then it follows that they are among the services that are unbound in China's Schedule in the cross-border mode of supply.

B. Mode 3

27. China's market access and national treatment commitments in Mode 3 of subsector (d) are limited to foreign financial institutions. Thus, even if the United States were to prove that the services at issue in this dispute are classifiable under subsector (d) – the premise of this entire section – it would still need to demonstrate that the terms, limitations, and conditions inscribed in China's Schedule for Mode 3 do not preclude the U.S. claims in this dispute.

28. The United States appears to have three conflicting theories in respect of China's Mode 3 commitments for subsector (d): (1) that network operators like Visa and MasterCard are "foreign financial institutions" within the ordinary meaning of that term, and are entitled to market access under Mode 3 according to the same terms, limitations, and conditions that apply to other foreign financial institutions; (2) that network operators like Visa and MasterCard are not "foreign financial institutions" and are not subject to *any* of the terms, limitations or conditions on market access inscribed in China's Mode 3 entry; or, (3) that network operators like Visa and MasterCard are not "foreign financial institutions", but are subject to the terms, limitations, and conditions on market access in Mode 3 as if the term "foreign financial institution" were synonymous with the term "financial service supplier". China will begin with the theory that network operators like Visa and MasterCard are financial institutions.

29. As China discussed in response to Question 61 from the Panel, network operators like Visa and MasterCard are not "financial institutions" within any understanding of this term. Nor is CUP a "financial institution" under Chinese law. But even if one were to accept the proposition that network operators are "financial institutions", or the equally erroneous proposition that the term "financial institution" is synonymous with the term "financial service supplier", the United States would still need to demonstrate that its claims in this dispute are consistent with the terms, limitations, and conditions inscribed in China's Schedule. The United States contends that "the only limitations China may impose are in connection with legitimate prudential regulation and the limitations explicitly listed in China's Schedule – the now defunct restrictions on geographic scope and use of domestic currency, *and ongoing requirements applicable to banks*." Yet the United States never explains what it considers these "ongoing requirements" to be, and why they are only "applicable to banks."

30. China's Mode 3 market access entry for subsectors (a) through (f) clearly specifies the conditions that foreign financial institutions must satisfy in order to engage in local currency business under any of these subsectors. If the United States is correct that network operators like Visa and MasterCard are "financial institutions", or that the term "financial institution" is synonymous with the term "financial service supplier", then the licensing conditions inscribed in the market access column are applicable to these service suppliers. These conditions are applicable to "foreign financial institutions", not just "banks". Moreover, it is clear that the United States is claiming a right of market access to engage in "local currency business" under subsector (d).

31. Perhaps in recognition of the problems that it faces in Mode 3, it appears that the United States is trying to preserve the alternative theory that network operators like Visa and MasterCard are *not* "financial institutions" and, as a result, are not subject to *any* limitations or conditions on market access and national treatment. This theory leads to the absurd conclusion that entities that are not financial institutions have an unlimited right to enter the Chinese market for the purpose of supplying regulated banking services, while the types of

financial institutions that actually supply these services are required to satisfy additional conditions on market access.

32. In sum, no matter what theory the United States ultimately adopts on Mode 3, it has no place to land. The correct answer is that network operators like Visa and MasterCard are not financial institutions of any sort, and therefore have no right of market access under China's Mode 3 commitments, even accepting the classification of the services at issue under subsector (d). But even if Visa and MasterCard were financial institutions, the United States would still need to demonstrate that "EPS suppliers" satisfy the conditions on market access and national treatment inscribed in China's Schedule for engaging in local currency business. This it cannot do.

C. Conclusion to Section II

33. Even if the United States were to establish that the services at issue in this dispute are classifiable under subsector (d), it has failed to prove that China undertook relevant market access and national treatment commitments in Mode 1 and Mode 3 in respect of these services. As China explained in its first written submission, this is the second juncture at which the U.S. claims in this dispute fail in their entirety.

III. THE UNITED STATES HAS FAILED TO DEMONSTRATE A MONOPOLY BASED ON THE MEASURES AT ISSUE

A. The U.S. "Monopoly" Claim Under Article XVI:2(a) Must Be Based on Measures that Are Within the Terms of Reference

34. The United States is well aware that the specific legal instruments that it identified in the panel request do not support its "monopoly" claims in this dispute, and so it now contends that there are "measures" at issue in this dispute that exist *independently* of any particular legal instrument. Those "measures" are the six alleged "requirements" that it invented for the purpose of this dispute.

35. The situation before the Panel is highly reminiscent of the "total prohibition on the cross-border supply of gambling and betting services" that Antigua alleged to exist in *US – Gambling*. Like Antigua, the United States appears to be arguing that there are "measures" that the Panel can evaluate independently of the content of any particular law or regulation. Like the "total prohibition", the six "requirements" are meant to describe the *effect* of an *unknown and unspecified* set of laws and regulations, of which the instruments identified in the panel request are merely "illustrative".

36. In *US – Gambling*, the panel and Appellate Body flatly rejected this approach to identifying the measures at issue, and the Panel should do the same here. Among other considerations, the panel in *US – Gambling* noted that "Article 6.2 of the DSU requires that measures be 'specifically' identified in a panel request", a standard that cannot be met where the complaining Member

purports to challenge any conceivable law or regulation that might be construed as having a particular "effect".

37. While the analogy to *US – Gambling* seems more apt, one could also see the United States as alleging that the six "requirements" constitute *unwritten* "rules or norms of general and prospective application" that are capable of being challenged as independent measures on an "as such" basis. But in *US – Zeroing (EC)*, the Appellate Body held that a Member seeking to challenge an unwritten rule or norm "must clearly establish, through arguments and supporting evidence, at least that the alleged 'rule or norm' is attributable to the responding Member; its precise content; and indeed, that it does have general and prospective application." The Appellate Body considered that there is a "high threshold" for such claims. The United States has not even remotely met that high threshold. It has presented no evidence whatsoever that these alleged "requirements" exist independently of the identified instruments.

38. The six independent "measures" that the United States has invented are not "specific measures at issue" within the meaning of Article 6.2 of the DSU and are not within the Panel's terms of reference under Article 7 of the DSU. The Panel must therefore reject this attempt by the United States to base its claims on anything other than the legal instruments specifically identified in the panel request. It is on the basis of these measures that the U.S. claims must succeed or fail.

B. The United States Has Failed to Establish a "Monopoly" on the Basis of Measures that Are Within the Terms of Reference

39. Turning to the measures that are within the terms of reference, the United States has failed to prove its claim under Article XVI of the GATS, even under its own theory of how to classify the services at issue and interpret China's commitments.

40. It is worth recalling the six "requirements" that the United States set out to prove in this dispute: (1) requirements that mandate the use of CUP and/or establish CUP as the sole supplier of EPS for all domestic transactions denominated and paid in RMB; (2) requirements on issuers that payment cards issued in China bear the CUP logo; (3) requirements that all ATM and POS terminals in China accept CUP cards; (4) requirements on acquiring institutions to post the CUP Logo and be capable of accepting all bank cards bearing the CUP logo; (5) broad prohibitions on the use of non-CUP cards; and, (6) requirements relating to China, Macao, and Hong Kong that mandate the use of CUP. Of these six alleged requirements, the United States has failed to demonstrate that four of them have anything to do with the maintenance or adoption of a limitation on market access "in the form of" a monopoly or exclusive service supplier arrangement.

41. Requirements 2, 3 and 4 relate to the use of the CUP logo and the ability of financial institutions to process transactions made with CUP cards. As China explained in its responses to questions from the Panel, these measures establish a

common national network for processing domestic interbank payment card transactions by ensuring that all interbank payment cards and POS devices adhere to a common technical standard, and by requiring all banks that issue interbank payment cards to be members of a common network. Because the United States has failed to establish that these measures impose "quantitative, or 'quantitative-type'" limitations on market access, they are irrelevant to the U.S. claim under Article XVI:2(a).

42. With respect to the sixth alleged requirement, concerning Hong Kong and Macao, the United States has failed to establish how this requirement is relevant to China's market access commitments for subsector (d). Pursuant to Article XVI:2 of the GATS, a Member's market access commitments impose limitations on the measures that a Member may maintain or adopt "either *on the basis of a regional subdivision or on the basis of its entire territory*, unless otherwise specified in its Schedule". In other words, a Member's Schedule implicates the provision of services *in the territory of that Member*. In the current dispute, this means that China's commitments relate only to the provision of services *in China*, and not to the supply of services in the territories of other Members. For this reason, there is no legal basis to find that the measures relating to Hong Kong and Macao contain "quantitative, or 'quantitative-type'" limitations on market access within the scope of Article XVI:2(a).

43. Having dispensed with requirements 2-4 and requirement 6, this leaves the first of the alleged requirements, *i.e.*, "requirements that mandate the use of CUP and/or establish CUP as the sole supplier of EPS for all domestic transactions denominated and paid in RMB", and the fifth of the alleged requirements, *i.e.*, the "broad prohibition on the use of non-CUP cards". China will address these two requirements collectively as measures that the United States believes to require the processing of domestic, RMB-denominated interbank payment card transactions over the CUP network.

44. Exhibit CHI-74 accompanying China's response to Question 22(a) from the Panel is a table that indicates all of the provisions of the measures: (1) that were in effect on the date of establishment of this Panel; and (2) that the United States has cited in support of its allegation that CUP has a "monopoly" on the processing of domestic interbank payment card transactions. In the last column of this table, China explains why each of the five provisions cited by the United States does not require domestic interbank payment card transactions to be processed over the CUP network.

45. Unable to demonstrate the existence of a "monopoly" on the face of the measures at issue, the United States resorts to creative juxtapositions and rewordings of different measures. For example, the United States interprets Article I.2 of Document No. 153 to state that "China Union Pay is *the* domestic clearance organization". Based on this misinterpretation, it concludes that "CUP is the *only* 'domestic clearance organization'", even though the word "only" is nowhere to be found in the text. In fact, Article I.2 states that "China Union Pay is *a* domestic clearance organization", not that it is "the" domestic clearance organization, let alone "the *only*" domestic clearance organization. But this does

not stop the United States from carrying its misinterpretation over to a different document, Document No. 53, where it interprets the terms "domestic clearing channels" and "domestic RMB clearing organizations" to refer *exclusively* to CUP. Document No. 53 does not even refer to CUP by name, much less confer any sort of monopoly upon it.

46. The fact that the United States must resort to this sort of manipulation of the measures merely confirms that it is unable to prove its case under Article XVI:2(a). Not a single one of the provisions cited by the United States even remotely imposes a quantitative or quantitative-type limitation on market access "in the form of" a monopoly or exclusive service supplier arrangement. For these reasons, the Panel must reject the U.S. claim under Article XVI:2(a), even assuming that all of the services at issue are classifiable under subsector (d) and that the United States has established the existence of relevant market access commitments.

IV. THERE IS NO BASIS FOR THE U.S. NATIONAL TREATMENT CLAIMS IN THIS DISPUTE

47. The parties do not dispute that an entry of "unbound" in the market access column means that a Member has reserved the right to adopt or maintain any of the types of measures listed in Article XVI:2. Nor do the parties dispute that the types of measures listed under Article XVI:2 can be either discriminatory or non-discriminatory (except for Article XVI:2(f), which is inherently discriminatory). It follows that a Member that has left a particular subsector and mode of supply unbound is free to adopt or maintain measures under Article XVI:2, including measures that are discriminatory, and that any such measure cannot simultaneously be the subject of a claim under Article XVII. Allowing such a claim would be contrary to the meaning of the term "unbound", and contrary to the intention, reflected in Article XX:2, to leave measures of the type listed under Article XVI:2 governed exclusively by the entry in the market access column.

48. The United States does not have a meaningful response to this conclusion. In response to Question 69(b) from the Panel, it asserts that "[i]f a Member had no commitments with regard to Article XVI, but a full commitment with regard to Article XVII, that Member could not retain a market access restriction that was simultaneously inconsistent with national treatment." It claims that, in these circumstances, the "Member could come into … compliance with its obligations by removing the national treatment inconsistency, while leaving the market access limitation in place."

49. The "solution" proposed by the United States merely begs the question of how to evaluate limitations on market access that are also discriminatory. Consider, for example, limitations on the participation of foreign capital under Article XVI:2(f). This is a limitation on market access that is inherently discriminatory, and one that a Member is allowed to adopt or maintain if its market access entry is unbound. Given its inherently discriminatory nature, how

could a Member "remov[e] the national treatment inconsistency, while leaving the market access limitation in place"? The discrimination *is* the market access limitation; it cannot be removed "while leaving the market access limitation in place".

50. The impossibility of what the United States is proposing demonstrates that its interpretation of how Articles XVI and XVII relate to each other is in error. The agreed meaning of the term "unbound", as well as the clear intention behind Article XX:2, is to have measures of the type listed in Article XVI:2 governed by the entry in the market access column, including in any respect in which they might be seen as discriminatory.

V. CONCLUSION

51. For the foregoing reasons, China respectfully requests that the Panel reject the U.S. claims in this dispute

ANNEX E

ORAL STATEMENTS OR EXECUTIVE SUMMARIES THEREOF, OF THE PARTIES AT THE SECOND SUBSTANTIVE MEETING

Contents		Page
Annex E-1	Executive summary of the oral statement of the United States at the second substantive meeting	5661
Annex E-2	Executive summary of the oral statement of China at the second substantive meeting	5668

ANNEX E-1

EXECUTIVE SUMMARY OF THE ORAL STATEMENT OF THE UNITED STATES AT THE SECOND SUBSTANTIVE MEETING

I. INTRODUCTION

1. The United States has shown that China's measures prevent foreign suppliers from supplying the service that enables credit, charge, debit and other payment card transactions to occur in China for *all* transactions where the card is issued in China and used in China. These transactions constitute the overwhelming number of transactions in China, whether they be RMD-payment card transactions or transactions using foreign currency denominated payment cards issued in China. Instead, China has granted one Chinese domestic company, China UnionPay, Co. Ltd. ("CUP"), a monopoly to supply the service. China's written and oral submissions show nothing to the contrary. In fact, in its defense thus far, China has largely avoided substantive discussion of the challenged measures.

II. EPS FOR PAYMENT CARD TRANSACTIONS IS A SINGLE, INTEGRATED SERVICE THAT FALLS WITHIN THE ORDINARY MEANING OF "ALL PAYMENT AND MONEY TRANSMISSION SERVICES, INCLUDING CREDIT, CHARGE AND DEBIT CARDS..." (SUBSECTOR (D))

2. The United States has demonstrated that EPS for payment card transactions is a single, integrated service that is properly classified under subsector (d) in China's Schedule. EPS is supplied as coherent whole, and this service enables cardholders' banks to pay merchants' banks the amount they are

owed. EPS suppliers provide an efficient, timely and reliable means to facilitate the transmission of funds from the holders of payment cards who purchase goods or services to the individuals or businesses that supply them. The network, rules and procedures, and operating system provided by an EPS supplier enable payment card transactions to occur. EPS suppliers receive, check and transmit information that the parties need to conduct the transactions, and enable the transmission of funds between participating entities. Each component of EPS is critical to effectuate payment card transactions. The customers of EPS suppliers – the entities that are participating in the payment card transactions – demand and rely on EPS as a complete, integrated, and unified service.

3. The clear language of subsector (d) compels the conclusion that EPS falls within the ordinary meaning of "payment and money transmission services" as one type of "*all*" such services. The illustrative list that explicitly provides that the services in subsector (d) "include[s] credit, charge and debit cards" underscores that EPS is integral to the processing of credit, charge, debit and other payment card transactions.

III. THE SERVICE AT ISSUE IS NOT "SETTLEMENT AND CLEARING SERVICES FOR FINANCIAL ASSETS, INCLUDING SECURITIES, DERIVATIVE PRODUCTS, AND OTHER NEGOTIABLE INSTRUMENTS"

4. China's arguments regarding subsector (d) are anchored to a flawed premise, cannot be reconciled with the text of its commitments, and are contrary to how the service at issue operates in practice. Moreover, China's position hinges on an exceedingly narrow reading of subsector (d). China's interpretation fails to give meaning to the word "all" in the sectoral description of "all payment and money transmission services, including credit, charge, and debit cards…" At the same time that it reads out the word "all" and pushes for an extremely narrow reading of subsector (d), however, China advocates an overly broad interpretation of "settlement and clearing services for financial assets" that is inconsistent with its proper context.

5. China continues to assert that certain elements of EPS for payment card transactions constitute separate services that are classified in a sector, item (xiv) of the GATS Annex on Financial Services, for which China has made no market access or national treatment commitments. China's overly broad reading is also combined with an incorrect understanding of the services in item (xiv) that fails to account for fundamental, recognized differences in the operation and risk profile of financial services under item (xiv) and services related to retail payment processing, such as EPS for payment card transactions.

6. The ordinary meaning of the services described in item (xiv) is evidenced by the words, the illustrative list in item (xiv), the additional context provided by paragraph 5 of the Annex on Financial Services, and other sources, including the United Nations, the OECD, the World Bank, International Monetary Fund ("IMF"), Bank for International Settlements ("BIS"), and BIS Committee on

Payment and Settlement Systems ("CPSS"), which all confirm that the ordinary meaning of item (xiv) does not include EPS for payment card transactions. Moreover, even if one were to erroneously attempt to disaggregate the component parts of EPS, no element of EPS falls within item (xiv). In short, the same rules of treaty interpretation that compel the conclusion that EPS for payment card transactions fall within subsector (d) also compel the conclusion that EPS for payment card transactions do not fall within item (xiv).

7. The ordinary meaning of the term "financial assets" that China has put forward is incorrect and contradicted by several sources. The United States has cited to the IMF's explanation that "a financial asset is negotiable if it is actively or inactively traded in a secondary market." In addition, the United States identified the Uniform Commercial Code ("UCC") definition of "financial asset," which is in accord with the IMF's explanation. Similarly, the BIS CPSS "glossary of terms used in payments and settlement systems" clearly illustrates that the terms "clearing" and "settlement" each have different meanings in the respective payment and securities contexts, confirming that context is crucial and all the terms in item (xiv) must be taken into account in determining the ordinary meaning of "settlement and clearing services for financial assets, including securities, derivative products, and other negotiable instruments."

8. The BIS CPSS glossary definitions relating to payments systems, including EPS for payment card transactions, are drawn from different source documents than those for securities settlement systems. China's interpretation of "financial asset" fails to account for the fact that "settlement and clearing services for financial assets" is a substantially different financial service than EPS for payment card transactions, which is a type of retail payment service. The CPSS has explained that "[r]etail payments are generally classified as cash payments or non-cash payments," which are subclassified into "cheque payments, direct funds transfers and card payments." The United States provided a detailed explanation of the many practical differences between the systems used to settle and clear investment instruments of the kind referenced in item (xiv) and the systems used to settle and clear retail payment instruments, like payment cards.

9. Because credit card receivables can be used to create asset-backed securities, China also argues that there is "no distinction whatsoever between the issuing bank's claim against the cardholder and the acquiring bank's claim against the issuing bank." China is wrong here too. The assets that are used to create credit card asset-backed securities are *not* the obligations between issuing and acquiring banks that are processed by EPS suppliers on a daily basis. The relevant assets are the *loans* that are extended from the issuing bank to the cardholder. EPS suppliers are not involved in the processing of such loans.

10. China cites the Basel Committee on Banking Supervision, Report on Special Purpose Entities (Exhibit CHI-76) ("Basel Report"), for the proposition that credit card receivables are financial assets. However, the Basel Report makes it clear that the "assets" are not the obligations between the issuing and acquiring banks, but instead are receivables that generate income or cash flow

(that is, the loan). Thus, this source actually supports the proposition that the "financial assets" are *the loans between the issuing bank and the cardholders*.

11. China's argument that clearing and settlement services for certain types of retail payment instruments such as checks are covered by item (xiv) is also flawed. Item (xiv) covers only those types of "negotiable instruments" that qualify as "financial assets," and instruments such as personal checks do not fall within that category. The System of National Accounts (SNA), an international standard system of national accounts, prepared jointly by the United Nations, the OECD, the World Bank, the IMF, and the European Commission, distinguishes between financial claims that are negotiable and those that are not, and according to the SNA the term "negotiable instrument' does not include retail payment instruments such as checks.

12. Finally, paragraph 5(a) of the Annex provides additional context that supports the U.S. interpretation. The terms "financial assets" and "negotiable instruments" also appear item (x) of the Annex, which covers, "Trading for own account or for account of customers, whether on an exchange, in an over-the-counter market or otherwise." As used in item (x), these terms refer to tradeable investment assets, rather than "interbank claims for payment." Thus, the context for item (xiv) indicates that "negotiable instruments" and "financial assets" are not retail payment vehicles like payment cards. Additional context is item (viii) of the Annex, which contains the most specific and accurate description of the service for purposes of classifying EPS for payment card transactions.

IV. CHINA'S MODE 1 AND MODE 3 COMMITMENTS FOR "ALL PAYMENT AND MONEY TRANSMISSION SERVICES, INCLUDING CREDIT, CHARGE AND DEBIT CARDS..."

13. It is plain from the text that China has taken mode 1 market access commitments for "all payment and money transmission services, including credit, charge and debit cards..." The word "Unbound" in the market access column of its Schedule is qualified. The phrase "except for the following" is further elaborated by two sentences that describe elements of the service within subsector (d) for which China has taken mode 1 commitments. The qualifying phrase and specific elaboration following the word "Unbound" must be given meaning.

14. Meanwhile, China's reaction to the U.S. response underscores its attempt to conflate the classification of a service in a particular subsector, on the one hand, with the interpretation of market access limitations, on the other. China states that "the United States needs the service at issue to be in two places at once: in subsector (d) and in subsectors (k) or (l)." Sequence is critical to a proper analysis. Step one is to classify the service: the service at issue is a single, integrated service that falls within subsector (d). Step two is to discern China's commitments for subsector (d), such as China's mode 1 commitments. This is a separate and distinct exercise from step one. Yet China continues to muddle the discussion of these separate steps.

15. China's arguments fail to give any meaning to the extensive language qualifying the term "Unbound" in its mode 1 commitments. They essentially reduce to the single point that all of the extensive language qualifying the term "Unbound" in its mode 1 market access commitments was provided simply to confirm language already existing elsewhere in China's Schedule. According to China the additional wording should be given no meaning whatsoever. If China wished to be fully "Unbound," that is, not to have *any* mode 1 commitments, it should not have qualified its commitments; rather it should have left the word "Unbound" unqualified. However, as its Schedule reflects, China did not do so. It is not credible to argue that the additional language is merely for greater certainty to repeat China's commitments in subsectors (k) and (l). Such an argument fails to give meaning to this treaty language. Perhaps knowing this, China implores the Panel to "imagine" instead different treaty language rather than the actual words in its Schedule.

16. Elements of CUP's own activities are described in terms similar to the "excepted" elements that are set out in China's mode 1 market access commitments, and China's regulatory system similarly describes a primary activity of CUP as exchanging information among financial institutions. Moreover, the concept that a service may include elements of "provision and transfer of financial information, and financial data processing" was recognized, for example, in paragraph 8 of the Uruguay Round Understanding on Commitments in Financial Services. The provision and transfer of financial information and data processing is central to the supply of many different financial services, and, according to the Understanding, signatory WTO Members cannot frustrate their commitments by, for example, blocking the ability to communicate and process information.

17. With respect to China's mode 3 market access commitments for subsector (d), the presence of the term "financial institution" in China's schedule does not create a separate and independent limitation. The Schedule states that "[c]riteria for authorization to deal in China's financial services sector are solely prudential." There is nothing in China's Schedule that indicates it may condition the supply of a service on the criteria listed in the market access commitment column and also require that another Member's supplier meet additional (and unspecified) criteria to be recognized as a "foreign financial institution." Such a limitation would have needed to be imposed explicitly in its Schedule, and China did not do so. Finally, even if it were the case that the term "financial institution" somehow served as a limitation in China's Schedule, the definition of "financial institution" offered by China is too narrow. Many definitions are much broader, and some explicitly include "an operator of a credit card system."

V. CHINA'S MEASURES ESTABLISHING AND SUPPORTING CHINA UNIONPAY'S MONOPOLY ON THE SUPPLY OF EPS ARE INCONSISTENT WITH ARTICLE XVI OF THE GATS

18. China's measures limit the number of suppliers of EPS. The United States identified 19 instruments in the U.S. panel request and is challenging each of them independently. The United States has also identified six separate categories of requirements that constitute six separate measures that are implemented through several instruments operating in conjunction:

- Requirements that mandate the use of CUP and/or establish CUP as the sole supplier of EPS;
- Requirements that RMB denominated payment cards issued in China bear the CUP logo;
- Requirements that all automated teller machines ("ATM"), merchant card processing equipment, and POS terminals in China accept CUP cards;
- Requirements on acquiring institutions to post the CUP logo and be capable of accepting all payment cards bearing the CUP logo;
- Broad prohibitions on the use of non-CUP cards; and
- Requirements pertaining to card-based transactions in China, Macao and Hong Kong.

19. These measures establish and maintain CUP's monopoly and limit the number of suppliers of EPS for payment card transactions and are inconsistent with China's obligations under Article XVI of the GATS.

VI. CHINA'S MEASURES ARE INCONSISTENT WITH ARTICLE XVII OF THE GATS

20. The measures at issue affect the supply of services and accord less favorable treatment to foreign suppliers of EPS, and are inconsistent with China's obligations under Article XVII of the GATS. Some measures impose a limitation such that CUP is the sole entity that can process certain transactions, such as domestic RMB transactions. This of course means that foreign suppliers of EPS are prevented from supplying the service at all. Other measures promote CUP's position in the marketplace such as by imposing certain requirements on every key player in a card-based electronic payment transaction. The United States has explained how China's measures affect every aspect of a card-based electronic payment transaction and the key players, including issuers (all cards issued in China for domestic RMB transactions must bear the CUP logo), merchants (all merchant card processing equipment and POS terminals must accept CUP cards), and acquiring institutions (which must post CUP logo and accept CUP cards).

VII. CONCLUSION

21. The United States respectfully requests that the Panel find that China's measures are inconsistent with China's obligations under Article XVI:1 and XVI:2(a) and Article XVII of the GATS. The United States again thanks the Panel for its continued service in this dispute and looks forward to responding to any questions the Panel may have.

ANNEX E-2

EXECUTIVE SUMMARY OF THE ORAL STATEMENT OF CHINA AT THE SECOND SUBSTANTIVE MEETING

I. INTRODUCTION

1. It is not my intention this morning to review China's arguments as they relate to all of the issues in this dispute. As a result of the questions posed by the Panel after the first meeting and the parties' subsequent submissions, the key issues in this dispute are now reasonably well defined. I intend to focus my remarks on those key issues and, in particular, on the positions that the United States has taken in respect of those issues.

II. CLASSIFICATION: ITEM (XIV) OF THE ANNEX LIST

2. The only issue that remains in dispute in respect of item (xiv) of the *Annex* list is whether interbank claims for payment are among the "financial assets" that are covered by item (xiv). China has definitively established that the ordinary meaning of the term "financial assets" includes cash and any right to receive cash. An acquiring bank's right to receive payment from an issuing bank is indisputably a "financial asset" within this ordinary meaning.

3. In its second submission, the United States continues to search for *some* definition or usage to support its position that the term "financial assets" is limited to what it calls "investment instruments". The United States cites only two "sources" in support of its interpretation: the Monetary and Financial Statistics Guide prepared by the IMF, and the definition of the term "financial assets" in Article 8 of the U.S. UCC. Neither one of these supports the U.S. position.

4. The United States cites a passage from the Monetary and Financial Statistics Guide that explains the types of financial assets that the IMF considers to be *negotiable* for statistical purposes. The United States fails to explain why this *statistical* definition of *negotiability* is relevant to the interpretation of the term "financial assets" in item (xiv). That omission aside, the more important point is that the IMF defines the term "financial assets" – the *operative* term in item (xiv) – to include "*all* financial claims". Moreover, the Monetary and Financial Statistics Guide cited by the United States, as well as the System of National Accounts maintained by the IMF, are expressly based on the International Financial Reporting Standards. As China has previously explained, those standards define the term "financial asset" to include "cash" and any "contractual right to receive cash".

5. As for Article 8 of the U.S. UCC, the United States has yet to explain why U.S. municipal law is relevant to the process of discerning the common

intention of the Members with respect to the meaning of item (xiv). But setting aside its interpretative irrelevance, the United States neglects to point out that the subject matter of Article 8 is expressly limited to investment securities. Naturally, the definition of the term "financial assets" in Article 8 is tailored to the subject matter of that article. The limitation that the United States seeks to impose upon the ordinary meaning of the term "financial assets" is entirely arbitrary.

6. Lacking any support for its position in the ordinary meaning of the term "financial assets", the United States spends *eight pages* of its second submission describing alleged differences between the clearing and settlement of "investment instruments" and the clearing and settlement of retail payment instruments. What the United States never explains is why any of these alleged differences *matter* for the purpose of determining the ordinary meaning of the term "financial assets" in item (xiv).

7. The last refuge for the United States is its so-called "contextual" interpretation of the term "financial assets", based on the three examples provided in item (xiv). First, the United States asserts that because "payment cards" are "not similar" to securities or derivative products, and "are not negotiable instruments", they are not "of the same type of financial assets as the items included in the illustrative list" and therefore are not covered by item (xiv). The United States knows that this is not the issue in dispute. Network operators do not clear and settle "payment cards". They clear and settle interbank claims for payment that arise under four-party payment card models. Whether such *claims for payment* are financial assets within the meaning of item (xiv) is the only interpretative issue in this case. As China has shown, all legitimate interpretative tools demonstrate that interbank claims for payment are "financial assets" within the ordinary meaning of that term.

8. The second key point is that the U.S. "contextual" interpretation is based entirely on a misinterpretation of what that context means. The critical underpinning of the U.S. "contextual" approach is to deny that the term "negotiable instruments" in item (xiv) includes cheques and other types of retail payment instruments. It is understandable why the United States must take this position. To acknowledge the obvious fact that cheques are negotiable instruments would destroy not only the U.S. position that item (xiv) is limited to "investment instruments", but also its position that all clearing and settlement services relating to payment instruments are implied by interpretative necessity in item (viii).

9. The United States adds to the litany of contradictions in the very next section of its submission, when it points to item (x) of the *Annex* list as an "illustrative list" of what it considers to be the types of financial assets that are covered by item (xiv). Apparently overlooked by the United States is the fact that item (x)(A) of this list explicitly refers to "cheques" as among the "negotiable instruments" and "financial assets" that are included within this category. This fatally undermines the U.S. insistence that the drafters of the

Annex list meant to exclude cheques from the ordinary meaning of the terms "financial assets" and "negotiable instruments".

10. One final point about the U.S. "contextual" argument deserves highlighting. In addition to all of its other flaws, the U.S. interpretation does not come to terms with the fact that the illustrative list in item (xiv) is a *non-exhaustive* list of "financial assets". The U.S. interpretation of item (xiv) not only misinterprets the meaning of the three examples that are provided, it then treats those three examples as if they were the *only types* of "financial assets" that are covered by item (xiv). As China has shown, this is not the role that illustrative lists play in the process of treaty interpretation.

III. CLASSIFICATION: SUBSECTOR (D)

11. Like its interpretation of item (xiv), the U.S. interpretation of subsector (d) has become an exercise in how many inconsistencies and contradictions the United States can maintain simultaneously. The United States contends that all of the services at issue are in subsector (d), but then argues that the same services are actually described by subsectors (k) and (l). It agrees that the subsectors in a Member's Schedule are mutually exclusive, but then argues that subsectors can become "embedded" in other subsectors by "necessity". In its attempt to reconcile these inconsistent positions, the United States unwittingly creates oxymorons like "auxiliary central services" and "optional essential services".

12. In its second submission, the United States places significant emphasis on the proposition that the services at issue in this dispute "constitute one integral, indivisible service." As a factual matter, the United States is mistaken in its premise. In fact, it is common for the network infrastructure of a payment card system to be supplied separately from the clearing and settlement services that banks use to reconcile and discharge their obligations toward each other. For example:

- In Australia, most ATM and EFTPOS networks are owned by specific banks. As a result of interconnection agreements, these networks effectively operate as a single national network. ATM and EFTPOS transactions are not cleared and settled over this network. Instead, banks clear and settle payment card transactions on a bilateral basis, using a gross settlement system operated by the Australian Payments Clearing Association and the Reserve Bank of Australia.
- In Canada, the principal network for ATM and EFTPOS transactions is operated by Interac, a non-profit association owned primarily by Canadian banks. Interac provides the front-end authorization network for ATM and EFTPOS transactions. These transactions, however, are cleared and settled through the Automated Clearing and Settlement System (ACSS), a different

system operated by the Canadian Payments Association. The ACSS clears and settles all types of interbank claims, including not only ATM and EFTPOS transactions, but also paper-based cheques.

13. France, Germany, Italy, Japan, the Netherlands, and Sweden are just a few other examples of countries where the network infrastructure is supplied separately from clearing and settlement services. The fact that Visa and MasterCard happen to bundle certain services into a single service offering does not mean that all network services are provided on this basis or that the bundling of these services is required as a matter of operational necessity.

14. In addition to its factual inaccuracy, the U.S. theory is based on the notion that any set of services that is supplied on a "bundled" basis *must* be classified as a single service, at least if *some* service suppliers happen to provide the services on this basis. But the manner in which a service supplier combines and prices services does not change their classification as distinct services. For example, a hotel might include a tour of the local sights as part of a package price, but this does not change the fact that it is providing both hotel services and tour services. Nor can it be the case that the same service takes on a *different* classification *only* in those cases where a particular service supplier happens to bundle it with another service. This would violate the principle of mutual exclusivity.

15. In sum, there is no reason, either as a matter of fact or as a matter of law, why the services at issue in this dispute can or should be classified into one and only one subsector. The clearing and settlement services at issue in this dispute, in particular, are plainly recognizable as a distinct and separately classifiable service under item (xiv) of the *Annex* list.

IV. COMMITMENTS: MODE 1

16. The U.S. position on how to classify the services at issue is now directly in conflict with its position that China made relevant Mode 1 commitments in respect of those services. In its second written submission, the United States has strongly reaffirmed its position that all of the services at issue in this dispute are classifiable under subsector (d). Yet at the same time, the United States maintains that *every aspect* of what it calls "electronic payment services" fits within the description of subsectors (k) and (l).

17. The U.S. theory that China undertook Mode 1 commitments in respect of the services at issue rests entirely on the proposition that the services described in one subsector can become "embedded" in another subsector to the extent that they are "integral" to the provision of the latter service. As China has explained, this theory is flatly inconsistent with the principle of mutual exclusivity, and the Panel must reject it for this reason alone.

18. The U.S. position, if accepted, would make a mockery of China's actual commitments for subsectors (a) through (f). Both the text and context of China's

Schedule establish that the intention behind these commitments was that the banking services listed in subsectors (a) through (f) would be supplied by foreign financial institutions operating in China on a commercial presence basis.

19. According to the United States, network operators like Visa and MasterCard could provide *all* of the services at issue in this dispute with "no or a very limited physical presence in China". Moreover, entities like Visa and MasterCard could provide these services in China even though they are not financial institutions. In other words, services that were meant to be supplied on a *commercial presence* basis by *financial institutions* would be supplied on a *cross-border* basis by service suppliers that are *not* financial institutions.

20. Other than in the case of subsector (d), the United States appears to understand the nature of China's commitments for these subsectors. In response to question 28 from the Panel, the United States provided examples of a financial institution that provides a core banking service in China on a commercial presence basis and, in conjunction with that service, provides certain other services on a cross-border basis that the United States considers to be within the description of subsectors (k) or (l). The United States would presumably agree that, in each instance, the core banking service is unbound in Mode 1. In the case of subsector (d), however, the United States has yet to identify any service at issue in this dispute that would be unbound in Mode 1. According to the United States, *all* of the services at issue fit within the exception and could be supplied on a cross-border basis. There is no "core" service to be supplied on a commercial presence basis – the services *are* the exception.

21. The exception to China's unbound market access entry for subsector (d) only becomes relevant if there is something in subsector (d) to begin with – that is, if there is some service that the service supplier is legitimately supplying in China on a commercial presence basis. If the United States believes that there *is* such a service, and is able to identify what it is, that service is necessarily unbound in Mode 1. Otherwise, the United States can no longer maintain that subsector (d) has any relevance to this dispute.

V. COMMITMENTS: MODE 3

22. The United States still has not committed to a single, coherent theory of how China's commitments in Mode 3 relate to the services and service suppliers at issue in this dispute. There is one thing, however, that is reasonably clear: the United States *knows* that China's market access commitments for subsector (d) are limited to foreign financial institutions. This is the only plausible explanation for why the United States continues to insist that Visa and MasterCard are financial institutions, even though they are not financial institutions under any commonly understood definition of that term, and even though Visa and MasterCard routinely deny any such status.

23. The problem for the United States, however, is that Visa and MasterCard are *not* financial institutions. Once this is properly taken into account, the U.S.

claims to market access under subsector (d) simply evaporate, in both Mode 3 *and* Mode 1. As I discussed earlier, China's commitments for subsectors (a) through (f) contemplate that foreign financial institutions will provide these services in China on a commercial presence basis. For the exception to China's unbound market access entry in Mode 1 even to be relevant, the service supplier at issue must be providing one or more of these services in China on a commercial presence basis. Because Visa and MasterCard are not financial institutions, they have no right of market access in Mode 3. It follows that they have no right of market access in Mode 1 that could even potentially be relevant to the services that they provide.

24. For these reasons, even if the services at issue were properly classifiable under subsector (d), which they are not, in no event do China's commitments in Mode 1 or Mode 3 extend to service suppliers that are not financial institutions.

VI. CONCLUSION

25. It is easy to lose sight of the fact that there are at least three distinct layers to this dispute: classification, commitments, and the consistency of the measures at issue. For all of the reasons that China has set forth in its submissions, China considers that the United States has failed to meet its burden of proof in respect of the classification of the services at issue. China considers that the failure of the United States to meet its burden of proof in respect of classification should lead the Panel to dismiss the U.S. claims in their entirety.

26. Even if the Panel were to conclude that some or all of the services at issue in this dispute are classified under subsector (d), the Panel should find that the United States has failed to prove that China undertook relevant commitments in Mode 1 and Mode 3. This, too, would require the Panel to dismiss the U.S. claims in their entirety.

27. It is only if the Panel were to find that some or all of the services at issue are classified under subsector (d), *and* that China undertook relevant commitments in either or both modes of supply, that the Panel would need to evaluate the consistency of the measures at issues with those commitments. Here, too, the United States has failed to prove its case. As China detailed in its second written submission, the United States is now grasping at straws, arguing that the six alleged "requirements" are freestanding "measures" that the Panel can evaluate independently of any of the specific legal instruments identified in the panel request. The United States has been forced to take this approach – which it so strenuously opposed in *Gambling* – because the measures that are *actually* at issue in this dispute plainly do not support its claims. Thus, even in this scenario, the Panel would need to dismiss the U.S. claims in their entirety.

28. China respectfully submits that this is the order of analysis that the Panel should follow. At every juncture in this analysis, the end result is the same: the United States has failed to prove its claims in this dispute, and the Panel must therefore reject those claims in their entirety.

ANNEX F

REQUEST FOR A PRELIMINARY RULING

Contents		Page
Annex F-1	Executive summary of China's request for a preliminary ruling	5675
Annex F-2	Executive summary of the United States' submissions in response to China's request for a preliminary ruling	5677
Annex F-3	Executive summary of China's comments on the United States' submissions in response to China's request for a preliminary ruling	5689

ANNEX F-1

EXECUTIVE SUMMARY OF CHINA'S REQUEST FOR A PRELIMINARY RULING

I. THE U.S. PANEL REQUEST DOES NOT PROVIDE A BRIEF SUMMARY OF THE LEGAL BASIS OF THE COMPLAINT SUFFICIENT TO PRESENT THE PROBLEM CLEARLY

1. China hereby requests a preliminary ruling by the Panel with respect to the consistency of the U.S. panel request with Article 6.2 of the Understanding on Rules and Procedures Governing the Settlement of Disputes ("DSU"). Article 6.2 of the DSU provides, in relevant part, that "[t]he request for the establishment of a panel shall … identify the specific measures at issue and provide a brief summary of the legal basis of the complaint sufficient to present the problem clearly."

2. The Appellate Body has held that "in order for a panel request to 'present the problem clearly', it must plainly connect the challenged measure(s) with the provision(s) of the covered agreements claimed to have been infringed, so that the respondent party is aware of the basis for the alleged nullification or impairment of the complaining party's benefits." The Appellate Body has further held that the sectors and subsectors set forth in a Member's schedule of specific commitments under the General Agreement on Trade in Services ("GATS") are mutually exclusive. Thus, by operation of law, any given service that is the subject of a claim under the GATS must fall into one, and only one, sector or subsector of the responding Member's schedule of specific commitments. It follows that, in order to "present the problem clearly" under Article 6.2 of the

DSU, the panel request must identify the specific sector or subsector that allegedly encompasses the service at issue or, if there are multiple services at issue, plainly associate those services with the specific sector or subsector that allegedly encompasses each service.

3. The foundation of the U.S. panel request in this dispute is a lengthy definition of the services that it alleges to be at issue – what it calls "electronic payment services". This is a term of the United States' own making – it does not correspond to any of the service subsectors set forth in China's Schedule of Specific Commitments ("Schedule"). The lack of any such correspondence is evidenced by the fact that the United States cites three different and mutually exclusive subsectors in China's Schedule as the legal basis for its claims. These subsectors are, in brief: (1) "all payment and money transmission services"; (2) "provision and transfer of financial information, and financial data processing and related software by supplier of other financial services"; and (3) "advisory, intermediation and other auxiliary financial services".

4. The nature and extent of China's market access and national treatment obligations in the three subsectors identified in the panel request depend upon the particular subsector involved, as well as the mode of supply. Notwithstanding these differences in China's legal obligations, the U.S. panel request fails to explain, even concisely, how its definition of "electronic payment services" relates to China's specific commitments in any one of the three subsectors, and fails to provide any indication of which mode (or modes) of supply the United States considers to be at issue. In these critical respects, the U.S. panel request fails to connect the challenged measures to the provisions of the covered agreements that the United States relies upon as the legal basis for its claims.

5. In light of these deficiencies, the U.S. panel request has failed to "present the problem clearly" as required by Article 6.2 of the DSU. In order to address China's due process concerns, and in order to avoid prejudice to either party, China respectfully requests that the Panel issue a preliminary ruling at the earliest opportunity.

ANNEX F-2

EXECUTIVE SUMMARY OF THE UNITED STATES' SUBMISSIONS IN RESPONSE TO CHINA'S REQUEST FOR A PRELIMINARY RULING

I. INTRODUCTION

1. Each day around the world, credit, charge, debit, and other payment cards are used in hundreds of millions of transactions where cardholders purchase a vast array of goods and services, ranging from groceries, clothing, and gasoline, to airplane tickets, hotel accommodations, and dining at restaurants. In terms of both volume and value, the amount of goods and services subject to payment card transactions is staggering. The services that enable, facilitate, and manage the transfer of funds between cardholders and merchants – commonly known as electronic payment services ("EPS") – are essential to processing the several hundred million card-based electronic transactions that occur daily around the world. These services are vital to the operation of a modern economy.

2. When China joined the World Trade Organization ("WTO") in 2001, it made important commitments with respect to electronic payment services. In 2005, China explicitly recognized that "the RMB bank card operation shall be opened to the outside world in an all-around manner." In the financial services sector, as set out in China's Schedule of Specific Commitments on Services, China undertook both market access and national treatment commitments with respect to electronic payment services. Under the terms of its Schedule, China was required to fully implement these commitments as of December 2006. Yet, despite China's commitments to provide both market access and national treatment for "all payment and money transmission services, including credit, charge and debit cards" for domestic currency transactions, China continues to maintain a government-mandated domestic monopoly, enabling only its domestic champion, China UnionPay, Co. Ltd. ("CUP" or "China UnionPay"), to provide these services, thereby blocking participation by foreign suppliers.

3. China itself acknowledged in 2005 that "the bank card industry of our country is facing a comparatively big challenge" because its WTO commitments were to take effect in 2006. Yet despite the December 2006 deadline for the implementation of its WTO commitments, China failed to remove the measures that form the basis for CUP's monopoly on the supply of EPS for RMB payment card transactions (*e.g.*, those using credit card, charge card, and debit cards). Not only did China fail to eliminate the monopoly, it also adopted additional measures to lock in CUP's dominance. Statements from PBOC and CUP officials suggest that China did not dismantle CUP's monopoly because China wanted more time to establish and solidify CUP's presence overseas before it would eventually have to face competition from foreign EPS suppliers in China.

4. Since December 2006, China has steadfastly refused to allow foreign suppliers of electronic payment services to process RMB payment card transactions and has enacted numerous barriers to establishing the processing infrastructure, network, rules, and procedures that are essential to the supply of EPS, and hence necessary for foreign suppliers' processing of such card-based transactions in China. Meanwhile, operating from its protected home market monopoly position, CUP has been rapidly expanding its card acceptance and issuance internationally since 2003. Unlike foreign suppliers of electronic payment services in China, CUP is able to have full and unencumbered access to the domestic payment card market in a growing number of foreign countries in which it has chosen to operate (now numbering more than 110). In other words, foreign EPS suppliers in China do not have the same market access in China that CUP enjoys abroad.

5. China failed to open its market as required by its WTO obligations. The measures that provide for CUP's monopoly position remain in place, and China has introduced reinforcing measures to strengthen and entrench the CUP monopoly. This monopoly structure ensures that CUP is the sole entity that can provide EPS for RMB transactions in China – the vast majority of all transactions in China.

6. The United States enumerated its concerns regarding China's measures in the U.S. panel request. Nonetheless, on July 5, 2011, China filed a request for a preliminary ruling with respect to the consistency of the U.S. panel request with Article 6.2 of the *Understanding on Rules and Procedures Governing the Settlement of Disputes* ("DSU"). Yet the U.S. panel request is in writing, indicates that consultations were held, identifies the specific measures at issue, and provides a brief summary of the legal basis of the complaint sufficient to present the problem clearly. China's procedural challenge is baseless. The U.S. panel request is fully consistent with DSU Article 6.2.

II. PROCEDURAL HISTORY OF CHINA'S PRELIMINARY RULING REQUEST

7. On July 5, 2011 China filed a request for a preliminary ruling on the consistency of the U.S. panel request with DSU Article 6.2. In its submission, China requested that the Panel adopt procedures and a timetable to provide for separate submissions, a hearing, and findings by the Panel on China's request before the United States had had an opportunity to provide its first submission. However, China failed to explain why it would suffer prejudice from receiving the U.S. response in the U.S. first submission, an approach consistent with the customary practice in responding to preliminary ruling requests. Nor did China explain how its request would avoid prejudice to the United States and its interest, as the complaining party, in presenting its case in a coherent manner. Rather, China's request would require the United States to address certain key aspects of its case in advance and separate from other key aspects. And China failed to address the delay in the Panel proceedings caused by its request, a delay

that China itself had successfully argued to a prior panel as grounds for denying a similar request.

III. THE U.S. PANEL REQUEST SATISFIES THE REQUIREMENTS OF DSU ARTICLE 6.2

A. The Requirements of DSU Article 6.2

8. Article 6.2 of the DSU provides in part as follows:

> The request for the establishment of a panel shall be made in writing. It shall indicate whether consultations were held, identify the specific measures at issue and provide a brief summary of the legal basis of the complaint sufficient to present the problem clearly.

9. The Appellate Body has described the requirements of DSU Article 6.2 as follows:

> When parsed into its constituent parts, Article 6.2 may be seen to impose the following requirements. The request must: (i) be in writing; (ii) indicate whether consultations were held; (iii) identify the specific measures at issue; and (iv) provide a brief summary of the legal basis of the complaint sufficient to present the problem clearly.

10. In analyzing whether a panel request complies with DSU Article 6.2, the Appellate Body has stated that "compliance with the requirements of Article 6.2 must be determined on the merits of each case, having considered the panel request as a whole, and in the light of attendant circumstances." Compliance with the requirements of DSU Article 6.2 must be determined by considering the panel request as a whole, and not simply on the basis of isolated portions of the panel request.

B. The U.S. Panel Request is in Writing, Indicates that Consultations Were Held, Identifies the Specific Measures at Issue, and Provides a Brief Summary of the Legal Basis of the Complaint Sufficient to Present the Problem Clearly

11. The U.S. panel request meets each of these requirements under Article 6.2 of the DSU. The panel request identifies the specific measures being challenged, the specific commitments at issue in China's schedule, and the specific obligations that are the subject of the U.S. complaint. In addition, the U.S. panel request specifies, with precision, the services at issue: "electronic payment services for payment card transactions." The United States also provides in its panel request a detailed narrative of the claims it is making as an additional basis for China to understand "the legal basis of the complaint." The

U.S. panel request contains information "sufficient to present the problem clearly."

12. China's argument essentially reduces to the assertion that the United States needed to "explain how or why the United States considers the challenged measures to be inconsistent with China's specific commitments." China also states that "[t]he foundation of the U.S. panel request in this dispute is a lengthy definition of the services that it alleges to be at issue – what it calls 'electronic payment services'" and that "[t]his is a term of the United States' own making." China further argues that the term electronic payment services "does not correspond to any of the service subsectors set forth in China's Schedule of Specific Commitments."

13. As an initial matter, China is wrong factually. First, as explained in detail in this submission, the description of the sector at issue in this dispute that is set out in the U.S. panel request – "electronic payment services" for "payment card" transactions – is drawn from industry sources and reflects the broad and common understanding within this sector. Suppliers of the services at issue in this dispute who work within this sector are described as supplying, or characterize themselves as supplying, "electronic payment services" and as operating within the "global payments industry." The sector that services credit, charge, debit, and other payment card transactions characterizes itself as providing "electronic payment services." China simply cannot credibly assert that the use of this term is somehow confusing or prejudicial.

14. An analogous issue was addressed in the context of a challenge to a product description in a panel request and the purported lack of clarity in terms of tariff classification. The panel in *EC – Computer Equipment* rejected the EU's argument regarding the purported lack of clarity of the term "LAN equipment" and found the definition "is sufficiently specific for the purposes of our consideration of this dispute." The panel in *EC – Computer Equipment* also rejected the same type of argument advanced in connection with the term "PC's with multimedia capability." The EU appealed these panel findings in that dispute on the basis that that the purported lack of clarity violated the EU's due process rights. The Appellate Body upheld the panel's findings, rejected the EU's alleged due process claims.

15. China's assertion that the term "electronic payment services" does not correspond to any of the service subsectors set forth in China's GATS schedule is equally unavailing. EPS fall within the definition of "*all* payment and money transmission services, including credit, charge and debit cards…" The language of item (d) of China's Schedule itself makes this clear.

16. EPS are at the center of all payment card transactions and without these services the transactions could not occur. EPS fall within the ordinary meaning of payment and money transmission services, within item (d) of China's Schedule. As set forth in the U.S. panel request, and as detailed in this submission, EPS involve the services through which transactions involving payment cards are processed and through which transfers of funds between

institutions participating in the transactions are managed and facilitated. EPS clearly fall within the ordinary meaning of "payment and money transmission service" as one type of "*all*" such services. Second, the phrase "all payment and money transmission services" is modified with an illustrative list that explicitly provides that it "include[s] credit, charge and debit cards." Visa, MasterCard, Discover, and American Express are names recognized around the world as credit, debit and charge cards. The reference to debit cards covers suppliers of EPS for debit card transactions like First Data, Pulse, NYCE, STAR, and PLUS.

17. And China is wrong as a legal matter as well. The "explanation" that China seeks goes beyond what is required by Article 6.2 of the DSU and instead asks the United States to provide China the U.S. *arguments* as to "why" China's measures breach the identified obligations. Similarly, China's arguments that the services do not fall within the specified sectors is a *defense* by China to the claims – a defense it will be free to make in its first written submission. There is no failure to satisfy the requirements of Article 6.2. And China's arguments in this regard demonstrate that China does in fact understand the matter raised in the U.S. panel request.

18. Also without merit is China's argument that "the United States cites three different and mutually exclusive subsectors in China's Schedule as the legal basis for its claims." Whether a complainant can prevail on separate claims advanced under potentially mutually exclusive subsectors in a Member's GATS schedule is a substantive legal issue to be decided on the merits based on the evidence and legal arguments presented to the Panel. Identifying potentially mutually exclusive claims in the U.S. panel request is not a failure under Article 6.2 to provide a summary of the legal basis of the complaint. In the three subsectors identified in the U.S. panel request, China undertook both market access and national treatment commitments for modes (1) and (3) as specified in its Schedule. The U.S. panel request thus puts China on notice as to China's market access and national treatment commitments, including the modes of supply, that are before the Panel.

19. In its request, China appears to acknowledge the claims in the U.S. panel request, but then seeks more – China seeks a detailed explanation of the U.S. legal arguments as to exactly how China's measures put it in breach of these commitments. In other words, China concedes that specific commitments and claims are identified in the U.S. panel request, but asks for more than what is required by DSU Article 6.2. With its request for a preliminary ruling, China seeks to have specific legal arguments presented as to how the measures at issue breach commitments identified in the U.S. panel request. China is not entitled to see how the United States will present its legal arguments in advance of the U.S. first submission. Yet, that is precisely what China seeks with its preliminary ruling request.

20. The U.S. panel request identifies that China undertook both market access and national treatment commitments with respect to item (d) "All payment and money transmission services, including credit, charge and debit cards..." In addition, the U.S. panel request identifies the specific measures being challenged

and the specific obligations that are the subject of the U.S. complaint. The United States also specifies with precision the service at issue: "electronic payment services for payment card transactions," and provides in its panel request a detailed narrative of the claims it is making in order to provide additional information for China to understand "the legal basis of the complaint." The U.S. panel request also indicates the following.

21. *China maintains requirements that mandate the use of CUP and/or establish CUP as the sole supplier of EPS for all domestic transactions denominated and paid in RMB.* China requires that all transactions denominated and paid in RMB in China be processed and cleared in RMB through CUP, and that where there is a choice, all domestic transactions on dual currency cards be routed in RMB through CUP.

22. *China maintains requirements that RMB denominated payment cards issued in China bear the CUP logo.* China requires that any bank cards issued in China for RMB purchases in China, including dual currency payment cards issued in China, must bear the CUP logo. This means that issuers – the institutions that issue payment cards to consumers – must have access to the CUP system, and must pay CUP for that access.

23. *China maintains requirements that all automated teller machines ("ATM"), merchant card processing equipment, and point of sale ("POS") terminals in China accept CUP cards.* China requires that all ATMs, merchant card processing equipment, and POS terminals in China be capable of accepting CUP cards. There are no equivalent requirements for non-CUP cards.

24. *China maintains requirements on acquiring institutions to post the CUP logo and be capable of accepting all bank cards bearing the CUP logo.* China requires that all acquiring institutions – the institutions that sign up merchants to accept payment cards – in China post the CUP logo and be capable of accepting all bank cards bearing the CUP logo. An acquiring institution, often a bank, provides POS terminal and processing equipment to merchants so it can process payment cards, maintains the merchant's account, handles relations with the merchant, and ensures that payments are properly credited to the merchant.

25. *China maintains broad prohibitions on the use of non-CUP cards.* China prohibits the use of domestically issued non-CUP payment cards where the issuing bank and acquiring bank are different. China also requires that all inter-bank transactions for all bank cards be handled through CUP.

26. *China maintains requirements pertaining to card-based electronic transactions in China, Macao and Hong Kong.* China requires that CUP be used to handle all RMB transactions in Macao or Hong Kong using bank cards issued in China. China also requires that CUP be used to handle any RMB transactions in China using RMB cards issued in Hong Kong or Macao.

27. The U.S. panel request also asserts that these measures are inconsistent with China's obligations under GATS Article XVI:1 and XVI:2 not to adopt or maintain measures of the types listed in Article XVI:2. The U.S. panel request also asserts that these measures are also inconsistent with China's obligations

under GATS Article XVII to accord to services and service suppliers of any other Member treatment no less favorable than that it accords to its own like services and service suppliers, in respect of all measures affecting the supply of services. Accordingly, the U.S. panel request is fully consistent with DSU Article 6.2, China's request is without merit, and the Panel should reject China's request and decide this case on its merits.

IV. THE U.S. PANEL REQUEST IDENTIFIES WITH PRECISION "ELECTRONIC PAYMENT SERVICES" FOR "PAYMENT CARD" TRANSACTIONS

28. The U.S. panel request identifies the specific measures at issue and provides a brief summary of the legal basis of the complaint that presents the problem clearly. As part of that summary, the United State also described the nature of the services at issue – "electronic payment services for payment card transactions." The United State further provides in the U.S. panel request footnotes that set out a description of those services and an illustrative list of payment cards. As explained above, this is more than adequate to satisfy the requirements of DSU Article 6.2. We also note that the description "electronic payment services" is known and customarily used by market participants. The United States further highlights the clarity of its panel request by presenting extensive evidence regarding the use of these terms.

29. Contrary to China's assertion that the description of the service as set out in the U.S. panel request is "a term of the United States' own making" the description is drawn from industry sources and reflects the broad and common understanding within this sector. Suppliers of the services at issue in this dispute who work within this sector are described as supplying, or characterize themselves as supplying, "electronic payment services" and as operating within the "global payments industry." In this submission the United States provides extensive evidence in support of this description of the sector at issue in this dispute and as specifically set out in the U.S. panel request – "electronic payment services" for "payment card" transactions.

30. A supplier of EPS enables cardholders' banks to pay merchants' banks the amount they are owed. Suppliers of electronic payment services supply, directly or indirectly, a system that typically includes the following:

- the processing infrastructure, network, and rules and procedures that facilitate, manage, and enable the transmission of transaction information and payments, and which provide system integrity, stability and financial risk reduction;
- the process and coordination of approving or declining a transaction, with approval generally permitting a purchase to be finalized or cash to be disbursed or exchanged;
- the delivery and transmission of transaction information among participating entities;

- the calculation, determination, and reporting of the net financial position of relevant institutions for all transactions that have been authorized in a given period; and
- the facilitation, management and/or other participation in the transfer of net payments owed among participating institutions.

31. Electronic payment services provide an efficient, timely and reliable means to facilitate the transmission of funds from the holders of payment cards who purchase goods or services to the individuals or businesses that supply them. The network, rules and procedures, and operating system that are part of the EPS architecture that allow processors of payment card transactions to pay merchants promptly the amounts they are owed, and to ensure that customers pay what they owe. EPS suppliers receive, check and transmit the information that the parties need to conduct the transactions, and manage, facilitate, and enable the transmission of funds between participating entities. The rules and procedures established by the EPS supplier give the payment system stability and integrity, and enable it to efficiently handle net flows of money among the institutions involved in card payments.

32. The two principal types of networks used in card-based electronic payment transactions are often referred to as either "open-loop" (or sometimes referred to as "four party" networks) and "closed-loop" (sometimes referred to as "three party" networks). EPS suppliers also provide their customers with certain guarantees to ensure the integrity of the electronic payment services, including, for example, instances where customers fail to honor payment cards or where issuers or acquirers fail to fund obligations.

33. In addition to the EPS supplier, other entities play a role in a payment card transaction:

- ***The issuing institution (or issuer).*** Issuing institutions solicit cardholders, establish individual credit limits, fix terms such as interest rates and fees, and issue payment cards. Debit cards are linked to the card holders' checking or savings account with the issuer, while credit cards provide an unsecured personal line of credit from the issuing bank. An institution seeking to issue cards must itself be capable of supplying EPS or must use an EPS supplier. Issuing institutions agree to adhere to specified rules that allow the EPS supplier to process transactions that use the cards issued by the bank. The issuer administers the cardholder's account and handles relations with the cardholder. The issuer is responsible for ensuring that the cardholder is able to pay, charging the cardholder for each purchase, and the transmission of funds to the EPS's settlement bank for settlement of payment obligations incurred by its cardholders.
- ***The acquiring institution.*** Acquiring institutions seek to "acquire" transactions on payment cards. Acquiring institutions, often a bank, provide point-of-sale terminals or payment card processing

equipment (*e.g.* a card swiper) to merchants so they can process payment cards. As with issuers, an acquiring institution must itself be capable of supplying EPS or must use an EPS supplier. Acquiring institutions also must adhere to specific rules governing transactions processed on the payment card transactions it has acquired. Acquiring institutions maintain merchant accounts, handle relations with the merchant, and ensure that payments are properly credited to the merchant.

- ***The settlement bank.*** In an open-loop (four party) network, the EPS's settlement bank manages the flow of money between issues and acquirers. Typically, issuers will transfer funds to the EPS's settlement bank, and the EPS's settlement bank will transfer funds to acquirers.

34. Outside of China, the competition to provide services for card-based electronic payment transactions is intense. EPS suppliers explain that they compete "in the global payment marketplace against all forms of payment, including paper-based forms (principally cash and checks)" and "card-based payments (including credit, charge, debit, ATM, prepaid, private-label and other types of general purpose and limited use cards)."

35. CUP is a significant and increasingly active participant in this competition and EPS suppliers describe CUP as a competitor. CUP's Articles of Association are explicit that the company is "to provide advanced electronic payment technologies and specialized services in connection with the inter-bank bank card information switching." CUP itself recently noted the global reach of its "payment services" around the world:

> As the bankcard association in China, China UnionPay operates the national inter-bank clearing and settlement system, develops the worldwide UnionPay Card acceptance network, promotes the issuance and usage of the UnionPay Card as well as other innovative payment solutions, so as to provide quality, efficient and safe payment services to cardholders. To date, the total number of the UnionPay Card issued both at home and aboard has exceeded 2.5 billion. The UnionPay network has been extended to all the cities and rural areas in China. In addition, China UnionPay has enabled the UnionPay Card acceptance over 110 countries and regions through extensive cooperation with about 400 financial institutions around the world.

36. As the discussion in above in section IV makes clear, the term "electronic payment services" as set out in the U.S. panel request is a commonly understood term for service supplied for payment card based electronic transactions, and, outside of China, there is intense global competition to provide these services, and CUP is an active competitor.

V. THE U.S. PANEL REQUEST IDENTIFIES SPECIFIC MEASURES OF CHINA THAT MAINTAIN CUP'S MONOPOLY ON THE SUPPLY OF EPS AND THAT AFFECT THE SUPPLY OF EPS BY FOREIGN SUPPLIERS

37. In addition to the narrative description of China's measures that maintain CUP's monopoly on the supply of EPS and that affect the supply of EPS by foreign suppliers, the U.S. panel request enumerated separate instruments. The U.S. panel request identifies the following:

- ***Requirements that mandate the use of CUP and/or establish CUP as the sole supplier of EPS for all domestic transactions denominated and paid in RMB.*** China imposes requirements that all transactions denominated and paid in RMB in China be processed and cleared in RMB through CUP, and that where there is a choice, all domestic transactions on dual currency cards be routed in RMB through CUP.
- ***Requirements on issuers that payment cards issued in China bear the CUP logo.*** China imposes requirements that any bank cards issued in China for RMB purchases in China, as well as any dual currency cards issued in China, must bear the CUP logo. In practice, this means that issuers must pay CUP for access to the CUP system.
- ***Requirements that all ATM and POS terminals in China accept CUP cards.*** China requires that all ATM, merchant card processing equipment, and point-of-sale terminals in China be capable of accepting CUP cards. There is no equivalent requirement for other non-CUP cards.
- ***Requirements on acquiring institutions to post the CUP Logo and be capable of accepting all bank cards bearing the CUP logo.*** China requires that all acquiring institutions in China post the CUP logo and be capable of accepting all bank cards bearing the CUP logo.
- ***Broad prohibitions on the use of non-CUP cards.*** China maintains broad prohibitions on the use of non-CUP cards for cross-region or inter-bank (cross-bank) transactions. China also requires that all inter-bank transactions for all bank cards be handled through CUP.
- ***Requirements in China, Macao, and Hong Kong.*** China also requires that CUP be used to handle all RMB transactions in Macao or Hong Kong using bank cards issued in China. In addition, China also requires that CUP be used to handle any RMB transactions in China using RMB cards issued in Hong Kong or Macao.

VI. THE U.S. PANEL REQUEST SPECIFIES THAT CHINA'S GATS SCHEDULE INCLUDES BOTH MARKET ACCESS AND NATIONAL TREATMENT COMMITMENTS WITH RESPECT TO "ALL PAYMENT AND MONEY TRANSMISSION SERVICES, INCLUDING CREDIT, CHARGE AND DEBIT CARDS..."

38. The Appellate Body has confirmed that the customary rules of treaty interpretation reflected in Articles 31 and 32 of the Vienna Convention apply to the interpretation of specific commitments in a Member's GATS Schedule. Article 31(1) of the *Vienna Convention* requires a treaty to be interpreted "in good faith in accordance with the ordinary meaning to be given to the terms of the treaty in their context and in the light of its object and purpose." The Appellate Body has stated that "the structure of the GATS necessarily implies two things. First, because the GATS covers *all* services except those supplied in the exercise of governmental authority, it follows that a Member may schedule a specific commitment in respect of *any* service. Second, because a Member's obligations regarding a particular service depend on the specific commitments that it has made with respect to the sector or subsector within which that service falls, a specific service cannot fall within two different sectors or subsectors. In other words, the sectors and subsectors in a Member's Schedule must be mutually exclusive."

39. EPS are at the center of all payment card transactions and without these services the transactions could not occur. EPS fall within the ordinary meaning of payment and money transmission services, within item (d) of China's Schedule. The language of item (d) itself makes this abundantly clear. First, as detailed extensively in this submission and described in greater detail below, EPS involve the services through which transactions involving payment cards are processed and through which transfers of funds between institutions participating in the transactions are managed and facilitated. EPS clearly fall within the ordinary meaning of "payment and money transmission services" as one type of "*all*" such services. Second, the phrase "all payment and money transmission services" is modified with an illustrative list that explicitly provides that it "include[s] credit, charge and debit cards." This explicit reference is in line with the recognition that EPS are integral to the processing of credit, charge, debit and other payment card-based electronic payment transactions, and without these services, payment card transactions could not occur. EPS suppliers such as Visa, MasterCard, and American Express are names recognized around the world as credit cards and charge cards. The reference to debit cards covers suppliers of EPS for debit card transactions like Visa, MasterCard, Discover, First Data, Pulse, NYCE, STAR, and PLUS.

VII. THE U.S. PANEL REQUEST SPECIFIES THAT CHINA'S MEASURES ARE INCONSISTENT WITH CHINA'S GATS MARKET ACCESS AND NATIONAL TREATMENT COMMITMENTS

40. In addition to identifying the service at issue, the specific measures at issue, and China's GATS commitments, the U.S. panel request specifies that China's measures that maintain CUP's monopoly on the supply of EPS and that affect the supply of EPS by foreign suppliers are inconsistent with China's obligations under GATS Article XVI:1 to accord services and services suppliers of any other Member treatment no less favorable that that provided for in China's Schedule and that China is maintaining or adopting measures set out in Article XVI:2. The U.S. panel request also states that these measures are inconsistent with China's obligations under GATS Article XVII to accord to services and service suppliers of any other Member treatment no less favorable than that it accords to its own like services and service suppliers.

VIII. CONCLUSION

41. The U.S. panel request is fully consistent with DSU Article 6.2. The U.S. panel request is in writing, indicates that consultations were held, identifies the specific measures at issue, and provides a brief summary of the legal basis of the complaint sufficient to present the problem clearly. Accordingly, the United States requests that the Panel reject in its entirety China's request for preliminary ruling.

ANNEX F-3

EXECUTIVE SUMMARY OF CHINA'S COMMENTS ON THE UNITED STATES' SUBMISSIONS IN RESPONSE TO CHINA'S REQUEST FOR A PRELIMINARY RULING

I. THE U.S. RESPONSE CONFIRMS THE INCONSISTENCY OF THE PANEL REQUEST WITH ARTICLE 6.2 OF THE DSU

1. The unprecedented scale of the U.S. response to China's request for a preliminary ruling – 64 pages of single-spaced text, with 62 accompanying exhibits – offers definitive proof that the U.S. panel request failed to "provide a brief summary of the legal basis of the complaint sufficient to present the problem clearly", as required by Article 6.2 of the DSU.

2. As far as China can discern, there is no material disagreement between the parties concerning the requirements of Article 6.2 or its associated jurisprudence. Apparently, the United States hopes that by supplying explanations and connections that are nowhere evident in the panel request, the Panel will be willing to overlook the fact that the U.S. panel request is deficient on its face. It is "well established", however, "that compliance with the requirements of Article 6.2 must be determined on the face of the request for the establishment of the panel and that defects therein cannot be 'cured' in the subsequent submissions of the parties during the panel proceedings."

3. In its response, the United States could have acknowledged the failure of the panel request to indicate which modes of supply are at issue, and attempted to defend this omission as consistent with the requirements of Article 6.2. Instead, the United States pretends that the panel request actually did put China on notice as to which modes of supply were at issue, stating that "[w]ith respect to each of the subsectors identified in the U.S. panel request, China undertook both market access and national treatment commitments for modes (1) and (3) as specified in its Schedule [and] [t]he commitments for each mode of supply for items (d), (k), and (l) in China's Schedule are specified therein."

4. As China understands this statement, the United States appears to be saying: (1) that it considers its claims to arise under Modes 1 and 3; and (2) that because Modes 1 and 3 are among the four modes of supply, the panel request "put China on notice" as to which modes of supply were at issue. Yet the panel request makes no reference whatsoever to the modes of supply. The fact that Modes 1 and 3 are among the four possible modes of supply did not, by itself, put China on notice as to which modes of supply were at issue and provide a sufficient basis for China to begin preparing its defence.

5. Furthermore, despite the belated explanations from the United States, the U.S. panel request remains unclear as to the legal relevance of the three distinct and mutually exclusive subsectors identified in the panel request. The United

States now asserts, categorically and unequivocally, that the entirety of what it calls "electronic payment services" is encompassed by subsector D, "all payment and money transmission services".

6. As with its belated indication of the modes of supply, the tone of the U.S. response is that it should have been self-evident to any reader of the panel request that the United States intended to encompass all of "electronic payment services" in subsector D. But taking two of the three subsectors off the table in a subsequent submission does not rectify the obvious lack of clarity in the panel request itself.

7. Indeed, the U.S. response only serves to deepen the confusion as to how the three subsectors relate to its claims in this dispute. Twice in its response, the United States implies that it intends to advance "separate claims" under each of the three subsectors identified in the panel request. If the United States intended to advance "separate claims" under three different and mutually exclusive subsectors, the time for setting forth these "separate claims" was in the panel request. But the panel request merely lists the three subsectors and makes an undifferentiated set of claims that the challenged measures are inconsistent with China's market access and national treatment commitments.

8. In sum, what Article 6.2 requires, and what is still missing from even the "amended" U.S. panel request, is a concise explanation of how the identified services relate to China's specific commitments in the identified subsectors and modes of supply. The inability of the United States to provide this explanation is further proof that the U.S. panel request does not "present the problem clearly" as required by Article 6.2.

II. CONCLUSION

9. There is now little doubt that the panel request provides an insufficient legal basis for this proceeding to continue. The course of action that is both prudent and required by Article 6.2 of the DSU is to require the United States to submit a revised panel request to the DSB.

ANNEX G

EXCERPT OF CHINA'S SCHEDULE

Contents		Page
Annex G-1	The People's Republic of China - Schedule of Specific Commitments, GATS/SC/135 – excerpt	5691

Modes of supply:
(1) Cross-border supply (2) Consumption abroad (3) Commercial presence (4) Presence of natural persons

Sector or sub-sector	Limitations on market access	Limitation on national treatment	Additional commitments
7. FINANCIAL SERVICES A. All Insurance and Insurance-Related Services[1]			
[…]	[…]	[…]	
B. Banking and Other Financial Services (excluding insurance and securities) Banking services as listed below: (a) Acceptance of deposits and other repayable funds from the public; (b) Lending of all types, including consumer credit, mortgage credit, factoring and financing of commercial transaction; (c) Financial leasing; (d) All payment and money - transmission services, including credit, charge and debit cards, travellers cheques and bankers drafts(including import and export settlement); (e) Guarantees and commitments;	(1) Unbound except for the following: . Provision and transfer of financial information, and financial data processing and related software by suppliers of other financial services; . Advisory, intermediation and other auxiliary financial services on all activities listed in subparagraphs (a) through (k), including credit reference and analysis, investment and portfolio research and advice, advice on acquisitions and on corporate restructuring and strategy. (2) None (3) A. *Geographic coverage* . For foreign currency business, there will be no geographic restriction upon accession. For local currency business, the geographic restriction will be phased out as	(1) None (2) None (3) Except for geographic restrictions and client limitations on local currency business (listed in the market access column),	For financial leasing services, foreign financial leasing corporations will be permitted to provide financial leasing service at the same time as domestic corporations.

[1] Any further authorization provided to foreign insurers after accession under more favorable conditions than those contained in this schedule (including the extension of grandfathered investments through branching, sub-branching or any other legal form), will be made available to other foreign service suppliers which so requested.

Sector or sub-sector	Limitations on market access	Limitation on national treatment	Additional commitments
(f) Trading for own account or for account of customers: foreign exchange.	follows: Upon accession, Shanghai, Shenzhen, Tianjin and Dalian; Within one year after accession, Guangzhou, Zhuhai, Qingdao, Nanjing and Wuhan; within two years after accession, Jinan, Fuzhou, Chengdu and . Chongqing; within three years after accession, Kunming, Beijing and Xiamen; Within four years after accession, Shantou, Ningbo, Shenyang and Xi'an. Within five years after accession, all geographic restrictions will be removed. B. *Clients* . For foreign currency business, foreign financial institutions will be permitted to provide services in China without restriction as to clients upon accession. . For local currency business, within two years after accession, foreign financial institutions will be permitted to provide services to Chinese enterprises. Within five years after accession, foreign financial institutions will be permitted to provide services to all Chinese clients. Foreign financial institutions licensed for local currency business in one region of China may service clients in any other region that has been opened for such business. C. *Licensing* . Criteria for authorization to deal in China's financial services sector are solely prudential (i.e., contain no economic needs test or quantitative limits on licenses). Within five years after accession, any existing non-prudential measures restricting ownership, operation, and juridical form of foreign financial institutions, including on internal branching and licenses, shall be eliminated. . Foreign financial institutions who meet the following condition are permitted to establish a subsidiary of a foreign bank or a foreign finance	foreign financial institution may do business, without restrictions or need for case-by-case approval, with foreign invested enterprises, non-Chinese natural persons, Chinese natural persons and Chinese enterprises. Otherwise, none.	

Sector or sub-sector	Limitations on market access	Limitation on national treatment	Additional commitments
	company in China: - total assets of more than US $10 billion at the end of the year prior to filing the application. . Foreign financial institutions who meet the following condition are permitted to establish a branch of a foreign bank in China: - total assets of more than US $20 billion at the end of the year prior to filing the application. . Foreign financial institutions who meet the following condition are permitted to establish a Chinese-foreign joint bank or a Chinese-foreign joint finance company in China: - total assets of more than US $10 billion at the end of the year prior to filing the application. . Qualifications for foreign financial institutions to engage in local currency business are as follows: - three years business operation in China and being profitable for two consecutive years prior to the application, otherwise, none. (4) Unbound except as indicated in horizontal commitments.	(4) Unbound except as indicated in horizontal commitments.	
. Motor vehicle financing by non-bank financial institutions	(1) Unbound except for the following: . Provision and transfer of financial information, and financial data processing and related software by suppliers of other financial services; . Advisory, intermediation and other auxiliary financial services on all activities listed in subparagraphs (a) through (k), including credit reference and analysis, investment and portfolio research and advice, advice on acquisitions and on corporate restructuring and strategy. (2) None (3) None (4) Unbound except as indicated in horizontal commitments.	(1) Unbound (2) None (3) None (4) Unbound except as indicated in horizontal commitments.	
. Other financial services as listed below: (k)Provision and transfer of financial information, and financial data processing and	(1) None (2) None (3) None (Criteria for authorization to deal in China's financial services sector are solely prudential (i.e.,	(1) None (2) None (3) None	

Sector or sub-sector	Limitations on market access	Limitation on national treatment	Additional commitments
related software by supplier of other financial services; (l) Advisory, intermediation and other auxiliary financial services on all activities listed in subparagraphs (a) through (k), including credit reference and analysis, investment and portfolio research and advice, advice on acquisitions and on corporate restructuring and strategy.	contain no economic needs test or quantitative limits on licenses). Branches of foreign institutions are permitted. (4) Unbound except as indicated in horizontal commitments.	(4) Unbound except as indicated in horizontal commitments.	
. Securities	(1) Unbound except for the following: . Foreign securities institutions may engage directly (without Chinese intermediary) in B share business. (2) None (3) (a) Unbound, except for the following: . Upon accession, representative offices in China of foreign securities institutions may become Special Members of all Chinese stock exchanges. . Upon accession, foreign service suppliers will be permitted to establish joint ventures with foreign investment up to 33 per cent to conduct domestic securities investment fund management business. Within three years after China's accession, foreign investment shall be increased to 49 per cent. Within three years after accession, foreign securities institutions will be permitted to establish joint ventures, with foreign minority ownership not exceeding 1/3, to engage (without Chinese intermediary) in underwriting A shares and in underwriting and trading of B and H shares as well as government and corporate debts, launching of funds. (b).Criteria for authorization to deal in China's financial industry are solely prudential (i.e., contain no economic needs test or quantitative limits on licenses). (4) Unbound except as indicated in horizontal commitments.	(1) None (2) None (3) None (4) Unbound except as indicated in horizontal commitments.	

ANNEX H

TABLE OF TRANSLATIONS OF LEGAL MEASURES AND OTHER INSTRUMENTS[1]

Contents		Page
Annex H-1	Table of translations of legal measures and other instruments referred to by the parties	5695

DOCUMENT NO.	TRANSLATION BY UNITED STATES	TRANSLATION BY CHINA	TRANSLATION AGREED BY PARTIES / TRANSLATION SUGGESTED BY UNOG
CUP's Articles of Association Exhibit US-20	*Art. 11* The purpose of the Company: by adopting advanced and practical technical means and scientific and flexible operational and managerial methods, to set up and operate a unified, highly efficient and safe inter-bank bank card information exchange network across the country, ensure the inter-bank common use of bank cards and the joint development of bank card business, provide specialized services with regard to the inter-bank bank card information exchange, improve the environment for bank card use, and promote the rapid development of China's bank card industry.	[No Chinese Exhibit]	[See the parties' translations]
	Art. 12 Upon being registered according to law, the business scope of the Company is as follows: (1) to establish and operate a single nationwide inter-bank bank card information switching network; (2) to provide advanced electronic payment technologies and specialized services in connection with the inter-bank bank card information switching; (3) and to engage in bankcard technological innovation; (4) to manage and operate the brand of "UnionPay";	[No Chinese Exhibit]	[See the parties' translations]

[1] This annex is available in English only, as it specifically relates to Chinese-to-English translations.

DOCUMENT NO.	TRANSLATION BY UNITED STATES	TRANSLATION BY CHINA	TRANSLATION AGREED BY PARTIES / TRANSLATION SUGGESTED BY UNOG
	(5) to formulate the code and technical standards for inter-bank bank card transactions, and to mediate and arbitrate any business disputes arising out of inter-bank transactions; (6) to organize trainings for the industry, business seminars and international exchange programs; and (7) to conduct related researches and consulting services; and to conduct such other related businesses as may be approved by competent authorities.		
Notification of Approval of CUP's Business Licence Exhibit US-29	*Business Scope* To establish and operate a single nationwide inter-bank bank card information switching network, to provide advanced electronic payment technologies and specialized services in connection with the inter-bank bank card information switching, and to engage in bankcard technological innovation; to manage and operate the brand of "UnionPay", to formulate the code and technical standards for inter-bank bank card transactions, to mediate and arbitrate any business disputes arising out of inter-bank transactions, to organize trainings for the industry, business seminars and international exchange programs, and to conduct related researches and consulting services; and to conduct such other related businesses as may be approved by the People's Bank of China.	[No Chinese Exhibit]	[See the parties' translations]
Document No. 8 Exhibit US-46 Exhibit CHN-62	*Art. 6* Matters in relation to individual RMB bank card clearing shall be organized and handled by the clearance banks and ChinaUnionPay Joint Stock Co., Ltd. Mainland residents may use individual RMB bankcards issued by the domestic banks to pay for travelling expenses (such as shopping, meals, accommodation, transportation, and medical expenses) in Macao and to withdraw small-amounts of cash in Macao dollars from ATM machines in Macao but may not withdraw Renminbi cash. RMB bankcards issued to Macao individual residents by participating banks or their subsidiaries can be used to pay	*Art. 6* Matters in relation to individual RMB bankcards are organized and handled by the Clearing Bank and China UnionPay Co., Ltd. A mainland resident may use an individual RMB bankcards issued by a mainland bank to make payments in respect of touring and consumption in Macao for shopping, catering, accommodation, traffic, medical care, etc., and may withdraw a small amount of MOP cash on ATMs in Macao, but may not withdraw RMB cash. A RMB bankcard issued by a Participating Bank or its	[See the parties' translations]

DOCUMENT NO.	TRANSLATION BY UNITED STATES	TRANSLATION BY CHINA	TRANSLATION AGREED BY PARTIES / TRANSLATION SUGGESTED BY UNOG
	for individual expenses in Mainland China and to withdraw small amounts of RMB cash from ATM machines in Mainland China.	subsidiary to a Macao resident may be used to make payments in respect of individual consumption in the mainland, and to withdraw a small amount of RMB cash on ATMs in the mainland.	
Document No. 16 Exhibit US-44 Exhibit CHN-60	*Art. 6* Matters in relation to individual RMB bank card clearing shall be organized and handled by the clearance banks and China UnionPay Joint Stock Co., Ltd. Mainland residents may use individual RMB bank cards issued by the domestic banks to pay for travelling expenses (such as shopping, meals and accommodation) in Hong Kong and to withdraw small amounts of cash in Hong Kong dollars from ATM machines in Hong Kong. RMB bankcards issued to Hong Kong individual residents by participating banks or their subsidiaries can be used to pay for individual expenses in Mainland China and to withdraw small amounts of RMB cash from ATM machines in Mainland China.	*Art. 6* Matters in relation to individual RMB bankcard clearing are organized and handled by the clearing banks and China UnionPay Co., Ltd. Mainland residents may use the individual RMB bankcards issued by mainland banks to make payments in respect of touring and consumption in Hong Kong for shopping, catering, lodging, etc., and may withdraw a small amount of HKD cash on ATMs in Hong Kong. The RMB bankcards issued by the participating banks or their subsidiaries to Hong Kong residents may be used in the mainland to make payments for individual consumption and withdraw a small amount of RMB cash on ATMs in the mainland.	*Art. 6 – **UNOG translation**:* The clearance of individual RMB bankcards will be organized and handled by the clearing banks and China UnionPay Co., Ltd. Mainland residents may use individual RMB bankcards issued by mainland banks to make payments in Hong Kong for such travelling expenses as shopping, meals and lodging, and may withdraw small amounts of cash in Hong Kong dollars from ATMs in Hong Kong. RMB bankcards issued to Hong Kong residents by participating banks or their subsidiaries may be used to make payments for individual expenses and to withdraw small amounts of cash in RMB from ATMs on the mainland.
Document No. 17 Exhibit US-52 Exhibit CHN-53	*Art. 5* Bank cards are classified into credit cards and debit cards. Bank cards may be classified into RMB cards and foreign currency cards according to the currency type; entity cards (commercial card) and individual cards according to the target of issuance; and magnetic cards and integrated circuit (IC) cards according to the information carrier.	*Art. 5* Bankcards include credit cards and debit cards. Bankcards can be classified into RMB cards and foreign currency cards according to different currencies of the cards; entity cards (commercial cards) and individual cards according to different issue targets; and magnetic cards and integrated circuit (IC) cards according to different information carriers.	[See the parties' translations]
	Art. 7 Debit cards may be classified into cards for transferring accounts (including savings cards, same as below), cards for special purposes and stored-value cards. Debit cards do not possess the overdrawing function.	*Art. 7* According to different functions, debit cards can be classified into account transferring cards (including stored value cards, similarly hereafter), special use cards and stored value cards. Debit	[See the parties' translations]

DOCUMENT NO.	TRANSLATION BY UNITED STATES	TRANSLATION BY CHINA	TRANSLATION AGREED BY PARTIES / TRANSLATION SUGGESTED BY UNOG
		cards do not have overdraw function.	
	Art. 8 The card for transferring accounts refers to the debit card which makes real-time deduction of accounts. It possesses such functions as transfer, settlement, depositing and withdrawing cash, and consumption.	*Art. 8* An account transferring card refers to a debit card which provides instant deduction service. It provides functions including account transferring and clearing, cash deposit and withdrawal, and consuming, etc..	[See the parties' translations]
	Art. 9 The card for special purpose refers to the debit card which is for any special purpose and used in certain specially designated areas. It possesses such functions as transfer, settlement, depositing and withdrawing cash. Special purpose refers to a purpose other than those in the industries of general merchandise, catering, restaurant and entertainment.	*Art. 9* A special use card refers to a debit card used in specific areas for specific purposes. Its provides functions including account transferring and clearing, cash deposit and withdrawal, etc.. Special use means being used other than in the industries of general merchandise, catering, dining and entertainment.	[See the parties' translations]
	Art. 10 Stored-value card refers to purse-style debit card which requires advance payment, and when the card-issuing bank transfers the money of the cardholder into this card upon the request of the cardholder and the money is deducted from the card when a transaction is made.	*Art. 10* A stored value card refers to prepaid wallet-style debit card which allows to transfer the cardholder's funds to the card for storage according to the cardholder's requirements and deduct money from this card directly when a transaction is made.	[See the parties' translations]
	Art. 27 [See agreed translation]	*Art. 27* [See agreed translation]	*Art. 27* – ***Translation agreed by parties***: Commercial banks, when acting as agents for overseas bankcard acquiring services, shall charge a merchant settlement commission, which shall be no less than four percent of the transaction amount.

DOCUMENT NO.	TRANSLATION BY UNITED STATES	TRANSLATION BY CHINA	TRANSLATION AGREED BY PARTIES / TRANSLATION SUGGESTED BY UNOG
	Art. 30 [See agreed translation]	*Art. 30* [See agreed translation]	*Art. 30* - ***Translation agreed by parties***: As for the account of a foreign currency entity card, funds shall be deposited by means of transferring from the foreign exchange account of the entity, and no cash in foreign currency may be deposited or withdrawn within the territory of China. The foreign exchange account of the entity shall satisfy the following conditions: (1) The account shall be opened according to relevant provisions issued by the People's Bank of China regarding the administration of foreign exchange accounts within the territory of China; (2) The specific items of payment shall be indicated accordingly within the scope of the revenue and expenditure of the foreign exchange account.
	Art. 48 [See agreed translation]	*Art. 48* [See agreed translation]	*Art. 48* - ***Translation agreed by parties***: Where losses are still not fully recovered after taking measures listed under Article 47, the issuing bank shall apply the Administrative Measures on Reserves for Uncollectible Accounts, issued by the Ministry of Finance.
	Art. 64 A commercial bank (or financial institution) within the borders of the People's Republic of China shall, when issuing any variety of bank card (except those with the mark of any international credit card organization), implement the technical standards prescribed by the state. As for an entity card, relief stamp of such characteristics as "DWK" shall be made at a proper place of the bottom left of the card. The following elements shall be indicated on the surface of a bank card: name of the primary legal person of the card-issuing bank,	*Art. 64* Any type of bankcard issued by a commercial bank (or financial institution) within the territory of the People's Republic of China shall follow the technical standards prescribed by the state, except for those bankcards affixed with logos of international credit card organizations. With regard to an entity card, a relief stamp of such characters as "DWK" shall be marked at a proper place at the lower left of the card. The following information	[See the parties' translations]

DOCUMENT NO.	TRANSLATION BY UNITED STATES	TRANSLATION BY CHINA	TRANSLATION AGREED BY PARTIES / TRANSLATION SUGGESTED BY UNOG
	uniform brand name, brand mark (except the cards for special purposes), card number (except IC cards), points of attention for the cardholder, customer service telephone number, signature bar for the cardholder (except IC cards), etc.	shall be indicated on the surface of a bankcard: name of the card-issuing bank, brand name of the card, brand logo (except for cards with special purposes), card number (except IC cards), user attention, customer service telephone number, and signature bar for the cardholder (except IC cards), etc.	
	Art. 65 As for the domestic circulation and use of bank cards issued by other financial institutions and overseas institutions approved by the People's Bank of China as qualified for operating bank card business, these Measures shall apply.	*Art. 65* These measures are applicable to the circulation and use within the territory of the PRC of the bankcards issued by other financial institutions which have been approved by the People's Bank of China for operating bankcard business, or the bankcards issued by overseas institutions.	*Art. 65* – ***UNOG translation***: [*If overseas financial institutions are indeed subject to regulation by the domestic authorities*]: These measures [shall] apply to the domestic circulation and use of bankcards issued by other financial and overseas institutions authorized by the People's Bank of China to conduct bankcard operations. [*Or, if overseas financial institutions are NOT subject to regulation by the domestic authorities*]: These measures [shall] apply to the domestic circulation and use of bankcards issued by other financial institutions authorized by the People's Bank of China to conduct bankcard operations, and to bankcards issued by overseas institutions.
Document No. 37 Exhibit US-40 Exhibit CHN-54	*Art. 1.2(i)* By the end of this year, all commercial banks shall, in accordance with unified standards and specifications of bank cards, complete transformation of their bank card processing system, and make technical preparations for accepting bank cards bearing the CUP logo.	*Art. 1.2(i)* Before the end of this year, all Commercial Banks shall complete the transformation of their own bankcard business processing systems according to requirements of the uniform standards and specifications for bankcards and make technical preparation for accepting the cards bearing the "Yin Lian" logo.	*Art. 1.2(i)* – ***UNOG translation***: All commercial banks shall complete the transformation of their internal bankcard business processing systems before the end of this year, in accordance with the requirements of the uniform standards and specifications for bankcards, and make technical preparations for accepting cards bearing the "Yin Lian/UnionPay" logo.
	Art. 1.2(ii) The head office of the National Bank Card Information Exchange and all city centers shall basically	*Art. 1.2(ii)* The transformation of the switching system of the National Bankcard	[See the parties' translations]

DOCUMENT NO.	TRANSLATION BY UNITED STATES	TRANSLATION BY CHINA	TRANSLATION AGREED BY PARTIES / TRANSLATION SUGGESTED BY UNOG
	complete transformation of the exchange system by October 1 of this year and conduct various system joint adjustment work in cooperation with member banks to realize transaction information inter-bank transfer for bank cards bearing the CUP logo by the end of the year.	Information Center ("General Center") and the switching systems of the urban centers shall be completed basically before October 1 this year. Cooperate with the member banks in the collaborative adjustment of systems and realize the cross-bank transmission of transaction information for the cards bearing the "Yin Lian" logo before the end of the year.	
	Art. 1.2(iii) All commercial banks and city centers which have adopted POS integrated management shall, in conjunction with progress made in their business processing system transformation, speed up the transformation of terminal equipments such as ATM, POS, etc., and strive to complete all transformation tasks by the end of 2002. Before the end of this year, transformation in all municipalities directly under the Central Government, provincial capitals and in Shenzhen, Dalian, Xiamen, Qingdao, Ningbo, etc. shall be basically completed. From the second quarter of this year, all terminal equipments such as ATM, POS etc. newly placed by all commercial banks (centers) shall comply with the requirements of unified standards and specifications, to avoid repetitive transformation.	*Art. 1.2(iii)* All commercial banks and the urban centers that apply the POS centralized management mode shall, according to the transformation progress of their own business processing system, hasten the transformation of the terminals, e.g. ATM and POS, and try to complete all transformation before the end of 2002. Before the end of this year, transformation shall basically be completed in the municipalities directly under the Central Government, the provincial capital cities and Shenzhen, Dalian, Xiamen, Qingdao and Ningbo, etc.. From the second quarter of this year, terminals, e.g. ATM and POS, which are newly launched by the commercial banks (centers), shall meet requirements of the uniform standards and specifications to obviate the need for further transformation.	[See the parties' translations]
	Art. 2.1(i) Bank cards issued by all commercial banks with inter-bank usability in China must bear the CUP logo at the specified position on the front of the cards, and all RMB credit cards issued solely for domestic use must also bear the CUP special anti-counterfeiting logo at the specified position, provided that special cards issued solely for specific regions or for specific usage shall not use the CUP logo:	*Art. 2.1(i)* All the bankcards issued by Commercial Banks for domestic cross-bank use must bear the "Yin Lian" logo printed uniformly at the designated position on the front of the cards. The RMB credit card limited to domestic interoperable use shall also bear the special anti-counterfeiting mark of the "Yin Lian" at the designated position.	[See the parties' translations]

DOCUMENT NO.	TRANSLATION BY UNITED STATES	TRANSLATION BY CHINA	TRANSLATION AGREED BY PARTIES / TRANSLATION SUGGESTED BY UNOG
		However, the "Yin Lian" logo shall not be used on the special usage cards which are limited to use in a certain region or a particular purpose.	
	Art. 2.1(ii) All terminals (such as ATM and POS) which join the nationwide bank card inter-bank processing network must be capable of accepting all bank cards bearing the CUP logo and must post the CUP logo; and	*Art. 2.1(ii)* The terminals, e.g. ATM and POS, which have joined the national bankcard cross-bank switching network, must be able to accept any type of bankcards with the "Yin Lian" logo, and must bear the "Yin Lian" logo.	[See the parties' translations]
	Art. 2.1(iii) All cards bearing the CUP logo must strictly abide by the unified technical specifications and all bank card issuers must provide corresponding cross-region and inter-bank services pursuant to the unified business specifications.	*Art. 2.1(iii)* All bankcards bearing the "Yin Lian" logo must be in strict compliance with uniform technical standards. Card issuing banks must provide corresponding cross-regional and cross-bank services as required by uniform business specifications.	[See the parties' translations]
	Art. 2.2(i) Starting this year, all commercial banks shall arrange the replacement of all bank cards which do not conform to the unified requirements and the CUP logo usage requirements and will basically complete the work by the end of 2003. Starting in 2004, all bank cards not bearing a CUP logo will not be used for cross-region or inter-bank transactions; and	*Art. 2.2(i)* From this year, all Commercial Banks shall make overall arrangements for the replacement of the bankcards that do not meet the uniform standards and the requirements for the use of the "Yin Lian" logo, and the replacement shall basically be completed before the end of 2003. From 2004, any bank's bankcards issued without the "Yin Lian" logo may not be used for cross-region or cross-bank transactions.	[See the parties' translations]
	Art. 2.2(ii) By the end of this year, all state-owned banks shall issue bank cards bearing the CUP logo in the five cities of Beijing, Shanghai, Guangzhou, Shenzhen and Hangzhou, and shall gradually issue these cards in other cities in consideration of their progress in terminal equipment transformation. Joint stock commercial banks, urban commercial banks and postal savings institutions shall endeavor to issue the bank cards bearing the	*Art. 2.2(ii)* Before the end of this year, the State-owned commercial banks shall introduce bankcards bearing the "Yin Lian" logo in the five cities of Beijing, Shanghai, Guangzhou, Shenzhen and Hangzhou before gradually spreading the same into other cities according to the transformation progress of the terminal acceptance equipments of the banks.	[See the parties' translations]

DOCUMENT NO.	TRANSLATION BY UNITED STATES	TRANSLATION BY CHINA	TRANSLATION AGREED BY PARTIES / TRANSLATION SUGGESTED BY UNOG
	CUP logo in the said cities this year.	Joint-stock and urban commercial banks and postal saving institutions shall also strive to introduce the bankcards bearing the "Yin Lian" logo in the aforementioned cities within the year.	
	Art. 3.1(i) Commercial banks which have opened bank card business in China must join the nationwide bank card inter-bank exchange network, to complete the interoperability of its bank card business processing system and nationwide bank card inter-bank processing network.	*Art. 3.1(i)* The commercial banks that operate bankcard business within the territory of China must join the national bankcard cross-bank switching network in order to realize the interoperability between their own bankcard business processing systems and the national bankcard cross-bank switching network.	[See the parties' translations]
Document No. 49 Exhibit US-62 Exhibit CHN-68	*Art. IV* [See agreed translation]	*Art. IV* [See agreed translation]	*Art. IV – **Translation agreed by parties***: A wholly foreign-funded bank or Chinese-foreign equity joint bank which plans to issue bank cards shall abide by the bank card business and technical standards as formulated by the People's Bank of China and meet the general requirements regarding the network for bankcard interoperability.
Document No. 53 Exhibit US-51 Exhibit CHN-71	*Art. V.2* Domestic card transactions inside China shall be settled in RMB through domestic clearing channels after subtracting the amount of cash in foreign currencies withdrawn over the counter. Any overdraft arising from domestic transactions shall be paid by the cardholder in RMB.	*Art. V.2* Transactions occurring within the territory of China with domestic cards shall, after the deduction of the amount of the cash in any foreign currency withdrawn over the counter, be cleared in RMB through domestic clearing channels. Any overdrawn amounts arising from domestic transactions shall be paid in RMB by the card holder.	[See the parties' translations]
	Art. V.3 If, for any reason, the clearing of transactions made inside China with domestic cards is made through an international bank card organization, the card-issuing financial institution may, after clearing in foreign currency,	*Art. V.3* Where transactions occurring within the territory of China with domestic cards are cleared through an international bankcard organization for a particular reason, upon the completion	*Art. V.3 - **UNOG translation:*** Where, under special circumstances, domestic-card transactions occurring within China are cleared through an international bankcard organization, the

DOCUMENT NO.	TRANSLATION BY UNITED STATES	TRANSLATION BY CHINA	TRANSLATION AGREED BY PARTIES / TRANSLATION SUGGESTED BY UNOG
	purchase exchange with the RMB funds to make up the foreign exchange that has been used in the clearing. "Clearing through an international bank card organization" refers to two circumstances: the clearing of domestic transactions made with domestic foreign currency cards through a international bank card organization; and "wrong throw", in which the clearing is made through an international bank card organization due to the merchant service institution's mistreating a domestic home-foreign currency card as a foreign currency card, which, when used within the territory of China, shall be regarded as a RMB card.	of the clearing in foreign currencies, the card-issuing financial institutions may use the RMB repaid by the card holders to purchase foreign exchanges to reimburse for the foreign exchange paid in advance. A transaction might be cleared through an international bankcard organization under the following two circumstances: (1) Transactions occurring within the territory of China with domestic foreign currency cards are cleared through an international bankcard organization; (2) A "wrong throw" transaction, which refers to the circumstance where a transaction occurring within the territory of China with a domestic dual currency card, which should have been processed same as that of a RMB card, was mistakenly identified by an acquiring financial institution as a foreign currency card and thus processed through an international bankcard organization.	card-issuing financial institutions may, after completing the clearing in foreign currencies, purchase foreign exchange using the RMB repaid by the card holders to make up for the foreign exchange already advanced. Clearance through an international bankcard organization occurs under one of two circumstances: (1) where domestic foreign-currency card transactions occurring within China are cleared through an international bankcard organization; and (2) "wrong hand- off" transactions, in which domestic dual-currency cards, which should be treated as RMB cards, are mistakenly identified by the acquiring financial institution as foreign-currency cards and thus handed off to an inter-national bankcard organization for clearance.
	Art. VII.3 [See agreed translation]	*Art. VII.3* [See agreed translation]	*Art. VII.3* – ***Translation agreed by parties***: Domestic RMB card clearing organizations shall do a good job in the RMB clearing of domestic transactions of home-foreign currency cards. Card-issuing financial institutions must report the bank identification number of their cards to the domestic RMB card clearing organization for the acquiring financial institution to download. The merchant service financial institutions shall properly set up their bank card systems under which RMB cards precede others when being read.

DOCUMENT NO.	TRANSLATION BY UNITED STATES	TRANSLATION BY CHINA	TRANSLATION AGREED BY PARTIES / TRANSLATION SUGGESTED BY UNOG
Document No. 57 Exhibit US-41 Exhibit CHN-55	*Art. 1* All bank cards issued by commercial banks solely for domestic interoperable use must bear the CUP logo at the specified position at the lower right corner on the front of the cards, and all RMB credit cards issued solely for domestic interoperable use must also bear the CUP holographic anti-counterfeiting logo at the specified position at the lower right corner on the front of the cards. Commercial banks have the discretion to decide whether to place the CUP holographic logo on their RMB debit cards issued solely for domestic interoperable use, but shall not use any anti-counterfeit logo other than the CUP holographic anti-counterfeit logo.	*Art. 1* The bankcards issued by the commercial banks only for domestic interoperable use must bear a uniform "Yin Lian" logo printed at the designated position on the lower right side of the card front. The RMB credit cards only for domestic interoperable use shall also bear the holographic anti-counterfeiting mark of the "Yin Lian" logo at the designated position on the lower right side of the card front. With respect to the RMB debit cards only for domestic interoperable use, the commercial banks may decide by themselves whether to use the holographic anti-counterfeiting mark thereon, but no anti-counterfeiting mark other than the holographic anti-counterfeiting mark of the "Yin Lian" logo may be used.	*Art. 1* - ***UNOG translation***: Bank cards issued by all commercial banks solely for domestic interoperable use must bear the uniform "Yin Lian/UnionPay" logo printed at the specified position at the lower right corner on the front of the cards, and the "Yin Lian/UnionPay" holographic anti-counterfeiting logo shall also be added at the specified position at the lower right corner on the front of RMB credit cards issued solely for domestic interoperable use. Commercial banks have the discretion to decide whether to place a holographic anti-counterfeiting logo on their RMB debit cards issued solely for domestic interoperable use, but shall not use any anti-counterfeit logo other than the "Yin Lian/ UnionPay" holographic anti-counterfeit logo.
	Art. 2 All "dual account" bank cards issued by any commercial banks for both domestic and foreign interoperable use must bear the unified CUP logo at the specified position at the upper right corner on the front of the cards.	*Art. 2* The "dual-account" bankcards issued by the commercial banks for both domestic and foreign interoperable use must bear a uniform "Yin Lian" logo printed at the designated position on the upper right side of the card front.	*Art. 2* - ***UNOG translation***: "Dual-account" bankcards issued by all commercial banks for both domestic and foreign interoperable use must bear a uniform "Yin Lian/UnionPay" logo printed at the designated position on the upper right side of the card front.
	Art. 3 From the issuance date of this Circular, bank cards which are newly issued by commercial banks upon application with cross-region or inter-bank use function must comply with the unified 'Business Specifications for Interoperable Service of Bank Cards' and relevant technical standards. The commercial banks must submit to PBOC a card sample which complies with the use requirements of CUP logo in accordance with the requirements of this Circular.	*Art. 3* From the date of issuing this Circular, all bankcards for cross-regional or cross-bank use that are newly issued by commercial banks upon their application, must comply with requirements of the "Business Specifications for Bankcard Interoperability" and other relevant technical standards, and, a sample card that complies with the requirements for the use of the "Yin Lian" logo must be submitted to the People's Bank of China according to requirements of this Circular.	[See the parties' translations]

DOCUMENT NO.	TRANSLATION BY UNITED STATES	TRANSLATION BY CHINA	TRANSLATION AGREED BY PARTIES / TRANSLATION SUGGESTED BY UNOG
	Art. 4 In order to effectively prevent risks to the bank card business from various counterfeiting activities, the CUP holographic anti-counterfeit logo is produced by designated agents and operated under special control. The Zhongchao Credit Card Plant under China Banknote Printing and Minting Company is responsible for unified production and sales. By July 1, 2001, China Banknote Printing and Minting Company shall complete various product designs and related production preparation for the CUP holographic anti-counterfeit logo. The National Bank card Office is responsible for the use of the CUP logo and for making specific management rules on printing, marketing, transportation and other management work of the CUP holographic anti-counterfeit logo and shall also be responsible for supervising the implementation of such rules.	*Art. 4* To effectively prevent the risks to bankcard business arising from forgery, the holographic label for anti-counterfeiting of "Yin Lian" will be made and sold by the credit card factory under China Banknote Printing and Minting Corporation through fixed-point production and operation under special control. Before July 1, 2001, China Banknote Printing and Minting Corporation shall complete the product design and related production preparations for the holographic label for anti-counterfeiting of "Yin Lian". The National Bankcard Office is responsible for formulating specific management measures regarding the use of the "Yin Lian" logo and the printing, sales and transportation of the holographic label for anti-counterfeiting of "Yin Lian" and shall supervise the implementation thereof.	[See the parties' translations]
	Art. 5 All commercial banks shall take the job of promoting CUP logo use and acceptance seriously and gradually reduce the role of their own bank card brands in the market. Starting January 1 2004, all POS terminals and merchants in the bank card acceptance market must have the CUP logo posted.	*Art. 5* All commercial banks shall carefully promote the use and acceptance of the "Yin Lian" logo, and gradually phase out the role of their own card brands on the acceptance market. From January 1, 2004, all terminals and merchants in the bankcards acceptance market must bear the "Yin Lian" logo.	[See the parties' translations]
	Art. 6 Regional bank card interoperability logos produced and designed regionally shall be gradually abolished. Starting January 1, 2002, no bank cards allowed to bear any regional interoperability logo. Starting January 1, 2004, the specially engaged merchants of bank cards and terminal equipment such as ATM, POS, etc. shall not bear any regional card interoperability logo.	*Art. 6* Logos designed and produced by each region for its regional interoperability of bankcards shall be phased out gradually. From January 1, 2002, logos for regional interoperability of bankcards shall not be used by bankcard merchants or on bankcard terminals such as ATM or POS.	[See the parties' translations]

DOCUMENT NO.	TRANSLATION BY UNITED STATES	TRANSLATION BY CHINA	TRANSLATION AGREED BY PARTIES / TRANSLATION SUGGESTED BY UNOG
Document No. 76 Exhibit US-56/ US-63 Exhibit CHN-56	*Paragraph 2 of the Notice* The Business Practices shall apply to all commercial banks, postal savings and remittance bureaus and rural credit cooperatives which are participating in bankcard service in China, all Interoperating Bank cards and relevant cross-bank business;	*Paragraph 2 of the Notice* The Specifications apply to all commercial banks, postal saving and remittance bureaus and rural credit cooperatives which operate bankcard business within the territory of China, as well as to all networked bankcards and relevant cross-bank business.	[See the parties' translations]
	Paragraph 3 of the Notice [See agreed translation]	*Paragraph 3 of the Notice* [See agreed translation]	*Paragraph 3 of the Notice – **Translation agreed by parties***: From the date of implementation of the Business Practices to the end of Year 2001, all acquiring banks that have been participating in bank card acceptance business shall meet the relevant requirements of the Business Practices; the card- issuing Banks shall start compulsory businesses, and shall complete the bank card processing system reform in combination with the implementation of technical standards of various bank cards. All Bank Card Information Exchange Centers shall complete the system reform within a stipulated period of time, and shall carry out information switching and processing for relevant cross-bank service.
	Paragraph 4 of the Notice Before the establishment of a unified bank card industry organization, the State Bank Card Office shall be responsible for the interpretation of the Business Practices, and shall organize to amend the same according to business development needs.	*Paragraph 4 of the Notice* Before the establishment of the industrial organization for interoperability of bankcards, the National Bankcard Office ("NBCO") is responsible for interpreting the Specifications and organizing amendment thereof according to the business development.	[See the parties' translations]

DOCUMENT NO.	TRANSLATION BY UNITED STATES	TRANSLATION BY CHINA	TRANSLATION AGREED BY PARTIES / TRANSLATION SUGGESTED BY UNOG
	Paragraph 5 of the Notice [See agreed translation]	*Paragraph 5 of the Notice* [See agreed translation]	*Paragraph 5 of the Notice* – ***Translation agreed by parties***: From the date of implementing the Specifications, all bankcard business rules that are inconsistent with the Specifications shall be abolished.
	Appendix, Chapter I, Art.1.1 Purpose These Business Practices aim to promote the bank card interoperable service in China, to establish a business practice system for bank card interoperation, to regulate bank card cross-bank operation, to improve the bank card utilization environment, to achieve the use of bank cards throughout the country, and to promote the development of bank card business.	*Appendix, Chapter I, Art.1.1* Purpose The purpose of these Specifications is to promote the interoperability of our bankcard business, establish a system of business specifications for the bankcard interoperability, standardize the cross-bank business operations of bankcards, improve the environment for use of bankcards, achieve the nationwide use of bankcards and boost the development of the bankcard business.	[See the parties' translations]
	Appendix, Chapter I, Art.1.3 [See agreed translation]	*Appendix, Chapter I, Art.1.3* [See agreed translation]	*Appendix, Chapter I, Art.1.3* – ***Translation agreed by parties***: These Business Practices apply to each of the commercial banks and non-bank financial institutions participating in bank card interoperable services, various types of interoperated bank cards and relevant cross-bank businesses.
	Appendix, Chapter I, Art. 2.1 [See agreed translation]	*Appendix, Chapter I, Art. 2.1* [See agreed translation]	*Appendix, Chapter I, Art. 2.1* – ***Translation agreed by parties***: After applying for membership of a BJO and becoming its formal member, a Bankcard Financial Institution will be eligible to apply for participation in bankcard interoperability business and becoming a network member.

DOCUMENT NO.	TRANSLATION BY UNITED STATES	TRANSLATION BY CHINA	TRANSLATION AGREED BY PARTIES / TRANSLATION SUGGESTED BY UNOG
	Appendix, Chapter I, Art. 4.1 Purpose The purpose is to regulate and develop the domestic bank card acquiring market, to facilitate customers acquiring and training, and to set up a unified bank card network logo while carrying out interoperating business.	*Appendix, Chapter I, Art. 4.1* Purpose To standardize and develop domestic bankcard acceptance market and facilitate the acceptance and training of merchants, a uniform bankcard networking logo will be created concurrently with the implementation of networked interoperability business.	[See the parties' translations]
	Appendix, Chapter I, Art. 4.2 Network Logo The logo of the network is comprised of the Chinese character of "UnionPay" and a graph symbolizing the united network, which has been formulated by the United Association and registered with the trademark registration bureau. The United Association possesses the ownership in and the use and management right of the logo, and promulgates administrative measures for the production, utilization etc. of the network logo.	*Appendix, Chapter I, Art. 4.2* Networking Logo Composed of the Chinese characters of "Yin Lian" and the pattern symbolizing the network, the networking logo is made by BJO and registered with the trademark bureau. Its ownership and use management right both belong to BJO, which will draw up the management measures for the making and use of the networking logo.	[See the parties' translations]
	Appendix, Chapter I, Art. 4.3 Use right of logo The Interoperating Members automatically obtain the right to use the logo as from the date on which cross-bank business is officially carried out thereby upon approval of the United Association.	*Appendix, Chapter I, Art. 4.3* Logo Use Right Networked members obtain the logo use right automatically starting from the day their cross-bank business is launched formally with the approval of BJO.	[See the parties' translations]

DOCUMENT NO.	TRANSLATION BY UNITED STATES	TRANSLATION BY CHINA	TRANSLATION AGREED BY PARTIES / TRANSLATION SUGGESTED BY UNOG
	Appendix, Chapter I, Art. 4.4 Use of logo A. The network logo is used by Interoperating Bank cards of all Interoperating Members, terminal equipment and processing premises, advertising and promoting materials for bank card business of each Interoperating Member, etc. B. Each Interoperating Member shall use the network logo according to the requirements, and shall not change the logo without permission. C. While providing training for the Designated Merchants, the Interoperating Members must promote the united network logo and provide training in relation to the logo, and must instruct the customers to accept all bank cards bearing the united network logo. D. The Interoperating Members shall obtain the written consent of the United Association if they make use of the logo beyond the scope of the interoperable business.	*Appendix, Chapter I, Art. 4.4* Use of Logo A. The networking logo is used for all networked bankcards, terminals and acceptance sites of all networked members as well as the advertising publicity they conduct for bankcard business. B. Networked members shall use the networking logo as required and shall not take the liberty to change it. C. When training their merchants, networked members must publicize the networking logo, train them in the use of it and require them to accept all bankcards bearing the logo. D. Networked members must obtain the written approval of BJO before using the logo outside the networked interoperability business.	[See the parties' translations]
	Appendix, Chapter I, Art. 5.2.1 Qualification of interoperability The Bank-Card Financial Institutions shall first join the United Association in order to apply for interoperability, and the other Professional Service Institutions shall obtain specific acknowledgement from the United Association in order to apply for interoperability.	*Appendix, Chapter I, Art. 5.2.1* Network Access Eligibility A Bankcard Financial Institution that applies for network access must join the BJO first. Other specialized service institutions that apply for network access must obtain the special approval of BJO.	[See the parties' translations]
	Appendix, Chapter I, Art. 5.2.2 Requirement for system The Interoperating Banks shall have secure and highly efficient computer processing system, and shall meet the technical specifications and standards of the National Bank Card Networks.	*Appendix, Chapter I, Art. 5.2.2* Requirement for System A Networked Bank must have a secure and efficient computer processing system that meets the technical specifications and standards of the National Bankcard Center.	[See the parties' translations]

DOCUMENT NO.	TRANSLATION BY UNITED STATES	TRANSLATION BY CHINA	TRANSLATION AGREED BY PARTIES / TRANSLATION SUGGESTED BY UNOG
	Appendix, Chapter I, Art. 5.2.3 Business requirements An Interoperating Bank can be either an Issuing Bank or an Acquiring Bank, and can be both an Issuing Bank and an Acquiring Bank. If an Interoperating Bank is an Issuing Bank, when interoperating, it must comply with relevant industry standards for card and usage standard under *Bankcards Issuer Identification Code and Card Number, Bankcards Magnetic StripInformation Formats and Use Specifications, China Financial Integrated Circuit (IC) Card Specifications*; if it is an Acquiring Bank, when interoperating, its terminal equipments must comply with the requirements of *Bankcard Magnetic Strip Specifications of Sales Point Terminals (POS)* and other relevant regulations; meanwhile, its terminals for acceptance of IC cards shall comply with terminal standards under *China Financial Integrated Circuit (IC) Card Specifications*.	*Appendix, Chapter I, Art. 5.2.3* Requirements for Business A Networked Bank can be either a card-issuing bank or an acquiring bank or both. For network access as a card-issuing bank, it must observe relevant standards of the industry for cards and use thereof, including the *Identification Codes and Card Numbers of Bankcard-issuing Banks*, the *Specifications for the Format and Use of the Information on the Magnetic Stripes of bankcards* and the *Specifications of China for Financial Integrated Circuit (IC) Cards*; for network access as a card acquiring bank, it must have terminals that meet the requirements of the *Specifications for Points of Sales (POS) of Bank Magnetic Stripe Cards* and other relevant regulations, while the terminals that accept IC cards must also meet the criteria for terminals set out in the *Specifications of China for Financial Integrated Circuit (IC) Cards*.	[See the parties' translations]
	Appendix, Chapter II, Art. 1.2 Unified Logo The Unified Network Logo must be posted on the machines and equipment of any merchant developed by each Interoperating Member in accordance with relevant regulations of interoperability, and shall be posted on the merchant's cash machines.	*Appendix, Chapter II, Art. 1.2* Uniform Logo The machines and equipment of the merchants developed by networked members must be affixed with the uniform networking logo according to the regulations on networked interoperability, which must be placed or pasted on the checkout counter of the merchants.	[See the parties' translations]
	Appendix, Chapter IV, Art. 1.4 Principles of Settlement The national cross-bank funds settlement of bank cards shall be based on the settlement data provided by the Information Exchange Center. The settlement data of the Information Exchange Center shall be generated from transaction records of the	*Appendix, Chapter IV, Art. 1.4* Clearing Principle The national fund clearing of the cross-bank business of bankcards is based on the clearing data of the Information Switching Center, which are generated on the basis of the central	[See the parties' translations]

DOCUMENT NO.	TRANSLATION BY UNITED STATES	TRANSLATION BY CHINA	TRANSLATION AGREED BY PARTIES / TRANSLATION SUGGESTED BY UNOG
	Information Exchange Center and from the settlement documents submitted by Acquiring Banks. If the accounts of the Interoperating Members are inconsistent with those of the Information Exchange Center, the date of the Information Exchange Center shall be used as a basis for settlement first and, if any error is discovered after the settlement, such error shall be handled in accordance with relevant provisions of Errors Correction.	transaction records and the clearing documents uploaded by the acquiring banks. When a networked member cannot reconcile its account with the Information Switching Center, clearing shall take place first on the basis of the data of the Information Switching Center. If any error is found after the clearing, the relevant provisions on error handling shall apply.	
	Appendix, Chapter IV, Art. 3.2 Cross-bank transaction settlement not through the Headquarter Center Bank card cross-bank transactions transmitted only through the Regional Center (and not through the Headquarter Center) shall be handled by a Regional Center and its Interoperating Members by reference to measures for settlement of cross-bank transactions transmitted through the Headquarter Center.	*Appendix, Chapter IV, Art. 3.2* Clearing of Transactions That Do not Go through General Center The cross-bank transactions of bankcards that are diverted only through a regional center (rather than through the General Center) are handled by the regional centers and their networked members according to the clearing methods for the cross-bank transactions diverted through the General Center.	[See the parties' translations]
	Appendix, Chapter X Supplemental Provisions All bank cards referred to in these Business Practices shall adopt the definitions and classifications in the *Measures for the Administration of Bank Card Business* by PBOC. These Business Practices are not applicable to the situation where a foreign currency card issued outside China is used in China. The State Bank Card Office will be responsible for the interpretation of these Business Practices. These Business Practices shall be implemented as from the date of promulgation by PBOC.	*Appendix, Chapter X* Supplementary Provisions The bankcards mentioned herein are subject to the definition and classification in the *Administrative Measures for Bankcard Business* of the People's Bank of China. These Specifications do not apply to the domestic interoperable use of the foreign currency cards issued outside China. These Specifications shall be interpreted by NBO. These Specifications are implemented as from the day they are released by the People's Bank of China.	[See the parties' translations]

DOCUMENT NO.	TRANSLATION BY UNITED STATES	TRANSLATION BY CHINA	TRANSLATION AGREED BY PARTIES / TRANSLATION SUGGESTED BY UNOG
	Schedule: Definitions of Terms Unified Network Logo is comprised of the unified brand name of the domestic bank cards (namely the Chinese characters of "China UnionPay") and the symbolized logo of the united network, has been registered with the trademark office, and the ownership and usage management right thereof belongs to the United Association. The United Association will promulgate the measures for the promulgation, use and management of the logo of interoperability separately.	*Schedule: Definitions of Terms* "Networking logo" consists of the uniform brand name of domestic bankcards (i.e. the Chinese characters of "Yin Lian") and the design that symbolizes interoperability network. It is registered with the trademark office, with its ownership and use management right belonging to BJO, which will separately formulate the measures for the production, use and management of the networking logo.	*Schedule: Definitions of Terms* - ***UNOG translation***: The network logo comprises the uniform brand name for domestic bank cards (the Chinese characters *yinlian* 银联) and the design symbolizing the united network, as registered with the trademark office. All rights of ownership and use belong to the Association of Interoperable Bank Card Service (AIBCS), which will separately define measures for the production, use and management of the logo.
Document No. 103 Exhibit US-1 Exhibit CHN-65	Section II.5(1) Consolidating and improving the achievements of networking use: We should earnestly summarize and spread the working experience of networking use in recent years, where the range of networking use shall be further extended to all the cities at and above the prefecture-city level and economically-developed cities at the county level. We should ensure that all bankcard machines satisfy the relevant criteria and standards of networking use, strictly abide by the principle of "one counter, one machine" so as to realize the sharing of resources. We should improve the technical standards for using RMB bankcards as soon as possible and strengthen the popularization of the technical standards of RMB bankcards that are formulated according to the international criteria. Those RMB bankcards as newly issued by any commercial bank shall meet the said technical standards and shall complete the work of changing the present non-standardized bankcards as soon as possible.	*Section II. 5(1)* Consolidate and heighten the results of the networked interoperability. Carefully sum up and spread the experience in the networked interoperability efforts made in recent years, further expand the scope of networked interoperability to all prefecture-level and higher-level cities and economically-developed county-level cities; ensure that all bankcard machines meet the specifications and standards for networked interoperability, strictly observe the principle of "one machine one counter" and realize the sharing of resources; lose no time to improve and implement the Chinese technical standard for RMB bankcards, intensify the popularization of the Chinese technical standard for RMB bankcards formulated according to international standards. The new RMB bankcards issued by commercial banks must meet the technical standard. The replacement of the existing cards that do not meet the standard shall be completed as soon as possible.	[See the parties' translations]
	Section III …By 2006, the RMB bank card operation shall be opened to the	*Section III* …When the RMB bankcard business is opened	*Section III* - ***UNOG translation:*** -+The RMB bankcard

DOCUMENT NO.	TRANSLATION BY UNITED STATES	TRANSLATION BY CHINA	TRANSLATION AGREED BY PARTIES / TRANSLATION SUGGESTED BY UNOG
	outside world in an all-around manner, and accordingly the bank card industry of our country is facing a comparatively big challenge and we should make use of the limited time to enhance the international competitiveness of our industries.	completely to the outside world by the end of 2006, the Chinese bankcard industry will be faced with serious challenges and must capitalize on the limited time to enhance its international competitiveness…	business opens fully to the outside world at the close of 2006, posing greater challenges to the Chinese bankcard industry; the limited time [remaining] must be used to boost that industry's competitiveness.
Document No. 129 Exhibit US-53 Exhibit CHN-59	*Art. 3.2(i)* [See agreed translation]	*Art. 3.2(i)* [See agreed translation]	*Art. 3.2(i)* – ***Translation agreed by parties***: All commercial banks and postal saving and remittance bureaus should further speed up the standardization of terminals and the development of cross-bank business, and should, before the end of 2003, in all prefecture-level and higher-level cities, realize resource sharing of all terminals such as ATM and POS and the cross-bank and cross-region use of various types of non-special- purpose bankcards.
	Art. 3.2(ii) Universal use of bank cards bearing the CUP logo. All RMB bank cards newly issued by all commercial banks and all postal savings and remittance bureaus must conform to the unified business specifications and technical standards and must bear the unified CUP logo; all commercial banks and all postal saving and remittance bureaus must formulate specific plans for replacement of and specific working requirements on the remaining bank cards not bearing the CUP logo and mustfile the replacement plans and other materials with the PBOC before August 20, 2003.	*Art. 3.2(ii)* Overall popularization of the "Yin Lian" logo cards. All types of RMB bankcards newly issued by the commercial banks, postal saving and remittance bureaus, must comply with uniform business specifications and technical standards, and shall bear the uniform "Yin Lian" logo as stipulated; for the existing cards without "Yin Lian" logo, the commercial banks, postal saving and remittance bureaus shall draw up replacement plans and clarify work requirements, and materials such as the replacement plans shall be reported to PBOC for record before August 20, 2003.	[See the parties' translations]
	Art. 3.4 Fully improve the efficiency of error processing in inter-bank bank card transactions. (i) China Unionpay Joint Stock Co., Ltd. shall, in conjunction with all commercial banks, further supplement and perfect error processing management measures	*Art. 3.4* Improve the efficiency of error handling in the cross-bank transactions of bankcards (i) China UnionPay Co., Ltd. shall join the commercial banks in further supplementing and	[See the parties' translations]

DOCUMENT NO.	TRANSLATION BY UNITED STATES	TRANSLATION BY CHINA	TRANSLATION AGREED BY PARTIES / TRANSLATION SUGGESTED BY UNOG
	and implementation rules, establish a scientific and effective error processing procedures, clarify the responsibilities of the parties involved in error processing and specify the task assignment at each link. (ii) All commercial banks, postal saving and remittance bureaus and China UnionPay Joint Stock Co., Ltd. Shall continue to improve the technical processing methods, strengthen the supervision and inspection of error processing at each link and improve the efficiency of error processing. (iii) Pay special attention to complaints handling, improve the efficiency of complaints handling and provide better services to cardholders	improving the management measures for error handling and the detailed rules for implementation thereof, establishing a scientific and effective flow of error handling, clarify the responsibilities of those participating in error handling and detail the division of work at all links. (ii) The commercial banks, postal saving and remittance bureaus and China UnionPay Co., Ltd. shall continue to improve technical processing means, strengthen the urging and inspection of all links of error handling and improve the efficiency of error handling. (iii) Attach great importance to complaint handling, improve the efficiency of complaint handling and provide better service for cardholders.	
Document No. 142 Exhibit US-55 Exhibit CHN-69	*Art. II.3* Protecting the information safety of cardholders. Card issuers shall set up an effective information safety protection system to protect the information safety of cardholders. They shall provide clients with safe and reliable services for setting and changing passwords and make sure that clients can change their passwords over the counter, through telephone banking or in other expedite and safe ways. They shall hide part of the card number on the account statements or other service vouchers (except those printed out over the counter) issued to cardholders. Bank cards issued by card issuers shall meet the requirements of the Bank Card Specifications (JR0052-2099) and the Technical Specifications on Bankcard Interoperability (JR0055-2009). Card issuers shall give priority to the issuance of IC bank cards which adopt the PBOC 2.0 Standards so as to improve the anti-counterfeiting ability of bank cards. For large transactions, upon the consent of cardholders, card issuers may make confirmations with or give risk alerts to cardholders or	*Art. II.3* Protect the security of card holders' information. Card-issuing institutions shall establish an effective information security protection system to protect the security of cardholder information. They shall provide applicants with safe and reliable services for setting and modifying password, which should be able to be quickly and safely changed over the counter, through telephone banking or other channels. The card number on the bank statement and other service vouchers provided to cardholders shall be partially shielded (except the vouchers printed for counter business). Bankcards issued shall comply with the Specifications for Bankcards (JR0052-2009) and the Technical Specifications for Bankcard Interoperability (JR0055-2009). Card issuing institutions shall actively issue bank IC cards that	[See the parties' translations]

DOCUMENT NO.	TRANSLATION BY UNITED STATES	TRANSLATION BY CHINA	TRANSLATION AGREED BY PARTIES / TRANSLATION SUGGESTED BY UNOG
	take other risk control measures through phone calls or text messages. Where there is any risk of leakage of bank card information, the card issuer shall contact the cardholder and suggest that the cardholder change the card or password as soon as possible. If it cannot reach the cardholder in the case of emergency, it can take measures to temporarily lock up the cardholder's account.	adopt PBOC 2.0 Standard to enhance the anti-counterfeiting capability of the cards. Subject to cardholders' consent, card-issuing institutions may take risk management measures for large-amount transactions, such as making confirmation or giving risk reminders for cardholders through telephone or short message. Where there is any risk of leakage of bankcard information, card-issuing institutions shall contact the cardholder in question and suggest him/her to change the card or change its password as soon as possible. If the cardholder cannot be contacted, the card-issuing institution can take measures to temporarily lock the cardholder's card.	
	Art. II.5 ...Card issuers shall timely submit the risk information on bank cards to the credit system of the People's Bank of China, and voluntarily submit the same to the bank card risk information sharing system of China Unionpay, so as to make full use of such information sharing mechanisms to prevent and control risks	*Art. II.5* ...Card-issuing institutions shall promptly report relevant bankcard risk information to the credit system of PBOC and the bankcard risk information sharing system of China UnionPay to makes full use of the sharing mechanism for risk prevention.	[See the parties' translations]
	Art. III.7 ..Acquiring institutions shall set up strict rules for the real name examination and on-site investigation of merchants, make full use of the identity information on-line check system, the credit system of the People's Bank of China and the bank card risk information sharing system of China Unionpay to verify the identities of the legal representatives of persons in charge and the authorized representatives of merchants…	*Art. III.7* …Acquiring institutions shall establish a strict system of real name examination and site investigation for absorption of merchants. They shall fully utilize the online identity information examination system, the credit system of PBOC and the bank risk information sharing system of China UnionPay to verify the personal identity of the legal representative or leader and authorized operator of a merchant...	[See the parties' translations]
	Art.III.8 …When finding that any merchant illegally accepts bank cards, the acquiring institution shall timely	*Art.III.8* …If any merchant is found to accept bankcards in suspected violation of	[See the parties' translations]

DOCUMENT NO.	TRANSLATION BY UNITED STATES	TRANSLATION BY CHINA	TRANSLATION AGREED BY PARTIES / TRANSLATION SUGGESTED BY UNOG
	make investigation, verification and correction.....Once it is confirmed that the merchant has committed any of such illegal acts, the acquiring institution shall immediately terminate its bank card transactions, report it to the public security department, report the relevant information to the People's Bank of China, submit the relevant information on the merchant and its legal representative or person in charge to the credit system of the People's Bank of China, and voluntarily submit it to the bank card risk information sharing system of China Unionpay...	regulations, the acquiring institution shall make timely investigation and verification for correction.....for any merchant with confirmed acceptance of counterfeit cards, illegal information copying, cash-out of fraudulency, the acquiring institution shall immediately terminate its bankcard transactions, report the same to the public security department and PBOC and submit the information of the merchant and its legal representative or leader to the credit system of PBOC and the bankcard risk information sharing system of China UnionPay...	
	Art. III.11 ...Acquiring institutions shall correctly set and register the relevant merchant information with China Unionpay, submit correct information to China Unionpay at the time of transaction processing, and make sure that the card acceptance terminals can fully and accurately read and transmit the card verification code.	*Art. III.11* ...Acquiring institutions shall correctly set and register with China UnionPay the information of relevant merchants, upload accurately to China UnionPay during transactions processing. Meanwhile, they shall ensure that the acceptance terminals can read and transmit card verification code completely and accurately	[See the parties' translations]
	Art. V.15 Improving the Anti-risk Service Level of China Unionpay Setting up and improving the bank card risk prevention and control system. China Unionpay shall set up a transaction data recording, analyzing and monitoring system, make more efforts in monitoring and analyzing suspicious transactions, and make comprehensive and dynamic assessment and categorized management of transaction risks, so as to protect the safety of accounts and transaction information...China Unionpay shall strengthen the standard administration of its branches and subsidiary companies, implement the relevant bank card business standards and technical norms, separate the inter-bank clearing business, acquiring business and outsourcing service	*Art. V.15* Raise the Risk Prevention Service Level of China UnionPay Establish and improve bankcard risk prevention and controls system. China UnionPay shall establish the system for the recording, analyzing and monitoring of transaction data, strengthen the supervision and analysis of suspicious transactions, make comprehensive and dynamic assessment and conduct classified management of transaction risks to protect the security of accounts and transaction information...China UnionPay shall strengthen the standardization management of its branches and subsidiaries, strictly	[See the parties' translations]

DOCUMENT NO.	TRANSLATION BY UNITED STATES	TRANSLATION BY CHINA	TRANSLATION AGREED BY PARTIES / TRANSLATION SUGGESTED BY UNOG
	business from each other and assume the compensatory liability for cases or losses caused by its poor management of acquiring business or outsourcing service business…	implement the business specifications and technical standards related to bankcard, separate cross-bank clearing business, acquiring business and outsourcing service business, assume compensation responsibility for the cases and losses resulting from its poor management on acquiring business and outsourcing service business…	
	Art. V.16 …China Unionpay shall coordinate all member institutions in setting up a work mechanism for preventing bank card risks and an information sharing platform so as to provide good services for member institutions to submit information on suspicious bank card transactions and violation of laws and regulations and use the bank card risk information sharing system, and make continuous efforts to improve the bank card risk information sharing mechanism…	*Art. V.16* …China UnionPay shall coordinate the member institutions to establish the working mechanism for preventing bankcard risks and a information sharing platform, provide them with good services in reporting the information on bankcard transactions that are suspicious and violate laws and regulations and using the bankcard risk information sharing system, continuously improve the mechanism of sharing bankcard risk information…	[See the parties' translations]
	Art. VI.18 …The People's Bank of China shall, together with the Ministry of Public Security, set up a long-term effective mechanism for cracking down on bank card crimes as soon as possible, coordinate the forces and resources of both of them as well as those of commercial banks and China Unionpay, jointly set up an office for jointly combating bank card crimes, and keep smooth intelligence channels.	*Art. VI.18* …PBOC shall, together with the Ministry of Public Security, establish a long-term regime as soon as possible for the joint penalization of bankcard crimes, coordinate the strength and resources of the two departments and the commercial banks and China UnionPay, set up the office for the joint penalization and keep the information channel unblocked.	[See the parties' translations]

DOCUMENT NO.	TRANSLATION BY UNITED STATES	TRANSLATION BY CHINA	TRANSLATION AGREED BY PARTIES / TRANSLATION SUGGESTED BY UNOG
Document No. 149 Exhibit US-50 Exhibit CHN-70	*Art. 2(5)(iii)* Strictly control the opening of bankcard acceptance terminals. The acquiring institutions may not allow the non-CUP and non- PBOC 2.0 pre-payment cards issued by other enterprises to be accepted at any POS terminals.	*Art. 2(5)(iii)* Strictly control the opening of bankcard acceptance terminals. No acquiring institutions may, through the bankcard acceptance terminals, accept non-"Yin Lian" or non-PBOC2.0 standard prepaid cards issued by non-financial institution enterprises.	*Art. 2(5)(iii) - **UNOG translation**:* Strictly control access to bankcard terminals. No acquiring institutions may allow non-"Yin Lian/UnionPay" and non-PBOC2.0 standard prepaid cards issued by non-financial social enterprises to be accepted at bankcard terminal equipment.
Document No. 153 Exhibit US-49 Exhibit CHN-66	*Art. 1.2* ...At the present time, China UnionPay is the domestic clearance organization which specializes in the RMB bank card inter-bank information routing and exchange. Its main responsibility is to set up and operate a secure and efficient bank card inter-bank information routing and exchange network to achieve the inter-bank use of bank cards. China UnionPay shall focus on this main business, improve the network service level and enhance the management and operation of the brand "China Unionpay".	*Art. 1.2* ...China UnionPay is a clearing organization within China that currently specializes in the cross-bank information exchange for RMB bankcards. Its primary responsibility is to establish and operate a secure and efficient network for the cross-bank information exchange of bankcards, and to realize the cross-bank interoperability of bankcards. China UnionPay shall focus on this primary business, improve its network services and strengthen the management and operation of the "Yin Lian" brand.	*Art. 1.2 - **UNOG translation***: China UnionPay is currently the domestic clearing organisation specialising in RMB bank card inter-bank information routing and exchange. Its main responsibility is to set up and operate a secure and efficient bank card inter-bank information routing and exchange network to bring about bank card inter-operability among banks. China UnionPay shall focus on this primary business, conscientiously improve the level of network service, and enhance the management and operation of the "Yin Lian/UnionPay" brand.
	Art. 1.3 Regarding the third party service providers of merchant acquiring business. The third party service providers are the legal person enterprises which engage in non-core business of the bank card acquiring business entrusted by merchant acquiring institutions on the basis of making their own operation decisions and taking full responsibility for their own profits and losses. Since the bank card information exchange system concerns the security of financial information and payment system, engagement in bank card information exchange services is subject to a system of strict access and management. No third party service provider shall engage in bank card information exchange services.	*Art. 1.3* About the third party service providers for merchant acquiring business. Third party service providers refer to those legal entities that are entrusted by merchant acquiring institutions to carry out the non-core business in the bankcard acquiring business and are independent in operation and responsible for their own profits and losses. Since the bankcard information switching system is significant to the security of financial information and the payment system, there is strict access and administrative system for engaging in bankcard information switching business; thus, no third party	[See the parties' translations]

DOCUMENT NO.	TRANSLATION BY UNITED STATES	TRANSLATION BY CHINA	TRANSLATION AGREED BY PARTIES / TRANSLATION SUGGESTED BY UNOG
		service provider may engage in the bankcard information switching business.	
	Art. 2.2 POS terminals placed by the acquiring institutions or by third party service providers must conform to the business specifications and technical standards of cross-network interoperability, be posted with the unified CUP logo, and be capable of accepting all bank cards bearing the CUP logo. For the acquiring institutions which cannot accept all bank cards bearing the CUP logo or intentionally set obstacles against the bank cards issued by others, customers, merchants and issuers are entitled to report and file complaints to PBOC.	*Art. 2.2* The POS machines placed by merchant acquiring institutions or by third party service providers entrusted by merchant acquiring institutions, shall be in accordance with business specifications and technical standards of networked interoperability, bear the uniform "Yin Lian" logo and be able to accept all "Yin Lian" logo cards. With respect to merchant acquiring institutions that cannot realize the acceptance of all "Yin Lian" logo cards or intentionally set obstacles against bankcards that are not issued by its own bank, customers, merchants and card-issuing institutions have the right to report and complain to the People's Bank of China.	[See the parties' translations]
	Article 4, second paragraph Merchant acquiring institutions shall take precautions against acquiring risks in conducting POS direct connections business, and strengthen daily training to the direct connection merchants. Merchant acquiring institutions shall comply with the principle of interoperability in conducting POS indirect connection business, open all acquiring equipment to CUP cards, and strictly comply with the unified inter-bank business specifications and technical standards.	*Article 4, second paragraph* While carrying out POS business of direct connection, a merchant acquiring institution shall guard against acquiring risks and strengthen the daily training of merchants of direct connection; while carrying out the POS business of indirect connection, it shall meet the principle of networked interoperability, open acquiring machines to all China UnionPay cards and strictly observe uniform cross-bank business specifications and technical standards.	[See the parties' translations]
	Article 5, second paragraph After being approved by PBOC, China UnionPay may set up branches in regions where there is a market demand, in accordance with the company's overall plan to provide bank card information exchange and clearance services. A nationwide inter-bank transaction	*Article 5, second paragraph* With the approval of the People's Bank of China, China UnionPay may set up affiliates in regions with market demand according to its own overall plan to provide bankcard information switching and clearing	[See the parties' translations]

DOCUMENT NO.	TRANSLATION BY UNITED STATES	TRANSLATION BY CHINA	TRANSLATION AGREED BY PARTIES / TRANSLATION SUGGESTED BY UNOG
	network shall be formed as soon as possible.	services and form an cross-bank transaction network system that covers the whole country.	
	Article 5, third paragraph In order to regulate the payment clearance services market, and strengthen the administration of information routing and exchange, the current professional service platform established by China UnionPay in non-CUP branch regions and engagement in inter-bank POS transaction information transfer shall be directly managed and operated by China Unionpay, and shall not be indirectly managed or operated through authorization.	*Article 5, third paragraph* To standardize the payment clearing service market and strengthen the management of information transfer, the professional service platforms that have been set up by China UnionPay in regions without China UnionPay branch to engage in the transfer of POS cross-bank transaction information shall be managed and operated directly by China UnionPay, which shall not manage and operate the professional service platforms indirectly through authorization.	[See the parties' translations]
	Art. 6, third paragraph [See agreed translation]	*Art. 6, third paragraph* [See agreed translation]	*Art. 6, third paragraph – **Translation agreed by parties***: …When dual currency credit cards and debit cards are used in Hong Kong, Macao and other countries/regions where the CUP network exists, the Chinese issuing banks should support routing through the CUP network and open the RMB accounts related transactions and clearing services to the CUP network…
	Art. 6, third paragraph (last sentence) …No organizations should set any obstacles or cause any interference.	*Art. 6, third paragraph (last sentence)* …no institution may set any obstacle and intervene thereto.	[See the parties' translations]

DOCUMENT NO.	TRANSLATION BY UNITED STATES	TRANSLATION BY CHINA	TRANSLATION AGREED BY PARTIES / TRANSLATION SUGGESTED BY UNOG
Document No. 219 Exhibit US-47 Exhibit CHN-63	*Art. III* A Renminbi card acquiring institution in a border area shall regulate the merchants' execution of contracts, and clarify in the relevant Renminbi card acquisition agreement that no merchant shall use the sales slip, sales settlement slip, the "UnionPay" mark or the POS for the purposes not covered by the acquisition agreement, bring the POS outside the territory for use, authorize a third party to handle the Renminbi card business or transfer such business to the third party, counterfeit another merchant transaction as its own merchant transaction to carry out liquidation with the acquiring institution, or use fictitious POS transaction to draw cash for clients.	*Art. III* The acquiring agreement of relevant RMB cards shall clearly stipulate that merchants shall not use the purchase slips, purchase statements, "Yin Lian" logo and POS terminals for purposes outside the scope delimited by acquiring agreement; shall not take any POS set abroad; shall not entrust or transfer the business of accepting RMB cards to any third party; shall not use the transactions of other merchants to pass for the transactions of their own for clearing with the acquiring institution; shall not use POS machines to fabricate transactions so as to withdraw cash for customers.	*Art. III* - ***UNOG translation***: RMB card acquisition agreements shall clearly stipulate that merchants must not use sales slips, purchase receipts, the Yin Lian/UnionPay logo or POS terminals for purposes outside the scope of those agreements, must not take POS devices for use outside the country, must not entrust or transfer the handling of RMB card business to a third party, must not pass off other merchants' transactions as their own for clearance with the acquiring institution, and must not use POS terminals to fabricate transactions so as to withdraw cash for customers.
Document No. 254 Exhibit US-48 Exhibit CHN-64	*Art. 3* Where RMB bank cards issued by domestic banks are used for paying expenses or withdrawing cash in Hong Kong dollars or Macao dollars in Hong Kong or Macao, the issuers shall process clearing in RMB with China UnionPay Joint Stock Co., Ltd. (hereinafter "China UnionPay") and China UnionPay shall, after purchasing foreign exchanges from the designated foreign exchange banks, process clearing in Hong Kong dollars or Macao dollars with the acquiring banks in Hong Kong and Macao;	*Art. 3* If a RMB bankcard issued by a Mainland Bank is used in Hong Kong or Macau for consumption or withdrawal of HKD or MOP cash, the card- issuing bank shall use RMB to clear with China UnionPay Co., Ltd. (hereafter referred to as "China UnionPay"). China UnionPay shall then purchase foreign currency from designated foreign exchange banks and clear with Hong Kong/Macau acquiring banks in HKD or MOP.	[See the parties' translations]
	Art. 4 [See agreed translation]	*Art. 4* [See agreed translation]	*Art. 4* – ***Translation agreed by parties***: Where the RMB bank cards issued by Hong Kong or Macao participating banks are used for paying expenses or withdrawing RMB cash in Mainland China, the issuers shall process the clearing in RMB with the Mainland acquiring banks through the clearing banks and China UnionPay.

DOCUMENT NO.	TRANSLATION BY UNITED STATES	TRANSLATION BY CHINA	TRANSLATION AGREED BY PARTIES / TRANSLATION SUGGESTED BY UNOG
	Art. 17 Banks in Mainland China shall, in accordance with "the notice" and this circular, handle relevant business and clearing through the clearing banks and China UnionPay, and shall not directly carry out RMB transactions with other Hong Kong or Macao Institutions.	*Art. 17* Mainland banks shall, as required by the Announcements and the Circular, operate and clear relevant business through clearing banks and China UnionPay, and shall not make RMB transactions with other Hong Kong/Macau institutions directly.	[See the parties' translations]

Cumulative List of Published Disputes

Argentina - Definitive Anti-Dumping Duties on Poultry from Brazil

Complaint by Brazil (WT/DS241)

Report of the Panel DSR 2003:V, 1727

Argentina - Definitive Anti-Dumping Measures on Imports of Ceramic Floor Tiles from Italy

Complaint by the European Communities (WT/DS189)

Report of the Panel DSR 2001:XII, 6241

Argentina - Definitive Safeguard Measure on Imports of Preserved Peaches

Complaint by Chile (WT/DS238)

Report of the Panel DSR 2003:III, 1037

Argentina - Measures Affecting Imports of Footwear, Textiles, Apparel and Other Items

Complaint by the United States (WT/DS56)

Report of the Appellate Body DSR 1998:III, 1003

Report of the Panel DSR 1998:III, 1033

Argentina - Measures Affecting the Export of Bovine Hides and the Import of Finished Leather

Complaint by the European Communities (WT/DS155)

Report of the Panel DSR 2001:V, 1779

Award of the Arbitrator under Article 21.3(c) of the DSU DSR 2001:XII, 6013

Argentina - Safeguard Measures on Imports of Footwear

Complaint by the European Communities (WT/DS121)

Report of the Appellate Body DSR 2000:I, 515

Report of the Panel DSR 2000:II, 575

Australia - Measures Affecting the Importation of Apples from New Zealand

Complaint by New Zealand (WT/DS367)

Report of the Appellate Body DSR 2010:V, 2175

Report of the Panel DSR 2010:VI, 2371

Australia - Measures Affecting Importation of Salmon

Complaint by Canada (WT/DS18)

Report of the Appellate Body DSR 1998:VIII, 3327

Report of the Panel DSR 1998:VIII, 3407
Award of the Arbitrator under Article 21.3(c) of the DSU DSR 1999:I, 267
Report of the Panel - Recourse to Article 21.5 of the DSU DSR 2000:IV, 2031

Australia - Subsidies Provided to Producers and Exporters of Automotive Leather

Complaint by the United States (WT/DS126)
Report of the Panel DSR 1999:III, 951
Report of the Panel - Recourse to Article 21.5 of the DSU DSR 2000:III, 1189

Brazil - Export Financing Programme for Aircraft

Complaint by Canada (WT/DS46)
Report of the Appellate Body DSR 1999:III, 1161
Report of the Panel DSR 1999:III, 1221
Report of the Appellate Body - Recourse to Article 21.5 of the DSU DSR 2000:VIII, 4067
Report of the Panel - Recourse to Article 21.5 of the DSU DSR 2000:IX, 4093
Report of the Panel - Second Recourse to Article 21.5 of the DSU DSR 2001:XI, 5481
Decision by the Arbitrators - Recourse to Arbitration by Brazil under Article 22.6 of the DSU and Article 4.11 of the *SCM Agreement* DSR 2002:I, 19

Brazil - Measures Affecting Desiccated Coconut

Complaint by the Philippines (WT/DS22)
Report of the Appellate Body DSR 1997:I, 167
Report of the Panel DSR 1997:I, 189

Brazil - Measures Affecting Import of Retreaded Tyres

Complaint by the European Communities (WT/DS332)
Report of the Appellate Body DSR 2007:IV, 1527
Report of the Panel DSR 2007:V, 1649
Arbitration under Article 21.3(c) of the DSU DSR 2008:XX, 8581

Canada - Certain Measures Affecting the Automotive Industry

Complaint by the European Communities (WT/DS142); Complaint by Japan (WT/DS139)
Report of the Appellate Body DSR 2000:VI, 2985
Report of the Panel DSR 2000:VII, 3043

Award of the Arbitrator under Article 21.3(c) of the DSU DSR 2000:X, 5079

Canada - Certain Measures Concerning Periodicals

Complaint by the United States (WT/DS31)

Report of the Appellate Body DSR 1997:I, 449

Report of the Panel DSR 1997:I, 481

Canada– Continued Suspension of Obligations in the EC – Hormones Dispute

Complaint by the European Communities (WT/DS321)

Report of the Appellate Body DSR 2008:XIV, 5373

Report of the Panel DSR 2008:XV, 5757

Canada - Export Credits and Loan Guarantees for Regional Aircraft

Complaint by Brazil (WT/DS222)

Report of the Panel DSR 2002:III, 849

Decision by the Arbitrator under Article 22.6 of the DSU and Article 4.11 of the *SCM Agreement* DSR 2003:III, 1187

Canada - Measures Affecting the Importation of Milk and the Exportation of Dairy Products

Complaint by New Zealand (WT/DS113);
Complaint by the United States (WT/DS103)

Report of the Appellate Body DSR 1999:V, 2057

Report of the Panel DSR 1999:VI, 2097

Report of the Appellate Body - Recourse to Article 21.5 of the DSU DSR 2001:XIII, 6829

Report of the Panel - Recourse to Article 21.5 of the DSU DSR 2001:XIII, 6865

Report of the Appellate Body - Second Recourse to Article 21.5 of the DSU DSR 2003:I, 213

Report of the Panel - Second Recourse to Article 21.5 of the DSU DSR 2003:I, 255

Canada - Measures Affecting the Export of Civilian Aircraft

Complaint by Brazil (WT/DS70)

Report of the Appellate Body DSR 1999:III, 1377

Report of the Panel DSR 1999:IV, 1443

Report of the Appellate Body - Recourse to Article 21.5 of the DSU DSR 2000:IX, 4299

Report of the Panel - Recourse to Article 21.5 of the DSU DSR 2000:IX, 4315

Canada – Measures Relating to Exports of Wheat and Treatment of Imported Grain

Complaint by United States (WT/DS276)

Report of the Appellate Body DSR 2004:VI, 2807

Report of the Panel DSR 2004:VI, 2887

Canada - Patent Protection of Pharmaceutical Products

Complaint by the European Communities (WT/DS114)

Report of the Panel DSR 2000:V, 2289

Award of the Arbitrator under Article 21.3(c) of the DSU DSR 2002:I, 3

Canada - Term of Patent Protection

Complaint by the United States (WT/DS170)

Report of the Appellate Body DSR 2000:X, 5093

Report of the Panel DSR 2000:XI, 5121

Award of the Arbitrator under Article 21.3(c) of the DSU DSR 2000:IX, 4537

Chile - Price Band System and Safeguard Measures Relating to Certain Agricultural Products

Complaint by Argentina (WT/DS207)

Report of the Appellate Body DSR 2002:VIII, 3045

Report of the Panel DSR 2002:VIII, 30127

Award of the Arbitrator under Article 21.3(c) of the DSU DSR 2003:III, 1237

Report of the Appellate Body - Corrigendum DSR 2006:XII, 5473

Recourse to Article 21.5 of the DSU by Argentina

Report of the Appellate Body DSR 2007:II, 513

Report of the Panel DSR 2007:II, III, 613

Chile - Taxes on Alcoholic Beverages

Complaint by the European Communities (WT/DS87), (WT/DS110)

Report of the Appellate Body DSR 2000:I, 281

Report of the Panel DSR 2000:I, 303

Award of the Arbitrator under Article 21.3(c) of the DSU DSR 2000:V, 2583

China - Measures Affecting Imports of Automobile Parts

Complaints by Canada, European Communities, United States (WT/DS339, WT/DS340, WT/DS342)

Reports of the Appellate Body DSR 2009:I, 3

Reports of the Panel DSR 2009:I, 119

China - Measures Affecting the Protection and Enforcement of Intellectual Property Rights

Complaint by United States (WT/DS362)

Report of the Panel DSR 2009:V, 2097

China - Measures Affecting Trading Rights and Distribution Services for Certain Publications and Audiovisual Entertainment Products

Complaint by United States (WT/DS363)

Report of the Appellate Body DSR 2010:I, 3

China - Measures Related to the Exportation of Various Raw Materials

Complaint by United States, European Union and Mexico (WT/DS394, WT/DS395, WT/DS398)

Reports of the Appellate Body DSR 2012:VII, 3295

Reports of the Panel DSR 2012:VII, 3501
DSR 2012:VIII, 3933

Colombia - Indicative Prices and Restrictions on Ports of Entry

Complaint by Panama (WT/DS366)

Report of the Panel DSR 2009:VI, 2535

Arbitration under Article 21.3(c) of the DSU (Award of the Arbitrator) DSR 2009:IX, 3819

Dominican Republic - Measures Affecting the Importation and Internal Sale of Cigarettes

Complaint by Honduras (WT/DS302)

Report of the Appellate Body DSR 2005:XV, 7367

Report of the Panel DSR 2005:XV, 7425

Arbitration under Article 21.3(c) of the DSU (WT/DS302/17)

Report of the Arbitrator DSR 2005:XXIII, 11663

Egypt - Definitive Anti-Dumping Measures on Steel Rebar from Turkey

Complaint by Turkey (WT/DS211)

Report of the Panel DSR 2002:VII, 2667

European Communities and Certain member States - Measures Affecting Trade in Large Civil Aircraft (WT/DS316)

Report of the Appellate Body DSR 2011:I, 7
Report of the Panel - Part I DSR 2011:II, 685
Report of the Panel - Part II DSR 2011:III, 1477

European Communities and its member States - Tariff Treatment of Certain Information Technology Products

Complaint by United States, Japan and Chinese Taipei (WT/DS375, WT/DS376, WT/DS377)

Report of the Panel DSR 2010:III, 933
Report of the Panel (Annexes) DSR 2010:IV, 1567

European Communities - Anti-Dumping Duties on Imports of Cotton-Type Bed Linen from India

Complaint by India (WT/DS141)

Report of the Appellate Body DSR 2001:V, 2049
Report of the Appellate Body (Recourse to Article 21.5 of the DSU by India) DSR 2003:III, 965
Report of the Panel DSR 2001:VI, 2077
Report of the Panel - Recourse to Article 21.5 of the DSU DSR 2003:IV, 1269

European Communities - Anti-Dumping Duties on Malleable Cast Iron Tube or Pipe Fittings from Brazil

Complaint by Brazil (WT/DS219)

Report of the Appellate Body DSR 2003:VI, 2613
Report of the Panel DSR 2003:VII, 2701

European Communities - Anti-Dumping Measure on Farmed Salmon from Norway

Complaint by Norway (WT/DS337)

Report of the Panel DSR 2008:I, 3

European Communities – Conditions for the Granting of Tariff Preferences to Developing Countries

Complaint by India (WT/DS246)

Report of the Appellate Body DSR 2004:III, 951
Report of the Panel DSR 2004:III, 1037
Award of the Arbitrator under Article 21.3 (c) of the DSU DSR 2004:IX, 4313

European Communities – Countervailing Measures on Dynamic Random Access Memory Chips from Korea

Complaint by Korea (WT/DS299)

Report of the Panel DSR 2005:XVIII, 8671

European Communities - Customs Classification of Certain Computer Equipment

Complaint by the United States (WT/DS62, WT/DS67, WT/DS68)

Complaint by the United States - Ireland

Complaint by the United States - United Kingdom

Report of the Appellate Body DSR 1998:V, 1851

Report of the Panel DSR 1998:V, 1891

European Communities - Customs Classification of Frozen Boneless Chicken Cuts

Complaint by Brazil and Thailand (WT/DS269, WT/DS286)

Report of the Appellate Body DSR 2005:XIX, 9157

Complaint by Brazil (WT/DS269)

Report of the Panel DSR 2005:XIX, 9295

Complaint by Thailand (WT/DS286)

Report of the Panel DSR 2005:XX, 9721

Arbitration under Article 21.3(c) of the Understanding on Rules and Procedures Governing the Settlement of Disputes DSR 2006:XII, 5441

European Communities - Definitive Anti-Dumping Measures on Certain Iron or Steel Fasteners from China

Complaint by China (WT/DS397)

Report of the Appellate Body DSR 2011:VII, 3995

Report of the Panel DSR 2011:VIII, 4289

European Communities - Export Subsidies on Sugar

Complaint by Australia, Brazil, Thailand (WT/DS265, WT/DS266, WT/DS283)

Report of the Appellate Body DSR 2005:XIII, 6365

Complaint by Australia (WT/DS265)

Report of the Panel DSR 2005:XIII, 6499

Complaint by Brazil (WT/DS266) DSR 2005:XIV, 6793

Report of the Panel

Complaint by Thailand (WT/DS283)

Report of the Panel DSR 2005:XIV, 7071

Arbitration under Article 21.3(c) of the Understanding on Rules and Procedures Governing the Settlement of Disputes (WT/DS265/33, WT/DS266/33, WT/DS283/14)

Award of the Arbitrator DSR 2005:XXIII, 11579

European Communities - Measures Affecting Asbestos and Asbestos-Containing Products

Complaint by Canada (WT/DS135)

Report of the Appellate Body DSR 2001:VII, 3243

Report of the Panel DSR 2001:VIII, 3305

European Communities - Measures Affecting the Approval and Marketing of Biotech Products

Complaint by United States, Canada, Argentina (WT/DS291, WT/DS292, WT/DS293)

Report of the Panel DSR 2006:III, 847

European Communities - Measures Affecting the Importation of Certain Poultry Products

Complaint by Brazil (WT/DS69)

Report of the Appellate Body DSR 1998:V, 2031

Report of the Panel DSR 1998:V, 2089

European Communities – Measures Affecting Trade in Commercial Vessels

Complaint by Korea (WT/DS301)

Report of the Panel DSR 2005:XV, 7733

European Communities - Measures Concerning Meat and Meat Products (Hormones)

Complaint by Canada (WT/DS48);
Complaint by the United States (WT/DS26)

Report of the Appellate Body DSR 1998:I, 135

Report of the Panel (Canada) DSR 1998:II, 235

Report of the Panel (United States) DSR 1998:III, 699

Award of the Arbitrator under Article 21.3(c) of the DSU DSR 1998:V, 1833

Decision by the Arbitrators under Article 22.6 of the DSU (Canada) DSR 1999:III, 1135

Decision by the Arbitrators under Article 22.6 of the DSU (United States) DSR 1999:III, 1105

European Communities – Protection of Trademarks and Geographical Indications for Agricultural Products and Foodstuffs

Complaint by the United States (WT/DS174)

Report of the Panel DSR 2005:VIII-IX, 3499,4083

Complaint by Australia (WT/DS290)

Report of the Panel DSR 2005:X-XI, 4603,5121

European Communities - Regime for the Importation, Sale and Distribution of Bananas

Complaint by Ecuador; Guatemala; Honduras; Mexico; and the United States (WT/DS27)

Report of the Appellate Body DSR 1997:II, 589

Report of the Panel (Ecuador) DSR 1997:III, 3

Report of the Panel (Guatemala, Honduras) DSR 1997:II, 695

Report of the Panel (Mexico) DSR 1997:II, 803

Report of the Panel (United States) DSR 1997:II, 943

Award of the Arbitrator under Article 21.3(c) of the DSU DSR 1998:I, 3

Decision by the Arbitrators under Article 22.6 of the DSU (US) DSR 1999:II, 725

Report of the Panel - Recourse to Article 21.5 of the DSU (European Communities) DSR 1999:II, 783

Report of the Panel - Recourse to Article 21.5 of the DSU (Ecuador) DSR 1999:II, 803

Decision by the Arbitrators under Article 22.6 of the DSU (Ecuador) DSR 2000:V, 2237

Second Recourse to Article 21.5 of the DSU by Ecuador

Report of the Appellate Body DSR 2008:XVIII, 7165

Report of the Panel DSR 2008:XVIII, 7329

Recourse to Article 21.5 of the DSU by the United States

Report of the Appellate Body DSR 2008:XVIII, 7165

Report of the Panel DSR 2008:XIX, 7761

European Communities - Selected Customs Matters

Complaint by United States (WT/DS315)

Report of the Appellate Body DSR 2006:IX, 3791

Report of the Panel DSR 2006:IX, 3915

European Communities - The ACP-EC Partnership Agreement - Recourse to Arbitration Pursuant to the Decision of 14 November 2001 (WT/L/616)

Award of the Arbitrator DSR 2005:XXIII, 11667

European Communities - The ACP-EC Partnership Agreement - Second Recourse to Arbitration Pursuant to the Decision of 14 November 2001

Award of the Arbitrator (WT/L/625) DSR 2005:XXIII, 11701

European Communities - Trade Description of Sardines

Complaint by Peru (WT/DS231)

Report of the Appellate Body DSR 2002:VIII, 3359

Report of the Panel DSR 2002:VIII, 3451

European Communities - Trade Description of Scallops

Complaint by Canada (WT/DS7);
Complaint by Chile (WT/DS14);
Complaint by Peru (WT/DS12)

Report of the Panel (Canada) DSR 1996:I, 89

Report of the Panel (Chile, Peru) DSR 1996:I, 93

European Union - Anti-Dumping Measures on Certain Footwear from China

Complaint by China (WT/DS405)

Report of the Panel DSR 2012:IX, 4585

Guatemala - Anti-Dumping Investigation Regarding Portland Cement From Mexico

Complaint by Mexico (WT/DS60)

Report of the Appellate Body DSR 1998:IX, 3767

Report of the Panel DSR 1998:IX, 3797

Guatemala - Definitive Anti-Dumping Measures on Grey Portland Cement from Mexico

Complaint by Mexico (WT/DS156)

Report of the Panel DSR 2000:XI, 5295

India – Additional and Extra-Additional Duties on Imports from the United States

Complaint by United States (WT/DS360)

Report of the Appellate Body DSR 2008:XX, 8223

Report of the Panel DSR 2008:XX, 8317

India - Measures Affecting the Automotive Sector

Complaint by European Communities (WT/DS146)
Complaint by the United States (WT/DS175)

Report of the Appellate Body DSR 2002:V, 1821
Report of the Panel DSR 2002:V, 1827

India - Patent Protection for Pharmaceutical and Agricultural Chemical Products

Complaint by European Communities (WT/DS79); Complaint by the United States (WT/DS50)

Report of the Appellate Body (United States) DSR 1998:I, 9
Report of the Panel (European Communities) DSR 1998:VI, 2661
Report of the Panel (United States) DSR 1998:I, 41

India - Quantitative Restrictions on Imports of Agricultural, Textile and Industrial Products

Complaint by the United States (WT/DS90)

Report of the Appellate Body DSR 1999:IV, 1763
Report of the Panel DSR 1999:V, 1799

Indonesia - Certain Measures Affecting the Automobile Industry

Complaint by European Communities (WT/DS54); Complaint by Japan (WT/DS55, WT/DS64); Complaint by the United States (WT/DS59)

Report of the Panel DSR 1998:VI, 2201
Award of the Arbitrator under Article 21.3(c) of the DSU DSR 1998:IX, 4029

Japan - Countervailing Duties on Dynamic Random Access Memories from Korea

Complaint by Korea (WT/DS336)

Report of the Appellate Body DSR 2007:VII, 2707
Report of the Panel DSR 2007:VII, 2809
Arbitration under Article 21.3(c) of the DSU DSR 2008:XX, 8553

Japan - Measures Affecting Agricultural Products

Complaint by the United States (WT/DS76)

Report of the Appellate Body DSR 1999:I, 277
Report of the Panel DSR 1999:I, 315

Japan - Measures Affecting Consumer Photographic Film and Paper

Complaint by the United States (WT/DS44)

Report of the Panel DSR 1998:IV, 1179

Japan - Measures Affecting the Importation of Apples

Complaint by the United States (WT/DS245)

Report of the Appellate Body DSR 2003:IX, 4391

Report of the Panel DSR 2003:IX, 4481

Report of the Panel - Recourse to Article 21.5 of the DSU DSR 2005:XVI, 7911

Japan - Taxes on Alcoholic Beverages

Complaint by Canada (WT/DS10);
Complaint by the European Communities (WT/DS8);
Complaint by the United States (WT/DS11)

Report of the Appellate Body DSR 1996:I, 97

Report of the Panel DSR 1996:I, 125

Award of the Arbitrator under Article 21.3(c) of the DSU DSR 1997:I, 3

Korea - Anti-Dumping Duties on Imports of Certain Paper from Indonesia

Complaint by Indonesia (WT/DS312)

Report of the Panel DSR 2005:XXII, 10637

Recourse to Article 21.5 of the DSU by Indonesia

Report of the Panel DSR 2007:VIII, 3375

Korea - Definitive Safeguard Measure on Imports of Certain Dairy Products

Complaint by the European Communities (WT/DS98)

Report of the Appellate Body DSR 2000:I, 3

Report of the Panel DSR 2000:I, 49

Korea - Measures Affecting Imports of Fresh, Chilled and Frozen Beef

Complaint by Australia (WT/DS169);
Complaint by the United States (WT/DS161)

Report of the Appellate Body DSR 2001:I, 5

Report of the Panel DSR 2001:I, 59

Korea - Measures Affecting Government Procurement

Complaint by the United States (WT/DS163)

Report of the Panel DSR 2000:VIII, 3541

Korea - Measures Affecting Trade in Commercial Vessels

Complaint by the European Communities (WT/DS273)

Report of the Panel DSR 2005:VII, 2747

Korea - Taxes on Alcoholic Beverages

Complaint by the European Communities (WT/DS75)
Complaint by the United States (WT/DS84)

Report of the Appellate Body DSR 1999:I, 3

Report of the Panel DSR 1999:I, 44

Award of the Arbitrator under Article 21.3(c) of the DSU DSR 1999:II, 937

Mexico - Anti-Dumping Duties on Steel Pipes and Tubes from Guatemala

Complaint by Guatemala (WT/DS331)

Final Report of the Panel DSR 2007:IV, 1207

Mexico - Anti-Dumping Investigation of High Fructose Corn Syrup (HFCS) from the United States

Complaint by the United States (WT/DS132)

Report of the Panel DSR 2000:III, 1345

Report of the Appellate Body - Recourse to Article 21.5 of the DSU DSR 2001:XIII, 6675

Report of the Panel - Recourse to Article 21.5 of the DSU DSR 2001:XIII, 6717

Mexico - Definitive Anti-Dumping Measures on Beef and Rice - Complaint with Respect to Rice

Complaint by the United States (WT/DS295)

Report of the Appellate Body DSR 2005:XXII, 10853

Report of the Panel DSR 2005:XXIII, 11005

Mexico - Definitive Countervailing Measures on Olive Oil from the European Communities

Complaint by the European Communities (WT/DS341)

Report of the Panel DSR 2008:IX, 3179

Mexico - Measures Affecting Telecommunications Services

Complaint by the United States (WT/DS204)

Report of the Panel DSR 2004:IV, 1579

Mexico - Tax Measures on Soft Drinks and Other Beverages

Complaint by the United States (WT/DS308)

Report of the Appellate Body DSR 2006:I, 3

Report of the Panel DSR 2006 I, 43

Philippines - Taxes on Distilled Spirits

Complaint by European Union and United States (WT/DS396, WT/DS403)

Reports of the Appellate Body DSR 2012:VIII, 4163

Reports of the Panel DSR 2012:VIII, 4271

Thailand - Anti-Dumping Duties on Angles, Shapes and Sections of Iron or Non-Alloy Steel and H-Beams from Poland

Complaint by Poland (WT/DS122)

Report of the Appellate Body DSR 2001:VII, 2701

Report of the Panel DSR 2001:VII, 2741

Thailand - Customs and Fiscal Measures on Cigarettes from the Philippines

Complaint by the Philippines (WT/DS371)

Report of the Appellate Body DSR 2011:IV, 2203

Report of the Panel DSR 2011:IV, 2256

Turkey - Measures Affecting the Importation of Rice

Complaint by United States (WT/DS334)

Report of the Panel DSR 2007:VI, 2153

Turkey - Restrictions on Imports of Textile and Clothing Products

Complaint by India (WT/DS34)

Report of the Appellate Body DSR 1999:VI, 2345

Report of the Panel DSR 1999:VI, 2363

United States - Anti-Dumping Act of 1916

Complaint by the European Communities (WT/DS136)

Decision by the Arbitrators under Article 22.6 of the DSU DSR 2004:IX, 4269

Complaint by Japan (WT/DS162)

Report of the Appellate Body DSR 2000:X, 4793

Report of the Panel (European Communities) DSR 2000:X, 4593

Report of the Panel (Japan) DSR 2000:X, 4831

Award of the Arbitrator under Article 21.3(c) of the DSU DSR 2001:V, 2017

United States-Anti-Dumping Administrative Reviews and Other Measures Related to Imports of Certain Orange Juice from Brazil

Complaint by Brazil (WT/DS382)

Report of the Panel DSR 2011:VII, 3753

United States-Anti-Dumping and Countervailing Measures on Steel Plate from India

Complaint by India (WT/DS206)

Report of the Panel DSR 2002:VI, 2073

United States - Anti-Dumping Duty on Dynamic Random Access Memory Semiconductors (DRAMS) of One Megabit or Above from Korea

Complaint by Korea (WT/DS99)

Report of the Panel DSR 1999:II, 521

United States - Anti-Dumping Measures on Certain Hot-Rolled Steel Products from Japan

Complaint by Japan (WT/DS184)

Report of the Appellate Body DSR 2001:X, 4697

Report of the Panel DSR 2001:X, 4769

Award of the Arbitrator under Article 21.3(c) of the DSU DSR 2002:IV, 1389

United States - Anti-Dumping Measures on Oil Country Tubular Goods (OCTG) from Mexico

Complaint by Mexico and United States (WT/DS282)

Report of the Appellate Body DSR 2005:XX, 10129

Report of the Panel DSR 2005:XXI, 10225

United States - Anti-Dumping Measures on Polyethylene Retail Carrier Bags from Thailand

Complaint by Thailand (WT/DS383)

Report of the Panel DSR 2010:IV, 1841

United States – Anti-Dumping Measure on Shrimp from Ecuador

Complaint by Ecuador (WT/DS335)

Report of the Panel DSR 2007:II, 425

United States - Anti-Dumping Measures on Stainless Steel Plate in Coils and Stainless Steel Sheet and Strip from Korea

Complaint by Korea (WT/DS179)

Report of the Panel DSR 2001:IV, 1295

United States – Certain Measures Affecting Imports of Poultry from China

Complaint by China (WT/DS392)

Report of the Panel DSR 2010:V, 1909

United States - Continued Dumping and Subsidy Offset Act of 2000

Complaint by Australia, Brazil, Canada, Chile, the European Communities, India, Indonesia, Japan, Korea, Mexico and Thailand (WT/DS217)

Report of the Appellate Body DSR 2003:I, 375
Report of the Panel DSR 2003:II, 489
Award of the Arbitrator under Article 21.3(c) of the DSU DSR 2003:III, 1163
Complaint by Brazil
Decision by the Arbitrator under Article 22.6 of the DSU DSR 2004:IX, 4341
Complaint by Canada (WT/DS234)
Decision by the Arbitrator under Article 22.6 of the DSU DSR 2004:IX, 4425
Complaint by Chile (WT/DS217)
Decision by the Arbitrator under Article 22.6 of the DSU DSR 2004:IX, 4511
Complaint by European Communities (WT/DS217)
Decision by the Arbitrator under Article 22.6 of the DSU DSR 2004:IX, 4591
Original Complaint by India - Recourse to Arbitration by the United States under Article 22.6 of the DSU (WT/DS217)
Decision by the Arbitrator DSR 2004:X, 4691
Original Complaint by Japan - Recourse to Arbitration by the United States under Article 22.6 of the DSU (WT/DS217)
Decision by the Arbitrator DSR 2004:X, 4771
Original Complaint by Korea - Recourse to Arbitration by the United States under Article 22.6 of the DSU ((WT/DS217)
Decision by the Arbitrator DSR 2004:X, 4851
Original Complaint by Mexico - Recourse to Arbitration by the United States under Article 22.6 of the DSU (WT/DS234)
Decision by the Arbitrator DSR 2004:X, 4931
United States - Continued Existence and Application of Zeroing Methodology
Complaint by European Communities (WT/DS350)
Report of the Appellate Body DSR 2009:III, 1291
Report of the Panel DSR 2009:III, 1481
United States - Continued Suspension of Obligations in the EC Hormones Dispute

Complaint by European Communities, United States and Canada (WT/DS320)

Report of the Appellate Body DSR 2008:X, 3507

Report of the Panel DSR 2008:XI, 3891

United States - Countervailing Duties on Certain Corrosion-Resistant Carbon Steel Flat Products from Germany

Complaint by European Communities (WT/DS213)

Report of the Appellate Body DSR 2002:IX, 3781

Report of the Panel DSR 2002:IX, 3835

United States - Countervailing Duty Investigation on Dynamic Random Access Memory Semiconductors (DRAMS) from Korea

Complaint by Korea (WT/DS296)

Report of the Appellate Body DSR 2005:XVI, 8131

Report of the Panel DSR 2005:XVII, 8243

United States - Countervailing Measures Concerning Certain Products from the European Communities

Complaint by European Communities (WT/DS212)

Report of the Appellate Body DSR 2003:I, 5

Report of the Panel DSR 2003:I, 73

Recourse to Article 21.5 of the DSU by the European Communities

Report of the Panel DSR 2005:XVIII, 8950

United States - Customs Bond Directive for Merchandise Subject to Anti-Dumping/Countervailing Duties

Complaint by Thailand, India and United States (WT/DS343, WT/DS345)

Report of the Appellate Body DSR 2008:VIII, 2781

Report of the Panel DSR 2008:VIII, 2933

United States - Definitive Anti-Dumping and Countervailing Duties on Certain Products from China

Complaint by China (WT/DS379)

Report of the Appellate Body DSR 2011:V, 2869

Report of the Panel DSR 2011:VI, 3143

United States - Definitive Safeguard Measures on Imports of Certain Steel Products

Complaint by Brazil (WT/DS259);
Complaint by China (WT/DS252);
Complaint by European Communities (WT/DS248);
Complaint by Japan (WT/DS249);
Complaint by Korea (WT/DS251);
Complaint by New Zealand (WT/DS258);
Complaint by Norway (WT/DS254);
Complaint by Switzerland (WT/DS253)

Report of the Appellate Body DSR 2003:VII, 3117

Report of the Panel DSR 2003:VIII, 3273

United States - Definitive Safeguard Measures on Imports of Circular Welded Carbon Quality Line Pipe from Korea

Complaint by Korea (WT/DS202)

Report of the Appellate Body DSR 2002:IV, 1403

Report of the Panel DSR 2002:IV, 1473

Award of the Arbitrator under Article 21.3(c) of the DSU DSR 2002:V, 2061

United States - Definitive Safeguard Measures on Imports of Wheat Gluten from the European Communities

Complaint by the European Communities (WT/DS166)

Report of the Appellate Body DSR 2001:II, 717

Report of the Panel DSR 2001:III, 779

United States - Final Anti-Dumping Measures on Stainless Steel from Mexico

Complaint by Mexico (WT/DS344)

Report of the Appellate Body DSR 2008:II, 513

Report of the Panel DSR 2008:II, 599

Arbitrator under Article 21.3(c) of the DSU DSR 2008:XX, 8619

United States - Final Countervailing Duty Determination with Respect to Certain Softwood Lumber from Canada

Complaint by Canada (WT/DS257)

Report of the Appellate Body DSR 2004:II, 587

Report of the Panel DSR 2004:II, 659

Recourse by Canada to Article 21.5 of the DSU

Report of the Appellate Body DSR 2005:XXIII, 11355

Report of the Panel DSR 2005:XXIII, 11399

United States - Final Dumping Determination on Softwood Lumber from Canada

Complaint by Canada (WT/DS264)

Report of the Appellate Body DSR 2004:V, 1917

Report of the Panel DSR 2004:V, 1981

Arbitration under Article 21.3(c) of the DSU (WT/DS264)

Report of the Arbitrator DSR 2004:X, 5011

Report of the Appellate Body - Recourse to Article 21.5 of the DSU by Canada DSR 2006:XII, 5087

Report of the Panel - Recourse to Article 21.5 of the DSU by Canada DSR 2006:XII, 5147

United States - Import Measures on Certain Products from the European Communities

Complaint by the European Communities (WT/DS165)

Report of the Appellate Body DSR 2001:I, 373

Report of the Panel DSR 2001:II, 413

United States - Imposition of Countervailing Duties on Certain Hot-Rolled Lead and Bismuth Carbon Steel Products Originating in the United Kingdom

Complaint by the European Communities (WT/DS138)

Report of the Appellate Body DSR 2000:V, 2595

Report of the Panel DSR 2000:VI, 2623

United States - Import Prohibition of Certain Shrimp and Shrimp Products

Complaint by India (WT/DS58);
Complaint by Malaysia (WT/DS58);
Complaint by Pakistan (WT/DS58);
Complaint by Thailand (WT/DS58)

Report of the Appellate Body DSR 1998:VII, 2755

Report of the Panel DSR 1998:VII, 2821

Report of the Appellate Body - Recourse to Article 21.5 of the DSU (Malaysia) DSR 2001:XIII, 6481

Report of the Panel - Recourse to Article 21.5 of the DSU (Malaysia) DSR 2001:XIII, 6529

United States – Investigation of the International Trade Commission in Softwood Lumber from Canada

Complaint by Canada (WT/DS277)

Report of the Panel DSR 2004:VI, 2543
Report of the Appellate Body - Recourse to Article 21.5 of the DSU by Canada DSR 2006:XI, 4865
Report of the Panel - Recourse to Article 21.5 of the DSU by Canada DSR 2006:XI, 4935

United States - Laws, Regulations and Methodology for Calculating Dumping Margins ("Zeroing")

Complaint by European Communities and the United States (WT/DS294)
Report of the Appellate Body DSR 2006:II, 417
Report of the Panel DSR 2006:II, 521
Recourse to Article 21.5 of the DSU by the European Communities
Report of the Appellate Body DSR 2009:VII, 2911
Report of the Panel DSR 2009:VII, 3117

United States - Measure Affecting Imports of Woven Wool Shirts and Blouses from India

Complaint by India (WT/DS33)
Report of the Appellate Body DSR 1997:I, 323
Report of the Panel DSR 1997:I, 343

United States - Measures Affecting the Cross-Border Supply of Gambling and Betting Services

Complaint by Antigua (WT/DS285)
Report of the Appellate Body DSR 2005:XII, 5663
Report of the Panel DSR 2005:XII, 5797
Arbitration under Article 21.3(c) of the DSU (WT/DS285/13) Award of the Arbitrator DSR 2005:XXIII, 11637
Report of the Appellate Body - Corrigendum DSR 2006:XII, 5475
Recourse to Article 21.5 of the DSU by Antigua and Barbuda
Report of the Panel DSR 2007:VIII, 3109
Recourse by the United States to Arbitration under Article 22.6 of the DSU
Decision by the Arbitrator DSR 2007:X, 4163

United States - Measures Affecting Imports of Certain Passenger Vehicle and Light Truck Tyres from China

Complaint by China (WT/DS399)

Report of the Appellate Body DSR 2011:IX, 4811

Report of the Panel DSR 2011:IX, 4945

United States - Measures Relating to Shrimp from Thailand

Complaint by Thailand, India, United States (WT/DS343, WT/DS345)

Report of the Appellate Body DSR 2008:VII, 2391

Report of the Panel DSR 2008:VII, 2545

United States - Measures Relating to Zeroing and Sunset Reviews

Complaint by Japan (WT/DS322)

Report of the Appellate Body DSR 2007:I, 3

Report of the Panel DSR 2007:I, 97

Arbitration under Article 21.3(c) of the DSU

Report of the Arbitrator DSR 2007:X, 4160

Recourse to Article 21.5 of the DSU by Japan

Report of the Appellate Body DSR 2009:VIII, 3441

Report of the Panel DSR 2009:VIII, 3553

United States - Measures Treating Export Restraints as Subsidies

Complaint by Canada (WT/DS194)

Report of the Panel DSR 2001:XI, 5767

United States - Preliminary Determinations with Respect to Certain Softwood Lumber from Canada

Complaint by Canada (WT/DS236)

Report of the Panel DSR 2002:IX, 3597

United States - Restrictions on Imports of Cotton and Man-made Fibre Underwear

Complaint by Costa Rica (WT/DS24)

Report of the Appellate Body DSR 1997:I, 11

Report of the Panel DSR 1997:I, 31

United States - Rules of Origin for Textiles and Apparel Products

Complaint by India (WT/DS243)

Report of the Panel DSR 2003:VI, 2309

United States - Safeguard Measures on Imports of Fresh, Chilled or Frozen Lamb Meat from New Zealand and Australia

Complaint by Australia (WT/DS178);
Complaint by new Zealand (WT/DS177)

Report of the Appellate Body DSR 2001:IX, 4051

Report of the Panel DSR 2001:IX, 4107

United States - Section 110(5) of the US Copyright Act

Complaint by the European Communities (WT/DS160)

Report of the Panel DSR 2000:VIII, 3769

Award of the Arbitrator under Article 21.3(c) of the DSU DSR 2001:II, 657

Award of the Arbitrator under Article 25 of the DSU DSR 2001:II, 667

United States - Sections 301-310 of the Trade Act of 1974

Complaint by the European Communities (WT/DS152)

Report of the Panel DSR 2000:II, 815

United States - Section 211 Omnibus Appropriations Act of 1998

Complaint by the European Communities (WT/DS176)

Report of the Appellate Body DSR 2002:II, 589

Report of the Panel DSR 2002:II, 683

United States- Section 129(c)(1) of the Uruguay Round Agreements Act

Complaint by Canada (WT/DS221)

Report of the Panel DSR 2002:VII, 2581

United States - Standards for Reformulated and Conventional Gasoline

Complaint by Brazil (WT/DS4);
Complaint by Venezuela (WT/DS2)

Report of the Appellate Body DSR 1996:I, 3

Report of the Panel DSR 1996:I, 29

United States – Subsidies on Upland Cotton

Complaint by Brazil (WT/DS267)

Report of the Appellate Body DSR 2005:I, 3

Report of the Panell DSR 2005:II- III- IV- V- VI, 297

Recourse by Brazil to Article 21.5 of the Understanding on Rules and Procedures Governing the Settlement of Disputes

Report of the Appellate Body DSR 2008:III, 809

Report of the Panel DSR 2008:III- IV- V- VI, 997

Recourse to Arbitration by the United States under Article 22.6 of the DSU and Article 4.11 of the *SCM Agreement* (Decision by the Arbitrator) DSR 2009:IX, 3871

Recourse to Arbitration by the United States under Article 22.6 of the DSU and Article 7.10 of the *SCM Agreement* (Decision by the Arbitrator) DSR 2009:IX, 4083

United States - Sunset Review of Anti-Dumping Duties on Corrosion-Resistant Carbon Steel Flat Products from Japan

Complaint by Japan (WT/DS244)

Report of the Appellate Body DSR 2004:I, 3

Report of the Panel DSR 2004:I, 87

United States – Sunset Reviews of Anti-Dumping Measures on Oil Country Tubular Goods from Argentina

Complaint by Argentina (WT/DS268)

Report of the Appellate Body DSR 2004:VII, 3341

Report of the Panel DSR:2004:VIII, 3421

Arbitration under Article 21.3(c) of the DSU (WT/DS268/12)
Award of the Arbitrator DSR:2005:XXIII, 11617

Recourse by Argentina to Article 21.5 of the Understanding on Rules and Procedures Governing the Settlement of Disputes (WT/DS268)

Report of the Appellate Body DSR 2007:IX, 3529

Report of the Panel DSR 2007:IX, 3615
DSR 2007:X, 3829

United States - Tax Treatment for "Foreign Sales Corporations"

Complaint by the European Communities (WT/DS108)

Report of the Appellate Body DSR 2000:III, 1619

Report of the Panel DSR 2000:IV, 1675

Report of the Appellate Body - Recourse to Article 21.5 of the DSU DSR 2002:I, 55

Report of the Panel - Recourse to Article 21.5 of the DSU DSR 2002:I, 119

Decision by the Arbitrator under Article 22.6 of the DSU and Article 4.11 of the *SCM Agreement* DSR 2002:VI, 2517

Report of the Appellate Body - Second Recourse to Article 21.5 of the DSU by the European Communities DSR 2006:XI, 4721

Report of the Panel - Second Recourse to Article 21.5 of the DSU by the European Communities DSR 2006:XI, 4761

United States - Transitional Safeguard Measure on Combed Cotton Yarn from Pakistan

Complaint by Pakistan (WT/DS192)

Report of the Appellate Body DSR 2001:XII, 6027

Report of the Panel DSR 2001:XII, 6067